For Lila King and Christina Bosanko

Religion, Theory, Critique

RELIGION, THEORY, CRITIQUE

*Classic and Contemporary
Approaches and Methodologies*

EDITED BY
RICHARD KING

Columbia University Press
New York

Columbia University Press
Publishers Since 1893
New York   Chichester, West Sussex
cup.columbia.edu
Copyright © 2017 Columbia University Press
All rights reserved
Library of Congress Cataloging-in-Publication Data
Names: King, Richard, 1966– editor.
Title: Religion, theory, critique: classic and contemporary approaches and
    methodologies / edited by Richard King.
Description: New York: Columbia University Press [2017] | Includes bibliographical
    references and index.
Identifiers: LCCN 2016058609 | ISBN 9780231145428 (cloth: alk. paper) |
    ISBN 9780231145435 (pbk.: alk. paper) | ISBN 9780231518246 (e-book)
Subjects: LCSH: Religion.
Classification: LCC BL41 .R367 2017 | DDC 200.7—dc23
LC record available at https://lccn.loc.gov/2016058609

Columbia University Press books are printed on permanent
and durable acid-free paper.

Printed in the United States of America

Cover design: Jordan Wannemacher

Contents

Preface

This edited collection seeks to explore the academic study of religion not as the study of a preexisting and established object but rather as a discursive field that produces its object of study in the very process of engaging in the language game of "religion." In an edited volume of this size, with so many different authors and perspectives to consider, one cannot—indeed *should* not—expect any uniformity of perspective or single position to prevail. Nevertheless, as an overall editorial project, the volume seeks to move forward our understanding of both the history of the field of the comparative study of religion and its possible future directions by drawing attention not only to the contingent, constructed, and "imagined" aspects of the field but also to theoretical trends in the late twentieth and early twenty-first century that are impacting upon the self-understanding of the field by its scholarly practitioners. Note that in talking about work within the study of religions as imagined (with the appropriate nod toward the work of Jonathan Z. Smith), I am not implying that such work is false (though there is an important dimension of such work that is indeed "made up" or constructed in particular ways) but rather drawing attention to the creative role of the scholar's imagination in the construction of the field and its object(s) of study. The academic study of religion is of course not a special case in this regard. Academic fields constitute their objects through engagement with specific language games. The stability of such discourses often results in a reification and naturalization of their objects in the process, though this need not be the case. Part of the unmasking of strong disciplinary claims to provide solid, "objective," and incontestable "scientific" knowledge is precisely to point out ways in which one might imagine such constructions and scholarly fields unfolding differently. Rather than a sign of intellectual weakness or vapid generality, the multidisciplinary and comparativist lenses of the contemporary study of religion remain tangible intellectual strengths in that they make scholarship within the field especially receptive to an awareness of the limitations of narrow disciplinary perspectives and cultural blind spots as well as furnishing opportunities to observe the otherwise largely unseen Western and modernist assumptions that continue to define contemporary academic discourses.

All methodological approaches to the study of religion have embedded within them a series of paradigmatic assumptions about religion and how it might be examined and these presuppositions frame the horizon of investigative possibility for each disciplinary lens. This volume is about the diverse ways in which religion can and has been theorized and seeks to draw out some of the theoretical presuppositions that have framed the dominant ways that religion has been understood and studied in the Academy.

The volume is organized into sections intended to explore how the category of "the religious" has been implicated in a series of elisions (for example, religion/secular/sacred, religion/society/culture). As editor, I have chosen this approach for two reasons. First, to demonstrate that however one characterizes "religion," it always remains defined in relation to a series of cognate *and* oppositional categories that establish both its clarity and its usefulness as a conceptual placeholder within discourse. However, in establishing the nature and identity of something called "religion," the term remains bound up not only with its cognate relatives ("the sacred," "faith," "belief," "devotion," "ritual," "myth," and the like) but also with that which it is deemed *not* to be ("the secular," "magic," "science," "philosophy," "society," and the like). In this sense, "religion" is a signifier that is stabilized in discourse as a meaningful conceptual placeholder through a complex network of repeated elisions and differentiations. "Religion" is not a special or unique case in this regard, though it has played a crucial role in defining and concretizing national and cultural identities across time and space and defining the relationship of "the West" to "the rest." As such, its ongoing interrogation is a crucial component of any comparative study of cultures/civilizations. Second, organizing sections according to underlying themes, elisions, and assumptions about "the religious" seeks to avoid an approach that might further entrench disciplinary differences and authority claims (from areas such as psychology of religion, sociology of religion, anthropology of religion, and the like), since the process whereby these disciplinary fields become "naturalized" is itself an object of discussion and debate within this volume. Nevertheless, each respective disciplinary lens has constituted its own field of intellectual analysis and has generated a set of approaches and issues that intersect with broader concerns and methods but that also develop their own set of questions and sense of internal coherence. Consequently, contributions are organized in a way that would be recognizable to those seeking to examine the study of religions in terms of established disciplinary approaches.

The volume is organized into twelve broadly thematic parts. After an overview essay exploring both the history and the potential future direction of the field of the study of religion, part 1 offers some discussion of formative historical influences on the emergence of the field of Religious Studies. The part does not attempt to offer a comprehensive overview of the early history of the field, since this work is carried out across multiple sections within the volume, but can be better characterized as a series of interventions by the contributors to the question of the formation of the field itself. Part 2 explores the great naturalistic thinkers emerging during the European Enlightenment who sought in various ways to "bring religion down to earth." Having explored the critical perspectives of Hume, Feuerbach, Nietzsche,

Marx, and Freud, the part finishes with a critical discussion of what has become known as the "new atheism."

Most textbooks on the study of religion treat the subject matter from within a wholly Euro-American conceptual framework. In part 3 this approach is disrupted by contributions exploring the category of religion and its deployment in a variety of non-Western contexts. How has "religion" as a concept been translated into cultural contexts where it had no previous history? How might the examination of African, Asian, or Islamic traditions change our understanding of the operational assumptions embedded in discourses about religion? In part 4, we explore the range of broadly psychological approaches that have been taken to the study of religion. How has the religious been conceived when examined as a primarily experiential or psychological phenomenon. This section contains analysis and discussion of key classical thinkers such as Freud, James, and Jung but also examines more recent developments and interest in contemporary neuroscience and the study of religion. What can a study of neuroscience bring to our understanding of religious experience and what are the limitations of such approaches?

No discussion of the study of religion can proceed without some consideration of the central role of language and translation involved in generating comparative or cross-cultural data and claims about the religious. Part 5 brings together analysis of the deployment of the category of religion within Anglo-American debates within the philosophy of religion with pieces on the importance of structuralist linguistics and structuralist theories of religion. This part also provides a critical analysis of dominant theories of myth and religion, and the part is completed with a contribution on the many ways in which the category of religion has functioned as a mode of translation of "the Other" into a modern, Western conceptual framework.

Part 6 of the volume provides contributions on the intersections between religion, society, and culture. Here authors explore the representation of religion within classical sociological work, in contemporary social theory, and in classical and contemporary discussions within anthropology. In the final contribution to this part we explore the understanding of religion and media at work within contemporary mainstream approaches to cultural and media theory.

Part 7 focuses upon classical and contemporary discussions of ritual and theories of religious action. Contributions explore classical theories of ritual and the myth-ritual debate, as well as contemporary discussions of action and performance as constitutive elements of what are usually taken to be religious phenomena.

In part 8, the historical significance of the history of religions or phenomenological school within the comparative study of religion is explored and also subjected to critical analysis. After an introductory overview on phenomenology as a philosophical movement, contributors explore the key assumptions and approaches of the phenomenological approach to religion in general as well as in specific thinkers such as Mircea Eliade. The section is completed with two pieces offering a critical interrogation of assumptions at work within phenomenological approaches to the study of religion.

Part 9 examines the impact of European continental (especially French) philosophical writers upon contemporary theoretical discussions within the study of religion. Contributions explore this influence through an examination of post-Marxist writers and individual pieces on the French thinkers Pierre Bourdieu, Jacques Derrida, and Michel Foucault. Finally, the broader perspective of contemporary continental philosophy and the much vaunted "return of the religious" in such writing is explored.

Part 10 engages the intersections between religion, gender, and sexuality with an overview piece on feminist approaches to the study of religion and discussions of the impact of French feminist thinking on debates within religious studies, in particular the work of figures such as Cixous, Kristeva, and Irigaray. This part is completed with a contribution calling for scholars to take seriously the intersections between constructions of sexuality, gender, and religion and the impact of queer theory on debates within the study of religion.

In part 11 the role of colonialism and race is examined in relation to theories of religion. After examination of colonialism in "the Americas" and apartheid South Africa in the production and representation of "religion," the reader will find a discussion of the work of W. E. B. Du Bois, Frantz Fanon, and Oliver Cromwell Cox in exploring the theoretical imbrications of race and religion. Questions considered in this part include the theoretical intersections of black cultural studies, critical race theory, and religion before asking the question "what might a 'Black Religious Studies' look like?"

Finally, in part 12, we find three reflective pieces examining contemporary issues and themes in relation to the category of religion: The first discusses the formation of the contemporary category of religion in the early modern period, the trope of "religious violence," and the role that such discourses have played in the authorization of the modern, secular nation-state. This is followed by a contemporary discussion of globalization and religion and a contribution exploring the links between religion and economy.

Acknowledgments

M any people have contributed to the completion of this volume, which has been a long time in production. I would like to thank the many authors and contributors to this work for their patience as the project suffered unforeseen delays as I worked to commission late contributions and replacement pieces and also negotiated a trans-Atlantic move that pushed back the intended publication date. This work grew out of two initiatives: first, the long-term interest of Wendy Lochner of Columbia University Press in commissioning a new, research-driven textbook on the study of religion and, second, the theories of religion project that I organized as Senior Research Fellow for the Center for the Study of Religion and Culture (CSRC) at Vanderbilt University from 2007 to 2009. Special mention should be made of the co-directors of the CSRC at that time, Professors Volney Gay and Doug Knight (both of Vanderbilt), for their unswerving support and encouragement. The Center for the Study of Religion and Culture should also be acknowledged directly for providing crucial financial support in the development of this project. Due respect and acknowledgment should also be given for the excellent contributions made by Dr. David Dark, Dr. Margaret Adam, and Taylor Weaver in editing an unruly manuscript at crucial periods of its history.

Religion, Theory, Critique

The Copernican Turn in the Study of Religion

RICHARD KING

The academic future of religion as a concept will need to focus on deconstructing the category and analyzing its function within popular discourse, rather than assuming that the category has content and seeking to specify what that content is.
—William Arnal[1]

Debates within the field of religious studies, particularly since the 1990s, have increasingly focused on the "hidden" (one might even say "dark") side of the "discipline"—that is, the cultural, political, and social processes that brought this particular academic field into existence, and the politics of its ongoing transformation. This interest in the way in which the field has been constructed, most strikingly exemplified by those who have sought to "denaturalize" the concept of religion as a category that maps seamlessly onto the diverse social and cultural fabrics of the world, received much of its initial impetus from the impact of feminist criticism upon the academy and its canons of knowledge. Since then a plethora of new "critical" perspectives have emerged, from those labeled by the (slightly problematic and triumphalist) prefix "post-" (for example, postmodernism, poststructuralism, postcolonialism) to other critical trends such as queer theory and critical race theory. Theoretical debate within the comparative study of religions is currently going though a process of engaging with these various intellectual trends—to which there are (and no doubt will continue to be) a variety of responses.

These trends have led to a widespread "postmodern" suspicion of grand narratives—of the universalist claims of an older generation of scholars to be able to speak in broadly essentialist terms about something called "religion." Indeed this anxiety about generating cross-cultural claims has cast doubt upon the very possibility of a *comparative* study of religion. Such concerns are crucial to the ongoing development of the field, but they do not create an impasse that prevents the possibility of a self-critical and nuanced comparativism to take place. Indeed, I shall conclude this introductory chapter with an argument for the necessity of something resembling "the comparative study of religion" as a vital intellectual pursuit within a globalizing academy.

Despite this, mainstream textbooks on the study of religion have lagged behind in their grasp of the intellectual implications of such research for an understanding of both the history of the field and its ongoing formation and development. This volume is an attempt to bring together a variety of scholars and perspectives within an organizational framework that seeks to pay attention to the ways in which both historical and contemporary scholarship within the study of religion produces the very thing that they purport to study, namely, "religion."

Generally speaking, the impact of these trends upon the field (as upon the humanities as a whole) has been to establish a stronger hold for what one might call "constructivist" or historicist understandings of cultural and religious forms. This trend, most famously outlined in Berger and Lückmann's *The Social Construction of Reality*,[2] published in 1966, has become something of an established "truth" or orthodoxy in the humanities and social sciences by the turn of the twenty-first century, though the implications of this standpoint are played out in different ways and with different degrees of emphasis in a variety of approaches. (There is a difference, for instance, between the position as found in the work of early structuralists such as Lévi-Strauss and the more radical rendering of the constructivist line by "poststructuralist" writers such as Derrida and Foucault.)[3]

At the same time as the constructivist position has established itself as a truism of sorts within the academy, there are also trends that seek to interrogate the implications of the constructivist or historicist position in the light of its own intellectual and cultural roots. In the field of the study of religion, some of these reflect conservative reactions (on behalf of traditions) to what is widely perceived to be a form of "multicultural relativism" (see, for instance, the work of John Milbank), while other critics have been motivated by a concern to move intellectual debates about "religion" beyond a narrowly Eurocentric history and frame theoretical discussions in a cross-cultural, cross-disciplinary, and "globalized" conversational space.[4] To what extent, such diverse thinkers ask, is the modern liberal acceptance of the constructed nature of cultures built upon a much older legacy of historicist thought that derives from the European Enlightenment and its critique of tradition, and that, in the field of the study of religions, has been most strongly expressed in terms of naturalistic accounts of religion (by European thinkers such as Hume, Kant, Nietzsche, Feuerbach, Marx, and Freud)? To what extent do "secularist" accounts of religion offer an account that is unfairly "reductive" of the object of study (in this case, the reputed object "religion")? An earlier rendition of such concerns about the implications of "naturalistic reductionism" precipitated the rise of the phenomenological approach to the study of religion, which gained such prominence in the late twentieth century (under the leadership in North America of figures such as Joachim Wach and Mircea Eliade) and which in institutional terms helped spawn the rise of autonomous "religious studies" departments in the United States and United Kingdom in the late 1960s and early 1970s.

The phenomenology of religion (or "history of religions" school as it has sometimes been called) has come under increasing fire by recent waves of "critical theory" scholarship within the study of religion for the political associations of some of its primary advocates, for its romanticism, for its methodological naiveté and

for its crypto-theological tendencies. The issue that precipitated the rise of the phenomenology of religion, however—that is, the search for an approach to the study
of religions that does not offer a straightforwardly theological (read: "emic," or
insider) account on the one hand or a dogmatically secular, social-scientific (read:
"etic," or outsider) account on the other—remains a key tension within the field.
All scholars working on religion in the contemporary academy will place themselves (or *be placed* by their academic peers and readers) at different points on the
spectrum between these two poles.

Increasingly contemporary scholars of religion, influenced by feminist, poststructuralist, postcolonial, and queer theories, have sought to denaturalize the established categories of scholarly analysis—those terms and approaches that have
been mostly taken for granted by an earlier generation. Most often this work has
been done by highlighting the politics underlying the deployment of such theories,
particularly in relation to processes of "othering" or exclusion (usually along gender, sexual, racial, or colonial lines). One does not have to be a card-carrying member of any of these intellectual trends to be impacted by the series of questions and
challenges that they bring up for the field as a whole. It is in this context that contemporary theorizing about religion is now taking place.

A second trend in the academy at the beginning of the twenty-first century is a
move (at least rhetorically) toward interdisciplinarity. This trend has led to the development of transinstitutional and cross-disciplinary centers but their status as
long-term, stable entities remains unclear because they do not conform to the traditional spatial division of knowledge in the academy, which has been based on
departmental and disciplinary specialization. As Andrew Haas has suggested:

> The wider institution, however much it espouses a nominal notion of interdisciplin-
> ary studies, is not set up for the ground-breaking disruption and dispersal of a pure
> interdisciplinarity. The academy functions by virtue of its disciplines, not in opposi-
> tion to them. Precise and defining boundaries are set rigidly in place through the cre-
> ation of institutional compartments—faculties, departments, schools and colleges—
> that become dividing lines of bureaucratic organization by which each discipline is
> held in check and every field of study demarcated one against the other. . . . The
> University resists and will continue to resist any interdisciplinarity that disrupts the
> structural logic upon which it has prided itself for so many centuries. . . . The acad-
> emy loves to applaud interdisciplinary rhetoric, and does so by employing this lan-
> guage of interdisciplinarity itself. But we know that this kind of rhetoric only goes so
> far. It must of necessity go only so far if the academy is to remain what it is.[5]

Despite this tension, contemporary work within the field of the study of religion continues to reflect this growing interest in stepping beyond the boundaries of
specific disciplinary regimes. At the end of *The Order of Things*, Michel Foucault
famously evokes the image of a human face drawn in the sand that is slowly disappearing as the waves wash over it.[6] For Foucault the death of God heralded by
Nietzsche (and the scholarly displacement of theology as queen of the sciences in
the academy) has led to God's *temporary* replacement by "Man" (and the

establishment of the "sciences of man" as the replacement of the science of God, theology). This, he suggests, is little more than an aftereffect (an "aftershock" if you will) of the death of God. Similarly, this "Man" (actually a white European male) is destined to be displaced as a figure on which to establish the foundations of scientific knowledge and history.

Whether one sees the move toward interdisciplinarity in terms of Foucault's prophecy of the demise of the sciences of man, or more simply as evidence of an attempt to redress previously unacknowledged inequalities and move away from narrow academic specialization, or even as evidence of the undermining of academic specialization and disciplinarity linked to the rise of managerialist and business-oriented models of university research, it remains the case that the mainstream knowledge-disciplines of the academy, grounded as they have been in the European Enlightenment's reconfiguration of knowledge in the eighteenth, nineteenth, and early twentieth centuries, are now being shaken up by a succession of critical waves that are hitting the shore of our "postmodern," "postcolonial," hypertextualized, ecologically conscious, and rapidly globalizing world. What will come out of these shifts is not yet clear. The interdisciplinary trend, however, has been most striking in scholarship that seeks to bridge the traditional divide between the "arts/humanities" and the "natural sciences"—particularly in work that explores and even disrupts an easy separation of the "nature/culture" divide upon which such a division of knowledge has been based. This is most striking, for instance, in debates about science and religion (especially the interface between cognitive science and religion), as well as in poststructuralist and feminist theories that focus on the idea of the thinking body (and that seek to read the body as both a "natural" given of our experience but also as an *already cultured* vehicle for framing that experience).

"CRITICAL RELIGION" AND THE COPERNICAN TURN IN THE STUDY OF RELIGIONS

Religion is not a native term; it is a term created by scholars for their intellectual purposes and therefore is theirs to define. It is a second-order, generic concept that plays the same role in establishing a disciplinary horizon that a concept such as "language" plays in linguistics or "culture" plays in anthropology. There can be no disciplined study of religion without such a horizon.[7]

Although important intellectual precedents can be found in the work of Giambattista Vico (1668–1744), in many respects the epistemological foundation for modern Western theories of social constructivism can be found in Immanuel Kant's work *The Critique of Pure Reason* (1781). Kant sought to initiate what he called a "Copernican Turn" in our understanding of human experience by demonstrating how our perception of the world is preconditioned by certain a priori categories (most notably, time and space). His analysis also offered an analysis of the constructed nature of our experience of reality, conditioned as it is not just by a priori and framing categories of the intellect, but also through the agency of the mind in organizing and synthesizing the sensory manifold that presents itself to us through the mediation of our sense organs. This realization, which for Kant related to a universal human subject, has echoed through subsequent European intellectual thought and, with increasing attention paid to gender, ethnic, race, and class identities, formed the intellectual foundations for the emergence of the social-constructivist paradigm that is now largely regnant within the humanities.

What we have seen in scholarship in the study of religion since the 1990s, however, is a similar "Copernican turn." Just as Kant asks us to consider that the world of objects "out there" is actually framed by certain a priori categories that determine our perception of the world, we should recognize that the study of religion as a multidisciplinary field is not concerned with the examination of a stable phenomenon "out there" called "religion," and that the object is itself constituted according to certain framing cultural assumptions. The impact of post-Kantian social constructionism and a wave of critical theories that have moved through the arts and humanities (namely, third-wave feminism, postmodernism, poststructuralism, postcolonialism, queer theory, and the like) has been to highlight the ways in which the object of study is itself constructed in the act of examination itself.

As with the Copenhagen interpretation of quantum mechanics (associated with the physicist Niels Bohr), scholars influenced by a wave of critical theories have increasingly come to appreciate that what one chooses to measure (and how) determines to a significant degree what it is that one will find. This is no more a denial of an "objective reality" out there than Bohr's theory is a denial of the reality of an electron, but what it does mean is that the kind of object one considers "religion" to be and the kinds of claims one makes about that object are significantly determined by the disciplinary lens and formative assumptions that ground that analysis in the first place. Unlike quantum mechanics, however, we are dealing here with human-engineered macroevents—complex networks of cultural phenomena that have been classified, for better or worse, under the rubric of "the religious." Nevertheless, where this shift in approach within the field of the study of religions creates a parallel with the insights of quantum mechanics is in the recognition that the closer one studies the phenomenon of "religion," the more its stability as a singular object with a fixed "essence" dissolves before one's eyes.

Critical theories of religion remain diverse both in their implications and in their underlying presuppositions and can range from approaches heavily influenced by the critical theory of the Frankfurt, Neo-, and Post-Marxist schools, to trends influenced by various strands of feminist, poststructuralist, postcolonial, and queer theories. The type of constructivism embedded in such approaches can vary from those that see critical theory as an acknowledgment of the role of interpretation and "prior judgment" in the selection of empirical data to approaches that disavow what is seen as subservience to a positivistic appeal to "empirical data" altogether. For the latter strand of critical theorists, the "naive" subservience of "theory" to the demand for empirical verification is premised on a mistaken understanding of the role of theory. Thus, according to Wendy Brown:

Theory is not simply different from description; rather it is incommensurate with description. Theory is not simply the opposite of application but carries the impossibility of application. As a meaning-making enterprise, theory depicts a world that does not quite exist, that is not quite the world we inhabit. But this is theory's incomparable value, not its failure. Theory does not simply decipher the meanings of the world but recodes and rearranges them in order to reveal something about the meanings and incoherencies that we live with. To do this revelatory and speculative work, theory must work to one side of direct referents, or at least it must disregard the conventional meanings and locations of those referents. Theory violates the self-representation of things in order to represent those things and their relation—the world—differently. Thus, theory is never "accurate" or "wrong"; it is only more or less illuminating, more or less provocative, more or less of an incitement to thought, imagination, desire, possibilities for renewal.[8]

Not all critical theorists would be prepared to relinquish a representational function for theory, even if one acknowledges that it is naive to assume that there is such a thing as "raw data" free from an interpretive grid or set of framing assumptions.[9] For scholars like Brown, however, the point of theory is precisely to offer a *counterhegemonic* vision of the world, an approach that makes the social and political location of all thinking overt by way of a refusal to obscure power dynamics and agendas from sight by an authoritative appeal to "scientific neutrality" or empirical objectivity. On this view, the authority claims of a certain kind of "social-scientific" empiricism that claims to represent "the facts" are to be refused in favor of a positive (rather than a positivistic) reimagining of the social world about which it speaks. Thus Brown argues:

Insofar as theory imbues contingent or unconscious events, phenomena, or formations with meaning and with location in a world of theoretical meaning, theory is a sense-making enterprise of that which often makes no sense, of that which may be inchoate, unsystematized, inarticulate. It gives presence to what may have a liminal, evanescent, or ghostly existence. Thus theory has no kinship with the project of "accurate representation"; its value lies instead in the production of a new representation, in the production of coherence and meaning that it does not find lying on the ground but which, rather, it forthrightly fashions. Similarly, theory does not simply articulate needs or desires but argues for their existence and thus literally brings them into being. As theory interprets the world, it fabricates the world (*pace* Marx! especially Marx!); as it names desire, it gives reason and voice to desire, and thus fashions a new world of desire; as it codifies meaning, it composes meaning. Theory's most important *political* offering is this opening up of a breathing space between the world of common meanings and the world of alternative ones, a space of potential renewal of thought, desire and action.[10]

Whatever one's view of the relationship between the enterprise of a "critical theory" that seeks to locate itself and others in a network of cultural, epistemological, and political networks and an appeal to "empirical data," this type of critique can be characterized, as Kocku von Stuckrad has argued, by a recognition of the "recursive contingency" of intellectual work. Thus,

Reflexive critique is more than mere critique of ideology. It takes seriously what I called the recursion of contingency, because this method is ready continuously to call into question the very ground on which it stands. By fostering multiple perspectives and approaches to its subject, it makes visible dynamic networks of identities and meanings. Academic concepts are generated in a communicative and discursive procedure, in which the variables change constantly under temporal and local conditions. The reasons for us to hold certain scientific propositions are highly contingent but not arbitrary. Scholarly meanings are the result of processes of negotiation.[11]

When we come to consider the history of scholarship in the study of religion from this perspective, it is remarkably easy to notice that what counts as evidence of "religion" varies quite considerably from writer to writer and across different disciplinary thresholds. Just as Max Müller, following the prevailing philological and Orientalist paradigm of his day, tended to search for "the religious" in mythological, textual, and doctrinal sources with an emphasis on the classic literary expressions of intellectual elites, William James, at the forefront of the emerging field of psychology, focused on individual experiences as the core of the religious subject matter. If we look at the work of scholars such as Robertson Smith and Victor Turner, we find an emphasis on ritual performances and communal practices. These foundational approaches and assumptions continue as ongoing legacies of approach and perspective within the field and within specific disciplines.

From this vantage point it should become clear from even a basic familiarity with the diversity of scholars contained within mainstream canonical accounts of the history of the study of religion that such intellectual figures represent not so much different approaches or lenses to the examination of an easily identifiable, singular, and stable object of analysis "out there" called "religion" as diverse attempts to construct the very object they are purporting to analyze. In many cases it is far from clear that scholars of "religion" are even discussing the same phenomenon in their accounts. What I wish to argue, therefore, is that what unites the field of the study of religion is neither a singular, essentialized, and stable object of study ("religion") nor even the shared emergence of a distinctive disciplinary practice or enterprise ("the history of religions" or "religious studies"), but rather an ongoing commitment to the reproduction of the language game of "religion" itself. It is conversations about this category—about how it is to be defined and conceived (as belief, sacred text, practice, community, experience, and so on), about how it is to be evaluated, understood, embraced, or rejected, that bring scholars of "religion" together into a distinctive field. Sustained scholarly conversation about "religion" is itself what constitutes the field of the study of religion.

Our first task then as critical scholars of "religion" is to examine how the category of "religion" has been deployed within scholarly (and other) works, to understand how disciplinary lenses, institutionalized training (the "sciences"), and cultural assumptions have framed the conditions of possible knowledge within the academy. This involves an analysis of not only the manifold ways in which scholars of religion have construed and constructed their object of study but also how they have construed themselves in relation to it. This, as Jonathan Z. Smith argued in *Imagining Religion* (published in 1981), should be the primary orientation of the critical scholar of religion. However, if one examines the plethora of student textbooks and histories of the study of religion, one rarely finds such a critical

enterprise presented as the sine qua non of understanding the field of the comparative study of religion. Most textbooks assume that there is an easily identifiable
and stable object out there called "religion" and proceed from this assumption to
outline how various scholars and disciplinary approaches have sought to examine
that object. The task of developing a critical history of religion, or what Timothy
Fitzgerald has called the "Critical Religion" approach, requires us to ask instead
how discourses of religion construct the very object that they seek to explain.

COLONIALISM AND WESTERN MYTHS OF ORIGIN
FOR THE STUDY OF RELIGIONS

Most accounts of the emergence of the study of religions emphasize their roots in
the naturalistic accounts of religion of the Enlightenment period. Most often the
roots of the comparative study of religion are linked to the establishment of a disciplinary "science" (distinct from theology) in the work of nineteenth-century figures such as Max Müller (1823–1900) and Cornelius Tiele (1830–1902) and the
institutional beginnings of *Religionswissenschaft* in Europe. In that sense, the
modern study of religion is linked to a growing awareness of the historical and
socially constructed nature of religion and its truth-claims. This association is a
key feature of what one might call the secularist account of the emergence of the
study of religions and is prevalent in textbook accounts of the history of the field.
Ivan Strenski's *Thinking About Religion* (2006), for instance, locates the "birth" of
the field in the emergence of naturalistic/historicist accounts of religion in sixteenth-
century European thinkers such as Herbert of Marbury and Jean Bodin. Thus,

> It is true that from place to place, in rare outbursts of creative curiosity, people have
> asked such basic questions about the nature, value and justification of religion. But
> these were fleeting episodes in the spotty history of human curiosity, that left behind
> no major books or treatises, no sustaining institutions or "schools," no lasting cul-
> tural influences in the forms of lines of enquiry or major questions about religion. On
> the contrary, religion did not become a real arena of problems, rigorously interro-
> gated and systematically researched, until fairly late in the history of the West. There
> would never have been the study of religion as we know it, unless religion itself had
> first become a problem in some sustained way.[12]

One of the problems with Strenski's account, which is generally representative
of mainstream histories of the study of religion, is that it finds exactly what it sets
out to discover while remaining largely unaware of the role of the investigator's
own operating assumptions in the imagined reconstruction of the legacy with
which she or he then identifies. Another problem with such accounts is that they
generally lack the presence of any non-Western voices, except perhaps as objects of
study. This is perhaps not all that surprising since the category of "religion" is indeed, as Strenski notes, a "problem" that emerged in early modern Europe. Consequently, in this narrow regard at least we do not find any "theorists of religion" in

"foreign lands" precisely because "religion" was neither a category nor an operating assumption in the intellectual and cultural traditions of non-European civilizations. This realization, however, should cause us to reflect upon our own operating assumptions and the implications of their universalization through the language game of "religion."

In contrast to such accounts, there are potentially a great number of "non-Western" antecedents of the modern study of religion that would be worth acknowledging on a global historical scale. Jonathan Z. Smith has argued that the scriptocentric and philological emphasis of much of the modern work carried out in the field of the study of religion suggests its roots not so much in the Enlightenment but in the Renaissance:

> If some alien, unfamiliar with the fierce eighteenth and nineteenth century taxonomic controversies concerning the classification of the academic disciplines, were to observe scholars of religion in action, it would have no difficulty identifying the class to which they belong. With respect to practice, the history of religions is, by and large, a philological endeavor chiefly concerned with editing, translating and interpreting texts, the majority of which are perceived as participating in the dialectic of "near" and "far." If this is the case, then our field may be re-described as a child of the Renaissance.[13]

This characterization of the field of course ignores or underplays other strands and approaches that focus less attention upon texts as the key to understanding "religion." However, if the study of religion is at least partly about the classification and analysis of doctrinal treatises and worldviews, then we must consider the global scholarly practice of doxography as an important element in the broader history of the field. In that context, Irenaeus of Lyons (c. 115–202 CE) and his work *Against Heresies* must be considered an important historical precedent. Beyond a specifically Christian context we should also consider the works of classical Chinese, Indian, Greek, and Jewish philosophers and doxographers. Thus, one might point to classical Greek writers such as Hecataeus of Miletus (c. 550–476 BCE), Herodotus (484–425 BCE), and Xenophon (c. 430–354 BCE) as important precedents. In this context we should also consider the long history of intellectual debate, analysis, and contestation that characterized Indian (Brahmanical, Buddhist, Jain, Islamic), Jewish, Persian, and Chinese (Daoist, Confucian, Buddhist) intellectual traditions. What of the intellectual experiments in debate and analysis across and between different traditions in the court of the Mughal emperor Akbar (1542–1605 CE) or the documentation and analysis of different schools in Chinese scholars such as Wei Shou (506–572 CE)?

One response to such attempts to globalize the history of the field is to reassert European exceptionalism through an appeal to the specifically "secularist" roots of the modern study of religion. On this view, the necessary "objectivity," detachment, or critical distance required to count as an antecedent of the modern study of religion first occurred in the European Enlightenment. Of course this involves a rather selective historical consciousness that privileges Western "modernity" by way of the binary opposition of the secular and the religious that is itself encoded in the secularist standpoint. If the modern "study of religion" is understood as rooted in the Enlightenment tradition of humanistic critique then much earlier figures such as Xenophanes (b. 570 BCE), the reputed founder of the Eleatic school, should be considered an important antecedent with his critique of the anthropomorphism of Greek polytheistic beliefs. Indeed, we find that Xenophanes is often cited by modern writers wishing to emphasize the "naturalistic approach" as the distinctive orientation or contribution of the modern comparative study of religion. As Xenophanes famously remarked: "the Ethiopians make their gods snubnosed and black; the Thracians make theirs gray-eyed and red-haired. . . . And if oxen and horses and lions had hands, and could draw with their hands and do what man can do, horses would draw the gods in the shape of horses, and oxen in the shape of oxen, each giving the gods bodies similar to their own."[14]

Some see this as the precursor of projectionist accounts of religion (that is, ones that locate the origin of religion in human projections onto the natural world, rather than divine revelation). However, the focus on classical Greek thought (along with the historical jump to much later European thinkers) in such historiographies reinforces classic Orientalist accounts that focus upon ancient Greece as the foundation of democracy, philosophy, and Western civilization as a whole. Such Eurocentric accounts ignore the history of "naturalistic" criticism of theism that has been present in non-Western cultures for millennia. It is difficult, for instance, to read Mimamsaka, Jain, Buddhist, and Indian materialist critiques of theistic belief systems without recognizing that there has been a long and vibrant tradition of critical reflection and contestation of theistic beliefs in existence in Indian civilization for thousands of years. Consider, for instance, the following words, attributed to Brhaspati, the reputed founder of an ancient school of Indian materialism (*jadavāda*):

> There is no heaven, no final liberation, nor any soul in another world, nor do the actions of the four castes, orders etc., produce any real effect. The *Agnihotra* (fire sacrifice), the three Vedas, the ascetic's three staves, and smearing oneself with ashes, were made by nature as the livelihood of those destitute of knowledge and manliness. If a beast slain in the *Jyotistoma* rite will itself go to heaven, why then does the sacrificer not offer his own father immediately? . . . While life remains let a man live happily, let him eat ghee (clarified butter) even if he runs into debt. When the body turns to ashes, how can it ever return again? If he who departs from the body goes to another world, how is it that he does not come back again, restless because of love for his kindred? Hence it is only as a means of livelihood that the Brahmin priests have established here all these ceremonies for the dead—there is no other fruit anywhere. The three authors of the Vedas were buffoons, knaves and demons.[15]

One of the key challenges for a global perspective on the history of the study of religion is to determine what cultural corollaries of "religion," if any, one should examine in non-Western cultures. Generally, as I have been arguing, indigenous intellectual discussions of such potential corollaries in "non-Western" civilizations are ignored in the production of mainstream historiographical accounts of religious studies, resulting in a highly Eurocentric account of the field as a human intellectual endeavor. One response to this might be to argue that this is acceptable on the perfectly reasonable grounds that the modern study of religion is in fact a "peculiarly Western" enterprise and conversation. This after all is the burden of Strenski's assertion that only in Europe did "religion" constitute a "problem" to be addressed. However, such reticence in the extension of the category of "religion" to non-Western contexts soon dissipates when scholars seek to generate universal claims about the *import* of their work beyond a Western horizon. Suddenly evidence of "religion" can be pinpointed in the various cultures of the world and the category can be deployed in a way that maps seamlessly across time and space. This begs the obvious question: if the study of religion began as a specifically European cultural conversation (which at one level it undeniably did since it was in Europe that the language of "religion" originated and initially prevailed before it was exported more widely in the colonial era), what issues remain when scholars then seek to universalize the scope of that language game to include cultures, civilizations, and practices where the category of religion has had, until European colonial engagement, no history or critical purchase? If "religion" works as a description of, say, eighth-century-CE Confucianism and Vedic sacrificial practice in the fifth-century BCE or is a useful category for understanding fifteenth-century North African ritual practices, then why are indigenous examples and traditions of intellectual analysis and discussion of such cultural phenomena not also considered part of the global legacy of the study of religions? Again the answer, whether explicitly stated or implicitly assumed, involves an appeal to the exceptionalism of modern Western secularism. It is only with the rise of the secularist approach and the distancing it requires from its object of study that the modern study of religion becomes fully attainable and this, so it is claimed, is a distinctive feature of the European Enlightenment. However, after what I am calling "the Copernican turn in the study of religion" has taken place, the two arguments that undergird the secularist authority claim become moot. First, that secularism is a "neutral" account of the world standing apart from all other ("religious") worldviews, and second, that only a secularist standpoint can provide the required objectivity and "critical distance" from its object of study to constitute the foundational basis for the comparative study of religion.

What remains in place, however, is the claim that it is with the rise of Enlightenment secularism that the modern study of "religion" begins, but this has now been seen for what it is, namely, a tautological claim. "Religion" can be studied only from this point because it is now clear that the birth of "the religious" as a distinctive and substantive modern category is the twin birth of the formation of "the secular." What brings the modern study of religion into existence is precisely the development and adoption of the category of "the religious" as a substantive noun believed to designate specific and discrete cultural phenomena "out there" in the world, and in a very tangible sense this only becomes possible through its formal separation from a realm thereby labeled "the secular." However, this will provide neither the authority claim nor the purificatory function that is required for the secularist approach to establish itself in its state of exceptionalism. On the contrary what this demonstrates is that "the secular" and "the religious" function as binary opposites in the context of Western forms of modernity. As Derrida (and long before him the Buddhist philosopher Nāgārjuna) would remind us, both sides of this binary are dependent upon each other to establish their ground but are therefore also undermined by this in their sui generis claims to purity and self-sufficiency. As Bruno Latour has argued, the constitution of authority claims with regard to "science" within a variety of intellectual disciplines involves an attempt at a purification of the field from that which it is not, but in a way that must always fail because each act of purification draws attention to the role of the excluded in the very constitution of the foundationally "pure" subject itself.[16] Secularist accounts of religion, therefore, remain dogged by the constitutive presence of that which they dare not partake—most obviously "the religious," which in that sense constitutes a repressed disciplinary memory of their twin birth and mutual dependence. There is now quite a substantial literature from the work of Ernst Feil, Peter Harrison, Timothy Fitzgerald, Richard King, Russell McCutcheon, William T. Cavanaugh, and the like that places the emergence of this particular understanding of "religion" and "the religions" as substantive nouns drawn in contrast to a realm known as "the secular" in the context of early modern European thought and the Enlightenment.[17] This has led to a body of contemporary academic literature that seeks to rethink the "formations of the secular" as well as the role played by its foil—the category of "religion," as a key ideological lynchpin in the privileging of Westernized models of modernity.[18]

Thus, the development of avowedly "secularist" philosophies, worldviews, and approaches is indeed linked to the emerging recognition of a distinct realm known as "the religious." An awareness of the mutual imbrication of the secular and the religious as categories, however, renders deeply problematic the attempt to create a transcendentally pure and foundational platform for secularism to stand "above" the religions, since the recognition of mutual imbrication brings "the secular" back "down to earth" (ironically) to the level of those traditions and worldviews that, through oppositional definition, constitute the very ground of secular identity itself. In this way modern secularism becomes seen for what it is, namely, as one of a number of diverse worldviews, but one characterized specifically by the way in which it builds its case for distinctiveness, exceptionalism, and foundational originality by classifying all other worldviews that it encounters as "religious." In perhaps the strangest twist of the tale, insofar as secularists make transcendental authority claims about the truth of their position they end up replicating an ideological separation of "universal truth" from "superstitious belief" that precisely characterized earlier eras of Christian triumphalism that secularism was itself seen as overcoming.

However, even if one concedes that the study of religion as a field is indeed a modern European invention, this is not merely the story of a hermetically sealed European awareness of the historicity of "religion" emerging from the fracturing of Christendom after the Protestant Reformation. The academic invention of the study of religion is also driven by the explosion of data from the missionary and colonial exploration of "new worlds" in Asia, Africa, and the Americas. Although his account focuses exclusively on European writers and locates the rise of the modern study of religion in the European Enlightenment, J. Samuel Preus remarks that

> The discovery of non-European cultures put into sharp relief the parochialism of Christianity's universalist ambitions. For a while, religion (or at least Christianity) was exempt from the expanding naturalism. The very last bastion of theology (or religious thought) was, and is, the claim to be able to explain *itself* on "its own terms." As I shall try to show, the birth of the modern study of religion occurred at the point where that claim was effectively challenged—where the same procedures for explanation that seemed accurate and fruitful in the realms of nature and social institutions were now applied to religion itself. Only on such an assumption could the modern study of religion build.[19]

Despite the nod to "non-European cultures," the role of the colonial encounter of Europe with other civilizations has been significantly underplayed in accounts of the history of the field. As David Chidester remarks:

> Standard histories of the study of religion have been almost exclusively preoccupied with the questions, issues, or modes or analysis that were internal to the development of a set of European academic disciplines. As a result, the real story remains untold. . . . The disciplinary history of the study of religion is also a history of discipline, a dramatic narrative of the discourses and practices of comparison that shaped subjectivities on the colonized peripheries and at European centers.[20]

The irony here is that the parochialism that Preuss and other secular critics see as embedded in the "universalist ambitions" of Christianity is mirrored in their own scholarship and self-representation of the history of the field. This can be seen first in the lack of sustained attention paid to the role of the encounter with "non-European cultures" in the emergence of the modern study of religion. Second, the "parochialism" of Christianity's "universalist ambitions" is replicated in the failure of the mainstream secularist narrative to acknowledge the possibility of "non-Western" contributions to *historical* and *contemporary* theoretical debates and analysis. Despite such assumptions, I would suggest not only that the emergence of the field of the study of religion cannot be understood without a recognition of the ways in which it was significantly impacted by European encounters with various "non-Christian others," but also that it remains possible, once we question the universalist pretensions of "Western theory," to engage intellectual thought beyond "the West" without having to accept the accusation of "going native."

Indeed, one could even go so far as to argue that what I have rhetorically described as "the Copernican turn" in the field—that is, the challenge to the universalist provenance of established Western terms such as "religion," "faith," "belief," "experience," and the like—is occurring in response to the end of European colonialism—that is, to the challenge offered by the postcolonial "non-West" to Western claims to universality.[21] Earlier I offered an account of contemporary "critical theories of religion" which suggested that an important feature of such approaches has been the gradual unfolding and radicalization of the implications of the Kantian epistemological project in the form of a social-constructivist understanding of human culture. As Clifford Geertz (following Max Weber) once suggested, "man is an animal suspended in webs of significance he himself has spun."[22] However, even this contemporary challenge to established categories and paradigms within the study of religion is not *merely* an internal product of the constructivist turn in post-Kantian theoretical debates in the West. It is, I would argue, also representative of a gradually unfolding cultural and political effect in the late twentieth and early twenty-first centuries—an intellectual aftershock if you will, brought about by the dissolution of European colonialism and the ideologies, categories, and paradigms that supported it.[23]

Consider for a moment the profound implications of this perspective. On this reading of history, the challenge to European parochialism brought about by the colonial encounter with other civilizations *began* with the assault on the universalist truth-claims of European Christianity, but with the end of formal colonial rule in the late twentieth century now *continues* by impacting the authority claims of Western secular universalists to have cornered the market on "critique" and "theory." This, I would argue, is a sign of the unraveling of the project of a singular, universal "modernity" grounded in the confident belief in the inevitable secularization of the world. We have not yet been able to envision a clear way forward after this "secularization of secularism" itself. However, it remains a necessary and vital task if we are to make sense of the rapidly shifting geopolitical context of the early twenty-first century.

BEYOND THE SCIENCE WARS: RE-CONCEIVING THE COMPARATIVE STUDY OF RELIGIONS

The trope of the "science of religion" has been a powerful narrative strand within the field of the comparative study of religion since the late nineteenth century. Mainstream (broadly secularist) histories of the development of "religious studies" or the comparative study of religion focus on claims to found a comparative "science of religion" that would seek to avoid the perceived subjectivist pitfalls of "insider," theological positioning. Such approaches continue to resonate in particular institutional contexts. The "science of religion" trope is represented in the field by ongoing spats that continue to this day about the relationship of religious studies and theology, in the decision to locate the birth of religious studies in the Enlightenment traditions of naturalism, anticlericalism, and the works of the "masters of suspicion" (Nietzsche, Marx, Freud), in "social-scientific" and "empirical" approaches to the study of religions, and in the contemporary application of insights from biological and cognitive science to the study of religion.

However one positions oneself in the field in terms of this spectrum of opinion, there is a need to think beyond the highly policed cold war between "theology" and the social-scientific or "secular" study of religion that has dominated the study of religion for much of the twentieth century. This opposition is built upon a binary opposition of the secular and the religious that is itself a constitutive feature of dominant Western discourses of modernity. As such, it is far from an ideologically neutral account of the world. It also does not constitute the only way to imagine either the history or the future of the field of study.

There are many problems with the standard secularist account of the emergence of the study of religion. I have focused so far on the colonial dimensions of such accounts. I will now briefly mention two further problems.

The first problem is an acute form of disciplinary amnesia, particularly with regard to the origins of the field.[24] We have seen this already in the disavowal of non-European precedents for the field and the tendency to represent European intellectual developments as sui generis events only marginally affected by the encounter with non-European peoples. However, even within a narrowly European perspective, mainstream accounts of the rise of the comparative study of religion tend to occlude the pioneering work of missionaries and comparative theologians (such as Ernst Troeltsch and Rudolph Otto) in the collection of valuable data and in theoretical developments within the subject area.[25] When scholars within the accepted canon of writers sometimes exhibit explicit theological orientations or "biases" in their work (such as the declarations of the superiority of Christianity in the writings of figures such as Max Müller and Rudolph Otto), these are usually represented as imperfect struggles to reach later standards of self-awareness and critical objectivity. In these contexts such "founding fathers" (and they are almost always white men) are often represented, within a broadly liberal and progressivist narrative, as important figures in an unfolding story of the progressive development of a more truly scientific, neutral, and objective approach to the study of religion. In this way the post-Darwinian evolutionist assumptions that are so often noted in the works of early scholars in the comparative study of religion are absent in contemporary accounts of "religion" (where such claims would be open to the accusation of colonialism and ethnocentrism), but persist in accounts of the development of the field itself as part of a progressivist narrative about the gradual emergence of an "objective" science grounded in a "neutral" secular approach that does not privilege any tradition or religion over another. Thus, as Masuzawa notes,

> It is of course one of our contemporary habits of thought to deem such religiously compliant—and in fact, denominationally particular—interests as *pre*scientific, which is also our way of saying *un*scientific. To regard such a narrowly confessional orientation as a throwback, therefore, presumes a certain self-understanding of the position of science, or what has been baldly called the ideology of scientific progress. This scientistic ideology is predicated, or so it seems, on a certain form of anticlericalism, or as some religious advocates would argue, antireligionism. In any event, it may not be prudent for us today to swallow whole either the scenario of progress or any version of scientific triumphalism if we hope to claim evenhandedness and analytic equilibrium. What should be noted here, then, is not the backwardness of these texts, but rather the complex and multifaceted appeal they were making to their prospective readers, who must have been clerical and state authorities.[26]

As Urs Apps has demonstrated, even influential fields of study in the eighteenth and nineteenth centuries such as comparative linguistics, philology, and orientalism—often deemed to be important influences on the emergence of a comparative "science of religions"—are themselves implicated in a series of broadly Christocentric debates about religion, the origins of language, and the status of biblical accounts of human origins.[27] The strong theological roots and precedents for the modern study of religion are ignored or underplayed in most mainstream accounts amid concerns about "contaminating" the field with its excluded other. One of the functions of this emphasis upon "weeding out" the earlier errors and theological biases of classical authors is to inscribe greater authority and objectivity to the "more enlightened" contemporary scholar of religion. With the benefit of hindsight, we are now able to see the errors of our flawed intellectual heroes and avoid their mistakes. However, the problem with such attempts to inscribe modern scholarship with greater authority and objectivity (after all, some might argue, if we are not in some sense getting "better" at the work of scholarship, what is the justification for continuing with it?) is that such claims obscure and preserve the platform of Christocentric assumptions about the nature of "religion" that continue to inform scholarship in the contemporary study of religion. In this way the rhetoric of objectivity, neutrality, and "science" can often shield and distract us from seeing the ongoing replication of a series of theological and Eurocentric assumptions about the world that lie embedded within post-Enlightenment secularism but that remain largely occluded from view (and therefore insulated from potential criticism) by the rhetorical force of the appeal to scientific progress and objectivity.

An additional problem with secularist accounts of the study of religion is that the desire for a demonstration of some measure of neutrality and objectivity in the development of a "science of religion" also tends to turn our attention away from other registers at work in scholarship within the field. Thus, all of the key thinkers in canonical histories of the field of the comparative study of religion—Müller, James, Durkheim, Weber, Eliade, and so on—also participated in another important intellectual legacy, one that is often neglected in mainstream accounts, namely, the role of the comparative study of religion as a forum for cross-cultural discussion, *civilizational* analysis, and *cultural critique*. In his classic overview of the history of the field, Jacques Waardenburg notes that scholarship within the study of religion, from its inception, has tended to oscillate between two extreme concerns:

> On the one hand there were those who, for lack of a better expression, may be called the idealists. They had a fundamentally positive appreciation of religion and they held certain ideas about its historical development and its crucial role in society and culture. These scholars were keen to discover the truths, norms and values by which other peoples had lived or were living, especially if such truths were neglected in the modern West. . . . The other extreme motivation was represented by those researchers who, on the contrary, were suspicious of religion as a phenomenon and denied the claims of truth not only of the different religions but also of the idealists' constructs. On the contrary, they were keen to discover the "real" factors operative behind religious behavior and representations.[28]

As Hans Kippenberg has argued, the emergence of the history of religions as an academic field in Europe and North America has been bound up with debates about how to evaluate and respond to processes of modernization and industrialization and diverse attempts by scholars to theorize Western "modernity."[29] Similarly, Wouter Hanegraaf reads the history of the "science of religions" not so much as a struggle between theology and a secular "religious studies" but rather as a struggle between two competing intellectual trends (Isaiah Berlin's Enlightenment and a "Counter-Enlightenment"), represented more significantly in terms of two different emotional responses to secular modernity—one positive, the other highly critical.[30]

Much of the classic scholarship within the field was concerned not just with defining a legitimate "science of religions" but also with defending and contesting various conceptions of what it is to be "modern." This goal of understanding "ourselves" through a comparative analysis of "the other" has been a vital element in debates about religion and "the religions" from its inception. The "other," whether conceived as "the Orient," "the archaic or primitive, or "the non-Western," has functioned as a mirror for Western scholars to debate, defend, and contest the conditions of Western modernity itself. This has played itself out in terms of different constituencies and debates, from the defense of the particularity and superiority of the West to counterdiscourses (often deeply resonating with Romanticist elements in Western culture, literature, and philosophy) that explore the "exotic Other" precisely as a means of finding that which is perceived to be lacking or lost in their own civilization. In this context we also see the rise of discourses about "religion" and "humanity" that search for commonalities as a theological exercise in peace-making and solidarity across cultures (the notion of the humanities more generally and "religious studies" more specifically as "bringing people together") or in mapping out "essential differences" between different cultures, religions, or groups (as in Samuel Huntington Jr.'s famous, but deeply flawed, "clash of civilizations" thesis).

Consider, for instance, the work of Émile Durkheim, deeply concerned by the challenges of anomie and the task of maintaining forms of social solidarity in the context of the rise of contemporary individualism in modern society. The author explains in *The Elementary Forms of the Religious Life* that his discussion of animism and totemism is fundamentally driven by the cultural project of understanding the modern: "like every positive science, it has as its object the explanation of some actual reality which is near to us."[31] Similarly, in his foreword to the *Protestant Ethic* (1920), Max Weber explains his interests by locating and describing himself as follows:

> A product of modern European civilization, studying any problem of universal history, is bound to ask himself to what combination of circumstances the fact should be attributed that in Western civilization, and in Western civilization only, cultural phenomena have appeared which (as we like to think) lie in a line of development having *universal* significance and value. Only in the West does science exist at a stage of development which we recognize to-day as valid.[32]

Whatever the specific ideological position taken by such classic scholars (and similar examples could be given for all of the major figures in the history of the comparative study of religion), an important part of the "cultural work" performed by such scholarship has been to provide an informed commentary—sometimes a defense, at other times a critique—of "the present"—that is, of the prevailing cultural forms, beliefs, and modes of behavior that characterize modern, Western civilization. This strand or emphasis within the field continues within contemporary scholarship, sometimes explicitly and sometimes in a largely undertheorized and unconscious manner. Thus we see enormous intellectual energy expended by some in defense of the modern European Enlightenment tradition and against "theological incursions" (Donald Wiebe, Bruce Lincoln), or anxieties about potentially disturbing aspects of modern Western society (such as Robert Bellah's Durkheimian concerns about individualism and contemporary "habits of the heart," or Carrette and King's critique of the rise of capitalist spiritualities—itself echoing Weber's concerns about the "iron cage" of modern capitalism).[33] In some scholars of religion we find an outright denunciation of modernity for its loss of a sense of "the sacred" (as in Mircea Eliade's concerns with the "terror of History"), in others a prescription of a return to a particular understanding of Christian tradition as a remedy for contemporary woes (as in John Milbank's "radical orthodoxy").

Despite recent hesitation to engage in comparative study in an age of uncertainty and suspicion about "grand narratives," the legacy of cultural critique and debate about the conditions, limits, and possibilities of prevailing models of modernity that has characterized scholarship in the study of religions highlights the ongoing social and intellectual relevance of such work as well as the ongoing significance of *comparative* work within the field in general. To follow Max Müller's comparativist axiom ("he who knows one, knows none"), I would argue that anyone seeking to engage in cultural critique or civilizational analysis (or what, in a slightly different vein, Ninian Smart used to call "worldview analysis") lacks a sufficiently broadened perspective from which to comment on modernity and its various forms if they make no recourse to *historical* and *non-Western* contexts since these serve as the primary sites of *difference* from which one may view dominant Western models of modernity in their historical and cultural specificity. In that sense there is a vitally important role for the comparative study of religion in the modern academy as the primary scholarly location for the exercise of a truly comparative humanities—that is, an informed, multivocal, and critical reflection on what it is to be human and what it might be to be modern.

NOTES

This is an expanded and updated version of an article that first appeared in the *Journal of Method and Theory in the Study of Religion* 25 (2013): 137–59. Reproduced with permission.

1. William Arnal, "Definition," in *Guide to the Study of Religion*, ed. Willi Braun and Russell T. McCutcheon (London: Bloomsbury Academic, 2000), 30.
2. Peter Berger and Thomas Lückmann, *The Social Construction of Reality* (New York: Doubleday, 1966).

3. See Andrew Abbott, *Chaos of Disciplines* (Chicago: University of Chicago Press, 2001). He provides a useful discussion of the history of "social constructionism" and the various shades of interpretation involved in this position.

4. See, for instance, Richard King, *Orientalism and Religion: India, Postcolonial Theory and the "Mystic East"* (London: Routledge, 1999); Arvind Mandair, *Religion and the Specter of the West* (New York: Columbia University Press, 2009).

5. Andrew Haas, *Poetics of Critique: Interdisciplinarity of Textuality* (Farnham, UK: Ashgate, 2003), 4–5.

6. Michel Foucault, *The Order of Things: An Archaeology of the Human Sciences* (New York: Pantheon, 1970).

7. Jonathan Z Smith, "Religion, Religions, Religious," in *Critical Terms for Religious Studies*, ed. Mark C. Taylor (Chicago: University of Chicago Press, 1998), 281–82.

8. Wendy Brown, *Edgework: Critical Essays on Knowledge and Politics* (Princeton: Princeton University Press, 2005), 81.

9. Indeed some would argue for a necessary recognition of the givenness of our own embodied materiality as the basis for both the limits and the grounds of possibility for any theory of social construction. For a useful discussion of this, see Manuel A. Vásquez, *More Than Belief: A Materialist Theory of Religion* (Oxford: Oxford University Press, 2011).

10. Brown, *Edgework*, 82.

11. Kocku von Stuckrad, "Discursive Study of Religion: From States of the Mind to Communication and Action," *Journal of Method and Theory in the Study of Religion* 15, no. 3 (January 2003): 268.

12. Ivan Strenski, ed., *Thinking About Religion: An Historical Introduction to Theories of Religion* (Hoboken: Blackwell, 2006), 1.

13. Jonathan Z. Smith, "A Twice-Told Tale: The History of the History of Religions' History," *Numen* 48, no. 2 (January 2001): 133.

14. Xenophanes, fragments 15 and 16, quoted in John Mansley Robinson, *An Introduction to Early Greek Philosophy* (Boston: Houghton Mifflin, 1968), 55.

15. Mādhava, *Sarvadarśanasamgraha*, trans. E. B. Cowell and A. E. Gough (Delihi: Motilal Banarsidass, 1996). Cited in the first chapter of the *Sarvadarshanasamgraha*, a fourteenth-century doxography composed by the Indian philosopher Mādhava in his discussion of the materialist school of thought (known as the Cārvakas).

16. Bruno Latour, *We Have Never Been Modern*, trans. Catherine Porter (Cambridge, Mass.: Harvard University Press, 1993).

17. Ernst Feil, ed., *On the Concept of Religion* (Binghamton, N.Y.: Global, 2000); Peter Harrison, *"Religion" and the Religions in the English Enlightenment* (Cambridge: Cambridge University Press, 2002); Timothy Fitzgerald, *The Ideology of Religious Studies* (Oxford: Oxford University Press, 2000); Timothy Fitzgerald, *Discourse on Civility and Barbarity: A Critical History of Religion and Related Categories* (Oxford: Oxford University Press, 2007); Timothy Fitzgerald, ed., *Religion and the Secular: Historical and Colonial Formations* (London: Equinox, 2007); Timothy Fitzgerald, *Religion and Politics in International Relations: The Modern Myth* (London: Continuum, 2011); King, *Orientalism and Religion*; Richard King, "Philosophy of Religion as Border Control: Globalization and the Decolonization of the 'Love of Wisdom' (*Philosophia*)," in *Postcolonial Philosophy of Religion*, ed. Purushottama Bilimoria and Andrew

Irvine (Berlin: Springer, 2010), 35–52; Richard King, "Imagining Religions in India: Colonialism and the Mapping of South Asian History and Culture," in *Secularism and Religion-Making*, ed. Arvind Mandair and Markus Dressler (Oxford: Oxford University Press, 2011), 37–61; Russell McCutcheon, *Manufacturing Religion: The Discourse on Sui Generis Religion and the Politics of Nostalgia* (Oxford: Oxford University Press, 1997); William T. Cavanaugh, *The Myth of Religious Violence: Secular Ideology and the Roots of Modern Conflict* (Oxford: Oxford University Press, 2009).

18. See, for instance, the recent works of Talal Asad, *Formations of the Secular: Christianity, Islam, Modernity* (Stanford: Stanford University Press, 2003); William Connolly, *Why I Am Not a Secularist* (Minneapolis: University of Minnesota Press, 2000); Charles Taylor, *A Secular Age* (Cambridge, Mass: Belknap Press of Harvard University Press, 2007); John Milbank, *Religion and Social Theory: Beyond Secular Reason*, 2nd ed. (Hoboken: Wiley, 2006); Fenella Cannell, "The Anthropology of Secularism," *Annual Review of Anthropology* 39 (2010): 85–100; Charles Hirschkind and David Scott, eds., *Powers of the Secular Modern: Talal Asad and His Interlocutors* (Stanford: Stanford University Press, 2006).

19. J. Samuel Preus, *Explaining Religion: Criticism and Theory from Bodin to Freud* (Atlanta: Scholars Press, 1996), xv–xvi.

20. David Chidester, *Savage Systems: Colonialism and Comparative Religion in Southern Africa* (Charlottesville: University of Virginia Press, 1996), xiii.

21. For more discussion on this, see King, "Imagining Religions in India."

22. Clifford Geertz, *Interpretation of Cultures* (New York: Basic Books, 1973), 5.

23. See King, "Philosophy of Religion."

24. Jeremy Carrette, *Religion and Critical Psychology: The Ethics of Not-Knowing in the Knowledge Economy* (London: Routledge, 2007).

25. On the pioneering work of missionaries, see Chidester, *Savage Systems*.

26. Tomoko Masuzawa, *The Invention of World Religions; Or, How European Universalism Was Preserved in the Language of Pluralism* (Chicago: University of Chicago Press, 2005), 69.

27. Urs Apps, *The Birth of Orientalism* (Philadelphia: University of Pennsylvania Press, 2010).

28. Jacques Waardenburg, *Classical Approaches to the Study of Religion: Aims, Methods and Theories of Research, Introduction and Anthology* (Berlin: Walter de Gruyter, 1973), viii–ix.

29. Hans G. Kippenberg, *Die Entdeckung der Religionsgeschichte: Religionswissenschaft und Moderne* (München: C. H. Beck, 1997).

30. Wouter J. Hanegraaf, "Defining Religion in Spite of History," in *The Pragmatics of Defining Religion: Contexts, Concepts and Contests*, ed. Jan Platvoet and Arie Molendijk (Leiden: E. J. Brill, 1999), 337–78.

31. Emile Durkheim, *The Elementary Forms of the Religious Life*, 2nd ed. (London: George Allen and Unwin, 1976), 1.

32. Max Weber, *The Protestant Ethic and the Spirit of Capitalism*, trans. Talcott Parsons (London: Routledge, 1992), 13.

33. Jeremy Carrette and Richard King, *Selling Spirituality: The Silent Takeover of Religion* (London: Routledge, 2005).

PART I

Historical Foundations/Genealogies

2

Nominalist "Judaism" and the Late-Ancient Invention of Religion

DANIEL BOYARIN

In the scholarly literature as it stands today, there are two almost directly opposed stances to the category "religion," especially religion as a form of identity. On the one hand, we find still many—if not most—writers writing as if "religion" were an essential category, something as essentially human as language or walking, and the only relevant question being what kind of religion any given human group or human individual "had" or adhered to, usually expressed in terms of his (*sic*) beliefs or faith (or, occasionally, whether it is possible for human beings to survive without any religion at all). On the other hand, we find too, although not quite as frequently, a recognition that religion is a historical and thus historicizable category, not an essence but a particular kind of institution, something like literature or science and thus no more universally applicable to all human societies than they are. Typically, for scholars holding this view, religion is not found before the Enlightenment. Thus Jonathan Z. Smith wrote famously that religion "is solely the creation of the scholar's study" and hence it "has no existence apart from the academy,"[1] while Talal Asad declared that there can be no "universal definition of religion . . . because the definition is itself the historical product of discursive processes."[2] Another slightly earlier Smith, Wilfred Cantwell, wrote famously, "I have not found any formulation of a named religion earlier than the nineteenth century."[3] I would suggest that the subject in question in these authors is not *religion* so much as the concept of *religions*, the thesis that there are different species of a genus, religion, disembedded from other practices and discourses that make up cultures (whether that genus is held to be a universal possession of humans or not), different answers to a question phrased: What religion are you; or, to what religion do you adhere?[4] This genus is usually defined as having gods, beliefs (= faith), and various practices of service to those gods. The claim made by Cantwell Smith is that this genus itself is only a product of modern analysis, whether ecclesiological or anthropological. My own researches and reflections have led me to a third position, one like the Smiths and Asad in that I, too, regard "religion" as a culturally specific, nonuniversal, historicizable category, but unlike them in that I consider "religion" to be an essential category of Christian self-understanding and of the constitution of Christianity itself and thus a product of late antiquity and not of modernity or the Enlightenment. I wish to propose here that while, indeed, "religion" may be the product of the scholar's study, it was a late-ancient scholar (or rather group of scholars) who created it and that consequently studying the genealogy of the historical product that is the definition of "religion" is, contra Asad, a study of late-antique (and not only modern) discursive processes. That episcopal scholar's study, then, had enormous impact on discursive processes that made a significant difference (for good or ill) in the lives of millions of human beings.

IOUDAISMOS AND *CHRISTIANISMOS* BEFORE RELIGION

One of the first questions to be asked in claiming that there was no religion before Christianity is the question of Judaism, since it is typically reckoned, both by lay folk and by scholars, that the religion, Christianity, grew out of and away from a prior religion, Judaism. Indeed, it almost seems counterintuitive to even think of denying such a proposition. Yet, to start thinking of such a denial, it seems highly significant that there is no word in premodern Jewish parlance that means "Judaism." When the term *Ioudaismos* appears in non-Christian Jewish writing—to my knowledge only in 2 Maccabees—it doesn't mean Judaism the religion but, as Steve Mason has demonstrated definitively, loyalty to Judaic practices in response to Hellenizing, behaving as a Greek.[5] After that, it is used as the name of the ascribed Jewish religion only by writers who do not identify themselves with and by that name at all, until, it would seem, well into the nineteenth century.[6] It might seem, then, that "Judaism" has not, until some time in modernity, existed at all, that whatever moderns might be tempted to abstract out, to disembed from the culture of Jews and call their religion, was not so disembedded and did not ascribe particular status by Jews until very recently.[7]

In order to even make sense of this claim, I need first to articulate the meaning or rather the possible meanings of the counterclaim, that there was such a thing as Judaism in the first century. I can think almost of no better place to start than with the realist/nominalist divide. This, as is well known, consists of an argument as to whether or not universals are "real" objects or only collections of particulars to which our minds/languages ascribe a name (hence nominalism). The argument in favor of the existence of Judaism would have to be a realist one, asserting that the practices, corporeal, verbal, and textual, that Jews engaged in were instances of a real universal, Judaism, and indeed that some of those practices were legitimately so and others not. I would assert that notwithstanding the position taken about such universals in the nonhuman world, such as "green," for human products or categories such as "religion" or "Judaism" *only* a nominalist position is tenable. Since there is no way of even characterizing the particulars that would enter into the category "Judaism," there is no possible universal in the world to which it could apply. Unless we seriously entertain the notion of ideas in the mind of God, we must recognize that there can be no thing "Judaism" until it is, in fact, a social fact and thus named as such by humans.[8] It is the case, moreover, that it only exists for those humans for which it is named. Universals of this sort only exist insofar as they are named as such by a group of humans within a human language. If "Judaism" had no name for ancient, late-ancient, and medieval Jews, there was no such object in the world for Jews. If others, but not Jews, have a name for it, it is an object in their sociocultural world, not that of Jews.

The lack of existence of the word (for Jews) is a more or less established fact. If there was no word for it in the ancient Jewish conceptual world, without the assumptions of a realist ontoepistemology there can have been no object, for the only conceptual objects that exist are names. On the other hand, as we shall see below, "Judaism" comes to be named by Christians as such very early on to serve Christian discursive needs. Quite paradoxically, "Judaism" thus exists for Christians but not for Jews until modernity. This point can be documented from the third century on, as we shall observe in the research of Mason.[9] There remains, to be sure, another possible, perhaps even plausible—maybe even unavoidable—use for the term "Judaism," namely, to name an object in *our* conceptual world that helps us make sense of an ancient world that is not ours and does not know of this object.[10] There just seem to be times when scholars (including me) need to abstract from the practices of the ethnic group, Jews, certain particular practices and group them as "religious" in order to make assertions about what was or was not the case, what was or was not possible within that abstraction, or to compare them to this or that set of practices by others. In this sense, "Judaism" is produced over and over in the scholars' studies, and at the very least must be defined by each scholar who is using the term, or else he or she is likely to simply fall into whatever the nineteenth century defined as "Judaism" and assume it as a "real" category that is certainly an anachronism for Jews of the first, second, third, or fourteenth century.

Reiterating my point above, I would insist that a category cannot exist in a culture unless it is named as such, since categories have no existence other than as a human practice of category making. To designate that object and make it clear that it is only a product of *my* study in my work, I will always enclose the word "Judaism" in quotation marks until I can find a better neologism, one that does not imply in any possible way a "real" object, an object that is historical or ontological, before the term comes to be used by Jews as a name for their own "religion." Taking my nominalism seriously, I insist that there is no category, "Judaism," in the world but that it is a name we give to an aggregate of objects that we sometimes find analytically convenient to group together. One frequently encounters at this point an alleged counterexample, namely, the ancient economy. Even though, it is suggested, ancient folks did not have a word that is equivalent in extension to our economy, we nevertheless study economies in antiquity. This alleged counterexample, however, only strengthens my claim insofar as it is clear, even now, that an economy is a purely discursive object and thus also the product of economics as a discourse, a product of the scholars' study just as much as I am claiming for "religion." Ancient economies are thus the product of economic histories. This does not devalue such discourses, but they must be recognized for what they are, analytical tools and not entities in the world. This has, perhaps, more consequences for the study of "religion" than for the study of economics.

In my usage, moreover, when I choose to use it, the scholarly term "Judaism" will designate all the expressions of that which we *now* name "religion": dealings with gods, sacralization of objects and people, beliefs and practices taken to be enjoined by sacralized people in the name of gods that are attested for the ethnic group called Jews in antiquity and the Middle Ages. Until and only when and where there is another name for people of the Jews who believe in Jesus, such people are also designated Jews in my work and their "religion" is, then, "Judaism," which only means that insofar as it makes sense at all to speak of Jews having a religion, there is no reason for Jewish followers of Jesus to be left out of it. Again, the caveat: "Judaism," when it refers to a time before it was named at all, is *only* a product of the modern scholar's study; after it was named as such by Christian writers, it is an element within a Christian system of culture and language, not within the Jews' at all; only when Jews start naming their own "religion" as "Judaism" could one say that a religion called "Judaism" exists for the Jews.

THE THIRD-CENTURY INVENTION OF "JUDAISM" BY TERTULLIAN

In his recent article, Steve Mason has decisively demonstrated that which other scholars (including me) have been bruiting about in the last few years, namely, that there is no "native" term that means "Judaism" in any language used by Jews of themselves until modernity, and, moreover, that the term *Ioudaioi* is rarely if ever used by people to refer to themselves as "Jews."[11] In a fascinating demonstration, Mason shows that the term *Ioudaismos/Iudaismus* only comes to mean "Judaism" in the mid-third century (with the Latin actually preceding the Greek), when the practices and beliefs of the Jews are separated polemically by Tertullian from their landedness, their history, "all that had made it compelling to Judaizers," and *Iudaismus* means now "an ossified system flash-frozen with the arrival of Jesus."[12] This is not, of course, a historically accurate representation of the state of the Jewish people at the time (after all, a certain heyday of Palestinian Jewish life, the time of the Mishna), as Mason shows eloquently. His explanation for Tertullian's new usage is equally convincing:

> By about 200 C.E. the Church was making headway as a popular movement, or a constellation of loosely related movements. In that atmosphere, in which internal and external self-definition remained a paramount concern, Tertullian and others felt strong enough to jettison earlier attempts at accommodating their faith to existing categories, especially efforts to portray themselves as Judaeans, and to see commitment to Christ as *sui generis*. Rather than admitting the definitive status of the established forms and responding defensively, they began to project the hybrid form of *Christanismus* on the other groups to facilitate polemical contrast (σύνκρισις). The most important group for Christian self-definition had always been the *Ioudaioi*, and so they

were the groups most conspicuously reduced to such treatment, which generated a static and systemic abstraction called Ἰουδαϊσμός/*Iudaismus*.[13]

The clear and critical conclusion to be drawn from this argument is consonant with my thesis in *Border Lines* that "Judaism" as the name of a "religion" is a product of Christianity in its attempts to establish a separate identity from something else that they call "Judaism," a project that begins no earlier than the mid-second century and only in certain quarters (notably Asia Minor), gathers strength in the third century, and comes to fruition in the processes before and following the Council of Nicaea.

Thus, bearing out in much greater detail some of the philological points that I made with reference to the semantics of *Ioudaismos* in context with *Hellenismos* and *Medismos*, Mason entirely supports the conclusion drawn there (without, however, mentioning it) that there is no "religion" (or even way of life) called *Ioudaismos* in antiquity.

Where I disagree with Mason is in his acceptance of Wilfred Cantwell Smith's conclusion that "early western civilization was on the verge, at the time of Lactantius [d. ca. 325 CE], of taking a decisive step in the formulation of an elaborate, comprehensive, philosophic concept of *religio*. However, it did not take it. The matter was virtually dropped, to lie dormant for a thousand years,"[14] to which Mason comments decisively: "It is only western modernity that knows this category of religion."[15] In the next section of my argument, I will present evidence that Smith (and thus Mason) is wrong on precisely this point, that a robust notion of "religion" both existed and was necessary for the existence of a transethnic Christendom. Mason himself has given us the material for a hypothesis. First of all, to sum up, he has shown how by the third century Christian writers are using both *Ioudaismos/Iudaismus* and *Christianismos/us* to refer to belief systems abstractable from cultural systems, kinship networks, and coterritoriality. Second, he has argued that the later meanings of "religion"—the allegedly modern ones—are prepared for in antiquity by the concept of a "philosophy" as a system of beliefs and practices "voluntarily" adopted and maintained (which is not to imply that not adopting or maintaining such a system didn't have negative consequences; "voluntary" here is not necessarily voluntary). These two elements—the latter one ignored by me till now to the detriment of my argument—I now strongly suggest led to a late-ancient development of something quite close to our modern notion of religion.

"NO RELIGION IN A SWAMP," OR, RELIGION IN A FIFTH-CENTURY SCHOLAR'S STUDY

In early Latin, *religio* certainly did not mean anything like what we mean when we say "religion." Carlin Barton writes:

> *Religio* is, like pudor, a whole system of emotional, psychological, and behavioral responses to bonds and obligations and their transgressions. It is part of the

internalized homeostatic systems by which the Romans governed themselves until the civil war period. It is in that period that *religio* becomes, in the works of Cicero, a disciplinary system, imposed by the state magistrates, authorized and reinforced by the gods. For Cicero, the threat to the state from the violence of the civil wars caused him to look for ways to reinforce the authority structures of the state. For him, more fear, more inhibition, more anxiety with regard to the gods and their spokesmen, the magistrates and priests, were necessary. So, while Cicero uses *religio* in all of its ancient usages, he often explicitly calls it the "cult of the [state authorized] gods" and makes the priests and magistrates to oversee and enforce that cult of which they are the most important part.

It was Cicero, and especially the book of Cicero's widely-read by Christians, De natura deorum,[16] that gave Minucius Felix, Lactantius and Augustine—and probably Tertullian and Ambrose as well, the word that would become "religion."[17]

In other words, some (at least) of the important semantic features of our usage of "religion" were already in place in Cicero's post–Civil War writing, and these were picked up and developed further by Latin Christian writers of the second to the fifth centuries. I, accordingly, find inconclusive Asad's declaration that "When the fifth-century bishop of Javols spread Christianity into the Auvergne, he found the peasants 'celebrating a three-day festival with offerings on the edge of a marsh.' . . . '*Nulla est religio in stagno*,' he said: 'There can be no religion in a swamp.' For medieval Christians, religion was not a universal phenomenon."[18] It may be that there can be no religion in a swamp, but this does imply that there can be religion other than Christianity, whether true or false. If he meant that there cannot be any Christianity in a swamp, he could have said that; I would suggest that he is implying rather that the practices of these swamp-dwellers don't even rise to the level of "paganism." In other words, I am suggesting that there are other criteria for the existence of "religion" as a concept than universality, criteria sufficient to mark the usage as very close, if not identical, to modern usage of the term. As David Chidester has amply demonstrated, Christians who explicitly did recognize the existence of other religions, "Judaism, Islam, and Paganism," nevertheless were quite capable as late as the beginning of the nineteenth century of denying that the indigenes of southern Africa had any religion at all, even an idolatrous one.[19] As he shows there, these early "ethnographers" would observe various ceremonies but insist that they were not "religion," and by this they did *not* mean that they were not Christian.[20] The concept of "religion" is not dependent, as is sometimes claimed, on the Enlightenment assumption that "religion" is simply a natural faculty of all human groups, that all humans have "religion." Some humans may have "religion," some may not, but "religion" in its modern sense of an organized and authorized system of beliefs and practices about gods not essentially tied to a particular ethnos or place already existed in Christian late antiquity.

By the end of the fourth century and in the first quarter of the fifth century, we can find several texts attesting how Christianity's new notion of self-definition via "religious" alliance was gradually replacing self-definition via kinship and land.[21]

These texts, belonging to very different genres, indeed to entirely different spheres of discourse—heresiology, historiography, and law—can nevertheless be read as symptoms of an epistemic shift of great importance. As Andrew Jacobs describes the discourse of the late fourth and early fifth centuries, "Certainly this universe of discourses engendered different means of establishing normativity: the disciplinary practices of Roman law, for instance, operated in a manner quite distinct from the intellectual inculcation of historiography or the ritualized enactment of ortho-doxy. Nevertheless, the common goal of this discursive universe was the reorgani-zation of significant aspects of life under a single, totalized, imperial Christian rubric."[22]

This construction of "Christianness" primarily involved the invention of *Chris-tianity* as a "religion," disembedded, in Seth Schwartz's words, from other cultural practices and identifying markers.[23] Susanna Elm shows that late-fourth-century Christians were already committed to the idea of "religions" in something very much like the modern sense and even understood quite well the difference between reli-gious definition and other modes of identity formation. She finds evidence for this claim as early as Julian, "the Apostate" who formed his "religion," Hellenism, in the 360s on the model of Christianity,[24] but there is evidence for this concept going back at least as far as Eusebius in the first half of the century.[25] Julian insists that only one who believes in "Hellenism" can understand it and teach it, as justifica-tion for his denial of the right to teach philosophy to Christian teachers. Vasiliki Limberis also emphasizes how, for all Julian's hatred of Christianity, his notion of religion and religious identity has been deeply structured by the model of Christi-anity.[26] As Limberis puts it: "Christians had never been barred from letters. Not only was this an effective political tool to stymie Christians, it had the remarkable effect of inventing a new religion and religious identity for people in the Roman empire."[27] I would slightly modify Limberis's formulation by noting that Julian did not so much invent a new religion as participate in the invention of a new notion of "religion" as a category, as a modality of identity formation, and as a regime of power/knowledge. She writes: "In particular, Julian echoes Christianity's *modus operandi* by turn-ing pagan practices into a formal institution that one must join."[28]

Although Julian seems never to have used any word that parallels our "religion," his usage of *Hellenismos*, in its contexts, certainly seems to add up to that meaning. At any rate, the great fourth-century Cappadocian theologian Gregory Nazianzen so understood him and retorted to Julian:

> But I am obliged to speak again about the word . . . Hellenism[:] to what does the word apply, what does one mean by it? . . . Do you want to pretend that Hellenism means a threskeia, or, and the evidence seems to point that way, does it mean a people, and the language invented by this nation. . . . If Hellenism is a threskeia, show us from which place and what priests it has received its rules. . . . Because the fact that the same people use the Greek language who also profess Greek religion does not mean that the words belong therefore to the threskeia, and that we therefore are naturally excluded from using them. This is not a logical conclusion, and does not agree with your own

logicians. Simply because two realities encounter each other does not mean that they are confluent, i.e. identical.[29]

I have modified Elm's translations here, substituting *threskeia* for the printed "religion," so as not to prejudice the case, but it seems clearly correct to translate *threskeia* as "religion" in something quite close to its modern meanings. Gregory has some sort of definition of an object that comes very close to the modern usage of the concept, very like the modern concept of "religion" in mind here, distinct from and in binary semiotic opposition to *ethnos*, contra the commonplace that such definitions are an early modern product.[30] In other words, it seems fair enough to consider his term *threskeia* as the semantic equivalent, or very close to that, of "religion" as it functions in our semantic systems. "Religion," that nominalistic category, named in both Greek and Latin, had been invented by the fourth century at the latest by Christians, enabling them to see and identify a "religion" called "Judaism" within their semantic system as well, but not yet within the semantic system of the Jews themselves. Since the term *threskeia* is quite rare in Greek prior to this time,[31] I suggest tentatively that it is a calque on the Latin *religio* in its latter meaning. Whether or not this is the case, I suggest that the catachresis in the language marks a catachresis in the (conceptual) world, an event that we might be tempted to regard as the invention of "religion."

Gregory knew precisely "what kinds of affirmation, of meaning, must be identified with practice in order for it to qualify as religion":[32] it must have received its rules from some place (that is, some book?—Gregory surely doesn't mean geographical locations, for then he would be playing into Julian's hands) and some priests. He separates the language, Greek, from the religion of the Greeks and claims that it, as well as many cultural practices associated with it, including philosophy, now effectively secularized, is not tied to the *threskeia* itself. In my view, this explicit definition makes it eminently defensible to translate the Greek term by our modern "religion," remembering that, for instance, there is not as yet, and won't be for over a millennium, a word in Hebrew with any such meaning.[33] While Gregory's definition of "religion" is, of course, somewhat different from the Enlightenment Protestant one (a difference oddly homologous to the difference between Catholicism and Protestantism between rules of priests and a "faith"), he nevertheless clearly has a notion of religion as an idea that can be abstracted from any particular manifestation of it; for Gregory, different peoples have different "religions" (Christianity and Hellenism), and some folks have none. Once again, we see his Greek approximating the later meanings of the Latin *religio*.

Gregory affords a definition of "religion" as clear as that of later comparatists (although quite different from them). A "religion" is something that has priests, rites, rules, and sacrifices. It is absolutely clear, moreover, from Gregory's discourse that, for this Christian, "the emergence of religion as a discrete category of human experience—religion's *disembedding*," in Seth Schwartz's terms[34]—has taken place fully and finally, as he explicitly separates religion from ethnicity and language. In Julian, in contrast, on the one hand, we find "Hellenism" described as something very like a modern religion, but, on the other hand, his tight association of his "Hellenism" with all of Hellenic practice is more akin to ancient national cults than to latter-day "religion." As Schwartz explicitly writes, "religion" is *not* a dependent variable of *ethnos*; indeed, almost the opposite is the case.[35] A corollary of this is that language itself shifted its function as identity marker.

As Claudine Dauphin has argued, by the fifth century linguistic identity was tied to religious affiliation and identity, and not to geographic or genealogical identification.[36] The fullest expression of this conceptual shift may be located in the heresiology of Epiphanius (fl. early fifth century), although his terminology is not entirely clear. For him, not only "Hellenism" and "Judaism" but also "Scythianism" and even "Barbarianism" are no longer the names of ethnic entities[37] but of "heresies," that is, "religions" other than orthodox Christianity.[38] Since Epiphanius's usage of the term "heresy" is quite idiosyncratic—the term is never applied to "Hellenism" elsewhere to the best of my knowledge—apparently what he means by "heresies" is often what other Greek writers of his time, such as Eusebius,[39] call *threskeiai* (and even Epiphanius uses this term elsewhere too): "<Hellenism originated with Egyptians, Babylonians and Phrygians>, and it now confused <men's> ways."[40] It is important to see that Epiphanius's comment is a transformation of a verse from the Pauline literature, as he himself informs us.[41] In Colossians 3:11 we find, "Here there cannot be Greek and Jew, circumcised and uncircumcised, barbarian, Scythian, slave, free man, but Christ is all, and in all." This is a lovely index of the semantic shift. For pseudo-Paul, these designations are obviously the names not of "religious" formations but of various ethnic and cultural and even social groupings,[42] whereas for Epiphanius they are the names of "heresies," by which he means groups divided and constituted by "religious"—in the sense that I have defined that word above—differences fully disembedded from ethnicities: How, otherwise, could the "heresy" called "Hellenism" have originated with the Egyptians?[43] Astonishingly, Epiphanius's "Hellenismos" seems to have nothing to do with the Greeks; it is Epiphanius's name for what other writers would call "paganism." Epiphanius, not surprisingly, defines "the topic of the Jews' religion [*threskeian*]" as "the subject of their beliefs."[44] For Epiphanius, as for Gregory, a major category (if not the only one) for dividing human beings into groups is "the subject of their beliefs," hence the power/knowledge regime of what we call, following Latin Christian usage, "religion."

Whatever the terminological issues involved, Epiphanius's meaning seems quite clear from context. The system of identities had been completely transformed during the period extending from the first to the fifth centuries. The systemic change resulting in "religious" difference as a modality of identity that began, I would suggest, with the heresiological work of Christians such as Justin Martyr works itself out through the fourth century and is closely intertwined with the triumph of orthodoxy. Orthodoxy thus not only is a discourse for the production of difference within, but functions as a category to make and mark the border between Christianity and its proximate, invented, other "religions," particularly a "Judaism" that it is too inventing.

ORTHODOXY AMONG THE RABBIS

It could be maintained, along with other scholars, that Christianity developed the notion of "orthodoxy" simply as a technology for defining what it was in a world in which such a thing, disembedded religion, had not existed before. I am using "orthodoxy" in the sense referred to by Rowan Williams when he wrote, " 'Orthodoxy' is a way that a 'religion,' separated from the locativity of ethnic or geocultural self-definition as Christianity was, asks itself: '[H]ow, if at all, is one to identify the 'centre' of [our] religious tradition? At what point and why do we start speaking about 'a' religion?' "[45]

Given that, as Williams argues, the notion of orthodoxy is almost exclusively significant for the development of a transethnic "religion" as a mode of identification, I argued in *Border Lines* that the apparent development of a similarly defined "Judaism" at the time of the Mishna, namely, rabbinic Judaism, was a product of the encounter with Christian orthodoxy. This part of my argument in that book came, rightly so, under considerable fire.[46] A much more broadly based historical contextualization of the development of rabbinic orthodoxy is necessary. The evidence for the development of a virtual orthodoxy as definitional for rabbinic Judaism, that is, the representation of Judaism as a nascent orthodoxy in the Mishna, stands up in my view and I will not rehearse it here, nor yet the exclusion of the *minim* (believers in a binitarian godhead) from that community of the orthodox. I would no longer, however, see this as a product of the impact of Christian developments (such as those of Justin and Irenaeus). On the other hand, the contrary thesis, defended by Alain Le Boulluec, that the notion of orthodoxy developed in Christian circles owing to the impact of the rabbinic developments, seems to me (still) equally untenable and based on outmoded assumptions about the historical fealty of rabbinic accounts of events long before their times. For one thing, as pointed out correctly by my critics, the rabbinic Judaism and earliest orthodox Christianity are way too close in time (and Christianity is still so insignificant institutionally) for *either* to have directly caused the development in the other. I would suggest now rather that we see both in such scholarly Christian writers as Justin and Irenaeus and in the equally scholarly producers of the Mishna the impact of the philosophical schools and their own developing notions of orthodoxy and authority.[47]

The correct generalization seems now to me that while for the nascent Church the use of such a model and the nascent notion of "heresy" that it offered was necessary for Christian self-definition for the reasons given by both Rowan Williams and Mason, since "Judaism" was supported by a vigorous and ongoing ethnic identity, nascent notions of heresy and orthodoxy were never crucial for rabbinic self-definition and ultimately fell into desuetude, as argued in my book.

I remain committed, and find nothing to contradict, my claim that the definition of "Judaism" as a religion served ongoing Christian discursive and polemical needs that were manifested in such documents as the Theodosian Code as well as some late-ancient Christian narratives of the conversion of Jews.[48] That Christian identification of Judaism as a religion has had ongoing and complex effects on Jewish self-definition then, from late antiquity until modernity. In the "definitive" formulation of rabbinic Judaism in the Babylonian Talmud, the rabbis rejected this option, proposing instead a distinct ecclesiological principle: "An Israelite, even if he [*sic*] sins, remains an Israelite [one remains a part of a Jewish or Israelite people whether or not one adheres to the Torah, subscribes to its major precepts, or affiliates with the community]." Whatever its original meaning, this sentence was understood throughout classical rabbinic Judaism as indicating that one cannot cease to be a Jew even via apostasy.[49] The historical layering of these two ideologies and even self-definitions by the rabbis themselves of what it is that constitutes an Israel and an Israelite provide for the creative ambivalence in the status of Judaism today. This thesis should not in any way, shape, or form be construed as a claim for greater tolerance of diversity among Jews than Christians.[50]

THE CHRISTIAN INVENTION OF RELIGION

Hegemonic Christian discourse also produced Judaism (and paganism, for example, that of Julian) as other religions precisely in order to cordon off Christianity, in a purification and crystallization of its essence as a bounded entity. Julian cleverly reverses this procedure and turns it against Christianity. In at least one reading of Julian's "Against the Galileans," the point of that work is to *reinstate* a binary opposition between Greek and Jew, Hellenism and Judaism, by inscribing Christianity as a hybrid. Eusebius's claim that Christianity is a religion halfway between Judaism and Hellenism now constitutes an argument that Christianity is a monstrous hybrid, a mooncalf: "For if any man should wish to examine into the truth concerning you, he will find that your impiety is compounded of the rashness of the Jews and the indifference and vulgarity of the Gentiles. For from both sides you have drawn what is by no means their best but their inferior teaching, and so have made for yourselves a border of wickedness."[51] Julian further writes: "It is worth while . . . to compare what is said about the divine among the Hellenes and Hebrews; and finally to enquire of those who are neither Hellenes nor Jews, but belong to the sect of the Galileans."[52] Julian, as dedicated as any Christian orthodox writer to policing borderlines, bitterly reproaches the "Galileans" for contending that they are Israelites and argues that they are no such thing—they are neither Jews nor Greeks but impure hybrids.[53] Here Julian sounds very much like Jerome when the latter declares that those who think they are both Jews and Christians are neither, or Epiphanius when he refers to the Ebionites as "nothing." This would make Julian's project structurally identical to the projects of the Christian heresiologists who, at about the same time, were rendering Christianity and Judaism in their "orthodox" forms the pure terms of a binary opposition, with the "Judaizing" Christians, the hybrids who must be excluded from the semiotic system, being "monsters." I suggest, then, a deeper explanation of Julian's insistence that you cannot mix Hellenism with Christianity. It is not only that Hellenism and Christianity are separate religions that, by definition, cannot be mixed with each other, but even more that Christianity is always already (if you will) an admixture, a syncretism. Julian wants to reinstate the binary of Jew and Greek. He provides, therefore, another instance of the discursive form that I am arguing for in the Christian texts of his time, a horror of supposed hybrids. To recapitulate, in Julian's very formation of *Hellenism* (or should I say *Hellenicity*?)[54] as a religious difference, he mirrors the efforts of the orthodox churchmen. This is another instantiation of the point made above by Limberis.[55] While he was protecting the borders between *Hellenism* and *Judaism* by excluding *Christianity* as a hybrid, Julian, it seems, was, unbeknown to himself, smuggling some Christian ideas in his very attempt to outlaw Christianity.

This interpretation adds something to that of Jacobs, who writes that

> the Christian reader could come to understand through the representation of the known and dominated figure of the Jew that Christians have power. The production of naturalized and totalized forms of Christian knowledge, significantly oriented around the paradigmatically known figure of the Palestinian Jew, delineated the first crude outlines of imperial Christian power. . . . The Jew emerges throughout the fourth century, the "Age of Constantine," as a malleable "shadow-other" of the Christian-in-power; in the totality of the new Christian worldview, power from the Christian is articulated though imperial power over the Jew of the "frontier zone" of the holy land.[56]

I am suggesting that the heretic can also be read as a proximate other, producing a hierarchical space between the Christian and the Jew. This point is at least partially anticipated by Jacobs himself when he writes that "Jews exist as the paradigmatic 'to-be-known' in the overwhelming project of conceptualizing the 'all in all' of orthodoxy. This comes out most clearly in the [Epiphanian] accounts of 'Jewish-Christian' heresies."[57] One way of spinning this would be to see heresiology as central to the production of Judaism as the "pure other" of Christian orthodoxy, while the other way of interpreting it would be to see Judaism as essential to the production of orthodoxy over against heresy. My point is that both of these moments in an oscillating analysis are equally important and valid. Seen in this light, orthodoxy itself, orthodoxy as an idea, as a regime (as opposed to any particular orthodox position), is not only or even primarily a mode for the oppression and exclusion of people called "heretics"—particularly as so many of these latter seem to be fictive—but essential to the very formation of Christianity as religion, qua religion, as an entity and form of identification that is autonomous of particular ethnicities, histories, genealogy, and language. In this sense, perhaps, "Judaism" is never—until modern times— a religion, except perhaps as the "other" of Christianity.

It may then be suggested, in conclusion, that Cantwell Smith was correct in not discerning any named "religion" before the nineteenth century, with the proviso that this is only true of groupings other than Christianity.[58] The Christian invention of Judaism in the third century and the confident talk of "religion" in both Latin and its hypothesized Greek equivalents in the fourth century by ecclesiastical writers would suggest that the notion itself, however, has much more ancient historical sources within Christian writing than are acknowledged by Cantwell Smith, Talal Asad, or J. Z. Smith.

NOTES

This paper was originally written and submitted in 2011. To be sure in 2014, I made certain revisions but in some ways it reflects my thinking of five years ago. I mention this simply because it will appear, insha'allah, at about the same time as work that goes in a somewhat different (albeit not totally incompatible) direction. The critical aspect about "Judaism" is now being developed into a book—*Judaism: A Genealogy*—that I am currently writing for Rutgers University Press for the Keywords in Jewish Studies series. The argument about the fifth century and Christianity will need the most rethinking. On the one hand, it is clear to me that something very important happened at that time; it is less clear to me now that it ought to be called the invention of religion. Much of my new thought is the product of the joint work undertaken in the last five years on *Imagine No Religion* with Carlin A. Barton (2016) for Fordham University Press. Jonathan Boyarin made some critical interventions as well, for which I thank him as always. It is clear to me that there remain unsolved, and as yet unsolvable (by me), terminological and conceptual problems, and I invite critical and suggestive response. Finally, I would like to thank Ruth Haber, who has been an indispensable research assistant for the last five years, as she moves on now to bigger and better things.

1. Jonathan Z. Smith, *Imagining Religion: From Babylon to Jonestown* (Chicago: University of Chicago Press, 1982), 11.
2. Talal Asad, *Genealogies of Religion: Discipline and Reasons of Power in Christianity and Islam* (Baltimore: Johns Hopkins University Press, 1993), 29. For discussion of these matters (and the placement of these two quotations side by side), see Elliot R. Wolfson, "Structure, Innovation, and Diremptive Temporality: The Use of Models to Study Continuity and Discontinuity in Kabbalistic Tradition," *Journal for the Study of Religions and Ideologies* 6, no. 18 (2007): 148.
3. Wilfred Cantwell Smith, *The Meaning and End of Religion* (London: SPCK, 1978), 61.
4. Cf. Steve Mason, "Jews, Judaeans, Judaizing, Judaism: Problems of Categorization in Ancient History," *Journal for the Study of Judaism* 38, no. 4–5 (2007): 482.
5. Ibid., 465–68.
6. John J. Collins, "Cult and Culture: The Limits of Hellenization in Judea," in *Hellenism in the Land of Israel*, ed. John J. Collins and Gregory Sterling (Notre Dame: University of Notre Dame, 2000), 39. The medieval *Yahadut* does not mean "Judaism" but the state of being Jewish, as I shall show, *Deo volonte*, in the book.
7. The reason that the term "Jews" is not scare-quoted in this project at any rate is that it certainly is an ancient category defined *then* by a group in which there was mutual recognition of identity. Thus one could be a "bad" Jew in the eyes of another without ceasing to be recognized as a Jew.
8. Note that this does not imply that particulars do not or did not exist. People obviously had intercourse before there was sexuality, and there is no reason to believe that people who did not have the same names for emotions did not feel them substantially as we do.
9. Mason, "Jews."
10. I write this paragraph in the wake of Seth Schwartz, as mentioned earlier.
11. Mason, "Jews."
12. Ibid., 473.

13. Ibid., 476.

14. Smith, *The Meaning and End of Religion*, 488.

15. Mason, "Jews," 489.

16. For the popularity of *De natura deorum* among Christians such as Tertullian, Minucius Felix, Lactantius, Arnobius, and Augustine, see Arthur Stanley Pease, introduction to *M. Tulli Ciceronis de natura deorum*, by Cicero (New York: Harvard University Press, 1979), 1:52–57; H. Bouillard, "La formation du concept de religion en Occident," in *Humanisme et Foi Chretienne: Melange scientifiques de Centenaire de l'Institut Catholique de Paris*, ed. C. Kannengiesser and Y. Marchasson (Paris: Editions Beauchsene, 1976), 453; Andrew Dyck, introduction to *De natura deorum: Book I*, by Cicero (Cambridge: Cambridge University Press, 2003), 14–15.

17. Personal communication, May 25, 2011.

18. Asad, *Genealogies*, 45.

19. David Chidester, *Savage Systems: Colonialism and Comparative Religion in Southern Africa* (Charlottesville: University Press of Virginia, 1996).

20. This point contradicts one observation frequently made of the supposed Enlightenment notion of "religion," to wit, that it assumes religion as a universal.

21. Hal A. Drake, "Lambs Into Lions: Explaining Early Christian Intolerance," *Past and Present* 153 (1996): 25. Drake's theory is germane to the hypothesis of this article. Limberis argues that for second-generation Christians this process was reversed in Vasiliki Limberis, "'Religion' as the Cipher for Identity: The Cases of Emperor Julian, Libanius, and Gregory Nazianzus," *Harvard Theological Review* 93, no. 4 (2000): 377. I am not entirely persuaded by her argument on this point but do not wish to entirely disallow it, either. One way of thinking about it would be to see who is left out of "us." In both the earlier rabbinic and orthodox Christian formations, exemplified by Nazianzen below, there are those tied to us by tradition, kinship, and land who are, nevertheless, not us; they are heretics. See also Rosemary Radford Ruether, "Judaism and Christianity: Two Fourth-Century Religions," *Sciences Religieuses/Studies in Religion* 2 (1972): 1–10; and Jacob Neusner, *Judaism and Christianity in the Age of Constantine: History, Messiah, Israel, and the Initial Confrontation* (Chicago: University of Chicago Press, 1987), who take related positions.

22. Andrew S. Jacobs, "The Imperial Construction of the Jew in the Early Christian Holy Land" (PhD diss., Duke University, 2001), 28–29. See also Jonathan Boyarin, *The Unconverted Self: Jews, Indians, and the Identity of Christian Europe* (Chicago: University of Chicago Press, 2009), 59.

23. Seth Schwartz, *Imperialism and Jewish Society from 200 B.C.E. to 640 C.E.* (Princeton: Princeton University Press, 2001), 179.

24. Susanna Elm, "Orthodoxy and the True Philosophical Life: Julian and Gregory of Nazianzus," *Studia Patristica* 37 (2001): 79–80. See also Limberis, "Cipher," 383.

25. The Eusebian material is complex and will require a separate treatment of its own in the monograph for which this is an exploratory drill.

26. Limberis, "Cipher," 378, 382, and throughout. This is true, as well, for those fourth-century Roman aristocrats who designed themselves "pagans."

27. Ibid., 386.

28. Ibid., 399. I accept Limberis's assent to Asad's critique of Geertz, but nevertheless see much more continuity and a shift toward something that could be called "religion" in the modern sense taking place precisely in these fourth-century echoes of Christianity.

29. Oration 4.5 and 96–109, quoted in Elm, "Orthodoxy and the True Philosophical Life." See also Limberis, "Cipher," 395.

30. Cf., for example, Asad, *Genealogies*, 40–41.

31. According to Liddell-Scott, less than one hundred total occurrences, of which about 90 percent are in one writer, Josephus. A full study of the semantics of this term in Josephus is being carried out for the larger project.

32. Asad, *Genealogies*, 45.

33. In future work I will be treating the semantics of Hebrew *dat* and *yahadut* and showing, *Deo volente*, that the first does not mean "religion," nor the second "Judaism."

34. Schwartz, *Jewish Society*, 179.

35. This point is not contradicted in any way by Denise Kimber Buell, "Race and Universalism in Early Christianity," *Journal of Early Christian Studies* 10, no. 4 (Winter 2002): 429–68. Buell's compelling analysis of second- and third-century texts indicates early Christianity's struggle to find a mode of identity, with notions of Christianness as a new ethnos/genos being very prevalent indeed. However, Buell herself marks a shift that takes place in the fourth century: "Beginning in the fourth century, ethnic reasoning serves to naturalize the equation of Christianness with gentileness, or Romanness, in part through the oppositional construction of non-Jewish non-Christians as 'pagans'" (Buell, "Race," 465). I would argue, however, that such a classification marks the undoing of an "ethno/racial" definition of Christianness, insofar as in general throughout the fourth century "pagans" were understood to be just as Roman as Christians. "Pagan" surely did not constitute an ethnic or racial designation but a religious one. Even in the earlier writings considered by Buell, where Christianity is defined as an ethnos or a genos, these terms are the dependent variable of "faith." This is decidedly not the case for Jews much before the Christian era or for Judaism since the early middle ages. Buell argues elegantly that Christian universalism should not be seen in opposition to or against the background of a putative Jewish particularism: "Seeing that early Christians defined themselves in and through race requires us to dismantle an oppositional definition of Christianness and Jewishness on the basis of race or ethnicity. Doing so may also contribute to resisting periodizations that mark an early and decisive split between Christianities and Judaisms. Not only do many early Christians define themselves as a people, even competing for the same name—Israel—but early Christians adapt and appropriate existing forms of Jewish universalism in formulating their own universalizing strategies in the Roman period. . . . Since ethnic reasoning also resonates with non-Jewish cultural practices of self-definition, it offers an analytic point of entry that treats both Jewish and non-Jewish frames of reference as integrally part of Christian self-definition, not as its 'background'" (Buell, "Race," 467). At the same time, notwithstanding Buell's reference to Isaiah as "emphasizing attachment to Yahweh as defining membership in Israel," I would suggest that the notion of "orthodoxy" as defining membership in the Christian community and the feints in that direction in rabbinic literature that define orthodoxy as the criterion for membership in Israel represent a "new thing." That new thing would ultimately be called "religion."

36. Claudine Dauphin, *La Palestine byzantine: Peuplement et populations* (Oxford: Archaeo-press, 1998), 133–55.

37. Which is not, of course, to claim that the notion of ethnic identity is a stable and fixed one, either. See Jonathan M. Hall, *Ethnic Identity in Greek Antiquity* (Cambridge: Cambridge University Press, 1997).

38. Epiphanius of Salamis, *The Panarion of Epiphanius of Salamis, Book I, Sections 1–46*, trans. Frank Williams (Leiden: Brill, 1987), 16–50. Cf., however, Eusebius, *Demonstratio evangelica* 1.2.1; Eusebius, *The Proof of the Gospel*, ed. and trans. W. J. Ferrar (London: SPCK, 1920), 9.

39. I will treat Eusebius at length, *Deo volente*, in the fuller work for which this essay is a preliminary study.

40. Epiphanius, *Panarion*, 17–18; David Frankfurter, *Religion in Roman Egypt: Assimilation and Resistance* (Princeton: Princeton University Press, 1998), 79. In another part of the Christian world, Frankfurter points out, for the fifth-century Coptic abbot Shenoute "*Hēllēne* did not carry the sense of ethnically 'Greek' and therefore different from 'Egyptian,' but simply 'pagan'—'not Christian.'" In Syriac, as well, "Aramean" is no longer the designation of an ethnic or linguistic group but simply means what others call "pagan."

41. Epiphanius, *Panarion*, 9.

42. For a highly salient and crystal clear delineation of these terms, "ethnic" and "cultural," see Jonathan M. Hall, *Hellenicity: Between Ethnicity and Culture* (Chicago: University of Chicago Press, 2002), 9–19.

43. See discussion in Andrew S. Jacobs, *Remains of the Jews: The Holy Land and Christian Empire in Late Antiquity* (Stanford: Stanford University Press, 2004), 45–46; Aline Pourkier, *L'hérésiologie chez Épiphane de Salamine* (Paris: Editions Beauchesne, 1992), 85–87; and Frank Young, "Did Epiphanius Know What He Meant by 'Heresy?,'" *Studia Patristica* 17, no. 1 (1982): 199–205. As has been noted by previous scholars, for Epiphanius "heresy" is a much more capacious and even baggy-monster category than for most writers.

44. Epiphanius, *Panarion*, 24. "But to keep from getting side-tracked, bypassing the topic of the Jews' religion, and failing to touch on the subject of their beliefs, I shall give a few examples of them."

45. Rowan Williams, "Does It Make Sense to Speak of Pre-Nicene Orthodoxy?," in *The Making of Orthodoxy: Essays in Honour of Henry Chadwick*, ed. Rowan Williams (Cambridge: Cambridge University Press, 1989), 3.

46. Daniel Boyarin, *Border Lines: The Partition of Judaeo-Christianity* (Philadelphia: University of Pennsylvania Press, 2004). The following paragraphs represent a *revision* of my thesis in *Border Lines*, a revision occasioned by some very sharp and pointed critique by the respondents to the book in a symposium at the AAR, later published as a special forum in the journal *Henoch*: Virginia Burrus et al., "Boyarin's Work: A Critical Assessment," *Henoch* 28 (2006): 7–30. As a result of this criticism, as well as some other, I came to realize two great shortcomings in the argument of that book: (1) I had not in any way properly assessed or even really thought about the non-Christian, non-Jewish environment of the invention of "religion"; (2) insofar as I had done so, my statements about it were merely contradictory to my general thesis. In these few paragraphs here, I hope to sketch out a more satisfactory outline for a synthesis.

47. Élie Bikerman, "La chaîne de la tradition pharisienne," *Revue biblique* 59, no. 1 (1952): 44–54; John Glucker, *Antiochus and the Late Academy* (Göttingen: Vandenhoeck und Ruprecht, 1978); Albert I. Baumgarten, "The Pharisaic *Paradosis*," *Harvard Theological Review* 80 (1987): 63–77; all remain crucial for this point.

48. Daniel Boyarin, "The Christian Invention of Judaism: The Theodosian Empire and the Rabbinic Refusal of Religion," *Representations* 85 (2004): 21–57.

49. For instance, a Jew who "converts" to another religion does not have to convert back but only repent his or her sins in order to be accepted in the community again.

50. The claim that orthodoxy (as the necessary concomitant of "religion") was never meant, and should not be read, as a disparagement of Christianity. (As Joel Marcus most starkly represented it in an oral presentation: the Christians developed a disease, the Jews caught it for a while, then shook it off.) "Orthodoxy" is to be taken as neutral a term as "church" or "bishop" or "Jewish People," no more, no less and not the name for an intrinsically evil institution.

51. Julian, "Against the Galileans," in *The Works of the Emperor Julian*, trans. W. C. F. Wright (London: Heinemann Macmillan, 1913), 389.

52. Ibid., 319–21.

53. Ibid., 393–95. Fascinatingly, this perspective gives us another way of understanding Julian's intention to allow the Temple in Jerusalem to be rebuilt. A large part of his polemic consists, as we have seen, of charges that Christians are nothing, since they have abandoned Hellenism but not become Jews, given that they do not follow the Torah. He imagines a Christian answering him that the Jews, too, do not sacrifice as they are enjoined (ibid., 405–7). What better way to refute this Christian counterclaim and demonstrate that the only reason that Jews do not sacrifice is that they have no Temple than to help them rebuild their Temple and reinstitute the sacrifices?

54. Hall, *Hellenicity*, xix.

55. Julian, "Against the Galileans," 315. Wright, the translator, points out that Julian has Christlike figures in his own theology.

56. Jacobs, *Remains*, 53–54.

57. Jacobs, "Imperial Construction," 57.

58. Another term that needs careful semantic historicization in this context.

3

Bible/Religion/Critique

WARD BLANTON AND YVONNE SHERWOOD

If we were to imagine a joke or parable beginning with a chance encounter be-tween a religion scholar and a biblical scholar, then, in all likelihood, the punch line or lesson would be directed at the biblical scholar. In these late modern days, it is the biblical scholar who is on the back foot. She is likely to be seen as the red-faced exemplar of a parochially Protestant Christian understanding of religion—obsessed with origins and centered on scriptures. What starker incarnation of the sins of "scripturalism" than the anachronistic biblical scholar? One wonders whether her purpose is thus to remind us of a more hubristic age when we exported Protes-tant notions of religion and forced other religions to have "Bibles." Perhaps biblical scholars linger as signs of past sins or as an encouragement to repent again.

Not so long ago, the alternative to the American Society of Biblical Literature was not the American Academy of Religion but its forerunner, the National Asso-ciation of Bible Instructors, with the acronym "NABI": Hebrew for prophet. In this context, under the dominion of Bible, religion was folded back into the Book as, pa-rochially, "the beliefs, morals and practices encoded in Scripture."[1] Now it seems that we are witnessing an ironic return of that old scriptural motif of a late-born displacing the firstborn—now no longer safely contained in scripture but taking scripture as its target. For it is the American Academy of Religion that has the up-per hand: so much so that it could attempt to shed its fusty older brother in a fra-ternal schism patched up in 2011. In *practice* the center of gravity in departments with names like "Theology and Religious Studies" still tends to be overwhelmingly Christian. But in *theory* (that is to say, conceptually) "religion" is a far more confident and respectable academic term than "Bible"—and for good reason. After all, the two terms work very differently in narratives of secular modernity and the politics of the modern democratic state.

Stories of what it means to be modern or secular have always passed through their religious other, on which they are dependent. It would be extremely difficult to tell a narrative of becoming-modern while abstaining from any mention of reli-gion. Both the chronological watersheds on the way to the modern and the moral force pushing us toward the secular rely heavily on religion. It is a commonplace that the Reformation—understood as an individualist rebellion against the heavy hand of Church authority—set us on an inexorable path to more advanced or secular forms of Enlightenment. The need to protect ourselves against religious violence or fanaticism grounds the secular state.

One resilient mythology of the modern relies on the idea that once upon a time modernity slid off the edges of the Bible, becoming the mirror opposite of a point in time and space not seen as, precisely, *not* our own. Point zero for this epistemological break can be set at different times. We can date it from the discovery of the "Americas," revealing a whole new continent that the allegedly omniscient Bible and its *nabi*'s did not anticipate, from John Locke's quip that Genesis is not a document that carries much weight with the Chinese, or from freethinkers like Cyrano de Bergerac wondering how early Christian theologians and biblical authors could declare that "the Earth was flat as an oven, and swam on water like one half of a sliced orange"[2] —or myriad other starting points. But the result is always that the Bible, as the emblem and mascot of Christendom, retreats into the space of the old time, the time of tradition—"tradition" being the very antithesis of the modern. It comes to signify a lost world: the time of our believing, our naiveté, our past. If the modern, the time of now, involves, in the memorable words of Francis Bacon, emancipation from "devout adherence unto Antiquity" and the worship of "infallible" authorities, suffering from sclerosis, frozen like statues,[3] then the Bible becomes the ultimate sign of frozen antiquity. It is not just *in* the past; it *is* past per se. Even more significantly, by accepting that their task is essentially, and almost exclusively, the quest for nonmodern historical origins, biblical scholars tacitly accept and reinforce the identification of the Bible with and a more general cultural category of nonmodern pastness. By the same token, however, the parochialization of the Bible as the active making-past of the Bible was itself the testing ground of the viability of the "modern." As Karl Marx put it, the way to modernity emerged necessarily with signposts and milestones like "Locke displac[ing] Habbakuk,"[4] the emergence of one premised on the "antiquating" of the other. (The choice of that most foreign-sounding word "Habbakuk" perfectly illustrates the role of the Bible as an exotic theme park, Past Land, full of strange particularities and peculiarities. What could be less relevant than "Habbakuk" to the pressing concerns of Now?)

Given that "modernity" and "democracy" are slippery terms, it is perhaps no surprise that one of the clearest proofs of "modern democracy" has been imagined as the nondogmatic pluralization of religion to the point where it includes even the lack of religion, which is to say, atheism or Freethought as religion's publicly recognized other. This openness or acquisitiveness of religion as a category has led to repeated attempts to accommodate all religions (plural) in so-called Western legal systems—while simultaneously setting firm boundaries around plurality, which becomes restricted to a limited set of "world," or "world-class," religions.[5] Riding roughshod over some of the most elementary problems for first-year students of religious studies, legal criteria in England and Wales for the category known as "religion and belief" specify that in order to qualify a belief must be "genuinely held"; it must be a "belief" rather than an "opinion" or a "fact"; and it must be "serious," "weighty," and human-rights compliant.[6] Two frequently rehearsed examples of forms of believing that do not qualify are political beliefs (Marxism is often cited) and nonserious imposter religions, particularly "belief in Jedi Knights."[7]

While Christianity and its ever-plastic Bible are often seen as (vaguely and loosely) birthing and grounding democracy,[8] it is clear that the term "religion" has a skill set far more suited to the self-consciously modern polity and its self-consciously modern universities than does the Bible. Historically speaking, "religion" is imagined as the more expansive, irenic, and tolerant term. Unlike the Bible, it has the distinct advantage of being able to take an "s."[9] In received disciplinary definitions, religion confidently proclaims its advantages over the Bible and the Theology that the Bible ostensibly serves. Religion, the modern story goes, is an "anthropological not a theological category."[10] It is integral to the humanities or social sciences. It is not a dubiously numinous or transcendent other belonging to "Divinity." A central creed of Max Müller's study of religions—"to know one is to know none"—consolidates these disciplinary virtues precisely around the imagined (in)capacity to take an "s."

The confidence of the category of religion in comparison to the Bible is amply demonstrated in disciplinary parables told by religion scholars to stage an encounter between the Bible and Religion: "The Study of Religion and the Study of the Bible" (1971) by Wilfred Cantwell Smith or "Bible and Religion" (1999) by J. Z. Smith. Here, the Bible and biblical studies function rather as they do in myths of modernity. They serve as the figure of a limit that has been broken by modernity (and its disciplinary ally religious studies) and a ghostly specter of the past. Cantwell Smith's parable—to which we are tempted to give the subheading "The Parable of the Lost Biblical Scholar"—almost consciously deploys old biblical tales of the elder being displaced by the younger, or the division between the goats and the sheep, (disciplinary) death and (disciplinary) life. One day, a very old biblical scholar (most likely with a long white beard) comes knocking at the doors of the newly founded department of Religion, in a Liberal Arts department of the "future." He has an air of a ghostly anachronism and, relatedly, the aura of particularism or partiality about him. He represents the "questions, moods and methods of an earlier era" and is "bound to very particular sectors of the total religious history of mankind."[11] Triumphantly he pulls out his yellowing curriculum vitae to show that he can offer traditional Bible courses "on the whole calculated to turn a fundamentalist into a liberal" or, if he is a more sophisticated member of his species, even posttheological, purely historical courses, dealing in sophisticated contextual studies of the "ancient Near East or the first-century Eastern Mediterranean world."[12] The one who stands at the door is not impressed. The first option demonstrates the limits of an insider discourse: addressed by Christians to Christians, bouncing round and round in an echo chamber of internal positions and counterpositions. The second only loosely secularizes—and veils—this reification of the "Bible." The assumption that we should study these particularly tightly circumscribed times and places—rather than, say, classical India or medieval China or modern America—translates the privilege of scripture into secularized and universal terms of study, while bracketing out the whole question of the assumed uniqueness of this particular scripture, now expressed at one remove in particular geographical and temporal cordon of time and place.

Like the numerous figures of the blind in the Bible, Cantwell Smith's old Bible scholar cannot *see*. Specifically he cannot see the future: the importance of the futures or the afterlives of scripture. (He is no *nabi*.) About the ricocheting effects of the Bible as an "organized battery of symbols" and the "incredible ongoing career" of the Bible as an "agent," he has nothing to say.[13] Positively garrulous about antecedents, he does not see that the revelation of history begins once the parts are synthesized. This poor old lectured soul needs to be taught over and over again the fundamental truth that time's arrow points the other way. In short, he does not know that the future of biblical studies lies in studies of the Bible's futures—specifically in how the Bible has fired the imagination, and inspired the poetry, and formulated the inhibitions, and guided the ecstasies, and teased the intellects, and ordered the family relations and the legal chicaneries, and nurtured the piety of hundreds and millions of people in widely diverse climes and over a series of radically divergent centuries.[14]

Like the foolish bridesmaids who are too distracted to meet the bridegroom/messiah/future, he does not watch or pay attention.[15] The punch line of the parable is that the curator of historical fragments is turned away from this department of the future and dispatched elsewhere, to "Orientalist" departments, presumably with weeping and gnashing of teeth.

In J. Z. Smith's parable "The Bible and Religion," biblical studies is presented as an introverted, largely confessional "insider" zone. What passes for criticism is "an affair of native exegesis."[16] The "sort of accounts that, for other religious traditions, constitute data for the student of religion" frequently constitutes the end product here.[17] There is little space for translation, redescription, surprise, or any sense of difference from the phenomena in question. And since the only cognitive advantage of a discipline is difference, without the fresh air of difference, a discipline dies. Astutely, Smith observes that "The current, preservationist tactic of many biblical scholars to reduce any theory and its necessary entailments to a method, to a procedure for reading texts, contributes to this lack of effort at redescription." "Adapted" and softened versions of literary and social theories seem specifically designed to allow biblical scholars to steal the cache of theory and yet escape the "cost."[18] In a sonorous conclusion, Borges's parable "Exactitude in Science," published in 1946, is used to evoke this disciplinary space of deference without difference, inside without outside, heavily insulated from surprise or shock. Borges imagines that once, for a brief moment, in an unspecified empire, "the art of cartography attained such perfection that the cartographers guild struck a map of the empire whose size was that of empire, and which coincided point by point with it." However, the next generation, "who were not so fond of the Study of Cartography as their Forbears had been, saw that that vast Map was useless." It thus became a "relic of the discipline of geography." The "tattered ruin of the map" became a dwelling place for animals and beggars and howling winds in the "deserts of the west."[19] Borges's and Smith's imagery ironically evokes well-worn biblical tropes of devastation and apocalypse: glorious human reduced to dwelling places for jackals and howling creatures; uninhabitable spaces where no one can pitch his tent.[20] The tattered ruin of a map seems to evoke the specific sins or myopias of scripturalism: the folly and fragility of a discipline built on flimsy paper/text.

Our response to these parables is not to perpetuate the split and stand for Team Bible against Team Religion, or defensively so style ourselves as a younger, revamped version of biblical studies that can take its rightful place in volumes on theory/religion/critique and futuristic departments of religion and liberal arts. The two Smith parables make incisive diagnoses. Similar critiques and self-caricatures have been echoing inside the highly fractured discipline of Biblical studies in increasingly concerted ways. Smith's astute diagnosis of a "preservationist" tactic of "reduc[ing] any theory and its necessary entailments to a method, to a procedure for reading," has recently been amplified in critiques of "methodolatry" and the domestication of theory.[21] The campaign against the historical-critical has been so concerted that alternatives have been shaped (not always helpfully) by a dedication to being other-than-historical and breaking out of the museum.[22] The recent explosion of interest in the afterlives or reception of the Bible means that Cantwell Smith would now have viable candidates for his imagined post in biblical studies, as he somewhat prophetically reconfigured it back in 1971. In fact, study of the Bible's afterlives extends well beyond the limited regions he itemizes. No less than six out of eight (to "fire the imagination, and inspire the poetry, and formulate the inhibitions, and guide the ecstasies, and tease the intellects, . . . and nurture the piety") are firmly individualistic. The other two—"family" and law, or at least (somewhat pejoratively) "legal chicanery"—gesture very vaguely to something just on the periphery of the vision of the individual: a vague ghost of law, politics, and society, outside the center of operations for religion in the individual heart.[23] Cantwell Smith preaches a massive broadening out of the study of scriptures into "two millennia" and to "hundreds of millions of people" and urges consideration of the cultural force of scriptures. But then, bathetically, the punch line is that scriptures exert a rather gentle and private force on a limited list of domains, all set against a romanticized and exoticized backdrop of "diverse climes."[24]

Without getting into crude interdisciplinary fist-fights about who has the biggest log in their eye or who really has their eyes wide shut (confessing or praying), we want to argue that Cantwell Smith's strangely delimited view of scripture-as-religion highlights a far more interesting point lurking behind these parables: *namely, that the perceived lacks in biblical studies mirror structural problems in religious studies.* These are not simply minor issues such as, say, an insufficiently applied methodology, but major conceptual problems intrinsic to posing the question of "religion" (or indeed the Bible) in the modern world. When J. Z. Smith describes the domain of religious studies as "anthropological" and not "theological," or when he defines the true task of religious studies (as he conceives it) against the foil of biblical studies, the caricature of biblical scholarship is being used to exorcize a not yet properly academic relation to the object "religion" *within religious studies.* By describing the undifferentiated field of the Bible as a place where map is territory and there is not yet sufficient difference, he is calling for more differentiation and turbulence within religious studies. The deferential-pious world of biblical studies mirrors what he sees as the placid world of Eliadean religious studies, presided over by what Smith calls the "ontic primordium" of an atemporal universal "sacred"— always stable, always itself, outside the vacillations of history and the profane.[25] He wants to drag religion further "outside" its borders, to take it into forms more radically outside itself, more drastically alienated and demystified. By exorcising the ghost of a too-timid biblical studies, Smith seeks to recall religious studies to that which it has not been (yet) but which it really *is*. The effect is rather like the Hebrew prophets accosting the present Israel as an adulterous and syncretized version of a true self that is always yet to come.

For Cantwell Smith, in contrast, the contrast between Bible and religion works almost oppositely. As a site of historical fragments and simplistic and sterile "isms," biblical studies is the other to the true study of religion: human, personal, and integrative. The biblical scholar poring over fragments echoes Eliade's caricature of those history of religions scholars who "dream" of the "little speciality" and "would be satisfied with the smallest parcel"—to which Eliade retorts, in a strange fantasy of dismemberment evocative of the horrendous story of the Levite's concubine (Judges 19), "Indeed, what's the use of having a whole woman? An arm is enough, or a breast, or a knee?"[26] Unwittingly, Cantwell Smith also points to another major friction point within the field of religion. In his strangely circumscribed inventory of what is affected by that universal agent "religion"—imagination, poetry, inhibitions, ecstasies, family, law, intellects, piety—he provides a perfect example of a widespread liberal conceptualization of religion that has been increasingly under fire from scholars such as Russell McCutcheon, Tomoko Masuzawa, and J. Z. Smith. As his expansive and restricted list illustrates so perfectly, religion is often conceived, paradoxically, as a *strangely protected and delimited universal*, ubiquitous, yet confined to the private or the generic "human" ("human" as in the oft-rehearsed truism "human beings are spiritual animals" or "*Homo Sapiens* is also *Homo religiosus*.")[27] Structured around the human in this depoliticized, irenic sense, such a view positions religion as the New Theology, insofar as it promises to be a science of the "Total Man."[28] It allows the promising "s" of religion to fold back on itself in nothing more than an ecumenical theology of religious pluralism: myriad detemporalized and decontextualized instances of a fundamentally similar experience of "religion." A form of religious studies that produces religion as "*sui generis*, autonomous, of its own kind, strictly personal, essential, unique, prior to, and ultimately distinct from, all other facets of human life and interaction"[29]—and yet, simultaneously universal and universally human—is extremely useful for the politics of liberalism. (We can see a clear connection with the legal criteria for "religion or belief," pronouncing true religion to be "serious" and human-rights compliant: the perfect citizen.)[30] Arranged deferentially and paraphrastically around the "nonfalsifiable contents of religious experiences"[31] as "indeterminate or unmediatizable 'stuff,' "[32] it exactly replicates the work of the purely descriptive biblical scholar lampooned by J. Z. Smith.

The tendency of these two Smith parables to cast the Bible as religion's other—arranged in dichotomies of confessional versus professional, insider versus outsider, past versus present, subjective versus objective—simplifies the fractures on the inside of both vexed and schismatic disciplines. It also obscures the fact that the Bible and religion occupy a similarly productive strange place in the university and the modernities this institution both fashions and represents. Modernity is constituted around a founding allergy to religion, no less than its subsections, such as theology or the Bible. As Ninian Smart puts it, "having been dethroned as the Queen of Sciences, the study of religion has now become the Knave of Arts."[33] Following a restructuring at the University of Glasgow in 2011, Theology and Religious Studies found itself in a curiously named School of Critical Studies. One alternative proposal—the School of Literature, Language, and Religion (named after the three major subject areas)—was rejected because some colleagues felt deeply squeamish about being associated with religion, with its dubious flirtations with the numinous and dubious things that go bump in the night. This slightly strange institutional positioning looks like another parable of the place of religion in modernity—one written unconsciously. In modernity, religion is masked or subsumed under the distinctly modern practice of critique or the "critical." Religion can be included insofar as it bends over backward to translate itself out of "itself" into other terms entirely, insofar as affirms, constantly, that it is not simply "religious." The perceived softness of the word "religion" is a potential liability to arts and humanities faculties striving to demonstrate, in an ever-tighter battle for resources with the "hard" sciences, that they are sufficiently *robust*. Religion does not have the same exchange value as a word like "literature" or "history." It is possible to do a "literary" reading of the texts of religion or a "historical" reading of the archive of religion. But a "religious" reading of history or literature would suggest something weaker and dubiously partisan. It would imply something that belonged outside the university in a seminary or a "church." As the (soft and flimsy) arts are to the (hard) sciences, so religion is to the arts. The fact that the academic study of religion has named itself history of religions or religious science and constantly affirmed its rigor in contrast to theology and the Bible can be read as an attempt to compensate for this strange place of religion as, in some fundamental sense, modernity's outside or other. But this allergy should be critically analyzed, rather than defended against or overcome.

To cast the Bible as the confessional other to a more professional, essentially secular religious studies is to ignore how both disciplines awkwardly straddle both positions, legs akimbo. Religious studies is a conflicted space where religion appears as sui generis, utterly distinct—but also where it must be zealously hunted out of its privileged hiding place and translated into other terms entirely. J. Z. Smith portrays biblical studies as a place of excessive disciplinary piety without critical distance, whereas Wilfred Cantwell Smith portrays it as a robotic historicism or depersonalized science. This clearly demonstrates that biblical studies is in exactly the same position—a position fundamentally split from itself. Both fields are exceptionally expansive and interdisciplinary—but also exceptionally confined, folding back on themselves in a simple affirmation of the uniqueness of their object. Both open into myriad approaches, creating the impression that it is possible to say almost anything about religion or the Bible. And yet in both we find an aura of protective reverence hovering around the object of study that makes the object of study feel qualitatively different than, say, Shakespeare or the American Civil War. Both fields regularly erupt into laments that the modern discourse of religion or the Bible is inauthentic, alienated from its true object. (Ornithology is not flying; religious studies is a pale shadow of religion.) Both, equally regularly, issue clarion calls to return to the true work of demystification. J. Z. Smith's insistence on religion as an anthropological discipline and Russell McCutcheon's manifesto *Manufacturing Religion* find direct parallels in biblical studies in, say, Robert Oden's *The Bible Without Theology*, Jacques Berlinerblau's *The Secular Bible*,[34] and the Department of Biblical Studies at the University of Sheffield, founded in the late 1940s as a Department of Biblical History and Literature (emphatically not Theology). Works with apocalyptic titles such as Hector Avalos's *The End of Biblical Studies*[35] graphically perform the disciplinary being-toward-death that Richard King diagnoses as the "iatrogenic" effect of the study of religion (or the Bible) upon its object. Iatrogenesis is the damage or ill health caused by administering medical treatment. Efforts to make the discipline robust and healthy destroy religion as such, by constantly reiterating the fact that there is no such thing as religion as such.[36] This kamikaze dissolution of the very object of study only serves to draw attention to the strange place of religion or Bible in modernity, and the catch-22 in which they are placed. The devout secularization of the religious object attempts to deal head on with the perceived vulnerability of the category of religion as a place of special pleading or confession. It seeks to democratize, to generously puncture any residual haloes. But this only results in a more profound vulnerability—for it is surely time to close a department when the object of the discipline no longer exists.

Any caricature of biblical studies as "confessional," in any simple sense, brackets out its historical function as a massive machine for translating the "religious" or the "confessional" into something else. Biblical studies is essentially a big institutional edifice constructed around the production of what the historian Jonathan Sheehan has termed "the Enlightenment Bible." The Enlightenment Bible is a mode of understanding and working on the Bible that aspires to be a truly "catholic" or universal, appropriate for the university.[37] With its origins in the eighteenth century, it responded to the pressures of a posttheological era by the translating the dubiously partisan "theological" into universal, human cultural domains. If the answer to the question "Why should I read the Bible?" had previously been "because it reveals the means to your salvation," the Enlightenment Bible supplied a series of supplemental, even alternative, answers, meeting the challenge to the Bible's authority by dispersing that authority across different domains.[38]

As the institutionalized protector and propagator of the Enlightenment Bible, biblical studies grew into a massive disciplinary machine designed to extend the relevance of the Bible into an exhilarating range of disciplines—ancient history, philology, archaeology, long-dead languages of the ancient Near East, Greco-Roman literature and philosophy, ancient geography, numismatics, botany, linguistics, and so on and so forth. Irrespective of whether they preached on Sundays,[39] biblical scholars developed, and devoutly respected, a mode of discourse that displayed its critical credentials. Mutual mud-slinging between "insiders" and "outsiders" or confessors and professors masks the fact that all biblical scholars are constantly asserting—through great efforts of style and content—that their work is not homiletics but, emphatically, something else. The task is to write as if from the Kantian place of "philosophy" defined, in contrast to theology, as a vantage point from which one proves oneself "unintimidated by sacredness of the object."[40] One result is detailed articles examining various candidates for Jonah's fish or plant, or the true size of the city of Nineveh, or the geology of the mountain on which Abraham almost sacrificed his son[41]—sometimes with a coda of faith awkwardly tagged on the end.

One of the functions of this assiduously and tenaciously "critical" scholarship has been to limit the realm of critique and provide a major distraction from questions of the (im)morality and (in)humanity (which is to say, nondivinity) of the Bible, as raised so rudely by the so-called Deists. The eighteenth-century critics who provoked the crisis that led to the Enlightenment Bible posed the question of "integrity" in a various senses—including, particularly, the integrity of the human and divine authors of the Bible, who often appeared as less than gentlemen, "blasphemously" drifting down the social scale. Historical-critical scholarship effectively closed down the question of integrity until it became nothing more than a question of compositional wholeness. This could then split into myriad subquests—for the true biblical autographs, for putative sources, for the authorial intentions needed to unify the texts and infuse them with coherent meaning, and so on ad infinitum.

Such questions could happily keep biblical scholars occupied for eternity while at the same time keeping their labors at tangents to some of the major cultural challenges to the biblical text. As Legaspi comments, once biblical scholarship was thoroughly disciplined, "philologists strove to become scientific saints and ascetics." They "began to resemble the *Wissenschaftlicher* sketched so memorably by Max Weber: the socially alienated, science-intoxicated figure whose 'personality' is derived from intense devotion to his subject; his vocation internal because the old social and metaphysical dimensions of his work have largely lost their significance."[42] (Recall Cantwell Smith's ghostly biblical scholar, bound to the "questions, moods and methods of an earlier era"[43] without having noticed that his questions are no longer hardwired into questions of moral, existential, cultural, or political concern.) The work of translating the Bible out of specifically religious languages into solid disciplines available to all suggested that the new mode of Bible scholarship would be addressed to all, irrespective of a particular interest in religion. But at the same time, the relationship to confession was awkward, and biblical studies was never purely contentedly "secular," nor entirely happy with its most determinedly nonconfessional practitioners, who have always been "outsiders" in a sense. The modern Everyman ostensibly addressed by biblical scholarship turns out to be a very particular and, in the twenty-first century, rather rare creature. He is someone who seeks, for nondevotional reasons, to devote himself to the minutiae of this very particular text.

In many respects, *Bibelwissenschaft* and *Religionswissenschaft* come from the same womb. If religion, as Derrida puts it, "circulates in the world . . . like an English word [*comme un mot anglais*] that has been to Rome and taken a detour to the United States,"[44] institutionally it is born in the modern research university, with its doctoral seminar and the *Wissenschaftideologie*—a model exported to institutions like Johns Hopkins, Chicago, and Cornell from Schleiermacher's University of Berlin. As Legaspi argues, following the historian Thomas Howard, the very definition of the modern university was bound up with the transformation of theology: a transformation marked, not least, by the inauguration of the distinctly modern disciplines of biblical studies and history or science of religion.[45]

> Striking a Faustian bargain with the growing power of the state, [the modern research universities] maintained their religious and cultural inheritance by folding the authority of the Bible and of the Protestant theological tradition into the later programmes of *Verwissenshaftlichung* (scientization), *Entkonfessionalierung* (deconfessionalisation), *professionalisierung* (professionalization) and *Verstaatlichung* (nationalization).[46]

The study of Bible and religion was placed under the auspices of the state. In a climate of "academic mercantilism,"[47] the primary business of these disciplines became the production of peace and good citizenship. As Legaspi puts it, the task was "to head off religious extremism" —or, in Cantwell Smith's words, "turn a fundamentalist into a liberal."[48] Hence a strangely universal Bible, Christian but also relevant beyond the Christian, and also in a sense secularized: hence religious studies as an ally of liberalism and the science of a depoliticized, irenic "human" spirit as a fundamental attribute of Universal Man. As a "new [emphatically] postconfessional mode of biblical discourse, one that remained open to religion while opposed to interpretation consciously shaped by particular religious identities,"[49] the discipline of biblical studies shared in the same inaugural paradoxes as the study of religion.

It was through the gate of the Old Testament that scriptures first opened up to something like "religion" in the modern sense of an "anthropological" rather than a "theological" mode of study. And this was no accident. As well as forging connection through the transformative work of typology, Christianity has always dealt with the awkward appendix of the Old Testament by historicizing, localizing, and relativizing aspects of Old Testament "religion" (for example, sacrifice). Religious studies as the art of demystification or making-strange found a natural home in that portion of the canon that had, for centuries, been regarded as in some sense, tangential, alien, strange. The sixteenth-century *Antwerp Polyglot* (1569–1572) edited by Arias Montano contained an appendix volume, named, after Josephus, *Jewish Antiquities* (*Antiquitates Judaicae*), with treatises on translation, geography, architecture, liturgy, weights and measures, ancient coins, vestments, body gesture, artifacts, and relics. It looks like a veritable ethnography of the ancient Hebrews, particularly around the artifacts of sacrifice, displayed as in a museum. Crowded with different peoples and different gods, the Old Testament lent itself to serving as a forum for nascent "comparative religion." Comparative religion was born, in a sense, with rudimentary comparisons between the contemporary "heathen," the Greco-Roman "pagan," and the Hebrews. Thus, for example, Thomas Godwyn's *Moses and Aaron: Civil and Ecclesiastical Rites, Used by the Ancient Hebrewes* (1624) attempted the "clearing of many obscure Texts thorowout the whole Scripture" by showing "what Customes the Hebrews borrowed from Heathen people" and how "many Heathenish customes . . . have been unwarrantable imitations of the

Hebrewes."[50] Origin stories of religious studies and Old Testament studies pass through some of the same founding fathers (as in the Bible, the power of generation is with the father) or institutional fraternities. Abraham Kuenen, author of *The Religion of Israel to the Fall of the Jewish State* (published in Dutch in 1869–70) was a contemporary of C. P. Tiele, the putative founding father of the science of religion. He debated with Tiele over questions of taxonomy, and declared in the opening to *The Religion of Israel*: "the Israelitish is one of [the principle religions], nothing less, but nothing more."[51] Pivotal in the history of both disciplines are those eighteenth- and nineteenth-century polymath "orientalists" who double in Hebrew and Arabic, from Johann David Michaelis to Julius Wellhausen to William Robertson Smith.[52] Michaelis professionalized and "scientized" the kind of comparison in Goodwyn's *Moses and Aaron* by comparing Mosaic law and Bedouin customs.[53] He organized an expedition to "Arabia Felix" sponsored by the king of Denmark to shed light on the plants, animals, insects, language, and manners of the peoples of an Old Testament reconceived as a "remarkable fragment of Oriental antiquity."[54] Conducted by a six-man team including a botanist, a philologist, an illustrator, and an engineer/mathematician, the expedition was tasked with myriad quests, including the Arabic name for the ox-like creature in Job 39:9, the true botanical source of the "balm of Gilead" (Genesis 37:25; Jeremiah 8:22), and the tides at the outmost reaches of the Red Sea.[55] The relationship to Robertson Smith and his late-nineteenth-century explorations in *Kinship and Marriage in Early Arabia* or *The Religion of the Semites* is clear. As J. Z. Smith observes, whereas New Testament scholars seem allergic to the term "religion" even to the point where they would even chose "magic" over "religion," Hebrew Bible scholars almost habitually use phrases such as "religion of Israel," or "Old Testament religion," or "religion of the Semites."[56] The Old Testament and its related territories seem to serve as a natural habitat for "religion" and appropriately primitive territory to which to apply foundational terms such as "totemism."

Biblical studies and religious studies have a unique and important role in the modern university—not because of some dubiously essentialist sui generis status shrouding their object, but precisely because of the structural allergies between modernities and religions, and the unique and riven conceptual space for "Bible" and "religion" in the modern world. Tim Fitzgerald describes the university as the producer of rituals and liturgies designed to generate and sustain religious-secular distinctions:

> Universities can be thought of more as ritual institutions in the economy of contemporary affairs, something analogous to the monastic chanters of medieval times. The difference is that the rituals performed in the humanities and social sciences faculties of modern universities are generating the myth of the religion-secular distinction as objective knowledge achieved through disinterested rational procedures, whereas biblical exegesis in medieval monasteries would have been considered illegitimate if divorced from a more general commitment to the truth of the Bible and confessional practices such as prayer.[57]

Religious studies and biblical studies have served as major arenas for the production and maintenance of religious and secular distinctions. Thus these disciplines are crucial to one of the key contemporary debates in the humanities and social sciences: the so-called anthropology and genealogy of what is loosely called "the secular" (or "the modern") and, relatedly, the question "What is critique?"[58] Contributing to this discussion will involve moving outside standard histories of our subjects focused on our own disciplinary telos. Biblical studies, certainly, has had a surfeit of self-serving, introspective works of disciplinary stocktaking: stories of the evolution of the discipline structured around the fundamental pivot of "Before the Historical Method" and "After the Historical Method," with the baton being between the heroes and great men of *Wissenschaft*. Instead, as Cantwell Smith projects (albeit vaguely, through a mirror darkly, back in the 1970s), we need disciplinary histories that attempt to stand outside the "critical" movements they analyze and describe.[59] Specifically, we need to look at how our disciplines have constructed and produced what might be thought of as *secular effects, effects of being truly critical*. Foucault gives a few hints as to the forms of these new genealogies of Bible/religion/critique. Offering a provocative preliminary definition of critique as "the art of not being governed so much,"[60] he explores how critique, which always "exists in relation to something other than itself," could only emerge in contrast to a state of submission to authority: iconically religious authority. Thus inevitably histories of critique lead us to the Bible and through the Bible. "Befores" and "afters" in different modes of relation to the Bible are used to define the very essence of critique. As Foucault writes:

> At a time when the governing of men was essentially a spiritual art or an essentially religious practice linked to the authority of a church, to the magisterium of Scripture, not wanting to be governed in that way was essentially seeking in Scripture a relationship other than the one that was linked to the operating function of God's teaching. To not want to be governed was a certain way of refusing, challenging, limiting . . . the ecclesiastic *magisterium*. It was a return to Scripture, it was a question of what is authentic in Scripture, of what was actually written in Scripture, it was a question concerning the kind of truth Scripture tells, how to have access to this truth of Scripture in Scripture and perhaps despite what is written, until one arrives at the ultimately very simple question: Was Scripture true? In short, from Wycliffe to Pierre Bayle, I believe that critique was developed in an important, but of course not exclusive, part in relation in relation to Scripture. *Let us say that critique is historically biblical.*[61]

The results of such studies may well prove surprising. We may expect to find "the acceptance of the Bible's foreignness" presented as "an entry fee for modern subjectivity."[62] To be modern is in some sense to be alienated from the Bible: to be able to see the Bible (or at least parts of it) as exoticized, orientalized, repellent, strange. But more surprisingly, it seems that the Bible does not just give us an object against which critique flexes its muscles. Idioms and structures from the Bible and Christianity also provide the superior basis from which the Bible is criticized. It turns out that famous critics of religion such as Voltaire, Kant, and Heidegger presented their own critical thought as a kind of "purified" or "originary" version of Christianity, doing Christianity one better, as it were, in the polemical struggle to establish the parameters of religion itself.[63] The domain of "philosophy" in the modern sense (more universal and critical than religion) was partly grounded by asserting the power of critique against groups in the Christian tableau that represent myopia or limit (for example, the Pharisees). A truly *critical* spirit could be produced and certified by extending Pauline rhetoric about the "spirit" that exceeds the "letter" or the universal category of natural religion or natural law.[64] If criticism arises from the Bible against the Bible, this unsettles contemporary identities and "religious" and "secular" distinctions. It also helps us to understand why, in Western theories of "religion," Christianity can still seem to persist as a larger category than "religion"— somehow presiding over discussions of religion from its putative "outside." Until the results of such genealogies of our disciplines and modernities are in, we would be naive to assume that we know all that there is to know about hierarchies and relations between "Bible," "religion," and "critique."

NOTES

1. Jonathan Z. Smith "Bible and Religion," in *Relating Religion: Essays in the Study of Religion*, ed. Jonathan Z. Smith (Chicago: University of Chicago Press, 2004), 199.

2. John Locke, *Two Treatises of Government*, ed. Peter Laslett (Cambridge: Cambridge University Press, 1996), 243; Cyrano de Bergerac, *Journey to the Moon*, trans. Andrew Smith (London: Hesperus, 2007), 13.

3. Francis Bacon, *New Atlantis and The Great Instauration*, ed. Jerry Weinberger, 2nd ed. (Hoboken: Wiley, 2016). First published in 1620.

4. Karl Marx, *The Eighteenth Brumaire of Louis Bonaparte* (New York: International, 1963), 16–17.

5. Russell McCutcheon, *Manufacturing Religion: The Discourse on Sui Generis Religion and the Politics of Nostalgia* (New York: Oxford University Press, 1997), 104.

6. See *The Employment Equality (Religion or Belief) Regulations 2003* at www.legislation. gov.uk/uksi/2003/1660/contents/made. For discussion, including a discussion of the strangely persistent Kantian distinction between believing, opining, and knowing, see Yvonne Sherwood, "The Persistence of Blasphemy," in *Biblical Blaspheming: Trials of the Sacred for a Secular Age* (Cambridge: Cambridge University Press, 2012), 9–98.

7. "Jedi" is a specifically British example, referencing the campaign to have "Jedi Knights" returned as a qualifying "religion" in the 2001 census: 390,000 respondents—0.7 per cent of the population—declared their religion to be Jedi, thereby making Jedi the fourth major "religion" and proving, as the comedian Dara O'Briain quips, that "there are more nerds in the United Kingdom than there are Sikhs." Dara O'Briain, *Tickling the English: A Funny Man's Notes on a Country and Its People* (London: Penguin, 2010), 67.

8. See, for example, Yvonne Sherwood, "The God of Abraham and Exceptional States; Or, the Early Modern Rise of the Whig/Liberal Bible," *Journal of the American Academy of Religion* 76, no. 2 (2008): 312–43; Yvonne Sherwood, "On the Genesis of the Alliance Between the Bible and Rights," in *Biblical Blaspheming*, 303–32.

9. Of course the Bible can boast versions, even different canons—Jewish, Protestant, and Catholic—but this moderately plastic "s" still looks parochial compared to the fundamental commitment to plurality intrinsic to the very idea of religion, with an "s."

10. Jonathan Z. Smith, "Religion, Religions, Religious," in *Critical Terms for Religious Studies*, ed. Mark C. Taylor (Chicago: University of Chicago Press, 1998), 269.

11. Wilfred Cantwell Smith, "The Study of Religion and the Study of the Bible," in *Rethinking Scripture: Essays from a Comparative Perspective*, ed. Miriam Levering (Albany: State University of New York Press, 1989), 19.

12. Ibid.

13. Ibid., 21, 22.

14. Ibid., 21.

15. Matthew 25.

16. Smith, "Bible and Religion," 201.

17. Ibid.

18. Ibid., 206.

19. J. L. Borges, "Exactitude in Science," in *Collected Fictions*, ed. J. L. Borges (New York: Viking Penguin, 1998), 325, quoted in Smith, "Bible and Religion," 209.

20. Isaiah 14:17–22.

21. See Ward Blanton, "Escape from the Biblical Aura," in *Displacing Christian Origins: Philosophy, Secularity and the New Testament* (Chicago: University of Chicago Press, 2007); Stephen D. Moore and Yvonne Sherwood, *The Invention of the Biblical Scholar* (Minneapolis: Fortress, 2011), 31–41.

22. See, for example, George Aichele, Peter Miscall, and Richard Welsh, "An Elephant in the Room: Historical Criticism and Postmodern Interpretations of the Bible," *JBL* 128 (2009): 383–404.

23. Cantwell Smith, "The Study of Religion and the Study of the Bible," 21.

24. Ibid.

25. Jonathan Z. Smith, *Imagining Religion: From Babylon to Jamestown* (Chicago: University of Chicago Press, 1982), 42.

26. Mircea Eliade, *Journals III: 1970–1978*, trans. Teresa Lavendar Fagan (Chicago: University of Chicago Press, 1989), 329.

27. As asserted by Karen Armstrong, *A History of God* (New York: Vintage, 1999), 3. Armstrong writes: "men and women started to worship gods as soon as they became recognizably human."

28. McCutcheon, *Manufacturing Religion*, 38.

29. Ibid., xi.

30. See *The Employment Equality (Religion or Belief) Regulations 2003*, discussed above, note 6.

31. McCutcheon, *Manufacturing Religion*, 124.

32. Hent de Vries, "Introduction: Why Still 'Religion?,'" in *Religion: Beyond a Concept*, ed. Hent de Vries (New York: Fordham University Press, 2008), 5.

33. Ninian Smart, quoted in Eric Sharpe, *Understanding Religion* (London: Duckworth, 1983), 2.

34. Robert Oden, *The Bible Without Theology: The Theological Tradition and Alternatives to It* (San Francisco: Harper and Row, 1987); Jacques Berlinerblau, *The Secular Bible:*

Why Nonbelievers Must Take Religion Seriously (Cambridge: Cambridge University Press, 2005).

35. Hector Avalos, *The End of Biblical Studies* (Amherst, N.Y.: Prometheus, 2007).

36. Richard King, *Orientalism and Religion: Post-Colonial Theory, Indian and the "Mystic East"* (New York: Routledge, 1999), 42. King's discussion of *iatragenesis* overlaps with Derrida's discussion of autoimmunity in relation to religion. See Jacques Derrida, "Faith and Knowledge: The Two Sources of 'Religion' at the Limits of Reason Alone," in *Religion*, ed. Jacques Derrida and Gianni Vattimo (Stanford: Stanford University Press, 1996), 1–78.

37. Jonathan Sheehan, *The Enlightenment Bible: Translation, Scholarship, Culture* (Princeton: Princeton University Press, 2004); Michael C. Legaspi, *The Death of Scripture and the Rise of Biblical Studies* (New York: Oxford University Press, 2010), 32.

38. Sheehan, *The Enlightenment Bible*, xii.

39. As any Jewish biblical scholar will testify, the genealogy of Biblical Studies is decidedly Christian.

40. Immanuel Kant, *The Conflict of the Faculties*, trans. Mary J. Gregor (Lincoln: University of Nebraska Press, 1979), 53.

41. The analysis of the geology of Mount Moriah is, at this present time, a joke, as far as we know. The other examples actually exist. See Yvonne Sherwood, *A Biblical Text and Its Afterlives: The Survival of Jonah in Western Culture* (Cambridge: Cambridge University Press, 2000), 56–59.

42. Legaspi, *The Death of Scripture*, 31; Max Weber, "Wissenschaft als Beruf," in *Gesammelte Aufsätze zur Wissenschaftlehre* (Tübingen: J. C. B. Mohr, 1922), 524–55.

43. Cantwell Smith, "The Study of Religion," 19.

44. Derrida, "Faith and Knowledge," 29.

45. Thomas Albert Howard, *Protestant Theology and the Making of the Modern German University* (New York: Oxford University Press, 2006).

46. Legaspi, *The Death of Scripture*, 29.

47. Ibid., 35.

48. Ibid., 38; Cantwell Smith, "The Study of Religion," 19.

49. Legaspi, *The Death of Scripture*, 7.

50. Thomas Godwyn, *Moses and Aaron: Civil and Ecclesiastical Rites, Used by the Ancient Hebrewes* (London, 1655).

51. Abraham Kuenen, *The Religion of Israel to the Fall of the Jewish State* (London, 1873–75), 1:5; Smith, "Bible and Religion," 203.

52. For a rich and detailed study of German orientalism and biblical criticism, see Suzannne L. Marchand, *German Orientalism in the Age of Empire: Religion, Race and Scholarship* (Cambridge: Cambridge University Press, 2009).

53. J. D. Michaelis, *Mosaiches Recht* (*Commentaries on the Laws of Moses*), trans. Alexander Smith (London, 1814).

54. Sheehan, *The Enlightenment Bible*, 189.

55. For an account of the expedition, see Sheehan, *The Enlightenment Bible*, 186–91; and Thorkild Hansen, *Arabia Felix: The Danish Expedition of 1761–1767*, trans. James McFarlene and Kathleen McFarlane (London: Readers Union Collins, 1965).

56. Smith, "Bible and Religion," 201–2.

57. Timothy Fitzgerald, *Discourse on Civility and Barbarity: A Critical History of Religion and Related Categories* (Oxford: Oxford University Press, 2007), 10.

58. See, for example, Talal Asad, Wendy Brown, Judith Butler, and Saba Mahmood, *Is Critique Secular? Blasphemy, Injury and Free Speech* (Berkeley: University of California Press, 2009).

59. Cantwell Smith, "The Study of Religion," 24, 25.

60. Michel Foucault, "What Is Critique?," in *What Is Enlightenment? Eighteenth-Century Answers and Twentieth-Century Questions*, trans. Kevin Paul Geiman, ed. James Schmidt (Berkeley: University of California Press, 1996), 385.

61. Ibid.

62. Blanton, *Displacing Christian Origins*, 8.

63. Ibid., 85.

64. 2 Corinthians 3:1–7; Romans 2:14–15.

4

Hegel

On Secularity and the Religion-Making Machine

ARVIND MANDAIR

No philosopher of the 19 C or 20th C has had as great an impact on the world as Hegel. The only possible exception to this sweeping statement would be Karl Marx—and Marx himself was heavily influenced by Hegel. Without Hegel neither the intellectual or political developments of the last 150 years would have taken the path they did.
—Peter Singer, Hegel: A Very Short Introduction

Since David Strauss first coined the terms "Right Hegelians" and "Left Hegelians" in the mid-nineteenth century, perceptions about Hegel's intellectual legacy generally tend to have been split between two opposing interpretations of his work. The so-called Right Hegelians saw Hegel primarily as a religious philosopher whose ideas helped to revive a theistic version of traditional Protestantism. By contrast "Left Hegelians" argued that Hegel had shown how to unravel the structure of human consciousness, in the process demonstrating that religion was a mere by-product of the human mind and could be better understood if we reduced it to more basic processes such as psychology, society, economics, and so on. By laying bare the processes of thinking itself, Left Hegelians, including Marx, developed a form of secular critique that framed the way in which religion was thought about for almost two centuries, culminating in the secularization thesis: the idea that modernity and secularism would combine to eventually displace religion altogether from the public sphere.

Hegel, it seems, has suffered many different fates. Exorcized by thinkers as different in their orientations as Marx and Kierkegaard in the nineteenth century, left for dead by modern theologians such as Karl Barth, supposedly made redundant by analytic philosophers such as George E. Moore in the early twentieth century, and disavowed though surreptitiously deployed by postmodern theorists, it would appear that the death of Hegelianism has become part of conventional wisdom.

Yet such banal optimism about the death of Hegel has been shattered by a recent revival of interest in Hegel's key philosophical works within the humanities and social sciences. Hegel's philosophical resurrection seems to revolve around two main themes: (i) a broad shift in scholarly understanding of the relationship between religion and the secular, and related to this (ii) the revalued status of time and temporality (specifically the future) in relation to Hegel's system of dialectic.

As I argue below, these two themes are strongly interlinked. The first theme has been examined by Catharine Malabou in her recent book *The Future of Hegel*.[1] Arguing against the prevailing Heideggerian interpretation of Hegel, Malabou calls for a revaluation of time and temporality in Hegel's key works such as the *Phenomenology of Spirit*, his two Berlin lecture courses on the *Philosophy of History* and the *Philosophy of Religion*, and the *Science of Logic*. The dialectical process, Malabou argues, needs to be read not simply as an exercise in logic, but as a movement or plasticity that forms time itself: "The dialectical composition of such concepts as 'the future,' 'plasticity,' and temporality form an *anticipatory structure* operating within subjectivity itself as Hegel conceived it."[2] Malabou names this anticipatory structure "to see what is coming" (*le voir venir*), an expression that can refer at one and the same time to teleological necessity, to being sure of what is coming, and to the surprise of not knowing what is coming. Far from simply being a philosopher of history (understood as the overcoming and installation of past stages in human development), Hegel needs to be understood as a thinker who anticipated a certain future that seems to be unfolding right now. That future involves the vexed relationship between religion and the secular, or better still, what comes after religion and the secular as it relates to the future of democracy in an era of sharply accelerated globalization. The question that concerns us in this chapter is why in contemporary theory and in the politics of the global right and left, Hegel has become such a resource for understanding the intersections between politics, religion, and culture.

To answer this question I want to situate this reading of Hegel in relation to recent intellectual movements that have analyzed the key transformations in the enigmatic relationship between religion and the secular, as well as its practical implications for postcolonial cultures for whom the categories religion and secular are doubly problematic. This juxtaposition of the theoretical and the practical/political may help to justify Peter Singer's claim that Hegel has had an unrivaled impact on intellectual and political developments in the modern world.

HISTORICAL CONSCIOUSNESS, SECULAR CRITIQUE, AND THE WESTERN IMAGINARY

Recent years have seen significant alterations in the way that public spheres are perceived, as can be seen in the proliferation of phrases such as the "return of religion" or the "crisis of secularism." In accordance with this altered perception, scholarship in the study of religions has begun to adopt a less normative stance toward the secularization thesis, in the process redrawing the map of the religion-secular debate. For the sake of argument, it is helpful to identify several of the more important strands of scholarship that have contributed to this transformation. These include (i) the sociopolitical philosophy of secular liberalism championed by Charles Taylor and to some extent shared by thinkers such as John Rawls and Jürgen

Habermas, (ii) the discourse of "political theology" revived in part by postmodernist theologians and continental philosophers; (iii) Foucault's genealogical critique of power, particularly as it has been deployed by theorists of postcoloniality such as the literary critic Edward Said and the anthropologist Talal Asad.

While all three schools have responded to the challenges posed by the resurgence of religion within the dominant frameworks of modern liberal social democracy, what distinguishes the first two schools from the third is a specifically philosophical investment in the constitution of the modern Western imaginary. This philosophical investment hinges on the belief that there is an essentially historical difference between the West and the Rest. The term "historical difference," which I borrow from Dipesh Chakrabarty, signifies a cluster of related ideas that account for the co-emergence and codependence of religion and secularity in the West, and by implication, why these processes and the forms of cultural and political organization that it spawned (global capitalism, democracy, and so on) could not have emerged in the non-West.

Religion and secularity thus haunt each other such that religion, as it evolved in the West, has always been present in all secular phenomena, even when it appears to be absent, and secularity, in turn, has covertly continued a religious agenda. However, these oscillations between religion and secularity did not take place in a vacuum, but are tied to a series of theoretical developments that helped to create the current map of religion and the secular. These developments were instigated, at least in part, by a logic of reform that was embedded in the Protestant revolution. It was this logic of reform that not only helped to rupture the connections between society and religious life, but also created the rupture in consciousness that generated the individuated religion of devotion (Protestant interiority) that is so integral to our understanding of the secular age.[3]

The key theoretical developments include the following.[4] First, Luther's discovery of the divided self, that is to say, the form of consciousness that separates itself from itself. Second, Kant's discovery of the transcendental faculty of mind whose operative mechanism he termed "the schematization of the categories." This schema unified human experience through three interrelated ideas of reason—God, self, and world—and in so doing Kant laid the groundwork for the disclosure by his successors (such as Hegel) of the self-reflexive structure of self-consciousness. According to Mark C. Taylor, a self-conscious subject is one that "turns back on itself by becoming an object to itself. As a result self-as-subject and self-as-object are reciprocally related in such a way that each becomes itself through the other and neither can be itself apart from the other.[5] The self-conscious subject is therefore noncoincident with itself—it separates itself from itself. This paradoxical structure of self-relation (to be itself the self must separate itself from itself) is what we call self-representation. As Kant sees it, an important consequence of this representational mode of thinking associated with this self-conscious subject is that any object of thought must already be separated from itself. Thus when religion becomes an object of thought, the imperative to separate itself from itself constitutes its secularization. Through this mode of secularization the sanctity of religion is replaced by the sanctity of critique, which then becomes inviolable.[6]

The third development is Hegel's incorporation and reworking of this mode of self-relation into a comprehensive schema for organizing the ever-growing knowledge about other cultures in terms of the historical transition between religion(s), secularity, and the postsecular. It was with Hegel that the notion of historical difference became integral to the determination of the other. Hegel's genius was to integrate the possibility and definition of critical thinking (or critique) with the notion of historical difference. That is to say, religion/tradition can be defined as critical if from its very beginnings it is able to contest its own origins. The ability to separate oneself from one's origins, hence separation from religion or tradition, can be seen as a measure of secularity. In Hegel's reworking of this principle (see the following) the degree to which a culture or religion can carry out this self-separation at its origins not only defines history (and secularity), but also determines the degree to which it is different from other traditions and cultures.[7]

But how exactly did Hegel make the move from the structure of rational self-consciousness (the self-representing subject) to the nature of thinking (critique as a mode of secularization) and finally to a world-historical organization of human society? The key to this move is the complex interplay between, on the one hand, the universalization of the category of religion and, on the other hand, the deployment of a particular religion (Christianity) as the glue that holds together the movement between self-consciousness and secular thought and world-historical society. This move was continually reformulated in his key works, but its most familiar version is found in the *Phenomenology of Spirit*, published in 1806, in which the representational model of self-conscious subjectivity not only explains the relationship between Kant's ideas of reason (God, self, world), but equally accounts for the relationship between religion and secularity (qua history).

For Hegel, the structure of self-consciousness—the field on which the self represents itself to itself—mirrors the conceptual structure of the Incarnation and the Trinity. Taylor explains, "the triadic structure of Father-Son-Spirit is isomorphic with the triadic structure of self-consciousness: self-as-subject [= Father]. Self-as-object [= Son] and the inter-relation of the two [= Spirit]."[8] Since the figure of the Father, which symbolizes transcendence and separation as attributes of religion, is transfigured into that of the Son, it is possible to see how the oscillation between religion and secularity is mediated through the activity of the spirit. And because Spirit is described as that substance which is able to separate itself from itself in the moment of its origin (or what Hegel calls pure elevation, pure movement), the work of Spirit consists in nothing less than a pure relation, an infinitely transparent (or "generalized") translation that is able to move between self and other, subject and object, religion and secularity, infinitely and at will.

What is often forgotten about Hegel's reconstruction of the Kantian imaginary is that even though it universalized its self-referential mode of subjectivity on the basis of a particular religious culture (Christianity), it was not formed in a cultural vacuum. Its backdrop was the growing encounter between European and non-European cultures, an encounter that Hegel was not only aware of, but took an active part in reformulating, especially in his later works, which were written at a time of maximal colonial expansion.[9] Insofar as it represented the self-consciousness of the West, this imaginary was, from the outset, a comparative imaginary "that functioned according to a structured-structuring process."[10] At the very moment that the comparative imaginary was inscribed in and structured the "signifying practices that described, classified, annotated, analyzed, represented, prescribed and ordered the cultural and material world of its colonial subjects, in ways that have too often become naturalized,"[11] in that very moment and through the work of comparison, the very same imaginary was actively fleshing out the identity of European culture. The contours of the West and the non-West were thus codependent and coemergent. They were mutually fleshed out (translated) within and through this model of self-representation. It is possible to suggest that the comparative relation between West and non-West was, and continues to be, isomorphic with the relation between self-as-subject and self-as-object.[12] It was in fact a universalized or "generalized" translation in which the other was reduced to the same (self-as-object) or cast out of the purview of human consciousness altogether.[13] Through this generalized translation that constitutes the comparative relation between self and other (say, Europe and Africa/Asia), "the difference of the other no longer appear[ed] as a threat; a hindrance maybe, and a source of resistance to be quelled, certainly a source of evidence and experiences for reflection on the human condition and for forging the policies and the measures for the transformation of the world."[14]

To briefly restate the above point, the historical coemergence and codependence of religion and secularity, leading up to the contemporary map of these two categories, are inextricably bound to the development of the modern Western imaginary with its constitution of a particular structure of human consciousness. This in turn privileges a particular type of critical thinking as universal (one that grounds itself in self-separation) and a particular religion, Christianity, which acts as the pivotal "axis on which the history of the world turns."[15] Hegel's reference to the turning of the world seems to imply two things.[16] First, the potential for a culture to move from the lowest to the highest stages of religious evolution—typically from paganism to Christianity but also from religion, through secularity, to the postsecular. Second, the potential for changing the world ("world turning") is also an indirect reference to the logic of reform that was embedded within the Protestant revolution. For it is this logic of reform that enabled Christianity to overcome itself, to shift from corporeal practices toward states of interiority and, in the event, give rise to the disenchantment that led to secularism. It was precisely this logic that forced the rupture in consciousness that gave Luther his project. Thus the key to understanding the role of Christianity is the historical—specifically the notion of time central to the task of inheriting (that is, reforming) Christianity that is built into the perceived codependency of religion and the secular.

If the secular and the reform that gave rise to it represent the dynamics of religion's self-overcoming, its ability to turn the axis of the world, then (i) turning implies the movement of history, that is, temporality, (ii) the secular is incipient in religion from the moment that human consciousness emerges as a divided subjectivity. In other words, the relationship between religion and secularity is maintained by a particular notion of history. This notion of history is nothing other than the moment of emergence of a particular form of self-consciousness as the so-called critical attitude that not only came to define the very nature of modern Western man as the relational center of the world, but also constitutes itself as universal insofar as the twinned categories of religion and the secular, time and consciousness, are then inscribed onto every other culture through the work of imperialism.

In this way, prior to their actual colonization, all other cultures of the world (indeed the very possibility of pluralism) were mapped within a framework of historical development in such a way that Christianity provided the essential blueprint for the map and the historical evolution of world cultures inscribed within it. As Jonathon Sheehan suggests, it is through this emerging narrative arrangement of cultures on a world grid, that Christianity came to occupy all of the available sites of intellectual responsibility—"to possess the past. . . . as the originary author of the secular age and yet to disavow responsibility for it."[17] The crucial aspect in this is performed by the narrative itself. For it is the narrative that, on the one hand, recognizes other cultures as religion(s), and in that very moment of recognition sets them apart in a proper place, and on the other hand, inasmuch as it coincides with the transparent movement that is time (or history), ensures the Christian claim to the present (the secular age that we all live in), to its past (the history of the world's religion(s), or the religious history of the world), but also, and perhaps more importantly, to its postsecular future, which would entail a renewal of the secular by returning to its religious sources.[18]

HEGEL'S TRANSCENDENTAL APPARATUS: REMAKING RELIGIOUS PLURALITY

One of the keys factors that enabled the narrative movement from religion to the secular, and through to the postsecular, thereby connecting the world spatially and temporally, is the concept of *religion as a universal*. That philosophical interpretations of the religion-secular-postsecular relationship depended on the ability to conceptualize religion as a universal should not surprise us. Its antecedents can be found in the work of major thinkers of the Enlightenment such as David Hume in the mid-eighteenth century and, even more so, G. W. F. Hegel in the early nineteenth century.

One of the key problems for both Hume and Hegel was to find a reliable intellectual solution to the problem of pluralism and cultural difference as it was manifesting itself in the reports of explorers, missionaries, and orientalists. Although they both worked in different contexts, in different time periods, and with different materials at their disposal, for both Hume and Hegel the only proper solution to the problem presented by the increasing variety of non-Christian cultural beliefs and practices was to assimilate them to a category of religion modeled on a Protestant understanding of religion with "belief and practice at its conceptual center."[19] The closest that Hume comes to entertaining the idea of religion as a universal category can be seen in his *Natural History of Religion*, in which he traces the origin of religion to peculiarly human experiences of hope and fear, arguing that the "first obscure traces of divinity" grow out of "ordinary affections in human life."[20] But even in this influential treatise Hume is very clear to point out that while religion is common (all men potentially have religion) it is not necessarily universal.

While arguments for or against a universally applicable model of religion remain implicit in Hume's accounts, they are far more rigorously theorized by Hegel.

In his Berlin courses, published as the *Lectures on the Philosophy of History* and *Lectures on the Philosophy of Religion*, Hegel effectively constructed just such a model in the form of a comparative schema that could frame all empirical and explanatory knowledge of other cultures within a historicist vector much the same as the one recounted above. Hegel's main concern in the Berlin lecture courses was to counter the philosophical influences of Deism and the debates about natural religion. As Hegel saw it, discourses such as these, especially when deployed by the early orientalists, provided a potentially safe haven for oriental cultures, a means whereby they could adversely influence the European intellectual mindset, and in so doing could possibly displace or undermine the dominant vantage point of Christian European cultural identity. The problem for Hegel was how to differentiate between Christian religion as properly historical (and therefore capable of self-critique and secularization) and other, especially Asian, *religions* as lacking history. Hegel's answer was to establish a firm theoretical standpoint, the concept of religion-in-general, that could be used as a means for *comparing* oriental cultures (particular religions) by means of an ontotheological framework.[21] The term "ontotheology" refers to an essential continuity of different moments in the Western philosophical and theological traditions (specifically the Greek [-*onto*], the medieval-scholastic [*theo-*], and the humanist [*logo-* or *logic*]), a continuity that challenges the dominant secular Enlightenment story in which modernity and humanism constitute a radical break with prior religious tradition.[22]

Hegel's genius was to incorporate both *religion* (by reformulating the existing ontological proofs for God's existence) and *secularity* (through the vector of historicism) into the work of *comparing* different cultures.[23] According to the rules of his schema, the degree to which any culture can think coherently and clearly about "the transcendent" corresponds to its ability to emerge into history, that is, to elevate itself from a purely natural existence. This in turn is a measure of that culture's ability to think *critically*, as measured by its ability to separate itself from itself—and it also measures its degree of secularity. What becomes clear in any close reading of the Hegelian narrative is that the concept of religion-in-general is being fleshed out with the simultaneous inclusion and exclusion of oriental cultures within history (that is, inclusion within the domain of religion*s*, which is simultaneously exclusion from the domain of history/secularity).[24] Furthermore, the concept of religion as universal is fleshed out in a process that is paralleled by the refinement of a specific mode of thinking, the so-called critical attitude that is characteristic of the modern West, in which the operation of thought becomes indistinguishable from *generalized translation* as the ability to translate infinitely and at will between the universal and the particular.

In short, Hegel's ontotheological schema identifies reason with Christianity and thus closes the circular relationship between (i) historical consciousness, (ii) the assumed secularity of critique, and (iii) Western civilizational identity more securely than at any point in the history of philosophy. But more importantly, he can implement this circularity between history, critique, and secularity by identifying tangible others (Asia, Africa, and the like) as "religious," followed by their inclusion-exclusion within the order of knowledge and existence. In other words, by means of the law of history/critique/secularity Hegel is able to constitute a relation between European Christianity and its others. But it is a relation in which the other is excluded through its inclusion within the orders of knowledge and existence. This simultaneous exclusion-inclusion becomes a means for rendering the encounter with non-Western cultures politically harmless. This was achieved by installing these cultures at the lower end of a horizontal axis that charts the development (self-elevation) of cultures of the world from religion through secularity and eventually into the post-secular.[25] The dual purpose of this installation was to give them a comparable and recognizable identity, while through that very gesture subverting their potential for contributing in any way to modernity.[26]

In one sense Hegel's comparative schema (underpinned by the movement from religion to secular to postsecular) can be seen as part of a broader anxiety felt by European intellectuals about an originary diremption, a crisis of identity, at the heart of the intrinsically linked concepts of Europe, Modernity, and Christianity. In other words, Hegel's response to this anxiety was not just epistemological but deeply political, a point that is echoed by Michael Hardt and Antonio Negri in their influential work *Empire*.[27] According to Hardt and Negri, modernity was never a unitary concept, but rather appeared in two ways. The first mode was a radical revolutionary process that broke with the past and declared the immanence of world and life, positing human desire at the center of history. For Hardt and Negri, the philosophy of Spinoza provides a good example of this tendency toward immanence. But it could also be discerned in the supposedly "pantheistic" philosophies of oriental cultures, particularly those of India and China. Opposed to this, however, was a second mode of modernity, which deployed a transcendental apparatus to suppress the potential for liberating the multitude. In the struggle for hegemony between these two modes, victory went to the second and hence to the forces of order that sought to neutralize the revolutionary effects of modernity. This internal conflict at the heart of European modernity was simultaneously reflected on a global scale in the form of external conflict. The same counterrevolutionary power that sought to control the potentially subversive forces within Europe also began to realize the possibility and necessity of subordinating other cultures to European domination. Eurocentrism was born as a reaction to the potentiality of a newfound human equality.[28]

In many ways Hegel's reworking of the comparative imaginary of the West epitomizes this second mode of modernity. As Hardt and Negri point out, intellectual projects such as Hegel's "could not but take place against the backdrop of European expansion . . . and the very real violence of European conquest and colonialism." However, the real threat for Hegel was not physical but intellectual—a threat to the very design of the *concept*. Hence the ontotheological schema can be considered a diagram of power that at the same time provided a mechanism of power for controlling the constituent and subversive forces within Europe that championed a revolutionary plane of immanence, as well as a "negation of non-European desire." During Hegel's tenure, the thought of his rivals, such as Schelling and later Schopenhauer, must be considered good examples of "non-European desire."

The results of this transcendental apparatus—the new comparative schema—were far reaching. Deploying for the first time the terms "pantheism," "monotheism," and "polytheism" as "world-historical" or comparative categories, the schema provided an intuitive comprehension of the "meaning-value" of each culture that happened to be plotted on the axis.[29] The insidious aspect of this schema is not simply the representation of diversity, plurality, difference, time, and other(s) through a configuration of the "world," but more accurately the fleshing out and preservation of the particular constellations "Europe," the "West," "Christianity," and "the Secular" through the category of universal religion.[30] It is this move that allowed Hegel, and after Hegel a host of orientalists, missionaries, philosophers, anthropologists, historians, economists, and religionists, to apply models that recognized the diversity of world cultures in terms of similarity and difference. Non-Western cultures could be recognized as *religions* (and therefore similar to "our own," that is, Christianity, and as part of a broad human unity) but at the same time served to differentiate between humans and cultures precisely on the basis of their different religious elevation, their incompatibility with secular cultures of Europe. This ambivalent schema, which simultaneously *produces religions* of the world as a measure of their *historical* difference from the West, even as they are denied the ability to overcome or reform themselves except through a developmental process based on Western patterns, was put to use intellectually and practically during the colonial and postcolonial era.

Obviously, variations of this Eurocentric schema were located within the broader imperialist politics of modernization, understood as a civilizing mission when referring to the "Rest." Intellectually, aspects of it were incorporated into hermeneutic explanations about the essential nature of non-Western cultures that would eventually become seamlessly incorporated into the system of the emerging human sciences. Within an emerging world-religion discourse, the schema provided an intuitive comprehension of the "meaning-value" of cultures through a principle of "generalized translation"—a mechanism for bringing different cultures into a taxonomic system of equivalence, in which the relative meaning-values could be assigned to each culture in order for them to be exchanged or compared. By bringing the meaning-value of different cultures into a system of exchange-comparison, this approach effectively replaced the tangible problem of translation (and hence the anxiety of real encounter) with the work of representation proper to the political economy of the sign. Within the context of cultural exchange and comparison that begins to parallel commodity exchange in the political economy of empire, the system of exchange-comparison that is intrinsic to the comparative cultural imaginary of the West can be seen as a precursor of the system of global monetary exchange, which, as Karl Marx pointed out, developed at roughly the same time.[31]

In practice, the principle of "generalized translation" (which combined the twin assumptions that critique is secular[32] and that religion is a universal category) was transferred almost invisibly from philosophical texts into the work of orientalists and missionaries as the privileged interpreters and translators of key indigenous texts and cultural practices. From there it passed, again seamlessly, into the policy-making decisions of administrators, lawmakers, and educators during the colonial period, and then crucially into the reformist-cum-nationalist (religionizing and secularizing) projects of native elites in various parts of the colonial world.[33]

Of course, as we know only too well today, the work of the schema of generalized translation did not stop with the colonial era but can be seen in the centrality of historicism and secular critique that continues to underpin the contemporary human sciences in such a way that it continues to theoretically exclude non-Western cultures, to "ban them from entering signification (the realm of human intellectual and physical contact and interaction)" and yet at the same time to "retain, rename and elevate them in a benevolent second-order gesture as signification's spectral other."[34]

Because it is born out of a particular religion (Christianity), and in order to justify its claim to be a universal discourse that can maintain its promise of peace, the secular-historicist regime has to be able to *produce* religion in other cultural sites. Yet this could be done only by the assumption of religion as a universal. That is, religion has to have a logic that requires the translation of itself, which means that it performs an invisible violence toward every culture it encounters. Only then can it be desired by all and accepted without the imposition of direct colonial violence. Consequently the normative and dominant diagnosis of a West that is secular (and/or postsecular) versus a non-West that is nonsecular (and/or religious) remains persuasive. Indeed, as Dingwaney and Rajan argue, this occurs "even when recast in tones of politically correct self-reproach and postmodern interrogation among intellectuals in the Western academy, as, for example, in the following statement issued at a recent major Euro-American conference on "political theologies":

> Imagined to be universal in both relevance and application, the rigid boundaries by which secular social structures divide the public sphere of political processes from private commitments to the values inculcated by religious and spiritual traditions have proved, instead, a source of mounting resistance on the part of cultures in which the superiority of such structures is not self-evident.

The statement continues to insist on the urgency of understanding the "religiously informed resistance to pressures of secularization and cultural-political assimilation implicit in the continuing sources of tension between the 'secular' West and the developing societies imagined in the West as the 'beneficiaries of globalization.'"[35]

What Dingwaney and Rajan usefully draw attention to is the phenomenon of *religion-making*—the fact that "religion is still called on to serve as the distinguishing mark of such minority identity struggles. Even though the globalizing West may be blamed for such a development, it implicitly remains the secular [or postsecular (author's insertion)] party in this narrative."[36] As I have argued above, the mechanisms by which religion-making continues to do its work (historical difference, secular critique and its concomitant, the belief in religion as a cultural universal) can be attributed more to Hegel than to any other modern thinker.

NOTES

1. Catharine Malabou, *The Future of Hegel: Plasticity, Temporality and Dialectic*, trans. Lisabeth During (New York: Routledge, 2005).
2. Ibid., 13.

3. See Charles Taylor's extended discussion of this in *A Secular Age* (Cambridge, Mass.: Belknap Press of Harvard University Press, 2007).

4. See Mark C. Taylor, *After God* (Chicago: University of Chicago Press, 2008), chap. 2.

5. Ibid., 111.

6. A useful source here is Ananda Abeysekara, "The Impossibility of Secular Critique," *Culture and Religion* 11, no. 3 (2010).

7. For a detailed discussion of this, see Arvind Mandair, *Religion and the Specter of the West* (New York: Columbia University Press), chap. 2.

8. Taylor, *After God*, 159.

9. There are many scholarly works that highlight the importance of the colonial encounter with Hegel's philosophical work. Relevant works include: Wilhem Halbfass, *India and Europe: An Essay in Understanding* (Albany: State University of New York Press, 1988); J. L. Mehta, *India and the West: The Problem of Understanding* (Chico, Calif.: Scholar's Press, 1985); Jacques Derrida, *Glas*, trans. Richard Rand and John P. Leavey (Lincoln: University of Nebraska Press, 1986); Gayatri Spivak, *A Critique of Postcolonial Reason* (Cambridge, Mass.: Harvard University Press, 2000); Susan Buck-Morss, *Hegel, Haiti and Universal History* (Pittsburgh: Pittsburgh University Press, 2009); Arvind Mandair, *Religion and the Specter of the West: Sikhism, India, Postcoloniality, and the Politics of Translation* (New York: Columbia University Press, 2009).

10. Couze Venn, *Occidentalism* (London: Sage, 1997), 147.

11. Ibid.

12. See Naoki Sakai, "The Dislocation of the West," *Traces: A Multilingual Journal of Cultural Theory and Practice* 1 (2001): 71–94.

13. The term "generalized translation" is borrowed from Jacques Derrida. However, the sense in which I use it is somewhat wider than Derrida's. See also chapter 17 in this volume, "Translation." Jacques Derrida, "Theology of Translation," in *Eyes of the University: The Right to Philosophy II*, trans. Jan Plug (Stanford: Stanford University Press, 2004), 65.

14. Venn, *Occidentalism*, 147.

15. G. W. F. Hegel, *Lectures on the Philosophy of History*, trans. J. Sibree (New York: Dover, 1956), 319.

16. See also the helpful discussion in, Malabou, *The Future of Hegel*, 115–17.

17. Jonathan Sheehan, "When Was Disenchantment? History and the Secular Age," in *Varieties of Secularism in a Secular Age*, ed. Michael Warner, Jonathan van Antwerpen, and Craig Calhoun (Cambridge, Mass.: Harvard University Press, 2010), 240.

18. For similar arguments, see Gil Anidjar, "Secularism," in *Semites: Race, Religion, Literature*, Cultural Memory in the Present (Stanford: Stanford University Press, 2007), chap. 3.

19. Robert Baird, "Late Secularism," in *Secularisms*, ed. Janet R. Jakobsen and Ann Pellengrini (Durham: Duke University Press, 2009), 165–66.

20. David Hume, *Natural History of Religion*, ed. A. Wayne Clover (New York: Oxford University Press, 1976), 33.

21. See G. W. F. Hegel, *Lectures on Philosophy of Religion*, trans. and ed. Robert Brown (Oxford: Oxford University Press, 2009).

22. See Mandair, *Religion and the Specter of the West*.

23. Again, a particularly good example of this can be found in the *LPR* texts; see Mandair, *Religion and the Specter of the West*.

24. See discussion on this in Spivak, *A Critique of Postcolonial Reason.*

25. This axis is, of course, entirely virtual, an imagined function of the narrative itself.

26. Antonio Negri and Michael D. Hardt, *Empire* (Cambridge, Mass.: Harvard University Press, 2000), 74–77.

27. Ibid.

28. Ibid., chap. 2.1.

29. I borrow the term "meaning-value" from Lydia Liu, "The Question of Meaning-Value in the Political Economy of the Sign," in *Tokens of Exchange: The Problem of Translation in Global Circulations*, ed. Lydia H. Liu (Durham: Duke University Press, 1999), 13–44.

30. See Tomoko Masuzawa, *The Invention of World Religions; Or, How European Universalism Was Preserved in the Language of Pluralism* (Chicago: University of Chicago Press, 2005). A detailed explanation of Hegel's epistemo-political schema can be found in Mandair, *Religion and the Specter of the West*, 147–60.

31. A related discussion can be found in my chapter "Translation," chapter 17 in this volume.

32. For a particularly helpful probing of the relationship between secularity and critique, see Asad's essays in Talal Asad et al., *Is Critique Secular? Blasphemy, Injury and Free Speech* (Berkeley: University of California Press, 2009).

33. I am by no means suggesting that Hegel's schema (or Hegelian ideology) was uncontested during the last two centuries. Far from it. All I am suggesting is that when one looks for a convergence of the key ciphers that constitute Western civilizational identity—as rooted in a convergence of Christianity, the "critical attitude," historicism, secularism, liberalism, democracy, freedom, and so on—it is Hegel more than any other thinker who brings them all together in a way that others were not able to do. And despite the fact that Hegelian thought was contested so vigorously, his basic schema, far from disappearing, seems to have morphed into what might call the global/Western "social imaginary," partly through the more palatable and sophisticated renderings of his comparative schema, for example, by Karl Marx, Max Weber, Ernest Troeltsch, and any number of religionists during the twentieth century. Even today, if one looks closely at many of the postmodern and postsecular defenses of Western civilizational identity (for example, Slavoj Žižek, Mark C. Taylor, and Charles Taylor, among others), Hegel is still a primary point of reference.

34. Rey Chow, *The Age of the World Target: Self-Referentiality in War, Theory and Comparative Work* (Durham: Duke University Press, 2006). For a fuller discussion on this see also Mandair, *Religion and the Specter of the West.*

35. Anuradha Dingwaney and Rajeshwari Sundar Rajan, *The Crisis of Secularism in India* (Durham: Duke University Press, 2007), 3.

36. Ibid., 3–4.

5

Friedrich Max Müller and the Science of Religion

LOURENS VAN DEN BOSCH

INTRODUCTION

The scientific study of religion originated in the second half of the nineteenth century, a period marked by a widening of the cultural horizon as a result of progressing colonialism. However, it was also a period of unsettlement of Christian faith among educated people in Europe. First, a conflict was felt between science and religion and, second, one between history and revelation. These themes were raised in the work of Friedrich Max Müller (1823–1900), who argued for a scientific and impartial study of religion and coined the term "science of religion." Müller's views often refer to academic debates in England and Germany; some of the main players are mentioned here.

Charles Lyell (1785–1863) argued in his *Principles of Geology* that life on earth had existed for millions of years, refuting traditional biblical chronology. Subsequently, Charles Darwin (1808–82) developed an alternative theory of creation in his *Origin of Species*, proposing a theory of evolution based on natural selection. Thomas Huxley (1825–95) adjusted this theory into "survival of the fittest by natural selection," thus introducing progress. These scientists relegated biblical stories about creation and the like to the field of myth and legend. The conviction that science did not go well together with Christian creeds became more wide spread among educated people.

The center of Christianity was touched when the New Testament came under attack. Historical research developed methods to test the reliability of texts with respect to historical data. The Tübingen School with scholars like Ferdinand Baur (1792–1860) and Friedrich Strauss (1808–74) developed a "Higher Criticism of the Bible." They tried to show that the historical Jesus defied the Christ of faith. Revelation was relegated to history, where its meaning had to be discovered. As a consequence of this, Christianity had to compete with the other world religions. In this changing intellectual climate Müller developed an evolutionary approach to the study of religion, but derived his formative ideas from his study in Germany. A short sketch of his life may suffice.

A PHILOLOGIST BECOMES SCHOLAR
OF RELIGION

Müller was born in 1823 in an educated Lutheran family of officials in the service of the dukes of Dessau-Anhalt (Germany). After the untimely death of his father, Wilhelm Müller (poet of *Winter Journey* and the *Beautiful Miller's Daughter*, set to music by Franz Schubert), in 1827, young Max received ducal support, which enabled him to study at various universities. He studied philology and philosophy—particularly Kant and Hegel—at the University of Leipzig, where he wrote his thesis on Spinoza's *Ethica* in 1843. In these years he also developed a great interest in Sanskrit and its ancient literature.

In 1844, Müller went to Berlin to study the comparative grammar of Indo-European languages under Franz Bopp (1791–1867) and philosophy under Friedrich Schelling (1774–1854). Fascination with the Vedas brought him to Paris in 1845, where Eugène Burnouf (1801–52), specialist in Vedic texts, stimulated him to prepare a critical edition of the Rig-Veda. There he met Dwarkanath Tagore, a highly cultured Indian, who taught him about the Brahmo Samâj, a reform movement that wanted to undo Hinduism from its mythological accretions. Müller developed a great interest in these reform movements and became in touch with many of their leaders.

In 1846, Müller went to London to work in the library of the India Office, a treasury for Sanskrit manuscripts. There he collected the funds for his Rig-Veda project from the East India Company. He moved to Oxford, which was supposed to only be temporary, but he became enthralled by the city and stayed there for the rest of his life. Müller's edition of the Rig-Veda with Sayana's commentary appeared in six volumes between 1849 and 1874. He later often referred to the Rig-Veda, because it contained religious poetry expressive of the most ancient stages of mankind.

Müller, who was versed in German Romanticism and Idealism, functioned in England as an intermediary of German culture. In 1854, he became professor of European languages at a semiacademic institute. He focused his research particularly on linguistic origins and argued that the history of the human mind could be read in the records of language, thus introducing a kind of linguistic paleontology. Müller was passed over for the chair of Sanskrit in Oxford in 1860, because he was German and associated with modernism. He went on with linguistics and finally received a professorship in comparative philology at the University of Oxford in 1867, in recognition of his *Lectures on the Science of Language*. At that time, his interests were led toward the scientific study of religion. Colonial expansion had led to huge accumulation of materials for the study of the world religions. He wondered how to survey the whole field of religious thought, how to classify the religions of the past and the present, and how describe their main features adequately. This was the task he set himself for the rest of his life.

THE SCIENCE OF RELIGIONS AND THE RELIGIONS OF THE WORLD

Müller developed his view of religion in his *Introduction to the Science of Religion*. There he argued for the impartial and scientific comparison of the religions of the world. As a philologist, he focused on religions with written traditions and stated that the texts should be studied in their original languages with the methods that textual and historical research had developed. One should distinguish older from younger traditions, but remain aware of the continuity between past and present.

Müller acknowledged that it was impossible for one scholar to study all the texts in the original languages. In 1874, he proposed to the International Orientalist Congress in London that he edit a series of annotated translations of the authoritative texts, known as *Sacred Books of the East*, in which fifty-one volumes appeared between 1879 and 1901. He included in this series all those books that had been formally recognized by religious communities as the highest authorities in matters of religion. In making this decision, he founded his selection of texts on the acknowledgment of religious communities, thus distancing himself from criteria current in monotheistic traditions. However, the sponsors of the Oxford University Press rejected his proposal to include the Old and New Testament in the series, because it would place Christianity on a par with the other "book religions." Müller viewed Christianity as a historical manifestation of religion, but was convinced that it could stand the test of being compared with other religions.

The comparative method had produced many important results in the natural sciences. For this reason, scholars in the humanities started to apply this approach as well. Taking Goethe's well-known epigram that "he who knows one language knows none," Müller argued that he who knows one religion knows none. He stressed that empirical knowledge of a single religious datum did not lead to scientific knowledge. The diversity in religions made him wonder what the world religions shared in common and where they differed, and further, how they rise and decline. He took as a guideline: *divide et impera*. The classification and comparison of religious concepts were of central importance in achieving scientific knowledge about religion.

Müller proposed a classification of religions according to linguistic criteria. The discovery of a common origin of the Indo-European languages and peoples enabled him to search for common religious concepts. By comparing linguistically related concepts, he tried to reconstruct the main religious ideas of the Indo-European peoples. But it also enabled him to trace the historical progress of religious concepts in the course of time. He suggested a similar program for the Semitic languages and its peoples, so that a typology could be made of the original religions of both groups. The manifestation of God in nature was the most important feature of the Indo-European people, while the manifestation of God in history was essential for the religion of the Semitic people. With this approach, he followed in the footsteps of Johann Gottfried von Herder (1744–1803), Wilhelm von Humboldt (1767–1835), and Hegel, who had argued for a close relationship between religion, language, and *ethnos*. Müller tried to fortify their views by referring to comparative linguistics.

Müller distinguished two aspects in studying religion, a historical and a theoretical one. The historical dimension focused on religion as a doctrinal system, handed down in books, rituals, and so on. But religion also had a psychological dimension that could not be reduced to its concrete historical manifestations. Religions all sprang from the same sacred soil, the human heart. He initially defined religion as a mental disposition that, independent of sense and reason, enables man to apprehend the Infinite under different names and under different disguises. A vague sense of the Infinite was the first impulse behind all religion. Müller's debt to Friedrich Schleiermacher (1768–1834) is evident in this view, but he gave his own twist to it by arguing that all religions were human endeavors to express this feeling. He thus gave an anthropological foundation to religion.

Müller regarded the Vedas as essential to the study of the origin and growth of religion. These texts enabled him to trace the various attempts of naming the Infinite in ancient India: from the pristine concepts in the Rig-Veda to the elevated ideas of the Upanishads. The Rig-Veda represented religion in a primeval stage, through which other religions had already passed, enabling him to study the initial growth of a theogony, in which there was no clear-cut system of religion and mythology. The text showed far more convincingly than any special revelation how the human mind went from the perception of the great phenomena of nature to the conception of agents behind these phenomena, the gods of nature. Müller introduced the term "henotheism" in order to denote this vague notion of the Divine, evoked by the perception of nature. As a stage, henotheism preceded polytheism (belief in many separate gods connected with specific natural phenomena) and polytheism preceded monotheism (belief in one god).

Müller illustrated his view by the example of the sun, a natural phenomenon that became connected with the idea of order and regularity, with trust, and developed from a mere luminary into a creator, preserver, and ruler of the world, in fact into a divine Supreme Being. At the same time, the sun had to share this idea of being divine with gods to whom similar features had been attributed. Gradually, the deities were divested of their material characteristics and fused into the concept of one god as manifested in monotheistic traditions.

A detailed analysis of the history of religions and a comparison of religious ideas were the basis for Müller's philosophy of religion. With Schelling and Hegel, Müller agreed that the history of religions also was a history of God's gradual disclosure. God's spirit had its influence on the mind of man in all ages and everywhere; there was "Truth" in all religions. Müller, therefore, accepted religious plurality and gave it a basis by referring to Kantian epistemology, but he regarded it also as a challenge for reflection on the human condition. He believed history to be a site for divine education. Religious dialogue that was based on the sacred books of mankind might contribute to better understanding of the message underlying all religions. The religions of the past served to understand the present. They formed the basis for a universal religion, sometimes also denoted by him as a religion of humanity.

In his Gifford Lectures on natural religion (1888–92), Müller developed a philosophy of religion that culminated in theosophy with panentheistic features. True theosophy, the highest ken within the reach of the human mind, would lead to a new universal religion, to a new view of man, and to a new brotherhood. For this reason, Müller supported the World Parliament of Religions in Chicago in 1893.

MYTHOLOGY

One of Müller's central aims was to discover reason behind the unreason of mythology. He did not accept the assumption of contemporaries that there was little point in looking for deeper meaning in the myths of ancient Greece. He argued that these irrational myths called for a scientific explanation that allowed for their origin and development. The etymological method of comparative philology proved valuable in reconstructing the oldest strata of Indo-European mythology. Müller focused on common mythical traditions and tried to identify the names of the principal actors in myths. The correct etymology of their names offered a clue to solve many riddles. This convinced him that ancient mythology had a physical basis. A fixed symbolic order lay beneath the chaotic surface of mythology, which referred to the great regular phenomena in nature: day and night, sun and moon, dawn and dusk, light and darkness. Early mankind had selected these phenomena as metaphors of sacred reality, because regularity in nature suggested order and gave meaning to existence. On account of his stress on the physical aspects of early religion, Müller was regarded as the main protagonist of the Nature Myth School.

Müller used the myth of Daphne and Phoibos Apollo to show his approach to mythology. Apollo fell in love with Daphne, but she was afraid of him and fled from him, praying to her mother, the earth, to guard her. The earth took her in her lap and at the place where she had disappeared a laurel tree sprang up. The word *phoibos*, "bright shining," was originally an epithet of the sun, but it developed into an independent deity associated with the rising sun. This deity fused with Apollo. Daphne was etymologically related to the Sanskrit *ahanâ*, "dawn." The word went back to an Indo-European root *dah*, "to burn" or to "be bright." The nymph Daphne was thus originally dawn. The love of the rising sun for dawn and its tragic consequences could be seen every day at sunrise, the fading away of dawn on account of the fiery rays of the sun and her disappearance in the lap of the earth. All these elements belonged to common Indo-European mythology and had parallels in Vedic lore. The last part of the story, the change of Daphne into a laurel tree, was a pure Greek legend. The laurel was a much-sought-after firewood because of its bright burning qualities and was therefore called *Daphne*, derived from the same verbal root, *dah*. Thus the original meaning of the myth and its subsequent development was traced.

When the original meaning of the names was forgotten and these names became petrified and nontransparent, new interpretations became current. The *nomina* became *numina* and started to live their own life. Phoibos became a beautiful youth in love with an equally beautiful girl, Daphne, but it remained unclear why she had fled and had disappeared in the lap of the earth. When people no longer understood their metaphors, they went astray and became embezzled by their own language. Müller called this development a disease of language, which affected human thought. It was the task of philosophy to fight against this kind of mythology.

CRITICAL EVALUATION

Müller's theories of mythology came in the course of time under attack from many sides. Andrew Lang (1844–1912), for instance, was one of the first who argued that Müller did not explain the more violent aspects of mythology. He drew attention to the worldwide parallels in mythology and lobbied for comparative studies within the context of ethnology, the science promoted by Edward Tylor (1832–1917). The disease of language could not explain myths about murder, incest, rape, sodomy, or castration, and foreclosed the exploration of the darker aspects of human existence as embodied in myth. Müller's naturalistic view of mythology was therefore inadequate. He focused too much on the origin of myth and not enough on its historical development. Moreover, his linguistic approach prevented him from dealing with the various influences exerted by the social, cultural, and physical settings in which myths originated.

Müller's view of religion also did not stand the test of time, intertwined as it was with mythology and language. Cornelis Tiele (1830–1907), another founding father of the study of religion, was one of the first to criticize him. Religion is expressed not only in words, but also in rituals. Therefore, it should not be reduced to a sacred dialect of human speech, but it requires the study of rituals as well.

Müller's definition of religion was also refuted. Though he claimed it to be founded on religious materials, it was highly abstract and derived from philosophy. It was based on a subjective perception of the individual and did not take the social dimension of religion into account. It was rooted in protestant belief, in which words as vehicles of ideas are central to the interpretation of religion. Müller was a proponent of a theological view of the science of religion, a view that gave priority to the study of concepts expressed in words; he made the study of rites and other aspects of religion of subordinate importance.

Müller's aspiration to find a message for humanity in the history of religions pervaded his study of religion and caused flaws. He often mixed up descriptions of historical processes with theological interpretations that originated in his personal view of Christianity. This disqualified him in the eyes of later generations of scholars in the field. Nonetheless, his contributions to the science of religion have been of great importance.[1] He was one of the first scholars to propose a theory for a scientific study of religion and to promote its development. By lecturing publicly, he presented the new discipline to a broad, educated audience and fostered its goodwill. His publications stimulated many contemporary scholars, although the comparative study of religion moved away from the theology of religions he proposed.

NOTE

1. Lourens P. van den Bosch, "Friedrich Max Müller: His Contributions to the Science of Religion," in *Comparative Studies in the History of Religions*, ed. E. R. Sand and J. P. Sorenson (Copenhagen: Museum Tusculum Press, 1999), 11–39. For further readings, see J. R. Stone, ed., *The Essential Max Müller: On Language, Mythology and Religion* (London: Palgrave Macmillan, 2002); H. G. Kippenberg, *Discovering Religious History in the Modern Age* (Princeton: Princeton University Press, 2002); and E. J. Sharpe, *Comparative Religion*, 2nd ed. (London: Duckworth, 1986).

6

Classic Comparative Theology and the Study of Religion

HUGH NICHOLSON

THE LEGACY OF COMPARATIVE THEOLOGY

Max Müller's *Introduction to the Science of Religion*, the text that Eric Sharpe calls "the foundation document of comparative religion,"[1] refers to the new science it was trying to promote with a term that has long since passed out of circulation and is therefore apt to strike today's reader as somewhat odd, namely, "comparative theology."[2] The term actually was among the loosely allied set of terms—including the more familiar "science of religion," "history of religions," and "comparative religion"—used in the later part of the nineteenth century to designate the new and uncertain discipline that was then taking shape.[3] "Comparative theology" was distinguished from those other designations not, as one might expect, by an acknowledged theological commitment, but rather by its implicit restriction of the object of comparative study to the intellectual or doctrinal component of religion.[4] In this sense, "theology" formed the *object* of comparison, where comparison was understood to be a method of scientific discovery.[5] At the same time, however, theology—specifically, a form of Christian fulfillment theology—also functioned as the *subject* of comparison. For paradigmatic works of comparative theology such as James Freeman Clarke's *Ten Great Religions: An Essay in Comparative Theology*,[6] or F. D. Maurice's *Religions of the World and Their Relations with Christianity*,[7] an ostensibly fair and impartial study of the religions leads to the conclusion that Christianity fulfills and thereby renders obsolete all the others.[8] It should be added, however, that those works in the new science of comparative religion whose designations include the word "theology" were hardly unique in their use of comparison to proclaim the superiority of Christianity.

As indicated by Muller's reference to the then growing body of literature in comparative theology in the preface of his *Introduction*, comparative theology clearly belongs to the genealogy of the modern study of religion. Curiously, however, this considerable body of literature has been all but ignored in the standard histories of the discipline.[9] Tomoko Masuzawa suggests that this failure to acknowledge the importance of comparative theology in the disciplinary history of comparative religion reflects the discipline's interest in presenting itself as a legitimate, that is to say, nontheological, academic discipline.[10] By calling attention to the all-but-forgotten legacy of comparative theology, Masuzawa exposes the unacknowledged ideological nexus between the academic study of religion and liberal theology. In particular, the comparative theology of the late nineteenth century represents the "missing link" between today's pervasive and ostensibly unproblematic discourse of "world religions," on the one hand, and the nineteenth-century missiological concept of Christianity as the "world religion," on the other.

Generally speaking, comparative theological works seek to ground the normative claim that Christianity is the world religion—that it is, in other words, the one religion uniquely suited to serve as the religion of all humanity—in an apparently empirical distinction between those religions that have managed to spread outside their original cultural contexts and those that have not. This initial distinction between world (or universal) religions and national (or ethnic) religions prepares the ground for the eventual identification of Christianity as the world religion by narrowing down the field of candidates, typically, though with some exceptions, to Buddhism, Islam, and—of course—Christianity. Having whittled down the list of world religions—the concept here of "world religions" in the plural is clearly recognizable as the ancestor of the current pluralistic notion of seven to ten "world religions"—these works then proceed to argue that Buddhism and Islam are, in fact, only national religions in disguise, a demonstration that leaves Christianity—predictably—as the only legitimate claimant to the title. This form of argument beautifully illustrates the thesis that at the core of the seemingly innocent, pluralistic concept of world religions lies the normative missiological concept of Christianity as *the* world religion. Despite its claim to have made a clean break with the tradition of Christian apologetics by rejecting its central category of "revealed" religion, comparative theology differs from that tradition in little more than its style of presentation, specifically in its presentation of a foreordained theological claim as the natural result of impartial, scientific inquiry. The comparative method, in other words, here serves as little more than as a rhetorical technique to naturalize a claim of Christian absolutism.

The works of nineteenth-century comparative theology challenge today's interpreter to understand how their authors could reconcile a sincere belief in their impartiality with unabashed assertions of Christian superiority.[11] The key to solving this interpretive puzzle is to recognize that "world religion"—and therewith Christianity—was not seen as simply one type of religion, in which case the claim would be undeniably partial, but rather as religion itself in its essence. The concept of world religion, in other words, coincides with the unitary concept of religion that formed the object of the new science of comparative religion.[12] The theological demonstration that Christianity is the world religion, then, could plausibly be understood to be integral to the scientific study of religion.

That the concept of world religion coincides with the generic concept of religion becomes clear when we trace the genealogy of the distinction between world religion and national religion to the post-Enlightenment theological problematic of identifying an essence of religion transcending the "political" aspects of historical religions—sectarian strife, intolerance, and persecution.

THE LIBERAL QUEST TO DEPOLITICIZE RELIGION

The categories of world religion and national religion apparently first appear in an essay by the theologian J. S. Drey (1777–1853), the founder of the Tübingen School of Catholic theology.[13] In that essay, "Von der Landesreligion und der Weltreligion" (1827), the categories do not serve the purposes of empirical classification and comparison; from beginning to end the term "world religion" appears in the singular. Rather, they give expression to the claim that true religion transcends the kind of sectarian division and mutual antagonism that Europe witnessed in the sixteenth- and seventeenth-century Wars of Religion. The idea of the world religion—instantiated, albeit imperfectly, in the Catholic Church—embodies the principles of unity and peace, national religion, for which Roman civic religion and the paganisms of pre-Christian Europe serve as models, those of division and strife.[14] Ultimately, the categories reflect Drey's more immediate and practical concern that the Church disentangle itself from the affairs of the state.[15]

For Drey—and this is the essential difference between him and the later comparativists who appropriate his schema of world religion and national religion—the categories of world religion and national religion correspond, respectively, to the traditional Christian apologetic categories of revealed religion and natural religion. Christianity evidences its divine source and principle by overcoming the putatively natural tendency for nations and peoples to separate and fight with one another.[16] Drey's concept of world religion thus serves to highlight the salient characteristic of revealed religion—which is to say, true religion—namely, its capacity to reconcile the peoples of the world with one another.

Perhaps the best-known and most influential expression of this claim that true religion transcends the principle of political division is Friedrich Schleiermacher's (1768–1834) *On Religion: Speeches to Its Cultured Despisers* (the first edition of which was published in 1799). Schleiermacher's apologetic aim in this classic work is to show that what the "cultured despisers" despise about religion, namely, its tendency to engender sectarian strife and persecution, is adventitious to the essence of religion.[17] Schleiermacher's effort to "depoliticize" religion attains its clearest expression in the often-neglected Fourth Speech, "On the Social Element [*das Gesellige*] in Religion." There he develops a contrast between the "true church" and the "external religious society" that parallels Drey's later distinction between world religion and national religion. The true church embodies the principles of reconciliation and unity, the external religious society the principles of antagonism and separation. Like oil and water, these heterogeneous forms of religious association would naturally separate were it not for corruptive forces from without—in particular, an obtrusive state seeking to bring the Church under its influence—that force them together in an artificial unity.[18]

Despite his sharp criticism of the Enlightenment's attempt to abstract a lowest common denominator from the various historical "positive" religions,[19] Schleiermacher's notion of an unbounded form of religious community founded on a particular kind of religious intuition (his "sense and taste of the Infinite") represents a response to the same problematic that inspired Enlightenment figures like Herbert of Cherbury, John Toland, Matthew Tindal, and David Hume to develop the concept of natural religion. Both concepts represent attempts to identify an essence of religion transcending the sectarian controversies that ostensibly motivated and justified the Wars of Religion. As such, they can be seen as a reflex of the modern differentiation of cultural spheres in which the religious sphere "came fully into its own, specializing in 'its own religious function' and either dropping or losing many other 'nonreligious' functions it had accumulated and could no longer meet efficiently."[20]

We see, then, that the Enlightenment's concept of natural religion, which, according to Samuel Preus,[21] marks a paradigm shift from a theological to a "naturalistic" approach to the study of religion, stems from the same problematic of depoliticizing religion from which the theological concept of world religion developed. Despite this common source, the two concepts subsequently follow distinct, though parallel and sometimes convergent, trajectories. The theological trajectory inaugurated by Schleiermacher separates the essence of religion from the concept of natural religion. Drey formalizes this separation when he correlates his concept of world religion with the contrasting term of natural religion, namely, revealed religion. Comparative theology reverses this divergent tendency when it disarticulates Drey's categories of world religion and national religion from those of revealed religion and natural religion. By dissolving the link between revealed religion and world religion, comparative theology brings the latter concept in line with the Enlightenment tradition of natural religion. What appears as an unhappy confusion of science and theological commitment from the point of view of a "modernist" scholar like Preus who reads the history of comparative religion in terms of an antithesis between naturalistic and theological approaches to the study of religion can perhaps be seen from another perspective as the reconciliation of two cognate principles.[22]

FROM CHRISTIAN UNIVERSALISM TO RELIGIOUS PLURALISM

During the early decades of the twentieth century, the distinction between world religion and national religion gave way to the familiar notion of seven to ten world religions. In lieu of an analysis of the complex set of factors responsible for the emergence of the world religions discourse, we might mention two separate events that each herald, although in different ways, this transition from Christian universalism to religious pluralism.

The first of these markers was Ernst Troeltsch's late essay, "The Place of Christianity Among the World Religions" (1923),[23] the text of a talk he was supposed to deliver at Oxford had death not intervened. In this essay, Troeltsch reflects critically on his earlier historical and theological work, in particular on his previous understanding of the absolute validity of Christianity in terms of its putative ability to transcend the limits of a particular cultural or civilizational matrix. Against this understanding of Christianity as the world religion, Troeltsch now asserts that

Christianity is indissolubly wedded to European civilization,[24] a claim that likely reflects a concern with promoting European unity in the immediate aftermath of the Great War[25]—he was, after all, a German invited to give a lecture in Britain—as much as it does a heightened appreciation of the principle of historicity. Troeltsch, in other words, denies that Christianity can be a world religion in the objective, universalistic sense that the term had in the nineteenth century.[26]

A second event signaling the transition to pluralism was the World Parliament of Religions in Chicago in 1893. If Troeltsch's essay marks the demise of the nineteenth-century universalist concept of world religion, the Parliament did the same for its counterconcept, national religion. Against the intentions of the Christian organizers of the Parliament, the appearance of representatives of the various "national" religions on the world stage implicitly called into question the appropriateness of the category of national religion. In an announcement that would shortly prove prophetic for the study of religion, Rabbi Emil Hirsch declared at the conclusion of the conference that "the day of national religions is past. The God of the universe speaks to all mankind."[27]

The advent of the current pluralistic notion of world religions marks a sudden reversal from the nineteenth-century tendency to restrict the number of world religions, a tendency that, as we saw above, reached the point of revoking the universal status of Buddhism and Islam. Now the membership of the class of world religions is expanded to include the formerly national religions Hinduism and Judaism as well as the indigenous religions of China (Taoism and Confucianism) and Japan (Shinto).[28]

Prima facie, this reversal marks a change in the meaning of the term "world religions" from one that was more evaluative (that is, world religions as opposed to national religions) to one that was more neutral and objective (any major religion in the world).[29] There is a sense, however, in which the reversal marks the complete triumph of a normative-evaluative sense of the term over one that was more neutral and descriptive. As we have seen, the nineteenth-century concept of world religion(s) combined—or better, conflated—the normative notion of the religion appropriate for all humanity, on the one hand, and the more neutral, empirical notion of a religion that had spread beyond the confines of a particular nation or people, on the other. When the concept of national religion falls out of use, the contrast that sustained the latter, more descriptive dimension of meaning disappears. Isolated from its proper contrasting term, "world religion" ceases to be informative; it becomes little more than a quasi-emotive expression of recognition and respect. Once the designation "world religion" becomes more or less a direct expression of the liberal attitudes of tolerance and respect, it must be extended to all those religions that liberal scholars and theologians claimed to respect, including, of course, those previously designated as ethnic or national.

Although this extension of the title "world religion" to the former national religions lends the term a semblance of neutrality, this pluralistic usage is still far from neutral. The current usage preserves an intrinsic reference to the history, identity, and interests of Western civilization. A world religion is, in the words of J. Z. Smith, "a religion like ours, . . . a tradition that has achieved sufficient power and numbers to enter our history to form it, to interact with it, or thwart it."[30] The contemporary concept of world religion still marks a contrast with the innumerable local or indigenous "no-name" traditions that have yet to win recognition from a hegemonic global culture still centered in the West.[31] Seen from this perspective, the contemporary pluralist discourse of world religions harbors an essential ambiguity between an ostensibly neutral and inclusive sense (religions of the world) and a normative and exclusionary sense ("world" religions as opposed to the local religions) that is formally identical to that of its nineteenth-century predecessor.[32]

DOGMATIC THEOLOGY AS THE SCIENCE OF RELIGION'S CONSTITUTIVE OTHER

We have seen that an awareness of the genealogy of the discipline of comparative religion in the comparative theology of the late nineteenth century exposes the unacknowledged normative presuppositions of the current discourse of "world religions." There is yet another problematic feature of the discipline of religious studies that the comparative theology of the late nineteenth century helps us to recognize. This is its tendency to artificially enhance its profile as a scientific discipline by projecting a theological "other."[33]

To see this, we return to a problem I mentioned above, namely, how the comparative theologians of the nineteenth century could sincerely believe that their studies were fair and scientific. This phenomenon can be explained only when we recognize that comparative theology, as an expression of Christian liberalism, defined itself over against a tradition of exclusivist Christian apologetics. Whereas traditional apologetics had declared the non-Christian religions to be unambiguously false, comparative theology was prepared to recognize a positive, providential role for these religions in an economy of salvation. By rejecting the inherently tendentious apologetic categories of revealed religion and natural religion, the comparative theologians thought that they had eradicated the sort of dogmatic bias that interferes with scientific inquiry. From our present historical vantage point, however, a vantage point in which the continuities between the Christian fulfillment theology that informs comparative theology and traditional exclusivist apologetics are plainly evident,[34] we see that the comparative theologians had badly deceived themselves.

Comparative theology helps us to recognize this phenomenon of politically generated claims of scientific objectivity elsewhere, where it is less obvious. A paradigmatic example of a twentieth-century conception of comparative religion whose intellectual legitimacy is maintained by an oppositional contrast with a particular form of theology is the phenomenology of Friedrich Heiler. Heiler's conception of comparative religion as an inductive science rests on a fine distinction between, on the one hand, the discipline's specifically religious presuppositions, such as a reverence for all religions and a capacity for religious feeling,[35] and, on the other, certain a priori attitudes that are to be excluded in order to safeguard the discipline's inductive method.[36] This distinction between hermeneutically productive presuppositions and data-distorting prejudices corresponds to the distinction between liberal-ecumenical and dogmatic-confessional forms of theology, respectively. Thus

Nathan Söderblom and Rudolf Otto, two scholars who were quite open about their theological commitments, nevertheless serve for Heiler as models for the comparative study of religion because neither allowed his theological commitments to become rigid and dogmatic.[37]

The belief that hermeneutical presuppositions could be neatly separated from ideological prejudice could be maintained so long as one assumed a qualitative distinction between liberal-pluralist theology and more traditional forms of confessional theology. Recent critiques of the universalist presuppositions of the classic pluralist theologies espoused by scholars like Heiler,[38] however, have yielded the disconcerting realization that the relation between presupposition and prejudice is not so clear-cut and, accordingly, that the idea of an interpretive science of religion is more elusive than previously thought. The criticism that classic pluralist theology is inclusivist theology in disguise, in other words, has effectively dismantled the projective mechanism that had sustained the notion of the phenomenology of religion as an inductive science.

It has often been said that the exposure of the unacknowledged theologism in the classic models of comparative religion has prompted an identity crisis in the discipline. Many scholars have responded to this crisis by repudiating the "transcendental" approach epitomized by scholars such as Heiler and, more notably, Mircea Eliade in favor of a naturalistic approach that concerns itself with explaining (as opposed to merely interpreting) religious phenomena in terms of causal factors.[39] Whether this shift to a naturalistic approach will finally place the discipline of comparative religion on firm scientific foundations is a complex question that lies out of the scope of the present essay. A legitimate question to be posed in light of the foregoing analysis, however, is the extent to which the promise of the naturalistic approach is sustained by the oppositional contrast with the much-maligned transcendental approaches, that is, by the same kind of "othering" that deceived two previous generations of *Religionswissenschaftler* that their studies were impartial and scientific.

NOTES

1. Eric J. Sharpe, *Comparative Religion: A History* (La Salle, Ill.: Open Court, 1986), 35.

2. The term has recently been revived in theological circles, but there it is generally distinguished from the discipline variously designated as the history of religions, *Religionswissenschaft*, or comparative religion.

3. Henry Louis Jordan, *Comparative Religion: Its Genesis and Growth* (New York: Scribner's, 1905), 24–28.

4. Ibid., 27.

5. Max Müller, *Introduction to the Science of Religion* (London: Longmans, Green, 1882), 9; Jordan, *Comparative Religion*, 26. Müller maintained that comparison was the scientific inquiry. Jordan remarks that the designation "the comparative science of religion" "is clearly tautological."

6. James Freeman Clarke, *Ten Great Religions: An Essay in Comparative Theology* (Boston: Houghton Mifflin, 1899).

7. Frederick Denison Maurice, *The Religions of the World and Their Relations to Christianity* (London: John W. Parker, 1847).

8. In addition to Clarke and Maurice, we might mention the following works as examples of comparative theology: Frank Field Ellinwood, *Oriental Religions and Christianity* (New York: Charles Scribner's Sons, 1892); Samuel Johnson, *Oriental Religions and Their Relations to Universal Religion* (Boston: Houghton, Osgood, 1872–85); Samuel Henry Kellogg, *The Genesis and Growth of Religion* (New York: Macmillan, 1892); Abraham Kuenen, *National Religions and Universal Religions* (New York: C. Scribner's Sons, 1882); John Arnott MacCulloch, *Comparative Theology* (London: Methuen, 1902); George Matheson, *Distinctive Messages of the Old Religions* (New York: Anson D. F. Randolph, 1894); James Clement Moffat, *A Comparative History of Religions* (New York: Dodd and Mead, 1871–73); William Fairfield Warren, *The Quest of the Perfect Religion* (Boston: Rand Avery, 1887).

9. Tomoko Masuzawa, *The Invention of World Religions* (Chicago: University of Chicago Press, 2005), 72; Müller, *Introduction to the Science of Religion*, 43–44; Thomas Kuhn, *The Structure of Scientific Revolutions* (Chicago: University of Chicago Press, 1996), 137–141 An excellent example of this neglect is the standard work in the field: Sharpe's *Comparative Religion*, in which the treatment of comparative theology is confined to a brief explication of Müller's use of the terms. The neglect of comparative theology in contemporary histories of the discipline of comparative religion might be taken as an example of the phenomenon, discussed by Thomas Kuhn, of the tendency for scientists to write the history of their discipline "backwards," eliding those events in its history that do not conform to its present paradigm.

10. Masuzawa, *Invention*, 73–74.

11. Ibid., 103–4.

12. Matheson, *The Distinctive Messages of the Old Religions*, 40. According to its founders, the comparative science of religion was founded on the recognition of a common element in religion or, as Matheson put it, "that in addition to religions there is religion."

13. J. S. Drey, *Manual of the Science of Religion*, trans. Beatrice S. Colyer-Fergusson (London: Longmans, 1891), 54. Pierre Daniël Chantepie de la Saussaye credits as the source of these categories J. S. Drey, "Von der Landesreligion und der Weltreligion," in *Theologische Quartalschrift* (1827): 234–74, 391–435. See Masuzawa, *Invention*, 115.

14. Drey, "Von der Landesreligion," 260–261.

15. Ibid., 433; Masuzawa, *Invention*, 115.

16. Drey, "Von der Landesreligion," 272.

17. Friedrich Schleiermacher, *On Religion: Speeches to Its Cultured Despisers*, trans. Richard Crouter (Cambridge: Cambridge University Press, 1996), 27–28.

18. Ibid., 88, 80.

19. Ibid., 111.

20. José Casanova, *Public Religions in the Modern World* (Chicago: University of Chicago Press, 1994), 21; Bernd Oberdorfer, *Geselligkeit und Realisierung von Sittlichkeit: Die Theorieentwicklung Friedrich Schleiermachers bis 1799* (Berlin: Walter de Gruyter, 1995), 5.

21. J. Samuel Preus, *Explaining Religion* (New Haven: Yale University Press, 1987), ix–xii.

22. This second perspective would support the position of contemporary scholars like Talal Asad, Timothy Fitzgerald, and Russell McCutcheon who call into question the use of "religion" as a valid analytical category. See Talal Asad, *Genealogies of Religion: Discipline and Reasons of Power in Christianity and Islam* (Baltimore: Johns Hopkins University Press, 1993); Timothy Fitzgerald, *The Ideology of Religious Studies* (New York: Oxford University Press, 2000); Russell McCutcheon, "A Default of Critical Intelligence? The Scholar of Religion as Public Intellectual," *Journal for the American Academy of Religion* 65, no. 2 (1997), 443–68.

23. Ernst Troeltsch, "The Place of Christianity Among the World Religions," in *Christian Thought: Its History and Application* (New York: Living Age Books, 1957), 35–63.

24. Ibid., 53–55.

25. Aimee Burant, "Ernst Troeltsch and the Politics of 'Christianity': Context, Pragmatics, and Method in the Historiography of Modern Theology" (unpublished manuscript, 2007), 9–10.

26. Masuzawa, *Invention*, 318.

27. Rabbi Emil Hirsch, quoted in Diana L. Eck, *Encountering God* (Boston: Beacon, 1993), 28.

28. Jonathan Z. Smith, *Relating Religion* (Chicago: University of Chicago Press, 2004), 191.

29. Masuzawa, *Invention*, 310.

30. Jonathan Z. Smith, "Are Theological and Religious Studies Compatible?," *Bulletin/CSSR* 26 no. 3 (September 1997): 191–92.

31. Masuzawa, *Invention*, 114.

32. Friedrich Heiler, "The History of Religions as a Preparation for the Co-Operation of Religion in the Academy," in *The History of Religions: Essays in Methodology*, ed. Mircea Eliade and Joseph Kitagawa (Chicago: University of Chicago Press, 1959), 158. The concept of nationalistic religions still lies just beneath the surface in the pluralistic usage, as can be seen, for example, in the pluralist Friedrich Heiler's contrast between the "higher religions" and the "lower nationalistic religions of mankind."

33. On the tendency for the study of religion to project a theological other, see, for example, Linell E. Cady, "Territorial Disputes: Religious Studies and Theology in Transition," in *Religious Studies, Theology, and the University*, ed. Linell E. Cady and Delwin Brown (Albany: State University of New York Press, 2002), 111, 113; Catherine Bell, "Modernism and Postmodernism in the Study of Religion," *Religious Studies Review* 22, no. 3 (1996): 183, 187; Tyler Roberts, "Exposure and Explanation: On the New Protectionism in the Study of Religion," *Journal of the American Academy of Religion* 72, no. 1 (2004): 149; Paul Griffiths, "On the Future of the Study of Religion in the Academy," *Journal of the American Academy of Religion* 74, no. 1 (2006): 72.

34. John Hick, "The Non-Absoluteness of Christianity," in *The Myth of Christian Uniqueness*, ed. John Hick and Paul F. Knitter (Maryknoll, N.Y.: Orbis, 1994). The standpoint from which the distinction between fulfillment theology and exclusivist apologetics appears specious is that of classic pluralist theology, as exemplified in the work of John Hick.

35. Friedrich Heiler, *Erscheinungsformen und Wesen der Religion* (Stuttgart: W. Kohlhammer, 1949), 17.

36. Ibid., 14; cf. Sharpe, *Comparative Religion*, 244.

37. Heiler, *Erscheinungsformen*, 12; Heiler, "Die Bedeutung für die vergleichende Religionsgeschichte," in *Religionswissenschaft in neuer Sicht* (Marburg: N. G. Elwert, 1951), 23.

38. Examples of such critiques are Mark S. Heim, *Salvations* (Maryknoll, N.Y.: Orbis, 1995); Kathryn Tanner, "Respect for Other Religions: A Christian Antidote to Colonialist Discourse," *Modern Theology* 9, no. 1 (1993): 1–18; and the various essays in Gavin D'Costa, *Christian Uniqueness Reconsidered: Myth of Pluralistic Theology of Religions* (Maryknoll, N.Y.: Orbis, 1990), 192–212.

39. Preus, *Explaining Religion*; E. Thomas Lawson and Robert N. McCauley, *Rethinking Religion: Connecting Cognition and Culture* (New York: Cambridge University Press, 1990); Smith, "Are Theological and Religious Studies Compatible?," 60–61.

7

Religion, Religious Studies, and Shinto in Modern Japan

JUN'ICHI ISOMAE

POLITICAL CONNOTATIONS OF THE CONCEPT "RELIGION"

When Japan opened to the West in 1858 the concept of "religion" was imported into Japanese society with all its political connotations. At that time, Western countries required that Japan guarantee the religious freedom for all its residents in response to the ban on Christianity that was instituted in 1612. If the Japanese Constitution did not recognize religious freedom, it would not have been recognized as a "civilized country" by Western powers, which would have eventually come to threaten its political sovereignty.

In 1873 the Japanese government allowed all Japanese individuals the right to accept Christianity, although until 1858 it was only the non-Japanese residents who had been granted religious freedom. It was around this time that the Japanese word *Shūkyō* was employed as the word corresponding to the Western term "religion." The creation of such terminology was urged in order to forge a homogeneous discourse that would allow for the embracing of Christianity along with other religions in Japan, such as Buddhism, Shinto, and so on. It was around this time that the concept of "comparative religion," as seen in Max Muller's work, gained recognition among those Japanese intellectuals interested in religious issues. Through the method of comparative religion, Japanese intellectuals attempted to extract the homogenous essence of "religion" from diverse religions such as Christianity, Buddhism, and Shinto. At that time, however, the understanding of the concept of "religion" was not understood apart from the meaning of "worship of gods." At this time, the concept of "religion" (*shūkyō* in Japanese) no longer represented a simple attempt to match the terminology of Western countries, but became instead a central issue concerning the right of religious freedom. Thus, Japanese society began to internalize the Western concept of "religion" into the Japanese domestic context, regulated, as it were, by processes of Westernization as a whole.

Originally the Japanese term *shūkyō* developed as a Japanese rendering of the Chinese term *zongjiao*, which occurred in various Buddhist sutras where it had the doctrinal meaning of "teaching" (as in "the teachings of the Buddha" and the like). However, the new modern Japanese understanding of "religion," imported from the West, centered on doctrinal *belief* and reflected a Protestant conception of "religion" positing a founder, set of scripture, and a church. This was very different from the Japanese case, where "religious" practice is part of everyday life as manifest in certain ritual behaviors. With the promulgation of the Japanese Imperial Constitution in 1889, the concept of "religion" came to be located in the private sphere, while the concept of "ritual," overlapping with "morality," was placed in the public sphere, dependent as these were on the Western dichotomy of "religion" and "the secular." Within such a dichotomy, obviously Christianity (which in Japan meant Protestantism due to the energetic activity of American missionaries) was perceived as belonging to the private sphere of religion. Of course such a Protestant notion of "religion" is far removed from the cultural reality of Japan, a factor that helps to explain why today so few Japanese have adopted Christianity. Moreover, modern Buddhists present their tradition in a manner akin to Protestantism in an attempt to shake off the former image of Buddhism as little more than a ritual of funeral service in the early modern period. Funerals were a popular social custom for most Japanese even if they were not familiar with the teachings of Buddhism. The strategy of Shinto apologists, however, was to argue that Shinto belonged to public ritual as a form of morality, with its focus on one's national duty to serve the Japanese emperor. By so doing, it was hoped that Shinto would avoid being classified as a "primitive religion" in comparison with Christianity and Buddhism.[1] Lastly, Japanese folk traditions were categorized as "superstitions" that required eradication in order to enlighten (or modernize) Japanese society sufficiently so that it might be accepted as a "civilized country." The move to categorize Japanese religions in this way was driven by the influence of Social Darwinism, which pervaded Japanese intellectual society at this time, and which provided the ideal vehicle to move from "superstition" to "religion," and then from "religion" to "morality." Shinto—as morality, not religion—was placed at the pinnacle of social evolution because of its ritual character that lacked a clear doctrinal aspect (contra Protestantism), although there was the danger that it might thereby be judged as a "primitive religion" since it had no founder, scripture, or church.

Under political pressure from Western countries, the Japanese state imported the concept of "religion" along with the idea of religious freedom, while at the same time curtailing the freedom of the populace by relocating Shinto from the private realm of religion to the realm of public duty, national morality, and ritual. Paradoxically, such a strategy obviously utilizes the Western liberal dichotomy of "religion" and "the secular." However, since Japanese law did not officially include a formal proclamation of the separation of religion and the state in the strict sense, the boundary between the private and the public, here constituted as the distinction between "religion" and "morality," has always remained extremely fluid. First of all, the constitution allowed for imperial, *not* popular, sovereignty, which makes it very difficult to guarantee religious freedom for the people. The Japanese emperor was seen to be a living god above the law. In this sense, then, the ambiguous nature of Shinto allowed it to transcend the Western dichotomy of religion and the secular since Shinto was now reinvented as a form of emperor worship. Consequently this political ambiguity gave rise to an issue among intellectuals and religious believers about whether the worship of Shinto as a national duty violates religious freedom. This paradigm therefore inevitably leads to the question of whether or not Shinto is a religion, and if it is not, what exactly falls under the heading of "religion." In order to address this issue an academic discourse on religion evolved in Japan as the means to discuss the essence of "religion" and its precise definition as it existed among Japanese intellectuals.

THE EMERGENCE OF RELIGIOUS STUDIES

The first lecture on religious studies, or the "science of religion" (*Shukyogaku*), in Japan was given by Masaharu Anesaki (1873–1949) at the Imperial University of Tokyo in 1898.[2] In 1900 he published the first book on religious studies in Japanese, titled *General Introduction to the Science of Religion*, in which he defined what constituted religion: "Religion is not simply the history of a single confession or sect, but a concept based on the understanding that all religions are realities of the history of human civilization, and are, as products of the human mind, part of the same process of production."[3]

This definition is based on a psychological viewpoint that regards the relations between gods and humans as "products of the human mind." Under the influence of William James, Anesaki interpreted religious phenomena as the psychological product of human beings and maintained that, in spite of their differences, the various religions or confessions could be understood to be variants of the same phenomenon of "religion." Religion is therefore not part of a sacred realm or a transcendental sphere. Since everyone possesses some religious inclinations, it belongs to the mundane world and, moreover, is secularized in the sense of "privatization." No longer excluded from the secular, the sacred can be found within human interiority, through which Japanese individuals had strong ties with the authority of the Japanese nation-state as symbolized by the emperor.

Anesaki's status as the founder of religious studies in modern Japan is based on such a discourse. His first lecture on religious studies was held in 1898, and his professorship of religious studies was established at the Imperial University of Tokyo in 1905. Subsequently, another professorship of religious studies was established at Kyoto Imperial University in 1906, Tōhoku Imperial University in 1922, Kyūshū Imperial University in 1925, and finally Keijō (Seoul) Imperial University in 1927. In 1930, the Japanese Association for Religious Studies was founded and Anesaki was its inaugural president.

In contrast to Anesaki, Katō Genchi (1873–1965), who specialized in Shinto but was influenced by the work of C. P. Tiele, somewhat belatedly came forward with another definition of religion, one in which Shinto is emphasized as an indigenous religion: "The field of Religious Studies made huge progress when it no longer understood 'religion' exclusively as universal religion like Buddhism, Christianity and Islam, but also included tribal beliefs of primitive societies or national creeds that have prospered among common people since ancient times and regarded them with serious academic concern."[4] Needless to say, from this point of view, "One arrives at the understanding that a national religion, as, for instance, State Shinto, even if it does not possess all aspects of a universal religion or a private religion, is of foremost importance among all religions."[5] Katō's understanding further led him to an affirmative recognition of Shinto as a form of religion. Nevertheless, Katō was in full agreement with his colleague Anesaki in arguing that religious belief is consciously adhered to by the individual devotee and that this constitutes the core of any concept of religion.

In an attempt to overcome the limitation of this conceptualization, Yanagita Kunio (1875–1962), the founder of Japanese folklore studies, put forward an interpretation of Shinto that initiated yet another array of definitions of religion. In his article on Shinto in 1918, he wrote: "Any conclusion that shrines serve no other purpose than to pay respect to our forefathers or to exceptional personalities is not based on firm ground, I believe." He thereby criticized the viewpoint of the Japanese government, which interpreted all gods of the Shinto shrine as humans (hence the worship of the emperor). Likewise, he remained dissatisfied with the interpretations of Shinto scholars who understood shrines as nonreligious phenomena. Instead, he regarded "thinking about the gods that we actually find in rural villages, . . . which have neither a doctrine nor a founder," with the utmost respect. Influenced by the work of Émile Durkheim, Yanagita in his emphasis on communal practice rather than individual belief influenced a new generation of scholars, who from the 1930s onward began to revise the ideas of Anesaki and Katō. In the form of the religious ethnology introduced by Uno Enkū (1885–1949) or the religious anthropology introduced by Furuno Kiyoto (1899–1979), Yanagita's views gradually developed into the most widely held approach to the study of non-Western religions, which accompanied Japanese colonization as it spread to other Asian countries.

This practice-oriented view of religion had already spread in the West, as contact with developing countries intensified through colonialism. In modern Japan, interpretations according to the Protestant model still prevail, but practice-oriented understandings of religion have begun to erode the preeminent importance attached to religious belief in their exploration of the indigenous and colonial society under the reign of the Japanese empire. The word *shūkyō* has therefore developed multiple levels of meaning. With such a broad definition of the concept of "religion" as it existed around the 1920s, serious doubts began to be raised concerning the official doctrine of the "nonreligious" nature of Shinto. The concept of religion, therefore, held conflicting implications that were never resolved one way or the other. These "fluctuations surrounding the concept of religion" are still ongoing today, as Shimazono Susumu explains:

> The word "religion" was not simply introduced in its original meaning as soon as it began to be translated as *shūkyō*. . . . In today's Japanese society, there is much confusion as to what *shūkyō* actually means, especially when one asks what the main religion of Japan is. . . . In this sense, the Western concept of "religion" has not yet neatly

settled in Japan. Rather, it is widely recognized that there is a certain perplexity regarding the concept of "religion."[6]

"Morality" was also another term, similar to "religion," that was endowed with a number of meanings. While scholars in the tradition of the European or Western Enlightenment simply contrasted it with religion, adherents of Shinto used it more or less as a synonym for "National Body" or, more simply, the Japanese emperor system, which defied a precise definition. Especially from the 1920s onward, morality in the latter sense was emphasized by Shinto scholars and conservative circles. Morality embodied a public space that also subsumed the private realm. In the same way, the indigenous ritualism of Shinto transcended the distinction between the secular and the religious. In both cases, the framework of the European or Western Enlightenment was increasingly rejected. In this context emerged the new academic discourse of "Shinto Studies," which interpreted Shinto and the Japanese emperor system as the origin of the "National Body," which itself was perceived as the essence of the Japanese spirit and something that goes beyond any kind of Western categorization.[7] It is notable to point out that Shinto studies tended to emphasize the indigenous character of Shinto around the 1920s as a reaction to religious studies, which was perceived to be influenced by Western forms of knowledge. At the same time, Shinto was purged of traditional folk elements, which were rooted in everyday Japanese life by their abstraction as an expression of "national morality." Ironically, this conservative plan deprived Shinto of any *religious* validity, causing the Japanese populace to adhere to Shinto in the form of daily ritual.

In Japanese society before World War II, in which religion was part of state ideology, "religion" and "morality" were both highly ambiguous terms and were related to each other: a change in the meaning of one term was likely to bring about changes in the other term's meaning as well. All in all, they pointed to the extremely difficult choice between a collectivist and an individualistic conception of human life, and further, between moral and religious norms of human behavior. The following statement by José Casanova, whose work has served to problematize the public-private dichotomy deriving from the European or Western Enlightenment, may help us to understand the problem in the Japanese case:

> Modern walls of separation between church and state keep developing all kinds of cracks through which both are able to penetrate each other; . . . religion and politics keep forming all kinds of symbolic relations, to such an extent that [it] is not easy to ascertain whether one is witnessing political movements which don religious garb or religious movements which assume political forms.[8]

THE DECLINE OF RELIGIOUS STUDIES

After the Second World War, the American occupation forced the Japanese government to adopt the policy of the separation of religion and state, and provided an institutional framework of religion in relation to "nonreligious" Shinto in order to purge itself of such ambiguities. As a result, Shinto was no longer regarded as a matter of a morality within national duty but was transformed into a religion of personal choice within the larger milieu of religious freedom as defined by the new constitution. Ironically, at the same time, religious studies in postwar Japan came to decline in social significance because it lost its function and role as providing a critical discourse on Shinto's ambiguity in relation to the concept of "religion."

Hideo Kishimoto (1903–64), Anesaki's successor at the University of Tokyo, advised the American occupation army regarding the reformulation of Shinto, which was to be reconceived as a religion based on the idea of the separation of religion and the state. He also worked to reorganize the character of religious studies in Japan, taking the model of the American social and human sciences. In his book *Religious Studies* (1961), he writes: "Religious Studies aims to search for the meaning of religion as a cultural phenomenon. Its object of research is religious phenomena as human activity."[9]

According to Kishimoto, since the notion of "religion" had lost its sui generis status, religious studies could only be revived through the medium of the social and human sciences in postwar, secular Japanese society. Regardless of Kishimoto's endeavor after the war, in almost every one of the new national universities, which were established in every prefecture, as well as in the former imperial universities, departments of religious studies were not included because the lack of a conflict with Shinto obviated their necessity. Religious phenomena became an object of study in the fields of sociology, anthropology, and historical studies, rather than religious studies.

In the 1970s dissatisfaction with the theory of secularization prompted scholars of religious studies to question this theory, basing their fieldwork on new religions and Thomas Lückmann's theories. They argued that religious phenomena have always been rooted in Japanese society in a way very different from European post-Christian society. In other words, religion in Japan is not limited to the private sphere, but rather interpenetrates the public sphere, an approach that thereby repudiates the dichotomy of religion and the secular. Based on Western liberal secularism, the concept of "religion" had become obscured even though its representation remained within the constitution. As Kishimoto had predicted, the boundary between religion and culture had become unclear. In 1972, Kei'ichi Yanagawa (1926–90), professor at the University of Tokyo, proclaimed the bankruptcy of religious studies as the objective and systematic science to which Kishimoto adhered. Yanagawa said, "We do not need to insist that Religious Studies is a legitimate academic discourse any more. . . . What matters is what is of interest that can be found in religious phenomena themselves."[10]

Yanagawa attempts to overcome the binary thinking of objectivism and subjectivism within religious studies in order to emphasize the irrational positivity of religion against academic rationalism. His argument leads to the conclusion that the positionality of a scholar of religious studies approximates that of a religious believer because the objective neutrality seemingly held by academic discourse is something of an illusion. The claim to "neutrality" made it easier for Japanese scholars to have sympathy with new religious groups, even those like Aum Shinrikyo, whose members attempted to perpetrate mass murder in 1995 as part of their belief in the coming of Armageddon. Since this incident many scholars of religious studies in Japan have had to seriously confront the implications of their own academic discourse, as well as take into account the violent aspects of religion itself, especially when influenced by those informed by cultural studies and postcolonial perspectives to consider the positionality of scholars of religious studies in terms of political context. The decline of religious studies shows the transformation of the discursive formation of the concept of "religion" in postwar Japan, which did not assimilate to the model of a modern secular society under the new constitution. Under such social circumstances, scholars of religion in Japan have been searching for their place within the discourses of contemporary Japanese society.

NOTES

1. Jun'ichi Isomae, "State Shinto, Westernisation, and the Concept of Religion in Japan," in *Religion and the Secular: Historical and Colonial Formations*, ed. Timothy Fitzgerald (London: Equinox, 2007), 92–102.

2. Jun'ichi Isomae, "The Discursive Position of Religious Studies in Japan: Masaharu Anesaki and the Origins of Religious Studies," *Method and Theory in the Study of Religion* 14, no. 2 (2002): 21–46.

3. Masaharu Anesaki, *Shukyōgaku gairon* (General Introduction to the Science of Religion) (Tokyo: Senmon Gakkō Shuppanbu, 1900), 1.

4. Genchi Katō, *Shintō Seigi* (Essential Teaching of Shinto) (Tokyo: Dainippon Tosho, 1938), 294–95.

5. Ibid., 295.

6. Susumu Shimazono, "Nihon niokeru 'shūkyō' gainen no keisei" (The Formation of Religious Discourse in Japan), in *Nihonjin wa kirisutokyō o donoyōni juyō shitaka*, ed. Y. Tetsuo and O. Toshiki (Kyoto: International Research Center for Japanese Studies, 1998), 63.

7. Jun'ichi Isomae, "Tanaka Yoshitō and the Beginnings of *Shintogaku*," in *Shinto in History: Ways of the Kami*, ed. J. Breen and M. Teeuwen (Richmond: Curzon, 2000), 318–39.

8. José Casanova, *Public Religions in the Modern World* (Chicago: University of Chicago Press, 1994), 41.

9. Hideo Kishimoto, *Shūkyōgaku* (Religious Studies) (Tokyo: Taimedō, 1961), 2.

10. Keiichi Yanagawa, *Matsuri to Girei no Shukyo gaku* (Tokyo: Chikuma shobo, 1987), 718.

PART II

The Enlightenment Critique of Religion

8

David Hume on Religion

RANDALL STYERS

The seventeenth and eighteenth centuries saw dramatic social and intellectual change in Europe. In the wake of the bloody Wars of Religion following the fifteenth-century Reformation and also in response to the dramatic increase in new information arriving from the non-European world demonstrating the range of human cultural diversity, many important European thinkers turned new attention to the notion of "natural religion," a concept of religion freed from particularistic dogma and rituals. While many of the arguments supporting natural religion can be traced back far in ancient and medieval philosophy, a number of early modern theologians and natural philosophers rejuvenated efforts to find a grounding for religion in the natural order, sometimes as a "natural theology" that served to bolster Christian apologetics (by formulating rational proofs for the existence of God or other key theological claims) and sometimes as part of efforts to identify a common conceptual core underlying the range of different religious systems (such as Deist attempts to prune back religious particularity in favor of a more universally acceptable set of "common notions").

It is in this context that we come to the work of the Scottish philosopher David Hume (1711–76), one of the key figures in European intellectual history. Hume is commonly regarded as the greatest philosopher to write in English and one of the chief intellectual progenitors of modern empiricism. In a series of key works such as his *Treatise of Human Nature* and *An Enquiry Concerning Human Understanding*,[1] Hume rejected the pretensions of metaphysics in favor of what he saw as a constrained empirical inquiry into "the science of man," focusing particularly on the nature—and limitations—of human understanding. Hume's brand of empiricism, stressing the proper bounds of rational inference, led him to a bold new approach to questions of religion.[2]

Over his life Hume produced a range of important texts dealing with key religious issues. His *Natural History of Religion* (written between 1749 and 1751 and published in 1757) opens with this assertion: "As every enquiry, which regards religion, is of the utmost importance, there are two questions in particular, which challenge our attention, to wit, that concerning its foundation in reason, and that concerning its origin in human nature."[3] Hume addressed this first question—the foundation of religion in reason—in a number of texts as he responded to important developments in eighteenth-century theology and philosophy. And Hume addressed the second question—the origin of religion in human nature—in *The Natural History of Religion*, where he marked out a decisive new program for the scholarly study of religion.

Hume was a bitter critic of the superstition and emotionalism he saw in the popular religion of the "enthusiasts," but throughout his work he was also a particularly harsh opponent of efforts by rationalist philosophers and Deists to formulate a rational defense for religion. In the *Treatise*, he attacked contemporary a priori arguments for the existence of God (such as the "cosmological" version put forth by Samuel Clarke in his *A Demonstration of the Being and Attributes of God* in 1704) by rejecting the theories of causality underlying these arguments. In the *Treatise* and his *Dialogues Concerning Natural Religion* (published posthumously in 1779), Hume also challenged the foundational element of Descartes's version of the ontological argument for the existence of God—that the creator must be self-existent. Any attempt at logical deduction concerning the existence of God, Hume concluded, takes us beyond the capacities of human experience and understanding.

Hume was also sharply critical of a posteriori arguments for the existence of God, a mode of argument that might appear more aligned with his basic empiricism. In the *Dialogues Concerning Natural Religion*, one of the Hume's characters, Cleanthes, mounts a strenuous defense of the argument from design, asserting that there is an order to be found in the universe—"the curious adapting of means to ends"—and that the most coherent explanation for this order is that it derives from an intelligent creator with a mind analogous to the human mind.[4] Cleanthes goes on to claim that human beings can also infer important attributes concerning the nature of this creator by attending to the evidence within the created order.

Through the ensuing dialogue, though, Cleanthes's interlocutors—particularly Philo—raise a number of challenges to Cleanthes's argument, focusing on the weakness of the analogy between the order of the universe and that found in the products of human contrivance. The cosmos, Philo argues, is so different from the specific products of human design that Cleanthes's basic analogy holds little weight. And, Philo continues, even on its own terms this mode of reasoning can shed little light on the nature of the creator. (In section 11 of *An Enquiry Concerning Human Understanding* Hume voiced a similar conclusion, that God differs so radically from human nature and experience that human beings are unable to form any clear or distinct idea of God's nature or attributes.) In *The Natural History of Religion* Hume acknowledged that the argument from design is the most plausible of the arguments for the existence of God, and the interchange in the *Dialogues* appears to conclude that the argument from design might lead one reasonably to infer that a creator exists. But Hume was adamant that despite this thin conclusion, human beings can have no meaningful knowledge of that creator's nature or attributes. As Philo states it, the very most that can be inferred through the argument from design is that "the cause or causes of order in the universe probably bear some remote analogy to human intelligence."[5] And Philo voices Hume's basic skepticism concerning the claims of natural theology to draw grand conclusions about the creation and its creator: "A very small part of this great system, during a very short time, is very imperfectly discovered to us: and do we thence pronounce decisively concerning the origin of the whole?"[6]

To support his skepticism, Philo also invokes one of the classical philosophical arguments against theism, the argument from evil. The evil in the world, Philo asserts, affirmatively thwarts human attempts to draw meaningful conclusions about the attributes of the creator (such as divine power, goodness, or morality). Philo rejects the various attempts at theodicy put forward by his interlocutors, and he argues that if our logical directive is to proportion the cause to the effect, the flawed nature of the creation bars us from attributing any type of perfection to the creator: "there is no view of human life, or of the condition of mankind, from which, without the greatest violence, we can infer the moral attributes" of God.[7] As Philo concludes, "these subjects exceed all human capacity"; any attribution of perfection to the divine must be arrived at purely through "the eyes of faith alone"—not through reason.[8] Through these various arguments, Hume sought to dismantle the core rational arguments on behalf of natural religion.

Unlike rationalistic natural religion, theistic religious orthodoxy invokes special divine revelation as an additional basis for its religious truth claims, and Hume's attack on this mode of religious knowledge appears in his essay "On Miracles." Earlier philosophers (most notably Hobbes and Spinoza) had expressed skepticism about the notion of miracles, but others (including the great empiricist John Locke) had invoked miracles as evidence authenticating the claims of special revelation and the authority of the Christian scripture. Hume, in turn, rejected any effort to give miracle stories rational legitimacy. He begins his argument by defining a miracle as "a violation of a law of nature," and he proceeds to assert that since the evidence in support of a law of nature is uniform and pervasive (this is what makes the law a law), there can never be sufficient reliable evidence to give rational support to the claim that a law has been broken and a miracle has occurred.[9] Further, Hume catalogues the specific factors in human psychology and sociology that should make us skeptical about reports of miracles (such as the allure of the uncanny or the self-interested nature of such reports). As Hume states it: "No testimony for any kind of miracle has ever amounted to a probability, much less to a proof; and . . . even supposing it amounted to a proof, it would be opposed by another proof; derived from the very nature of the fact, which it would endeavor to establish. It is experience only, which gives authority to human testimony; and it is the same experience, which assures us of the laws of nature . . . no human testimony can have such force as to prove a miracle, and make it a just foundation for any such system of religion."[10] Thus, while Hume never goes so far as to assert that miracles are impossible, he concludes that there is never a rational basis for accepting reports of miracles. This leg of theistic orthodoxy falters.[11]

Hume attacked one additional element of the rational defense of religion in the *Treatise* and in his essay "Of the Immortality of the Soul" (published posthumously), as he considered traditional metaphysical arguments for the existence of an immaterial and immortal soul, a belief at the heart of doctrines of life after death. Against such claims, Hume argued that human identity lacks sufficient stability to constitute some type of substance; as he states it in the *Treatise*, consciousness is "nothing but a bundle or collection of different perceptions, which succeed each other with an inconceivable rapidity, and are in a perpetual flux and movement."[12] And further, if consciousness is simply a bundle of perceptions, and if perception ends at death (with the destruction of the sense organs), death entirely annihilates human identity. Hume also argues that since human thought and consciousness always appear in conjunction with matter and motion, and since thought itself involves bodily existence and experience, there is no basis for the claim that thought is the product of an immaterial soul. In any event, Hume asserts, religious accounts of life after death are so abstractly distant from the current human condition that they lack practical effect. In part 11 of the *Enquiry* he further argues that our experience in the present world provides no meaningful evidence to support the claim that eternal rewards and punishments will be fairly distributed in some future life after death. And in both the *Treatise* and his *Enquiry Concerning the Principles of Morals* Hume argues that a naturalistic account of human moral sensibilities demonstrates that religion and its teachings concerning an afterlife are unnecessary for the establishment and maintenance of morality. In fact, he says, religion often exerts a detrimental effect on morality, leading to moral and social decay and fanaticism.

Through these various arguments, Hume rejected all the prominent eighteenth-century theological and philosophical efforts to provide religion with a rational grounding, and these arguments illustrate a number of elements in Hume's thought that will be extremely significant in later methodological approaches to the study of religion. A double gesture is in play as Hume works to police the relation between religion and rationality. On the one hand, he agrees with his rationalist and Deistic opponents that the core of religion lies in assent to a set of coherent propositions. But Hume seeks to limit the scope of rationally defensible religion to one single principle: the "Assent of the Understanding to the Proposition that God exists."[13] Beyond this thin claim, he argues, any human effort to add content to religion becomes "absurd, superstitious, and even impious."[14] So Hume is here defining a mode of secular rationality (built on properly trained and refined passions) within which the only form of "rational" religion is one that abandons any relevance to meaningful human endeavor. To the extent religion exceeds that narrow bound, it also places itself beyond the realm of properly cultivated rationality.

The implications of this fundamental approach to religion become more explicit when we turn to Hume's *The Natural History of Religion*, a text that has exerted great influence on the scholarly study of religion. The central feature of Hume's *Natural History* is signaled in its title; religion is here to be studied as a phenomenon with a "natural history." While advocates of natural religion had sought to identify an innate grounding for religious belief, Hume aggressively rejected those efforts. Instead, he set out to explore the natural development of the human aspects of religion—its origins and change over time—without basing religion in either rationality, human instinct, or supernatural revelation. This deliberate effort to replace what Hume saw as quasi-theological modes of inquiry with a purely empirical method had extraordinary impact on the scholarly study of religion. Religion becomes one more object of study for Hume's broader "science of man."

Hume has multiple objectives in *The Natural History*. He begins by challenging the supposition that religious ideas are somehow innate or instinctive to human nature. In this regard, his "natural history" works to denaturalize religion by emphasizing its historical contingency and variability. He invokes the heterogeneity of religion to argue that since all human ideas derive from experience, even religious concepts are historical rather than innate. As he explains, there is a "universal propensity to believe in invisible, intelligent power," but while this propensity is "a general attendant of human nature," there are circumstances where it is lacking, and even when it does appear it is highly variable.[15] As Hume states it, "no two nations, and scarce any two men, have ever agreed precisely in the same sentiments."[16] Since religion is so irregular, it cannot be "an original instinct or primary impression of nature." Instead, it is a "secondary" development that "may easily be perverted by various accidents and causes."[17] So, he explains, in this text he will explore the origin of religious principles and consider the historical accidents and causes that can affect religion's development.

Hume then proceeds to formulate an account of the development of religion using various types of historical and psychological evidence (drawing particularly on classical sources). He argues that the initial stage of religious development is "polytheism or idolatry" (since the mind must move from inferior concepts toward superior ones).[18] This initial polytheism has its origins, he explains, in human weakness, fear, and ignorance. Religion arises from "the anxious concern for happiness, the dread of future misery, the terror of death, the thirst of revenge, the appetite for food and other necessities."[19] Fueled by this amalgam of unrestrained emotion and ignorant of the principles of cause and effect, early human beings come to suppose that the world is animated by invisible agents, and through the human tendency to anthropomorphize, these agents become personified in the "imagination." As religion develops, human beings seek to control fate by placating or cajoling these invisible agents through prayers or sacrifices. In line with his opening insistence that religion is not innate, Hume here argues that properly basic human experiences and emotional responses are given secondary religious interpretations.

As religious development proceeds, monotheism evolves from this initial primitive polytheism. Out of selfish interests, the votaries of a particular deity exaggerate their god's status (particularly in periods of distress or fear), and as one god comes to predominate the local pantheon, eventually these votaries conclude that their god is infinite. These followers arrive at that conclusion, though, "not by reason, of which they are in great measure incapable, but by the adulation and fears of the most vulgar superstition."[20] While theism is a significant achievement, its origin in human emotions makes it unstable, so that "men have a natural tendency to rise from idolatry to theism, and to sink again from theism into idolatry" as they seek to address their competing fears and anxieties.[21] And while theism is in many ways more intellectually advanced than polytheism, it also results in new tendencies toward religious intolerance and persecution, new corruptions of the human spirit, and new threats to rational thinking. Hume details a long litany of the moral and intellectual harm caused by theistic religion.

Through this account of religion, Hume works to identify what he sees as "the essential and universal properties of human nature" at work within the course of religious development.[22] He concedes that rational reflection might lead one to acknowledge a divine creator demonstrating "one single purpose or intention" in the natural order. But at the same time, this creator's intention remains "inexplicable and incomprehensible," and religion constantly disfigures the simple truth of the creator's existence.[23] As Hume states it: "Examine the religious principles, which have, in fact, prevailed in the world. You will scarcely be persuaded, that they are any thing but sick men's dreams: or perhaps will regard them more as the playsome whimsies of monkeys in human shape, than the serious, positive, dogmatic assertions of a being who dignifies himself with the name of rational."[24] So, Hume concludes, "The whole is a riddle, an enigma, an inexplicable mystery. Doubt, uncertainty, suspense of judgment appear the only result of our most accurate scrutiny, concerning this subject." The only escape from the mystery and confusion of religion is to be found in "the calm, though obscure, regions of philosophy."[25]

Throughout *The Natural History*, religion is framed primarily as a conceptual matter (involving the belief in invisible power), but religious development is driven not by reason or rational deduction, but by fear and ignorance. This mode of religion is deeply individualistic, a matter of the individual psyche with no accounting for human social interaction. At the same time, though, Hume also assumes that all human beings share a fundamentally common human nature; it is this supposition that makes cross-cultural comparisons relevant to his argument.

Hume's *Natural History* marks the transformation of religion into an object of historical and cultural study divorced from questions of any sort of supernatural truth or revelation. He sets out instead to utilize an empirical, comparative method in order to identify the origins of religion within human nature, to chart its development through human history, and to examine its consequences for human life. Rejecting the claim that religion is innate or instinctive (as maintained by advocates of natural religion and Deism), he argues instead that religion is characterized by heterogeneity and irregularity. His role as a scholar is to map the emotional conditions that give rise to religion and the various factors that affect its development. Through this very procedure, questions of religious truth have been supplanted by matters of contingency.

In his other works on religion, Hume rejects most every rational argument put forward in defense of religion, and he argues that morality needs no religious base. In *The Natural History*, he argues that religion can be accounted for by recourse to more fundamental, identifiable principles of human nature and that religion often exerts harmful effects on human life. In making these arguments, Hume works to define and exercise a mode of secular rationality utterly distinct from religious presuppositions, and he gives this secularized, scientific method jurisdiction over the study of religion. With this dramatic shift in method, Hume sets the stage for major new developments in the naturalistic study of religion over the coming century.

NOTES

1. See David Hume, *A Treatise of Human Nature*, 2nd ed., ed. P. H. Nidditch (Oxford: Clarendon Press, 1978), 10.

2. On Hume's significance more broadly, see J. Samuel Preus, *Explaining Religion: Criticism and Theory from Bodin to Freud* (New Haven: Yale University Press, 1987); Ivan Strenski, *Thinking About Religion: An Historical Introduction to Histories of Religion* (Oxford: Blackwell, 2006); and Stanley Tweyman, ed., *Hume on Natural Religion* (Bristol, UK: Thoemmes, 1996).

3. David Hume, "The Natural History of Religion," in *Principal Writings on Religion Including "Dialogues Concerning Natural Religion" and "The Natural History of Religion,"* ed. J. C. A. Gaskin (Oxford: Oxford University Press, 1993), 134.

4. David Hume, "Dialogues Concerning Natural Religion," in *Writings on Religion*, ed. Antony Flew (La Salle, Ill.: Open Court, 1992), 203.

5. Ibid., 291.

6. Ibid., 201.

7. Ibid., 265.

8. Ibid., 264–65.

9. David Hume, "An Inquiry Concerning Human Understanding," in *Enquiries Concerning Human Understanding and Concerning the Principles of Morals*, 3rd ed., ed. P. H. Nidditch (Oxford: Clarendon, 1975), 114–15.

10. Ibid., 127.

11. See also Stanley Tweyman, ed., *Hume on Miracles* (Bristol, UK: Thoemmes, 1996).

12. Hume, *A Treatise of Human Nature*, 252.

13. David Hume, "Letter To William Mure of Caldwell (1743)," in *Writings on Religion*, 17.

14. Hume, "Dialogues," 290.

15. Hume, "Natural History," 184.

16. Ibid., 134.

17. Ibid.

18. Ibid., 135.

19. Ibid., 140.

20. Ibid., 155.

21. Ibid., 158–59.

22. Ibid., 183.

23. Ibid.

24. Ibid., 184.

25. Ibid., 185.

9

Feuerbach on Religion

JAY GELLER

Ludwig Feuerbach (1804–72), having the good sense to marry well, was able to reconcile himself to the impossibility of attaining a university teaching position in any of the reactionary German states and retired in 1837 to the rural village of Schloss Bruckberg to pursue his historical-philosophical researches. Four years later (1841) he published *Das Wesen des Christentums* (*The Essence of Christianity*), which revealed that religion, in general, and Christianity, in particular, were nothing other than anthropology. It argued that Christianity's God was nothing other than the infinite collection of phenomenal qualities and capabilities that predicate humanity throughout time: "ignorance [that the consciousness, knowledge, of God is the self-consciousness, self-knowledge, of man] is fundamental to the peculiar nature of religion."[1] Because "the measure of the species is the absolute measure, law, and criterion of man,"[2] Feuerbach argued not that the concept of God is anthropomorphized, but that the essence of God is misrecognized human species-being. Further, by unnaturalizing the natural, theology both denies the identity of the deity and humanity and expropriates all that is positive in the human and attributes it to the divine: "To enrich God, man must become poor; that God may be all, man must be nothing."[3] Feuerbach saw his project as repudiating the illusions of theology while affirming the anthropological truth of religion. He saw it as a political intervention that pulled away the curtain of the ostensibly Christian theology, upon which the Prussian state of Friedrich Wilhelm IV also founded its authority. It was a call, as it were, for a transfer of power from the regent to the crown prince, humanity coming of age.

The Essence of Christianity created an uproar among the established theologians, philosophers, and politicians—and aroused the admiration of a group of similarly frustrated would-be academics, including, among others, Karl Marx. Yet what would be claimed by Feuerbach and initially endorsed by his cohort as "the philosophy of the future" had been reduced by the beginning of 1844, in the opening line of Marx's "A Contribution to the Critique of Hegel's Philosophy of Right. Introduction," to a mere (and uncredited) first, albeit necessary, step: "For Germany, the criticism of religion has been essentially completed, and the criticism of religion is the prerequisite of all criticism."[4] (See the discussion of Marx's exegesis and transformation of Feuerbach's critique below.)

While the direct impact of his religious criticism on the development of social theory had come to an end, Feuerbach continued to elaborate on the nature and history of religion. In his later work Feuerbach expanded his purview from human nature alone to the natural world. Further, he qualified his Hegelian understanding of Christianity as the ideal exemplar and culmination of the history of religious development; in that later work Feuerbach came to view Christianity through the lens of theistic religion rather than, as he had in *The Essence of Christianity*, vice versa. But his *Lectures on the Essence of Religion* (delivered in Heidelberg in 1848–49 and published in 1851) and their later incarnations, such as his would-be magnum opus *Theogonie* (1857),[5] found few followers; indeed, the one insight of Feuerbach's later work that remains widely cited—the celebrated apothegm "you are what you eat" or, in his punning original, "*Der Mensch ist, was er isst*" (lit. "Man is what he eats")—is rarely credited to him. Consequently, the so-called "projection" theory of religion promulgated by *The Essence of Christianity* remained for posterity Feuerbach's defining critique of religion.

FROM FOLLOWING IN HEGEL'S WAKE TO CELEBRATING AT HIS WAKE

Feuerbach was born in 1804, in Landshut, Bavaria, where his father was a professor of law at the university. Rather than following his father into the intricacies of criminal law, Feuerbach, having early on developed a strong inclination toward religion and its study, commenced his theological studies at the University of Heidelberg in 1823. A year later he moved to the University of Berlin with the intention of studying with Schleiermacher; however, he soon fell under the spell of the philosopher G. W. F. Hegel, eventually receiving his doctorate in philosophy. Hegel's speculative idealism privileged Self-Consciousness whereby the subject comes to recognize its self, to know its self, through its externalization and objectification; or as Feuerbach put it in *Essence*: "in the object which he contemplates, therefore, man becomes acquainted with himself."[6] Individual human consciousness reproduces the dialectical process whereby Absolute Spirit (or the Idea) comes to realize and know itself as the actual world. Christian theology narrates this same rational process; however, it employs an inadequate imagistic language that mistakes its representation (that is, God) for that which it represents (that is, Absolute Spirit's dialectical unfolding in and as nature and history).

Feuerbach, like many in his Hegel-influenced cohort (Bauer, Rüge, Stirner, Engels, Marx), came to recognize certain lacunae in Hegel's systematic determination of human experience. Exacerbating their dissatisfaction were the constraints placed on Hegel's work through its appropriation by both the state and the state (Protestant) church as a tool for their respective and mutual legitimation. In 1835, David Friedrich Strauss's *Life of Jesus*[7] had already pointed out that Hegelian thought still retained a remainder of mythic consciousness, a product of an earlier stage of cultural development, when it misrecognized the culmination of Absolute Spirit's historical realization of itself in the world as the individual rather than as the species, the human species. For Feuerbach this fundamental failure to recognize that human species-being is the true "*Ens realissimum*" (the most real Being)[8] was exacerbated by the way Hegelian speculative idealism privileged rational thought as determinative of the human while marginalizing external and internal sensuality (*Sinnlichkeit*). Further, by rendering the world and knowledge of the world (the Idea) as coextensive, mistaking the Idea for the world (the real is the rational), it occluded how the absolute that is humanity realizes itself in material, embodied relationships in time (the rational is real). Speculative idealism no less than Christian theology generated abstract entities out of fundamental human predicates: reason, motion, will. Feuerbach would invert the inverted world of speculative philosophy and theology.

Through his transformative method Feuerbach would restore human predicates to their original subject. His botanically figured formula for Christian salvation, "In the religious systole man propels his own nature from himself, he throws himself outward; in the religious diastole he receives the rejected nature into his heart again,"[9] would be reanimated by and as human self-consciousness. "God" is human species-being involuntarily and unconsciously become an object of thought and feeling to which humanity relates as a separate, heavenly being. Like a good Enlightenment thinker, Feuerbach assumed that "knowledge would set one free." By "unveiling ... the naked truth,"[10] the recognition that the deity is nothing other than its predicates and that its predicates are nothing other than human potential, the autonomy and authority claimed by the deity and its official enablers would return from whence it came: to humanity. "The necessary turning-point of history is therefore the open confession, that the consciousness of God is nothing else than the consciousness of the species."[11] The turning point, however, proved to be a fork as the readers of *Essence* pursued divergent interpretive trajectories.

ÜBER FEUERBACH OR EXTINGUISHING THE FIERY BROOK

While Feuerbach highlighted the contradiction inherent in theology (or reflection on religion), the misrecognition of the absolute identity of human and divine nature as absolute difference, Marx attended to the more fundamental contradictions that he claimed Feuerbach unveiled[12] but nevertheless overlooked—that these predicates and the social relationships that intrinsically rather than extrinsically condition them are themselves rife with distortions. Marx took Feuerbach's recognition that the objects of religion are the unconscious concretization of the species-being back to its Hegelian roots in the slave's unrecognized self-objectification in the products of his labor. Marx inverted Feuerbach's inversion of Hegel and emphasized the human praxis that created those objects such as religious ideas—"*Man makes religion*, religion does not make man"[13]—in order to address "the question which [Feuerbach] left unanswered: how did it come about that people 'got' these illusions 'into their heads.'"[14] Religion, Marx argues, is indeed an "an *inverted consciousness of the world*" because the producer of religion, man in "this state and this society," already lives in an "inverted world," a heartless, soulless, oppressive world of suffering that denies human realization.[15] According to Marx, Feuerbach's soteriological solution, the recognition of the illusory nature of religious representation, required another step: "To call on [people] to give up their illusions about their condition [of alienation] is to *call on them to give up a[n alienating] condition that requires illusions.*"[16] Consequently, rather than expending any further effort on deconstructing religious representation, Marxist analysis focused on the worldly processes and relationships and assumed that when they changed the representations would take care of themselves: "Pouf!"

PROJECTING FEUERBACH'S ROLE
IN THEORIES OF RELIGION

The interpretation of Feuerbach's theorizing about religion also followed another path. Feuerbach declaimed: "Man—this is the mystery of religion—projects his being into objectivity [*vergegenständlicht*], and then again makes himself an object to this projected image of himself [*vergegenständlichten*] thus converted into a subject."[17] George Eliot here translated Feuerbach's "object making" (*vergegenständlichen*) as "image projecting" (*vergegenständlichen*), using his ocular imagery in combination with Feuerbach's own privileging of sight (readily observed in his optical metaphors, visual verbs, and explicit statements).[18] Eliot's translation helped thematize Feuerbach's critique as the "projection" theory of religion; spotlighting projection also obscured both *Essence*'s philosophical background and the source of its appeal to his contemporaries (discussed above). This "projection" label also placed the emphasis on psychologization at the expense of the materialist, humanistic, and collective dimensions of his critique. The lenses of projection and psychologization focused upon religious ideas as icons of heavenly referents that did not exist rather than as signifiers of real and realizable human capacities and relationships, origins and ends of which are here on earth. These lenses allowed the omneity and superiority figured by those icons to be explained as psychological compensation for individual human lack rather than registering Feuerbach's emphasis upon human inadequacy as itself an effect of the misattribution of the source of value: human species-being. Hence, it seems a small step from Feuerbach's own commentary[19]—

> The yearning of man after something above himself is nothing else than the longing after the perfect type of his nature, the yearning to be free from himself, i.e., from the limits and defects of his individuality. . . . The child sees the nature of man above itself in the form of its parents . . . all feelings which man experiences towards a superior man, nay, in general all moral feelings which man has towards man, are of a religious nature—

to find oneself in Freud's *Future of an Illusion* (1927):[20]

> When the growing individual finds that he is destined to remain a child for ever, that he can never do without protection against strange superiors, he lends those powers the features belonging to the figure of the father; he creates for himself the gods whom he dreads, whom he seeks to propitiate, and whom he nevertheless entrusts with his own protection. Thus his longing for a father is a motive identical with his need for protection against the consequences of his human weakness. . . . which is primarily the formation of religion.

While Freud makes no mention of Feuerbach in the entire *Standard Edition* of his works, let alone in his explicit discussions of religion in, among others, *Future of an Illusion*, *Totem and Taboo* (1912–13), and *Moses and Monotheism* (1939),[21] Freud's adolescent correspondence with his friend Eduard Silberstein suggests that Feuerbach is clearly among the unnamed "other and better men" whose critiques of religion, Freud humbly notes, were "said before me in a much more complete, forcible, and impressive manner."[22] Freud tells his friend (November 8, 1874) that he is reading Feuerbach while attending philosophy courses, including one that "deals with the existence of God."[23] A mere five months later (March 7, 1875), Freud reports that Feuerbach is "one whom I revere and admire above all other philosophers."[24] On the other hand, when Freud made his allusion to Feuerbach in *Future of an Illusion*, he did add "All I have done . . . is to add some psychological foundation to the criticisms of my great predecessors."[25] Feuerbach's and Freud's projection theories may share certain formal characteristics; however, one must give Freud his due, and whatever one's judgment on the truth-claims of that psychological foundation, Freud's understanding of human emotional life is far more differentiated and subject to development than Feuerbach's presentation in *The Essence of Christianity*.

WHITHER FEUERBACH?

While Feuerbach has become but a sidebar in many histories of the critiques and theories of religion (as well as in accounts of Marx's antecedents), the historian and theologian Van Harvey has endeavored, in *Feuerbach and the Interpretation of Religion*, to unveil to contemporaries the importance of Feuerbach's corpus in its entirety for thinking about religion. Rather than focusing upon either the alienation of species-being or the "projection" (*vergegenständlichen*) thematized in Feuerbach's early writings and their reception histories, Harvey attends to the later works. His Feuerbach presents a more naturalistic, if no less psychological, theory, in which religion arises from the desire for happiness and fear of death by "a conscious, narcissistic ego aware of the vulnerability of its body,"[26] and thereby anticipates the psychoanalytic revisions of Otto Rank and Ernest Becker. Nevertheless, Feuerbach's legacy remains less in the specifics of his theorization than in shifting the critique of religion from the conscious deception by clerics (the priestly manipulation of the masses excoriated by the French Enlightenment) and the errant notions of the cognitively challenged (Hegel's depiction of fetish-worshipers incapable of rising above "sensuous arbitrariness").[27] More significant, he catalyzed the recognition that sociality, alienation, and corporeality shape the emergence of human religiosity.

NOTES

1. Ludwig Feuerbach, *The Essence of Christianity*, trans. George Eliot (Buffalo, N.Y.: Prometheus, 1989), 13.

2. Ibid., 16.

3. Ibid., 26.

4. Karl Marx, "A Contribution to the Critique of Hegel's Philosophy of Right: Introduction," in *Early Writings*, ed. Quinton Hoare, trans. Rodney Livingstone and Gregor Benton (New York: Random House, 1975), 243.

5. Ludwig Feuerbach, *Lectures on the Essence of Religion*, trans. Ralph Manheim (New York: Harper and Row, 1967); and Ludwig Feuerbach, *Theogonie*, ed. Harich Wolfgang (Berlin: Akademie, 1968).

6. Feuerbach, *Essence of Christianity*, 5.

7. David Friedrich Strauss, *The Life of Jesus Critically Examined*, ed. Peter C. Hodgson, trans. George Eliot (Ramsey, N.J.: Sigler Press, 1992).

8. Feuerbach, *Essence of Christianity*, xv.

9. Ibid., 31.

10. Ibid., xix.

11. Ibid., 270.

12. The repeated analogies to religious phenomena and processes as critiqued by Feuerbach in Marx's *Economic and Philosophic Manuscripts* (1844) demonstrate how Marx, when he looked to the ground rather than the heavens, had appropriated Feuerbach's critical algorithm; in Marx, *Early Writings*, 279–400.

13. Marx, "Contribution," 244.

14. Karl Marx and Friedrich Engels, *The German Ideology* (Moscow: Progress Publishers, 1976), 253.

15. Marx, "Contribution," 244.

16. Ibid.

17. Feuerbach, *Essence of Christianity*, 29–30.

18. For example, ibid., xiv, 8.

19. Feuerbach, *Essence of Christianity*, 281.

20. Sigmund Freud, *The Future of an Illusion*, ed. and trans. James Strachey (New York: Norton, 1961), 30.

21. Sigmund Freud, *Totem and Taboo*, trans. James Strachey (New York: Norton, 1950); and Sigmund Freud, *Moses and Monotheism*, trans. Katherine Jones (New York: Vintage, 1955).

22. Ibid., 45.

23. Sigmund Freud, *The Letters of Sigmund Freud to Eduard Silberstein, 1871–1881*, ed. Walter Boehlich, trans. by Arnold J. Pomerans (Cambridge, Mass.: Harvard University Press, 1990), 70.

24. Ibid., 96.

25. Freud, *Illusion*, 45.

26. Van A. Harvey, "Ludwig Feuerbach and Karl Marx," in *Nineteenth-Century Religious Thought in the West*, vol. 1, ed. Ninian Smart, John Clayton, Patrick Sherry, and Steven T. Katz (Cambridge: Cambridge University Press, 1985), 320; cf. Harvey, *Feuerbach and the Interpretation of Religion* (Cambridge: Cambridge University Press, 1995).

27. Georg Wilhelm Friedrich Hegel, *Lectures on the Philosophy of World History: Introduction*, trans. H. B. Nisbet (Cambridge: Cambridge University Press, 1981), 190.

10
Nietzsche
Life, Works, Reception
TYLER ROBERTS

The influence of Friedrich Nietzsche (1844–1900) on twentieth- and twenty-first-century continental philosophy and critical theory rivals that of Kant and Hegel. Son and grandson of Lutheran pastors, trained as a philologist at the University of Leipzig (after initially enrolling to study theology), Nietzsche was appointed professor of philology at the University of Basel at age twenty-four. While at Basel, his thinking deeply impressed by the philosophy of Arthur Schopenhauer and his close friendship with Richard Wagner, he published his first book, *The Birth of Tragedy* (1872). As these influences waned and his health deteriorated, Nietzsche resigned his academic post in 1879. For the next decade, he led a nomadic existence and wrote. Between 1878 and 1882, he published *Human, All Too Human*, *Daybreak*, and the first four books of *The Gay Science*. Then came the stylistic and conceptual departure of Nietzsche's best-known work, *Thus Spake Zarathustra*. Between 1885 and 1887, Nietzsche published what are perhaps his greatest works, *Beyond Good and Evil*, the remarkable fifth book of *The Gay Science*, and his most philosophically influential work, *On the Genealogy of Morals*. In 1888, in a furious burst of productivity that preceded a mental breakdown in January 1889, he wrote *Twilight of the Idols*, *The Antichrist*, *The Case of Wagner*, and *Ecce Homo*. Nietzsche died in 1900, having spent the last decade of his life as a mental and physical invalid.

The reception of Nietzsche by two philosophers, Martin Heidegger and Gilles Deleuze, has been particularly important for establishing his impact on twentieth- and twenty-first-century philosophy, theology, and religious studies. In an extended series of lectures on Nietzsche in the 1930s, Heidegger read Nietzsche's proclamation of the death of God as heralding the end of metaphysics. Not only did Heidegger's reading shape Nietzsche's early reception as an existentialist philosopher but, more important, it laid the groundwork for the astonishing readings of Nietzsche's thought that emerged in France starting in the 1960s. In 1963, Deleuze published his *Nietzsche and Philosophy*, which championed Nietzsche's thought as an affirmative challenge to Hegel's philosophy of totality. This is one of the initial moments of postmodernism, as Nietzsche's stylistic challenges to philosophical writing, his perspectivalist challenges to philosophical theories of truth, and his genealogical challenges to philosophies of history were developed and transformed not only by Deleuze, but also by Derrida, Foucault, and many other interpreters. Of particular importance for thinking about the study of religion, as we will see, is Nietzsche's genealogical method, a radical historicizing of concepts and values. As Foucault puts it, "the genealogist refuses to extend his faith in metaphysics, if he listens to history, he finds that there is 'something altogether different' behind things: not a timeless and essential secret, but the secret that they have no essence or that their essence was fabricated in a piecemeal fashion from alien forms."[1]

NIETZSCHE ON RELIGION

Against Religion

For modernists, existentialists, and many postmodernists, Nietzsche's pronouncement that God is dead makes it clear that Nietzsche was an atheist proclaiming the end or exhaustion of religion. And there is no doubt that Nietzsche is one of modernity's most vehement and incisive critics of religion and, in particular, of Judaism and Christianity. In much of his work, up to and including *Beyond Good and Evil*, Nietzsche argues that metaphysics, philosophy, and religion are all grounded in a "faith in opposite values," a faith that things of the highest value cannot have their origin in this transitory world but in some perfect or eternal realm.[2] For Nietzsche, though, all values, meanings, and practices have a material, worldly origin—they are "human, all too human." In his early works, Nietzsche brings this idea to bear on religion in a way that is close to Marx's criticisms of religion as a hermeneutic of suffering. Religion provides consolation, but only as it prevents us from examining the real causes of suffering and even imposes new forms of suffering, such as the intense guilt caused by the concept of sin. As Nietzsche puts it in *Daybreak*: "The worst sickness of mankind originated in the way in which they have combated their sicknesses, and what seemed to cure as in the long run produced something worse than that which it was supposed to overcome."[3]

By the time we get to the *Genealogy*, Nietzsche is condemning the faith in opposite values as "nihilism." If all values have a human origin, then the belief in absolute values that have an otherworldly origin must be a belief in "nothingness." But human beings, Nietzsche thinks, cannot bear the thought that life has no meaning and so would rather "will nothingness than not will."[4] In this book, Nietzsche also brings the genealogical method to bear on the issue of the origins and development of religion (though we can see this method emerging as early as early as *Human, All Too Human* in 1878). In essay 2 of the *Genealogy*, Nietzsche offers one of his most concise and interesting accounts of religion. The idea of gods, he claims, originates when social groups articulate a sense of debt—a "juridical duty"—toward their ancestors.[5] As time passes and as the power of the social group grows, the imagined power of the ancestors increases to the point where the ancestors are "transfigured" into gods. At the origin of religion, then, is a primarily juridical and economic relation to the gods. But Nietzsche goes on to argue that a crucial trans-formation takes place when this relationship is "moralized," that is, when it is re-interpreted by the bearers of "bad conscience" who found in the idea of a *moral* debt owed to a god a perfect vehicle for increasing the hatred and torture of self that is the goal of bad conscience.[6] This moralization finds its strongest and most influential expression in the concept of sin, where the debt to God is not simply something owed, but something owed due to a fault or transgression on the part of the debtor. For Nietzsche, this trajectory is of course perfected, brought to its "most gruesome pitch," in Christianity. The Christian concept of "original sin" means that only God can pay the debt that is owed to him through his own self-sacrifice on the Cross.

This moralization of religion is examined in more depth in the final essay of the *Genealogy*, titled "What Is the Meaning of Ascetic Ideals?" There, Nietzsche ar-gues that human beings need meaning and that the ascetic ideal has been made the most powerful, and nearly exclusive, meaning for human beings so far. The ascetic ideal posits an "other mode of existence" as the goal of this life, a goal that can be reached only by denying this life.[7] This ideal has come to dominate human life be-cause it has served the interests of the priests—here Nietzsche's original insight into religion as a form of life denial is bound up closely with a more traditional Enlight-enment perspective on the power of clerics and institutional religion—and because it has been a preservative force for the sick and decadent who would rather "will nothingness than not will."[8]

Nietzsche for Religion?

Though most readers of Nietzsche have been satisfied to view him as an atheist and critic of religion, others, especially recently, have offered more nuanced readings. Especially noteworthy among earlier interpreters is Paul Ricoeur's argument that the "hermeneutics of suspicion" in Marx, Nietzsche, and Freud must be incorpo-rated into any "mature faith."[9] We find variations on this idea in Merold Westphal and in Giles Fraser's account of Nietzsche's own "piety of unbelief." We also find versions of it in the secularist and postmodern theologies or a/theologies of Mark C. Taylor, Charles Winquist, and Carl Rashke.

In recent years, however, a number of book-length studies and volumes of es-says have appeared that directly challenge the received view of Nietzsche the athe-ist and antireligious thinker. As Julian Young puts it: "While most conclude . . . that Nietzsche was, *quite obviously*, an 'atheist,' I hold the he *never* was. Though athe-istic with respect to the Christian God, Nietzsche, I hold, ought to be regarded as a religious reformer rather than an enemy of religion."[10] These studies have focused on a range of themes in Nietzsche, including his Dionysian affirmation and his dis-ruptions of the religious/secular binary,[11] his religious communitarianism,[12] his pi-etistic, Dionysian faith,[13] his mysticism,[14] his soteriology,[15] and his transformative bodily practices.[16] If nothing else, these studies show that Nietzsche's criticisms of religion have to be reexamined in light of the much more complicated picture of the philosopher that is still in the process of emerging.

This brings us back to Nietzsche's fundamental genealogical warning against the assumption that the value or meaning of something is determined by its origin. Religion for Nietzsche clearly has been the vehicle, if not the cause, of some of the worst forms of self-degradation in human history. But he also claims that this is not the only use human beings have put to religion. Thus, in essay 2 of the *Genealogy*, immediately after some of his most scathing writing on the degradations of the Christian imagination, Nietzsche pauses to note that when we look at the Greeks, we find "more noble" interpretations of the concept of gods.[17] Although in the context of the *Genealogy*'s attack on Judaism and Christianity, the significance of this passage can be easily overlooked, it shows that for Nietzsche religion is not necessarily life-denying. It also reminds us of Nietzsche's fascination with and admiration of the Greeks and, in particular, of his discussions of Greek religion in *The Birth of Tragedy* and other early writings. There, as Julian Young has argued most recently, Nietzsche views Greek tragedy as "the most important moment in Greek religion."[18] For Nietzsche tragedy was ritual, not entertainment. It invoked Dionysus for the spectators/participants and produced for them a "metaphysical solace." Although Nietzsche later criticized *The Birth of Tragedy*, the Dionysian makes a return in the character of Zarathustra, in the fifth book of *The Gay Science*, in *Twilight of the Idols*, and in *Ecce Homo*. In these works, where religion, philosophy, and art come together, the Dionysian represents a creative and ecstatic principle of gratitude and affirmation. "Dionysian art," Nietzsche writes, is the "transfiguring power of intoxication," rooted in the noble soul's overabundant "gratitude and love."[19] In his notebooks from 1888, as he was preparing to write *Twilight of the Idols*, Nietzsche complained that Christianity had for two thousand years prevented the creation of new gods. But he goes on to say, "how many new gods are still possible! As for myself, in whom the religious, that is to say god-forming instinct occasionally becomes active at impossible times—how differently, how variously the divine has revealed itself to me each time! . . . I should not doubt that there are many kinds of gods.[20]

NIETZSCHE AND THE STUDY OF RELIGION

Nietzsche's work has not had as much of a direct influence on the study of religion as theorists such as Marx, Freud, or Durkheim. Nonetheless, his influence has been significant. With the new work on Nietzsche and religion, this influence promises to grow in at least three different directions. First, Nietzsche's most important contribution to the study of religion today is grounded in the genealogical method, particularly as mediated by Foucault, Edward Said, and Talal Asad and expressed in recent titles such as "Manufacturing Religion," "The Invention of World Religions," and "The Modern Myth of 'Hinduism.'" Genealogy has been particularly important in shaping new perspectives on the history of religious traditions and in exploring the history of the concept of religion itself. With respect to the former, genealogy exposes the way in which religious traditions are always contested and always being constructed in and through these contestations. It also can show, as we see, for example, in Richard King's treatment of Hinduism, how the very concept of "religious tradition" can be imposed on a rather decentralized religious history in a colonial context. Talal Asad's genealogical work examines the very effort to define religion and, as he puts it, the way "the theoretical search for an essence of religion invites us to separate it conceptually from the domain of power."[21] More generally, a genealogical approach to the study of religion itself leads us to inquire into the constellation of discourses and powers out of which this field has been established and institutionalized. Asad more recently has extended this approach to questions about the "formation of the secular."[22] He thereby makes the important point—anticipated in Nietzsche's argument that the will to truth of modern science is the latest form of the ascetic ideal—that the distinction between the religious and the secular, as it operates, for example, both in modern politics and in the modern study of religion, is clearly tied to questions of power and exclusion.

Second, Nietzsche can help us think about religion as an interpretive operation and, more particularly, about the operation of positing "gods" or "divinity." "What, then, is truth? A mobile army of metaphors, metonyms, and anthropomorphisms—in short, a sum of human relations which have been enhanced, transposed, and embellished poetically and rhetorically, and which after long use seem firm, canonical, and obligatory to a people."[23] In this, one of Nietzsche's most quoted lines, truth is produced, in history, through poetical and rhetorical processes, that is, through interpretations that are tied to particular social configurations of will and power. Tim Murphy has recently produced an incisive study of these processes as they pertain to Nietzsche's views on metaphor and religion. For Nietzsche, metaphor is *Übertragung*, a "carrying over." As Murphy elaborates, metaphor carries over a meaning or set of meanings from one domain to another in a process of "interpretive transfer." Moreover, these mappings for Nietzsche, the philosopher of will to power, are agonistic and thus seek to impose new meanings on old domains. From this perspective, Murphy argues, Nietzsche views religion as a metaphorical, cultural mapping operation. Among other things, this suggests that we might usefully shift the focus of our search for a definition of religion from content, where religion has to do with gods, ultimate meaning, or the "sacred," to "operation," that is, the cultural mapping operations characteristic of religious discourses. Murphy himself, in line with other contemporary theorists who study religion in terms of "social formation" (such as Bruce Lincoln), defines religion in terms of a "foundationalist" and "obsessively totalizing" operation.

Despite the usefulness of this general approach to religion, we need to ask whether the claim that religion is a totalizing operation can be supported by a reading of Nietzsche or by work in the history of religions. One reader of Nietzsche who would point us in a different direction is Peter Murray. His study of Nietzsche's "affirmative morality" views Nietzsche's Dionysus as a name for the "infinite otherness" of life and world. On this reading, "gods" in Nietzsche are clearly human creations, as in Feuerbach or Freud. Feuerbach's projection creates gods out of human essence and Freud's illusion is rooted in infantile wish. For both, then, gods are formed as, in Karl Barth's words, "reflected images and guarantees of the needs and capacities of man."[24] But for Murray, Nietzsche's Dionysus is different, a projection or creation that affirms the human *only* as it also affirms the limits of the human and in an affirmative relation to the otherness of the earth. This is the meaning of Nietzschean faith—be "true to the earth"—in which the idea of god, a "chthonic god," is "equal to that of faith in the totality of the process of becoming."[25]

Finally, one of most fascinating aspects of Nietzsche's work is the way he philosophizes not just about but through, with, and against the body. He proclaimed his affirmative vision as a philosopher who "danced" and he grounded it in the "great health." Eric Blondel, in another important study of metaphor in Nietzsche, argues that the body is Nietzsche's fundamental metaphor, that it is "an interpretive space."[26] In this and other ways, then, Nietzsche anticipated much of the academic, theoretical work of recent decades in religious studies and other fields that seeks to put the body at the center of cultural histories and theories. The genealogical work of both Asad and Foucault, which often focuses on issues of punishment and pain, can be traced directly to Nietzsche's concern with these same issues. As scholars of religion—who long have been focused on questions of belief and text—begin to explore different kinds of questions, about, for instance, forms of action, discipline and expression in ritual, movement, dress, sound, and smell, this recovery of the body as a topic or subject for study is of great significance. However, as Kimerer Lamothe warns in her study of Nietzsche, dance, and religion, we should be careful not to view the body simply as a site for the reception of discipline or to too quickly "textualize" the body. Lamothe argues that for Nietzsche the body is a generative source of knowledge and that for Nietzsche, and for dancers influenced by him, such as Isadora Duncan and Martha Graham, the "process of bodily becoming is a locus for discovering and exploring alternative forms of knowledge and alternative ideals of religion than those offered by the Christian values woven into western culture."[27] Whether as a critic of religion or as someone who anticipated postsecular forms of imagining the divine, Nietzsche remains one of our most provocative sources for thinking about religion.

NOTES

1. Michel Foucault, "Nietzsche, Genealogy and History," in *Language, Counter-Memory, Practice: Selected Essays and Interviews* (Ithaca: Cornell University Press, 1977), 142.

2. Friedrich Nietzsche, *Beyond Good and Evil*, trans. Judith Norman, ed. Rolf-Peter Horstmann (Cambridge: Cambridge University Press, 2002), 10.

3. Friedrich Nietzsche, *Daybreak*, trans. R. J. Hollingdale (Cambridge: Cambridge University Press, 1982), 33.

4. Friedrich Nietzsche, *On the Genealogy of Morals*, trans. Walter Kaufmann and R. J. Hollingdale (New York: Vintage, 1969), 97.

5. Ibid., 88.

6. Ibid., 91.

7. Ibid., 117.

8. Ibid., 97.

9. Paul Ricœur, *The Philosophy of Paul Ricœur: An Anthology of His Work*, ed. Charles E. Reagan and David Stewart (Boston: Beacon, 1978), 219.

10. Julian Young, *Nietzsche's Philosophy of Religion* (Cambridge: Cambridge University Press, 2006), 2.

11. See Peter Durno Murray, *Nietzsche's Affirmative Morality: A Revaluation Based in the Dionysian World-View* (Berlin: de Gruyter, 1999); Tyler T. Roberts, *Contesting Spirit: Nietzsche, Affirmation, Religion* (Princeton: Princeton University Press, 1998).

12. See Young, *Philosophy*.

13. Bruce Ellis Benson, *Pious Nietzsche: Decadence and Dionysian Faith* (Bloomington: Indiana University Press, 2008).

14. See Jill Marsden, "Lunar Rapture: Nietzsche's Religion of the Night Sun," in *Nietzsche and the Divine*, ed. Jim Urpeth and John Lippitt (Manchester: Clinamen Press, 2000); and Tyler Roberts, "Ecstatic Philosophy," in *Nietzsche and the Divine*, ed. Jim Urpeth and John Lippitt (Manchester: Clinamen Press, 2000).

15. Giles Fraser, *Redeeming Nietzsche: On the Piety of Unbelief* (London: Routledge, 2002).

16. Kimerer L. LaMothe, *Nietzsche's Dancers: Isadora Duncan, Martha Graham, and the Revaluation of Christian Values* (New York: Palgrave Macmillan, 2006).

17. Nietzsche, *Morals*, 93.

18. Young, *Philosophy*, 22; Roberts, *Contesting Spirit*; Murray, *Nietzsche's Affirmative Morality*.

19. Friedrich Nietzsche, *The Gay Science*, trans. Walter Kaufmann (New York: Vintage, 1974), 328.

20. Friedrich Nietzsche, *The Will to Power*, trans. Walter Kaufmann and R. J. Hollingdale (New York: Vintage, 1967), 534. See also Nietzsche, *Sämtliche Werke: Kritische Studien Ausgabe*, in *Bänden*, ed. G. Colli and M. Montinari (Berlin: de Gruyter, 1980), 13:523–26.

21. Talal Asad, *Genealogies of Religion: Discipline and Reasons of Power in Christianity and Islam* (Baltimore: Johns Hopkins University Press, 1993), 29.

22. Talal Asad, *Formations of the Secular: Christianity, Islam, Modernity* (Stanford: Stanford University Press, 2003).

23. Friedrich Nietzsche, "On Truth and Lie in an Extramoral Sense," in *The Portable Nietzsche*, ed. Walter Kaufman (London: Penguin: 1976).

24. Murray, *Nietzsche's Affirmative Morality*, 275.

25. Ibid., 232.

26. Eric Blondel, *Nietzsche, the Body and Culture: Philosophy as a Philological Genealogy* (Stanford: Stanford University Press, 1991), 238.

27. LaMothe, *Dancers*, 221.

11

Sigmund Freud on Religion

VOLNEY GAY

FREUD'S LIFE AND THOUGHT

Sigmund Freud (1856–1939), the most famous psychologist of the twentieth century, began his career as neuroscientist trained in the best laboratories of nineteenth-century Vienna. He hoped to continue as a bench scientist, investigating the structure of newly discovered neurones (as he called them) using marvelous new technologies. Lacking financial resources, Freud left the laboratory and entered private practice as a nerve specialist. By the middle 1890s he earned his living as a consultant and with Josef Breuer authored *Studies on Hysteria* (1895), a book on psychotherapy technique. In that book, Freud sought to extend his neurological training (and scientific values) to the study of the mental apparatus, the conscious and nonconscious systems of the brain-mind continuum. A gifted writer and clinical observer, Freud offered novel theories of hysteria, obsessional neuroses, depression, and character pathology and then normal psychology, especially dreams, but also the arts, religion, and politics.

By his death in 1939 Freud had become world-famous, the spokesman for modernity, and the creator of a school of thought that altered Western self-consciousness. To answer his critics, Freud sought to map clinical observations onto neuroscience, and link both sets of observations to the larger world of cultural artifacts. Freud examined religion to illustrate and support his scientific work.[1] Freud's influence has been so pervasive, his writings so numerous, and his progeny, psychoanalytic psychotherapists, so influential that he is subject to numerous, often conflicting, interpretations. His stock rises and falls depending upon political and scientific taste.

FREUD'S DEFINITION OF RELIGION

As expressed throughout this volume, scholars define the concept "religion" differently depending upon their conscious and unconscious commitments. In contrast to natural scientists, religionists struggle to define their subject *before* they investigate it: the essential features of a virus, for example, do not shift depending upon intellectual constructs, but the essential features of religion do. Thus, natural scientists use preliminary definitions confident that they can discover new truths about their subject matter. Religionists enjoy no such luxury. How we define religion conditions what we can discover about it. Yet, defining religion is not a mere academic pastime. In the United States, for example, the tax code, the Constitution, and state laws presume that "religion" refers to something distinctive and meaningful. Around the world, political conflicts between small and great powers turn on how each group defines its religious affiliations and identifications.

By offering a new, compelling construct of how the mind works and how it creates illusions, Freud inserted himself into these debates. Freud defined religion as the folk beliefs of European Jews and Christians—which he rejected. Like Karl Marx and Friedrich Nietzsche, his nineteenth-century intellectual compatriots, Freud sought to uncover truths hidden beneath religious language. Unlike them, Freud wrestled with religion throughout his career. Because it alone challenged psychoanalysis for dominion over the question of the mind, Freud viewed religion as a lifelong opponent. Consequently, in each stage of his work we find a major article or book on religion.

REALITY TESTING: THE CENTRAL FOCUS OF FREUDIAN THOUGHT

Numerous thinkers understood that the human mind operated in ways outside of conscious control; few explore these realms with Freud's courage. Freud's struggles to understand his own mind and then the minds of his patients reveal what Einstein describes as "anxious searching in the dark." These efforts culminated in his greatest book, *The Interpretation of Dreams* (1900). Analyzing his own dreams, Freud describes feelings of envy, pride, competition, petty jealousy, failure, narcissistic wounds, male-male eroticism, and more.

This confession-like quality of Freud's writing coincides with his steadfast refusal to seek metaphysical unity. Freud's lifelong goal was to ground clinical theory in the bedrock of neuroscience (a goal reanimated in the rise of twenty-first-century neuroscience). This requires us to eschew a central experience of most people: that they are distinctive and irreducible unities, singularities of experience captured in the concept "soul." Freud rejected this almost universal belief and that rejection drives his lifelong struggle with religion.

We can read the twenty-four volumes of *Standard Edition* of Freud's works as the development of a research program that required Freud to reject religious promises because they violate his earliest theory of the thinking process, the theory of the cathected neurone, which finds its most brilliant exposition in the "Project" of 1895. Lacking access to brain imaging studies, Freud had to imagine how the brain (or mental apparatus) *might* be constructed to account for manifest behavior. Having sworn allegiance to physiological reductionism, Freud rejected explanations of mental behavior at odds with the known laws of physics and chemistry. Following his Viennese teachers, Freud proposed that physiological needs and their psycho-logical concomitants, desires, were functions of the organism's basic tendency to perceive and then discharge stimuli arising both from within (for example, the ap-petites, or drives) and from without. The increasing pressure of stimuli toward dis-charge first issues in random body movements, for example, the infant screams and kicks. When an external source (the mother) reduces the painful state by effecting environmental changes, the event constitutes an experience of satisfaction: "A fa-cilitation is then formed between these cathexes and the nuclear neurones."[2]

This creates a physiological (neural) connection between a biological state (hun-ger), images of the formerly need-satisfying object (for example, the breast), and the memory of subsequent satisfaction. Renewed hunger evokes the memory-image of the breast and the infant initiates discharges against that hallucinated image. When hunger persists, the level of unbound cathexes (which means psychic energy) rises and the infant experiences pain. To avoid that pain, the organism must be educated to reality. Freud concentrated his considerable intellect upon explaining how hypothetical neural systems using psychic energy, made up of different kinds of neurones, carried out this form of reality testing, as he called it. All his major essays—beginning with "The Project" in 1895, through *The Interpretation of Dreams* (1900), to the essays on metapsychology (1911–17), through *Group Psychol-ogy* (1921) and *The Ego and the Id* (1923), to *Inhibitions, Symptoms, and Anxiety* (1926), to *New Introductory Lectures* (1933), to his posthumous essays on ego psy-chology—refine his model of reality testing and the *failures* of reality testing that occur in religion and other illusions.

For example, in the 1890s Freud noted that hysterical patients exhibited exces-sive emotions around seemingly neutral memories. He explained this mystery by demonstrating that the apparently neutral memory symbolizes a sexual trauma that occurred prior to sexual maturity. A young woman may exhibit hysteric symptoms when in the presence of clerks because she had been sexually molested as a child under similar circumstances[3] even though she was not traumatized at that time. Rather, Freud claims, the memory of the original assault becomes traumatic follow-ing the upsurge in sexual urges at puberty: "Although it does not usually happen in psychical life that a memory arouses an affect which it did not give rise to as an experience, this is never-the-less something quite usual in the case of a sexual idea, precisely because the retardation of puberty is a general characteristic of the organization."[4]

Freud abandoned this claim when he discovered that not all hysterics had suf-fered prepubertal (actual) traumata. However, in the same discussion, he distin-guishes between the ego's avoidance of unpleasure and the ego's task of creating side-cathexes in order to repair a breech in the mechanism itself. He says the ego necessarily suffers repeated unpleasure in order to (actively) effect the necessary side-cathexes, meaning "contained" energies, which prevent subsequent repetition of the original trauma: what he calls a "posthumous primary affective experience":

> If the trauma (experience of pain) occurs . . . at a time when there is already an ego, there is to begin with a release of unpleasure, but simultaneously the ego is at work too, creating side-cathexes. If the cathexis of the memory is repeated, the unpleasure

is repeated too, but the ego facilitations are there already as well; experience shows that the release (of unpleasure) is less the second time, until, after further repetition, it shrivels up to the intensity of a signal acceptable to the ego.[5]

All thinking, including self-awareness, grows out of drive inhibition. Since pleasure is the discharge of tension, it follows that inhibition is necessarily painful. Hence, as humans acquire the ability to think, they lose the immediacy of primary pleasure, and gain the displeasure of inhibition. The corollary is that the thinking ego, the primary organ of human adaptation, is the original source of alienation from the satisfaction of desire. One can learn the reality principle and hope for later satisfaction but that satisfaction is hypothetical, located in the as yet unavailable future. Hence, the central, irreparable human conflict is not that we must think in order to survive but that thinking makes us sick. By insisting upon instinctual renunciation, religions advance the cause of culture; religion is a form of cultural taxation upon the libido and freedom of individuals who are compensated by promissory notes of an afterlife.

FREUD'S CRITIQUE OF RELIGION: ILLUSORY WHOLENESS

Freud's critique of religion derives from his fixation upon the problem of reality testing. It is best exemplified in his texts on the ego, especially *Group Psychology and the Analysis of the Ego* (1921). There he attempts to show that the ego's dependent status vis-à-vis the drives and reality, as well as the painfulness of thinking, is mirrored in larger social structures, including religious groups. They too struggle against the drives, including aggression, and they do so in the face of major, real traumata— the loss of the archaic family with its all-powerful, idealized father who promised eternal protection from the terrors of life. The structure and content of religious repetition parallel the ego's repetitious attempts to bind excessive stimuli. The ego attempts to heal the trauma of oedipal loss by repetitiously acting out those moments of suffering until the pain "shrivels up to the intensity of a signal acceptable to the ego."[6] Religious institutions promise precisely the same relief, but at the cost of the ego's integrity.

It is difficult to overstress Freud's commitment to his physicalist program: at the end of *Totem and Taboo* (1912–13), his disquisition on archaic religion, he cites Goethe: "In the beginning was the Deed."[7] One finds the same commitment in last book, *Moses and Monotheism* (1939), an outlandish speculation about the origins of Judaism in real traumata. Freud argued that archaic Judaism is the social equivalent of the ego's creation of a side-cathexes with which it seeks to avoid repetition of the original loss: the idealized father is not dead; he lives eternally in the deathless image of God the Father. The superego gains its content from these ego identifications and id (instinctual) derivatives. The superego serves as an unconscious vehicle for cultural norms and cultural taboos, but it assumes that role through its genesis in real trauma (the oedipal loss, the death of the archaic father, and so on). Thus religious institutions have superego qualities—as purveyors of the "Thou shall not," for example—but their core structure parallels the ego, not the superego. They serve, therefore, adaptive tasks. For Freud, to become modern requires one to mourn the loss of archaic religious solutions to life's problems.

The ego's task of binding and so ameliorating the pain of real suffering is necessarily repetitious because the drives that animate the system—especially sex—are themselves cyclical. The ego's manifestation of repetition compulsion, which occasions the need for reanalysis,[8] is the dynamic source of religious institutions. Churches gain adherents because they relieve one of the tasks of self-control. They are ready-made defenses: "If the ego succeeds in protecting itself from a dangerous instinctual impulse, through, for instance, the process of repression, it has certainly inhibited and damaged the particular part of the id concerned; but it has at the same time given it some independence and has renounced some of its own sovereignty."[9] Becoming religious allows the ego to assume a defensive network elaborated over centuries and so constitutes a net gain. However, religion requires the ego to forgo many crucial acts of reality testing (one is forbidden to question dogma and so on) and this means the ego renounces part of its powers, part of its sovereignty. We can see this, again, in the repetitious and compulsive features of religion, which, while originally a function of the need to bind painful stimuli (loss of the father and the like), now operate independently and automatically: "If now the danger-situation changes so that the ego has no reason for fending off a new instinctual impulse analogous to the repressed one, the consequence of the restriction of the ego which has taken place will become manifest. The new impulse will run its course under an automatic influence—or, as I should prefer to say, under the influence of the compulsion to repeat."[10]

Even if one can do without institutionalized defenses and yet avoid unsocial and deviant actions, the ego is still damaged: "Intimately bound up with the id as it is, it [the ego] can only fend off an instinctual danger by restricting its own organization and by acquiescing in the formation of symptoms in exchange for having impaired the instinct."[11] With the attainment of thinking the ego is necessarily and permanently split off from direct satisfaction of the organism's strongest, oldest, and most intense desires. But dissolving the ego and seeking to return to such an undifferentiated state—as occurs in religious ecstasy—means forsaking the ego's major achievements, the adoption of the reality principle and mastery over the compulsion to repeat.

Freud never doubted that religious institutions offered solutions to human conflicts and that they did so by guaranteeing feelings of wholeness. On the contrary, it was precisely their ability to gratify fundamental human wishes that made them antithetical to the ego's toleration of real suffering and that prevented, therefore, real solutions to human misery. For Freud, the hermeneutic wish to recapture the satisfaction offered by religion can be achieved only in fantasy—in a living dream— which, like all dreams, placates the ego, assuages its losses, and allows it to assume a pose of completion and lack of conflict."[12]

Freud does not disdain the ubiquitous drive to achieve wholeness and completion of self. It is only when this drive overwhelms and obscures equally valid drives toward union with others that disorder occurs. By itself, the ego is not adequate to the tasks of unifying the personality and securing its safety. Although the outside world is a source of pain and frustration, it is also the realm of other people who, since the ego's birth in infancy, have helped affirm, maintain, and complete it. While the ego instantiates the essentially biological conflict between the anabolic and catabolic processes of life itself, the individual's conflict with the social world is "not a derivative of the contradiction—probably an irreconcilable one—between the primal instincts of Eros and death."[13]

RELIGION AND YEARNINGS
FOR TRANSCENDENCE

Shortly after Freud's death, Ernest Jones, his official biographer, compared Freud to the ancient Greeks who proclaimed "Know Thyself!"—the injunction carved over the temple at Delphi. In Jones's estimation, Freud was the first person to obey fully this demand. How did Freud do this, when others had tried and failed for two thousand years? Jones answers: "it must remain a cause for wonder. It was the nearest to a miracle that human means can compass, one that surely surpasses even the loftiest intellectual achievements in mathematics and pure science."[14] What Freud criticized—an un-self-conscious yearning for transcendence—reappears in Jones's adoration. The Freudian critique of religion as yearning and as a magic remains an essential part of the modern West; so too do its limitations remain part of our contemporary struggle.

NOTES

1. Unless otherwise noted, all Freud references are to volumes in *The Standard Edition of the Complete Psychological Works of Sigmund Freud*, 24 vols. (London: Hogarth and Institute for Psycho-Analysis, 1953–74). See also Sigmund Freud, *Gesammelte Werke* (Frankfurt: Fischer, 1960). Portions of this essay derive from my previous books and articles on Freud.

2. Sigmund Freud, *A Project for a Scientific Psychology* (London: Hogarth, 1955), 1:318.

3. Ibid., 1:353–56.

4. Ibid., 1:356.

5. Ibid., 1:359.

6. Ibid.

7. Ibid., 1:161.

8. Sigmund Freud, *Analysis Terminable and Interminable* (London: Hogarth, 1964), 23:211–53.

9. Sigmund Freud, *Inhibitions, Symptoms and Anxiety* (London: Hogarth, 1959), 20:153.

10. Ibid.

11. Ibid., 20:156.

12. Sigmund Freud, *The Interpretation of Dreams* (London: Hogarth, 1953), 4:550–72.

13. Sigmund Freud, *Civilization and Its Discontents* (London: Hogarth, 1961), 21:141.

14. Ernest Jones, *The Life and Work of Sigmund Freud* (New York: Basic Books, 1955), 2:423.

12

Karl Marx on Religion

TERRY REY

OVERVIEW

"Religion is . . . the opium of the people." Few things ever written on the topic have received as much attention or sparked as much controversy as this epic metaphor from Karl Marx, crafted in 1843. Many interpret the intended meaning of this phrase to be that human beings are suffering creatures in need of anesthesia and that religion's raison d'être is to fill that need. That is all true, but Marx in fact saw much more in religion than this. Even as he argued that human suffering is essentially what religion reflects, he also held that it is precisely what religion protests. Human suffering, meanwhile, is multiform and multilayered, Marx argued. It is sometimes subtle and sometimes acute, but always rooted in forms of *alienation* that are caused by unjust and literally dehumanizing economic forces. Instead of opium, Marx prescribed communism, and we know too well how that turned out. Yet despite the demise of communist regimes throughout the world, which has led many to question the worth of Marxist thought today, Marx's critiques of what is wrong with the world remain as compelling as when he first wrote them about a century and a half ago, be it his critique of religion, capitalism, or the state.

Although later in is his prolific career he seldom returned to the topic of religion, Marx did say a good bit more about it, rather pithily, in the very essay in which his famous opium reference appears. That essay, "Towards a Critique of Hegel's Philosophy of Right," is among the most influential of Marx's early writings, a collection of papers treating a range of subjects that he penned circa 1843 and 1844. In these texts we see Marx laying the foundation for his social philosophy at large, as here, in addition and related to his critique of religion, the young philosopher began to develop his theory of alienation, which is key to understanding his "relentless . . . hostility to religious beliefs, practices, and institutions."[1] This chapter examines the philosophical underpinnings of this hostility, and moves toward mapping out the contours and content of Marx's thinking about religion and how it relates to his larger intellectual project. It concludes with a brief suggestion about the relevance of Marx's sociology of religion for our own time.

TURNING HEGEL ON HIS HEAD
THROUGH A STREAM OF FIRE

Marx was born in the German Rhineland two years after the 1816 anti-Jewish laws drove his father to convert to Protestant Christianity in order to continue his legal practice there. Thus, although several prominent German rabbis were among Marx's ancestors and relatives, he was raised Protestant, albeit marginally, in a predominately Catholic region, and as an adolescent the future champion of atheism did display a marked poetic and spiritual temperament. By the time he had completed his undergraduate studies in law and begun working toward his doctorate in philosophy, however, the spirituality of that temperament had been burned away by his reading of Ludwig Feuerbach's great atheistic treatise *The Essence of Christianity*, which first appeared in 1841. The name Feuerbach literally means "fire stream" in German, a metaphoric opportunity that was not lost on the erstwhile poet Marx, who wrote that "there is no other road for you to *truth* and *freedom* except that leading *through* the stream of fire, Feuerbach is the *purgatory* of the present time."[2] *Truth* about what? *Freedom* from and *through* what? A *purging* of what? These are questions that Marx spent the better part of his life seeking to answer.

Although deeply compelled by the philosophy of G. W. F. Hegel and its explication of the dialectical cadence of history's unfolding, like Feuerbach before him, Marx was convinced that philosophy needed to be freed from the idealism of Hegel's ambitious and influential system of thought and purged of its underlying assumption that history is essentially some grandiose divine project. Identified by the term "dialectical idealism," Hegel's highly complex and far-reaching philosophical system is predicated upon the notion that history progresses dialectically in a triadic formula wherein truths meet contradictions and consequently surer truths emerge. Or, in Hegel's own terms, *thesis* meets its *antithesis* and a *synthesis* results.[3] Moving this entire historical dialectic is God (*Geist*, literally "Spirit" or "Mind"), who is ever moving toward self-realization in humanity's ongoing quest for higher truth. In this inherently theistic scheme of things, it is especially philosophy and religion—or, more precisely, the philosophy of religion—that leads the way toward God's ultimate self-realization, which is the absolute meaning and purpose of human existence. And, for Hegel, this self-realization was nearing its culmination with the emergence of Christianity as the world's dominant religion.

Four years after Hegel's death in 1831, the publication of David Strauss's *The Life of Jesus*[4] heralded the arrival of the school of philosophy in which Marx would take his own place, the Young Hegelians, which was inspired in part by Marx's mentor and friend Bruno Bauer. In the first of a series of influential treatises that used Hegel's dialectic to critique religion itself, and hence liberate the dialectic from its illusory idealism, Strauss argued both that there was nothing at all supernatural about the Gospels or Jesus's ministry and that the absolutism of Christianity in Hegel's philosophical system was fallacious and absurd because the infinite could not logically incarnate in the finite.

From Strauss, the Young Hegelian's atheistic torch was passed to Feuerbach, who asserted that Hegel's *Geist* is nothing more than a human product and thus God does not exist independent of human thought and desire. As such, theology amounts merely to anthropology, in the sense that humanity's most cherished values (for example, love, wisdom, righteousness, power, majesty, and so on) are infinitized and projected onto a mythic notion called God, which in turn legitimates the embodiment and pursuit of those vaules.[5] Feuerbach therefore concluded that "man has in fact no other aim than himself."[6] These words would have a resounding influence on Marx, who reflected them in his own stated conviction that "the more man puts into God the less he retains in himself."[7]

Thus fueled by Feuerbach, Marx ventured *to turn Hegel on his head* by cracking "the mystical shell" in Hegel to get at the "rational kernel," the dialectic, which Marx esteemed to be "the outstanding achievement of Hegel's phenomenology and of its final outcome, *the dialectic of negativity as the moving and generating principle . . .* that Hegel conceives the self creation of the human being as a process."[8] David McLellan describes this feature of Hegel's dialectic that so compelled Marx, that each "successive stage [of human progress] retains elements of the previous stage at the same time as it goes beyond them": "Hegel also talked of 'the power of the negative,' thinking that there was always a tension between any present state of affairs and what it was becoming. For any present state of affairs was in the process of being negated, changed into something else. This process was what Hegel meant by dialectic."[9]

With Hegel's idealism thus banished, Marx grounded this *dialectic* in the *material* social processes of human history. This history is defined by class struggle and by fluctuating periods of stability and instability, a progression fueled by the forces of human productivity and by economics. In this way, Marx departs from Hegel and moves ahead in forging his *dialectical materialism*, which in time would prove to be one of the most concretely influential developments in the history of human thought.

Meanwhile, though indebted to Feuerbach in his criticism of Hegel, Marx also criticized Feuerbach's materialism for being ahistorical and missing the *practical* dimension of human existence, that human beings are defined not by their thought but by their physical, "sensuous" action, their *practice*, the essence of which for Marx is *labor*:

> The chief defect of all hitherto existing materialism (that of Feuerbach included) is that the thing, reality, sensuousness, is conceived only in the form of the object, *or of contemplation*, but not as *human sensuous activity*, practice, not subjectivity. . . . Feuerbach wants sensuous objects, really distinct from the thought objects, but he does not conceive human activity itself as *objective* activity. . . . Hence he does not grasp the significance of "revolutionary," of "practical-critical" activity.[10]

And this is a serious problem for Marx, because, as he writes a few lines later in one of his most famous statements, "The philosophers have only *interpreted* the world, in various ways; the point however is to *change* it."

Although in Feuerbach "the *criticism of religion* is essentially complete,"[11] the criticism of *the cause* of religion remained unarticulated. This was the deeper problem that perplexed Marx, one that Feuerbach failed to address: the suffering that causes people to turn to religion in the first place. "Feuerbach, consequently, does not see that the 'religious sentiment' is itself a *social product*."[12] More specifically, for Marx, our "religious sentiment" is the product of *alienating* social forces. In the rapidly industrializing, urbanizing world in which Marx lived and wrote, capitalism had spawned the latest version of the class struggle that he viewed as constant across human history: the *proletariat* (working class) versus the *bourgeoisie* (managerial class). Three principle forms of alienation result from this: (1) humans are alienated from the product of their labor (they do not control what they produce); (2) humans are alienated from one another, laboring in competition rather than communally; and (3) humans are alienated from their very essence, or "species-being," as Marx terms it—that which distinguishes humans from all other species—which is our capacity to freely and communally labor to make and transform our world and life itself. Religion serves to mask all of these forms of alienation, and as such it contributes to their reproduction. And whereas other Young Hegelians were hopeful that Feuerbach's putative demonstration of the human creation of God would lead to our liberation from religion, Marx was of the mind that religion would only go away once its causes were eradicated: human suffering and alienation. Let us now take a closer look now at Marx's early writings on religion and how they relate to his philosophy of human existence at large.

RELIGION AND HUMAN SUFFERING IN MARX'S EARLY WRITINGS

For the better part of the 160-odd years that have passed since Marx penned his foundational manuscripts of the early and mid-1840s, social-scientific debate about religion has been predominated by three fundamental points of general consensus, which themselves of course take various forms in a wide range of analyses. As summarized by Rodney Stark and Roger Finke, they are: (1) "that religion is false and harmful"; (2) "that religion is doomed"; and (3) "that religion is an epiphenomenon."[13] Marx clearly held each of these positions quite firmly, and his critique of religion is commonly portrayed in light especially of the first of these. In its legitimation of the division of labor and the radical inequalities in wealth distribution that characterize the capitalistic world, Marx certainly found religion to be harmful. He saw this function of religion to be nothing new with the emergence of capitalism, moreover:

> The social principles of Christianity justified slavery in antiquity, glorified medieval serfdom, and, when necessary, also know how to defend the oppression of the proletariat, although they may do this with a pious face. The social principles of Christianity preach the necessity of a ruling and an oppressed class, and for the latter they have only the pious wish that the former will be benevolent. . . . The social principles of Christianity declare all vile acts of the oppressors against the oppressed to be

either just punishment for original sin and other sins, or suffering that the Lord in his infinite wisdom has destined for those to be redeemed.[14]

As such, religion as an opiate has two chief functions: (1) to anesthetize us to our suffering; and (2) to dupe us into understanding this suffering to be part of a divine plan or cosmic law (for example, the will of God or karma), rather than the product of material historical forces that it really is. This, for Marx, is the crux of the matter, and this indeed is the main message about religion that most readers take from him. But surrounding Marx's assertion that religion "is the opium of the people" are other intriguing ideas that receive neither further development in his work nor anything near the same degree of attention among his interpreters. Let us consider here more fully this extraordinary passage:

> *Man makes religion*, religion does not make man. Religion is indeed the self-consciousness and self-esteem of man who has either not yet won through to himself or has already lost himself again. But *man* is no abstract being squatting outside the world. Man is *the world of man.* . . . *Religious* suffering is at one and the same time the *expression* of real suffering and a protest against real distress. Religion is the sigh of the oppressed creature, the heart of a heartless world and the soul of a soulless condition. It is the *opium* of the people.[15]

The allusion to Feuerbach is clear in the claim that human beings make religion, yet Marx is also implying here the core of his humanistic philosophy: that human beings by nature are—or at least they should be—the producers of themselves and their own world, that is, their *species- being*. Furthermore, in claiming religion to be "the self-consciousness and self-esteem of man who has either not yet won through to himself or has already lost himself again," Marx means that religion is symptomatic of our alienation from our species-being. This alienation is the root cause of the suffering that makes people turn to religion to begin with. Thus while our opium to some degree alleviates our suffering in this "heartless world," it also misplaces our focus onto God instead of humanity, thereby further alienating us from what we as a species should be.

Often overlooked in Marx's famous critique of religion is the notion that religion is not only "the *expression* of real sufferings" but also "the protest against real suffering." But Marx never bothers explicating what precisely he means by the word "protest" here; it would seem that he was of the mind that religion had virtually nothing to offer in the way of "revolutionary praxis," or any practical means that could help change the world. Like several important Marxist thinkers after him, Marx's close friend and frequent coauthor Friedrich Engels deviated from Marx in this regard, writing at some length of the function of religion in challenging the social order in Central European history,[16] ideas that are echoed by the twentieth-century German Marxist philosopher Ernst Bloch.[17] In a similar vein, the great Italian communist thinker Antonio Gramsci saw some revolutionary potential in popular religion,[18] while the Polish-born German Marxist theorist Rosa Luxemburg called for an alliance between socialism and the church.[19]

Such an alliance has nowhere witnessed a greater concrete realization than in Latin America, where in the 1970s and 1980s liberation theology inspired the church to give a "preferential option to the poor." In the United States, furthermore, religion clearly played a central role in the Civil Rights Movement and forever changed the world's most powerful and wealthiest nation, and for the better at that. In a careful and sustained reading of Marx, John Raines—who himself was jailed in Little Rock during the movement for his pastoral work toward racial justice—goes so far as to claim that "for Marx the essence of religion is its voicing of 'suffering'—its crying out against the realities of exploitation and degradation."[20] As such, shouldn't those who wish to change the world turn to religion as a serviceable resource rather than seek to *abolish* it as a form of alienation? Perhaps by the "abolition of religion,"[21] in effect, Marx meant something else?

MARX, RELIGION, AND THE GLOBALIZATION OF HEARTLESSNESS

In Marx's claim that religion is both "*expression* of" and "*protest* against" suffering, we see at work the dialectic that runs through his entire philosophy. As Andrew McKinnon helpfully explains, it is important to be mindful of the historical (and future) implications of Marx's dialectical mode of thought, for in this light we can come to see that when Marx speaks of the "abolition" of religion he means something more like "transcendence." "For Marx, the criticism of religion, although essentially finished, is not an end in itself, but rather a means. Marx's concern is to take the latest developments of Hegelian philosophy, and turn them into praxis-oriented critique of the social world, one rooted in the '*categorical imperative* to overthrow all relations in which man is a debased, enslaved, forsaken, despicable being.'"[22]

This is not to suggest that Marx held out any hope for religion, for he seemingly believed that it would eventually die a slow death of desuetude as humanity progressed toward emancipation in the realization of our species-being. Like so many subsequent sociologists of religion who once subscribed to the secularization thesis, he was wrong about that, even though his own vision of religion's eventual disappearance was more sophisticated than most in terms of his broader vision that all forms of alienation, religion being chief among them, would disappear once human emancipation is achieved. Timelessly, and therefore more importantly, what Marx's critique of religion does suggest is that we must bring to the study of religion today an "attentiveness not only to heart and spirit, but also to the concrete heartless and spiritless situation in which heart and spirit are expressed. Religion . . . points beyond them to other possibilities."[23] In his broader vision of religion's eventual demise, Marx conceived of such possibilities as bringing to humanity "heaven on earth."[24]

With nearly half of the total global human population today subsisting on less than $2.50 a day and more than twenty thousand children dying daily as a result of poverty, heaven seems as far away from earth as ever. New and increasingly widespread and globalizing forms of heartlessness and soullessness embattle and embitter our species, with far too many people living unfree, alienated, and malnourished lives. Marx's philosophy helps us understand both how we got to this point and how we might transcend it. It also suggests that we should pay careful attention to the social and economic forces behind the global resurgence of religion in our age, just as we should listen attentively to Marx's ever-trenchant critique of the dehumanizing market forces of global capitalism.

NOTES

1. Delos B. McKown, *The Classical Marxist Critiques of Religion: Marx, Engels, Lenin, Kautsky* (The Hague, Netherlands: Martinus Nijhoff, 1975), 10. The term "relentless" may be challenged here: McKown offers ample evidence of a sustained hostility toward religion in Marx's writing, though in his personal life, according to his daughter Eleanor, Marx was known to frequently say, "Despite everything, we can forgive Christianity much, for it has taught us to love children." Samuel K. Padover, "Introduction: Marx's Religious Views," in *The Karl Marx Library*, vol. 5, *On Religion*, ed. Samuel K. Padover (New York: McGraw-Hill, 1974), ix–xxvii, xxvii.
2. Karl Marx, *Early Texts*, trans. and ed. David McLellan (New York: Barnes and Noble, 1972), 25, italics in original.
3. G. W. F. Hegel, *The Phenomenology of Spirit*, trans. A. V. Miller (Oxford: Oxford University Press, 1977).
4. David Friedrich Strauss, *The Life of Jesus: Critically Examined*, trans. George Eliot (Whitefish, Mont.: Kessinger, 2008).
5. For this reason, Feuerbach's philosophy of religion is commonly referred to as "projection theory."
6. Ludwig Feuerbach, *The Essence of Christianity*, trans. Marian Evans (London: Trubner, 1881).
7. Karl Marx, *Economic and Philosophic Manuscripts of 1844*, trans. Martin Milligan (New York: International Publishers, 1982), 108.
8. Marx, *Early Texts*, 164.
9. David McLellan, *Karl Marx: His Life and Thought* (New York: Harper and Row, 1974), 29.
10. Karl Marx, *Early Writings*, trans. Rodney Livingstone (New York: Vintage, 1975), 421–22.
11. Ibid., 243.
12. Ibid., 423.
13. Rodney Stark and Roger Finke, *Acts of Faith: Exploring the Human Side of Religion* (Berkeley: University of California Press, 2000), 28–29.
14. Karl Marx, "Social Principles of Christianity," in *Marx on Religion*, ed. John C. Raines (Philadelphia: Temple University Press, 2002), 184–85, 186.
15. Marx, *Early Writings*, 244.
16. Friedrich Engels, *The Peasant War in Germany* (Moscow: Progress, 1959).
17. Ernst Bloch, *Atheism in Christianity: The Religion of the Exodus and the Kingdom*, trans. J. T. Swann (New York: Herder and Herder, 1972).

18. Antonio Gramsci, *Selections from the Prison Notebooks*, ed. and trans. Quintin Hoare (London: Lawrence and Wishart, 1978). See also Dwight B. Billings, "Religion as Opposition: A Gramscian Analysis," *American Journal of Sociology* 96, no. 1 (1990): 1–31.

19. Rosa Luxembourg, *Socialism and the Churches*, trans. Juan Punto (Colombo, Ceylon: Young Socialist Publication, 1964).

20. John Raines, "Introduction," in Marx, *Marx on Religion*, 1–14, 8.

21. Marx, *Early Writings*, 244.

22. Andrew McKinnon, "Opium as Dialectics of Religion: Metaphor, Expression and Protest," in *Marx, Critical Theory, and Religion: A Critique of Rational Choice*, ed. Warren S. Goldstein (Boston: Brill, 2006), 21.

23. Ibid., 29.

24. Marx, *Early Texts*, 64.

13

"Religion" in the Writings of the New Atheists

TINA BEATTIE

This essay explores the representation of religion by thinkers associated with a movement sometimes referred to as "the new atheism." This is an antireligious ideology that emerged primarily in Britain and America during the late 1990s, as a response to the growing visibility and sometimes violent extremism of Islamism and fundamentalist Christianity.

Not all forms of atheism define themselves over against religious ideas. There is, for example, a fruitful engagement between postmodern theologians and the work of philosophical nontheists such as Alain Badiou, Gilles Deleuze, Jacques Derrida, Julia Kristeva, Gianni Vattimo, and Slavoj Žižek, all of whom are concerned with ways in which the idea of God and religious meanings function in their linguistic, psychological, and political contexts.[1] However, unlike their continental and postmodern counterparts, the new atheists are not concerned with questions about the complexity of language and the ambiguity of philosophical and theological claims to knowledge. Rather, in language that sometimes echoes that of their nineteenth-century scientific predecessors, they assert the irrefutable triumph of scientific rationalism over religion and the ethical superiority of atheism over faith in God, and many of them seek the elimination of all religious influences from public institutions and civil society, including schools and universities.

Yet like all movements that define themselves primarily in oppositional terms, the new atheists risk mirroring that which they claim to reject, for in their polemical absolutism they are sometimes indistinguishable from their more extreme religious counterparts. In what follows, I seek to demonstrate the shortcomings in their conceptualization of religion, and to illustrate how often they betray their own stated criteria of rationality and empirical evidence as the only reliable basis for knowledge. I conclude by appealing for a more nuanced appreciation of the complexity of religious traditions and a greater awareness of the extent to which all our accounts of meaning and truth constitute mythical and metaphorical interpretations of reality that allow us to position ourselves meaningfully within the world. This invites a more thoughtful and open-ended dialogue between atheists and religious believers, a willingness to acknowledge that our diverse cultural and linguistic contexts defy any single, definitive claim to truth or knowledge, and an acceptance that this openness can and often does go hand in hand with a personal religious commitment that embodies its values within the material practices of everyday life, which can give a reasoned account of itself if called upon to do so, and which is open to modification or change when presented with persuasive and well-reasoned challenges to the positions it holds.[2]

"THE NEW ATHEISM"

In 2006, the popular science writer Richard Dawkins published a polemical attack on religion, *The God Delusion*,[3] which went to the top of the best-seller lists in Britain and America. Christopher Hitchens's book *God Is Not Great: How Religion Poisons Everything*,[4] published in 2007, was also an immediate best seller, and books offering similar although more nuanced arguments by Sam Harris and Daniel C. Dennett have attracted a wide readership.[5] The philosopher A. C. Grayling is an advocate of the new atheism, as is the novelist Ian McEwan and the journalist and political commentator Polly Toynbee—one of the few women associated with the movement.

There are two main points to Dawkins's antireligious campaign. First, he argues that modern science, especially Darwin's theory of evolution by natural selection, provides a sufficiently compelling explanation of human origins to make it irrational to believe in God. Second, he holds religion responsible for corrupting human values and ethics throughout history, and for causing most of the violence in the world.

Although he had been pitting Darwinism against religion for some time (a conflict that is more apparent to Darwin's recent disciples than it was to Darwin himself),[6] Dawkins embraced a more militant form of atheism in the aftermath of the 9/11 attacks on America. This inspired others to join in what they saw as a clash between the rational scientific values of liberal modernity and the dangerous and violent influences of religion in all its forms. In a newspaper article in 2002, the novelist Martin Amis wrote, "Since it is no longer permissible to disparage any single faith or creed, let us start disparaging all of them. To be clear: an ideology is a belief system with an inadequate basis in reality; a religion is a belief system with no basis in reality whatever. Religious belief is without reason and without dignity, and its record is near-universally dreadful."[7] Amis's description of all religion as irrational, unreal, and immoral sums up claims that are made in one form or another by all the new atheists.

DEFINING "RELIGION"

At the heart of Amis's description of religion is a circular argument that one finds in most of the new atheist writings. The claim that religious belief is "without reason and without dignity, and . . . is near-universally dreadful," results in a tendency to dismiss any evidence of reasonable and ethical religious faith as not really religious at all, and to identify all irrational, unethical, and violent belief systems as de facto religions. Let me give some examples of this.

Sam Harris describes communism as "little more than a political religion."[8] Referring to Stalin and Mao, he argues that "Even though their beliefs did not reach beyond this world, they were both cultic and irrational."[9] In other words, the working definition of religion seems to be whatever is "cultic and irrational," so whatever is cultic and irrational must be a quasi-religion. Conversely, because all rational and ethical beliefs must be atheist, reasonable and ethical people are really atheists at heart, even if they believe themselves to be religious.

Like Harris, Dawkins refuses to accept that the savagery unleashed by atheist political ideologies in the twentieth century can in any way be attributed to atheism. He claims that "Individual atheists may do evil things but they don't do evil things in the name of atheism."[10] Even this concession is contradicted elsewhere, when he professes, "I do not believe there is an atheist in the world who would bulldoze Mecca—or Chartres, York Minster or Notre Dame, the Shwe Dagon, the temples of Kyoto or, of course, the Buddhas of Bamiyan."[11] Dawkins appears somewhat ignorant of twentieth-century history, when communist regimes destroyed vast numbers of religious buildings and shrines.[12] But while atheism is denied any motivating role when people do evil, religion is also denied any motivating role when people do good. Consider the following examples.

Dawkins gives an account of a television discussion with the obstetrician Robert Winston—described by Dawkins as "a respected pillar of British Jewry."[13] Winston told Dawkins that "he didn't really believe in anything supernatural," which leads Dawkins to conclude that Winston is confused when he calls himself Jewish:

> When I pressed him, he said he found that Judaism provided a good discipline to help him structure his life and lead a good one. Perhaps it does; but that, of course, has not the smallest bearing on the truth value of any of its supernatural claims. There are many intellectual atheists who proudly call themselves Jews and observe Jewish rites, perhaps out of loyalty to an ancient tradition or to murdered relatives, but also because of a confused and confusing willingness to label as "religion" the pantheistic reverence which most of us share with its most distinguished exponent, Albert Einstein.[14]

According to Dawkins's definition, any belief system that goes by the name of religion must make supernatural claims, for that's what religion is. Pantheism is therefore not a religion (even though many scholars would include it in that category), but Judaism is, and therefore Judaism must include belief in the supernatural. Because Winston does not believe in the supernatural, he is not really Jewish.

A more informed understanding of Judaism might force Dawkins to acknowledge that Judaism may not qualify as a religion according to his criteria, or that it is his definition of religion that is "confused and confusing." The position he attributes to Winston is not an aberration from traditional Judaism but a description that would be acceptable perhaps to the majority of observant Jews. Judaism does not entail a belief in the supernatural in the way that Dawkins implies. It is a way of life rooted in the overlapping narratives of many different communities and cultures that share a common story about their place within God's creation, and this finds expression in the communal observances, rituals, and ethics of Jewish life. This way of life provides the discipline, structure, and goodness that, according to Dawkins, Winston mistakenly identifies with being Jewish.

If we turn to Hitchens (1949–2011), we discover a similar resistance to any suggestion that, sometimes, religions inspire goodness and altruism in their followers. Dietrich Bonhoeffer was executed by the Nazis for his role in the attempted assassination of Hitler, and he is regarded by many as one of the greatest Christians of the twentieth century. He drew his inspiration and courage from a radical commitment to the Jesus Christ of the Bible beyond any religious, social, or moral status quo, but Hitchens attributes his willingness to die in resisting the Nazis to "an admirable but nebulous humanism."[15] Hitchens denies that there could be any Christian motivation for Nazi resisters such as Bonhoeffer and Martin Niemoller because "the chance that they did so on orders from any priesthood is statistically almost negligible."[16] Again, we see an insidious logic at work. According to Hitchens's definition, Christians act only on orders from priests; therefore Bonhoeffer and Niemoller were not acting because of their Christian beliefs.

Martin Luther King, another great twentieth-century Christian thinker and martyr, is given similar treatment. Hitchens points out that King quoted the Bible in "metaphors and allegories,"[17] rather than literally acting out its violent rhetoric, and he claims that "In no real as opposed to nominal sense . . . was he a Christian."[18] In other words, "real" Christians are violent biblical fundamentalists, and if good people claim to be Christians then they are either self-deluding or dishonest.

If Hitchens were to acknowledge that Christianity was the inspiration and motivation for the lives of Bonhoeffer, Niemoller, and King, he would have to conclude either that Christianity is not a religion at all or that religion is a more complex and multifaceted phenomenon than he once thought. He does neither. Instead, he clings to his conviction that religious people are by definition mad, bad, and dangerous by dismissing abundant evidence that many are in fact sane, good, and altruistic. What has become of the insistence on rationality and empirical evidence as the basis for belief? These attempts to categorize religion begin to sound a little like Humpty Dumpty speaking to Alice in Lewis Carroll's *Alice Through the Looking Glass*: " 'When *I* use a word,' Humpty Dumpty said, in rather a scornful tone, 'it means just what I choose it to mean—neither more nor less.' "[19]

CONTEXTUALIZING "RELIGION"

These confusions arise because the new atheists fail to acknowledge what a complicated, contested, and multivalent term "religion" is. They appear to have little awareness of recent developments in the field of religious studies, drawing most of their definitions and explanations from writers such as William James (1842–1910) and James Frazer (1854–1941). As is now well acknowledged, the modern concept of "religion" emerged during the nineteenth century, primarily as a way of categorizing and ranking the beliefs, values, and practices of non-Western cultures encountered during Britain's imperial conquests.[20] Perceptions of "religion" were filtered through a Eurocentric lens which assumed that the white, educated Western man with his Christian history and his objectifying and rationalizing mind was at the top of the evolutionary ladder, and women as well as all other cultures, races, and religions were inferior to him. His task was to educate and improve them as far as possible—which included ridding them of their religious superstitions and beliefs—and to assert his superiority by ruling them with a benign but authoritative paternalism.

An example of this is the pioneering English anthropologist Edward Burnett Tylor (1832–1917), who writes of the need "to obtain a means of measurement" in ethnological research in order to find "something like a definite line along which to reckon progress and retrogression in civilisation." This involves grading civilization according to the achievements of educated Europeans and Americans: "The educated world of Europe and America practically settles a standard by simply placing its own nations at one end of the social series and savage tribes at the other, arranging the rest of mankind between these limits according as they correspond more closely to savage or to cultured life."[21]

For Tylor, the ultimate purpose of ethnography is not simply to study the "primitive" religions of these societies, but to eliminate all traces of them from modern culture in the name of science and progress. He writes: "It is a harsher, and at times even painful, office of ethnography to expose the remains of crude old cultures which have passed into harmful superstition, and to mark these out for destruction. . . . Active at once in aiding progress and in removing hindrance, the science of culture is essentially a reformer's science."[22]

It is difficult not to see similar cultural prejudices at work among some of the new atheist writings, particularly in their treatment of Islam. Sam Harris represents Islam as an enemy of America because it is a worldview that is opposed to modern ideas of progress and reason. He writes that "many Muslims [are] standing eye deep in the red barbarity of the fourteenth century. . . . Any honest witness to current events will realize that there is no moral equivalence between the kind of force civilized democracies project in the world, warts and all, and the internecine violence that is perpetrated by Muslim militants, or indeed by Muslim governments."[23]

According to Harris, this necessarily entails a violent conflict in which Americans must accept war, torture, and the killing of the innocent as a necessary price they must pay to defend their values: "We will continue to spill blood in what is, at bottom, a war of ideas."[24] Harris goes further than some of his coatheists, but at least he makes clear that violence and killing are not the exclusive prerogative of religions. They are also part of the apparatus of the modern state.

Dawkins regards the *burqa* worn by some Muslim women as a particular symbol of darkness, ignorance, and superstition. Under the subtitle "The Mother of All Burkas," he describes the *burqa* as "a token of egregious male cruelty and tragically cowed female submission."[25] He goes on to use this as a metaphor for scientific inquiry:

The one-inch window of visible light is derisorily tiny compared with the miles and miles of black cloth representing the invisible part of the spectrum, from radio waves at the hem of the skirt to gamma rays at the top of the head. What science does for us is to widen the window. It opens up so wide that the imprisoning black garment drops away almost completely, exposing our senses to airy and exhilarating freedom.[26]

The idea that the scientific investigation of nature is comparable to stripping a woman of her clothes is not original. It has been a privileged metaphor ever since the scientific revolution of the sixteenth and seventeenth centuries, when the language of stripping and penetrating the female body was sometimes used to describe the scientific quest.[27]

METAPHORS, MYTHS, AND SYMBOLS

Scientists like Dawkins, no less than their religious counterparts, need metaphors, symbols, and analogies to think with.[28] If modern scholarship problematizes the concept of religion, it also calls into question the methods by which science gathers its evidence and establishes its claims, by demonstrating the extent to which all forms of knowledge and normative judgments are filtered through unacknowledged cultural, gendered, and ideological assumptions. To accept this is not to discredit our different ways of knowing, but to call for a more fluid and dynamic approach to what counts as knowledge. Academic disciplines and sciences help us to organize our studies and to focus our research, but when they seek to limit the horizons of knowing and to invalidate all but the most rational and empirical claims to truth and meaning, they diminish the imaginative wisdom and creativity of our species.

It is a delusion to believe that science offers an objective, value-free position from which to evaluate all claims to truth and meaning. The philosopher Mary Midgley argues that evolution has become a powerful quasi-religious myth by which atheists such as Dawkins confer meaning on the world. She refers to the "cosmic mythology"[29] associated with the theory of evolution, arguing that it is "not just an inert piece of theoretical science. It is, and cannot help being, also a powerful folktale about human origins."[30] Like any myth of meaning, scientific rationalism shapes our view of the world, but it also has the capacity to seduce its followers with its utopian promises and hubristic claims.

Religious narratives are our responses to vast questions that science will never be able to answer. Why is there something rather than nothing? How do we explain consciousness, which enables us to observe the world of which we are a part? In the words of the popular science writer and agnostic cosmologist Paul Davies,

The success of the scientific method at unlocking the secrets of nature is so dazzling it can blind us to the greatest scientific miracle of all: *science works*. Scientists themselves normally take it for granted that we live in a rational, ordered cosmos subject to precise laws that can be uncovered by human reasoning. Yet why this should be so remains a tantalizing mystery. Why should human beings have the ability to discover and understand the principles on which the universe runs?[31]

As a linguistic, meaning-making species, our defining essence is our capacity to discern order in the world, and to use language to create imaginative stories of possibility and meaning through that process of discernment. This is the means by which we weave our lives into an intelligible and meaningful cosmos, beyond the increasingly sterile debates between scientific atheists and Christian theologians who are often just as constrained by a narrow form of modern Western rationalism as those they are arguing against.[32]

In an interview with the playwright David Hare,[33] Archbishop of Canterbury Rowan Williams, describing his sense of tedium with regard to such debates, quotes St. Ambrose: "It does not suit God to save his people by arguments." Williams suggests that, "while I think it's necessary to go on rather wearily putting down markers saying, 'No, that's not what Christian theology says' and, 'No, that argument doesn't make sense,' that's the background noise. What changes people is the extraordinary sense that things come together." This making sense is not, he says, "a great theoretical system." It is rather that "you can see the connections somehow and—I tend to reach for musical analogies here—you can hear the harmonics. You may not have everything tied up in every detail, but there's enough of that harmonic available to think, 'OK, I can risk aligning myself with this.'"

This creative reading of the world, in which we attune ourselves to attend to the harmonics of the cosmos, is the basis of all great religions and all honest scientific research. The challenge we face today is to seek to better understand the kind of species we are in our capacity for dazzling genius and apocalyptic destructiveness, to ask how effectively our living stories about the world allow us to express the truthfulness of our condition, and to endeavor to reach out across differences of culture, creed, gender, and race, to create more fertile myths than those that are offered either by scientific rationalism or by religious extremism.

NOTES

1. Cf. John D. Caputo, "Atheism, A/theology, and the Postmodern Condition," in *The Cambridge Companion to Atheism*, ed. Michael Martin (Cambridge: Cambridge University Press, 2007), 267–82; Graham Ward, *The Postmodern God: A Theological Reader* (Oxford: Blackwell, 1997); Slavoj Žižek, *The Puppet and the Dwarf: The Perverse Core of Christianity* (Cambridge, Mass.: MIT Press, 2003). I refer to these thinkers as nontheists rather than atheists, because the word "atheist" implies a claim to knowledge based on belief (that there is no God), and the thinkers mentioned here are more subtle in their critique of traditional theism.

2. For a more detailed and extensive critique, see Tina Beattie, *The New Atheists: The Twilight of Reason and the War on Religion* (London: Darton, Longman and Todd, 2007). There is a growing body of literature written by supporters and critics of the New Atheists. For a very small selection of critical responses, see Francis S. Collins, *The*

Language of God: A Scientist Presents Evidence for Belief (New York: Free Press, 2006); John Cornwell, *Darwin's Angel: A Seraphic Response to "The God Delusion"* (London: Profile, 2007); Terry Eagleton, *Reason, Faith, and Revolution: Reflections on the God Debate* (New Haven: Yale University Press, 2010); Chris Hedges, *I Don't Believe in Atheists* (New York: Free Press, 2008); Peter Hitchens, *The Rage Against God: Why Faith Is the Foundation of Civilisation* (London: Continuum, 2010); Alister E. McGrath and Joanna Collicutt McGrath, *The Dawkins Delusion? Atheist Fundamentalism and the Denial of the Divine* (London: SPCK, 2007); Keith Ward, *Why There Almost Certainly Is a God: Doubting Dawkins* (Oxford: Lion Hudson, 2008).

3. Richard Dawkins, *The God Delusion* (London: Bantam, 2006). Dawkins also made a two-part documentary for Channel 4 television, with the title *The Root of All Evil?*, which was broadcast in January 2006, but renamed as *The God Delusion* when it was rebroadcast in 2010.

4. Christopher Hitchens, *God Is Not Great: How Religion Poisons Everything* (New York: Twelve, 2007). The first British edition had a less provocative title: *God Is Not Great: The Case Against Religion* (London: Atlantic Books, 2007).

5. Daniel C. Dennett, *Breaking the Spell: Religion as a Natural Phenomenon* (London: Allen Lane, 2006); Sam Harris, *The End of Faith: Religion, Terror, and the Future of Reason* (New York: Norton, 2004); Sam Harris, *Letter to a Christian Nation* (New York: Knopf, 2006).

6. Cf. Conor Cunningham, *Darwin's Pious Idea: Why the Ultra-Darwinists and Creationists Both Get It Wrong* (Grand Rapids: Eerdmans, 2010); Adrian J. Desmond and James Moore, *Darwin's Sacred Cause* (Boston: Houghton Mifflin Harcourt, 2009).

7. Martin Amis, "The Voice of the Lonely Crowd," *Guardian*, June 1, 2002, www.guardian.co.uk/books/2002/jun/01/philosophy.society.

8. Harris, *The End of Faith*, 79.

9. Ibid.

10. Dawkins, *The God Delusion*, 278.

11. Ibid., 283.

12. For more on this, see Tina Beattie, "Science, Religion and War," in *The New Atheists* (London: Darton, Longman and Todd, 2007).

13. Dawkins, *The God Delusion*, 19.

14. Ibid.

15. Hitchens, *God Is Not Great*, 7.

16. Ibid., 241.

17. Ibid., 175.

18. Ibid., 176.

19. Lewis Carroll, *Alice's Adventures in Wonderland and Through the Looking Glass* (London: Penguin, 2003), 186.

20. Cf. Timothy Fitzgerald, *The Ideology of Religious Studies* (Oxford: Oxford University Press, 2000); Russell T. McCutcheon, *Manufacturing Religion: The Discourse on Sui Generis Religion and the Politics of Nostalgia* (Oxford: Oxford University Press, 1997).

21. Edward B. Tylor, *Primitive Culture: Researches into the Development of Mythology, Philosophy, Religion, Language, Art, and Custom* (London: John Murray, 1920), 1:26.

22. Ibid., 2:453.

23. Harris, *The End of Faith*, 145.

24. Ibid., 53.

25. Dawkins, *The God Delusion*, 362.

26. Ibid.

27. See Beattie, *The New Atheists*, 65–67.

28. See Janet Martin Soskice, *Metaphor and Religious Language* (London: Clarendon Press, 1987).

29. Mary Midgley, *Evolution as a Religion: Strange Hopes and Stranger Fears* (London: Routledge, 2002), 34. See also Mary Midgley, *Science and Poetry* (London: Routledge, 2001); Mary Midgley, *Myths We Live By* (London: Routledge, 2003).

30. Midgley, *Evolution as a Religion*, 1.

31. Paul Davies, *The Mind of God: Science and the Search for Ultimate Meaning* (London: Penguin, 2006), 20.

32. See Beattie, *The New Atheists*, 9–11.

33. David Hare, "Rowan Williams: God's Boxer," *Guardian*, July 8, 2011, www.guardian.co.uk/uk/2011/jul/08/rowan-williams-interview-david-hare.

PART III

Religion Beyond the West

14

Indigenous African Traditions as Models for Theorizing Religion

EDWARD P. ANTONIO

The task of reflecting on the potential of indigenous African traditions to serve as models for theorizing religion is fraught with many difficulties. One difficulty is why this should be necessary at all. This is an important question because there is always the danger of positing these traditions as prototypes of religion. Evolutionary accounts of the history of religion made this mistake. It is a mistake that some anthropologists, missionaries, and African thinkers desirous to prove the religiosity of African cultures (and therefore their civilized status) have made. Some in granting the status of religion to African indigenous traditions have described them as "primal" religions.[1] Andrew Walls describes the meaning of the term "primal" as follows: "The word ['primal'] underlines two features of the religions of the peoples indicated: their historical anteriority and their basic, elemental status in human experience. All other faiths are subsequent and represent, as it were, second thoughts; all other believers, and for that matter non-believers, are primalists underneath."[2] Just before making this statement, Walls denied any intention to equate the primal with the primitive. He is right; the two do not necessarily mean one and the same thing. But he also denies "any evolutionistic undertones." Now, if we accept this, what are we to make of the language of all other faiths being *subsequent*, *second thoughts*, and of believers and nonbelievers being hidden primalists? Surely the use of the term "primal" to designate these traditions harks back to the late-eighteenth and the persistent nineteenth-century quest for theories of the origins of religion and belief that such origins could be determined by identifying, classifying, and describing the earliest (the primal) forms of religion. In addition to this, Walls and some of his followers make two further mistakes. The first one is that if we accept this understanding we are not only forced to subsume African traditions under the category of "religion" in a generalizing manner;[3] we are also forced to equate religion with belief and faith. I shall return to the problem of applying the term "religion" to African traditions. His second mistake is about the problematical way in which his description of these traditions is situated in the context of "faiths," "believers," and "nonbelievers." There is in fact a double mistake here: assimilating religion to faith and belief as if this is true of all religions, and assimilating primal traditions to religion on the one hand and to faith and belief on the other. This is a hugely problematical way of thinking about indigenous African traditions. The Africans I am familiar with do not talk about faith, belief, and lack of belief in relation to gods, spirits, and divinities. (Not only am I African, I have also had the privilege of living, for extended periods of time, in various African cultures such as in Mozambique, Zimbabwe, and South Africa. I also have reasonably close knowledge of Malawian, Zambian, and other Central African cultures.)[4] There is no evidence that African traditions are remnants of what religion originally looked like, which we must somehow understand if we want to theorize religion effectively. Thus, because there is no historical evidence establishing a prototypical or ideal-typical relationship between indigenous African traditions and religion, how the former can serve as models for theorizing the latter is not a straightforward matter. I shall leave aside the question of what we mean by "theory" and "model."[5] My approach here is as follows: since there is no prototype to work from, and since, as I argue below, the term "religion" is foreign to many African cultures, the movement of theorizing religion from the perspective of African traditions must be based on something else. I shall use the idea of a heuristic to provide such a basis.[6] A heuristic, as I use the term, is a clue or suggestion (a rule of thumb), a rough guide that aids the discovery of intelligibility and understanding in knowledge and interpretation. The heuristic question that guides this essay is: How can indigenous African traditions, taken in the context of their everyday expression, that is, before they are reduced to or defined in terms of religion, help us better understand the various phenomena ordinarily subsumed under this latter term? I shall proceed by identifying several areas where I think African traditions can helpfully throw some theoretical light on functions of religion.

The contribution of indigenous African traditions to the theorization of religion must be located in a number of places. First, its "otherness," which calls into question the category of religion itself. This otherness is a function of several things: (1) the social and cultural difference of these traditions themselves; (2) the manner in which that difference was taken as evidence of the absence of religion in Africa, indeed of the inapplicability of the category of religion to African traditions and cultures (here the otherness of African religions emerges as a colonial production);[7] (3) the extent to which African cultural practices refuse to be easily domesticated under the category of religion; and (4) the comparative difference with other religions and traditions. The constitutive otherness of African religion, which caused colonists so much trouble and colonial subjects so much anxiety, serves as a critique of the universality of the category of religion; it relativizes it by the sheer force of its existence.[8] The difference of African traditions contributes to a theory of religion insofar as it demands that any adequate theory or account of religion engage and take seriously both difference in general and the particular manifestations of that difference in African traditions. Taking this seriously means attending to the implications of these traditions for what can or cannot be said about the category of religion and its applicability to African cultures. Thus one important area where African traditions contribute to thinking about religion is that of the *absence* of the term "religion" in many African cultures. I suggest that instead of uncritically imposing the term on these cultures, scholars of religion interested in learning from Africa must grapple with the meaning of this absence and its significance in determining how the term "religion" came to be imposed on Africans. This absence should not be taken as an atavistic cipher, an embarrassing lack or sign of conceptual and moral backwardness, but rather as a powerful heuristic tool for answering questions about the possibility of "belief," ritual practice, morality, and social organization outside of the meaning of the term "religion." Acknowledging this absence as explanatory means coming to terms with the fact that Africans have raised questions of meaning and negotiated the cosmos on quite other terms than those typically associated with the term "religion" in Western thought. In fact, the idea that there is such a thing as religion and that it is universal, the idea that underwrites the efforts of many scholars of religions to see religion everywhere, is largely a Western obsession. Absence then circumscribes a moment of "postcolonial" critique that makes possible two different moves. In the first instance, it enables the interrogation of the applicability of religion to contexts where it is not ordinarily applicable. Then, in the second instance, it forces us to ask: "In the absence of religion, how did people comport themselves in ways that gave meaning and purpose to their being human?" (I leave aside here the peculiarity, in many African societies, of the notion that life somehow has or ought to have purpose and meaning. This is another Western obsession. It is exactly here that we run into problems. For here, we are faced with the temptation to ascribe "purpose and meaning" to nothing but the function of religion. But as soon as we do this, the absence of the African difference or rather the presence of the African difference appearing precisely as the absence of religion asserts itself and denies us this appeal to the category of religion.)

The insistence that African traditions must always be comprehended through religion betrays a desire for the reproduction of the "identical" at the expense of the "other." The identical here is what is posited as the essence of religion, whose meaning across cultures derives from its inherent translatability without difference (which is thus false translation because, in truth, all translations makes a difference) so that it always comes out at the end of any process of translation precisely as nothing other than religion. What I am suggesting is that if we want indigenous African traditions to serve as a model for theorizing religion, we must begin by allowing them to do so on the basis of their otherness or difference. African traditions contribute not by virtue of some imagined way in which they supposedly represent some form of "primal religion" but precisely by not being religion or by functioning in the mode described by Clifford Geertz as "the common-sense perspective," the perspective of the everyday.[9] Notice that, at least initially, I do not say the perspective of the "profane" or the "secular." This is because these terms already beg the question of religion and the absence or disappearance of religion, as well as the question of religion relative to other ways of being in the world. The import of my argument is that both sets of notions—religion and that against which it is usually defined, and the secular and the profane—are foreign, if not to much of sub-Saharan Africa, certainly to many societies in Southern and Central Africa.[10] The otherness of African indigenous traditions demonstrates for the possibility of theorizing religion not only the profound relativity or historical particularity (nonuniversality) of the category but also the fact that most of what is theorized under "religion" can be theorized in nonreligious terms in African traditions. This means that the contribution of the otherness of African traditions derives not from their supposed similarities to religion but from the difference inscribed in their human content.

There are, to be sure, many other ways in which African traditions can contribute positively, creatively, and productively to theorizing religion. I shall take, first of all, what I call the social aspects of indigenous African traditions. I want to distinguish these from cosmological aspects. The latter refer to the sky, god(s), earth, creation, and world. The social aspects range from beer drinking, hunting, and dancing to cooking and the everyday management of the homestead. It is precisely in this domain of the social aspects of indigenous belief that many Africans spend by far the bulk of their lives. Phenomena that we typically subsume under religion, phenomena such as gods, salvation, spirits, and many other cosmic realities, simply have no significance outside these social aspects. Many scholars of African religions have suggested that the everyday meaning of these social aspects, the significance of "the practice of everyday life," is entirely attributable to religion. Thus it is not uncommon for these scholars to claim that Africans are so totally religious that they entertain no distinction between the sacred and the profane. For Africans, the argument runs, everything is sacred and since everything is sacred Africans are formally incapable of distinguishing between the sacred and the profane.[11] Obviously the claim is logically incoherent, not to say, empirically false. But I will not engage with it here. What I am arguing is that what ordinarily passes for religion in Western understandings derives its equivalent meaning in the African context from everyday, immanent, this-worldly processes and interactions. Religious beliefs and practices do not refer to phenomena outside the world. They belong to what Geertz in a different context calls "the common-sense perspective." One way of naming how this contributes to the theorizing of religion is to emphasize, in the manner of the French philosopher Gilles Deleuze, this aspect of immanence. However, immanence is not proposed here as some sort of ideological claim against the existence of a transcendent god(s); rather, it is used descriptively, or even phenomenologically. What are described are the structures and the values that constitute the here and the now as the space of the everyday. The methodological significance of this for the study of religion is that religion must be sought in the everyday, not in some category of special or bounded activities. The experiences, entities, processes, practices, institutions, social objects, ideas, and concepts that we ordinarily associate with religion are all understood in terms of the immanent. This calls for a phenomenologically oriented ethnographic approach to the study of indigenous African traditions. One important implication of what I am suggesting is that in the context of these traditions "religion" is understood in terms of the everyday precisely because it radically belongs to the everyday.

The second way in which these traditions can serve as models for theorizing religion is in terms of their orientation toward what I will call their anthropological humanism.[12] The basic features of this humanism include personhood, community, hospitality, and health. Scholars of various African cultures have drawn attention to the manner and extent to which human relationships are central to indigenous traditions. The notion of being human, or *ubuntuism*, the belief that personhood is constituted intersubjectively, that is, through human relationships, is claimed by practitioners and scholars alike to be an organizing feature of African social imaginaries.[13] These relationships are defined in terms of belonging to community, and belonging to community is mediated through the ethical framework of hospitality.[14] Anthropological relationships represent the realm of interaction not only among humans but also among humans, nature, spirits, and god(s). This can be seen in the way in which these elements are invoked and socially addressed in everyday transactions. For example, ancestors or various spirits (nature or otherwise) are an integral part of the social configuration and their significance is always articulated through the form of existing communal relationships, and not through whatever cosmological status they might appear to have to outsiders. Furthermore, this principle of relationality is socially irreducible, that is to say, it is a fundamental category in terms of which human well-being is socially established and the modes of its achievement morally defined and prescribed.

This humanistic dimension of African traditions provides another heuristic tool for theorizing religion, namely, a pragmatic philosophical anthropology. To be sure, the study of religion is not a stranger to the investigation of ideas of the "self," selfhood, individuality, the person, the soul, and community. However, in most cases these ideas are treated as disparate themes and topics within the study of religion and hardly ever as convergent parts of a fundamental explanatory category that itself grounds the very nature of reality as an "organic" system of social relationships. I wish to stress two things at this point. The first is that theorizing religion on the model of such a fundamental philosophical anthropology requires making notions such as personhood, community, and relationality both a starting point and the substantive content of the process of theorizing. Second, such theorization must be informed and be inflected by the actual claims or the substantive content of the anthropological beliefs under investigation. If this is taken seriously, African traditions will have taught the study of religion the importance of privileging not gods, spirits, the cosmos, notions of salvation understood as the quest for the other world, and ritual as the bizarre performance of inarticulable abjection, but humanity as the space of relational encounter with otherness in the fullness of all its variety—human, natural, and spiritual. What is rich and fascinating about this is the possibility of a refusal of a Nietzschean and Feuerbachian humanism that is inscribed in its mode of conceiving of humanity. For Nietzsche, humanity is, among other things, the expression of the will to power; humanity is human, indeed, all too human, and is always at the mercy of this will to power. An African reading of Nietzsche is yet to happen. In Feuerbach our gods and the spirits with whom we claim to commune are nothing more than alienated projections of our psychological needs. However, in African indigenous traditions we are dealing with how the affirmation of human relationality is not exclusive of experiences of alienation.

This brings me to a discussion of the third way in which African traditions can serve as a model for theorizing religion. Affirmation and alienation are crucial categories for understanding the conception of relationality in African traditions. I take as an example the powerful phenomenon of divination that is almost universal in Africa.[15] Divination is a structure of beliefs, practices, processes, and relationships that is defined by the encounter of social and spiritual forces made possible, on the one hand, by the experience of evil and alienation in the world and, on the other, by the desire to overcome them. This structure comprises many different aspects such as the healing of physical ailments, the restoration of broken social relationships, the pacification of angry ancestors and other spirits, the explanation of the origins of evil, particularly social evil and misfortune, the marking and celebration of important events, and ascertaining and delineating the conditions of human well-being. The list is of course not exhaustive. Central to the nature of divination is the status and function of the diviner as a point of contact between humans, nature, and the spirit world. He or she diagnoses physical and social ills by consulting either with the ancestors or with other kinds of spirits.[16]

Divination can only take place as an intersubjective experience in which humans and spirits encounter each other on a dynamic continuum of moral exchanges reflexively mediated by the diviner. Divination has many goals, but here I want to mention only two. The first, which I call its penultimate goal, has to do with identifying the causes of social problems and prescribing remedies for their elimination. The second, its ultimate goal, I describe as providing a space for determining the preconditions of proper relationality and thus of what it means to be human. What heuristic implications does this have for theorizing religion? I think there are several: hermeneutic, psychoanalytic, and ethical. The diviner is an interpreter of the messages of the ancestors to their living relatives. He or she performs an important hermeneutical or interpretative function. This is a function that is common to many systems of divination throughout Africa. What I want to suggest is that this function provides an interesting model for thinking about the role of hermeneutics and the nature of human understanding in the study of religion. The second implication of divination for theorizing religion is the psychoanalytic role it plays in people's lives. A diviner is consulted about both social and personal misfortunes. His or her mode of diagnosing the causes of these problems always involves engaging his or her clients in an elaborate process of dialogue in which question and answer and his or her mediatory role between the ancestors and the living play a fundamental role. A psychoanalytic approach to the study of religion along the lines suggested by the role of the diviner is potentially productive of understanding what many religions articulate as their basic goal—human well-being in the very concrete terms of everyday experience rather than otherworldly projection. This is linked to the role ethics and morality play in divination. Divination is almost always a moral practice, concerned with how to create the conditions of rectifying relationships that have broken down. Human relationships are the exhaustive arena of moral concern. The diviner herself or himself must be morally exemplary to become and continue to operate as a diviner. Furthermore, divination is about explaining and communicating the moral expectations of the ancestors. This might help in theorizing religion by making the ethical and the moral important categories in the study of religion. Here the ethical and its social contexts constitute the data that the study of religion investigates through a phenomenological ethnography of everyday moral practices.

NOTES

1. Harold W. Turner, "The Way Forward in the Religious Study of African Primal Religions," *Journal of Religion in Africa* 12, no. 1 (1981): 1–15, www.jstor.org/stable/1581010. The term "primal" is linked to preliterate and prehistoric phases of human evolution and stands for indigenous, tribal, and traditional beliefs and practices.

2. Andrew Walls, *The Missionary Movement in Christian History: Studies in the Transformation of Faith* (New York: Orbis, 1996), chap. 10.

3. Thus, Kwame Bediako, "African and Christianity on the Threshold of the Third Millennium: The Religious Dimension," *African Affairs* (2000): 99, 303–323. See also R. C. Mitchell, *African Primal Religions* (Niles, Ill.: Argus, 1977).

4. I am aware that this raises the insider/outsider problem in the study of religion. I have no intention of addressing that problem here.

5. I do not have the space here to explore different meanings of "theory" and "model" in relation to their methodological significance for the study of both religion and indigenous African traditions. However, there can be no doubt that, epistemologically, these notions function in complex ways to structure the manner in which we set up the relationship between the category of religion and African traditions in the first place.

6. My understanding of heuristics is informed by Bernard Lonergan, SJ, *Insight: A Study of Human Understanding* (New York: Philosophical Library, 1956).

7. For an example from Southern Africa, see David Chidester, *Savage Systems: Colonialism and Comparative Religion in Southern Africa* (Charlottesville: University of Virginia Press, 1996).

8. On the putative universality of "Religion," see Jonathan Z. Smith, "Religion, Religions, Religious," in *Critical Terms for Religious Studies*, ed. Mark C. Taylor (Chicago: University of Chicago Press, 1998), 269–84.

9. Clifford Geertz, *The Interpretation of Cultures: Selected Essays* (New York: Basic Books, 1973), 119. See also Michel de Certeau, The *Practice of Everyday Life*, trans. Steven Rendall (Berkeley: University of California Press, 1984).

10. I do not mean that these societies do not distinguish between sacred and profane activities. They do. But the distinctions are not secured in through the category of religion but rather by common-sense, pragmatic, everyday concerns.

11. John S. Mbiti, *African Religions and Philosophy* (London: Heinemann Educational Books, 1969), 2. See also Jacob K. Olupona, "Major Issues in the Study of African Traditional Religion," in *African Religions in Contemporary Society*, ed. Jacob K. Olupona (New York: Paragon House, 1991), 28.

12. See, for example, Kwame Gyekye, *An Essay on African Philosophical Thought: The Akan Conceptual Scheme* (Cambridge: Cambridge University Press, 1987), 143ff.

13. Laurenti Magesa, *African Religion: The Moral Traditions of Abundant Life* (New York: Orbis, 1997), 64ff.

14. Newell S. Booth "Tradition and Community in African Religion," *Journal of Religion in Africa* 9, no. 2 (1978): 81–94.

15. Philip M. Peek, ed., *African Divination Systems: Ways of Knowing* (Bloomington: Indiana University Press, 1991).

16. See, for example, René Devisch, "Mediumistic Divination Among the Northern Yaka of Zaire," ibid.

15

Zongjiao and the Category of Religion in China

YA-PEI KUO

Throughout the twentieth century and well into the twenty-first century, "religion" continued to stir up controversies in China. The debate over whether Confucianism is a religion has lasted from the early 1900s to the present, generating scores of books and treatises in Chinese as well as other languages. Cultural elites of the Republican period (1911–49), such as Hu Shi, insisted that religion had never been important in Chinese civilization, while the Western-trained social scientists such as C. K. Yang saw an exceptionally rich religious life therein. In 1999 the government of the People's Republic of China declared Falungong a cult—and thus not a religion—and launched a relentless suppression of it. Criticism pointed to the crackdown as a violation of religious freedoms. At the core of these political, historical and cultural clashes lies one unsettled question—"What is religion?"

Part of the difficulty in finding a clear-cut answer is historical. The Chinese language did not possess an equivalent to the English term "religion" (as distinct from a corpus of teachings) until the turn of the twentieth century.[1] The lack of a proper term meant that religion was not cognitively demarcated from other realms of human activities. Religious motivations and outlooks, rather than articulating themselves in a distinctive voice, were often entwined in activities and discourses one might describe as secular. Scholars have noted that both the elites and the populace in premodern China viewed the human and superhuman worlds as one continuum. Many ostensibly worldly endeavors and practices were underpinned by a religious ethos.

The introduction of the term *zongjiao* (religion) into the Chinese language at the beginning of the twentieth century, in this context, signified an epistemological shift. The neologism gave recognition to religion as a category in its own right, indicating an awareness of its distinctiveness. This awareness, in turn, set in motion the sociopolitical process of marking religion off from other spheres of activities. The early twentieth century witnessed many social groups reforming themselves according to one or another officially approved definition of religion.[2] Meanwhile, society at large was to go through a cleansing of religious residues. Both the Republican government under the Nationalist Party and the PRC government under the Communist Party had an "antisuperstition" agenda of social reform. Outside its designated sphere, religion was supposed to play no role in modern society.

The continuous efforts to keep religion in its proper place, however, proved to be a messy and testing process. As Rebecca Nedostup's research shows, the National-ist Party's antisuperstition campaign of the 1930s failed not only due to confusions over the definition of the key concepts, but also because religion was too deeply imbricated in other aspects of social reality.[3] Top-down campaigns like this helped familiarize the populace with the new categories—*zongjiao* became a commonplace word in modern Chinese. Yet, the objective of demarcating and confining religion was never achieved. The so-called religious revival of the post-Mao era (1976 to the present) clearly demonstrates that many traditional practices and notions have remained vital and ubiquitous in Chinese society. After a century's investment of political capital and educational resources, how the modern categories mesh with these practices and notions continues to be hazy. According to the anthropologist Mayfair Mei-hui Yang, those who participated in the revival of deity temples, local festivals, and lineage organizations in the 1990s often wondered whether what they did fit the ticket of either religion or superstition.[4] Their wonder betrays an aware-ness of the categories, but also attests to the incomprehensibility of these catego-ries to grassroots social actors.

The project of creating a modern secular society, where religion's role is clearly outlined and checked, has proved to be a failure. The historical questions neverthe-less remain: Why was it attempted in the first place? What compelled the opinion leaders and politicians to contrive such a project? And what did they see in the con-cept of religion?

The term *zongjiao* had been in use since the medieval period. Instead of denot-ing a category, it merely meant "to revere a doctrine," "the reverence for a doctrine," or "the revered doctrine."[5] *Zongjiao* as a modern Chinese term was a borrowing from the Japanese word *shūkyō*. It was part of the linguistic circulation in East Asia: classical Chinese phrases were gleaned and recast to facilitate Japan's translation and importation of Western knowledge in the second half of the nineteenth century. The very same phrases then traveled back to China as new vocabulary.[6] Although Japan's influence on the emergence of the Chinese term is undeniable, tracing *zongjiao* to *shūkyō* was only half of the story. Scholars have agreed that in its early history, the term frequently implied simply Christianity. Anthony C. Yu, for exam-ple, claimed, "Whenever the Chinese term *zongjiao* was used, [Christianity] almost inevitably became its assumed standard referent."[7] Yu was writing about China, but his generalization may be applied to Japan. In the second half of the nineteenth century, both countries were set upon by Western powers and witnessed the advent of Christian missionary enterprise, aiming at nothing less than a total conversion of their peoples. This shared experience facilitated the linguistic trade.

Treaty negotiations, which recorded the inequality between these East Asian states and Western states, often involved religious questions. In 1858, for instance, Japan signed a "Treaty of Friendship and Commerce" with the United States of America, which assigned specific religious rights to American citizens in Japan. That same year, the Sino-American and Sino-English Treaties of Tianjin recognized the

Christian missionaries' right to preach their religion on Chinese soil. In both cases, finding an indigenous term for "religion" proved difficult. Japan's leaders settled on a Buddhist word *shūhō*, literally "sect law," as in the clause "Americans in Japan shall be allowed the free exercise of their religion."[8] The Qing government (1644–1911) came up with a different solution. In the Treaty of Tianjin the term "Christian religion" occurs in the following passage: "The principles of the Christian religion, as professed by the Protestant and Roman Catholic churches, are recognized as teaching men to do good." But in the official Chinese version, the phrase was conspicuously left out. In its place, "Protestantism [*Yesujidu shengjiao*] and Catholicism [*Tianzhujiao*]" are listed side by side as two teachings that both encouraged good deeds. These examples illustrate the linguistic lacuna in Japan's and China's legal and political dealings with the Western powers. To fill this gap, *shūkyō* was coined in Japan in the 1870s.[9] In China, the government and elites continued to understand religion through the preexistent category of *jiao* ("teaching," "doctrines"), until *shūkyō* was imported in the late 1890s.

The delay in coining a new term did not insulate China from the impacts of "religion." Officially banned in 1724, the teaching of Christianity became licit once more in 1858. Inspirational books and pamphlets, specially prepared for Chinese readers, began to circulate in coastal cities. Missionaries' self-narrative and representation also provided information about the Western practice and notion of religion.[10] In the 1860s and 1870s, frequent disputes between missionaries and Chinese converts, on the one hand, and the non-Christian Chinese, on the other, drove gentry-officials to devote more energy to religious issues. Thanks to the treaty system, Christianity enjoyed a privileged legal position in relation to other religions. Missionaries invoked the treaty rights to protect Christian communities when conflicts of any kind arose. The situation obliged Chinese elites to interrogate the Christian view of "religion." As it happened, much epistemological groping had taken place before the new term was coined.

Before the mid-nineteenth century, the indigenous category that grouped religions together was *jiao*.[11] Most systems that we nowadays would consider as religions bear the word in their appellations. Christianity for example, was called *yejiao*, literally, "the teaching of Jesus," and Confucianism was called *rujiao*, "the teaching of scholars." As Robert F. Campany has pointed out, rather than attributing agency to the doctrine proper, the use of *jiao* placed the emphasis on "the source of the teaching, the one who taught it." A more inclusive way of grouping, *jiao* differs from "religion" in its lack of a strong "contrastive" emphasis on being "opposed to other, non-'religious' kinds of things" such as superstition and magic. It places the illicit and the orthodox beliefs and practices in the same class without any categorical divide.[12]

Furthermore, *jiao* was supposed to work in tandem with the exercise of political power. Confucianism viewed education (*jiao*) and governance (*zheng*) as inseparable. They were each other's proper function, and both were the necessary components in the mission of bringing civilization to "all-under-heaven." Before the era of the nation-state, this civilizing pretension formed the ideological cornerstone of political legitimacy. To determine and inculcate the correct teachings was the state's rightful responsibility and prerogative. Conversely, the state had the exclusive authority to regulate religious affairs so as to ensure the functioning of the orthodoxy.

The dynastic state thus created a hierarchy within the category of *jiao*. Residing at the pinnacle was Confucianism, the ultimate orthodoxy and "prototype" of the category.[13] The question of the legitimacy of any given *jiao* can only be resolved by mapping it against the orthodox doctrines. The various forms of *jiao* could never be too far from them. Buddhism, *fojiao*, and Daoism, *daojiao*, were approved only to the extent that they complemented the basic moral tenets of Confucianism, rather than standing on an equal footing with it. Below Buddhism and Daoism were numerous religious groups associated with labels such as *Bailian jiao* (teachings of the white lotus), *Taiping jiao* (teachings of great peace). The imperial state viewed their deviations from the sanctioned teachings and practices as objectionable, but often had no choice but to tolerate them. Only when deviations became seditious would the label of *xiejiao*, literally, "straying teachings," would be doled out as the precursor of government crackdown.

This paradigm started to crumble in the late nineteenth century. In comparison with their sixteenth-century predecessors, Christian missionaries who arrived in China three centuries later came with a very different ideology. As a large number of Protestant evangelists entered the mission field, they saw in Chinese religions the same idolatry and ritualism that plagued Catholicism. They were more vocal and direct than the accommodationist Jesuits in their criticism of China's "heathen" culture. W. A. P. Martin, a prominent American Presbyterian in China, for example, ascribed the widespread worship of Buddhist and Daoist idols to a deficiency in China's orthodoxy. Confucianism needed to amend this flaw by developing doctrines that addressed the supermundane and honored the relationship between God and humans. In other words, it needed to become more like Christianity.[14]

Protestant missionaries also brought a particular narrative of history, which presented Protestantism as the spiritual force behind the secular power of Europe and America. In his influential catechism, W. A. P. Martin explained to his Chinese readers that Protestantism "communicated to people their heavenly mandate, encouraged them to devote themselves to improving the nation, and inspired them to study science." As a result, the people were content, society was orderly, and the nation grew wealthy and self-sufficient. The spread of Protestantism outside the West had the obvious effect of transforming the previously unruly societies. In Southeast Asia, India, and Burma, the reach of Christian missions coincided with the eradication of local "barbarism." Christianity was the civilizing force of the modern era.[15]

In reality, the nineteenth-century mission movement was deeply implicated in the expansion of imperialism. The Christian missionaries had different roots and objectives from those of the imperialist powers. However, the building of their global enterprise was unthinkable without the latter's infrastructure and protection. The official opening of China as a mission field, for instance, had to be attributed to the effect of the unequal treaty, forced upon the Qing government at the gunpoint of the Anglo-French alliance in 1858. Missionaries' rights to travel and evangelize were warranted not by Chinese laws, but by a series of such treaties. Legal cases involving missionaries and, later, Chinese converts were thus set apart from the normal procedure and supervised by a special central bureau. In 1862, the French legation even negotiated a special reduction of community levies for Chinese Catholics, a clause later extended to all Christians.[16]

The asymmetric relations of power between China and a "Christian West" nevertheless obliged the educated Chinese to consider Christianity as the force to be reckoned with, and to take serious interest in the "Christian way." Even those who were staunchly anti-Christian read missionary publications and watched their actions closely. Because of the global dominance of the Western powers, knowledge about Christianity became the currency for understanding the world and its history. In 1897, Kang Youwei, a reformist Confucian and a keen consumer of missionaries' publications, put forward an imperial memorial that proposed to separate Confucianism out from other state affairs. Confucianism needed its own organization that represented its political interest and acted as the Christian church's Chinese counterpart. Kang used the same Chinese term for the Christian church, *jiaohui*, to designate it. All conflicts pertinent to foreign religions would be administrated by the Confucian Church, and thus be contained within the arena of *jiao*. No longer would missionaries' complaints about China's religious discrimination escalate into the political crises that had in the past led to war. The Western doctrine of separation of church and state was adopted to fend off the encroachment of the Western religion.[17]

This strategizing exemplified how Christianity's long shadow shaped the conception of modern Confucianism and the category of *jiao*. Kang, in as early as 1891, started streamlining the complex Confucian legacy into a systematic set of doctrines, a more manageable canon of sacred texts, and a saintly figure as the symbol of its ultimate unity. In private writings, he readily admitted that his "reformation" was to prepare Confucianism for the inevitable showdown with Christianity.[18] From missionaries' publications, especially the Protestant discourse of heathenism, he derived that the global expansion of Christianity aimed at nothing less than a total domination of the world's spiritual life. Its spread heralded a time of vicious struggle. Confucianism had to resist by safeguarding its supreme teachings with new representation and organization. It also needed a strong secular state to back it up. All these were methods that had been employed and proved effective in the example of Christianity's advancement in the world.

This imagination of struggle for survival changed the lax attitude toward other religions in China. The state of being in combat necessitated a consolidation of the home base and a monopoly of political support. Echoing missionaries' disdain for idolatry, Kang criticized the government for granting imperial sanction to all kinds of worship and urged the throne to "convert all improper temples into Confucian temples and order men and women of every rank to worship and offer sacrifices to Confucius."[19] The Christianized view of Chinese religions justified the disparagement of other systems. Kang created a new category of "nonreligion," *wujiao*, in his writings. By this, he did not mean atheism. Rather, those belief systems demonstrating no potential of surviving the Christian conquest were to be displaced from the category of *jiao*.[20] Historically, Buddhism had showed its vigor by building a cross-regional following. However, because only one system would emerge as the victor of the struggle, when delineating the global future of religion, Kang also had to imagine this *jiao* being stamped out.

Kang's proposals of 1898 pioneered the political efforts to demarcate "religion" as a distinctive realm, and prefigured the hostile policies toward religious practices that failed to fit into the newly conceived category.[21] They represented a new paradigm for the political management of religions, a paradigm that took Christianity as the prototype and ranked others according to their proximity to it. *Zongjiao* was adopted to denote this new paradigm. After a century's circulation, the term today has become part of the daily vocabulary. The fitting of the paradigm into China's social context, however, is still a work in progress and a project full of glitches.

NOTES

1. Wilfred C. Smith, *The Meaning and End of Religion: A Revolutionary Approach to the Great Religious Tradition* (San Francisco: Harper and Row, 1962), 58.

2. Vincent Goossaert, "Republican Church Engineering: The National Religious Associations in 1912 China," in *Chinese Religiosities: Afflictions of Modernity and State Formation*, ed. Mayfair Mei-hui Yang (Berkeley: University of California Press, 2008), 209–32; Ji Zhe, "Secularization as Religious Restructuring: Statist Institutionalization of Chinese Buddhism and Its Paradoxes," in *Chinese Religiosities: Afflictions of Modernity and State Formation*, ed. Mayfair Mei-hui Yang (Berkeley: University of California Press, 2008), 233–60.

3. Rebecca Nedostup, *Superstitious Regimes: Religion and the Politics in Chinese Modernity* (Cambridge, Mass.: Harvard University Press, 2009).

4. Mayfair Mei-hui Yang, "Introduction," in *Chinese Religiosity: Afflictions of Modernity and State Formation*, ed. Mayfair Mei-hui Yang (Berkeley: University of California Press, 2008), 17.

5. For examples, see Anthony C. Yu, *State and Religion in China: Historical and Textual Perspectives* (Chicago: Open Court, 2005), 12–14; Chen Hsi-yuan, " 'Zongjiao'—yige Zhongguo jindai wenhuashi shang de guanjianci" (Zongjiao: A Key Term in the Cultural History of Modern China), *Xin shixue* 13, no. 4 (December 2002): 46–49.

6. Lydia H. Liu, *Translingual Practice: Literature, National Culture, and Translated Modernity-China, 1900–1937* (Stanford: Stanford University Press, 1995).

7. Yu, *State and Religion in China*, 8.

8. *Shūhō* had formerly been a term used only in Buddhism, denoting "a type of teaching or ethical restraint attached to a specific sect." See Jason Ānanda Josephson, "When Buddhism Became a 'Religion,' " *Japanese Journal of Religious Studies* 33, no. 1 (2006): 144.

9. Early examples of the use of *shūkyō* to translate "religion" can be found in the mid-1860s: see Suzuki Norihisa, *Meiji shūkyō shichō no kenkyū: Shukyōgaku kotohajime* (Studies in Meiji Religious Thought: The Beginnings of Religious Study) (Tokyo: Tokyo Daigaku shuppankai, 1979), 15–17. By the time of the 1870s debate on religious freedom (*shūkyō jiyū*), it had become a standard term in public discourse.

10. After the First Opium War (1939–41), the Qing authorities had adopted a more tolerant attitude toward the sectarian practice of Catholicism, which went underground and

took on specifically Chinese attributes after 1724. The opening of trade ports after the Treaty of Nanjing (1842) also gave foreign missionaries legal protection for religious activities on Chinese soil for the first time. These activities were supposed to be limited to the treaty ports. Still, the most zealous missionaries recruited Chinese coverts for evangelical work and sent them to the countryside.

11. Despite this accepted translation, there have been caveats against simply equating *jiao* with the modern notion of "teaching" or "doctrine." Anthony C. Yu, for example, emphasizes the religious connotations of *jiao* as being invested in "a set of activities, a form of ritual intended for efficacious communion and intercourse between the human and non-human realms." Yu, *State and Religion in China*, 22.

12. Robert F. Campany, "On the Very Idea of Religions (In the Modern West and in Early Medieval China)," *History of Religions* 42, no. 4 (May 2003): 307, 314–15.

13. For analyzing category construction through the "prototype effect," see Josephson, "Buddhism," 145–48.

14. W. A. P. Martin, *Tiandao suyuan* (Evidence for Christianity) (Taibei: Wenquan chubanshe 1967), 67a–b.

15. Ibid., 66a–67a.

16. The Qing government agreed in 1862 to exempt Chinese Catholics from those taxes that paid for local temple maintenance and construction, religious processions, and sacrificial offerings. It granted the same privilege to Protestants in 1881. See Roger R. Thompson, "Twilight of the Gods in the Chinese Countryside: Christians, Confucians, and the Modernizing State, 1861–1911," in *Christianity in China: From the Eighteenth Century to the Present*, ed. Daniel H. Bays (Stanford: Stanford University Press, 1996), 53–72.

17. Kang Youwei, "Qing shangding jiaoan falü, lizheng keju wenti, ting tianxia xiangyi zengshe wenmian, bing cheng *Kongzi gaizhi kao* zhe" (Memorial on Promulgating Religious Law, Correcting Examination Essay Style, Letting Villages and Cities Build Confucius Temples, and Submitting Confucius as a Reformer), in *Jiuwang tucun de lantu: Kang Youwei bianfa zouyi jizheng* (Blueprint for Saving China: Collection of Kang Youwei Memorials for Reforms), ed. Kong Xiangji (Taibei: Liehe baoxi wenhua, 1998), 124–25.

18. Kang Youwei, "Da Zhu Rongsheng shu," in *Kang Youwei quanji* (Complete Works of Kang Youwei), ed. Jiang Yihua and Wu Genliang (Shanghai: Shanghai guji chubanshe, 1990), 1:1037–43.

19. Kang, "Qing shangding," 125.

20. Kang, "Da Zhu," 1:1041.

21. Vincent Goossaert, "1898: The Beginning of the End for Chinese Religion?," *Journal of Asian Studies* 65, no. 2 (2006): 307–36.

16

Islamic *Dīn* as an Alternative to Western Models of "Religion"

AHMET T. KARAMUSTAFA

In a pioneering study published in 1962, the late Wilfred Cantwell Smith subjected the category "religion" to close scrutiny and argued that, far from being a universal concept found in all or most human cultures, "religion" was a specifically Western category with a peculiar history.[1] Cantwell Smith's remarks on the topic were highly original, and his book soon became a classic in the newly emerging field of religious studies, where a tradition of rigorous debate and discussion developed on the definition of religion and the proper methods for its academic study. Over the past two decades, these methodological issues have come under particularly intense scrutiny.[2] "Religion" has been explored as a peculiarly European concept of relatively recent, post-Enlightenment provenance, and its unquestioning application to non-European contexts has been questioned and even decried as an egregious instance of cultural colonialism.[3] In these debates, the discipline of religious studies has been criticized as academic "caretaking of religious traditions"[4] and as "the ideology of ecumenical liberal capitalism,"[5] and serious doubts have been raised about its academic integrity and social function.

Curiously, this soul-searching on the nature and definition of religion has occurred largely as an in-house Euro-American affair,[6] and apart from some notable exceptions,[7] there have been relatively few serious attempts to question the concept of religion from a comparative perspective. Yet, in his pioneering examination of "religion," Cantwell Smith, who was a specialist on Islam as well as a comparativist, had also contended that of all the living religious traditions of the world, Islam alone possessed a category, *dīn*, that was close to the Western "religion," and had offered tentative observations about what he termed the "special case of Islam."[8] His comments were penetrative and provocative, and the comparative method he adopted made it all too clear that the utility of "religion" as an analytical category could be reevaluated fully only when the category of religion was placed within the larger semantic context of its presumed parallels from non-Western cultural traditions.

Even though Cantwell Smith's penetrative examination of the history of the Western concept of religion had a formative impact on the development of religious studies as a separate academic field of study, surprisingly, only a few scholarly sequels to his account of the Islamic concept of *dīn* have appeared to this day.[9] Significantly, practically all of these later studies have focused solely on the uses of the category *dīn* in the Qur'ān, paying little or no attention to its historical development over time or to its undoubtedly complex cross-cultural journey across the numerous linguistic and cultural landscapes that came to be associated with the Islamic tradition. What shape would such a historical and critical scrutiny of *dīn* take, and how useful would it be?

First, a summary of just what the Qur'ān has to offer on *dīn* is in order.[10] With over ninety occurrences, *dīn* is a common qur'ānic word with two primary meanings: "judgment" and "cult or worship," more specifically, the "law" that governs such worship. In the former sense, the word is normally found in the phrase "Day of Judgment," referring to the Last Day in historical time when God will take account of human actions, after which all individuals will be consigned to either Heaven or Hell. In the latter sense, it occurs in a variety of contexts and generally denotes human obligations to God, or, to put it differently, God's expectations from and his commands to humans, often including acts of worship. These divergent meanings may have come about in Arabic as a result of its interaction with Persian and Aramaic in pre-qur'ānic times. In other words, as used in the Qur'ān, *dīn* was most likely a polysemous Arabized word of foreign origin (as already suggested by several pre-modern Muslim scholars themselves) with the aggregate meaning "God's directives for the conduct of human life on earth, which will form the basis of his judgment of humans on the Last Day in order to determine their status in the afterlife."

Even though *dīn* thus appears as the most kindred term for "religion" in the Qur'ān, the matter is not that simple. Not only are there several other words with closely related meanings such as *milla* (a community united by creed and cult), *'ibāda* (acts of worship), *islām* (surrender to God), and *sharī'a* (the law), but there is also the complicated question of the appearance of a whole array of "religious groupings" of indeterminate designation such as *ahl al-kitāb* (people of the book), Jews, Christians, Magians (Zoroastrians), Sabians (Mandaeans? Manichaeans?), *hunafā'* (pre-Islamic Arabian monotheists?), and *mushrik* ("polytheists/idolaters," or even "half-baked monotheists"). Indeed, "often, it is not clear if the qur'ānic concept indicates an actual, contemporary religious group identifiable as such to the qur'ānic audience, a pre-Islamic group or a theological concept."[11] In addition, there are quite possibly the Qur'ān's most positively charged key "religious" terms, *īmān* (belief, faith) and *mu'min* (believer, faithful). The latter, *mu'min*, occurs "almost a thousand times, compared with fewer than seventy-five instances of *muslim*," which demonstrates its centrality to the message of the Qur'ān.[12]

The landscape of religion in the Qur'ān, therefore, is complex and often quite puzzling. On the one hand, scrutiny of *dīn* and terms associated with it suggests that the Qur'ān presents a consistent vision of a single, continuous relationship between God and humanity in history, and it is this relationship that is depicted by the cluster of terms around *dīn*. This vision is "centered on the ideas of monotheism, preparing for the Last Day, belief in prophecy and revealed scripture, and observance of righteous behavior, including frequent prayer, expiation for sins committed, periodic fasting and a charitable and humble demeanor."[13] In this sense, theistic belief and practice would appear to be the natural form of religiosity for all humans. On the other hand, there is also a clear awareness, and acceptance, of the various manifestations of this God-humanity relationship, throughout history and contemporaneously with the Qur'ān, in the form of multiple socioreligious communities lined up at different points along the spectrum of monotheism. The Qur'ān would seem to be aiming at reviving the naturally theistic state of humanity over against its multifarious deviations from this optimal state by instigating a "believers' movement" through the agency of Muhammad.[14]

Dīn in the Qur'ān thus appears as the name of both a natural aspect of the human condition as "believers" in a relentlessly monotheistic universe and, simultaneously, of the different manifestations of this "natural disposition to monotheism" in the form of actual human groupings. This peculiar duality of its meaning (along with its foreign origin as a word) might explain why it does not have a plural form in the Qur'ān (later, it acquired the plural *adyān*). To the extent that *dīn* and its conceptual relatives signify "religiosity," then, the Qur'ān makes humans into inherently theistic beings, and the concept *dīn* simultaneously entails both elements of belief (prophecy, revelation, afterlife) and practice (worship and righteous behavior, including militancy when necessary). Humans organize themselves into socioreligious communities (the most common word for such communities being *umma*), though this organization occurs normally as a result of divine intervention in human history in the form of divinely appointed "messengers" sent to particular peoples with the basic monotheistic message, often as "revealed books."[15] Each such community has a specific history, which determines the place of the community and its members in the soteriological spectrum ranging from salvation to damnation.

The historical development of *dīn* is infinitely more complicated than its qur'ānic meaning. The natural instinct of scholars of Islam would be to trace the ramifying trajectories of the term along the various paths and byways of the enormous textual tradition of qur'ānic, legal, theological, and mystical expertise generated by Muslim elites over the course of the past millennium and a half. This is a daunting task, and, not surprisingly, it has not yet been attempted, except in piecemeal fashion. What we already know suggests that Muslim specialists on *dīn* (religious scholars and mystics) have designated the movement led by Muhammad as Islam (with a capital "I") and tended to see it as the "true" *dīn*. In their eyes, the community of *muslim*s, the Muslim *umma*, which came about as a direct result of God's last major redemptive intervention in human history, achieved the most efficacious combination between the affairs of this world (*dunya*) and the demands of the other world (*ākhira*). This view emphatically foregrounds Islam but still leaves room for other, albeit mostly historically corrupted or deficient, *dīn*s, and thus allows for a plurality of human orientations to God. This scholarly perspective on *dīn*, like the qur'ānic one, is decidedly theistic (though scholars did not agree on a single conception of God) and generally insistent on some combination of belief and righteous behavior (though scholars cultivated many different formulas of this combination). Significantly, *dīn* functioned at both the individual and the collective level and in both the private and the public sphere, once again with many different configurations. Crucially, scholarly and mystic specialists on *dīn* were not united among themselves, and inner Islamic diversity was a patent reality throughout Muslim history. Nevertheless, such specialists of all stripes clearly viewed *dīn* as a natural phenomenon in a naturally monotheistic cosmos, much as *dīn* appeared in the Qur'ān.

As an example, let us look at a single trajectory: conceptions of *dīn* as a private affair according to the Murji'a, the Malāmatiyya, and the Hanafī legal school.[16] Questions about the nature of faith surfaced very early in Islamic history, and the debates on these questions soon congealed into different trends that unfolded along different historical trajectories. One of these trends, the Murji'a (second century of Islam), formed around the reluctance to define faith in terms of concrete human acts, ritualistic or otherwise, or, more directly, around the view that faith was a state of the heart that remained a private affair between the individual believer and the Divine. The historical path of this particular orientation to faith takes the researcher from its beginnings in the Murji'a, through its close association with the Hanafī legal school (from the third century of Islam), to its merger with the Malāmatiyya (fourth century of Islam), a mystical trend originating in northeastern Iran that was theologically akin to the Murji'a. This trajectory, which can be traced all the way to the present in areas where the Hanafī legal school has been prevalent, demonstrates that there were powerful trends within Islam that equated faith with inner piety. Indeed, it is possible to argue that a conceptualization of Islam as a private affair between God and each and every human being—a pietistic orientation that is not fundamentally different than the generic Protestant theistic understanding of religion as a relation between the individual believer and God—has occupied a central role in the unfolding of the Islamic tradition. This recognition of the existence of powerful privatizing currents within mainstream Islam suggests that the post-Enlightenment construal of religion as a private affair of the individual had long-standing counterparts in the Islamic tradition.

It would, however, be deceptive to limit the history of *dīn* to a semantic delineation of its history as a key term in scholarship and learning on Islam. Moving beyond Muslim scholarship on Islam and mystical thought, there is a clear need to probe other intellectual arenas, from literature to philosophy and from historiography to science. Here, the picture is more colorful and the spectrum of opinion much broader, ranging from skepticism and outright denial of revelation and prophecy— as exemplified, for instance, by the philosopher-physician Abū Bakr al-Rāzī (d. 925 or 935) and the poet and writer al-Ma'arrī (d. 1058)—to curiosity about inner diversity within Islam as well as *dīn*s other than Islam.[17] On this last front, it is well known that premodern Islam possessed rich intellectual traditions of heresiography and polemics that were directed at internal sectarian/heretical developments and sometimes at external, non-Muslim "religious" communities.[18] In addition, much more can be discovered about Muslim perceptions of other *dīn*s in general, outside works of heresiography and polemical tracts.[19] All this literature needs to be probed with the purpose of uncovering the operative categories such as *dīn* that were used by Muslim authors to demarcate the boundaries of the various communities they discussed in their works.

As an example for notions of *dīn* beyond the legal and theological realm, we can turn to the views of the Persian sage/mystic philosopher ʿAzīz-i Nasafī (d. after 680/1280), who envisioned *dīn* as a pragmatic necessity.[20] This thirteenth-century thinker introduced a conception of *dīn* that was radically different than the piety-based conception of Islam at work in the Murjiʾī-Malamatī-Hanafī theological orientation mentioned above. Nasafī viewed human life as a continuous struggle to achieve perfection in which individual human souls attempt to develop themselves to the highest level of the "spiritual" domain of existence (which is, nevertheless, inextricably interconnected with the "physical" domain). However, only very few humans—sages, prophets, and saints—ever come close to achieving this goal on their own (this he termed the theory of the "perfect man"), while the great majority rest content with simply following this small group of nearly perfect individuals. Indeed, *dīn* is the name of recipes issued by the perfect few for the use of the great majority of humankind; in short, it is nothing other than a set of guidelines for the conduct of human life to be adopted by most as a matter of pragmatic necessity. Nasafī had monistic views about the cosmos, and seen in this context, such a conception of *dīn* as a pragmatic framework for human conduct proves to be quite different from the theistic understanding of *dīn* as a natural human propensity toward monotheism.

Not surprisingly, the scholarly and intellectual visions of *dīn* were never fully translated to social reality, and the attempt to scrutinize the history of *dīn* ultimately needs to break out of the confines of the intellectual realm to social and cultural history. Studying the history of *dīn* on the level of practice on the ground with an eye toward distilling conceptions of *dīn* that actually informed daily life is an enormous challenge, but there are hopeful signs that progress is being made on this front.[21] In this process, it is crucial to pay adequate attention to communities that have been marginalized or excluded, by both premodern Muslim and modern scholars, as being "heretical," "heterodox," or even outright "un-Islamic" because the recipes of Islam produced by normative works of scholarship often failed to include them.

As an example of such communities, let us consider the case of the Alevis of present-day Turkey. In brief, the emergence of Alevis dates back to the earliest phase of the simultaneous Islamization and Turkification of the Anatolian peninsula, roughly from the beginning of the twelfth to the end of the fifteenth century. The influx of large numbers of western Turks, most of them pastoralist nomads, into Anatolia triggered a long process of de-Hellenization in the peninsula that went hand in hand with increasing Turkification. Although some Turks that came to Anatolia had already "Islamized" for several generations, others were in rather early stages of Islamization. The same applied to the indigenous Kurdish populations of the Eastern Anatolian highlands, whose exposure to Islam up until that point had been minimal and sporadic. Many Turkish nomads and Kurds of this period came to adopt various permutations of the form of Islam fashioned and deployed by popular Sufi saints (dervishes commonly known as *abdals*) that was centered on a divinization of the human through veneration of 'Alī, the cousin and son-in-law of the Prophet Muhammad, hence the name Alevi.

Significantly, this 'Alī-centered Islam, though definitely tinged with Shi'ism, did not produce a class of learned authorities: there were no religious scholars who staked out a claim to authority on the basis of their scholarship, nor was there a developed literary/scriptural tradition that spelled out the doctrinal and practical parameters of Alevi Islam. In the absence of legal and theological scholarship that characterized urban Islamic environments, Alevis of the countryside developed their identity around oral teachings imparted to adherents through communal rituals, generically known as *cem*, in the form of gatherings that featured music, dance, alcoholic drinks, and shared food. Such rituals as well as regulation of communal affairs were overseen by a class of hereditary ritual specialists and communal elders known as *dede* (grandfather), many of whom claimed descent from 'Alī. During the Ottoman period, Alevi communities continued to maintain a distinct distance from Islamic scholarly discourses and canonical practices, and believed that they had captured the true core of Islam, shorn of its legalistic and deceptive accretions fabricated by self-absorbed scholars and mystics, including divisive definitions of *dīn* that falsely divided humanity into mutually exclusive socioreligious communities. According to them, the correct path was simply love and acceptance.[22] Such an implosion of *dīn*, not uncommon in vernacular forms of Islam, certainly needs to be included in the complex, hitherto largely unexplored history of the concept and its permutations in Islamic history.

As this rapid survey of the different chapters of the discursive and practical history of *dīn* demonstrates, it is an enormous task to scrutinize this concept with an eye toward comparing it with "religion." This task is rendered even more complicated in the modern period by the actual intertwining of the two concepts largely through the application of post-Enlightenment conceptions of religion to Islam by both Muslim and non-Muslim scholars and activists over the past two centuries. This intertwining is intricate and complex, and scholars have barely started to pay attention to it. The pitfalls of viewing Islam through the spectacles of historically specific (in particular Protestant Christian) understandings of religion have been noted,[23] and preliminary attempts are being made to explore the ways in which the category of religion informs modern Muslim understandings of *dīn*.[24] However, the modern reconfiguration of Islam as a "world religion,"[25] the deployment of this concept in Muslim and non-Muslim conceptions of Islam, and the casting of Islam as the mirror opposite of privatized religion that leaves no room for secularism all require in-depth analysis.[26]

An example of the modern imbrication of *dīn* and religion that is difficult to unpack is a sophisticated articulation of the philosophy of *dīn* by the Ottoman scholar Elmalılı Muhammed Hamdi (d. 1942). Elmalılı, who was one of the last great Ottoman scholars, worked with a thoroughly traditional theological definition of *dīn* that dated at least as far back as the fourteenth century: "*dīn* is a divine institution that leads those possessed of intellect to the absolute good through the use of their free will." However, Elmalılı reinterpreted this definition through an impressive set of intellectual maneuvers and argued that Islam, which he saw as the *dīn* of truth, is synonymous with freedom from coercion and freedom of conscience. The path of reasoning that led him to this conclusion, utterly traditional in many ways, is interesting in itself, but his conclusion is striking in its approximation to the post-Enlightenment discourses of human rights and individual freedom. The fact that Elmalılı was intimately familiar with contemporary European philosophy of religion makes his reinterpretation of the traditional Islamic theology of *dīn* a fascinating instance of the complex process through which *dīn* and religion became intertwined.[27]

With a rich and long history, Islamic *dīn* is certainly a powerful reminder that "religion" is not a naturally universal category. At the very least, close scrutiny of *dīn* leads to a serious reconsideration of the legitimacy of characterizing Islam as a "religion." Indeed, it is clear that "religion," in any of the specific forms it took in Western history, is not an automatically suitable category to use in describing Islam. This conclusion not only enriches the ongoing discussions on the history and global applicability of the concept of religion within the academic discipline of religious studies; it also compels us to work toward alternative conceptualizations of Islam that would do justice to the historical record and self-images of this major tradition. In addition, a reconceptualization of Islam as a category other than "religion" (and *dīn* would work perfectly here) promises to transform prevalent perspectives on a host of significant issues of current interest such as secularization and democratization in Muslim communities, Muslim understandings of the discourse of human rights and gender equality, "religious" pluralism, and "religious" conflict. It challenges the ways in which Islam is currently studied in academic settings and brings to greater relief the necessity of moving the scholarly scrutiny of Islam out of the confines of the departments of Middle and Near Eastern languages and civilizations as well as religious studies into the broader canvas of humanistic and social-scientific research in all its richness and diversity.

NOTES

1. Wilfred Cantwell Smith, *The Meaning and End of Religion* (Minneapolis: Fortress, 1991).

2. Talal Asad, *Genealogies of Religion: Discipline and Reasons of Power in Christianity and Islam* (Baltimore: Johns Hopkins University Press, 1993); Hent de Vries, *Philosophy and the Turn to Religion* (Baltimore: Johns Hopkins University Press, 1999); Hans G. Kippenberg, *Die Entdeckung der Religionsgeschichte: Religionswissenschaft und Moderne* (München: C. H. Beck, 1997); Tomoko Masuzawa, *The Invention of World Religions; Or, How European Universalism Was Preserved in the Language of Pluralism* (Chicago: University of Chicago Press, 2005).

3. S. N. Balagangadhara, *"The Heathen in His Blindness": Asia, the West, and the Dynamic of Religion* (Leiden: Brill, 1994); Richard King, *Orientalism and Religion: Post-Colonial Theory, India and "the Mystic East"* (London: Routledge, 1999).

4. Russell T. McCutcheon, *Critics Not Caretakers: Redescribing the Public Study of Religion* (Albany: State University of New York Press, 2001).

5. Timothy Fitzgerald, *The Ideology of Religious Studies* (New York: Oxford University Press, 2000).

6. Daniel Dubuisson, *L'Occident et la religion: Mythes, science et idéologie* (Bruxelles: Editions Complexe, 1998); Kippenberg, *Die Entdeckung der Religionsgeschichte*; De Vries, *Philosophy and the Turn to Religion*; Ernst Feil, *Religio: Die Geschichte eines neuzeitlichen Grundbegriffs vom Frühchristentum bis zur Reformation* (Göttingen: Vandenhoeck und Ruprecht, 1986–2001).

7. Fitzgerald, *The Ideology of Religious Studies*; Hans-Michael Haussig, *Der Religionsbegriff in den Religionen: Studien zum Selbst- und Religionsverständnis in Hinduismus, Buddhismus, Judentum und Islam* (Berlin: Philo, 1999); King, *Orientalism and Religion*; Balagangadhara, "The Heathen in His Blindness."

8. Smith, *The Meaning and End of Religion*.

9. Haussig, *Der Religionsbegriff*; Patrice C. Brodeur, "Religion," in *The Encyclopaedia of the Qur'ān*, ed. Jane Dammen McAuliffe (Leiden: Brill, 2001–05), 4:395–98; Yvonee Yazbeck Haddad, "The Conception of the Term *Dīn* in the Qur'ān," *Muslim World* 64 (1974): 114–23; Jane Dammen McAuliffe and Clare Wilde, "Religious Pluralism," in *The Encyclopaedia of the Qur'ān*, ed. Jane Dammen McAuliffe (Leiden: Brill, 2001–05), 4:399–419.

10. Brodeur, "Religion"; McAuliffe and Wilde, "Religious Pluralism."

11. McAuliffe and Wilde, "Religious Pluralism," 404.

12. Fred Donner, *Muhammad and the Believers, at the Origins of Islam* (Cambridge, Mass.: Belknap Press of Harvard University Press, 2010), 57.

13. Ibid., 68–69.

14. Ibid.

15. Daniel A. Madigan, *The Qur'ān's Self-Image: Writing and Authority in Islam's Scripture* (Princeton: Princeton University Press, 2001).

16. Wilferd Madelung, *"Murdji'a,"* in *The Encyclopaedia of Islam*, 2nd ed. (Leiden: Brill, 1960–2009), 7:605–7; Ahmet T. Karamustafa, *Sufism: The Formative Period* (Edinburgh: Edinburgh University Press, 2007), 48–51.

17. Sarah Stroumsa, *Freethinkers of Medieval Islam: Ibn al-Rāwandī, Abū Bakr al-Rāzī and Their Impact on Islamic Thought* (Leiden: Brill, 1999); G. J. H. Van Gelder, "Abū 'Alā' al-Ma'arrī," in *Encyclopedia of Arabic Literature*, ed. Julie Scott Meisami and Paul Starkey (London: Routledge, 1998), 1:24–25.

18. Keith Lewinstein, "Notes on Eastern Ḥanafite Heresiography," *Journal of the American Oriental Society* 114 (1994): 583–98.

19. Yohanan Friedmann, *Tolerance and Coercion in Islam: Interfaith Relations in the Muslim Tradition* (Cambridge: Cambridge University Press, 2003); Jacques Waardenburg, ed., *Muslim Perceptions of Other Religions: A Historical Survey* (Oxford: Oxford University Press, 1999).

20. 'Azīz Nasafī, *Persian Metaphysics and Mysticism: Selected Treatises of 'Azīz Nasafī*, trans. Lloyd Ridgeon (Richmond: Curzon, 2002).

21. Leor Halevi, *Muhammad's Grave: Death Rites and the Making of Islamic Society* (New York: Columbia University Press, 2007); Daniella Talmon-Heller, *Islamic Piety in Medieval Syria: Mosques, Cemeteries and Sermons Under the Zangids and Ayyūbids, 1146–1260* (Leiden: Brill, 2007).

22. Markus Dressler, "Alevīs," in *Encyclopaedia of Islam, Three*, ed. Gudrun Krämer, Denis Matringe, John Nawas, and Everett Rowson, Brill Online, 2011, http://referenceworks.brillonline.com/entries/encyclopaedia-of-islam-3/alevis-COM_0167.

23. Carl W. Ernst, *Following Muhammad: Rethinking Islam in the Contemporary World* (Chapel Hill: University of North Carolina Press, 2003).

24. Abdulkader Ismail Tayob, "Religion in Modern Islamic Thought and Practice," in *Religion and the Secular: Historical and Colonial Formations*, ed. Timothy Fitzgerald (London: Equinox, 2009), 177–92; Abdulkader Ismail Tayob, "Divergent Approaches to Religion in Modern Islamic Discourses," *Religion Compass* 3 (2009): 155–67; Markus Dressler, "Religio-Secular Metamorphoses: The Re-Making of Modern Alevism," *Journal of the American Academy of Religion* 76 (2008): 280–311.

25. Masuzawa, *Invention*.

26. Elizabeth Shakman Hurd, *The Politics of Secularism in International Relations* (Princeton: Princeton University Press, 2007); Asad, *Genealogies of Religion*.

27. Karamustafa, "Elmalılı Muhammed Hamdi Yazır's (1878–1946) Philosophy of Religion," *Archivum Ottomanicum* 19 (2001): 273–79.

17
Translation
ARVIND MANDAIR

At a time when scholars in the study of religion have become increasingly self-conscious about the key concepts of their discipline, it seems strange that "translation" has not appeared in recent scholarly collections as a term that merits critical reflection in the study of religion. Yet the last few years have seen a greater number of translations of "religious" texts than at any other time. Why, then, has translation not been considered on a par with other key concepts or "critical terms" in the study of religion?[1]

One reason for this apparent oversight may be that no two words seem more connected, and the relationship between them more transparent, than the terms "religion" and "translation." Another reason might be that "translation" has been figured in a particular way in religious studies, as if the translation *of* religion was an inevitable process. Or that religion is a cultural universal that continues to be successfully translated (that is, without too much resistance) across cultures, a phenomenon for which there has been and continues to be ample evidence in the form of the unproblematic reciprocation of equivalent terms or meanings in other languages and hence their commensurability.

Notwithstanding the fact that the definition of *religio* itself has changed, this implicit belief in the translatability of religion has in some sense marked much of the Western history of reflection on translation. The belief in religion's natural translatability is evident in certain prevalent themes, for example, the idea exemplified by the Italian aphorism "traduttore, traditore," that translation constitutes a betrayal of fidelity, or the theme of the inherent chaos of human communication exemplified by the myth of Babel, which signifies both the impossibility of translating among the irreducible multiplicity of languages and the desire for attaining the completion and purity of the original logos.[2] We see this, for example, in some of the earliest reflections on the problems associated with translation in the classical era for which the translation between Greek and Latin languages was the dominant theme. The earliest words for the function of translation were *hermeus* and *metaphora* in Greek and *interpres* in Latin.[3] Both imply the sense of an intermediary that transports meaning between two distinct and autonomous languages and speakers. Likewise the long history of Bible translation with its ambivalent practices (for example, that the passage into other languages implies fundamental loss, corruption, and wastefulness, counterbalanced by the constant need for translation in order to make new converts) signals the fundamental problem of mediating between one and many as a problem of language and religion simultaneously (that language is one yet languages are many: religion is one yet religions are many).[4] If anything, George Steiner's periodization of the history of Western translation theory around the figures of Cicero, Schleiermacher, Jakobson, and Benjamin underscores this belief in a basic metaphysical regime. Steiner argues that the evolution of Western theories of translation from antiquity to the present day has been determined by the underlying premise that the underlying structure of language is universal and communication is common to all men.[5] Consequently the history of translation in the West has been driven by theories of linguistic hospitality, which have effectively tried to limit the danger associated with the approach of the foreign language. Central to this premise is a fundamental metaphysical assumption that privileges the One over the Many, Unity over Plurality, Host over Guest, and equates Oneness and Unity with the sphere of the native, one's own-most, which in turn marks it as Universal. By contrast, Plurality is equated with the figure of the stranger or foreigner and carries the stigma of particularity.

It is noteworthy that Steiner's exposition of the metaphysical assumptions of Western translation converges with the work of religious studies scholars such as Jonathan Z. Smith who speculate about the "expansion of the use and understanding of the term 'religion' that began in the sixteenth century."[6] Recent theories about the evolution of "religion" as a universal concept suggest that the term emerged as a way of *excluding* the non-Christian others but ended up being pluralized ("religions") by the late nineteenth century as a term for *including* non-Christian others into a framework that allowed Europeans to systematically map the state of cultures and civilizations of the world. This major expansion of the term "religions" began to take effect at a time when European identity was being nationalized and redefined in relation to a growing knowledge of Asian cultures, which in turn was being accumulated through travel accounts and orientalist and missionary treatises empowered by colonial expansion. One of the main mechanisms for systematizing and ordering the growing database of knowledge about others is the philosophical schemas of representation developed by thinkers such as Kant and Hegel.[7]

In order to construct a philosophical universalism at the heart of their schemas of representation, both Kant and Hegel devised structures of representation that, in addition to being deployed by missionaries, anthropologists, and orientalists in the nineteenth century, eventually became part of a new academic discipline: the modern study of religion(s) that included philosophy of religion and the history of religions. Central to both of these disciplines is the ability to represent difference in the form of other religions in relation to a European self-identification that accords to itself the ability to simultaneously give meaning to, and overcome, the signifier "religion." Though rarely recognized, this demarcation of cultural difference (other religions) is based on a concept of religion that is determined by a particular concept of translation, and vice versa, a concept of translation determined by a particular concept of religion. The specific concept referred to here is the concept of identity, which assumes an all-important role in facilitating a meeting point between the nature of thought and the nature of things. No sooner than identity is posited (or presupposes itself) as the ideal relationship between thought and its object, three things happen: (i) concepts themselves can only be thought in terms of identity; (ii) thinking itself becomes a "regime of representation," which in turn becomes synonymous with unhindered translatability; (iii) difference cannot be thought outside of identity.[8]

It could be suggested, therefore, that the concept of difference proper to the pluralization of religions is dependent on an assumed translatability (that is, the assumption of some sort of equivalence or fundamental commensurability) between self and other. Not only is the other translatable in terms of the unity of the self, but the difference between self and other is already determined by identity. This understanding of translation as a "regime of representation" in which identity is assumed to be the condition for thinking difference becomes axial to the study of religion(s) and the study of language(s) in the nineteenth and twentieth century. During this phase of scholarly activity, translation operates as a metaphor for cultural/religious encounter. This is especially evident in the drive to pluralize religious studies after the 1960s, as can be seen in the proliferation of "sacred-text" translations. Texts are designated "sacred" or "holy" if they have a nonworldly or metaphysical component that resists translation but nevertheless requires translation.[9]

But how exactly does the nonworldly or metaphysical come to be assumed as the ground for equivalence between the host culture (usually Western) and the guest culture (usually non-Western)? More importantly, why is it reciprocated by the guest culture or text in such a way that it appears as religious? That is to say, how and when did non-Western texts become "religious" or nonworldly? It is worth noting here that even the more recent phase of translation theory and practice, which has heralded important shifts in the paradigm for studying translation from biblical studies through linguistics and into cultural studies (particularly postcolonial) studies, has not taken the relationship between religion and translation seriously. The reason for this is that something crucial has remained unexamined in the modern schema of religious pluralization and encounter. What remain unexamined in the "regime of representation" are (i) the role of scholars, missionaries, administrators, and politicians in constructing equivalence and reciprocity between texts, cultures, or concepts, and (ii) a model of globalization with European Latinity as its sole driving force and as its target. If this is the case, then it is necessary to ask, "In whose terms, for what linguistic constituency, and in the names of what kinds of knowledge or intellectual authority" does the model of translation underpinning the study of religion operate insofar as it assumes equivalence and reciprocity of the other?[10]

It is here that the work of translation theorists in Asian studies[11] who have cast doubt on the conventional translation practices grounded in representation can be shown to intersect productively with the work of religious studies scholars who have cast doubt on the idea of religion as a cultural universal.[12] There is now an emerging consensus among many scholars of religion that "religion" is not a term that all cultures understood in the same way and that the thesis of its supposed universality was constructed in the modern period not least as a result of colonial encounters between Europeans and Asian cultures. Thus, if we juxtapose recent theories of translation with recent theories of religion, one of the questions that emerge is to what extent the concept of religion and the concept of translation helped to mutually construct each other in the era of colonial modernity. To what extent did theories about the nature of language(s) affect theories about the nature of religion(s)? For example, to what degree was the putative translatability of religion grounded in a be-lief in monolingualism—the idea that the essential characteristics of one's own lan-guage, or mother tongue, are its identity and unity, that it is a boundarified entity and, ipso facto, that the language of the other, the other's mother tongue, must also be characterized by unity and identity? What was invested in the positing of the monolin-gualism thesis by European scholars in their translations and cultural interactions with non-Western texts and speaker, and why, as a consequence of this, were Asian speakers obliged to reciprocate the monolingual model even though such reciproca-tion did not reflect the reality of their language situation? Moreover, to what ex-tent was the economy of *language* relations (the positing and reciprocation of equivalence) dependent on the *political* economy of empire?

In order to pursue these interlinked questions more thoroughly, it will be helpful to examine a specific case that illustrates how this phenomenon might have come about. Among the many cases in modern Asian studies that one could choose from, I would like to focus on the case of precolonial India, which, like other East Asian contexts, has no equivalent term for "religion" in the native lexicon. After the colo-nial event, however, indigenous elites begin to reciprocate the colonial demand for a native equivalent to "religion." Subsequently "religion" begins to circulate in the neocolonial lexicon as if it were a native concept. The question that arises here is whether the apparent reciprocity between English and Indian languages is the re-sult of a given economy of historical exchange, or whether it is simply a matter of finding equivalent meanings that are assumed to exist naturally in both languages, followed by their transportation and circulation between languages.[13]

A closer look at the state of language relations prevalent in colonial North India suggests that equivalents were in fact created through historical exchange.[14] Prior to their arrival in India, the British found a complex and confusing language situa-tion. Fully expecting to find distinct homogenous languages that corresponded to distinct religious and cultural identities, what they actually encountered was a het-erogenous lingua franca, an undifferentiated blend of several vernaculars with vary-ing admixtures of Sanskrit, Persian, and Arabic, but with no strict correspondence to a distinct religio-cultural identity shared by Muslims, Hindus, Sikhs, and others. The British initially referred to this hybrid language as "Moors," "Indostan," and eventually "Hindustanee." Believing this native language to be a degenerate form of an originally pure Sanskrit that was corrupted by contact with Islamic culture, orientalists such as William Jones, Charles Wilkins, and later John Gilchrist began the process of mapping linguistic terms in order to retrieve the original mother tongues and teach them back to the natives. By removing Islamic influences from Hindustani, particularly Persian and Arabic terms, so that there was a correspon-dence between one language and one religion, the orientalists believed they were also purifying the religious identities of the Hindus. This was achieved in practice by Romanizing and then codifying these languages by creating new grammars that were institutionalized through seminaries. The immediate effect of these grammars was to accelerate language acquisition among first-language users such as military personnel and administrators. Second, it helped to fix and standardize the fluid nature of spoken languages and created modern standard versions such as Urdu and Hindi. The model adopted for standardizing the languages was English. As Bernard Cohn notes, teachers such as John Gilchrist "would explain the English term as best he could to the Hindustanis," who would then "furnish the synonymous vocables in their own speech."[15] As the fixed standard according to which the fluid languages would be reformulated, the effect of English cannot be underestimated. Whereas prior to the colonial encounter the norm for the Indian languages was a form of translation in which the speaker was constantly exposed to the incommensurality of different languages, soon after the initial contact the earlier kind of encounter was displaced by another: the encounter between the unity and fixed identity of English versus the fluid heterogeneity of the Indian, which thereafter would be forced to reciprocate by conforming to the apparently stable identity of the English.

What grammars and dictionaries did was to fix the naturally translational existence of indigenous languages with a schematic *representation of* translation.[16] To have a representation of translation means that the Englishman possesses a predetermined definition of what translation is, such that he is already assured of the nature or thingness of the language encountered.[17] Despite the Englishman's assurance, it is only the representation of translation that gives rise to the possibility of figuring out the unity of his own language against the supposed unity of the Indian. The discursive apparatus that replaces the temporality of becoming governing indigenous language relations with a regime of translation consists in an operation of thinking whose logic is governed by the law of noncontradiction, that is, an image of thought that disables and displaces the fluid situation where naturally self-differentiating languages come into encounter with a stance where the other is ordered by making it knowable to the self. What happens in the formation of this schema is that the threatening chaos of encounter is secured. It is made stable and fixed. This securing of stability demands that an encounter that threatens to overwhelm the host/receiving/target language (corresponding to the horizon of the self) is transposed onto something that stands as identical. From this moment on, the self-differentiating potential of languages in translation will have been shifted onto a schema through which their natural mobility or capacity to make new relations is slowed down and ultimately presented to the self as an object. Thus the standard (English) is based ultimately on the self-certainty of one's own cultural horizon, namely, the English self or character. This already-formed horizon is the essential component of what Naoki Sakai calls the "schema of co-figuration,"[18] which is the discursive apparatus whereby a community constitutes itself as the self or standard by making visible the figure of an imaginary other—in this case the imagined purity of Indo-Aryan-derived Hindi from the hybrid mélange of Hindustani languages. Hence the fixing of heterolingual Hindustani into monolingual Hindi occurs only when the other is perceived as constituted by a contamination that requires purification. Thus the two imagined unities—English and Hindi—now begin to resemble each other in a process that is entirely spectral.

In order to institutionalize Hindi (henceforth written in the Devanagri script) and Urdu (which continued to be written in the Perso-Arabic script) as two autonomous linguistic entities, the British put into place a major educational infrastructure which included the following two parts. The first part was the founding of Fort William College in Calcutta in 1800 for the purpose of teaching British and Indian administrators.[19] With Gilchrist driving the college's language policy, the tasks of teaching the two newly created languages were given respectively to Lallujilal, a Hindu from Gujerat, and to Mir Amman, a Muslim from Delhi. The initial reluctance of the natives to speak these languages (particularly Hindi), combined with the shortage of materials for teaching them, was eventually overcome by Christian missionaries, who composed and propagated extensive missionary literature in Hindi and implemented the first printing presses in India. The second part was the creation of a vast network of Anglo-Vernacular mission schools in which the native elites were exposed to English along with a vernacular language (Hindi for Hindus, Urdu for Muslims, and by the late 1870s Punjabi for Sikhs) as early as eleven years of age.

Taken together these institutional measures enabled the teaching of "national" or vernacular languages under a blueprint that "produced cultural difference on a world map as an already translated fact and pretended to speak for that difference in a universalizing idiom."[20] Within this educational process, the native elites were expected to internalize the pedagogical mechanism and as result willingly reciprocate (that is, enter into a form of largely unequal exchange) Hindi terms for English. As Lydia Liu argues, in such a system of exchange, "characterized by vastly unequal conditions of power, difference was both produced as a value and at the same time victimized by translating it as a lesser value, or non-universal."[21] For example, the word "religion" is upheld by the English as a signifier denoting civilization, morality, and the "the good." But within the colonial economy of historical exchange, the indigenous equivalents such as "dharma" or "Hindu" are already devalued as signifiers of lack because religion had been postulated by orientalists and missionaries as something that may have existed in India but had to be recovered through the processes of improvement, reform, and modernization. Also in the indigenous languages the term "Hindu" was considered a marker of civilization and geography rather than religion. Clearly the inadequate term "Hindu" could only be brought into exchange via an ascription of desire for the signifier "religion," whose linguistic, cultural, and political value would be guaranteed by a combination of Christianity and empire. This desire then enters into the native enunciation through their response to the English demand for the term "religion."

But how does a particular signifier (for example, "Hindu") become manufactured into an equivalent of something else (for example, "religion") during the process of circulation? And how does this act of translation articulate the condition of unequal exchange? In her article "Meaning-Value and the Political Economy," Liu provides a way of answering these questions by drawing upon Marx's seminal analysis of money and capital, which in turn makes an insightful comparison between the production of value in economic transactions and the production of meaning-value in linguistic exchange (translation).[22] Marx's theory of economic exchange elaborates on a much older Aristotelian notion of exchange that presupposes a common measure of value, or "universal equivalent."[23] According to Marx, parties in an exchange "cannot bring their commodities into relation as values and therefore as commodities except by comparing them with some one or another commodity as the universal equivalent."[24] Within an economic transaction money is precisely this common measure by which the value of different commodities is compared, and although money may have a material form (for example, gold), it is also a symbol or signified whose materiality is irrelevant. Money is therefore no different from language insofar as in both the signified is an idea "embodied in a material signifier." The sign, which is immaterial and material at the same time, becomes the medium that establishes and maintains the identity and value of everything within the system of exchange. Hence the "act of monetary exchange, like linguistic exchange, depends on a socially recognized universal equivalent [Gold, God, English, and so on] which seems to homogenize everything, or to reduce everything to a common denominator."[25]

According to Mark C. Taylor, Marx's notion of a socially recognizable universal equivalent that secures the unity-in-difference that transforms opposition into reciprocity is borrowed from Hegel's *Logic*.[26] Marx's description of capital as a "self-renewing circular course of exchanges" is actually a secularized version of an older theological principle: the notion of the Absolute, of God as Unmoved Mover, conceived in Western tradition through the metaphorics of the centered circle that "presupposes its end as the goal and has its end also as the beginning."[27] Stated differently, the principle that connects linguistic transaction to economic transaction, linguistic economy to political economy, is religion. It is precisely this triadic connection between language, religion, and political economy that is at work in the contexts of colonial and postcolonial India due to the fact that Indians have continued to reciprocate terms such as "God," "Religion," and "Faith" from within their conceptual resources through a process that remains largely uninterrogated because it seems entirely natural. More closely examined, however, this process of reciprocation can be attributed to nothing less than the faculty of speech itself—the very faculty that allows each and every response to take place. By interrogating this response, and by implication interrogating how certain words come to mind whereas others are interdicted, the very focus of the question of translation can be shifted in a different direction: How do agents of circulation consent to such an exchange of words when one of them does not have an equivalent to exchange in the first place, and when the process is fundamentally unequal? How does one subsequently enter into this economy of exchange? And why does agreement or giving of consent appear as natural? Insights in the work of Jacques Derrida (specifically the essays "Theology of Translation" and "Faith and Knowledge: The Two Sources of 'Religion' at the Limits of Reason Alone") and Jean-Luc Nancy (specifically the essay "A Deconstruction of Monotheism") help to address some of these questions.[28]

In "Theology of Translation" Derrida speculates on a particular moment in German Romanticism, suggesting that "a certain thinking about *Bildung*," indeed, "all the modifications of *bilden* [form, formation, figure, co(n)-figuration, schematization, and so on], are inseparable from what one could call precisely the imperative of translation."[29] There is, Derrida suggests, an "onto-theological dimension, a problematics of onto-theology that is located at the founding of a certain concept of translation."[30] This ontotheological dimension of translation can be found in the operation of cofiguring that is central to the work of the imagination (*Einbildungskraft*), but is in fact nothing more than the objectification of translation, the "totalizing gathering together" of the imagination into an "art of generalized translation."[31] Such "generalized translation" corresponds to an assumed "originary unity" of the imagination, the assumption that there is but "one world" into which two languages, language speakers, are thrown together in the schema of cofiguration. But it is precisely because of this assumed "originary unity" that "generalized translation" is already a disavowal of translation as such. As a result the "generalized translation" that takes place in any schema of cofiguration, in any schematization as such, is in fact a *representation of* translation, that is, the objectification of translation. The final destination of this objectification is to think the inaccessible and, in so doing, to give expression to what cannot be accessed, namely, the Unknown.[32]

The theme of "generalized translation" is broached again, albeit in a different manner, in Derrida's essay "Faith and Knowledge: The Two Sources of 'Religion' at the Limits of Reason Alone." This essay gives us a glimpse of how the assumption of a "fundamental translatability" is at work in the colonial institutions such as the Anglo-Vernacular (A/V) school. In "Faith and Knowledge" Derrida points to the theological underpinnings of the social contract involved in all linguistic acquisition and encounter, indeed in all human addressivity.[33] The role of the "interdict" is crucial here.[34] Objectively the interdict corresponds to the regime of translation imposed by the prestige of the English language as "official," as Law, mediated through the agency of language instructors in the A/V school.

From the standpoint of the native elites subjected to this Law, the interdict operates as a self-censorship that comes into effect by prohibiting a certain kind of speech from being articulated. Instead the interdict specifies access to uncensored identifications while in that very moment actively repressing other identifications. It can be regarded as the native's willing agreement to submit to language as Law (or to the Law as language). Through such submission one responds to the other and in thus responding will have entered into a relation with the other. Yet the very possibility of this response is premised on a confidence trick. One responds to the other as if one had already mastered language, and as if, in responding, one is in control of meaning or communication. Although Derrida doesn't reveal his source, he is clearly indebted to Lacan's notion of the Unconscious structured like a language. We could therefore say, in pastiche of Lacan, that the subject cannot *acquire* language but only *accede* to it. In effect this is another way of saying that one does not master language; rather, one is mastered *by* language, which of course provokes a question: Why does one's subjection to language/Law *appear* as a freely given response to the other? Lacan would say that the subject has to let himself into the other's word by investing a certain degree of faith in the other simply on the basis of the words he speaks, and without any correspondence between facts and proofs, this creates a minimal social relation between speaking beings.[35] But what guarantees the investment of belief or good faith in the other? Stated differently, what guarantees that the native's response will be recognized by the other, and through such recognition deemed by the other to be a response-able subject, a subject who has a similar self-consciousness to his own?

For Derrida the very fact that we require language to speak to another and for another to respond means that speaking/responding is unavoidable insofar as speech/response provides the possibility of the social bond or what might be regarded as the minimal form of community: the self in relation to an-other (the not-self). Thus the subject cannot respond and there can be no responsibility unless there is first of all an agreement already in place, a given-word, a sworn faith, without some kind of testimonial pledge, a legal binding that invokes the sacred: "No response without a principle of responsibility: one must respond to the other, before the other and for oneself. And no responsibility without a *given word*, a sworn faith, without a pledge, without an oath, without some *sacrament* or *ius iurandum*."[36]

There was, it seems, no question of the native's *not* responding. By responding the native promises to tell the truth and asks the other to believe that he is also an other. But a promise cannot properly take place even though promising is inevitable as soon as the native opens his mouth: "From the moment I open my mouth, I have already promised; or rather . . . the promise has seized the I that promises to speak to the other. . . . This promise is older than I am."[37] Language, like Lacan's symbolic order, precedes those who speak it or those through whom it speaks. For the colonized native subjected to the Law of English as Law, there could never be any question of not responding to the other, for "language has started without us, in us and before us. This is what theology calls God, and it is necessary, it will have been necessary to speak."[38] The connection between God and the possibility of speech/response is better explained in the text of "Faith and Knowledge," where Derrida provides an important clue as to what is really going on. He warns that:

> Before even envisaging the semantic history of testimony, of oaths, of the given word (. . . indispensable to whomever hopes to think religion under its proper or secularized forms), before even recalling that some sort of "I promise the truth" is always at work, and some sort of "I make this commitment before the other from the moment that I address him, even and perhaps above all to commit perjury," we must formally take note of the fact that *we are already speaking Latin*. We make a point of this in order to recall that the world today speaks Latin (most often via Anglo-American) when it authorizes itself in the *name* of religion.[39]

What Derrida seems to suggest here goes beyond the issue of Latin's linguistic hegemony. The reference to Latin is a pointer toward a structural principle around which an entire tradition (religious, intellectual, cultural, and political) continues to gravitate. At the core of this structure there is enshrined a sacred principle that Derrida calls an "*a priori* ineluctable" or inescapable presupposition: that at the very moment of our coming to speech, at the very moment that an "I" addresses or responds to another "I" (and therefore to an other), the self engenders the figure of God as a witness, "quasi-mechanically" as it were. The very emergence of our speech presupposes that God can be called upon as a witness, albeit the Supreme Witness, who testifies to the legality or correctness of the self's relation to an other, indeed to the inviolability of the *distance* between self and other: "Presupposed at the origin of all address, coming from the other to whom it is also addressed, the wager of a sworn promise, taking immediately God as its witness, cannot not but have already. . . . engendered God quasi-mechanically."[40]

According to this model of language, speech begins by presupposing the existence of God, which is also the condition for his absence or nonexistence. Without God, or with a God who is nonexistent, there is no absolute witness and therefore no ground for a proper relationship between self and other. With God, or a God who exists, we have the existence of a third, a mediator who guarantees even the minimal social bond between self and other, even when and perhaps most importantly when the self/I commits perjury, when I lie to the other, or when the pledge is at its most secular. Derrida refers to this fiduciary structure as a "transcendental addressing machine."[41] As such the fiduciary is effectively a mechanism that allows God to be invoked as an "originary unity," the transcendent One, but does not stop Him from being called upon at will and put to good use.

Quite simply, the fiduciary can be regarded as a "performative experience of the act of faith," without which there can be no address to the other. Constituted on the "soil of bare belief,"[42] the fiduciary not only underlies everything to do with religion or the religious, but insofar as it is also a principle of "generalized translatability," it underpins the generalized "institutional translation of the theology of translation" into the secular domain. Thus seemingly different notions as belief/faith, religion, and secularism are thoroughly interconnected, thoroughly translatable, one could say, because they are rooted in a peculiarly Christian concept of the world. As such, the fiduciary can only be spoken of universally in relation to other cultures through the phenomenon of Latinity and its globalization, or *globalatinization*, to use Derrida's neologism.[43]

Globalatinization in all of its manifestations is the result of presupposing a "concept of fundamental translatability [which] is linked poetically to a natural language"[44] *that itself resists translation.* Today *globalatinization* enables the fiduciary, the core mechanism of Christianity and its language, to retain its hegemony due to the conceptual apparatus of international law, capitalist economics, global political rhetoric that works in effect as a "generalized rhetoric or translatology," and (though Derrida doesn't specifically mention this) the various modes of multiculturalism. It can be seen as the global re-Christianization of the planet through the discourse of secular conceptuality. Wherever the conceptual apparatus of international law, capitalist technology, and politics (as well as multiculturalism) dominates, it speaks through the discourse of religion, and specifically, as Jean-Luc Nancy emphasizes, monotheism. Indeed as Nancy suggests, "if the capitalist and technological economy constitutes the general form of value or sense today," it does so by way of "a worldwide reign of a monetary law of exchange (or general equivalency) or the indefinite production of surplus value within the order of this equivalency."[45] Yet this "monovalence of value" is indissociable from the apparently atheistic "transcription of the monoculture whose monotheistic conception it carried: explicitly the culture of

Rome and its European and modern expansion."[46] Thus for Nancy, as for Derrida, monotheism is not restricted to a religious history. Rather it continues to determine the present insofar as it constitutes "the provenance of the West qua globalization" over which hovers the specter of nihilism. It is therefore important to realize that "the West is Christian in its depths"[47] and that, through this "Christian occidentality, an essential dimension of monotheism in its integrality is set into play. And it is urgent to realize this insofar as the Westernized world has replaced all values with the generalized equivalence that Marx designated as merchandise."[48]

But what is it that connects "monotheism to the monovalence of the general equivalency"? The answer, as alluded to above, is the mechanism that Derrida calls "generalized translation." This is the fundamental mechanism of the global fiduciary that translates monotheism into the objectification of knowledge in the humanities according to the "rhythm of techno-science," and because state structures depend essentially and concretely on the performativity of sciences and technosciences, this fundamental mechanism also translates into "what has rightly been called the military-industrial-complex of the modern State," and even beyond that to the economic rationality of capitalism.[49]

Though not always obvious, the process of *globalatinization* repeats a mechanism—the "theology of translation"—that was put into play at the microlevel in the Anglo-Vernacular school, a mechanism variously described as the manufacture of consent, native-informancy, or mimicry. Indeed, what the term *globalatinization* highlights is the indissociability of a "fundamental translatability" between the religious and the secular, two spheres that figure prominently in the native elites' acceptance of and resistance to the colonial symbolic order. As a result of an implicit "theology of translation" the concepts of secularism and religion are peaceably imposed (or violently *self*-imposed) on all things that remain foreign to what these words designate. This is best seen when we look at the continued translation of the concepts of religion and secularism within the South Asian context, through the medium of violence. In other words, violence mediates the movement between secularism and religion best seen in the complex relations between the secular state and nonstate actors and between state/media and the academy.

NOTES

1. See Mark C. Taylor, *Critical Terms for the Study of Religion* (Chicago: University of Chicago Press, 1999). An otherwise excellent volume, it misses out on "translation" as a "critical term."

2. For example, see Willis Barnstone, *The Poetics of Translation: History, Theory and Practice* (New Haven: Yale University Press, 1993), 42; George Steiner, *After Babel* (Oxford: Oxford University Press, 1992).

3. Richard Kearney, introduction to *On Translation*, by Paul Ricoeur (New York: Routledge, 2006), xiii.

4. This is comprehensively covered in Barnstone, *The Poetics of Translation*; and Steiner, *After Babel*.

5. Steiner, *After Babel*, 76–112.

6. Jonathan Z. Smith, "Religion, Religions and the Religious," in Taylor, *Critical Terms for the Study of Religion*, 269–84.

7. See, for example, remarks about Hegel and Kant in the following works: Gayatri Spivak, *Postcolonial Reason: Toward a History of the Vanishing Present* (Cambridge, Mass.: Harvard University Press, 1999); Arvind Mandair, *Religion and the Specter of the West: Sikhism, India, Postcoloniality, and the Politics of Translation* (New York: Columbia University Press, 2009); Lydia Liu, *Tokens of Exchange: The Problem of Translation in Global Circulations* (Durham: Duke University Press, 1999); Lydia Liu, *Translingual Practice: Literature, National Culture and Translated Modernity— China 1900–1937* (Stanford: Stanford University Press, 1995); Naoki Sakai, *Translation and Subjectivity: On Japan and Cultural Nationalism* (Minneapolis: University of Minnesota Press, 1997).

8. The classic version of this argument can be found in Gilles Deleuze, *Difference and Repetition*, trans. Paul Patton (London: Athlone, 1994).

9. This phase of translation activity begins with Max Muller's translation of the *Religious Books of the East* and the like, but a more recent version of it is the volume by Lynne Long, *Translation and Religion: Holy Untranslatable?* (Buffalo: Multilingual Matters, 2005).

10. Liu, *Translingual Practice*, 1.

11. Such as Lydia Liu, Naoki Sakai, James Hevia, and Tejaswini Nirinjana, among others.

12. A list of such scholars who have provided a more critical understanding of religion is too long to reproduce here. This subfield of religious studies has expanded considerably since the 1990s and could be said to constitute a mode of inquiry that is often referred to as "critical religion studies." Scholars who have contributed significantly to this field include Jonathan Z. Smith, S. N. Balagangadhara, Talal Asad, Daniel Dubuisson, Russell McCutcheon, Timothy Fitzgerald, Naomi Goldenberg, Tomoko Masuzawa, Richard King, and many others.

13. Liu, "The Question of Meaning-Value in the Political Economy of the Sign," in *Tokens of Exchange*.

14. The following works provide useful introductions to the language situation of colonial North India: Bernard Cohn, *Colonialism and Its Forms of Knowledge: The British in India* (New Delhi: Oxford University Press, 1997); Christopher King, *One Language, Two Scripts: The Hindi Language Movement of North India* (New York: Oxford University Press, 1996); Ranajit Guha, *Dominance Without Hegemony* (New Delhi: Oxford University Press, 1988); Vasudha Dalmia, *The Nationalization of Hindu Traditions* (New Delhi: Oxford University Press, 1997).

15. Bernard Cohn, *Colonialism and Its Forms of Knowledge* (New Delhi: Oxford University Press, 1997), 33.

16. For a fuller discussion, see Mandair, *Religion and the Specter of the West*, chap. 1.

17. My use of the term "English*man*" is more than just an indicator that most colonial translations were done by men. It points to the gendered logic of translation, which operates according to an image of thought that is phallocentric precisely because it fixes or spatializes the movement of time.

18. Naoki Sakai, *Translation and Subjectivity: On "Japan" and Cultural Nationalism* (Minneapolis: University of Minnesota Press, 1997).

19. For details on the work of John Gilchrist, see Cohn, *Colonialism and Its Forms of Knowledge*; and Dalmia *The Nationalization of Hindu Traditions*.

20. Lydia Liu, "The Question of Meaning Value in the Political Economy of the Sign," in *Tokens of Exchange*, 19.

21. Liu, *Tokens of Exchange*, 13–41.

22. Ibid.

23. Karl Marx, *Grundrisse: Foundations of the Critique of Political Economy*, trans. Martin Nicolaus (New York: Pelican, 1973), 134.

24. Karl Marx, quoted in Mark C. Taylor, *Confidence Games: Money and Markets in a World Without Redemption* (Chicago: University of Chicago Press, 2004), 107.

25. Marc Shell, *Money, Language and Thought: Literary and Philosophic Economies from the Medieval to the Modern Era* (Baltimore: Johns Hopkins University Press, 1993), 107.

26. Taylor, *Confidence Games*, 108.

27. Ibid., 109.

28. Jacques Derrida, "Theology of Translation," in *Eyes of the University: Right to Philosophy* 2, trans. Jan Plug (Stanford: Stanford University Press, 2004); Jacques Derrida, "Faith and Knowledge: The Two Sources of 'Religion' at the Limits of Reason Alone," in *Religion*, ed. Jacques Derrida and Gianni Vattimo (Cambridge: Polity, 1998), 1–78; Jean-Luc Nancy, "A Deconstruction of Monotheism," in *Dis-Enclosure: The Deconstruction of Christianity*, ed. Jean-Luc Nancy, trans. Bettina Bergo (New York: Fordham University Press, 2008), 29–41.

29. Derrida, "Theology of Translation," 65.

30. Ibid.

31. Ibid., 78–79.

32. Sakai, *Translation and Subjectivity*, 34.

33. Derrida, "Faith and Knowledge," 26–30.

34. Derrida, *Monolingualism of the Other* (Stanford: Stanford University Press, 1998), 30–33.

35. Willie Appollon, "Theory and Practice in the Psychoanalytic Treatment of Psychosis," in *Lacan and the Subject of Language*, ed. Ellie Ragland-Sullivan and Mark Bracher (London: Routledge, 1991), 117–19.

36. Derrida, "Faith and Knowledge," 26.

37. Jacques Derrida, "How to Avoid Speaking: Denials," in *Languages of the Unsayable: The Play of Negativity in Literature and Literary Theory*, ed. Sanford Budick and Wolfgang Iser (New York: Columbia University Press, 1989), 14.

38. Ibid., 29–30.

39. Derrida, "Faith and Knowledge," 27.

40. Ibid.

41. Ibid.

42. Jacques Derrida, "Above All, No Journalists," in *Religion and Media*, ed. Hent de Vries and Samuel Weber (Stanford: Stanford University Press, 2001), 65.

43. Derrida, "Faith and Knowledge."

44. Derrida, "Theology of Translation," 69.

45. Nancy, "The Deconstruction of Monotheism," 31.
46. Ibid.
47. Ibid., 32.
48. Ibid., 34.
49. Derrida, "Theology of Translation," 78.

PART IV
Religion as Experience

18

The Psychology of Religion

JEREMY CARRETTE

The psychology of religion is a complex interdisciplinary area of study. It formally emerged in late-nineteenth-century European and American thought as part of the scientific endeavor to explain religious attitudes and behavior, governed and guided by notions of modern individualism. The scope and nature of its project are complicated by its diversity, its cultural location, the politics of science, and its unexamined philosophical assumptions.

The complexity of the area is further increased by the uneasy historical relationship between the different interdisciplinary domains and their competing claims. There is a conceptual struggle about the continuity or discontinuity between psychology and previous modes of thinking about the self. For example, the longer traditions of thinking about the self from the history of philosophy and theology shape the emergence of some early forms of psychological knowledge, as can be seen in Wilhelm Wundt's folk psychology[1] or Stanley Hall's religious psychology.[2] There is also a debate about the relationship between aspects of Germanic theology, such as Schleiermacher's (1768–1834) idea of religious consciousness, and forms of introspective psychology. Psychologists who want to avoid any apparent contamination between theological ideas and supposed scientific methods fiercely reject any apparent crossover of ideas between the different disciplinary realms, but it is this tension that pervades the subject. There is an attempt to conceal a priori concepts of self from informing the assumed neutral ideal of scientific empiricism.

In a similar fashion, the study of religion has gone through various phases of ambivalence toward psychology as one of its founding disciplines. This uneasiness is caused by the fact that psychology shifts allegiance between the social, human, and natural sciences. Eric Sharpe[3] attributes the tensions between the two fields to the impact of behaviorism on the psychology of religion, which reduced religion to secondary phenomena, but the problem rather relates to a more fundamental historical problem of its knowledge claims and its relation to the philosophy of self-knowledge and cultures of measurement.

The psychology of religion is pulled in different directions by the various competing methodologies and their associated institutional authority. It has therefore become incumbent on the various protagonists of the psychology of religion, as Antonie Vergote's inescapably contentious essay on the subject recognizes, to "define the boundaries" and delimit the "competence and possible scope of the psychology of religion."[4] Each exponent of the psychology of religion holds different forms of allegiance to a type of knowledge about psychology and this defines and shapes what constitutes the "psychological" and what it can say about "religion." This means that each psychological approach makes a religious object that is measurable and identifiable in terms of the philosophical assumptions of the method. It means that there are different meanings associated with the idea of the "psychological" and different forms of understanding of how the psychological relates to a natural science object. In other words, psychological forms of knowledge are contentious and compete against each other for authority and power in making truth claims about how we know and what we are within the domain of religious thought.

We thus find all sorts of appeals to the "strict definition," "the real conception," and what "should" be called the psychology of religion.[5] Not surprisingly, the power relations between the two fields mean there are different kinds of relationship between religion and psychology, including reductionist, dialogical, and pastoral engagements. This creates slightly different disciplinary domains. The specific scientific claims of the "psychology of religion" are seen as distinct from "religious psychology" and "pastoral psychology," though there is some methodological slippage between these subsets of knowledge. The dances of engagements employ the conjunctions "and," "of," "as," and "with" between the two subjects, which reveals not only the shifting power relationship but deeper problems about the foundations of the subject.[6]

It can also be argued that psychology helps determine the object of religion, rather than psychology making a set of observations about religion from the position of psychological knowledge.[7] This means that different types of psychology create slightly different ideas about the "religious" object of study according to the method and philosophical judgment implicit in the knowledge claims. For example, there is a difference between the claim that religious symbols reflect unconscious wish fulfillments (psychoanalysis) and the claim they are innate structures of the mind (cognitive science). The competing edges of the psychology of religion can be explained by the fact that this area of knowledge is determined by the interaction of three underlying forms of knowledge: philosophy, physiology, and politics. It is *philosophical* in that it holds assumptions about the kinds of knowledge we can have about the self, individual, mind, and body; it is *physiological* in that it attempts to use methods of the natural sciences to anchor its philosophical claims; and it is *political* insofar as the knowledge claims about the self, individual, and mind are of social importance and culturally varied. It is also *political* because the way you view the individual will shape how you can govern individuals.[8]

PSYCHOLOGY, SCIENCE, AND INTERPRETATION

The nature of the psychology of religion is further complicated by its competing claims to be a scientific discipline. The first problem relates to the fact that psychology is not a coherent set of practices or agreed-on positions, but a set of miscellaneous theories, methods, and practices, including a spectrum of positions from folk psychology and psychoanalysis to behaviorism and neuroscience. Peter du Preez accurately captured this complex diversity in his Kuhnian analysis of psychology, when he stated, "psychology is more like gang warfare than harmonious family life."[9] Any attempt to reconcile the positions within the broad scope of psychological theory and method is always set to failure, because, as Howard Kendler concludes in his study of the data and methods of psychology, they employ "irreconcilable orientations."[10] This diversity of positions creates a complex shaping of the object of analysis as the psychological data (experience, behavior, cognition) reconfigures the religious phenomena. The second problem is that each tradition of psychology is determined by a set of philosophical assumptions about the nature of "science" and the correct "scientific" way to study the object of religion, and that set of assumptions also reflects the historical deployment of the idea of science in various periods of the nineteenth and twentieth centuries. Science, as Fuller shows,[11] is a variable form with competing Enlightenment (falsifiability) and positivist (verifiability) forms. It holds complex ethical choices and is—as is often forgotten—a human and social enterprise: not least linked to public policy and the history of error.[12]

In the light of these unresolved tensions, psychology has been variously marked out as a "fragile" or an "ambiguous" science.[13] This is because there is a failure to establish a natural science object, except in those instances where psychology becomes more biological and physiological in nature. The problem is that the language shifts—somewhat uncritically—between the various forms of psychological studies. The aim is often to aspire to the social imaginary of rational deduction (so-called objective studies) and neglects the value of the interpretative formation (so-called subjective/social studies) and, in turn, it forgets a whole array of positions in between these options where the object of study is conditioned by the interpretative concept. The notion and importance of the "empirical" shift between these positions and, in the end, what we witness is different appeals to "science" as a validating order, which cover over hidden philosophical values, accounts of truth, and models of being human.[14] It is perhaps hard to imagine that there may not be much difference between the appeal of Freud to science and the appeal of a neuroscientist; both assume the authority of the institution of science and interweave nonscientific languages in order to claim a scientific reading of religion.

The appeal to science also involves psychology in the polemical nature of the science-religion debate and issues of reductionism. The main problem relates to the question of naturalism and metaphysics. Here the assumption is that belief and metaphysical claims can be explained within different types of psychological analysis. There are, of course, different ideological concerns within the psychological community, from the desire to sustain a metaphysical reality to the desire to eradicate it. This can be seen from the early differences between such writers as William James (1842–1910), with an open attitude to religious truth, and James Leuba (1867–1946), an early exponent of a scientific naturalism. This difference is regularly played out in the history of the psychology of religion. It can be seen more recently in the difference between someone like Fraser Watts, a Christian psychologist working in the tradition of science, and writers like Pascal Boyer, who seeks to find a contemporary naturalistic model built from cognitive science.[15]

SCIENCE, POLITICS, AND TEXTBOOKS

Caught between questions of philosophy, belief, science, institutional allegiances, and ideologies of the self, every introductory textbook weaves a narrative about the subject—mostly without awareness—to support their own agenda and criteria of valid knowledge. For example, David Wulff takes an uncritical descriptive and inclusive position in his major account of the psychology of religion, where he attempts to defend and define a broad and diverse disciplinary space,[16] whereas B. Spilka et al. and M. Argyle take a clear empirical stand.[17] Jonte-Pace and Parsons give up trying to fix the subject and allow for multiple forms of relation and hold a politic of knowledge from empiricism to feminism and cultural theory.[18] The theoretical divisions mean that there are clear and distinct competing traditions and groups of literature, covering psychoanalytical, humanistic, developmental, cognitive, and neuroscientific models. Each area of knowledge has little time for the other and rarely seeks to cross-reference the other. The aim is rather to offer political dismissal of the different areas of work, through either direct challenge or epistemic avoidance. It means the psychology of religion is—at best—diverse and conceptually muddled and—at worst—a philosophically imprecise area of knowledge. In response to the existing confusions, there have been a number of critical responses to psychological thinking about religion and an opening up of the area to its philosophical and interdisciplinary questions of power.[19] The introduction of critical forms of the psychology of religion takes the subject back to its historical, philosophical, and methodological problems.

In the end, the psychology of religion remains an incoherent and dislocated field with ever-diminishing professional positions and numerous theoretical heads buried in the sands of unexamined assumptions of knowledge. "Disappointment," as Belzen has argued, seems "endemic to the field."[20] It fails to find a comfortable home in the study of religion or psychology and its affiliated subareas often emerge in idiosyncratic places, often under a new nomenclature, such as the emergence of cognitive science in anthropology or philosophy (for example, Whitehouse in anthropology and Boyer in philosophy). The idea of the psychological thus breaks up into diverse subareas with different ways of speaking, such that the language reflects subtle shifts of meaning. For example, we find studies of the self (humanistic), mind (cognitive/developmental), psyche/soul (psychoanalysis/archetypal psychology), and brain (neuroscience). This reveals the way the field contains competing narratives and epistemological confusions in the slips and jumps between these regions of description.

There are also ingenious rhetorical games played through the history of the subject that are used to displace and dismiss competing areas of psychology. This means that types of psychological language are employed against others. For example, as Fromm poignantly writes:

> Academic psychology, trying to imitate the natural sciences and laboratory methods of weighing and counting, dealt with everything except the soul. . . . Psychology thus became a science lacking its main subject matter, the soul; it was concerned with mechanisms, reaction formations, instincts, but not with the most specifically human phenomena: love, reason, conscience, values.[21]

The attitudes to science and the nature of constructing what constitutes a science thus lie at the heart of the engagement between psychology and religion. All these different gestures to science say more about the attitude to the category of religion and how individuals wish to order the world than careful claims from the philosophy of science.

EPISTEMOLOGY, HISTORY, AND THE PSYCHOLOGY OF RELIGION

It is necessary for a critical introduction to the field of the psychology of religion to address the central problem of its knowledge claims in the area of the study of religion. We can achieve this critical purchase on the subject by focusing on the historically complex idea of introspection and raising the question of *how* we think about, or achieve some understanding of, ourselves (as defined by the psychological) inside the categorical space of religion. The psychology of religion can therefore be approached according the criteria of history and epistemology.

This approach demands we ask some preliminary philosophical questions. How do we know ourselves as human beings and how do we assess the ways of our knowing? How do such forms of self-knowledge and examination allow us to understand and interpret the practices and thoughts deemed to be "religious"? There are many ways of knowing and examining what we are and the problem of the psychology of religion is that the discourse of the religious itself has a purchase on truth-claims about self-knowledge that compete with psychological knowledge, which arguably is also formed by implicit Christian models of self-knowledge. The psychology of religion thus forms its own object of the religious as psychological. Making something into a fixed object of analysis sets up a relation of power by controlling the apparatus of knowledge or way something is known. It is, of course, equally possible to reverse the relation and make psychology the object of cultural introspection or individualism. We can make sense of these paradoxical and convoluted epistemological issues by framing the psychology of religion according to a philosophical question of how self-knowledge moves from religious/philosophical to scientific domains of knowledge. The distinctive shift to the scientific in the psychology of religion is based on the nature of psychological *measurement* and how the religious is captured under such logic. Those working in the institutions and professional orders of the psychology of religion often ignore such epistemological questions, because they do not wish to undermine or question the discourse that provides them with such authority. However, the diversity and internal confusions within the area of the psychology of religion require such a critical task. Much is then revealed in exploring the nature of introspection and measurement as critical categories for understanding the psychology of religion.

FROM INTROSPECTION TO MEASUREMENT

Although the term "introspection" is not formally employed until the modern era, and by John Locke in particular, its Western roots as a practice clearly go back to the Delphic principle "Know thyself" (*Gnothi Seauton*), though the Greek tradition of self-knowledge and self-examination is a complex one and different from a psychological tradition of the measured self.[22] The greatest exposition of the Christian introspective tradition must to some extent be taken back to Augustine, not only in his *Confessions* (397–98), but in his work *On the Trinity* (400–16), where he expounds various models of the mind according to the Trinity.[23] As Charles Taylor has argued: "It is hardly an exaggeration to say that it was Augustine who introduced the inwardness of radical reflexivity and bequeathed it to the Western tradition of thought."[24] Taylor's discourse of the self in Western thought supports a revival of Augustinian thought in the modern period and somewhat neglects the complex models of self in Thomas Aquinas and the problem of self-knowledge in both the modern and the medieval period. Jerrold Seigel specifically seeks to counter Taylor's account of the self in Western thought and illustrates that it is not only present theory but historical analysis that is caught in the philosophical struggle of truth about the self and the nature of introspection.[25] The question is, what, if anything, is constitutive of the modern sense of the psychological self?

Christian forms of introspection were developed according to models of self-examination in the long monastic traditions of the West, not least in the writings of Cassian and Ignatius. However, the Lutheran formation of self-examination brought a shift to the long tradition of inner reflection in Christianity by radicalizing the relationship of self in a demand for a new inner ethical relation to God. In line with this, the German Protestant tradition held within it the more immediate roots of psychological introspection by providing a structure and intensity of thinking about the self. It was Schleiermacher's *The Christian Faith* (1821) that brought forward the Protestant tradition of inwardness to new levels with his pietistic theological claims to "God consciousness" and the "feeling of absolute dependence."[26] The historical importance of these Western introspective traditions and other culturally powerful traditions of self-examination (in, for example, Buddhism) is the open-ended modeling of self according to various philosophical and theological assumptions. The problem for a post-Enlightenment tradition of scientific analysis of the self is that these models of introspection did not provide a stable self for measurement. The resolution of these problems and the desire to create a fixed and stable object of inquiry and close down the philosophical ambiguities, or the vague, transcendent horizons of meaning in theology, are a key part of the debate of whether the field of the psychology of religion is an open or closed scientific arena. The defining feature of the emergence of the psychology of religion was the introduction of measurement to account for the practices of self, which stabilized the self as a knowable entity that could be captured.

According to Danziger, modern psychology in the work of Wilhelm Wundt begins with the establishment of a "methodical" way of examining subjective events.[27] Wundt, following Brentano, makes the distinction between "actual introspection" (*Selbstbeobachtung*) and "inner perception" (*innere Wahrnehmung*). This distinction between simply watching the inner world and some systematic approach led to the experimental condition by trying to create the conditions for observing subjective events as external events. Although, as Danziger makes clear, Wundt believed there was another type of nonexperimental psychology, *Völkerpsychologie* (a kind of folk or social psychology), it was soon overshadowed by the domination of the experimental method.[28] "The triumphal progress of the natural sciences," as Danizger indicates, "helped to promote the belief that their methods were the *only* methods for securing useful and reliable knowledge about anything."[29]

The attempt by Wundt to hold different strands of psychological thought together and his attempt to locate psychology within a wider cultural process reflect the central politics of knowledge within the area of the psychology of religion. Jacob Belzen has mapped out some of these tensions in his evaluation of the psychology of religion in Wundt's *Völkerpsychologie*, showing the ways Wundt can help in overcoming the problematic nature of individual psychologies that ignore cultural processes in the study of religion. Like Danziger, but within the historical study of the psychology of religion, Belzen's critique focuses on the problem of psychology as a discipline adopting what he calls "methodological monism": the move toward a natural science experimental method, including statistical analysis.[30] There were models of psychology that resisted such approaches, but this only creates greater ambiguity between what constitutes the psychological knowledge and what carries older ideas of the self from philosophy and theology.

The key moment of the psychology of religion is then the ways in which a methodical study of human beings was employed to read religion and the central philosophical adoption of measurement as the key approach to study religion. It is therefore this philosophical shift to measurement that defines something of the psychology of religion, because even in works that would in time be rejected as valid science (Freud, Jung, Maslow, and so on) they all appeal to the context of science and its hallmarks of measured knowledge. It is an open question as to whether the models of self in Christian or Buddhist cultures offer a challenge to the measured self of psychology and whether measurement precludes an a priori model of self. To understand something of this problem we need to explore the issue of psychological measurement and ask how we measure psychological aspects of something categorized as "religion."

PSYCHOLOGY AND CULTURES OF MEASUREMENT

As Belzen suggests, a key part of the psychology of religion is the application of the methods of "general" psychology to the realm of "religion."[31] However, he believes this too creates a series of additional problems: applying invalid psychological models, using valid psychology but wrongly applying it to religion, or using a flawed application of valid methods. The idea of what constitutes "valid" knowledge and "valid" application is central to the psychological evaluation of religion, because the idea of religion is contentious itself. The question remains as to who gives the validation and approval. Valid knowledge is often framed as that which has undergone the rigorous test of scientific analysis, but these tests are themselves open to error and unresolved philosophical judgments. It is not that communities of scholars simply choose a valid type of knowledge, but rather they adopt agreed-on scientific principles, which they seek to employ in different domains that they assume to be measurable. Scientific method may be valid, but whether it is useful for psychology is the central contention.

The history of errors in psychology, as Joel Michell argues, is part of all science, but this becomes a greater concern when these errors remain part of the very practice of a knowledge community.[32] Errors in the psychology of religion remain suppressed to service knowledge regimes and communities. Georges Canguilhem[33] believed that much of psychological knowledge was set up to determine the normal and the pathological in the social order and this gave benefit to the established powers. But much of the psychology of religion is also trying to locate religion in the conditions of measurement. The majority of the studies of the psychology of religion are trying to identify the psychological attributes of religion and measure what they deem "religiosity"—the characteristics of religion. The methods established by Edwin Starbuck in his *The Psychology of Religion: An Empirical Study of the Growth of Religious Consciousness*, published in 1899,[34] determine a tradition of thinking about the psychology of religion as an empirical science. Starbuck's landmark text in the area of the psychology of religion attempts to "carry out the well-established methods of science." Making links with the natural sciences of astronomy and chemistry, Starbuck wants, in Newtonian fashion, to mark out the "lawful universe" in relation to the "facts of religion," but he—like many after him—cannot find any distinction between the religious and the nonreligious in mental life.[35] The psychology of religion is always plagued by the fact that psychological attributes defy religious classification and that pretension to avoid this enigma only succeeds in making a mockery of the scientific method.

Nonetheless, Starbuck's empirical method is supported by writers such as Benjamin Beit-Hallahmi and Michael Argyle in their work *The Psychology of Religious Behaviour, Belief and Experience*.[36] Here they assert: "The psychology of religion is, *by definition*, empirical." Acknowledging a tradition of thinking from Starbuck, they want to find what would count as a "good *measure* of religiosity."[37] Wulff likewise wants to support the examination of religion according to what I will call the "measurable thesis." But what this entire tradition of thinking in the psychology of religion ignores is the philosophical error of making psychological attributes and categories—within the field of religion—measurable. In this respect, the history of the psychology of religion can be seen through its subterranean history of diagrams and figures: the attempt to represent the religious inside mathematics.[38]

From Starbuck in the 1890s to the cognitive science in the 1990s diagrams form the statistical camouflage for the philosophical errors of measurement. The approach was pioneered by Starbuck, who claimed that "the use of the charts was found to assist, in lessening the personal equation."[39] But the use of the charts, diagrams, and figures tends more to reveal the desire to be an objective science and benefit from such knowledge claims than a clear articulation of data, because Starbuck's text is caught in the problem of categories, interpretation, and the notion of the individual. The aspiration to the "purely empirical" is trapped,[40] as Starbuck partly recognizes, in his "unavoidably selective" ideas and the "limits within which the inductions are valid."[41] However, this history also reveals the error of making psychological reality and religion a quantifiable entity. The psychology of religion can still provide valuable insights, but only by recognizing the basis of its epistemological claims. The future of any study in the psychology of religion must as a matter of course carry out the critical task of examining the claim that its concepts are scientific and the hidden errors that enable groups of scholars to sustain their community.

In Ludwig Fleck's groundbreaking study *Genesis and Development of a Scientific Fact* (1935),[42] he shows how scientific ways of approaching an object are shaped by the collective ideas of the time. This recognition of the socially determined scientific fact reveals the way the psychology of religion is continually shaped by a set of assumptions about valid knowledge in each historical wave of observation and experimentation. In this vein, Kurt Danziger recognizes, in his analysis of measurement in psychological knowledge, that the measurable requires the marking out of what can be measured: "The individuals who are counted must be endowed with countable attributes."[43] This creates the problem of what counts as data for the psychology of religion. Putting aside the problems of what counts as religion, the data becomes extremely precarious. Rather than having clearly defined objects for observation, the psychologists of religion stabilize the data with a theoretical assumption about the data. The empirical in this sense, to follow Flick, is already conceptually located and these concepts are validated by a series of institutional orders of power.[44] What we see through each theoretical shift of the psychology of religion is a variety of appeals to constructed data, which assumes a given entity, such as the working notions of "character," "cognition," "experience," and "unconscious," or, where the object is material, an assumption that "mind" can be mapped on to "brain."

The fact that the psychology of religion is caught inside a long history of physiology, philosophy, and politics is fundamentally a question about the empirical and scientific within the field. However, as Michell makes clear in his book *Measurement in Psychology*: "But if research in the history and philosophy of science over the past half-century has shown anything of value, it has shown that the methods that scientists use to test their hypotheses are not transparent windows on the world."[45] He rightly argues that any critical account of method must examine the empirical and conceptual. It is these two areas that illustrate the values that operate within measurement. Thus, in the fields of psychology in particular, the empirical is already theoretical.

Michell stands in a tradition of thinking from Immanuel Kant that showed that psychological factors were not measurable according natural science methods. According to Michell, the use of quantitative and experimental methods in psychology originated with the German scientist G. T. Fechner in his work *Elements of Psychophysics*, published in the 1860s,[46] and was entrenched in S. S. Stevens's *Handbook of Experimental Psychology*, published in 1951.[47] In the latter work, Stevens sought to *assign* numerals according to a rule rather than following the traditional view of measurement based on the view that "numbers are only identified when relations of ratio are considered."[48] Can we classify psychology and religion according to ratio? The key question, as Michell asks, is: "What are the marks of quantity?"[49] Michell's work disentangles a complex error of measurement in psychological science, but the continued persistence of this central approach is more disturbing in terms of how the persistence of the error provided a scientific camouflage, which had wider social benefits. As Michell argues: "As a bonus, they [psychologists] feel safe to continue to market their practices as applications of scientific measurement and to reap the ensuing rewards."[50] What this means is that psychologists assumed that psychological attributes such as intelligence, cognitive abilities, and personality traits could be measured. In the context of religion, there was also the assumption that psychological attributes related to religion could be isolated, something William James had long shown to be an error. By returning to the founding fathers of psychology and religion we see the logical problems that are carried into the subject.

The move from the general history of introspection to the setting up of conditions for controlled measurement reveals something of the problem of knowledge in the psychology of religion. It is thus important to realize that the psychology of religion is determined by—what we can call—different "cultures of measurement" in each respective historical phase of scientific validity. In the nineteenth century we find the birth of the questionnaire method of empirical measurement, in the twentieth century we find the birth of the case study measurement, and in the late twentieth century and twenty-first century we find the birth of a kind of ideological measurement of cognition, not least in the "Decade of the Brain" in the 1990s. These forms of measurement shape the nature of experience and the representation of the experience of religion according to wider philosophical presuppositions, such that measuring religiosity and puberty in Starbuck's original work from 1899 assumes religion is based on *individual* choice, measuring the unconscious in Freud and Jung assumes religion is an *individual* dynamic, measuring cognitive inputs in the work of Whitehouse assumes religion is *individual* thought. These different types of psychological knowledge all reflect the central underlying philosophical construct through which religion is made measurable: the isolation of the individual unit from the noise of linguistic, social, and political concepts of knowledge.

The explorations of William James, Jung, spirituality, and cognitive theory in this section of the work on the psychology of religion are all marked with a problem of knowledge about the individual as a central aspect of psychological knowledge. Psychological measurement of the individual is an arbitrary division of knowledge that reflects the claim that it results in an isolation of knowledge. The notion of the private individual as a unit of observation had opened the problem of the relation of the individual to the social and the somewhat false distinctions made to sustain the individual as a unit of measurement.[51] The psychology of religion is by default determined by a series of a priori assumptions about the nature of self/mind in Western thought and the closure about the self/mind and the self-other boundary of more socially orientated models, which can eradicate the non-Western notions of self and histories of self-examination outside of the rationalist and imperialist Western model of individualism.

CONCLUSION: IDEOLOGY AND CRITIQUE

There is no neutral presentation of the psychology of religion and this critical outline reflects my return of the subject to the philosophical traditions of epistemology. It makes a claim not for relativistic acceptance of all types of knowledge as equal, but for critical examination of all knowledge within terms of a historical and epistemic critique in order to find the truth of claims to knowledge in the psychology of religion. It seeks to locate psychological studies of religion in such philosophical orders of critique, to draw out the implicit values and hidden errors. By interrogating the idea of science and the deployment of empirical claims to truth we see that much remains hidden in the ideas of psychology and religion. The question to be asked is, what do all the results of the psychology of religion reveal? What is the use value of this area of knowledge? The aspiration is to measure, because the measurable is seen as the mark of truth, but if the Kantian tradition of Danziger and Michell is right, then it might be that the psychology of religion is not a science of measurement at all, but rather a continuation of complex lines of imaginative introspection within diverse cultures and traditions. It might be that the future task of those within the psychology of religion is to reposition knowledge in the best forms of critical thinking in philosophy and the history of ideas. It will then be possible to see how our empirical claims reflect our will to power.

NOTES

1. W. Wundt, *Elements of Folk-Psychology: Outline of a Psychological Development of Mankind*, trans. E. L. Schaub (London: Allen and Unwin, 1916).
2. G. S. Hall, *Adolescence: Its Psychology and Its Relations to Physiology, Anthropology, Sociology, Sex, Crime, Religion and Education* (New York: D. Appleton, 1904); and, G. S. Hall, *Jesus, The Christ, in the Light of Psychology* (New York: D. Appleton, 1923).
3. E. Sharpe, *Comparative Religion: A History* (London: Duckworth, 1986), 98.

4. A. Vergote, "What the Psychology of Religion Is and What It Is Not," *International Journal for the Psychology of Religion* 3, no. 2 (1993): 74.

5. D. Wulff, *Psychology of Religion: Classic and Contemporary* (New York: Wiley, 1997), 15; J. Belzen, "The Future Is in the Return: Back to Cultural Psychology of Religion," in *Religion and Psychology: Mapping the Terrain*, ed. D. Jonte-Pace and W. Parsons (London: Routledge, 2001), 45.

6. Jonte-Pace and Parsons, *Religion and Psychology*, 3–6.

7. J. Carrette, *Religion and Critical Psychology: Religious Experience in the Knowledge Economy* (London: Routledge, 2007).

8. M. Foucault, "Afterword: The Subject and Power," in *Michel Foucault: Beyond Structuralism and Hermeneutics*, ed. H. L. Dreyfus and P. Rabinow (London: Harvester Wheatsheaf, 1982).

9. P. du Preez, *A Science of Mind: The Quest for Psychological Reality* (London: Academic Press, 1991), 29.

10. H. Kendler, *Psychology: A Science in Conflict* (Oxford: Oxford University Press, 1981), 371.

11. S. Fuller, *Science* (Buckingham: Open University Press, 1997), 26–27.

12. K. Danziger, *Constructing the Subject: Historical Origins of Psychological Research* (Cambridge: Cambridge University Press, 1990); Kendler, *Psychology*, 9; J. Michell, *Measurement in Psychology: A Critical History of a Methodological Concept* (Cambridge: Cambridge University Press, 1999), xi.

13. W. James, *Psychology: Briefer Course* (Cambridge, Mass.: Harvard University Press, 1985), 334; Kendler, *Psychology*, 3; R. A. Wilson, *Boundaries of the Mind: The Individual in the Fragile Sciences* (Cambridge: Cambridge University Press, 2004).

14. Carrette, *Religion and Critical Psychology*.

15. F. Watts, *Theology and Psychology* (Aldershot, UK: Ashgate, 1994); P. Boyer, *The Naturalness of Religious Ideas* (Berkeley: University of California Press, 1994); P. Boyer, *Religion Explained: The Human Instincts That Fashion Gods, Spirits and Ancestors* (New York: Basic Books, 2001).

16. D. Wulff, *Psychology of Religion*.

17. Spilka et al., *The Psychology of Religion: An Empirical Approach* (New York: Guilford Press, 2003); M. Argyle, *Psychology and Religion: An Introduction* (London: Routledge, 1999).

18. Jonte-Pace and Parsons, *Mapping*.

19. Ibid.; Carrette, *Religion and Critical Psychology*.

20. J. Belzen, "A Way out of the Crisis? From Völkerpsychologie to Cultural Psychology of Religion," *Theory and Psychology* 15, no. 6 (2005): 828.

21. E. Fromm, *Psychoanalysis and Religion* (New Haven: Yale University, 1978), 6.

22. W. Lyons, *The Disappearance of Introspection* (Cambridge, Mass.: MIT Press, 1986).

23. Augustine, *De Trinitate: Nicene and Post Nicene Fathers* (Edinburgh: T and T Clark, 1988). Original version written circa 420.

24. C. Taylor, *Sources of the Self: The Making of Modern Identity* (Cambridge, Mass: Harvard University Press, 1989), 131.

25. J. Seigel, *The Idea of the Self: Thought and Experience in Western Europe Since the Seventeenth Century* (Cambridge: Cambridge University Press, 2005), 41–52.

26. Friedrich Schleiermacher, *The Christian Faith* (London: T and T Clark, 1999).

27. Danziger, *Constructing*, 35.

28. Ibid., 37.

29. Ibid., 41.

30. Belzen, "Way Out," 825.

31. Ibid., 831.

32. Michell, *Measurement*, xi.

33. G. Canguilhem, *The Normal and Pathological* (New York: Zone, 1989). Originally published in 1966.

34. E. D. Starbuck, *The Psychology of Religion: An Empirical Study of the Growth of Religious Consciousness* (New York: Walter Scott, 1899).

35. Starbuck, *The Psychology of Religion*, 5; W. James, *The Varieties of Religious Experience* (Glasgow: Collins, 1960), 27; E. Lawson and R. N. McCauley, *Bringing Ritual to Mind: Psychological Foundations of Cultural Forms* (Cambridge: Cambridge University Press, 2002), 9.

36. B. Beit-Hallahmi and M. Argyle, *The Psychology of Religious Behaviour, Belief and Experience* (London: Routledge, 1997).

37. Ibid., 40, emphasis added.

38. See Carrette, *Religion and Critical Psychology*; J. Carrette, "Religion out of Mind: The Ideology of Cognitive Science," in *Soul, Psyche, Brain: New Directions in the Study of Religion and Brain-Mind Science*, ed. K. Bulkeley (New York: Palgrave Macmillan, 2005), 242–61.

39. Starbuck, *The Psychology of Religion*, 14–15.

40. Ibid., 11.

41. Ibid., 13.

42. L. Fleck, *Genesis and Development of a Scientific Fact* (Chicago: University of Chicago Press, 1979).

43. Danziger, *Constructing*, 136.

44. Ibid., 147.

45. Michell, *Measurement*, 1.

46. G. T. Fechner, *Elements of Psychophysics*, ed. Davis Howes and Edwin Boring, trans. H. Alder (New York: Holt, Rinehart and Winston, 1966).

47. S. S. Stevens, *Handbook of Experimental Psychology*, 4 vols. (New York: Wiley, 1951).

48. Michell, *Measurement*, 18.

49. Ibid., 19.

50. Ibid., 22.

51. Carrette, *Religion and Critical Psychology*.

19

William James and the Study of Religion

A Critical Reading

JEREMY CARRETTE AND DAVID LAMBERTH

INTRODUCTION

William James (1842–1910) is a canonical thinker for the study of religion. Born in New York City, he was the oldest child of Henry James Sr., the son of an Irish immigrant who succeeded in business in Albany. The family included his famous novelist brother Henry James Jr. (1843–1916) and the diarist Alice James (1848–1892), his sister. His other two brothers, Garth Wilkinson and Robertson, served in the American Civil War (1861–65), and much of William James's life reflects the post–Civil War American context.[1]

He rose to fame for writing one of the founding texts of psychology, *The Principles of Psychology* (1890), and initiating, along with Charles Sanders Peirce and John Dewey, the American philosophical tradition of pragmatism, most notably in his *Pragmatism, a New Name for Some Old Ways of Thinking*, published in 1907. His Gifford Lectures at the University of Edinburgh, *The Varieties of Religious Experience* (1902), widely read then and now, continue to shape and define the study of religion.

James's work is part of the late-nineteenth-century response to the shifting relationship between science and religion in a Darwinian world, but also one reshaped by the philosophical reorganization of knowledge in a post-Kantian critical context. James responds to these changes by construing and advancing a creative dialogue among the German physiologists (Helmholtz, Wundt), the French post-Kantians (Renouvier, Bergson), and the British Empiricists (Locke, Hume), including debates with the British philosophers John Stuart Mill and Herbert Spencer and the psychologist Alexander Bain, among others. James's father, Henry James Sr. (1811–82), was a major figure in his early formation due in part to his decision to take the family abroad to pursue a European education when James was a young teen. The influence of Henry Sr.'s own philosophical-theological thinking, which was shaped in succession by Protestant revivalist thinking, Swedenborgianism, and socialist ideals, is much debated. Ralph Waldo Emerson, the New England Transcendentalists, and the philosophy of Charles Peirce are also important strands for understanding the work of James. James's formal studies included the Lawrence Scientific School in Cambridge, Massachusetts, after which he completed the requirements for the MD at Harvard Medical School, though he never sought licensure as a physician.

After an unsettled start to early adulthood, due to depression and uncertainty about his choice of career, James began teaching at Harvard University, first in physiology (1872), then psychology (1889), and finally philosophy (1897). Notably, James was responsible for establishing one of the first experimental psychology laboratories in the world. Despite the apparent progression from physiology to philosophy, James's work always integrated these different facets, as well as religious and theological dimensions, and thus reflects a nineteenth-century transdisciplinary approach that is grounded from his earliest thinking in a metaphysical framework about the nature of consciousness and the relations of thought to the world.[2]

There are two central trends in the reception of James by the study of religion. First, within religious studies, James has mainly been interpreted through the dominant lens of key psychological observations, a reflection of his reception inside American psychology of religion in the twentieth century and the way it developed as a subfield of religious studies. This relates to a second trend. Analysis of James's thinking about religion tends to be restricted to his *The Will to Believe* (1897), essays on the right to believe in a changing world of science, and his Edinburgh Gifford Lectures, *The Varieties of Religious Experience* (1902). While the former has stimulated a set of discussions on "belief" in the philosophy of religion, it is the readings of *The Varieties* that have led to the reduction of James to a psychological rendition. Although they too have much to do with religion and the study thereof, his other major works, *The Principles of Psychology* (1890), *Pragmatism* (1907), *The Meaning of Truth* (1909), *A Pluralistic Universe* (1909), and his posthumous works *Some Problems in Philosophy* (1912) and *Radical Empiricism* (1912), have routinely been omitted from deeper consideration in discussions about the study of religion.

These selective readings of James result in distinctively different disciplinary approaches and receptions from psychologists, philosophers, and scholars of religion.[3] This critical outline argues that James has largely been misread in the study of religion. We contend that the richness and range of James's thinking for considering religious issues have largely been overlooked. This essay proposes a more integrated and expansive reading of James, one open to appreciating the wider transdisciplinary and metaphysical questions that his work offers. Through this approach there is scope for a greater critical engagement with contemporary themes in the study of religion. The key argument is that a dynamic critical force of James's thinking has been lost through selective readings. Nevertheless, there is potential for recovering the richness of James's texts.

READING JAMES AND READING JAMES'S RECEPTION: THE DISCONNECTION IN THE STUDY OF RELIGION

The reason James has been misread is related to the nineteenth-century-inspired disciplinary appropriation of his work and the reinforcement of these ways of reading in the postwar institutionalization of religious studies.[4] The framing of James within the study of religion is exhibited clearly in Eric J. Sharpe's history of comparative religion. Although Sharpe recognizes that James's "popularity stems more from his work as a philosopher than his purely psychological theories" and that "it would be wrong to think of him as anything other than a speculative philosopher," Sharpe situates James in the lineage of figures who established the psychology of religion, alongside G. Stanley Hall, James H. Leuba, Edwin Diller Starbuck (see chapter 18 of this volume).[5] James has thus been packaged for the twentieth-century study of religion as offering a "prototype" for the psychology of religion.[6] While it is true that James's thought is rooted in the history of psychology and concerned throughout with psychological issues and evidence, his published work and positions resist any such simple demarcation. Nevertheless, the study of religion embraced James most firmly as a psychologist and only then perhaps as a philosopher. This reception also meant there was distortion in the presentation of his work, which has been manifested by taking *The Varieties of Religious Experience* as the single guiding text to his thinking on religion. This was reinforced by engagements in the philosophy of religion that took claims about the veridicality and character of mysticism, and related experiences, as the central claim and contribution from James. The reception was also shaped by the fact the James's major work emerges in the era following the 1893 World Parliament of Religions. The fact that he attends to interreligious themes through his work on mysticism gave added force to the selectivity of concepts and ideas, associating James inaccurately with what came to be known as the perennial philosophy.[7]

The "science of religion" agenda delineated in James's eighteenth Gifford lecture and the popularity of *The Varieties* gave further impetus to the emphasis on the thematic of mysticism within the study of religion. Grace Jantzen has shown that James's model of mysticism shaped the dominant reading of what constitutes "mysticism" in the philosophical and popular imagination of the twentieth century, as well as showing how readers failed to appreciate its modernist construction.[8] What has not been given sufficient notice is that James only proposed his four marks of mysticism (ineffability, the noetic quality, transiency, and passivity) "for the purposes of the present lectures," as a means of pursuing the more narrow question of whether religious propositional claims have broad warrants for truth.[9] James concludes that they do not. Nonetheless, writers like Evelyn Underhill, in her own study of mysticism, framed the Jamesian legacy soon after *The Varieties*.[10]

The philosophical reception of religious experience also focused on *The Varieties* and *The Will to Believe* and little else besides, even though some of James's most serious philosophical work, which he connected directly with religion, lay elsewhere (radical empiricism and pragmatism). In effect, James was positioned to get the least out of his texts, and his full scope of contributions was fragmented and only selectively used. The reigning assumption in this reception was that James through *Varieties* offered a definitive definition (religion as private, individual, and subjective feelings) and a definitive method (the evidentiary consideration of religious experiences). In the process of construing this narrow interpretation, his wider philosophical perspectives and cross-disciplinary thinking were marginalized. James was aware of the potential problems in the "postscript" of *The Varieties* when he recognized "that my general philosophical position received such a scant a statement as hardly to be intelligible to some of my readers."[11] Lamberth has detailed both the connections of James's original plan for *Varieties* to radical empiricism and the reasons for James's failure to deliver it.[12] It is by locating James's work in his wider metaphysical understanding of pluralism and radical empiricism that we can enrich and rediscover the value of James for the contemporary study of religion.

CRITICAL READINGS: JAMES AS "CRITICAL PHILOSOPHER"

Reading James's reception within the study of religion reveals how his thought has been constrained. Nonetheless, there is an opportunity to read James anew, to free him from the disciplinary agendas of the twentieth-century study of religion and open a critical and creative thinker out in order to expand our horizons of thought. If we appreciate that there is a larger philosophical vision behind James's interventions, and a deep metaphysical and methodological commitment to pluralism, which is of contemporary relevance, we begin to see something new emerge. James's thinking about religion enables us to make at least two major reconfigurations for the study of religion.

James's Definition of Religion

In the nineteenth- and twentieth-century formation of the study of religion, there was a sustained desire to seek out definitions, methods, and approaches to support a budding, ambiguously interdisciplinary field. One weakness of this approach is that it extracted selected claims from nuanced and complex thinkers like James to support narrow disciplinary agendas. The key product of this approach was that the definition of religion became the distinguishing mark to position a thinker. Contrary to the work of anthologists and popular misrepresentations, *William James never gave a single definition to religion.* He always prefixed his claims about religion, as we noted in relation to mysticism, with hypothetical specifications such as the phrase "for the purposes of these lectures."[13] It is precisely here that we see the importance of positing James's thinking inside his novel and open metaphysical understanding, in which James understood and emphasized the contextual and functional nature of concepts. As James made clear as early as 1879: "Every way of classifying a thing is but a way of handling it for some particular purpose."[14] The occlusion of the contextual and temporal aspects of James's writing about religion results in a false solidification and narrowing of his thinking on the subject. We see this clearly in analyzing his working definition of religion in *The Varieties*, where he stated: "Religion, therefore, as I now ask you arbitrarily to take it, shall mean for us *the feelings, acts, and experiences of individual men in their solitude, so far as they apprehend themselves to stand in relation to whatever they may consider the divine.*"[15]

In many textbooks the crucial phrase "as I now ask you arbitrarily to take it" is omitted, and the provisional, contextual, and pragmatic application of the specification is lost. Although James has been criticized for using unclear terms, there is in his writing an awareness of the problems of using broad categories like religion. Ahead of his time, James asserts there is "no one essence" to the idea of religion.[16] James's critical and contextual reading of "religion" shows that contemporary debates about the category, and critiques of early essentialism in the classics of the field, themselves actually overlook the more careful foundational assessments in a thinker like James. A return to what James actually thought and wrote affirms the need for epistemological care and contextual self-awareness as much as empirical commitments.

The first way to reread James is to appreciate the fluidity of categories established in his "stream of consciousness" functional philosophy, a philosophy premised on a multiplicity of relations, some of which are empirically factual, and not merely created by the mind. This approach has been followed by Carrette who rereads James's deployments of the category of religion in order to retrieve the hidden tropes behind the dominant psychological and belief categories of religion.[17] Carrette uses James's metaphysics of relations to reveal how James can establish a multidimensional model of what constitutes "religion."[18] As James makes clear: "Religion has meant many things in human history."[19] We need to resist positioning James into one of a neat set of boxes and see how his thinking reflects a series of metaphysical insights and tensions. In this way, *The Varieties* becomes not simply a descriptive text, but one elaborating a series of metaphysical issues that cannot be separated from the wider trajectory of his thinking. It illustrates the need for an integrated reading that spans *The Principles* and *A Pluralistic Universe*.

Similarly, Lamberth has drawn attention to James's interest in what religion functions for in human life, both individually and socially, as a key both to interpreting James correctly and to making him useful for contemporary work.[20] This emphasis connects *The Varieties*'s concern with transformation to *Pragmatism*'s linking of religion to the social program of meliorism, a project of bettering the world according to our ideals.[21] By also attending to James's recognition of the plurality of rationality, Lamberth develops James's views to construct a functional account of religion as a dynamic means of reconciling the various rational demands in our lives, both individually and socially. This reading not only integrates and extends James's thinking, but also contributes significantly to critical discussions about how to think theoretically about religion without falling into the problems of definitions and essences.

One of the implications of taking James's situational definition of religion in *Varieties* as definitive is that James's gets positioned into a simple "individualistic" reading of religion.[22] While James upholds the importance of individuality, his emphasis on the individual is built into a broader social understanding of religion and interconnected nature of individuals. Many have failed fully to appreciate how James's thinking is built on social ideals. Cotkin has shown the social aspect of James's heroic ideal, Lamberth has shown how James's philosophical thinking is built on a social analogy, and Richardson has shown how *Varieties* holds a distinct social welfare analysis in its discussion of sainthood.[23] But these are only part of the picture. Within James's pragmatism there is a distinct social consciousness and program for public morality (meliorism) that he envisions in critical connection with religion. This line of thought is also evident in James's early ethical and evolutionary thinking and his later reaction against American imperialism.[24] This opening up of James to the social dimension of religion enables us to counteract the limited, individualistic, and subjectivist reading that has dominated until recently.[25]

The Science of Religion Enigma in James

In *The Will to Believe* James seeks to defend "the legitimacy of religious faith" and entertains the emerging ambitions for a "science of religion" in order to achieve this outcome.[26] James is clear that forms of religious belief—those that avoid dogmatic expression—have practical and ethical value. It is, however, not at all clear how James conceives such a "science" emerging and what the nature of such a project would be. Writers such as Henry Levinson believe that James "construed the *Varieties* as a rudimentary work in the science of religion," with a distinct method.[27] This view is supported by Proudfoot, who underlines a project to command equal weight to the natural sciences.[28] Other writers, such as Eugene Taylor, suggest that James's "science of religion" refers to "the development of a cross-cultural comparative psychology of subconscious states."[29] There is certainly a commitment to the "subliminal" in James's work, but there is also a "critical activity" after the things, as James states, "I myself a few moments ago pronounced."[30]

The "critical activity" in James is significant and often missed. Readers too frequently forget how nuanced and aware James is as a "critical philosopher."[31] Beyond the question of how committed James was to the science of religions idea, there are serious problems in extrapolating James's science of religions idea from his wider philosophical attitude and program. James read Max Mueller, and likely borrowed the "science of religion" idea from him. But in *Varieties* James is overt that his work is only "the beginning," something that might "eventually" have authority like the physical science. We might note, too, that James concluded that psychology "is no science, it is only the hope of a science."[32] This sense of a provisional "hope," with regard not only to psychology but to the even more nascent "science of religion," is significant. James is not limited in his purview of religious life, and he is careful in his qualifications. He "held out the notion" of "an impartial science of religion" and offered a "doorway" into the subject.[33] The science of religion in James, however, is not a foregone conclusion and is something he never completes. Lamberth's reading of *Varieties* qualifies speculation around the science of religions idea, suggesting that it was "post hoc" in the late chapters of *The Varieties*.[34] Lamberth also points out the fact that James "does not return substantively in print to the idea of a science of religion," likely because of his competing and eventually overriding interest in a pluralistic metaphysics.[35]

The pluralistic signal is pertinent in assessing James's reading of a science of religion. Lamberth enables us to see the importance of the stages of the discussion and provides useful qualifications. The science of religion discussion, although flagged much earlier in his career, remains a speculative trope at the end of *The Varieties*. Significantly, in the "Conclusion" to *The Varieties* we see a careful and detailed qualification of the science of religion option. First, the science of religions approach requires recognition of the "relations of theoretic to the active life."[36] There are limits for James within the science of religion approach, namely, that "knowledge about a thing is not the thing itself."[37] James follows this assertion with an important qualification, one ignored in the ambitions of those who aspire to the empire of science of religion. James asserts that "the science of religions may not be an equivalent for living religion; and if we turn to the inner difficulties of such a science, we see that a point comes when she must drop the purely theoretic attitude." Here the shift to pragmatism and meliorism as the more viable frame seems to be in view. There are further difficulties in the science of religions approach, not only those of reductive materialism, which James noted at the beginning of *The Varieties*, and the fact that sciences themselves are "full of conflicts."[38] In the "Conclusion" to *Varieties* James states that his "personal" and "experiential" approach is intended to counter scientific reductionism. It is important within the diversity of assessments, therefore, to consider the deeper context. After suggesting both a science of religions and the importance of the subliminal in psychology, James's "Conclusion" ends with a discussion of "over-beliefs" (conceptual extensions made to make sense of things) and the "more" (that which is beyond us), as well as his recognition of "partial systems" and "plurality," both of which also entail a critique of "science."

James manifests a strong desire to make "religion" into something of continuing viability in the modern world. From his earliest work he insisted on linking "science" and "religion," particularly through an appeal to empirical observation, and he continuously sought to bridge the two. He wanted to show that "empiricism" can be the friend of religion and even announced a "new era of religion" insofar as it embraced empiricism.[39] But James did not mean the empiricism that came to dominate through logical and scientific positivism. Instead, the empiricism James had in view was a radical one, since it placed experience within the world of fact, which itself includes felt and observed relationality.[40] The "empirical" in this sense thus stands over against mainstream "science" and checks its limits. This qualification of "science" is important and marks the last parts of *The Varieties*; James himself there places "science" in quotation marks.[41]

Strikingly, one of the duties of a "science of religions" is to keep religion and the study thereof in "connection" with other sciences.[42] But we also see that James's own "over-belief" (at least in 1902) is one that affirms "many worlds of consciousness" and questions the "sectarian scientist's attitude" and "scientific laws."[43] Science, even as it carries "the scientific name," can get caught in "humbug." As James declares: "the total expression of human experience, as I view it objectively, invincibly urges me beyond the narrow 'scientific' bounds."[44] If we are to understand the science of religions suggestion, we need to contextualize James's thinking in terms of his rejection of dogmatic thought in theology, philosophy, and science, as well as his commitment to radical empiricism, the immediacy of feeling, relationality, and experience.[45] James is critical of dogma wherever it emerges—in science, philosophy, or theology. In the last analysis of James's whole trajectory of thought, the "reconciling hypothesis" of the science of religion is superseded by his final "pluralistic hypothesis."[46] A "science of religion" can only provide limited understanding, and limited methods, because for James any closed system of understanding restricts knowledge. These are the themes of his Hibbert Lectures, *A Pluralistic Universe*, a text Lamberth has shown as the culmination of James's thinking.[47]

CONCLUSION: THE PRODUCTIVE VALUE OF REREADING JAMES

The centenary of William James's death in 2010 has brought a renewed focus on his work, and thus suggested critical rereading. Particularly, it offers a chance to overcome the disciplinary regimes that reduce James's texts to some of their parts, whether in psychology, philosophy, or religion. The challenge is to read James again with a new critical consciousness, beyond and through those disciplinary spaces. The ideas expressed here reflect just some examples from the wider work of Carrette and Lamberth on how to conduct such a rereading, attentive to his philosophical attitude and metaphysical approach to knowledge and reality. But there are also other, new critical depths within James's thinking potentially available, particularly since the completion in 2007 of *The Correspondence of William James*, depths that will further widen and clarify the scope of his thinking and provide a context for appreciating his personal concerns and intentions alongside his published aims.[48] James's vision for modern knowledge, as for life, was one that sought always to keep "the doors and windows open."[49] His critical challenge for us is to overcome the desire, in an age of modern imperialism, to capture things within closed systems of knowledge. Instead, we must recognize our thinking and action as of a piece, situated in a plural and open world that is, nonetheless, our own evolving environment. James sought to put knowledge to work, as a means of bettering life. For James the most "pregnant of all the dilemmas of philosophy" was that between the "one and the many," and in this we see the mark of the competing desires that drive all our knowing and acting.[50] The challenge and promise of reading James, particularly for the study of religion, are to explore the critical depth of the plurality of this many-sided universe, against those who wish to build the empire of the "one" in whichever field of study.

NOTES

1. G. Cotkin, *William James: Public Philosopher* (Urbana: University of Illinois Press, 1989).
2. J. Carrette, *William James's Hidden Religious Imagination* (New York: Routledge, 2013).
3. Jeremy Carrette, ed., *William James and the Varieties of Religious Experience* (London: Routledge, 2005).
4. D. Lamberth, "Putting 'Experience' to the Test in Theological Reflection," *Harvard Theological Review* 3, no. 1 (January 2000): 67–77.
5. Eric Sharpe, *A Comparative History of Religion* (Chicago: Open Court, 1986), 108.

6. D. Wulff, *Psychology of Religion: Classic and Contemporary Views* (New York: Wiley, 1997).

7. A. Huxley, *The Perennial Philosophy* (New York: Harper and Brothers, 1945).

8. G. Jantzen, "Mysticism and Experience," *Religious Studies* 25 (September 1989): 295–315.

9. William James, *The Varieties of Religious Experience* (Glasgow: Collins, 1960), 367; D. Lamberth, *William James and the Metaphysics of Experience* (Cambridge: Cambridge University Press, 1999), 122.

10. E. Underhill, *Mysticism: The Nature and Development of Spiritual Consciousness* (Oxford: Oneworld, 1999).

11. James, *Varieties of Religious Experience*, 495.

12. Lamberth, *Metaphysics of Experience*.

13. James, *Varieties of Religious Experience*, 28.

14. William James, *The Will to Believe, and Other Essays in Popular Philosophy* (New York: Dover, 1987), 63.

15. James, *Varieties of Religious Experience*, 31.

16. Ibid., 26.

17. Carrette, *Hidden Religious Imagination*.

18. Ibid.; J. Carrette, *William James on Religion* (London: Equinox, forthcoming).

19. James, *The Will to Believe*, 51.

20. Lamberth, *Metaphysics of Experience*; D. Lamberth, *Religion: A Pragmatic Approach* (Cambridge: Cambridge University Press, forthcoming).

21. S. Shamdasani, "Psychologies as Ontology-Making Practices: William James and the Pluralities of Psychological Experience," in *William James and the Varieties of Religious Experience*, ed. J. Carrette (London: Routledge, 2005), 27–44.

22. C. Taylor, *Varieties of Religion Today: William James Revisited* (Cambridge, Mass.: Harvard University Press, 2002).

23. Cotkin, *Public Philosopher*; D. Lamberth, "Interpreting the Universe After a Social Analogy: Intimacy, Panpsychism, and a Finite God in a Pluralistic Universe," in *The Cambridge Companion to William James*, ed. Ruth Anna Putnam (Cambridge: Cambridge University Press, 1997), 237–59; R. Richardson, *William James in the Maelstrom of American Modernism* (Boston: Houghton Mifflin, 2006), 410–11.

24. William James, "Great Men and Their Environment," in *The Will to Believe* (New York: Dover, 1880), 216–54; William James, "The Moral Philosopher and the Moral Life," in *The Will to Believe* (New York: Dover, 1891), 184–215; William James, "Remarks at the Peace Banquet," in *Memories and Studies* (Sioux Falls, S. Dak.: NuVision, 2008), 113–15; William James, *Pragmatism*, in *Pragmatism and Other Writings* (London: Penguin, 2000), 1–132.

25. Carrette, *Hidden Religious Imagination*; Carrette, *Varieties of Religious Experience*.

26. James, *The Will to Believe*, x, xii.

27. H. S. Levinson, *Science, Metaphysics and the Chance of Salvation* (Missoula, Mont.: Scholars Press, 1978), 183.

28. W. Proudfoot, *William James and a Science of Religions* (New York: Columbia University Press, 2004), 2.

29. E. Taylor, review of *William James and a Science of Religions*, by Wayne Proudfoot, *Religious Studies* 41, no.4 (December, 2005): 488.

30. James, *Varieties of Religious Experience*, 462.

31. Ibid., 480.

32. Cf. William James, *Psychology: The Briefer Course* (Notre Dame: University of Notre Dame, 1985), 335; James, *Varieties of Religious Experience*, 433.

33. James, *The Varieties of Religious Experience*, 486, 488.

34. Lamberth, *Metaphysics of Experience*.

35. Lamberth, *Religion*.

36. James, *Varieties of Religious Experience*, 467.

37. Ibid.

38. Ibid., 468.

39. William James, *A Pluralistic Universe* (Lincoln: University of Nebraska Press, 1996).

40. William James, "A World of Pure Experience," in *Essays in Radical Empiricism* (New York: Dover, 2003), 21–47. William James, *The Meaning of Truth*, in *Pragmatism and the Meaning of Truth* (Cambridge, Mass.: Harvard University Press, 1996), 314.

41. James, *Varieties of Religious Experience*, 488.

42. Ibid., 486.

43. Ibid., 493.

44. Ibid.

45. Ibid., 430.

46. Ibid., 500.

47. D. Lamberth, "*A Pluralistic Universe* a Century Later: Rationality, Pluralism, and Religion," in *William James's Transatlantic Conversation*, ed. J. Rasmussen, and M. Halliwell (Oxford: Oxford University Press, 2014); Lamberth, *Metaphysics of Experience*; Lamberth, "Interpreting the Universe."

48. Richardson, *Maelstrom of American Modernism*; E. K. Sutton, "Marcus Aurelius, William James and the 'Science of Religions,'" *William James Studies* 4 (2009): 70–89; E. K. Sutton, "When Misery and Metaphysics Collide: William James on 'the Problem of Evil,'" *Medical History* 55, no. 3 (July 2011): 389–92.

49. William James, *Some Problems of Philosophy* (Lincoln: University of Nebraska Press, 1996), 100.

50. Ibid., 114.

20

Rudolf Otto and the Idea of the Holy

GREGORY ALLES

Rudolf Otto (1869–1937) was a German Protestant theologian and philosopher of religion best known for seeing the source of religion in what he called "numinous" experience. This term refers to an experience of, in his terms, a *mysterium tremendum et fascinans* ("an awe-inspiring yet fascinating mystery"). Otto claimed that most if not all people come equipped with a device that makes this experience possible, a *sensus numinis* (a "sense for, or ability to be aware of, the numinous"). He exercised considerable influence on the study of religion in the middle of the twentieth century, and the word "numinous," which he coined, has since found its way into the vocabulary of scholars of literature and the arts. The phrase *mysterium tremendum* also now appears as an entry in the *Oxford English Dictionary*.

OTTO'S LIFE AND WORLD

Otto grew up in a well-to-do, devout north German family. Like many others of his generation, he wrestled in his youth with the results of nineteenth-century science and scholarship, especially Darwinian evolution and the historical study of the Bible. As a young university student of theology, he felt compelled to abandon the traditional Christianity with which he grew up and embraced instead a kind of Protestant theology that sought religious truth in the experience of individual persons, above all, individual Christians. This shift ultimately culminated in his identification and analysis of the numinous.

From his early days Otto was an inveterate traveler. In 1911–12 he made a "world tour"—actually a trip through North Africa, India, China, Japan, and Russia—that marked a shift of his attention away from the philosophy and toward the comparative study of religion. Subsequently, he learned Sanskrit and published translations of a number of texts as well as comparative studies of Indian religions and Christianity. Following the publication of his most famous book, *The Idea of the Holy*, in the fall of 1916 (dated 1917), he became professor of systematic theology at the University of Marburg, a position from which he retired in 1927, citing reasons of ill health. In autumn 1936 he fell, or perhaps jumped, from a tower and died of complications the following March.

Otto is most remembered today for a single book, *The Idea of the Holy: An Inquiry Into the Non-Rational Factor in the Idea of the Divine and Its Relation to the Rational* (1917, English translation 1923). Most accounts of it, however, tend to be overly simple. Other major publications include (dates of English translations in brackets): *Naturalism and Religion* (1904 [1907]), *The Philosophy of Religion Based on Kant and Fries* (1909 [1931]), *Mysticism East and West: A Comparative Analysis of the Nature of Mysticism* (1926 [1932]), *India's Religion of Grace and Christianity Compared and Contrasted* (1930), *Religious Essays: A Supplement to the Idea of the Holy* (1931), and *The Kingdom of God and the Son of Man: A Study in the History of Religion* (1934 [1943]).

In addition to being a scholar, Otto was active in politics from his student days onward, serving as a representative in the Prussian legislature during World War I and founding in the 1920s a group to promote world peace through interreligious understanding, the Religiöser Menschheitbund (Religious League of Humanity). He also founded a museum for religious artifacts that still exists, the Religionskundliche Sammlung at the University of Marburg.

AN APOLOGIST FOR RELIGION

Otto began his academic career as an apologist. He wanted to argue that, despite the advances of the natural sciences and history, it still made sense to be religious. He was influenced above all by two thinkers, Friedrich Schleiermacher (1768–1834) and, after 1904, Jakob Friedrich Fries (1773–1843), both heavily indebted to German Pietism.

In *Naturalism and Religion* (1904), Otto took on Darwinian evolution and mechanistic explanations of the world. He accepted the results of science but claimed that science by itself was insufficient. For example, natural selection is able to explain evolution without invoking final causes (purposes, intentions), but human action still requires them. Human brains may be material objects, but one cannot account for the experience of consciousness in terms of the mechanistic interactions of chemicals. Most fundamentally, Otto insisted that every scientific explanation is accompanied by mystery. Why is there something rather than nothing, and why is the universe as it is and not somehow different? As Otto's thinking developed, this "mystery" not only made it justifiable to be religious but also provided the key to understanding religion.

Five years later, Otto wrote *The Philosophy of Religion*, a book intended to introduce theology students to the thought of Fries. Among other points, Otto emphasized that all knowledge rests ultimately upon *Gefühl*. The word is related to the English word "feeling," but Otto meant it in a cognitive rather than an emotive sense, as in a "hunch" or "feeling," in the sense of "a feeling that . . . " Even the rules of logic, he claimed, rest upon the sense or feeling we have that they are correct. At the same time, Otto reconceived of theology. Modern theology, he claimed, was not dogmatic but scientific. It was a *Religionswissenschaft*, a "science of religion," and as such it had three branches: the philosophy of religion, which, similar to Kant's analysis of knowledge, showed what made religion possible; the psychology of religion, which examined how religion manifested itself in internal experience; and the history of religions, which detailed the unfolding of religion in the human species over time. *The Idea of the Holy* was Otto's major contribution to the descriptive psychology of religion.

THE HOLY AS A COMPLEX CATEGORY

The Idea of the Holy was never intended to be a comprehensive account of religion. It merely analyzed the experience upon which all religion allegedly rests. Otto claimed that this experience was captured by a category that was unique to religion, the category of "the Holy."

A century before Otto, Fries had developed an "anthropological" approach to philosophy. That is, he did not think that it was possible to prove the truth of metaphysical principles. The most one could do was show that all (human) minds shared them. In this demonstration, introspection played a large role. Otto's approach to the Holy was similar. No one could actually *demonstrate* that the Holy was ontologically real. All anyone could do was to note the presence of the experience in most normally functioning human minds. In contentious words, Otto invited readers who could not recall such an experience simply to stop reading. Like a person blind from birth trying to understand color, they were trying to understand an experience that was beyond them.

For Otto, the "Holy" was a complex category. Over time it had acquired the meaning of "morally pure,"[1] but originally, Otto claimed, it had no moral content. Consider "the Holy One of Israel" killing Uzzah simply because in doing a good deed he happened to touch a holy object, the Ark of the Covenant.[2] Otto called this original, nonmoral dimension of the Holy the "numinous." No one could actually describe this dimension. Instead, somewhat as in the well-known Zen image of a finger pointing at the moon, all anyone could do was point toward it and try to evoke it.

In "pointing toward" the numinous, Otto used three Latin words: *mysterium, tremendum,* and *fascinans*.[3] The numinous is a *mysterium*. It is not simply something that many of us do not understand, like the circuitry of a computer's central processing unit. It is completely different (in Otto's German, *ganz anders*) from anything that we know and can know. It is, further, a *mysterium tremendum*, a mystery that makes us feel as if we are nothing—a feeling more basic than Schleiermacher's feeling of absolute dependence—and fills us with awe and dread. Finally, it is a *mysterium fascinans*. It attracts as well as repels us, for in the numinous human beings encounter love and grace.

Despite all that, Otto insisted that the numinous could not really be expressed in concepts. That is what he meant when he called it "nonrational": it was beyond human thought and reasoning. Nevertheless, as a Christian theologian, he also insisted that the Holy had a rational side, for people, especially in "higher" religions, consistently associated it with specific concepts. Clearly these two claims are contradictory. To explain the relationship between the nonrational and the rational, the inconceivable and human conceptualization, Otto borrowed a term from Kant, "schematization," which refers to the way in which we associate concepts with perceptual experiences, and a psychological "law of association," according to which some feelings routinely arouse other, similar feelings. Certain aspects of our encounter with the numinous, he said, tend to evoke identifications that, although not entirely proper, nonetheless recur. For example, the power of the Holy—for theists, God's power—is utterly different in quality, not just in quantity, from the various kinds of power that we can conceptualize, such as the power of nature or of a human ruler. Nevertheless, the *mysterium tremendum* reminds people of those other kinds of power. As a result, they speak of the Holy as being "powerful."

Another rational dimension of the Holy belongs, Otto claimed, to the realm of value. We are all aware of the meaning of "Holy" as something "morally pure." What is at stake here for Otto, however, is something greater than mere purity. For him, the Holy is a category of absolute, ultimate value. When human beings sense its presence, they also sense their own utter worthlessness. They are, in Jewish and Christian terms, "sinful."

The relationship between the Holy and human experience is, then, a subtle one. On the one hand, Otto insists, various experiences can evoke a sense of the numinous in those who are attuned to it. Hieratic language, already suggested by Otto's use of Latin, is one common means to do so. Examples include the way Christians use Hebrew phrases whose meanings they do not understand and the apparent nonsense syllables in various mantras. Otto also sees a particularly close relationship between the Holy and a characteristic of profound art, the sublime. The latter, Otto says, suggests the numinous. To his mind, however, art has even more direct ways to express the numinous: darkness, silence, and—more common in Asian than in European art—emptiness. As examples, he cites Gothic cathedrals, quietly profound music, and Chinese painting. On the other hand, while a sense of the Holy is evoked by experience, the Holy is not something that one learns from experience. It is a category a priori, one that we bring to experience—if, that is, we detect it at all. All of its dimensions, nonrational, rational, and the relationship between the two, are in our minds prior to experience. They are only "called" by our experiences, the way certain sequences of events "call" the a priori category of "causality." (Obviously, Otto did not use programming terminology.) In other words, the Holy is a structure of human consciousness; it is built into the operating system of the mind. Ever the Kantian, Otto referred to this as a specific mental faculty. He called it the "faculty of divination," or *sensus numinis*, what in more contemporary language we might call a "numinous detection device."

COMPARING RELIGIONS

Only a few of Otto's later publications directly expanded upon the ideas advanced in *The Idea of the Holy*. The most notable was a collection of essays published in

English under the title *Religious Essays*. Other later writings went in different directions. Perhaps the most important were comparative.

Mysticism East and West and *India's Religion of Grace and Christianity* probably seemed to make larger contributions at the time when they first appeared than they do today, because less was known then about the religions of India.[4] The first volume compares the German mystic Meister Eckhart with the Indian philosopher Śankara (ca. 800 CE); the second compares notions of salvation in Indian traditions of *bhakti* and Protestant Christianity. In the end, Otto's finds that Christianity is superior to Indian traditions. Śankara lacks Meister Eckhart's active engagement with the world, while the Indian *bhakti* traditions lack a parallel to the cross.

The Kingdom of God and the Son of Man is not comparative per se, but it does discuss two different religious strands, Jewish and "Aryan." These two combine, Otto claims, in the person and teachings of Jesus. Otto presents Jesus not as a rabbi but as a charismatic evangelist-*cum*-exorcist. In his teaching Jesus replaced the Jewish tradition of "the day of YHWH" as taught by John the Baptist with a notion of the Kingdom of Heaven that had Iranian and Indo-Iranian roots. In retrospect it is somewhat eerie that a book published in Germany in 1934 would emphasize a charismatic individual utilizing Aryan traditions to proclaim a new kingdom (*Reich*) and bring salvation (*Heil*). Otto was, however, careful to emphasize the essential contribution of Judaism to Christianity at a time when the German Christians were trying to de-Judaize Christianity altogether,

RECEPTION, CRITICISM, REJECTION

By the time of Otto's death, theologians in Germany had almost entirely rejected his attempt to conceive of theology as a "naturalistic" *Religionswissenschaft*. In their view it was not possible to discover religious truth by studying human thought and behavior—or better, since they associated "religion" with human effort and activity, one could not discover God's Truth that way. That was because, in the words of Karl Barth, there was an "infinite qualitative distinction" between the divine and the human; God's Truth, the truth of the Gospel, necessarily irrupted into the world through revelation as the Word of God. To such theologians, Otto's museum of religions was nothing but a house of idols.

Otto's thought found a more favorable reception among scholars who wished to study religions comparatively, such as Friedrich Heiler, Gustav Mensching, and Ernst Benz. In this context it resonated with similar emphases on experience and holiness among thinkers as disparate as William James, Nathan Söderblom, and Alfred North Whitehead. After the Second World War a distinctive, independent academic enterprise devoted to the study of religions developed virtually throughout the globe. Although Otto's ideas had taken shape in order to defend religion for liberal practitioners, scholars now turned to those ideas to justify the new academic field. If religion resulted from an experience that was ultimately sui generis and in principle not reducible to or expressible in any other terms, they argued, then it required a separate academic discipline. At the same time, creative writers and artists also took up the term "numinous." Given Otto's concern with the sublime and the alleged ability of art to evoke numinous awareness, perhaps that was inevitable.

By the end of the twentieth century, however, Otto's influence had waned. Several factors are probably responsible. First, his ideas have internal inconsistencies. For example, if the Holy really is *wholly* other, it would be impossible for human beings to talk about it at all or even to apprehend it preconceptually. Again, it would seem contradictory to assert both that the Holy reminds people of natural things *and* that it does not share at all in the qualities of these natural things. Furthermore, the closer one looks, the harder it is to make sense of Otto's ideas about schematization. In each of these cases, the exaggerated rhetoric of religious insiders would seem to have impeded meaningful analysis.

Second, as normative discourse, it may make some sense to claim that true religion is rooted in numinous experience (provided one accepts that claim). As a description of everything that we are inclined to call religion, it does not. As Ninian Smart pointed out, Otto's account of the numinous is not even a reasonably accurate description of what we call mystical experience. Note, too, that scholars of religions have also become much more careful about distinguishing their work from theology.

Third, scholars sympathetic to Otto moved in other directions. For example, Joachim Wach sought fundamental types of what he called "religious expression" that bore no recognizable genetic relationship to either Otto's or his own account of religious experience. Mircea Eliade lauded Otto but wanted instead to examine the basic forms in which the Sacred manifested itself in the realm of the profane.

Fourth, a "linguistic turn" that occurred in many areas of thought in the mid-twentieth century emphasized the role of language in constructing and evoking experience, making any appeal to a primary, preconceptual, and in principle nonconceptualizable experience suspect.

Fifth, as Jonathan Z. Smith has pointed out, assigning religion to the internal recesses of an abstracted, atomized individual seems inadequate when faced with the view of religion as social formation emphasized by French theorists in the tradition of Durkheim. Later developments in the sociology of religion, such as rational choice and network theories, have only made Otto's move less tenable.

Sixth, the emergence of postmodern and poststructural thought and critical theory has called into question any notion that there is an "essence" of religion, much less the essence described by Otto. These trends have also critically interrogated the political agendas that previously sustained such claims.

Finally, and most recently, people studying consciousness and cognition have rejected fundamental moves that Otto's analysis of the Holy presupposes. Otto's claims about impossibility notwithstanding, neuroscientists have sought to correlate religious experience with physical events in the human brain. Cognitive scientists working on the level of mental activity have, like Otto, emphasized types of processing "hardwired" into the brain, but they do so not in terms of a peculiar kind of phenomenological experience but in terms of kinds of concepts and processes associated with the memory, transmission, and social perdurance of concepts.

Elements of Otto's program may still be found. One example may be work on *Religionsästhetik*, the study of how religion utilizes and affects the senses, which is an active concern on the continent of Europe. These directions are pursued, however, largely apart from any attention to Otto's thought.[5]

NOTES

1. This is perhaps stronger in German than in English. German-speakers use the word *heilig*, "Holy," when English-speakers use the word "saint." For example, in German Saint Elizabeth is *die heilige Elisabeth*.

2. 2 Samuel 6:6–8.

3. Later scholars of religious studies have also used the phrase *mysterium fascinosum*, presumably without realizing that before the modern era this Latin word was a *hapax legomenon*, that is, a word used only once, and that it seems to have been used in the sense of "having a large *fascinum*," that is, a large penis (*Oxford Latin Dictionary*, ed. P. G. W. Glare, s.v. *fascinosus, -a, -um*).

4. Otto tends not to use the term "Hinduism." For example, in *The Idea of the Holy* the word "Hindu" appears twice, but otherwise Otto speaks of "Indian religion(s)" (four times), "the Indian pantheon" (twice), "Indian gods" (once), "Indian mysticism" (once), "the Indian Sankhya system" (once), "Indian terminology" (once, speaking about the words *rakṣas* and *Brahman/Brahmā*), "the Indian world" (once), and "the Īśvara of India" (once)—but never Hinduism.

5. For further reading, see Philip C. Almond, *Rudolf Otto: An Introduction to His Philosophical Theology* (Chapel Hill: University of North Carolina Press, 1984); Todd A. Gooch, *The Numinous and Modernity: An Interpretation of Rudolf Otto's Philosophy of Religion* (Berlin: de Gruyter, 2000); Rudolf Otto, *The Idea of the Holy*, trans. John W. Harvey (London: Oxford University Press, 1973); Melissa Raphael, *Rudolf Otto and the Concept of Holiness* (New York: Oxford University Press, 1997).

21

Jung on Religion

VOLNEY GAY

Carl Gustav Jung (1875–1961), a Swiss psychiatrist, tried to account for the persistence of archaic religion and other behaviors contrary to norms of rationalist metaphysics and rationalist psychologies. He also developed the notion of psychological types and the concepts of introversion and extraversion. For a short time he aligned himself with Sigmund Freud but they parted company on the issue of the psychology of religion. Freud saw religion as an infantile holdover; Jung saw it as a symbolic expression of the hidden structures of the mind. Humans could no more forsake religion, Jung argued, than they could forsake breathing air.[1]

Freud said that the mind is tripartite: a conscious level sits upon a preconscious level, and both rest upon the unconscious (sometimes called the system Unconsciousness, or Ucs.). Jung, an assiduous student of Freudian theory from around 1902 to 1910, accepted this tripartite model but added to it a deeper level, the collective unconscious. The origins of this latter concept appear in Jung's earliest studies of psychiatric patients when he wrote about "psychic constellations" and "complexes."[2] He later subsumed both terms under the rubric "archetype." Jung showed that schizophrenic patients' fantasies replicated those seen in the dreams of normal people and that both were surprisingly similar to the myths of Western, Eastern, and archaic religions. Accounting for this fact defined Jung's greatest book, *Symbols of Transformation*, and his life's work: "I took it upon myself to get to know 'my' myth, and I regarded this as the task of tasks."[3]

Like Freud, Jung distinguished between two types of thinking: thinking with words and thinking with images or symbols, the latter being the more ancient and evocative: "When an idea is so old and so generally believed, it must be true in some way, . . . it is psychologically true."[4] He adds, "One could almost say that if all the world's traditions were cut off at a single blow, the whole of mythology and the whole history of religion would start all over again with the next generation."[5]

Modern peoples have inherited biologically based tendencies toward mythological thinking and thus archaic fantasies are objective, factual presences: "The God-image thrown up by a spontaneous act of creation is a living figure, a being that exists in its own right and therefore confronts its ostensible creator autonomously."[6]

Symbols of Transformation is a five-hundred-page tour de force of scholarship and imagination wound around a few pages of reverie by a young American woman, code-named Miss Miller, whose musings and wishes—sparked by a voyage on the Black Sea—were published in 1898. When *Memories, Dreams, Reflections (MDR)*, his shockingly honest autobiography, appeared fifty years later, Jung revealed that he composed *Symbols of Transformation* during a tumultuous time when he feared for his sanity.[7] Jung treats Miss Miller's fantasies as a kind of test case, an unpolished gem onto which he mapped the world's religious and literary heritage and thereby revealed universal themes. To her banal publication Jung linked ancient myths, world religions, philosophy, poetry, and the highest and lowest arts. Each springs from a common, shared foundation, the collective unconscious, and each shows iterations of the contents of the Collective, the archetypes.

Archetypes (or "original shapes") are forms of the instincts; there are, therefore, as many archetypes as there are instincts. (Indeed, any animal with rudimentary consciousness must have archetypes.) Archetypes are universal, precognitive structures that shape all subsequent human efforts at self-consciousness, ranging from Miss Miller's musings to the Sistine Chapel, the Bhagavad Gita, the Hebrew Bible, and every so-called primitive religion. For example, because human biology entails the capacity or entity we call "self," all religious systems reveal instances of the Self archetype using numinous and poetic imagery to do so. Thus numerous mystics, poets, and religious authorities, as well as primitive philosophers, assert that in the depths of the human psyche dwells a "sun-god" image or that the sun is a god, indeed, the chief god. Jung agrees: libido, the sun, and the high god are iterations of a single, underlying archetype, the Self. In sharp contrast to Freud's focus upon sexuality, Jung says that "Libido is . . . the name for the energy which manifests itself in the life-process and is perceived subjectively as conation and desire."[8]

Because individuals and their cultures must deal with human biological realities represented by the archetypes, coherent persons and cultures will be religious: "Religion is one of the greatest helps in the psychological process of adaptation."[9] This separates Jung from Freud and it distinguishes his system and values from those of his mentor. Freud used terms like "castration anxiety" and "incest barrier"; Jung used terms like "sacrifice" and "conservative adherence to earlier attitudes."[10]

THE ADVENT OF ANALYTICAL PSYCHOLOGY

Like Freud, most modern people abjure belief in spirits and seek always for the biological source of disease. Modern patients speak about their neuroses as if their psychical disorders were actual maladies; yet, at the same time they reduce them to the merely imaginary. In the same way, modern peoples—including rationalist theologians—reject traditional dogma. Jung says that they are dead wrong. Dogma lives and changes through time yet is always essentially the same because it emerges out of the collective unconscious; dogma represents an honest and brave confrontation with biological truths. For that reason, neurotic disorders are as real and as cancerous as the neurotic fears them to be. As he noted in his first studies of the Word Association Test (WAT), Jung says that unconscious complexes seen in modern mental illnesses act within the patient as if they were autonomous beings. This phenomenological truth emerges from the archetypical origins or psychological conflicts.

In a similar way, Jung used phenomenology to distinguish ordinary dreams from great (archetypal, or AT) dreams; the former derive from conflicts between the ego and the personal (so-called Freudian) unconscious, the latter derive from conflicts between the ego and the collective unconscious. More so, AT dreams reveal the separate and independent existence of an unconscious and automatic mechanism that attempts to compensate for the errors and exaggerations of consciousness. Thus, a man's exaggerated focus upon hypermasculine attributes will evoke from the collective unconscious archaic images of the anima, the contrasexual AT of men (which corresponds to the animus, the contrasexual AT of women.)

AT dreams always have religious and numinous qualities. AT dreams appear throughout *MDR* and they demarcate moments in Jung's life when he comes to a point of decision and crisis. Like Dante's portrait of the poet about to confront hell itself in *The Divine Comedy* (set on the night before Good Friday, 1300), AT dreams prefigure the ego's confrontation with powers and needs deeper than mere consciousness. From secret, tormenting dreams that he shared with no one, through his youth, Jung's dreams occurred, he says, at turning points when he had to confront the duality of his inner world, his number one personality (what he later termed the Ego) and his number two personality (an aspect of the Self). For example, after dreaming about a gigantic radiolarian (a circular, single-celled creature) Jung's doubts about his choice of career—between the arts and the sciences—were resolved. After he had developed AT psychology, Jung interpreted the radiolarian—with its circular, organic, and natural structure—as an AT symbol of wholeness and individuation. Like numerous religious images of balance and completion—such as the Cross or the Star of David—this dream image prefigures the goal of life, the individuation of the Self.

While Jung refused to include his autobiography in his collected scientific works, the book is a treasure trove of Jung's inward thoughts and illustrations of his key concepts. For example, early in *MDR* Jung describes his intense suffering in grade school. Through a brilliant series of creative acts, he fashioned a secret representation of himself, a carved manikin, and gave it a magic stone. When troubled or depressed, he could examine the manikin in secret and comfort himself. Jung recalled these stories when he composed *Symbols of Transformation* in 1910. In those creative moments he says, "I knew I was worthy of myself."[11]

SIGMUND FREUD AND THE RECOVERY
OF ARCHAIC RELIGION

Jung never claimed that his ideas were new: in fact he argued precisely the opposite. Yet they were new to the twentieth century. He felt that it was given to him to
rediscover these concepts (or truths), while others, equally gifted and even more
brilliant, like Nietzsche, fell into psychological illness. Jung preserved himself against
their fate by his psychiatric training and by spiritual exercises. This let him confront
ghostlike terrors: "These conversations with the dead formed a kind of prelude
to what I had to communicate to the world."[12] Those communications began in
moments of near-hallucinatory experience well represented in his essay "Septem
Sermones ad Mortuo" (Seven Sermons to the Dead), half-incantation, half-lecture,
which he published as an appendix to *MDR*.

Jung mounted vivid and passionate defenses of theological dogma and vivid and
heartfelt attacks on modern rationalism and mediocre intellectuals. His modern patients, especially scientists who shared the biases of Freud and others, showed, Jung
says, that their abhorrence of the inner world of AT symbols—their attacks upon
"naive" religion—emerged from their defense against the pull of the collective unconscious. Thus modern peoples dream in images that were common parlance two thousand years ago. However, lacking access to a sophisticated (ancient) wisdom, these
archaic images terrify them. All such images and the AT dreams in which they appear
are religious phenomenon. They represent the AT drive toward rebalancing the psyche.
As Jung never tires of saying, religions are, on the whole, psychotherapeutic systems.

A similar irrepressible urge toward rebalance occurs at the level of cultural representation. This principle drives Jung's analysis of the Christian dogma of the Trinity.
This dogma is limited, Jung says, not only because it is restricted to one sex (male),
but also because it is also unbalanced: three is unstable; four is stable. Through
his vast readings, his self-analysis, and the study of his patients' dreams, Jung became convinced that the quaternity archetype—a universal symbol of balance and
completion—had been suppressed in the West. Because the psyche seeks equilibrium,
we must expect to find in contemporary religiosity representations of female deities
and finally recognition of the divine female. When fully acknowledged culture as a
whole will recognize the quaternity. Thus, Jung argued, the ancient dogma of the
Trinity, a central facet of the Church's teaching, cannot remain unchallenged. Jung
adds another dimension to the Trinity: *to somaton*, which means "the earth" or "the
body." Jung developed his thoughts on the Trinity in an essay published in 1937. In
1950 the Catholic Church raised Mary to the status of Queen of Heaven.[13] Jung took
this as a confirmation of his views, views that originated in his boyhood struggles
with the Trinity and with his father's stubborn form of rationalist Lutheranism that
did not ponder the mystery of how three could also be one. It also illustrates his
claim that extrasensitive persons, like artists and mystics, prefigure in their individual
visions spiritual crises that will emerge later in the larger culture.

Feelings of sublime harmony, and similar religious experiences, are difficult to
explain by rationalist values; instead, Jung says we should note them as signs of a
genuine encounter with AT symbols. Thus, our feelings are of the utmost importance

in ascertaining the degree to which a dream or vision or other artifact is archetypal. In all such instances—as he did with Miss Miller's fantasies—Jung adds to the patient's associations his own, more learned associations drawn from classical literature and arcane subjects. Thus, he says that the quaternity is an archetypal entity, and while it is "entirely absent from [contemporary] dogma," it must reappear.[14] In a similar way, modern patients reveal in their dreams AT images that are not overtly religious. Describing one patient's religiosity and his specific Christian identity, Jung says that at the center of the patient's mandala (sacred circle) "we find no trace of a deity . . . but, on the contrary, a mechanism."[15] In fact, Jung says, in most patients one finds no deity at the center of their mandalas. Jung nevertheless says that such visions are religious and that that factor which instantiates the greatest power is rightly called "God."[16] Great philosophic figures, like Friedrich Nietzsche, grasped one half of the mystery of modernity, that it was vapid and unbalanced. Because they denied the reality of the collective unconscious and its universal contents, their lives were tragically incomplete.

ANSWER TO JOB (1952), CW 11

In his somber introduction to this study of the book of Job, an ancient Jewish text, Jung affirms his notion that his science is phenomenological. He also defends the validity of religious experiences against rationalist criticisms. Because the archetypes are forms of the instincts, they are the actual entities that produce experiences of the divine. Jung says that Job's greatness lies in his theological beliefs: that Yahweh is both a unity and an antinomy. Jung finds this appealing and he highlights Yahweh's dual personality and his irrational responses to Job. Each seemingly irrational action reveals Yahweh's growth, his individuation from a divided self into a coherent and individuated Self. Job's independent existence establishes and maintains Yahweh's. While superior to other deities, Yahweh is a young god whose development parallels the rise of human consciousness during an axial period. Yahweh's internal development requires the presence of superior beings. Yahweh's immorality and his animal nature characterize the dreams and visions of analytic patients when they confront for the first time their innermost archetypes. Like them, Yahweh needs the help of someone who is more mature than he. That someone else is his blameless servant, Job, who serves as the vehicle for Yahweh's individuation

Pursuing this radical reading of Job, Jung advances well beyond the Old Testament text and suggests an inherent dynamism within Western spiritual development. He links Sophia, Eve, Lilith, and the Virgin Mary together in a grand description of Yahweh's ineluctable development from a semiconscious deity to the New Testament visions of Jesus to the Assumption of Mary. Through Christ's character and his death on the Cross, Job's suffering was understood finally by the god who had up to that point remained partly unconscious. This may seem to be Christian apologetics, yet Jung argues that he is not championing Christianity over Judaism or other religions. Rather, he argues that the Western understanding of God's totality requires a synthetic treatment of the Christ story that emphasizes the mythical nature of Christ himself. For example, speaking of the Lord's Prayer, and the metaphysical implication of asking God to not lead one into evil, Jung affirms the Catholic over the Protestant reading. Because they disavow Satan and the Holy Ghost and because they demythologize scripture, Protestants rationalize it into common-sense dictums and such. This obedience to modernism strips the prayer and similar Jewish and Christian texts of their original archetypal powers.

In a similar way, the seventh petition of the Lord's Prayer and Christ's prayer—"My Father, if it be possible, let this cup pass from me"—illustrates the theme of the running together of opposites and the duality of God's nature.[17] That the book of Job corresponds to Ezekiel's visions and that Gautama the Buddha lived at the same time in India suggest parallel events in the development of world religion; each is an instance of synchronicity. Each is a "Son of Man."[18]

POST JUNG, HIS INFLUENCE

Jung was a commanding personality and, like Freud, he inspired followers, publications, journals, and annual conferences devoted to his thought and its extension. Religionists have read Jung with care and some, like Mircea Eliade, founder of the academic journal *History of Religions*, were influenced by Jung's core concepts. Through the twentieth century Jung found much less favor than Freud in European and American universities. For example, Claude Lévi-Strauss rejected Jung's notion of the archetypes because it focused upon semantic contents, not upon structural relations. Jung's influence has been pervasive in popular culture and popular religion, especially among European and American Catholics and Episcopalians. The latter have instituted adult education courses and well-attended retreats whose participants read Jung alongside traditional religious texts. In a related way, Jung's deep empathy for cultural variations and traditional stories finds amplification in science fiction and fantasy.

Intellectual elites tend to dismiss science fiction (and its many cousins) as lesser than high culture—like the novel, opera, and theater. People who, unlike students, can choose what they want to hear and see flock to movies that have AT themes. Here are the top ten most popular American films of all time:[19]

Gone with the Wind (1939)
Star Wars (1977)
The Sound of Music (1965)
E.T.: The Extra-Terrestrial (1982)
The Ten Commandments (1956)
Titanic (1997)
Jaws (1975)
Doctor Zhivago (1965)
The Exorcist (1973)
Snow White and the Seven Dwarfs (1937)

Two of these films are outright space stories (*Star Wars*, *E.T.*); two are outright religious (*The Ten Commandments*, *The Exorcist*); three are idealized love stories set amid total war (*Gone with the Wind*, *The Sound of Music*, *Doctor Zhivago*); one is about the universal theme of love and death in the face of annihilation by drowning (*Titanic*); one is about the universal theme of human intelligence against animal savagery (*Jaws*); and, finally, one is a folk tale with magical powers, evil witches, and singing dwarfs (*Snow White*). We find that AT themes dominate each of these beloved films, and this fact would surely make Jung happy.

NOTES

1. His scientific papers appear in Carl Jung, *Collected Works of C. G. Jung*, 20 vols. (Princeton: Princeton University Press, 1953–79). Hereafter referred to as *CW*.

2. Carl Jung, *The Psychology of Dementia Praecox*, in *CW* 3, 1–37.

3. Carl Jung, *Symbols of Transformation*, in *CW* 5.

4. Ibid., 7.

5. Ibid., 25.

6. Ibid., 60.

7. Jung's autobiography: Carl Jung, *Memories, Dreams, Reflections* (New York: Random, 1962), hereafter referred to as *MDR*.

8. Ibid., 125.

9. Ibid., 155.

10. Ibid., 155–56.

11. Ibid., 45.

12. Ibid., 192.

13. *CW* 11, 171.

14. *MDR*, 73.

15. *MDR*, 80.

16. *MDR*, 81.

17. Carl Jung, *Answer to Job*, in *CW* 11, 560–758, 659.

18. Ibid., 421.

19. www.boxofficemojo.com/alltime/adjusted.htm.

22

Religion and the Brain

Cognitive Science as a Basis for Theories of Religion

ILKKA PYYSIÄINEN

BRAIN AND MIND

Whether religion is "in the brain" is not a unique problem of religionists; a similar question can be asked about all of human activities, such as politics or music, for example. Solutions to the mind-body problem vary, of course. First, it has been suggested that all mental states reduce to neural activity in the brain, everything else being mere illusion.[1] Another option is to think that mental phenomena are real and that they somehow "emerge from" or "supervene on" physical events in the brain, although it is no easy task to describe the mechanisms by which this apparently mysterious ontological transformation actually takes place.[2]

The standard cognitivist (functionalist) argument says that mental states are realized in the brain that supports them, but that mental phenomena could just as well be realized in any other type of material basis. They should therefore be defined by their functional roles, not by the particular type of material basis in question.[3] Such "multiple realizability" has its problems, though. Neuroscientists neither identify "brain states" in such a fine-grained manner as Putnam and others had imagined, nor describe mental states as loosely as the argument of multiple realizability presupposes.[4] According to Bechtel, as long as one uses a comparable grain on both the brain and mind side, there will be a relatively neat mapping between the mental and the neural.

In what follows, I suggest that such multilevel mechanistic explanation as developed by William Bechtel and Carl Craver[5] might be successfully applied in the cognitive science of religion (CSR). This requires some rethinking of the very concept of religion, however.

RELIGION

Religion is studied from a variety of perspectives. History of religion(s) often deals with the past development of this or that particular "religion"; anthropology of religion mostly interprets religious beliefs and practices as an integral part of a specific culture; religious studies often focuses on the description and conceptual analysis of varying belief traditions; comparative religion very much continues on the lines of the old phenomenology of religion in exploring recurrent patterns and structures in the world's religious traditions; sociology of religion is interested in social groups and religion and society at large; and psychology of religion investigates the psychological correlates of religious behavior and experience.[6]

The question can well be raised whether there really is a thing called "religion" and whether the various approaches and disciplines actually interpret and explain only different dimensions or aspects of a single entity.[7] Some say: no![8] Although there is an important truth in this criticism, discussions on the definition of religion alone can never replace empirical exploration of religious phenomena.[9] First, religion can well be studied without a commonly accepted definition of the concept of "religion," as the long history of the discipline testifies; second, formulating a general definition of "religion" cannot be the ultimate goal because a single definition never answers all relevant questions about religion.

Some might try to argue that, although the definition is neither a precondition nor an ultimate goal, *attempts* at formulating a definition of religion are the engine that keeps the study of religion going. In such a view, the study of religion is based on conceptual analysis and is similar to a philosophy of life. By the same token, much empirical work is left to be done within other approaches. The cognitive scientists of religion are among the most outspoken defenders of explanatory research and empirical testing of hypotheses.[10] It is not an abstract and generalized "religion" that is studied but certain recurrent patterns of human behavior and experience.

Scholars within so-called neurotheology, just as some biologically oriented scholars of religion, for their part, have made claims about the neural basis and evolution of religion and religious experience as if religion were a unitary entity with an essence.[11] Religion is assumed to be found in the brain and to have evolved in time. Although scholars study some such particular phenomena as belief in supernatural agents or vague feelings of presence, these are supposed to tell something about a more general phenomenon called "religion." Yet it is highly problematic to reason from a single type of experience to religion in the abstract. Religious experience, for example, has been located either in the temporal or in the frontal lobes of the brain, depending on whether the prototypical experience is a vague feeling of presence[12] or learned ways of thinking that feel like something.[13] Religion thus looks very different depending on which of these two explanatory strategies one chooses.

Ann Taves points out that what neurotheologians actually study are "experiences *deemed* religious";[14] religiousness thus is not an inherent characteristic of experience. This argument also holds for claims about the evolution of religion: we are talking about the evolution of things deemed religious.[15] Such a nonessentialist understanding of "religion" by and large follows from the realization that religion is natural human behavior and that as such it is not supported by any special, "religious" cognitive mechanisms.[16] This immediately leads us back to the question of the proper level of analyzing religion.

LEVELS AND MECHANISMS

The standard model of CSR[17] is often regarded as reductionist in the sense of rejecting the assumption of culture as a specific ontological level that provides explanatory schemes that could not be produced simply by studying the ideas and actions of individuals.[18] Religion thus is explained with reference to cognitive mechanisms and structures in the minds of individuals.[19] Such psychological reductionism is yet counterbalanced by antireductionism with regard to neuroscience: cognitive mechanisms are not reduced to neural mechanisms.[20] McCauley's argument for this is that exploring phenomena at both the neural and the cognitive levels has benefited both neuroscience and cognitive science; advance at one level often provokes new developments also at the other level.[21]

However, there are differing levels and differing ways of identifying levels[22] and the cognitive level is not completely autonomous. If we rely on the general rule "Reduce whenever possible," then everything would reduce to quantum phenomena.[23] Yet the cognitive level has been regarded as foundational in the CSR. While the *explanans* thus is cognitive, it is not always clear what the *explanandum* is supposed to be. In Lawson and McCauley's theory it is the intuitive knowledge of ritual structures: our general cognitive structures explain the fact that we have intuitions about the efficacy of various types of rituals.[24] Pascal Boyer, for his part, has developed a model of the differential spread of traditions in human populations,[25] which is reminiscent of Dan Sperber's epidemiology of representations.[26] Boyer then applies the model to explain various *types* of religious behaviors as listed on the first page of his book;[27] the volume then ends with "The full history of all religion (ever)," consisting of two and a half pages.[28] The *explanandum* thus is something like "Why is there religion in general?" or "How are particular types of (religion-like) behaviors possible?" The scholar thus answers population-level questions that need not have any direct bearing on the motivations of individuals.[29]

Here cognitive mechanisms explain recurrent types of behavior (belief included) in the sense that the typical structure and function of cognitive mechanisms make certain types of concepts and behaviors easier to acquire and thus more likely to become widespread.[30] As Justin Barrett argues, cognitive theories have not been applied to *particular* problems, with scholars rather studying "why religious rituals appear the way they do *generally*, why people believe on gods generally," and so forth. This is also often accompanied by attempts to solve only theoretical problems and to do this by conceptual analysis alone.[31] This, however, may easily make CSR not so different from the conceptual analysis of religion motivated by definitional problems. The theoretical apparatus may be richer and carefully tested, but its application remains speculative.

On the other hand, when research consists of a strictly empirical testing of hypotheses, the question arises of what exactly is the difference between cognitive science (in general) and the cognitive science of religion. If cognitive scientists of religion are only interested in the same mechanisms and processes as other cognitive scientists, then these two fields merge. Another option is that CSR uses cognitive science in explaining particular instances of religious behavior. As Craver puts it: "Proving an etiological explanation involves not merely revealing the causal nexus in the past light cone of the *explanandum phenomenon*. It involves, in addition, selecting the relevant interactions and processes and picking out the relevant features of those processes and interactions."[32]

The mechanisms that make religious behavior possible exist at widely differing levels of size, ranging from molecular structures to culture.[33] This makes the study of religion challenging and also calls for more interdisciplinary projects. The important thing is not that many different disciplines contribute to the study of religion but rather that we learn to conceptualize the objects of study in new ways. We need not decide whether "religion" is in the head or outside of it, because the components of the relevant mechanisms cut across different levels. It is not even necessary to think that any such thing as "religion" exists; it is enough that we explain individual phenomena that fall within the range of what is commonly referred to as "religion."

What needs to be more carefully considered is whether mere epidemiology is enough as a program for the study of religion. To the extent that we also wish to explain particular instances of religion, whether in the history, anthropology, or sociology of religion, the cognitive science of religion could benefit from insights in such disciplines as neurobiology and neuropsychology. I do not mean "neurotheological" ideas of specifically religious structures in the brain but, rather, basic neuroscience dealing with neural mechanisms of ordinary emotions and cognitions that yet contribute to religious behavior.[34]

Brain research can, for example, bring new data to bear on such issues as hyperactive agent detection,[35] feelings of loneliness and religious sociality,[36] and emotions of pleasure and disgust in the acceptance of statements as being true or false,[37] to name a few examples. Taking such research into account seems to require an abandoning of the "multiple realizability" thesis, although functional decomposition remains necessary as a method.[38] However, combining humanistic study of religion with experimental sciences is not an easy task, and our discipline may be currently undergoing a long and winding process of transformations.[39]

NOTES

1. Patricia S. Churchland, *Neurophilosophy: Toward a Unified Science of the Mind/Brain* (Cambridge, Mass.: MIT Press, 1998); Paul M. Churchland, *A Neurocomputational Perspective* (Cambridge, Mass.: MIT Press, 1989); Paul M. Churchland, *The Engine of Reason, the Seat of the Soul: A Philosophical Journey Into the Brain* (Cambridge, Mass.: MIT Press, 1995).

2. Cf. Carl Craver, *Explaining the Brain: Mechanisms and the Mosaic Unity of Neuroscience* (New York: Oxford University Press, 2007), 211–17; William Bechtel, *Mental Mechanisms: Philosophical Perspectives on Cognitive Neuroscience* (New York: Routledge, 2008).

3. Hilary Putnam, "Reductionism and the Nature of Psychology," in *Mind Design*, ed. John Haugeland (Cambridge: Cambridge University Press, 1985), 205–19; David Lewis,

"Psychophysical and Theoretical Identifications," *Australasian Journal of Philosophy* 50, no. 3 (1972): 249–58.

4. William Bechtel and Jennifer Mundale, "Multiple Realizability Revisited: Linking Cognitive and Neural States," *Philosophy of Science* 66, no. 2 (June 1999): 175–207; Richard Brown, "What Is a Brain State?," *Philosophical Psychology* 19, no. 6 (2006): 729–42; Bechtel, *Mental Mechanisms*, 31, 70, 137–42.

5. Craver, *Explaining the Brain*; Bechtel, *Mental Mechanisms*; Carl Craver and William Bechtel, "Top-Down Causation Without Top-Down Causes," *Biology and Philosophy* 22, no. 4 (2007): 547–63; see Robert N. McCauley, "Reduction: Models of Cross-Scientific Relations and Their Implications for the Psychology-Neuroscience Interface," in *Philosophy of Psychology and Cognitive Science*, ed. Paul Thagard (Amsterdam: North Holland/Elsevier, 2007), 105–58.

6. See, Ninian Smart, *Worldviews: Crosscultural Explorations of Human Beliefs* (New York: Charles Scribner's Sons, 1983); Brian Morris, *Anthropological Studies of Religion: An Introductory Text* (Cambridge: Cambridge University Press, 1987); William E. Paden, *Religious Worlds* (Boston: Beacon, 1994); Jeppe Sinding Jensen, *The Study of Religion in a New Key* (Aarhus: Aarhus University Press, 2003); Tomoko Masuzawa, *The Invention of World Religions; Or, How European Universalism Was Preserved in the Language of Pluralism* (Chicago: University of Chicago Press, 2005); J. Milton Yinger, *The Scientific Study of Religion* (London: Macmillan, 1970); Bernard Spilka et al., eds., *The Psychology of Religion: An Empirical Approach* (New York: Guilford, 2003).

7. See, Benson Saler, *Conceptualizing Religion: Immanent Anthropologists, Transcendent Natives, and Unbound Categories* (New York: Berghahn, 2000); Ilkka Pyysiäinen, *How Religion Works: Towards a New Cognitive Science of Religion* (Leiden: Brill, 2001), 1–5; Armin Geertz, "Definition, Categorization, and Indecision; Or, How to Get on with the Study of Religion," in *Unterwegs: Neue Pfade in der Religionswissenschaft/New Paths in the Study of Religions; Festschrift in Honour of Michael Pye on His 65th birthday*, ed. Christoph Kleine, Monika Schrimpf, and Katja Triplett (München: Biblion, 2004), 109–18; Matthew Day, "The Undiscovered and Undiscoverable Essence: Species and Religion After Darwin," *Journal of Religion* 85, no. 1 (2005): 58–85; Ann Taves, "Religious Experience and the Brain," in *The Evolution of Religion: Studies, Theories, and Critiques*, ed. Joseph Bulbulia, Richard Sosis, Erica Harris, Russell Genet, Cheryl Genet, and Karen Wyman (Santa Margarita, Calif.: Collins Family Foundation, 2008), 211–18.

8. Timothy Fitzgerald, *The Ideology of Religious Studies* (New York: Oxford University Press, 1999).

9. See Pascal Boyer, *The Naturalness of Religious Ideas: A Cognitive Theory of Religion* (Berkeley: University of California Press, 1994), 29–34.

10. See ibid.; Justin L. Barrett, "In the Empirical Mode: Evidence Needed for the Modes of Religiosity Theory," in *Mind and Religion: Psychological and Cognitive Foundations of Religion*, ed. Harvey Whitehouse and Robert N. McCauley (Walnut Creek, Calif.: AltaMira Press, 2005), 109–26; Justin L. Barrett, "Keeping 'Science' in the Cognitive Science of Religion," in Bulbulia et al., *The Evolution of Religion*, 295–301.

11. See Taves, "Religious Experience and the Brain"; Ann Taves, "Ascription, Attribution, and Cognition in the Study of Experiences Deemed Religious," *Religion* 38, no. 2 (2008): 125–40; Joseph Bulbulia et al., *The Evolution of Religion*.

12. Michael A. Persinger, *Neuropsychological Bases of God Beliefs* (New York: Praeger, 1987).

13. Nina P. Azari et al., "Neural Correlates of Religious Experience," *European Journal of Neuroscience* 13, no. 8 (2001): 1649–52.

14. Taves, "Religious Experience and the Brain"; Taves, "Ascription, Attribution, and Cognition."

15. Ilkka Pyysiäinen, "Introduction: Religion, Cognition, and Culture," *Religion* 38, no. 2 (2008): 101–8; see Pascal Boyer, "Prosocial Aspects of Afterlife Beliefs: Maybe Another By-Product," *Behavioral and Brain Sciences* 29, no. 6 (2006): 466.

16. Boyer, *The Naturalness of Religious Ideas*; Robert N. McCauley, "The Naturalness of Religion and the Unnaturalness of Science," in *Explanation and Cognition*, ed. Frank C. Keil and Robert A. Wilson (Cambridge, Mass.: MIT Press, 2000), 61–85.

17. Pascal Boyer, "A Reductionistic Model of Distinct Modes of Religious Transmission," in Whitehouse and McCauley, *Mind and Religion*, 3–29.

18. Pascal Boyer, "Cognitive Aspects of Religious Symbolism," in *Cognitive Aspects of Religious Symbolism*, ed. Pascal Boyer (Cambridge: Cambridge University Press, 1993), 6–13.

19. E. Thomas Lawson and Robert N. McCauley, *Rethinking Religion: Connecting Cognition and Culture* (Cambridge: Cambridge University Press, 1990); Pascal Boyer, *Religion Explained: The Evolutionary Origins of Religious Thought* (New York: Basic Books, 2001).

20. Robert N. McCauley, "Intertheoretic Relations and the Future of Psychology," *Philosophy of Science* 53 (1986): 179–99; Robert N. McCauley, "Explanatory Pluralism and the Co-Evolution of Theories in Science," in *The Churchlands and Their Critics*, ed. Robert N. McCauley (Cambridge, Mass.: MIT Press, 1996), 17–47; McCauley, "Reduction."

21. McCauley, "Intertheoretic Relations"; Robert N. McCauley and William Bechtel, "Explanatory Pluralism and Heuristic Identity Theory," *Theory and Psychology* 11 (2001): 736–60.

22. Craver, *Explaining the Brain*; Bechtel, *Mental Mechanisms*.

23. Ilkka Pyysiäinen, "Reduction and Explanatory Pluralism in the Cognitive Science of Religion," in *Changing Minds: Religion and Cognition Through the Ages*, ed. István Czachesz and Tamás Bíró (Leuven: Peeters, 2012).

24. Lawson and McCauley, *Rethinking Religion*; Robert N. McCauley and E. Thomas Lawson, *Bringing Ritual to Mind: Psychological Foundations of Cultural Forms* (Cambridge: Cambridge University Press, 2002), 8–16.

25. Pascal Boyer, *Tradition as Truth and Communication* (Cambridge: Cambridge University Press, 1990); Boyer, *The Naturalness of Religious Ideas*.

26. Dan Sperber, "Anthropology and Psychology: Towards an Epidemiology of Representations," *Man* 20 (March 1985): 73–89; cf. Harvey Whitehouse, *Modes of Religiosity: A Cognitive Theory of Religious Transmission* (Walnut Creek, Calif.: AltaMira Press, 2013).

27. Boyer, *Religion Explained*.

28. Ibid., 326–28.

29. See Andre Ariew, "Ernst Mayr's 'Ultimate/Proximate' Distinction Reconsidered and Reconstructed," *Biology and Philosophy* 18, no. 4 (2003): 553–65.

30. See Boyer, *Religion Explained*, 298.

31. Barrett, "Keeping 'Science' in the Cognitive Science of Religion," 298. For two exceptions, see Petri Luomanen, Ilkka Pyysiäinen, and Risto Uro, eds., *Explaining Christian Origins and Early Judaism: Contributions from Cognitive and Social Science* (Leiden: Brill, 2007); Ilkka Pyysiäinen, *Supernatural Agents: Why We Believe in Souls, Gods, and Buddhas* (New York: Oxford University Press, 2009).

32. Craver, *Explaining the Brain*, 78.

33. Pyysiäinen, "Reduction and Explanatory Pluralism."

34. See Antti Revonsuo, "On the Nature of Explanation in the Neurosciences," in *Theory and Method in the Neurosciences*, ed. Peter K. Machamer, Rick Grush, and Peter McLaughlin (Pittsburgh: University of Pittsburgh Press, 2001), 45–69.

35. Raymond A. Mar et al., "Detecting Agency from the Biological Motion of Veridical vs Animated Agents," *Social Cognitive and Affective Neuroscience* 2 (2007): 199–205.

36. Jaak Panksepp, "The Neuroevolutionary and Neuroaffective Psychobiology of the Prosocial Brain," in *The Oxford Handbook of Evolutionary Psychology*, ed. R. I. M. Dunbar and Louise Barrett (New York: Oxford University Press, 2007), 145–62.

37. Sam Harris, Sameer A. Sheth, and Mark S. Cohen, "Functional Neuroimaging of Belief, Disbelief, and Uncertainty," *Annals of Neurology* 63, no. 2 (2007): 141–47; see Michael A. Persinger, "Are Our Brains Structured to Avoid Refutations of Belief in God? An Experimental Study," *Religion* 9, no. 1 (2009): 34–42.

38. Bechtel, *Mental Mechanisms*, 31, 70, 137–42.

39. See Pascal Boyer, "Science, Erudition and Relevant Connections," *Journal of Cognition and Culture* 3, no. 4 (2003): 344–58.

23

A Critical Response to Cognitivist Theories of Religion

STEVEN ENGLER AND MARK QUENTIN GARDINER

Cognitive science of religion (CSR) sits somewhat uneasily in a section called "religion and the brain." Most work in the field holds, at least implicitly, that religion is rooted in or constrained by evolved and brain-based cognitive processes, for example, analyzing the "functional origins of religious concepts . . . in evolved minds" and characterizing "religious thought and behavior as by-products of brain function."[1] However, there are three distinct claims to be sorted out here. (i) Religion is subject to or constrained by universal cognitive processes.[2] (ii) The relevant constituents, constraints, or precursors of religion are reducible to neurophysiological phenomena, that is, are "hardwired" in the brain.[3] And (iii) these cognitive features emerged through adaptive evolutionary processes. Strictly speaking, CSRs focus on (i); a cognitive theory of religion is not necessarily committed to an evolutionary or brain-based view. For example, Lawson and McCauley's foundational work, *Rethinking Religion*, carefully brackets (ii) and (iii).[4]

Thus, it is useful to distinguish CSRs from both evolutionary approaches to religion and neurophysiological approaches.[5] Work in the former area tends to differ in two important ways from CSRs: it focuses on religious behavior where CSRs tend to focus on religious belief; and it argues that religion evolved as a result of its adaptive function(s) (for example, promoting group solidarity) where CSRs tend to see religion as a side effect of "ordinary," nonreligious, cognitive adaptations (for example, erring on the side of safety by seeing signs of intentional beings around us even when none is actually there).[6] Neurophysiological work (investigating correlations between religious states and brain states) has been relatively nonproductive to date, largely because of difficulties over sorting out cause and correlation (or by making "a fundamental category error" that marks a failure to learn an important lesson from William James) and because of a tendency to converge with neurotheology.[7] Although important work is being done at the intersection of evolutionary and cognitive approaches, CSRs tend to eschew explicit discussion of the biological foundations of religion.[8]

Paying attention to the aims and scope of CSRs immediately counters a number of prima facie critiques.[9] (i) To simply claim that CSRs are reductionist or ideologically loaded, given that all theories share these characteristics to some extent, would fail to clarify exactly how and why this is a problem. (ii) To argue that they are culture-blind or too narrowly focused on one set of factors that influence religion would also miss the mark: like most productive theoretical work, CSRs explicitly focus on a limited range of religious phenomena and pertinent data; they do not claim to explain all things religious, or to replace or negate all other approaches. Nonetheless, CSR approaches should be expected to harmonize as much as possible with established or promising approaches to these other phenomenon and data. (Proponents have often been overly positive in self-appraisal and overly dismissive of other approaches to the study of religion.)[10] Moreover, though CSRs have arguably suffered from an insufficiency of solid cross-cultural data, this situation is being addressed.[11] (iii) To claim that CSRs offer no purchase on the study of specific religions would ignore the work of scholars who have done just that.[12] (iv) To argue that CSRs undermine the justification of religious belief would ignore the fact that CSRs offer limited and partial explanations.[13] (v) Arguing that CSRs reify and naturalize the culturally and historically contingent category of "religion" (using "a western folk category in the analysis of 'mind' ")[14] would fail to acknowledge that CSRs use "religion" as a pragmatic marker for more basic and reductive categories of analysis.[15] More nuanced critiques along all these lines might raise important questions, but CSRs are too often discounted without due attention to what they actually say. Critical evaluation must begin by taking CSRs seriously, at least to the extent that its core claims are represented fairly, with due reference to a broad spectrum of the literature.

The claim that CSRs constitute a "science" underlines their naturalistic, materialistic premises and their appeal to scientific methods, above all some empirical testing of hypotheses. Yet CSRs make for an odd science.[16] First, it is difficult to hold that there is or could be a distinct "cognitive science of religion": rather, it seems that a limited range of religious phenomena are susceptible to empirical study under the umbrella of certain established sciences, especially cognitive psychology and evolutionary anthropology. Second, CSRs sit uneasily within the academic study of religion: very few of the scholars working in the field are trained scientists, and most scholars of religion would not comfortably read a scientific paper in, for example, cognitive psychology (conversely, most cognitive psychologists ignore CSRs). Third, and crucially, much work in the field is armchair science: it does not generate and test hypotheses; it uses ideas drawn from published work in CSR (and occasionally related psychological work) as interpretive tools. Relevant ethnographic[17] and historical works generally use selected ideas from CSRs to analyze data after the fact.[18] The accumulation of examples is sometimes offered as support for claims instead of more "scientific" empirical evidence.[19] This blurs the distinction between experimental/scientific and text-based/humanistic approaches: the "science" of CSRs is often not the product of experimental method but an interpretive frame applied like others in the humanistic study of religion. At the very least, more explicit discussion of the complex relation between interpretation and explanation and of the empirical leverage of retrodiction, as opposed to prediction, is needed.[20]

Many potential criticisms of CSR simply reflect the early state of research in the field. CSRs began in the early 1990s and, with relevant empirical work increasing but still slight, have still not grappled effectively with a number of foundational issues. To date, theorizing roams far beyond the field's narrow and sketchy base of empirical findings: "The field is rife with . . . examples of under-supported psychological claims."[21] (Polemics aside, there is simply not enough data on the table to warrant titles like *Religion Explained* or *How Religion Works*.)[22] Key planks of theoretical platforms in the field lack empirical support. For example, the idea of a cognitive optimum is well supported (for example, that religious narratives tend to have one or two counterintuitive elements, no more and no less), but the evidence that this offers a mnemonic advantage is ambivalent and far from conclusive.[23] Support for the religious role of a cognitive module that posits agency in the case of ambiguous sensory data is similarly weak: "to date, no experimental evidence exists in support of this agency detection device playing any role in religious belief formation or transmission."[24] Basic concepts in the field (for example, "counterintuitive") are difficult to operationalize: as a result, some of the sparse empirical work in the field simply fails to contribute to effective theory building. There is still no consensus, or clear evidence, regarding the number, nature, and scope of, and the relations between, the various hypothesized modules or systems. In this area, the field remains at the stage of contemplating possible hypotheses: for example, empirical studies of cognitive constraints on representations of ritual action lead Sørensen, Liénard, and Feeny to "speculate that specific systems dedicated to the processing of information about Agent and Instrument might explain" their findings.[25]

Given its tentative, though promising, empirical base, it is not surprising that the field's theories remain somewhat up in the air. This applies at several levels. In terms of key hypotheses, for example, Anders Lisdorf critiques Justin L. Barrett's influential concept of a "Hyperactive Agency Detection Device" (HADD) (which fine-tuned Stewart E. Guthrie's earlier discussion of anthropomorphism).[26] Lisdorf shifts emphasis from agency to intentionality and concludes, "we should be wary of supplying ultimate explanations for phenomena whose proximate explanations are not sufficiently worked out. . . . The functions needed to explain the hyperactive intentionality detection are much more complicated than previously assumed."[27] In terms of more general models, McCauley and Lawson's and Whitehouse's competing cognitive theories of ritual both rest on "psychological claims in search of psychological evidence."[28] Underdetermination of theory is also prominent at a more basic level. Almost all CSRs lean strongly on a modular theory of mind, that is, the view that the mind has distinct systems that address specific tasks. However, some CSRs adopt holistic and embedded/situated views of cognition.[29] The result is "two different theoretical models of religious thought," a result that underlines the dependence of CSRs on theoretical debates within other fields.[30] These are symptoms of the current state of development of CSRs. Well-designed, replicable, empirically grounded work is beginning to patch together a fuller picture of religion's relation to cognition.

Matthew Day points to a potentially more serious problem.[31] Arguably, evolutionary theories can never offer a proper explanatory account of reality, given the complexity of the biological and ecological processes that they attempt to describe: that is, there is something in the stochastic nature of evolutionary/biological explanations that makes them unsuitable for the general law conception of science. Day argues that CSRs may face a similar problem:

> [if] cognitive theorists of religion . . . precisely identify the social, cognitive or neuro-logical forces that complicate religious cognition in ways that mean there is still only *some likelihood* that a given concept will exist and be transmitted in a given cultural context . . . [then] not only would the empirical generalization of the cognitive science of religion not approximate the timeless truths of scientific laws, but whatever empirical generalizations we do offer would be so conditioned by qualifications, exceptions and disjuncts that . . . these generalizations may not be very general at all.[32]

Day raises the possibility that the gap between empirical data and theory may never close: "it may be the case that a comprehensive, genuinely explanatory theory of religion is simply out of our reach."[33]

Jeremy Carrette makes a series of criticisms in his examination of "the 'conceptual' politics of cognitive theory and religion."[34] (i) CSRs often reinvent the wheel in "an academic ritual of amnesia and reinvention."[35] (ii) They fail to recognize that "there is no such singular object called religion or 'God' in the material world, but rather a semantic space, which is caught in the politics of representation."[36] (iii) "They remain to a large extent locked inside simple—early—models of cognition," individualistic rather than "more dynamic models of the mind."[37] (iv) They hide behind the allegedly neutral discourse of "science": "*cognitive* is . . . used as a scientific strategy to preclude . . . the ideological and political"; the *cognitive* has the aura of "science" by its conceptual apparatus inside the misleading brain-mind hypothesis."[38] And (v) they are complicit with regnant economic and political systems: they "flourish, not only because cognitive science supports a mechanistic and reductionistic worldview, but also because it orders human identity for a use-value in the present political system";[39] "Cognitive concepts have a currency because they are the dominant ideological language of the market and they therefore flow through the social apparatus more easily."[40]

Carrette's externalist critique raises important questions regarding the ideological presuppositions and positioning of the field. Of course, he does not focus on the issue of whether CSRs are correct or not; he does not engage them on their own ground. As a result, he does not examine their arguments. At the same time, he notes that CSRs do not reflect on their own sociopolitical positioning. It follows that scholars in that subfield will ignore his examination of "the link between politics and models of ourselves" that occupies a different level.[41] They talk science; he talks ideology; Carrette's argument in part presumes that they lack a common ground for further discussion. However, he lumps CSRs together, despite important differences among them, in part because he engages a narrow range of work in the field. As a result, it remains unclear whether certain CSRs would escape all or some of his critiques: for example, those that bracket the characterization of cognitive constraints in terms of neurophysiology, or those that adopt holistic and embedded/situated views of cognition.

Like almost all theoretical work in the study of religion, CSRs generally fail to discuss semantics. This is a critical lacuna that is only beginning to be addressed.[42]

Minimally, CSRs, like all theories of religion, need to give an account of how believers understand their own beliefs, and how scholars of religion should understand the contents of those beliefs. Surprisingly little has been written about the basic semantic commitments of cognitive theorists, with the notable exception of Lawson and McCauley, who defend what they call a "reflexive holism" to frame their syntactic representations of ritual form,[43] and Saariluoma, who argues for what he calls a "constructivist" semantic theory of conceptual content.[44]

A "semantic critique" of CSRs would argue that their basic methodological presuppositions stand in tension with various constraints on promising accounts of meaning. According to traditional or classical theories of meaning, the meaning of a term is given by its referent. The immediate problem for the cognitivist approach is to give an account of these referents. CSRs reject (or at least bracket) the idea that the referent of "god" is an actually existent transcendent being and similarly should reject the idea that knowledge of "god" (or, rather, an understanding of the concept of "god") can be grounded in certain kinds of sui generis religious experience. Religious understanding is to be grounded in more or less "ordinary" experience of the sort investigated empirically by cognitive psychology. The referents of the terms of religious discourse seem then to be ontologically reducible to cognitive events/processes in the human mind/brain, and the meaning of religious terms would similarly be analytically reducible to the language of cognitive science. Problems with giving a coherent semantic account of the meaning of "god" as reducible to such events/processes will constitute problems for the cognitivist approach to the study of religion.

One such problem is that the cognitivist might be committed to a problematic interpretation of the utterances and practices of believers.[45] This would entail that the (second-order) beliefs that believers have about the content of their own (first-order) beliefs are false. When a believer says, "God blesses this marriage," she believes that this statement of belief makes reference to a transcendent being, when in fact at best it would make reference to a cognitive event/process in the mind/brain. This consequence would be problematic for a number of reasons. For example, it seems unwise to assume widespread ignorance and deception in one's study participants. (Note that this is not the "normal" assumption of error that atheistically or agnostically inclined scholars could be comfortable with—that is, it is not merely the error of believing falsehoods, but rather of failing to even grasp one's own utterances.) Second, it suggests a methodological disaster. If CSRs take the beliefs of practitioners as data, this presupposes that the researcher has access to the content of those beliefs. But, (i) what *is* the content of those beliefs, and (ii) *how* does the CSR gain access to them? On the premise that the accounts of believers are not to be taken at face value, the content is *not* supplied by the believer, and it would be difficult to see how the ethnographic and cross-cultural socio-psychological approaches many proponents of CSR have taken would be relevant. On the other hand, if the content of the beliefs is to be supplied by the theory (as outlined above), then the original beliefs cannot serve as data for the theory on pain of circularity.

Of course, the traditional model of meaning (along with its usual ally, the "correspondence theory of truth") is problematic.[46] Alternative accounts are possible, most notably broadly functionalist or holistic models, which seek to explain the semantic meaning in terms of the role expressions play in an overall account of linguistic competence. CSRs need to provide a semantic framework that is (i) plausible on the face of it (that is, is consistent with advances in philosophical and linguistic semantics), and (ii) consistent with the basic constraints and assumptions of the cognitivist approach. To date, the only attempts we are aware of have run afoul of (i).[47] What is at stake is to provide a cognitive account of the content of religious discourse. What CSRs generally offer is something very different: an account of the origin and transmission of religious ideas, as well as the functions those ideas have typically had when embedded in cultural traditions. At best, the failure to provide an adequate semantics is a methodological and theoretical lacuna. At worst, it is a potentially decisive argument against CSRs. An inability in principle to provide such an account would suggest that, at best, the cognitivist approach is limited to providing a (perhaps interesting and even true) theory of the human psychological origin of religious belief, while falling far short of providing a theory of religion itself.

NOTES

This chapter was written in 2009 and revised in 2011. Thanks to Michael Stausberg for comments on a previous draft.

1. Pascal Boyer, "Functional Origins of Religious Concepts: Ontological and Strategic Selection in Evolved Minds," *Journal of the Royal Anthropological Institute* 6 (2000): 195–214; Pascal Boyer, "Religious Thought and Behaviour as By-Products of Brain Function," *Trends in Cognitive Sciences* 7, no. 3 (2003): 119–24.

2. The cognitive processes investigated by CSRs are held to be universal in the sense that they are shared by all human beings who are free from significant mental incapacities.

3. Jeppe Sinding Jensen, "Doing It the Other Way Round: Religion as a Basic Case of 'Normative Cognition,'" *Method and Theory in the Study of Religion* 22, no. 4 (2010): 322–29. The reductionism is thrown into sharp relief by comparison to the "normative cognition" model offered as supplementary or alternative to the "standard" model.

4. E. Thomas Lawson and Robert N. McCauley, *Rethinking Religion: Connecting Cognition and Culture* (Cambridge: Cambridge University Press, 1990); see also Steven Engler and Mark Q. Gardiner, "Religion as Superhuman Agency: On E. Thomas Lawson and Robert N. McCauley (1990), *Rethinking Religion: Connecting Cognition and Culture*," in *Contemporary Theories of Religion: A Critical Companion*, ed. Michael Stausberg (London: Routledge, 2009), 22–38.

5. For CSRs, see Justin Barrett, "Is the Spell Really Broken? Bio-Psychological Explanations of Religion and Theistic Belief," *Theology and Science* 5, no. 1 (2007): 57–72. For evolutionary approaches, see David Sloan Wilson, *Darwin's Cathedral: Evolution, Religion, and the Nature of Society* (Chicago: University of Chicago Press, 2002); and Richard Sosis and Candace S. Alcorta, "Signaling, Solidarity and the Sacred: The Evolution of Religious Behavior," *Evolutionary Anthropology* 12 (2003): 264–74. For

neurophysiological approaches, see Andrew B. Newberg, Eugene G. D'Aquili, and Vince Rause, *Why God Won't Go Away: Brain Science and the Biology of Belief* (New York: Ballantine, 2001).

6. Håkan Rydving, "A Western Folk Category in Mind?," *Temenos* 44, no. 1 (2008): 75n6, 80, 88. This ambivalence between adaptionist and nonadaptionist approaches is correlated with another crucially tension among CSRs: that between theorists who emphasize "counterintuitiveness" (for example, Boyer, Pyysiäinen) and those who emphasize intuitive aspects of human cognition (for example, Guthrie, Bulbulia).

7. Jeremy Carrette, introduction to *The Varieties of Religious Experience: A Study of Human Nature*, by William James, centenary ed. (London: Routledge, 2002), 1.

8. Jesse M. Bering, "The Folk Psychology of Souls," *Behavioral and Brain Sciences* 29 (2006): 453–98; Joseph Bulbulia, "The Cognitive and Evolutionary Psychology of Religion," *Biology and Philosophy* 19 (2004): 655–86.

9. Emma Cohen et al., "Common Criticisms of the Cognitive Science of Religion—Answered," *Bulletin of the Council of Societies for the Study of Religion* 37, no. 4 (2008): 112–15.

10. Armin W. Geertz, "Cognitive Approaches to the Study of Religion," in *Textual, Comparative, Sociological, and Cognitive Approaches*, ed. Peter Antes, Armin W. Geertz, and Randi R. Warne (Berlin: Walter de Gruyter, 2004), 2:347–400.

11. Rydving, "A Western Folk Category," 82–85.

12. Jon Abbink, "Ritual and Environment: The *Mosit* Ceremony of the Ethiopian Me'en People," *Journal of Religion in Africa* 25 (1995): 163–90; Harvey Whitehouse, *Inside the Cult: Religious Innovation and Transmission in Papua New Guinea* (Oxford: Oxford University Press, 1995); Harvey Whitehouse, *Arguments and Icons: Divergent Modes of Religiosity* (Oxford: Oxford University Press, 2000); Brian Malley and Justin L. Barrett, "Does Myth Inform Ritual? A Test of the Lawson-McCauley Hypothesis," *Journal of Ritual Studies* 17, no. 2 (2003): 1–14; Theodore M. Vial, *Liturgy Wars: Ritual Theory and Protestant Reform in Nineteenth-Century Zurich* (London: Routledge, 2004); Luther Martin, "Performativity, Narrativity, and Cognition: 'Demythologizing' the Roman Cult of Mithras," in *Rhetoric and Reality in Early Christianities*, ed. Willi Braun (Waterloo: Wilfred Laurier Press, 2004), 187–218; Roger Beck, *The Religion of the Mithras Cult in the Roman Empire: Mysteries of the Unconquered Sun* (Oxford: Oxford University Press, 2006); Emma Cohen, *The Mind Possessed: The Cognition of Spirit Possession in an Afro-Brazilian Religious Tradition* (Oxford: Oxford University Press, 2007).

13. Michael Murray, "Four Arguments that the Cognitive Psychology of Religion Undermines the Justification of Religious Belief," in *The Evolution of Religion: Studies, Theories, and Critiques*, ed. ed. Joseph Bulbulia, Richard Sosis, Erica Harris, Russell Genet, Cheryl Genet, and Karen Wyman (Santa Margarita, Calif.: Collins Foundation Press, 2008), 365–70; Barrett, "Is the Spell Really Broken?"

14. Rydving, "A Western Folk Category," 88–89.

15. Jesper Sørensen, "Cognition and Religious Phenomena—a Response to Håkan Rydving," *Temenos* 44, no. 1 (2008): 114–17.

16. Steven Engler, review of Pyysiäinen and Anttonen, *Current Approaches in the Cognitive Science of Religion*, and McCauley and Lawson, *Bringing Ritual to Mind*, *Numen* 51, no. 4 (2004): 354–58.

17. Whitehouse, *Inside the Cult*; Whitehouse, *Arguments and Icons*; Cohen, *The Mind Possessed*.

18. Vial, *Liturgy Wars*.

19. Rydving, "A Western Folk Category," 82–85.

20. Some work in this area has been done. See, for example, E. Thomas Lawson and Robert N. McCauley, "Interpretation and Explanation: Problems and Promise in the Study of Religion," in *Rethinking Religion: Connecting Cognition and Culture* (Cambridge: Cambridge University Press, 1990); and Jeppe Sinding Jensen, "Explanation and Interpretation in the Comparative Study of Religion," *Religion* 39, no. 4 (2009): 331–39.

21. Nicholas J. S. Gibson and Justin L. Barrett, "On Psychology and Evolution of Religion: Five Types of Contribution Needed from Psychologists," in Bulbulia et al., *The Evolution of Religion*, 334.

22. Pascal Boyer, *Religion Explained: The Evolutionary Origins of Religious Development* (New York: Basic Books, 2001); Ilkka Pyysiäinen, *How Religion Works: Towards a New Cognitive Science of Religion* (Leiden: Brill, 2001).

23. Justin L. Barrett, "So Counterintuitiveness Helps Explain Religion: What's the Evidence?," paper presented at the Annual International Meeting of the American Academy of Religion, Chicago, Ill., November 2, 2008.

24. Gibson and Barrett, "On Psychology," 334.

25. Jesper Sørensen, Pierre Liénard, and Chelsea Feeny, "Agent and Instrument in Judgements of Ritual Efficacy," *Journal of Cognition and Culture* 6, no. 3–4 (2006): 463.

26. Anders Lisdorf, "What's HIDD'n in the HADD?," *Journal of Cognition and Culture* 7, no. 3–4 (2007): 341–53; Justin L. Barrett, "Exploring the Natural Foundations of Religion," *Trends in Cognitive Sciences* 4, no. 1 (2000): 29–34; Stewart Guthrie, *Faces in the Clouds: A New Theory of Religion* (Oxford: Oxford University Press, 1993).

27. Lisdorf, "What's HIDD'n," 350–51.

28. McCauley and Lawson, *Rethinking Religion*; Robert N. McCauley and E. Thomas Lawson, *Bringing Ritual to Mind: Psychological Foundations of Cultural Forms* (Cambridge: Cambridge University Press, 2002); Harvey Whitehouse, *Modes of Religiosity: A Cognitive Theory of Religious Transmission* (Walnut Creek, Calif.: Altamira Press, 2004); Whitehouse, *Inside the Cult*; Whitehouse, *Arguments and Icons*; Gibson and Barrett, "On Psychology," 334.

29. Steven Mithen, "Cognitive Archaeology, Evolutionary Psychology and Cultural Transmission, with Particular Reference to Religious Ideas," in *Rediscovering Darwin: Evolutionary Theory and Archaeological Explanation*, ed. C. Michael Barton and Geoffrey A. Clark (Arlington, Va.: American Anthropological Association, 1997), 67–86; Steven Mithen, "The Supernatural Beings of Prehistory and the Eternal Storage of Religious Ideas," in *Cognition and Material Culture: The Archaeology of Symbolic Storage*, ed. Colin Genfrew and Christ Scarre (Cambridge: McDonald Institute for Archaeological Research, 1998), 97–106; Jensen, "Doing It the Other Way Round"; Matthew Day, "Religion, Off-Line Cognition and the Extended Mind," *Journal of Cognition and Culture* 4, no. 1 (2004): 101–21.

30. Matthew Day, "The Ins and Outs of Religious Cognition," *Method and Theory in the Study of Religion* 16, no. 3 (2004): 250.

31. Matthew Day, "Let's Be Realistic: Evolutionary Complexity, Epistemic Probabilism, and the Cognitive Science of Religion," *Harvard Theological Review* 100, no. 1 (2007): 47–64.

32. Ibid., 61, emphasis in original. See also Carrette, introduction to *Varieties of Religious Experience*, lxi; Jeremy Carrette, *Religion and Critical Psychology: Religious Experience in the Knowledge Economy* (London: Routledge, 2007), 166.

33. Day, "Let's Be Realistic," 63.

34. Jeremy Carrette, "Religion Out of Mind: The Ideology of Cognitive Science and Religion," in *Soul, Psyche, Brain: New Directions in the Study of Religion and Brain-Mind Science*, ed. Kelly Bulkeley (New York: Palgrave Macmillan, 2005), 245.

35. Ibid., 247.

36. Ibid., 244. See also Carrette, introduction to *Varieties of Religious Experience*.

37. Carrette, *Religion and Critical Psychology*, 165, 179.

38. Ibid., 191, 227n19, emphasis in original.

39. Carrette, "Religion Out of Mind," 257.

40. Carrette, *Religion and Critical Psychology*, 201.

41. Carrette, "Religion Out of Mind," 243.

42. On semantics and religion, see Terry F. Godlove Jr., *Religion, Interpretation, and Diversity of Belief: The Framework Model from Kant to Durkheim to Davidson* (Cambridge: Cambridge University Press, 1989); Lawson and McCauley, "Interpretation and Explanation"; Nancy K. Frankenberry, ed., *Radical Interpretation in Religion* (Cambridge: Cambridge University Press, 2002); Nancy K. Frankenberry and Hans H. Penner, eds., *Language, Truth, and Religious Belief.* (Atlanta: Scholars Press, 1999), especially essays by Godlove and Penner; Steven Engler and Mark Q. Gardiner, "Ten Implications of Semantic Holism for Theories of Religion," *Method and Theory in the Study of Religion* 22, no. 4 (2010): 275–84. Jeppe Sinding Jensen, "Meaning and Religion: On Semantics in the Study of Religion," in *Regional, Critical and Historical Approaches*, ed. Peter Antes, Armin W. Geertz, and Randi R. Warne (Berlin: Walter de Gruyter, 2004), offers the best introduction and overview. Jensen's key theoretical work, *The Study of Religion in a New Key: Theoretical and Philosophical Soundings in the Comparative and General Study of Religion* (Aarhus: Aarhus University Press, 2003), offers a uniquely ambitious attempt to theorize religion in light of semantic considerations.

43. McCauley and Lawson, *Rethinking Religion*; see also Engler and Gardiner, "Religion as Superhuman Agency."

44. Pertti Saariluoma, "Does Classification Explicate the Contents of Concepts?," in *Current Approaches in the Cognitive Science of Religion*, ed. Ilkka Pyysiäinen and Veikko Anttonen (London: Continuum, 2002), 229–59.

45. J. L. Mackie, *Ethics: Inventing Right and Wrong* (Harmondsworth, UK: Penguin, 1997). Much depends here on clarifying the neurophysiological status of cognitive "modules." There is an analogy here, though not a strict one, to an "error theory" in metaethics. Following J. L. Mackie an error theory would hold (i) that religious language makes assertions about the world (as opposed to being, for example, merely emotive), (ii) that there do not, in fact, exist any genuine entities picked out by the religious vocabulary, and, consequently, (iii) that all religious claims are literally false, in the same way that

"Santa Claus lives at the North Pole" turns out to be literally false. Similarly, CSRs arguably imply that much religious language is false.

46. Mark Q. Gardiner and Steven Engler, "Charting the Map Metaphor in Theories of Religion," *Religion* 40, no. 1 (2010): 1–13.

47. Engler and Gardiner, "Religion as Superhuman Agency."

PART V

Religion, Language, and Myth

24

"Religion" in Anglo-American (Analytical) Philosophy of Religion

LUDGER VIEFHUES-BAILEY

THE SCOPE OF ANALYTICAL PHILOSOPHY OF RELIGION

Despite its nearly exclusive concern with topics related to Christian theology, analytical philosophy of religion (APR), like analytical philosophy in general (AP), constitutes a varied field in which philosophers with at times conflicting metaphysical and methodological commitments converse.[1] Thus, we cannot assume that sets of agreed-upon metaphysics or methodologies describe the type of philosophy under review. A more promising approach to characterizing APR, and to analyzing which conceptions of "religion" operate within its texts, begins with Michael Dummett's idea of a common analytical tradition (AT). According to Dummett, a philosopher of religion is part of AT if her works fulfills the following two criteria: first, she appeals to a certain lineage of writers (originating with Russell, Moore, and Frege, and continuing with those, like Wittgenstein, who refer to them, or those who refer to the ones who refer to them). Second, she adopts a certain philosophical style.[2] Whereas Dummett himself does not explain what constitutes this characteristic style, I will argue that his "stylistic criterion" in fact reveals an "institutional criterion." A philosopher appealing to the requisite lineage of writers belongs to AT if she works in the context of the institutions of professional philosophy dominant in the United States and United Kingdom.

Analyzing the notions of religion operative in exemplary texts of APR will show how this particular Anglo-American philosophical professionalization leads to a deprofessionalization with regard to the field of religious studies (RLST). Unlike philosophers who work within the so-called continental context, self-described analytics do not engage the now decades-long critical evaluation of the concept of religion within the field of religious studies. Thus, to see how religion is conceptualized in the exemplary texts under consideration, we cannot turn to extensive hermeneutical discussions. Rather, we have to examine the conceptual choices that produce the operative concept of religion in a given text. Contrasting these choices with those of scholars in RLST will yield insights into the conceptions of religion shared in many texts of APR and into the price these conceptions exert on the projects pursued by APR.

In particular, I will demonstrate how the texts of APR allow readers to see religion either as a cultural system or as a concern for an individual consciousness. This rhetorical construction, as well as the focus on the logical and epistemic structure of propositional beliefs, obscures the focus on the social interactions within which religious beliefs are formed and lived. While communal practices of knowledge production are central for the arguments of Hick, Alston, and Swinburne, whose works we will examine among others, these authors do not engage in a detailed analysis of such practices. A more sustained conversation with the perspective of other scholars in religious studies, as well as a hermeneutical self-examination, would help APR to further its own goals of clarifying and evaluating the meaning of religious beliefs.

PROFESSIONALIZATION AND DEPROFESSIONALIZATION

First, why should we assume that an institutional criterion lurks behind the stylistic one? *Pace* Dummet, observing the texts of AT we find not one single but a multiplicity of styles ranging from a penchant for using formal logic, to attention to linguistic distinctions prevalent in ordinary English, to Wittgensteinian aphorism.[3] Nevertheless, Joshua Ross admits that he found Dummett's idea, that "style" delineates the body of AP, helpful to explain his own reaction to a lecture on Levinas that he had heard. The method of presenting ideas, the allusions to other philosophers (like Hegel and Rosenzweig), he writes, left him alienated, feeling confronted with a mode of philosophizing meant for the "inner circle of adherents."[4] In contrast, Ross concludes that texts in the lineage of AT use a style so broad as to encompass "*all* other schools as well—provided only that they are writing for *fellow professionals*."[5] Implied in his text is therefore the judgment that AP is the type of philosophy that is written in a style accessible for all professional philosophers. Yet, the universal quantifier Ross uses in this statement evidently excludes the authors of the continental lineage whose philosophical method left him excluded.

As a second example for the institutional criterion, let me point out how it operates in Dean Zimmerman's characterization of APR. He describes both AP and APR as pluralistic and modest enterprises in which philosophers engage who hold multiple and divergent metaphysical outlooks. Importantly, Zimmerman concludes, analytical philosophers are required to take into considerations views that seem "crazy" to them.[6] There is, however, one notable exception. The requirement that the analytic philosophers entertain "crazy" views does not extend to those of philosophers outside of the analytic lineage. Zimmerman observes that "almost invariably" analytic philosophers consider the philosophical claims of those in the lineage going back to Heidegger (and those who respect and aim to inherit it, without fully endorsing all of its claims or methodology) to be misguided and "impenetrable."[7] What motivates this exclusion of philosophers in the continental lineage from the scope of "crazy" views to be considered, as in Zimmerman's text, or from the circle of understandable philosophy, as in Zimmerman and Ross? Apparently, the so-called continentals do not count as fellow professionals.

While perhaps surprising intellectually, from the perspective of institutional politics this is an accurate description of the current state of affairs in professional philosophy. As John Searle notes, "indeed, analytic philosophy is the dominant mode of philosophizing . . . throughout the entire English-speaking world."[8] Most professional philosophy departments and major associations in the United States do not extensively value philosophers working in the continental lineage, who have usually found a home in literature departments. Thus, it makes sense that Zimmerman stresses the professional pedigree of APR and the fact that most philosophers of religion in this tradition work in philosophy departments, as opposed to those in departments of religion.[9] In sum: implied in the notion of "style" is the aforementioned institutional criterion. *A text is written in the style of AT if it uses modes of philosophical expression that the institutions of professional philosophy in the English-speaking world adjudicate as suitably clear as opposed to "impenetrable."* Let me flag here the question of what counts as the right kind of clarity, since it makes little sense to assume that there is "clarity" *in and of itself.* The logical structure of the sentence (G) "there is only one God" can be made pristinely clear by formalizing it into (G'): $\exists x\,(Px\,\&\,\forall y\,(Py \rightarrow y=x))$, where we let P be the predicate "instantiates the property of divinity." Such clarity however does not provide insight into the religious meaning of G (were we to hear [G] uttered in, say, a prayer).

A consequence of this particular philosophical professionalization under the auspices of the dominant styles of AT is, however, APR's deprofessionalization in relationship to RLST. APR is practiced without profitable connections to the institutions of the American study of religion.[10] Zimmerman sees this professional split as a problem since it limits the positive influence that APR can have on the discipline of theology. Thus, he invites theologians to articulate "Christian doctrine in ways that an analytic philosopher can understand."[11] (Note that the onus in Zimmerman's invitation for cooperation lies on the theologians—and other professional religionists, by extension. They have to adopt modes of thinking and argument that can meet the requirements of intelligibility that have been institutionalized in APR.) Whereas philosophers affiliated with the American Academy of Religion pursue textual lineages more broadly than those defining AT and participate in the conversations of RLST, the practitioners of APR risk a certain professional isolation.

This risk is particularly acute, given the vibrant debates about how to conceptualize "religion," the phenomenon that constitutes the subject matter of APR.[12] Without engaging these literatures, APR is in danger of analyzing artifacts that reflect more the lineage of problems of professional Western philosophy than the practices and beliefs that we, in the wider academy, currently consider as "religious." In other words, if APR presents itself as the best philosophical practice for "clarifying the meaning of religious claims and for assessing the reasons for and against the truth of those claims," it would be important to know what constitutes a *religious* claim.[13]

At stake is not only Blaise Pascal's famous distinction between the generic notion of God in the thought of the philosophers and the vibrant particularity of God in the testimony of the biblical prophets—a distinction that according to the theologian Hans Urs von Balthasar already tormented late medieval Christian philosophical theology, and one that the philosopher William Weischedel sees as foundational for the modern philosophy of religion.[14] Rather, the problem is whether APR can engage in a self-critical dialogue such that its own particular theological and conceptual presuppositions can be critiqued. The goal is not to arrive at a truly generic philosophy of religion but to provide an enriched and self-critical philosophical imagination that can be helpful for the very projects that APR pursues.

OSCILLATION BETWEEN SYSTEM AND PRIVACY

Consider how John Hick conceives of the essential characteristics of religious phenomena in his influential *An Interpretation of Religion*. Despite Hick's claim that "religion" is a family-resemblance concept without one unifying "common essence," he nevertheless identifies the "generic concept" of salvation/ liberation as a characteristic for contemporary religion.[15] He argues that religious activity shifts from concerns with the maintenance of communities to a concern for individual salvation/liberation after an alleged revolution in human consciousness during the so-called axial age (ca. 500 BCE to 500 CE). Built into Hick's use of the axial age is a dual opposition: (1) one between collective and individual religion, and (2) one between social stability and transformation. The concern for salvation and change is understood as an individual quest originating in the consciousness of great religious women or men.[16]

In RLST we find other instances where, as in Hick's work, the function of soteriological religion is allocated to the side of the individual and that of social maintenance to the side of communal religion. Contrasting Hick with other authors who engage this distinction can highlight what kind of notion of religion operates in his thought. The Buddhist studies scholar Richard Gombrich, for example, understands soteriological religion as primarily a matter of individual beliefs, which are only secondarily related to a system of ethics and right practices. Communal religion represents society's self-awareness. Such religion exists in the minds of individuals but it leaves no room for "individual initiative, primarily it is a pattern of action."[17] Gombrich and others, such as Melford Spiro, however, do not privilege one of these functionalities of religious practice over others. Far from describing different types of religious entities, they are heuristic devices helping us organize the various functions that religious symbols and practices can and do play in the lives of practitioners. It would be difficult, for example, to attribute the feeding of monks, which is part of what Milford Spiro describes as kammatic Buddhism, as representative of either soteriological or communal religion. Feeding monks is an act that comes with the promise of the accrual of merit for a better rebirth, and thus is part of the so teriological orientation that Spiro detects as prevalent among the Buddhist villagers he studies. At the same time, the practice of offering food to monastics also functions in the establishment and maintenance of social bonds among villagers and between villagers and monks. In short: *If we compare other uses of the soteriological/communal religion distinction with Hick's uses of it, we see that his strategy produces two types of religion (as opposed to two functions of the same phenomenon): archaic and contemporary religion. This move allows him to shape a concept of religion, in which the religious phenomenon is generically centered on events affecting and resulting from changes in an individual religious specialist.*

This particular conception of religion provides the basis for Hick's epistemological argument. The soteriological transformation of an individual consciousness is the result of this individual's religious experience. In it she encounters the Real, that is, "the supposed unity-of-reality-and-value that is thought of as God, Brahman, the Dharma, Sunyata or the Tao." Hick construes individual religious experience in analogy to perceptual experience as a composite of external informational input and mental categories that organize this input into a meaningful experience.[18] His creative extension of Kantian epistemology allows Hick to claim that, despite their various phenomenological contents, religious experiences can relate the same external reality. Moreover, drawing on Richard Swinburne's "principle of credulity" (PC), Hick defends religious experience as prima facie innocent until proven guilty. Absent specific grounds for doubt, a religious person is justified in trusting that her religious experience represents indeed things as they are. For Hick, a religious claim is one that originates in an individual experience that is structured by traditional and culture-specific categories. In this model, individual experience, as it is created through the categories available in a given religious tradition (Christianity, Judaism, Hinduism, Islam, Buddhism), secures that the religious belief connects with the appropriate reality and thus can have a positive truth-value.

Let me flag the unclear status of the role of community in Hick's picture. On the one hand, Hick positions individual experience in contrast to the goals and practices of communal religion, as we have seen. On the other hand, in pointing to cultural and traditional contexts in which such individual experience is processed, Hick imagines religious communities as neatly separated interpretive systems that neither overlap nor interact with one another. In Hick's understanding of religion, instances of cultural and religious hybridism, as studied in numerous anthropologies of religion, cannot become visible. Inversely, the strategy of presenting Islam, Christianity, Buddhism, and Judaism as homogenous cultural systems obscures the selectivity with which Hick presents the essential religious features of each of these (cf. Reçber).[19] Thus religion appears split in Hick's picture both as a phenomenon located in individual consciousness and as one located in separated cultural systems.

Community makes a third appearance in Hick's philosophizing, namely, through his application of Swinburne's principle of credulity. The standards by which we decide whether or not an experience can count as trustworthy representation of what is the case are community-specific. Swinburne and Hick, for example, characterize the imbibing of consciousness-altering substance as a defeater of PC. They see no obligation to judge the experience of such a person to be epistemically trustworthy. Yet, how do the philosophers adjudicate religious experiences that are related to practices of extreme fasting, to those of prolonged meditative regiments, or to the ritual inhaling of special herbs, and so on? Hick and Swinburne understand the ideal religious phenomenon as that which results from the experiences of an individual who has separated himself to the highest degree possible from communal interference and who contemplates the absolute in maximal quietude. At the same time, the communal location of this very epistemic ideal remains unexamined and it is noteworthy that in Hick's actual analysis, the experiences of women and peoples outside of hegemonic European and US cultures remain unacknowledged.[20] This lack of self-examination glosses over an epistemological problem: What is the relationship between societal practices that establish trustworthiness and our epistemic practices of knowledge production?

I have spent time with Hick's work because it shares salient features of its strategies of conceptualizing religion with other contemporary works of APR: the oscillation between religion as system or as matter of individual experience and the neglect of a detailed analysis of religion as the product of shared social practices. For example, in William Alston's *Perceiving God* we find a similar use of Swinburne's idea of epistemic trustworthiness, one that focuses not on individual beliefs but on systemic epistemic practices.[21] Wholesale cultural practices are to be evaluated as trustworthy, such as Christian mystical perceptual practice (CMP), the focus of Alston's work. He defends the right of the practitioner to trust the outcome of these epistemic practices that, in the case of CMP, lead to what is claimed to be a perception of the God. Alston uses the term "doxastic practice" to refer to our systemic ways of forming beliefs and of evaluating them based on the systems of background knowledge that are implied in these practices. We can consider such beliefs as prima facie justified until we find reasons to override this trust. However, what constitutes such overriders depends on the relevant background knowledge. Alston examines mystical perceptual practices such as CMP. They are firmly established in their cultures and their output cannot be shown to sufficiently indicate their individual unreliability, since they come with their own culture- and practice-specific overrider systems.[22] For the practitioner of each of these practices, it is rational to engage in them and to consider them as prima facie justified. This allows the practitioner, according to Alston, to "sit tight" and to continue her practice. If the practice is sufficiently socially established, if it is self-supporting (that is, produces the religious fruits that it promises), and if it does not run into contradictions with other socially established doxastic practices, then a belief formed through this mystical practice (MP) is justified.

In contrast to Hick, Alston emphasizes the social nature of our epistemically trustworthy practices. Only those practices that are socially established can be considered as candidates meriting epistemic trust—presumably because they have reliably produced what they claimed to produce. Yet, *we find again the split between "religion as individual experience" and "religion as system" that characterized Hick's conception of religion.* On the one hand Alston discusses the religious phenomenon primarily in analogy with individual sensory perception. CMP (along with other such MPs) is built on the model of sensory perception. Here, as in Hick, religious beliefs originate in an individual's experiential encounter with Ultimate Reality.[23] On the other hand, Alston talks about the "major world religions" or "major systems of religious beliefs" (Hinduism, Buddhism, Islam, Christianity, and Judaism) as providing identifiable and characteristic sets of systemic doxastic practices.[24]

Given that the study of religion as a field has witnessed a sustained critique of the idea that it makes sense to organize the multiplicity of religious life into the categories of major "world religions," the Alstonian philosopher should wonder whether the idea of religious system is viable.[25]

Alston is not alone in reconstructing religious traditions as coherent and high-level systems, such as Buddhism, Hinduism, and Christianity. For example, David Basinger critiques the tendency of most APR on the topic of religious diversity to focus on high-level intrasystemic diversity, contrasting, for example, the claims of "theistic systems" with those of "a-theistic religious systems." Highlighting inner religious diversity, Basinger cautions against this focus. Like his colleagues in APR, however, Basinger keeps the system-language alive. He assumes the existence of *the* Christian belief system, *the* Jewish belief system, and so on—systems that are identified by sets of internally shared beliefs.[26]

More recent anthropological work about the hybridity of religious practices can further undermine the idea of religious systems, which are defined by characteristic doxastic practices and, at the same time, expand on Alston's idea. For example, Jean DeBernardi's study of spirit media in Malaysia shows the hybrid and changing nature of the practices of spirit possession in which these media engage.[27] In her case studies we find that practitioners merge so-called Buddhist, Hindu, and Christian symbols and practices. Yet, the media and their clients seem to derive the promised benefit from the practices, which would attribute to them the status of a self-supporting practice in Alston's sense. Moreover, these practices are socially established in specific strata of their respective societies. In short, the hybrid nature of these practices further challenges the project of finding system-specific doxastic practices. Instead, what we see are local practices of belief formation and their localized social support.

Cases like these do not disable Alston's argument about the prima facie justification of beliefs produced by doxastic practices that are socially entrenched and thus pragmatically judged to be reliable. Rather, analyzing this anthropological material would allow him to highlight the fact that such practices are best understood not as unchanging mechanisms inherent in religious systems but rather as malleable and contested social activities. Acknowledging the social embeddedness would help to clarify the relationship between the social establishment and the epistemic status of a religious belief. Such clarification will bring with it a shift in what constitutes a paradigmatic case of religious knowledge production. Instead of focusing on an isolated individual's experience, the philosopher is asked to consider the *social* activities of, for example, spiritual direction or of the gurukula and monastic communities. At these sites, we can analyze how religious (and at times political) institutions shape and discipline the relevant doxastic practices that are aimed producing religious knowledge. *Taking these practices as paradigmatic of what constitutes a religious phenomenon would avoid the split between "religion as individual experience" and "religion as cultural system." Moreover, such a paradigmatic shift would require a deeper philosophical analysis of how our practices of knowledge production are intertwined with other social practices.*

RELIGION AND STATEMENTS OF FACTS
OR EXPRESSIONS OF ATTITUDES

The previous discussion also shows how the texts of APR are centrally concerned with evaluating the epistemic status of religious beliefs, which are assumed to have a discernible logical structure. This focus on the logical and epistemic structure of religious beliefs is a reaction to how logical positivists, such as Russell and Ayer, dismissed or defended religious claims. For example, in his famous lecture "Why I Am Not a Christian" (1927), Bertrand Russell distinguishes between emotional attachments and arguments about fact and identifies the former as the real reason why people "accept religion."[28] A. J. Ayer had famously argued that religious statements were meaningless, because they were impossible to verify. Devoid of propositional content, these statements express a religious person's emotive or practical attitudes.[29] In the 1950s, philosophers turned Ayer's critique into a defense by arguing that religious statements are best understood not as providing descriptions of how things objectively are, but as expressions of personal attitudes toward the world.[30] For example, in a debate with Antony Flew, R. M. Hare argued that religious beliefs expressed a fundamental attitude toward the world (something he calls a "blik") and not an explanatory hypothesis that could be proved or disproved.[31]

In contrast, Hick, Alston, and most current practitioners of APR hold that religious beliefs are best analyzed as statements of facts and not as expressions of values. The fortunes of logical positivism have waned (and with it those of verificationism or falsificationism); yet the underlying disentanglement of statements of facts from expressions of attitudes still operates in the work of the later defenders of religious beliefs. Consequently, religion in these texts appears as primarily concerned with believing certain propositional claims. Yet, the problem arises of how can we understand and evaluate such beliefs outside the varied contexts of their practice, including those of expressing attitudes and values? For example, Norman Malcolm concludes his defense of the logical soundness of Anselm's ontological proof for the existence of God with the following observation: This proof can only be "thoroughly understood by someone who . . . views it from the *inside* . . . and who has, therefore, some inclination to *partake*, in that religious form of life." We may find, contra Kant and many others, that the logical structure of the argument is unproblematic. For example, we can follow Malcolm in his refutation of Kant's critique of a necessary being and still lack a full understanding of what Anselm means by the concept of a "being a greater than which cannot be conceived." Clarifying its meaning would require understanding "the phenomena of human life that give rise to it."[32] And such a life contains interrelated practices of referring and of expressing convictions, values, and attitudes.

Malcolm, like most practitioners of AP, assumes that the ontological argument will not suffice to induce a "living faith" in the reader.[33] Maximally, these arguments can show that the philosophical objections to the rationality of religious beliefs are insufficient. Likewise, Plantinga states that his "ontological argument triumphant" is not a "successful piece of natural theology," because not everybody may accept its premise that for all possible worlds, there is at least one world in which it is possible that there is a maximally great being that is omniscient, omnipotent, and perfectly good. Plantinga admits that his argument can only show that "there is nothing contrary to reason in accepting this premise."[34] While his proof can show that a religious person is not irrational in believing that God exists, a nonbeliever cannot be compelled by the argument to endorse this belief. Even Richard Swinburne's reconstruction of the cosmological argument in *The Existence of God* does not aim to provide rational certainty.[35] Rather, his aim is to show—by using Bayes's theorem, which assigns probability to an event by weighing evidence and background knowledge related to it—that it is more probable that God exists than that God does not exist. The technical question of how to assign numerical values to factor in the evidence derived from, say, Jesus's resurrection aside, Swinburne's program can highlight why the proofs of APR are not religiously compelling, despite their pristine logical structure. We have to know what constitutes evidence, how to weigh it, and how to relate it or distinguish it from background knowledge—and we have to know what constitutes the right kind of background knowledge. All of this requires, however, a thorough understanding of the meaning of the claims in question, to echo Malcolm.

The focus on religious beliefs independent of their lived context leads to the odd situation that the philosopher can produce the pristine logical clarity of a statement's structure without elucidating its meaning. Yet, if we believe Hilary Putnam, among others, we may consider that what constitutes the meaning of a statement is not secured by its truth-values alone. *Rather, it is a remnant of positivism to construe beliefs as being fixed in their reference, and thus in their truth-evaluable content, independent of the context in which these beliefs are held or expressed.*[36] If we want to understand what beliefs (religious or not) are about, we need to explore the practical contexts within which they appear. Thus, gaining an understanding of what a religious statement means, such as a belief in something extremely "good," requires contextualizing it. Why does she see her illness as a test for her faithfulness to God and not as evidence against God's good will or existence? What counts for her as evidence for her belief in the afterlife—and how does her use of evidence for religious claims differ from her use of evidence in, for example, predicting the weather?

Wittgenstein, in his "Lectures on Religion," worries about questions like these in order to find out what constitutes the right understanding of a religious claim.[37] Critiques of Wittgenstein have argued that his concern with the lived context of a religious statement disallows him from correctly valuing religious statements as properly asserting claims about the world.[38] Yet, reflecting on these lectures, Genia Schönbaumsfeld has reiterated recently that Wittgenstein's *Philosophical Remarks* (PR) meant to undercut precisely the alternative between religious statements as statements of facts and religious statements as expression of attitudes. Like Malcolm, she points out that Wittgenstein does not deny that religious statements have cognitive content. Rather, his work highlights that we can understand this content only if "we understand the use to which the religious 'pictures' are put."[39] Thus, from a Wittgensteinian perspective, religious beliefs and practices are intertwined, as are beliefs about facts and attitudes toward the world. Wolterstorff's critique, like other, more sympathetic interpretations of Wittgenstein's alleged noncognitivism, turns on the idea that there is only one form of stating a fact: that is, the practice of stating empirical facts without purportedly expressing values.[40]

This insistence on the interrelation between social practices and cognitive content brings Wittgensteinian PR, which is currently situated at the fringes of APR, in close proximity to anthropological studies of religion and to feminist philosophy of religion. Shifting away from a focus on the justification of beliefs, the latter has developed a strong interest in analyzing the social and historically situated practices of belief formation. For example, in *Feminist Philosophy of Religion*, Pamela Sue Anderson distinguishes the weak objectivity of those blind to their own situatedness and biases from a strong objectivity, which requires a person to combine the hermeneutical awareness of one's own standpoint and its limitations with an attempt to epistemic empathy. Strong objectivity and the ability to think about a situation from the perspective of others is a communal practice aiming for the developing of less partial truth.[41]

The texts of APR under investigation face the charge of reflecting a perspective of weak objectivity. Adopting an Andersonian strong objectivity by engaging the perspectives of other scholars of RLST could help APR to develop a hermeneutical awareness of the kind of choices that inform the conceptions of religion operative in APR's text. Doing so will allow APR to better pursue its goal of clarifying and evaluating religious beliefs in their complexity.

NOTES

1. Peter Van Inwagen and Dean W. Zimmerman, *Persons: Human and Divine* (Oxford: Clarendon, 2007), 9.

2. Michael A. E. Dummett, *Origins of Analytical Philosophy* (London: Duckworth, 1993), 4–5.

3. A. C. Grayling, *Philosophy: A Guide Through the Subject* (Oxford: Oxford University Press, 1995), 5; Joshua Jacob Ross, "Analytical Philosophy as a Matter of Style," in *The Story of Analytic Philosophy: Plot and Heroes*, ed. A. Biletzki and A. Matar (London: Routledge, 1998), 65–67.

4. Ross, "Analytical Philosophy as a Matter of Style," 65–67.

5. Ibid., 68, italics mine.

6. Van Inwagen and Zimmerman, *Persons*, 7, 11.

7. Ibid., 6, 4.

8. John R. Searle, "Contemporary Philosophy in the United States," in *The Blackwell Companion to Philosophy*, 2nd ed., ed. N. Bunnin and E. P. Tsui-James (Oxford: Blackwell, 2003), 1.

9. Van Inwagen and Zimmerman, *Persons*, 4.

10. William J. Wainwright and Nicholas Wolterstorff, *God, Philosophy, and Academic Culture: A Discussion Between Scholars in the AAR and the APA* (Atlanta: Scholars Press, 1996).

11. Van Inwagen and Zimmerman, *Persons*, 12.

12. Tomoko Masuzawa, *In Search of Dreamtime: The Quest for the Origin of Religion, Religion and Postmodernism* (Chicago: University of Chicago Press, 1993); Tomoko Masuzawa, *The Invention of World Religions; Or, How European Universalism Was Preserved in the Language of Pluralism* (Chicago: University of Chicago Press, 2005); Richard King, *Orientalism and Religion: Post-Colonial Theory, India and the "Mystic East"* (London: Routledge, 1999); Jeremy R. Carrette and Richard King, *Selling Spirituality: The Silent Takeover of Religion* (London: Routledge, 2005); Timothy Fitzgerald, *The Ideology of Religious Studies* (New York: Oxford University Press, 2000).

13. William Hasker, "Analytic Philosophy of Religion," in *The Oxford Handbook of Philosophy of Religion*, ed. W. J. Wainwright (Oxford: Oxford University Press, 2005), 443.

14. Blaise Pascal and Léon Brunschvicg, *Pensées et Opuscules, Publiés Uvec une Introd: Des Notices et des Notes par Léon Brunschvicg, Classiques Hachette* (Paris: Hachette, 1959), 142–43; Hans Urs von Balthasar, Erasmo Leiva-Merikakis, Joseph Fessio, and John Kenneth Riches, *The Glory of the Lord: A Theological Aesthetics* (New York: Ignatius Press, 1982), 18; Wilhelm Weischedel, *Der Gott der Philosophen: Grundlegung einer Philosophischen Theologie im Zeitalter des Nihilismus* (Darmstadt: Wissenschaftliche Buchgesellschaft, 1971).

15. John Hick, *An Interpretation of Religion: Human Responses to the Transcendent*, 2nd ed. (New Haven: Yale University Press, 2004), 4, 36.

16. Ibid.

17. Richard Francis Gombrich, *Theravada Buddhism: A Social History from Ancient Benares to Modern Colombo*, Library of Religious Beliefs and Practices (London: Routledge, 1988), 26, 41.

18. Hick, *An Interpretation of Religion*, 36, 243.

19. Mehmet Sait Reçber, "Hick, The Real and Al- Aqq," *Islam and Christian-Muslim Relations* 16, no. 1 (2005): 3–10.

20. Pamela Sue Anderson, *A Feminist Philosophy of Religion: The Rationality and Myths of Religious Belief* (Oxford: Blackwell, 1997); Grace Jantzen, *Becoming Divine: Towards a Feminist Philosophy of Religion* (Bloomington: Indiana University Press, 1999).

21. William P. Alston, *Perceiving God: The Epistemology of Religious Experience* (Ithaca: Cornell University Press, 1991).

22. Ibid., 262.

23. Ibid., 190.

24. Ibid., 264, 266.

25. Masuzawa, *The Invention of World Religions*; Fitzgerald, *The Ideology of Religious Studies*, 2000.

26. David Basinger, *Religious Diversity: A Philosophical Assessment* (Aldershot, UK: Ashgate, 2002), 2.

27. Jean Elizabeth DeBernardi, *The Way That Lives in the Heart: Chinese Popular Religion and Spirit Mediums in Penang, Malaysia* (Stanford: Stanford University Press, 2006).

28. Bertrand Russell and Paul Edwards, *Why I Am Not a Christian, and Other Essays on Religion and Related Subjects* (New York: Simon and Schuster, 1967), 19.

29. A. J. Ayer, *Language, Truth, and Logic*, 2nd ed. (London: V. Gollancz, 1956).

30. R. B. Braithwaite, *An Empiricist's View of the Nature of Religious Belief* (Cambridge: Cambridge University Press, 1955).

31. Antony Flew and Alasdair C. MacIntyre, *New Essays in Philosophical Theology* (London: SCM Press, 1955), 100; Paul Matthews van Buren, *The Secular Meaning of the Gospel, Based on an Analysis of Its Language* (New York: Macmillan, 1966); Don Cupitt, *Taking Leave of God* (New York: Crossroad, 1981).

32. Norman Malcolm, "Anslem's Ontological Argument," in *Philosophy of Religion: An Anthology*, ed. C. Taliaferro and P. J. Griffiths (Malden, Mass.: Blackwell, 2003), 280, 279, italics in text.

33. Ibid., 280.

34. Alvin Plantinga, *God, Freedom, and Evil* (Grand Rapids: Eerdmans, 1977), 112.

35. Richard Swinburne, *The Existence of God* (New York: Oxford University Press, 1991).

36. Hilary Putnam, *The Threefold Cord: Mind, Body, and World* (New York: Columbia University Press, 1999), 5:118.

37. Ludwig Wittgenstein and Cyril Barrett, *Lectures and Conversations on Aesthetics, Psychology, and Religious Belief* (Berkeley: University of California Press, 1966).

38. Nicholas Wolterstorff, "Religious Epistemology," in *The Oxford Handbook of Philosophy of Religion*, ed. W. J. Wainwright (Oxford: Oxford University Press, 2005), 256.

39. John Preston, *Wittgenstein and Reason* (London: Blackwell, 2008), 68.

40. Kai Nielsen, "Wittgenstein and Wittgensteinians on Religion," in *Wittgenstein and Philosophy of Religion*, ed. R. L. Arrington and M. Addis (London: Routledge, 2001).

41. Anderson, *A Feminist Philosophy of Religion*, 76.

25

Structural Linguistics and Structuralist Theories of Religion

VOLNEY GAY

S tructural linguistics (more precisely, *formal* structuralist linguistics) refers to a theory of language that is associated with Ferdinand de Saussure (1857–1913) and that influenced generations of religionists and other humanist scholars who developed the structural theory of myth and related cultural forms, especially literature. Parallel to Saussurian linguistics was the work of Roman Jakobson (1896–1982) and the Prague Linguistic Circle, which he founded and which advanced *functional* structural linguistics. Jakobson argued that language includes semiotic elements that are iconic (that is, not arbitrary). Claude Lévi-Strauss (1908–2009), a creative French *philosophe*, drew upon both Saussure and Jacobson when he elaborated "structural anthropology." All three thinkers shaped the study of religion and myth.

The analysis of linguistic form (or structure) is as old as mathematics, logic, and grammar. Pre-Socratic philosophers like Parmenides (early fifth century BCE) reflected upon permanence and impermanence and Plato, a generation later, studied the concept of "form" and its eternal, essential nature. By the fifth century BCE, Sanskrit grammarians had formulated rules of Sanskrit morphology, including concepts analogous to morpheme and phoneme.[1] Because language is essential to science, philosophers ground their epistemology in a theory of language. A novel theory of language produces a novel school of thought: competing schools of literary theory, hermeneutics, phenomenology, theology, and political philosophy employ competing theories of language.

Joining these debates in the late nineteenth century, Ferdinand de Saussure published a brilliant treatise, *Mémoire sur le système primitif des voyelles dans les langues indo-européennes* (*Treatise on the Primitive System of Vowels in Indo-European Languages*), in 1878 at the age of twenty-two. His lectures on linguistics at the University of Geneva were published posthumously as *Course in General Linguistics* by his students in 1916. That single book shaped twentieth-century linguistics.

In *Mémoire* Saussure used methods advanced by historical linguists to study vowel patterns in reconstructed versions of Proto-Indo-European. Saussure showed that a class of vowels—the sonant coefficients—must have occurred even though evidence for them was lacking. Twenty years later, scholars discovered and translated Hittite texts that employed such vowels.[2] This stunning prediction prefigured Saussure's turn to formal structuralism (and it exemplifies the goals that Lévi-Strauss and other structuralists pursued, hoping to repeat Saussure's achievement).

While a master of historical methods, Saussure rejected the view that languages were organisms that had distinctive morphological histories and developmental lines: "Language was considered a specific sphere, a fourth natural kingdom."[3] Saussure defined language as "speech less speaking," grounded in arbitrary signs, and "bound to a community of speakers."[4] Without fixed, arbitrary relations between signified and signifier, reference and communication would be impossible. Because linguistic signs are not natural (iconic), we are not limited to fixed "meanings." Indeed, language (*la langue*) can be studied and understood independently of speech (*parole*). We can study dead languages, for example, because the rules that govern the representation of sound images (phonemes) systematically pertain to a fixed number of written symbols (graphemes).

Language lets us combine words, make new words, and express complex relationships between an infinite number of states of affairs. Using a consistent, arbitrary system, we can generate an infinite number of sentences the same way that knowing arithmetic lets us generate an infinite number of valid proposition, such as "5 + 10 = 15" in base ten notation. Language (*la langue*) is the set of transformational rules that govern all instances of speech (*parole*). "Language is comparable to a symphony in that what the symphony actually is stands completely apart from how it is performed."[5] Twenty high school bands playing Beethoven's Fifth Symphony cannot destroy it, no matter how hard they try.

For these reasons, we enjoy software that can translate speech into text. The magic that makes this possible is the fact that language users employ a small set of graphemes to represent a small set of phonemes. With sufficient computational power, software can "translate" spoken words into a likely representation of the speaker's intentions. Like chess-playing software, translation software replicates (or mimics) the rule-following heuristics that humans use. We can also trace changes in pronunciation, stress, word usage, grammar, and so on through history. This is a diachronic (evolutionary, historical) point of view—but it is not observing language per se.[6] Because of chance and other forces (political, historical, and social) speech evolves in unpredictable ways. For example, historians of English speech raise diachronic questions and seek to explain change using historical concepts. Whom do speech codes advantage or disadvantage?

DISTINCTIVE FEATURES AND PSEUDO DISTINCTIVE FEATURES

The term "distinctive feature" derives from Roman Jakobson's form of structural linguistics.[7] Distinct features are audible nuances that permit one to distinguish one acceptable sound (the phoneme) from another. For example, in English, the consonant sound denoted by "/p/" differs from the consonant sound denoted by

"/t/" by one distinctive feature, namely, what linguists call "labiality." In making the sound denoted by "/p/" one uses one's lips; while making the sound "/t/" one does not. Phonetic distinctive features permit English speakers to denote acceptable and nonacceptable sound classes, the phonemes, which are the minimum constitutive units of spoken languages. So too, visible distinctive features permit one to distinguish visual signs from one another: in printed English the grapheme /E/ is distinguished from the grapheme /F/ by the lower horizontal stroke. Hence, the lower horizontal stroke is a visual distinctive feature in English.

The concept of the phoneme makes possible the science of linguistics. By examining the structures that undergird all language use, we discover rules that regulate language. Like the discovery of the periodic table in chemistry, the discovery of the phoneme as the minimal unit of language demonstrated an underlying and universal pattern heretofore not recognized. Hence, without knowing Chinese, for example, we can assert that it must have a phonemic core out of which are generated all higher-level structures, like words and sentences.

Given the central place language holds in culture, the theory of the phoneme engendered applications to other forms of language. The theory of the phoneme also permitted linguists to sidestep traditional folk theories of language, which are obsessed with speech. These basic discoveries of scientific linguistics animated the French anthropologist Claude Lévi-Strauss and other structuralists. Using the phoneme as a heuristic model of cultural artifacts, Lévi-Strauss expanded the notion of distinctive feature and applied it to narratives, like religious myths, novels, and plays. In these contexts one no longer seeks acoustic or other physical distinctive features. Rather, one must seek distinctive sets of terms whose *meanings* are antithetical to one another. Thus Lévi-Strauss conflated semantics with phonemics. He assumes the following:

1. Human beings are distinct from other animals and from nature.
2. This distinction is based on or is the product of language.
3. Language is best understood as (a) the exchange of messages, (b) a system of transformations, and (c) universally the same everywhere.
4. Exchange and language are based on nonconscious or unconscious codes.
5. All human culture is based on exchange and is controlled by these unconscious codes.

Because all codes are ultimately arbitrary in their organization, they are vulnerable to disintegration. Through cultural rules, human beings invest their vulnerable sense of "meanings" in these codes. Hence, the codes are sacralized. They are reified as natural or as God's will or as revealed in the beginning of time. An inescapable tension springs up: we need the code and employ it yet we also perceive, however dimly, that reality slips through its structures. An honest person or culture perceives that a code "established by God" (for example) must be protected lest it disappear.

Myths represent and try to answer these kinds of existential puzzles. More accurately, we should say that myths and their attendant rituals instantiate our being in the world as creatures confined and defined by language. The logic of myths, or "mythologique" as Lévi-Strauss puts it, derives from their origins in a conceptual puzzle: How shall human beings bring to bear upon an apparently limitless world of differences, losses, terrors, and other disorganizations a semblance of pattern? This is a cognitive view of myths and it refers to specific contents, to nonarbitrary questions that arise not from language, but from experience. Drawing upon psychoanalysis, Marxism, and structural linguistics, especially Saussure, Lévi-Strauss claims to have elucidated the basic features of all myths and their numerous cognates.

Mythology confronts the student with a situation that at first sight appears contradictory. On the one hand it would seem that in the course of a myth anything is likely to happen. There is no logic, no continuity. Any characteristic can be attributed to any subject; every conceivable relation can be found. With myth, everything becomes possible. But on the other hand, this apparent arbitrariness is belied by the astounding similarity between myths collected in widely different regions. Therefore the problem: If the content of a myth is contingent, how are we going to explain the fact that myths throughout the world are so similar?[8]

Lévi-Strauss amalgamated Saussure's insight into the arbitrariness of language with Jacobson's theory of the phoneme. Adding these together, he articulated a table of constituent units (the minimal units of language) that extended from the smallest (the distinctive feature) to the largest (texts like the Mahābhārata, a Hindu epic of some 1.8 million words.)

Constituent units:

Phones	all possible speech sounds (or, for a written language, all possible marks)
Phonemes	strictly defined *classes* of sounds, /p/ vs. /b/; /l/ vs. /r/
Morphemes	interchangeable parts of words: (help, helper, helping, helpmate)
Sememes	meaningful components: bull: cow: calf = man: woman: child
Sentences	well-formed propositions

Bundles of Relations	sets of propositions that are logical analogues of one another: overvaluing
or Mythemes	blood relations vs. undervaluing blood relations
Myths	a complete set of mythemes, one among an infinite set of expressions of the same logical problem and attempts to overcome it

According to this table, myths are reflections upon core logical conundrums: they are symptomatic of a culture's deepest intellectual struggles with its conceptual apparatus. Sensing this, Lévi-Strauss says, we can tell when a story is mythical: "Whatever our ignorance of the language and the culture of the people where it originated, a myth is still felt as a myth by any reader anywhere in the world. Its substance does not lie in its style, its original music, or its syntax, but in the *story* which it tells. Myth is language, functioning on an especially high level where meaning succeeds practically at 'taking off' from the linguistic ground on which it keeps on rolling."[9] As he notes, in myth, the dictum "traduttori, tradittore"—that to translate a poem, for example, is to betray it—reaches its lowest truth-value. Because myths are reflections upon conceptual and logical conundrums, we can translate them fully and accurately just as we can translate the rules of chess into computer code.

The oddity of myths is that they seem arbitrary and illogical, yet they are astoundingly similar around the world and through time. This is so because they spring from the same cognitive puzzles: How did death come from life? Why are there two sexes? Why do I do that which I would not do? Are human beings categorically different from other animals? Can humans kill animals without moral sanction?

Lévi-Strauss says that to read a myth we are to "(1) define the phenomenon under study as a relation between two or more terms, real or supposed; (2) construct a table of possible permutations between these terms; (3) take this table as the general object of analysis."[10] Lévi-Strauss usually chooses the terms "nature" and "culture" as the basic antitheses. We could as well choose "male and female," "god and human," life and death," "war and peace," "Being and non-Being," or numerous other sets of antithetical terms. In choosing these terms we ineluctably assert that they designate wholly distinct entities or processes. Yet, on examination, we discover these are not, hence I term them pseudo-distinctive feature systems. By definition, the phoneme is a purely arbitrary sign of difference: it has no inherent meaning. But terms like "culture" and "nature" are rich with semantic content, associations, and their own peculiar history.

A simple table, constructed along the lines Lévi-Strauss indicates, illustrates the utility of his method. Consider a culture's struggle to define and regulate sexual contact between persons. We can set these issues into a table:

Using this table, we can locate all instances of sexual congress. We, or our tribe, can choose, for different reasons, to assign values—such as taboo and permitted—to each cell. Some of these reasons may be accidental, others motivated by unconscious anxieties, others motivated by sexist claims to dominance and power. Like the theory of the phoneme, these abstract tables map the logical space in which individual cultures elaborate their solutions to universal problems. No language uses all possible distinctive features to create its phonemes, so too no culture can or needs to exhaust these tables of logical possibility.

TABLE 25.1
Sexual Pairings: Two Persons

	MALE PARTNER	FEMALE PARTNER
MALE ACTOR	Taboo [or not]	Permitted [or not]
FEMALE ACTOR	Permitted [or not]	Taboo [or not]

Myths are narrations about these tables. Myths emerge continuously because myths "provide a logical model capable of overcoming a contradiction (an impossible achievement if, as it happens, the contradiction is real)."[11] For example, how did "Death" come from "Life"? For some children, how can a good mother engage in something "dirty" like sex? In the West, a basic conflict derived from monotheism is: "How can a good, omniscient, and omnipresent God create evil?" To respond to this logical dilemma Christians elaborated the myth of the God-Man. Regarding psychological theories of myths, including Freud's reflections on the Oedipal story, Lévi-Strauss says that such theories are themselves new versions of the same myth. Hence they are variations of the myth.

Lévi-Strauss brought to comparative mythology new power and scope. Suddenly one could escape the confines of a particular culture and its myths. He demanded that we look around the world for confirming or disconfirming instances of the same myth told by widely diverse peoples. Contrary to theories of myth that limited it to the "savage mind," Lévi-Strauss seemed to show that myths are subtle and complex reflections, using concrete metaphors, about the foundations of human thought. As he says continuously, "the kind of logic which is used by mythical thought is as rigorous as that of modern science."[12]

Myths are not infantile; they reveal logical tensions common to all reflection. In Western parlance, beginning with the Greek philosophers, such antinomies are at the foundation of logic. For example, the "Liar's Paradox" reveals something disturbing about the core concept "truth" in Western philosophy, namely, that we cannot define it. Briefly stated, the paradox can be expressed in a sentence S: (S) "This sentence is false." If, on the one hand, S is referring to itself, and if we assume it is true, then what it asserts is the case. What it asserts is that it is false; hence if it is true, then it is false. If, on the other hand, S is false, then what it asserts is not the case. What it asserts is that it is false; if this is not the case, then sentence S is true. In other words, we have shown that both possibilities of S's truth-value, that it is either true or false, lead to a contradiction.

This is more than a parlor trick. At the heart of Western philosophy and science is the concept of truth. That we struggle to define it shows how deep this problem lies. This famous paradox illustrates Lévi-Strauss's contention that logical antinomies are the engine of mythical reflection. Myth grows continuously "spiral-wise until the intellectual impulse which has originated it is exhausted."[13]

Following Lévi-Strauss's stunning works, scholars of religion and other humanistic forms, such as novels and movies, found a brilliant, new way to reread ancient and modern texts. Like Freud and Marx, his great predecessors, Lévi-Strauss offered a rigorous form of self-reflection. He rescued the study of mythology from its nineteenth-century restrictions and he brought to anthropology a new, vastly larger sense of human cognition and thought. A puzzle, or perhaps tragic limitation, ensues. For while we affirm the insights of structural linguistics, we cannot locate our feelings, our personal myths in that science. We speak *a* language, not Language. In *our* language we find our personal meanings, specific feelings, and memories that constitute our personal and collective identities. If our religion is like our language, then it is a source of meaning and value; yet it is not the only valid form of belief. There are other, equally valid religions as there are other valid languages. Lévi-Strauss shows that "primitives" are not primitive, that there is a common, human set of emotional and cognitive dilemmas, and that mythic systems are intertranslatable. How can people move toward a nonarbitrary, "natural," and universal religion if we can only speak our religion? These are among the tasks of theology, critical theory, and comparative religion.

NOTES

1. John Lyons, *Introduction to Theoretical Linguistics* (Cambridge: Cambridge University Press, 1968), 19–20.
2. Randy Allen Harris, *The Linguistics Wars* (New York: Oxford University Press, 1993), 261.
3. Ferdinand de Saussure, *Course in General Linguistics* (New York: Columbia University Press, 1959), 4.
4. Ibid., 77.
5. Ibid., 18.
6. Ibid., 90.
7. Roman Jakobson, C. Gunnar, M. Fant, and Morris Halle, *Preliminaries to Speech Analysis: The Distinctive Features and Their Correlates* (Cambridge, Mass.: MIT Press, 1951).
8. Claude Lévi-Strauss, "The Structural Study of Myth," in *Reader in Comparative Religion*, ed. W. A. Lessa and E. Z. Vogt, 3rd ed. (New York: Harper and Row, 1965), 291.
9. Ibid., 292.
10. Claude Lévi-Strauss, *Totemism*, trans. R. Needham (Boston: Beacon, 1962), 16.
11. Lévi-Strauss, "Structural Study of Myth," 301.
12. Ibid.
13. Ibid.

26

Imagining, Manufacturing, and Theorizing Myth

An Overview of Key Theories of Myth and Religion

DANIEL DUBUISSON

TRANSLATED FROM FRENCH BY WILLIAM MCCUAIG

Everyone knows that the study of myth is divided among various disciplines (history of religion, anthropology, semiology, sociology, psychology, and no doubt others as well). But that is not the only reason the concept of myth lacks a precise definition.[1] It can best be compared, in fact, to a malleable substance, like modeling clay. Protean and unstable, myths have been interpreted in different ways since antiquity, and in the modern era they have been harnessed to irreconcilable, and even clashing, theories.[2] So let us start from this position, which is akin to the radical historicism of Michel Foucault: the least appropriate way to think about the countless texts labeled as "myth" is to assume that they all correspond to an ideal type endowed with unchanging functions.[3]

This nominalist stance, which denies the existence of any timeless essence behind the word, is based on an overwhelming quantity of historical evidence, and would appear to be indisputable. So it is logical to focus on the word "myth" at the outset, and state firmly that it refers to nothing ascertainable: "a fish that dissolves into the ocean of mythology, myth is a form nowhere to be found."[4] Any attempt to define its preferred themes, describe its formal, narrative, or semiolinguistic properties, or enumerate its traditional functions soon forces one to recognize that no list of simple criteria allows us to separate out a category denoted "myth" from the mass of narrative texts spanning proverb, fable, and epic.

THE MYTH OF THE MYTH OF ORIGIN IN MYTHOLOGICAL STUDIES

So what accounts for the continuing—or rather amazingly expanded—notoriety of myth in the contemporary world? One loses count of the books that have been dedicated to it over the last sixty years. This paradox arises not out of the stability of its intrinsic qualities (we have just seen that it has none), but rather out of the qualities that authors as different as Mircea Eliade and Claude Lévi-Strauss have attributed to it a priori. In other words, these thinkers have themselves imagined and manufactured their own artifacts, and then gone on to erect their monumental oeu-vres around them. In these oeuvres they were free to develop theories of the most radical kind, since of course the ideal type of "myth" they had created was in each case extremely coherent a priori and displayed an array of properties (formal, se-miotic, functional, and even metaphysical) that were tailored to their intellectual projects. These *ideal* myths are consequently creations of a purely verbal or "po-etic" (from the Greek) kind, which is to say, they are fictive entities. Their only referents are ones they themselves have put in place. "They might be described in Stéphane Mallarmé's terms as 'knick-knacks of resonant inanity,' or with Bacon's word *fallacies*."[5] It is the rhetorical virtuosity of the interpreter alone that permits the a posteriori authentication of the definition assigned a priori to the ideal type of myth.[6] Whatever real facts or situations do happen to be mentioned are neces-sarily chosen and shaped to fit, in a reversal of the direction of any normal schol-arly protocol, since they are only there to illustrate the theory that was posited a priori. It would be like a novelist first inventing an unusual character, and then hunting in the newspapers for factual details in order to make him believable. This is where "the myth of myth" begins.[7]

In its conventional sense, the word "myth" designates primarily a narrative of a particular kind, one that evokes an origin, or primordial times, or simply a remote past. Since every human group lays claim to a distant, and often fabulous, origin, this somewhat banal sense is not in dispute.[8] Let us not forget, though, that to claim to utter the origin is always equivalent to uttering the world, its things and its be-ings, as they were at the dawn of time, meaning in the form of essences or perfect types. On that basis, moreover, we can observe two further slippages of an even more questionable kind. Our modern mythmakers have in fact conceived of myth *as if it were itself* an originary narrative form, an archaic tale anterior to all other narra-tive forms. As such (they let it be understood), myth amounts to a description of the archè (Greek), the true origin, the absolute principle of things. And with this piece of subtle equivocation as their stepping-stone, the same authors then let it be understood further that through the analysis of these antediluvian myths they are in a position to accede to these first principles themselves. Through the study of primitive myths,[9] contemporary mythology was thus laying claim to the miraculous ability to reach back to earliest times. At this stage confusion was well and truly lodged in the mind of the reader, since the ingenious mythologists had evidently introduced the same postulates as the basis of their conception of myth, and as the basis of their double system of analysis and interpretation.[10]

TOPOLOGY, CARTOGRAPHY, AND ARCHAEOLOGY

For the historian of ideas (mythological ones in particular), it is important to un-pack these scenarios with methodical care, for our authors have framed their con-ception of myth around their most cherished postulates. Now, these postulates are neither innumerable nor distributed at random. It helps to picture them as a simpli-fied topological system, in which each theory occupies a distinct position. Certain ones may come together to form small nebulae (Eliade, Carl G. Jung, Joseph Camp-bell, for example). The overall system comprises the ensemble of theories that have been proposed in a given epoch.[11] None of these theories is absolutely original, for they are always the result of more or less harmonious syntheses, in which influences (philosophical, religious, political, and so on), some of them very ancient, may have played a part. Thus, one will understand nothing about Eliade's theses if one over-looks their debt to Plato and ancient Gnosticism. Likewise, but at the other end of our spectrum, the atheism of Lévi-Strauss belongs to a current that goes back to Lucretius. To put it another way, contemporary theories of myth form an intelligible system, itself embedded in the long intellectual history of the West. The charting of this system is the most significant result we can hope to obtain from "compara-tive epistemology." The main purpose of such an epistemology is to establish

> an approach and a method that will reveal a supplementary way of looking at the history of thought. . . . It reveals its own "system" progressively, implied by the rules followed in the comparative analysis of other systems. It is a method: indifferent to metaphysics, yet concerned with showing as neatly as possible any metaphysical phenomena, complex or fragmented, that it may encounter in the course of its duty.[12]

In addition to the nominalist position just set forth, three magisterial theories have been developed in the domain of the contemporary study of mythology.

The first is grounded in a series of assertions that aim to be both rationalist and materialist. Among contemporary thinkers, Lévi-Strauss is no doubt the one who has gone furthest in the ambition to reconcile the sensible and the intelligible within a unified theory that is at the same time a coherent vision of the world and man.

The second is a little harder to pin down, since it claims a connection to a tran-scendent Reality—in other words, it ventures into a metaphysical domain lying beyond the bounds of science. Eliade remains its most celebrated, but also most controversial, representative.

The third shares the materialist approach of the first, but confines it to the social sphere (Georges Dumézil). It focuses on the inner workings of societies, where ide-ologies that justify the existing hierarchies, powers, laws, and traditions are elaborated.

These three theories are incarnated in "the three giants whose works remain the most important theoretical contributions and the most impressive concrete studies of myth that have been produced to this day."[13] Before we proceed to look closely at them, it is important to note that they are indeed opposed to one another, but in the manner of the great paradigms (a priorism, Platonism, materialism) that struc-ture the history of Western thought.[14] It is no less important to note that all three function in the same way, despite everything that divides them. They all utilize myth, and the interpretation of myth, to try to show that there is an overarching explana-tion, a key to understanding, to be found at the origin: an origin absolute and universal in the case of Lévi-Strauss and Eliade, and one belonging to Indo-European prehistory in the case of Dumézil.

A boundless ambition drives the oeuvre of Claude Lévi-Strauss, transcending the modesty of its purported object of study. For him, the analysis of primitive myth is a way to gain access to knowledge of the innermost mechanisms of the human mind, the ones that have always governed "cerebral organization" and "the architecture of the mind."[15] This ambition is philosophical in nature (Lévi-Strauss received solid philosophical training early in life, at the same time and in the same way as Jean-Paul Sartre), which is not a surprise: the plasticity of myth means it can be adapted to serve the most varied religious, political, social, and of course philosophical causes. No doubt this protean and polyvalent character is myth's most functional attribute. To attain this high ambition, Lévi-Strauss was forced to create a conceptual and methodological apparatus that may have been extremely abstract, but thereby gained remarkable coherence. Before examining its details, I emphasize once more that this ambition rests on an original postulate stated at the start of the 1950s: to bring sensible qualities and logical categories together under the same *superrationalism*.[16] To put it a bit more philosophically, as far as Lévi-Strauss is concerned the a-priorism of Immanuel Kant and the empiricism of David Hume ought not to clash. The two are, so to speak, simply incomplete, since neither has perceived that the same code and the same logical organization govern the objective qualities present in nature, the mechanisms of perception (especially the visual), the logical categories of the mind that thinks them, and the linguistic signs that express them verbally.[17] For Lévi-Strauss it is primitive myth that expresses most clearly this fundamental harmony, this profound unity, encompassing thought, language, and the material world. Challenging the opinion that, since the nineteenth century, has so often portrayed primitive myths as crude sketches, Lévi-Strauss affirms that, on the contrary, they express the ultrarational nature of thought.[18] What path did he follow in formulating this problem and supplying such an original solution to it?

In the first place, it is a philosophical problem of long standing, as old as Western philosophy itself since it already preoccupied Plato and Aristotle. The nature of the links that do, or do not, bind sensible qualities on the one hand to the categories of understanding on the other has obsessed Western philosophical reflection for twenty-five centuries. Additionally, though (and this is a quite separate point), Lévi-Strauss was profoundly influenced by modern linguistics (Ferdinand de Saussure, Nikolai Troubetzkoy, Roman Jakobson), which he saw as a model for his own approach. From structural linguistics he adopted three main features in particular. Lévi-Strauss's approach analyzes the terms' relations, rather than the terms themselves. It then posits that these logical relations are all grounded in oppositions (synchronic vs. diachronic, syntagmatic vs. paradigmatic, signifier vs. signified), and that the latter are themselves organized into systems. These three features, which are not normally present to consciousness, are made by Lévi-Strauss to serve as the basis of his structural analysis of myth. This is why it looks nothing like commentary of the traditional type, the paraphrase of the story line. In order to adhere as closely as possible to the notions of sign (Saussure) and phoneme (Troubetzkoy), Lévi-Strauss was compelled to undertake a full-scale analysis (Greek *analusis*, or "dissolution"), breaking the myth down into its elementary units and bracketing the significance of the actantial scheme and the story line. This analysis left Lévi-Strauss with nothing in the end but discrete elements (isolated signs) to be paired with one another according to the different figures of the binary code (opposition, the contrary, the congruous, alternance, the antithetical, and so on), a code that he saw as undergirding the functioning of thought. From his perspective, this logic brings to light the homologies between nature, thought, and language. Thus Lévi-Strauss outdoes Aristotle, Kant, Hume, and Karl Marx in his attempt to unify, through his vision of primitive myth, the qualities of the sensible world and the cognitive processes of the neurosciences.

The reader will have noted that Lévi-Strauss's version of myth lays no claim to and presents no element that could in any way be called religious. In fact, in its denial of any species of transcendence, it fits very well with radical materialism. Clearly this is not the case with Eliade, for whom in contrast myth is regarded as a fundamental religious fact.

The work and personality of Mircea Eliade have generated lively controversy for the last twenty years (a subject explored in detail in the contribution of Greg Alles, chapter 38 of this volume).[19] The reason is obvious: his fascist and anti-Semitic commitments in the 1930s, in connection with the Romanian Iron Guard.

Like Lévi-Strauss, but for other reasons, Eliade was fascinated by myths of origin and primitive and even prehistoric cultures.[20] He too believed that myths had had an originary function, but for him it had a radically different meaning, metaphysical and not logico-semantic. For Eliade, primitive man is a fundamentally religious being dwelling in a universe just as religious, since it is the permanent theater of numerous manifestations, or *hierophanies*, of the Sacred. For Eliade this term denotes a form of the absolute, but characterized by numerous pagan traits. Nature, life, fecundity are its most striking manifestations.[21]

This brief outline suggests that, if we are to disassemble the system built by Eliade with due care, we ought to look at it closely. The inspiration for his conception of myth actually came from within itself. His system is made of unverifiable metaphysical presuppositions, extravagantly hypothetical reconstructions of humanity's past and prehistory, cloudy notions, and rhetorical tropes aimed principally at seducing the credulous reader.[22] There are solid grounds for regarding it as more of an ideological fiction than a genuine scientific contribution.[23] The postulates required to put this system together are, like all postulates, undemonstrable. Those selected by Eliade fall into two categories, one related to supernatural realities, the other to highly improbable reconstructions of the early phase of human prehistory. As well as affirming the existence of this transcendental instance that, following Rudolf Otto, he calls the Sacred, Eliade brings another character onstage, whom he designates *homo religiosus*. This expression signifies that the human being is fundamentally religious, with the corollary that all religions possess a common origin and ground. In asserting this, Eliade is relying on a cliché that is also one of our oldest indigenous cultural prejudices. The conception of archaic humanity as marked by innate religious aspirations was already to be found in the Fathers of the Church, and it has since become a commonplace repeated by countless thinkers over the centuries, from Friedrich Schleiermacher to Jung by way of Kant, Ernest Renan, and, in the twentieth century, all the phenomenologists.[24] The attention of the reader is therefore drawn to the fact that, in opposition to this "religionist" current of thought, various authors have demonstrated more recently (a) that the two concepts, religion and religious, even when used in an academic context, retain the profound impression of their ethnocentrism and Christocentrism, (b) that they only achieved their definitive meaning in the West and in the nineteenth century, in other words at a time when the West was imposing its domination, and so its vision of the world and mankind, on all other cultures.[25] The view that the different human cultures are and always have been "religious" is thus the offshoot of a retrospective and ethnocentric illusion engendered by Western knowledge, starting in the nineteenth century. Its main ideological conclusion is the affirmation that all cultures rest on the same universal principles, whose development and expansion Western man has shown an incomparable capacity to promote.

Readers will have grasped by now that the primordial ages were turned into an idealized fantasy by Eliade. For him, humanity's golden age was a metaphysical age, and he assigns responsibility for the destruction of this original paradise to the invention of profane history by Judeo-Christianity, which in his eyes led to the desacralization of nature.[26] This idealization of the most distant past encompasses traditional agrarian societies, the essential role of their spiritual elites, and the great archaic liturgies, the bloody sacrifices, and the ritual orgies.[27] According to Eliade, an attentive reader of Wilhelm Mannhardt and James G. Frazer, the annual celebration of these bloody and orgiastic sacrifices favored the periodic regeneration of the cosmos. They perpetuated the vital forces animating it, promoting its eternal youth, fecundity, and power. The composition of this barbaric tableau relied on two rather straightforward procedures. The first was to adopt the exact antithesis of everything that Eliade, permanently marked by the years spent with the Romanian extreme right in the 1930s, detested in modern urbanized societies: democracy, human rights, the Enlightenment, science and materialism, ethnic mixing.[28] The second was to decontextualize the societies and cultures of the past, to empty them of everything that made up their historically existing reality. In fact, it was the totality of their contexts (social, political, juridical, economic) that Eliade sacrificed:

> *I must add that I will approach all these phenomena as a historian of religions, which is to say, I will not attempt to discuss their psychological, sociological, or even political contexts, meanings, or functions (leaving that to those who may be better qualified to do so).*[29]

> But [this little book] is not a study in the history of religions in the strict sense, for the writer, in citing examples, has not undertaken to indicate their historico-cultural contexts.[30]

This tableau received its final patina from Eliade's use of a style more expressive than precise, studded with phrases as magniloquent as they are hollow: "the experience of cosmic sanctity," "the total man," "the act of coming into being," "the sacrality of life," "a superior mode of being," "a new and charismatic cosmos," and so on. In this world of Baconian fallacies, reality is never simply the real; it is transfigured and becomes "total," "superior," or "absolute."

With this cosmic scenery in place, the last member of the cast—myth—is finally brought onstage. In fact, the role is an odd one: it derives all its essential elements from the backdrop already erected. As imagined by Eliade, myth conveys a true and ancient history, relating the creation of all or part of the world by supernatural beings. On this—eminently Frazerian—basis, myth also embodies an exemplary model, which men could repeat endlessly in their rites. The celebration of these carries them back into primordial time, and so allows them access to the Sacred. On top of that, Eliade sees mythological images, figures, and symbols as presenting an astonishing similarity to many of those found in the unconscious of individuals, because they all flow from mankind's experience of the Sacred.[31]

The most radical critique one can make of Eliade's system is simply to recontextualize all the elements that he—having carefully decontextualized them so as to be able to present them as atemporal simulacra—has included in it.[32] As each of them regains all of its proper historical depth and richness (social, cultural, linguistic, psychological), it immediately loses its aura of mystery and recovers the totality of its human dimensions. How true it is that to decontextualize is always to dehumanize.

As presented in the oeuvre of Georges Dumézil, myth is unlike its counterparts in either Lévi-Strauss or Eliade. In this author, you might say, myth comes back down to earth. For that matter, Dumézil himself stated that he was incapable of defining criteria for telling the difference between a myth and a tale.

He was not looking for some sort of absolute origin, in any case. With rare epistemological wisdom, he confined his investigation to the (linguistically homogeneous) Indo-European world, and as far as he was concerned, the only accessible origin must have been located toward the end of prehistory, at a time when the Indo-European world was more compact, its peoples less dispersed. His favorite research "tool" was obviously the comparative method. If two (at least!) historical documents (in Latin and Sanskrit, let's say, or Avestan and Irish Gaelic) present unquestionable resemblances, it is possible to postulate the existence of a prehistoric Indo-European prototype. And the hypothesis will carry even more weight if the observed resemblances occur not as minute and isolated traits, but rather as structural ensembles—a group of characters or divinities, for example.

In 1938, Dumézil determined the postulate on which he grounded most of his comparative research. It rests on the idea that the systems of social classification of India and Iran, the pantheons of pre-Capitoline Rome and Vedic India, and the archaic sacerdotal college of Rome all reflect the same ideology. For Dumézil, an ideology is a collective way of thinking and representing the world, in effect, a Weltanschauung. In his view, this ideology juxtaposed and hierarchized three specialized functions: magico-religious sovereignty, warfare, and the production of material goods. He saw these three functions reflected in highly precise social roles: that of the priest, that of the warrior, and that of the peasant. What was essential in myth was the ideology it expressed, and the key to any ideology was its social origin.

Subsequently he widened his documentation to include new material from the literatures of the ancient Celtic and Scandinavian worlds. But two enhancements imparted new life to Dumézil's system after the Second World War. For one thing, Dumézil realized that his "tri-functional ideology" presented a richer, more complex structure than the rather crude one he had first envisaged (three vertically stacked social functions). He showed that each of the two higher functions presented two aspects, both complementary and opposing. As for the third, it had its own specific characteristics (richness, multiplicity, health, fecundity, and so on). This "structural evidence," which swells in volume as the structure grows more complex, reinforced the "comparative evidence," which could hardly appear in two distant cultures, like Vedic India and archaic Rome, by chance or coincidence. For another thing, Dumézil argued that myth (or theology) and epic (or legendary history, as at Rome) were linked by mechanisms of transposition. Thus, for example, the principal heroes of the *Mahâbhârata* reproduce and transpose the tri-functional characters of various much more ancient Vedic divinities. Likewise the events recounted in this story of war echo a history of the close of a cosmic cycle. These developments led Dumézil to correct his earlier intuition. Albeit fundamentally social, the ideology of the three functions does not reflect any actual social organization in a mechanical way, but it does make it possible to think the social world.[33]

Dumézil chose to view the functions of ideology in an innocent light, by not assigning it any clearly political role. His approach may be contrasted in this respect with that of Roland Barthes, for whom myth is less an eternal object than a signifying form, originally closely tied to its own proper historical context of production, and corresponding in every case to precise political and ideological functions. Barthes emphasizes in particular that myth tends to transform historical signs into atemporal essences, the particular into the universal, "history into nature." What it tries to do, in sum, is to "immobilize the world."[34] The African as refracted through the (colonialist) myth is not a particular individual, a person; he is the immutable image of negritude, meaning an essentially inferior being, which is how the defenders of the civilizing mission of the West liked to think of him. So for Barthes, far from being religious, the ideological and thus political functions of "mythification" may, for example, be made to serve racist beliefs. In many respects the antithetical figures of the Jew and the Aryan as constructed by Alfred Rosenberg (*Der Mythus des zwanzigsten Jahrhunderts*) and the Nazi ideologues can be seen as examples of the process described by Barthes.[35] These mythical figures appear in a given historical situation, and spring from a generative process well summed up in the expression "essentialist thinking."[36] This process too consists of transforming historical figures into immutable types, and in order to do so, it resorts to "dehistoricization, universalization, decontextualization," and "generalization."[37]

Four important conclusions follow from the preceding analyses.

a. The fact that myth can be made to bear a logico-semantic structure and cognitive functions (Lévi-Strauss), or a fundamentally social dimension and functions of an ideological[38] (Dumézil) or even political (Barthes) kind, or yet again a supernatural origin and mystico-ritual functions (Eliade) demonstrates that myth is no more than an empty vessel, that it possesses neither "self-nature,"[39] nor universally valid properties and functions, whether religious or of any other sort. These theories, like the putatively organic linkage between myth and religion, all wear the aspect of ad hoc creations.

b. The theories form an intelligible system, nevertheless, and it is the heir of a long tradition. Despite their individual features and the numerous influences they have metabolized, the sociological materialism of Dumézil, the sociopolitical variety of Barthes, the rustic Kantism of Lévi-Strauss, and the mysticism of Eliade (like that of Campbell and Jung) are the modern descendants of three of the major paradigms that run through the intellectual history of the West (materialism, a priorism, and Platonic mysticism). For Dumézil and Barthes the reference is the real social world, for Lévi-Strauss it is the neurocognitive mechanisms of the mind, and for Eliade it is a mysterious transcendence.

c. Contemporary theories of mythology thus have in common the remarkable fact that they only address (the origins of) myths (of origin) the better to address notions that they themselves have located at the origin of things that they have imagined and theorized in advance, whether it be thought, society, or *homo religiosus*. The object they claim to study, myth, is actually constituted out of postulates, notions, and concepts that they themselves have manufactured a priori, and that are obviously the ones they will (re)discover as the upshot of their analyses.[40] Circularity, or the mirror effect, is inevitable here. Each of these theories achieves its goals by imagining, in the manner of Sigmund Freud, a different version of the "myth of myth," the "religious" version being no more or less than one among them.

d. To this end, they have perfected very elaborate rhetorical and textual systems, endowed with truly cosmographic ambition, so driven do they all seem by the urge to erect "a grand theory or an overarching symbol system that could unify the world."[41]

Doubtless scientific (*sic*) theories and their objects of study have never been so closely aligned and so much . . . alike. But then, for the object to be perfectly reflected in theory, all you have to do is trim the mirror to the exact dimensions of its own reflection.

NOTES

1. Lincoln, B. *Theorizing Myth: Narrative, Ideology, and Scholarship* (Chicago: University of Chicago Press, 1999), ix.

2. Saloustios, *Des dieux et du monde* (Paris: Les belles lettres, 1960), 57–84; D. Dubuisson, *Dictionnaire des grands thèmes de l'histoire des religions* (Brussels: Complexe, 2004), 289–325.

3. Paul Veyne, *Did the Greeks Believe in Their Myths? An Essay on the Constitutive Imagination*, trans. Paula Wissing (Chicago: University of Chicago Press, 1988).

4. Marcel Detienne, *The Creation of Mythology*, trans. Margaret Cook (Chicago: University of Chicago Press, 1986), 239.

5. Francis Bacon, *The Advancement of Learning* (New York: Modern Library, 2001), xiii, 11; R. McCutcheon, *The Discipline of Religion: Structure, Meaning, Rhetoric* (London: Routledge, 2003), xii, 5.

6. D. Dubuisson, "Contributions à une poétique de l'œuvre," *Strumenti Critici* 85 (1997): 449–66.

7. R. Ellwood, *Politics of Myth: A Study of C. G. Jung, Mircea Eliade and Joseph Campbell* (New York: State University of New York Press, 1999), 171.

8. D. Dubuisson, "Pourquoi et comment parle-t-on des origines?," *Graphè* 4 (1995): 19–31.

9. Which are not actually all that "primitive," especially in the context of the overall history of the human species. But there was obviously an advantage to be gained by presenting them as the most archaic evidence of human thought and religious activity.

10. D. Dubuisson, *Twentieth Century Mythologies: Dumézil, Lévi-Strauss, Eliade*, trans. Martha Cunningham (London: Equinox, 2006), 3; Lincoln, *Theorizing Myth*, 95.

11. Dubuisson, *Twentieth Century Mythologies*; R. Segal, *Theorizing About Myth* (Amherst: University of Massachusetts Press, 1999); Lincoln, *Theorizing Myth*. The death of J. G. Frazer in 1941 marks the end, in a sense, of an epoch that began in the middle of the nineteenth century with the "naturalistic mythologies" (M. Müller, followed by A. Kuhn, M. Bréal, and the like), and with the agrarian mythology of W. Mannhardt, thronged with his celebrated *Vegetationgeister*. The position of G. Dumézil, who was born in 1898, is interesting in this respect. He began his career under the aegis of Frazer, and only found his own path toward the end of the 1930s, under the influence of the sociological theories of Marcel Mauss and Marcel Granet, in particular.

12. Dubuisson, *Twentieth Century Mythologies*, 1, 3.

13. Lincoln, *Theorizing Myth*, 141.

14. Segal, *Theorizing About Myth*, 3; D. Dubuisson, *The Western Construction of Religion: Myths, Knowledge, and Ideology*, trans. William Sayers (Baltimore: Johns Hopkins University Press, 2003), 116–44.

15. Claude Lévi-Strauss, *From Honey to Ashes*, trans. John Weightman and Doreen Weightman (London: Cape, 1973), 467.

16. Claude Lévi-Strauss, *Tristes tropiques*, trans. John Weightman and Doreen Weightman (New York: Atheneum, 1974), 58.

17. Claude Lévi-Strauss, *The View from Afar*, trans. Joachim Neugroschel and Phoebe Hoss (New York: Basic Books, 1985), 115, 118.

18. Lincoln, *Theorizing Myth*, 70–71.

19. I. Strenski, *Four Theories of Myth in Twentieth-Century History: Cassirer, Eliade, Lévi-Strauss and Malinowski* (Iowa City: University of Iowa Press, 1987); Dubuisson, *Twentieth Century Mythologies*; R. T. McCutcheon, *Manufacturing Religion* (New York: Oxford University Press, 1997), 27–100; McCutcheon, *The Discipline of Religion*, 191–212; S. Wasserstrom, *Religion After Religion: Gershom Scholem, Mircea Eliade and Henry Corbin at Eranos* (Princeton: Princeton University Press, 1999); T. Fitzgerald, *The Ideology of Religious Studies* (Oxford: Oxford University Press, 2000), 40.

20. Wasserstrom, *Religion after Religion*, 118.

21. Mircea Eliade, *The Sacred and the Profane: The Nature of Religion*, trans. Willard R. Trask (New York: Harcourt Brace and World, 1961), 12, 28, 63.

22. Wasserstrom, *Religion After Religion*, 246; Dubuisson, "The Poetical and Rhetorical Structure of the Eliadean Text: A Contribution to Critical Theory and Discourses on Religions," in *Hermeneutics, Politics, and the History of Religions: The Contested*

Legacies of Joachim Wach and Mircea Eliade, ed. Christian K. Wedemeyer and Wendy Doniger (Oxford: Oxford University Press, 2010).

23. Fitzgerald, *The Ideology of Religious Studies*, 31.

24. Eusebius Of Caesarea, *Preparation for the Gospel*, trans. E. H. Gifford (Grand Rapids: Baker Book House, 1981), 2.6:79–80.

25. McCutcheon, *Manufacturing Religion*, 201–2; Dubuisson, *Twentieth Century Mythologies*; Dubuisson, *The Western Construction of Religion*; King, *Orientalism and Religion* (London: Routledge, 1999), 11–14, 35–40; Fitzgerald, *The Ideology of Religious Studies* (Oxford: Oxford University Press, 2000), 5; Masuzawa, The *Invention of World Religions* (Chicago: Chicago University Press, 2005), xi–xiv; S. Engler, D. Miller and D. Dubuisson, "Review Symposium, Daniel Dubuisson, *The Western Construction of Religion*," *Religion* 36, no. 3 (2006): 119–78.

26. Dubuisson, *Twentieth Century Mythologies*, 209–19.

27. Ibid., 221–31.

28. Strenski, *Four Theories of Myth*, 212.

29. Mircea Eliade, *Occultism, Witchcraft and Cultural Fashions* (Chicago: University of Chicago Press, 1976), 47.

30. Eliade, *The Sacred and the Profane*, 18.

31. Dubuisson, *Twentieth Century Mythologies*, 274–75, 204. The most important of which were "borrowed" from the French esoterist René Guénon, in whom Eliade saluted a "learned and rigorous mind."

32. McCutcheon, *Manufacturing of Religion*, 13–18.

33. Dubuisson, *Twentieth Century Mythologies*, 9; Georges Dumézil, *Mariages indo-européens, suivi de Quinze questions romaines* (Paris: Éditions Payot, 1979) 89.

34. Roland Barthes, *Mythologies* (Paris: Éditions du Seuil, 1957), 202, 229.

35. L. Poliakov, *Aryan Myth* (New York: Basic Books, 1974); P. Lacoue-Labarthe and J.-L. Nancy, *Le mythe nazi* (Le Château: Éditions de l'aube, 1996), 51–60.

36. McCutcheon, *Manufacturing Religion*, 183.

37. Ibid., 28–180.

38. B. Malinowski, *Les argonautes du pacifique occidental* (Paris: Gallimard, 1989), 390. Close, no doubt, to the "normative influence of myth on usage" that B. Malinowski recognized in "these tales from long ago."

39. An echo of the Mûlamadhyamakakârikâ (15.1) of Nagârjuna: "The rise of self-nature by relational and causal conditions is not justifiable. For, such a self-nature will have a character of being made or manipulated."

40. McCutcheon, *Manufacturing Religion*, 19.

41. D. Dubuisson, *Anthropologie poétique (Esquisses pour une anthropologie du texte)* (Louvain: Peeters, 1996), 45–100; Dubuisson, *The Western Construction of Religion*, 195–213; Ellwood, *Politics of Myth*, 174; Dubuisson, "Contributions à une poétique de l'œuvre," 458–59.

PART VI

Religion/Society/Culture

PART VI

27

The Origins of the Sociology of Religion

The Problem of "Religion" and "Religions" in Classical Sociology

BRYAN S. TURNER

INTRODUCTION: ENLIGHTENMENT AND THE SCIENCE OF RELIGION

The Enlightenment prepared the groundwork for the emergence of the science of religion by treating religion as a discrete set of beliefs and practices that could be studied as social phenomena within a secular framework and with the assistance of human reason. In particular we can recognize Immanuel Kant's *Religion Within the Boundaries of Mere Reason*, which was published in 1793, as a decisive turning point in secular reflection upon religion.[1] Kant did not designate an independent branch of knowledge called the "philosophy of religion" and his essay as a contribution to ethics thereby escaped the censorship of the Church. Because it was not classified under "biblical theology," it could be read as an analysis of the "limits of reason." Kant's conclusions were nevertheless radical.[2] He argued that human beings, as moral agents, can exercise their duty only when they are free and in exercising these moral duties there is no need to posit a superior being and hence morality does not require religious presuppositions. When morality and religion become confused, the result is superstition or, worse still, idolatry in which human beings mistakenly believe they can influence God by sacrifice, petitions, and offerings. By separating morality from religious practice, Kant opened up the way toward a critical study of organized religion as the negation of human freedom. In short, Kantian philosophy prepared the way toward the interpretation of religion as human alienation, and it was this notion that became central to Karl Marx's commentary on religion via his engagement with G. W. F. Hegel.

While in intellectual terms the secular study of religion was an outcome of Enlightenment philosophy, the historical context of the science of religion cannot be entirely separated from European colonialism. In Western societies, the study of "religion" as a topic of anthropological inquiry was initially undertaken by theologians who wanted to understand how Christianity as a revealed religion could be or was differentiated from other religions. The problem of religious diversity arose as an inevitable consequence of growing colonial contact with other religious traditions such as Buddhism and with phenomena that shared a family resemblance, however distant, with organized religion such as fetishism, animism, and magic. Because the science of religion implies a capacity for neutrality, self-reflection, and criticism, it is often claimed that other religions that have not achieved this level of reflection and introspection do not possess an indigenous science of religion. While different cultures give religion a decisively local content, Pauline Christianity had become a world religion through a combination of missionary activity, colonial supremacy, and industrialization. This development was the context for Hegel's speculations about world history and the development of a global consciousness. For Hegel, religion and philosophy were both modes of access to understanding the Absolute, and philosophy of religion (*Religionsphilosophie*) was seen to be different from theology in that it was the study of religion as such. In Hegel's dialectical scheme, the increasing self-awareness of the Spirit was a consequence of the historical development of Christianity. The philosophical study of religion was interpreted as an important stage in the historical development of human understanding as such. In this sense, Christianity was, in Hegel's *Lectures on the Philosophy of Religion* of 1824, the "consummate religion."[3] Karl Marx appropriated these ideas but, criticizing Christian belief as a form of alienation, focused on the global thrust of industrial capitalism and celebrated the capacity of the transnational working class as a political force. The proletariat was now the material incarnation of the Universal Spirit through the medium of world capitalism.

In the early sociology of religion, the Weberian tradition was a response to Kant's idea that, as a moral and reflective faith, liberal Protestantism was a revolutionary social force. In this respect, *The Protestant Ethic and the Spirit of Capitalism* explored the unique relationship between the ascetic ethic of the Protestant sects and modernity. By contrast, the sociological tradition that we associate with Émile Durkheim and Marcel Mauss, while also influenced by Kant's epistemology, was not an attempt to study religions but an inquiry into the generic nature of religion. In *The Elementary Forms of the Religious Life*, Durkheim depended on missionary and administrative reports emerging from late-nineteenth-century colonialism to formulate a notion of the fundamental structures of religion. The foundations of the sociology of religion in this interpretation were created by an inquiry into the cultural uniqueness of the Protestant Reformation, on the one hand, and by an inquiry into the generic nature of religion as a system of elementary (or "primitive" in Durkheim's terms) classification, on the other. In the first tradition, the scientific question was posed by the historical consequences of Protestantism on the rationalization of society. In the second tradition, the issue was to understand how religion in some generic sense contributed to social classification and hence to social life as such.

In pre-Christian Roman society, religion (*religio*) was associated with the notion of scrupulosity or excess attention to the details of rituals. In Christian times, religion came to have a different meaning, because it began to assume a congregational organization and had to be contrasted with pagan practice. First, *relegere* from *legere* means "to pull together," "to harvest," or "to gather in," and second, *religare* from *ligare* means "to bind together." The first meaning directs our attention to the religious foundations of any social group that is gathered together and the second meaning encapsulates the disciplines or moral principles that are necessary for controlling human beings and creating a regulated moral life—indeed a particular mentality.[4] The first meaning indicates sociologically the role of the cult in forming human collectivities and social identity, while the second meaning points to the moral or regulatory practices of religion in the discipline of passions. These two etymological roots of the notion of religion further elucidate the separation in Kant's philosophical analysis between religion and morality. In Kant's essay on religion, there is a distinction between religion as cult (*des blossen Cultus*) in which individuals seeks worldly favors from God, especially health and wealth, through prayers, gifts, and sacrifice, and religion as moral action (*die Religion des guten Lebenswandels*) that commands human beings to change their personal behavior in order to lead a better life. Kant further elaborated this point by an examination of "reflecting faith" that compels humans to strive for salvation through faith alone rather than through the possession of a specialized body of religious knowledge. The implication of this Kantian distinction was that Protestant Christianity was the only genuine "reflecting faith," and in a sense therefore the model of all authentic religions. Kant's distinction was fundamentally about those religious injunctions that call human beings to moral action and hence demand that humans assert their autonomy and responsibility. This philosophical distinction can be translated into a division between prosperity cults, on the one hand, and austere, ascetic lifestyles on the other. In order to have autonomy, human beings need to act independently of God and without the support of ecclesiastical rituals and institutions. In a paradoxical fashion, Protestantism implies the "death of God" because it calls people to intellectual freedom and hence the Christian faith is ultimately self-defeating. If Christianity as a religion is successful, its adherents will no longer need it.

These Kantian principles were developed, however implicitly, in the sociology of Max Weber. In *The Sociology of Religion*, he distinguished between the religion of the masses and of the virtuosi. While the masses seek earthly comforts from religion, the virtuosi fulfill the ethical demands of religion in search of personal development, spiritual salvation, or enlightenment. The religion of the masses is associated with saints and holy men who satisfy their earthly needs, and hence charisma is constantly in danger of being undermined and corrupted by the popular demand for miracles and spectacles. More importantly, Weber distinguished between those religious orientations involving inner-worldly asceticism that reject the world by challenging its traditions and those religious orientations based on other-worldly mysticism that seek merely to escape from the world through mystical contemplation. The former religious orientation (primarily the radical Calvinistic sects) has had revolutionary consequences for society in, for example, the formation of rational capitalism. Through this process, Christianity gives rise to secularization, which spells out its own self-overcoming (*Aufhebung*), as it becomes progressively detached from revelation. Mysticism was more open to an accommodation with the secular needs of lay followers and hence exercised less leverage over the process of social change in human history.

In the regard to secularization, there is an important historical tension between religion and philosophy in terms of their often conflicting claims to truth. This tension involves the classical struggle between revelation and reason as different modes of understanding reality. The Enlightenment was significant in the development of classifications of religion, since the Enlightenment philosophers treated organized religion as a form of false knowledge. They emphasized the importance of rational self-inspection as a source of dependable understanding against revelation. In particular they rejected the idea that miracles could ever produce direct or valid knowledge of divinity. For Hume, Diderot, and Voltaire, Christianity was a form of irrational or mistaken knowledge of the world, and hence the Enlightenment greatly sharpened the distinction between revelation and reason as modes of apprehension of reality. The sciences of religion are a product of the Enlightenment in which knowledge of religion was important in the liberation of human beings from the false consciousness of revealed religion. Diderot was specifically critical of Christian institutions and Hume wrote somewhat ironically of the differences between monotheistic and polytheistic religions. The former religions are more likely to support authoritarian states, while the polytheistic traditions are more conducive to pluralism. The Enlightenment associated monotheism in general and Catholicism in particular with political intolerance, and advocated the separation of church and state as a necessary condition of individual liberties.

The connections between the Enlightenment and organized religion are, however, a good deal more complex than these introductory comments might suggest. When the Enlightenment philosophers spoke about "error," this was a code word for organized religions and hence Rousseau as a Deist could argue consistently that without faith there could be no virtue and without religion no morality. Rousseau invented the notion of a "civil religion" to describe a humanistic faith, free from the idea of human depravity, as the necessary buttress of civil society. In fact the main target of Rousseau's irony was the hypocrisy of the philosophers.[5] In a similar vein, Gabriel Bonnot de Mably, a central figure in republican thought during the French Revolution, argued that superstition was indispensable as social glue and cited the Roman Empire as an example. Mably suggested that we should learn to live with superstition until we have something better and more rational with which to replace it.[6] The Enlightenment philosophers were hostile to institutionalized Christianity, specifically the Roman Catholic Church, rather than to religion per se. In this respect these Enlightenment philosophers had much in common with the Cambridge Platonists and the latitudinarian movement of the seventeenth century, which sought to reject what it saw as the fanaticism of the Civil War and attempted to present Christian practice and belief as reasonable. There was therefore considerable philosophical (indeed theological) continuity between the Christian humanism of Erasmus and the Enlightenment. It also explains why their contemporaries suspected a political plot between Freemasonry and the Enlightenment with the aim of attacking the authoritarianism of the Church and the monarchy. There was consequently an important legacy of the Enlightenment that recognized, and frequently defended, the idea that religion played an important social role in society as a buttress of social *moeurs*. In this respect, we can detect an important continuity between Rousseau and the sociology of religion, especially in the work of Durkheim, who thought that the moral foundations of French society were being destroyed by egoistical individualism.

WEBER'S COMPARATIVE SOCIOLOGY OF RELIGION

Born in 1864 in Erfurt in Germany, Weber claimed to be influenced by both Friedrich Nietzsche and Karl Marx, but the Protestant piety of his mother and his wife Marianne Weber was equally significant. In his monumental biography of Weber, Joachim Radkau has shown how Weber's life and work were subconsciously organized around the personal tensions between the craving for a satisfactory secular and sensual life and the disciplined and ascetic world of academic study.[7] The contradictions in the religious life that he described in the Protestant Ethic thesis in many ways also described his own life. As a result of neurotic illness, Weber could not continue teaching as a professor and traveled throughout Europe seeking a cure. Eventually after a visit to America in 1904, he returned to his academic writing, producing a large collection of works on the comparative sociology of the religions. His most famous work—*The Protestant Ethic and the Spirit of Capitalism*—dates from this period. Weber died in 1920 and his sociology did not receive immediate acclaim. The study of Protestantism, which was translated by Talcott Parsons in 1930, has perhaps subsequently received too much attention in comparison to his studies for example of Judaism, Buddhism, or Confucianism. The Protestant Ethic was also originally treated as a rather simple but false causal argument that Protestantism caused capitalism. By contrast Weber was more concerned with what we would now call the cultural sociology of capitalism, namely, what cultural practices appear to be compatible, not narrowly with industrial capitalism, but more broadly with modernity. As a theorist of modernity, Weber's work has become more rather than less influential.

In the light of the Kantian background to German social science, we can plausibly claim that the thematic unity of Weber's work was the comparative sociology of religion, namely, an inquiry into the ways in which religious orientations toward the world did or did not lead to an ethic of world mastery, that is, to a process of rationalization. This particular interpretation of Weber depends significantly on the work of Friedrich Tenbruck, who argued that we should not treat the posthumous *Economy and Society* as the key text, but concentrate rather on Weber's writings on the economic doctrines of the world religions.[8] Thus in such works as the "Introduction" to the essays on the "Economic Ethic of the World Religions" and "the Author's Introduction" to *The Protestant Ethic and the Spirit of Capitalism*, Weber developed a comparative and historical conceptualization of these rationalization processes.[9] This development is wholly compatible with Weber's notion of interpretative sociology, because it was these constellations of meaning that generated specific worldviews that acted as the motivations for action. Weber developed the idea of an "interpretative sociology," or *Verstehende sociologie*. The much disputed notion of *verstehen* ("understanding") was an important part of his philosophy of social science in which he argued, against positivism, that the idea of causal laws of the natural sciences or the use of statistical correlations were never entirely adequate in the social sciences, because the social scientist has to take into account the intentions of social actors and the meanings with which they make sense of the social world. For example, in his study of Protestantism, he noted that there was a statistical correlation between Protestantism and business occupations in Germany, but the task of an interpretative sociology is to understanding the meaning of hard work, discipline, asceticism, and the calling for Protestants. While not rejecting either causal arguments or statistical analyses, Weber argued that "causal adequacy" could only be achieved by taking the meaning of actions into account. By understanding the meaning of religious values for action, Weber came to see modern society as the unintended and ironic consequence of Protestant piety.[10] This interpretation is also consistent with the idea of the fatefulness of world images in Weber's metatheory, because it was paradoxically the irrational quest for salvation that generated a rational framework for our being in the world.

Weber's analysis of the religious quest for salvation produced a theory of the norms that govern the practical conduct of life (*Lebensführung*). In his inquiry into religious conduct, Weber distinguished between a theodicy of good fortune (*Glück*) and a theodicy of suffering (*Leid*). In coping with misfortune and suffering, human beings project their conceptions of their personal experiences beyond the everyday material world. These experiences of contingent misfortune can eventually begin to undermine the rational or purposive categories of any pragmatic orientation to reality. There is no satisfactory rational explanation of suffering in this world where chance rather than virtue dominates. However, it was primarily within the monotheistic and ascetic religions that the rationalization of theodicy reached its ultimate expression. The development of the concept of a universal God as the framework of history and salvation produced a rational theodicy of reality as such. The legacy of the Judeo-Christian world, based upon the notions of ethical prophecy and monotheism, was crucial to the development of a radical solution to theodicy in terms of highly intellectual, rational soteriologies. For example, the intellectual rationalism of the Protestant sects was critical in pushing European civilization toward a pattern of religious individualism involving strict norms of personal discipline and conduct. However, the everyday needs for health and wealth that characterize the religious needs and orientation of the disprivileged and the downtrodden were very different from the motivations that drove the elite virtuosi.

Many of these issues in the interpretation of Weber's sociology have been further elaborated by Wilhelm Hennis, for whom the central theme in Weber's sociology was directed toward the analysis of personality and life orders.[11] The historical development of *Menschentum*, especially the rational civil servants of the state bureaucracy, was a central issue in Weber's sociology, namely, how certain cultural developments produced a particular type of personality and a particular rational conduct of life (*Lebensführung*) particularly in the idea of a calling as part of the constitutive question of modernity.[12] In this respect Weber followed Nietzsche in describing the Last Men as people who have closed their eyes to the tragedy of human existence by encasing themselves in a happy social cocoon.[13] In more precise terms, Weber's sociology addressed the historical origins of life regulation as rational conduct in the development of professional vocations in the modern world. Weber's analysis of the ascetic regulation of life is therefore simply one dimension of this analysis of *Lebensführung*, or the study of personality types arising from particular kinds of (religious) practice.

The rationalization theme to which Weber draws attention in the Protestant Ethic thesis involved a transformation of discipline and methodology relevant to particular forms of economic life regulation. Weber's analysis of rational capitalism was not so much concerned to explain its economic structure and functions but to understand the ways in which forms of capitalist economic activity had an "elective affinity" with specific forms of personality and life order. By "personality" Weber did not have in mind what we would now call "the personality system" within an empirical social psychology, but rather what kind of being would be produced by different life orders, that is, Weber asked an existential question from the perspective of German cultural values.

Weber's central question was about the ethical character of human existence and not about the narrow question of the cultural foundations of Western capitalism in the theology of the Protestant sects. These issues—human nature and rational capitalism, personal happiness and discipline, human nature and social conventions, charisma versus bureaucracy—were deeply embedded in Weber's personal life and were reiterated in Weber's sociology as themes about rational modernity. As a result we can better understand that "Weber was a *German* thinker, from the land of 'Dr Faustus.'"[14] The tragic problem of Weberian sociology is that the heroic personality of Protestant asceticism is no longer compatible with the secular world of capitalism. In 1905 at the end of *The Protestant Ethic and the Spirit of Capitalism*, Weber, in a nostalgic mood, asked himself what had happened to religious asceticism: "Today its spirit has fled from this shell—whether for all time who knows? Certainly, victorious capitalism has no further need for this support now that it rests on the foundation of the machine . . . the idea of the 'duty in a calling' haunts our lives like the ghost of once-held religious beliefs."[15] Modern society is the disenchanted garden in which a meaningful life has been replaced by mere routine, mechanical discipline, and technical efficiency. It is a world that Nietzsche criticized as a form of cultural nihilism. In Weber's mind, there may well have been a deliberate reference in the title of *The Protestant Ethic and the Spirit of Capitalism* to Nietzsche's *The Birth of Tragedy from the Spirit of Music* (in the 1866 edition *The Birth of Tragedy; Or, Hellenism and Pessimism*). Nietzsche's characterization of Greek tragedy in terms of the struggle between Apollo and Dionysus found an echo in Weber's idea that the birth of modern tragedy was the unintended or fateful consequence of the spirit of pietism.[16]

In summary, Weber was not interested in the problem of religion in general. It is partly for this reason that he, unlike Durkheim, dismissed the quest for an adequate definition of religion as a prerequisite for the sociology of religion. At the beginning of *The Sociology of Religion* Weber more or less precludes any such discussion: "To define 'religion' to say what it *is*, is not possible at the start of a presentation such as this. Definition can be attempted, if at all, only at the conclusion of the study.[17]

The essence of religion is not even our concern, as we make it our task to study the conditions and effects of a particular type of social behavior." This argument is very far removed from Durkheim's task, which was specifically concerned to delineate the "essence of religion."

DURKHEIM, RELIGION, AND THE SACRED AS CLASSIFICATION

While Weber came eventually to be regarded the giant of German sociology, Émile Durkheim was without parallel the founding father of twentieth-century French sociology. Born in 1858 at Epinal in Lorrain, in his own lifetime Durkheim also experienced many of the deep contradictions of French society, just as Weber's life expressed a deep ambivalence toward German society, especially German Protestantism. Although Durkheim's family tradition was deeply influenced by rabbinical Judaism, he was closely identified with the rational thought of secular republicanism.[18] He was concerned by the decline of social solidarity in late-nineteenth-century France, which was going through a rapid period of urbanization and economic change; the new emphasis on individualism and secularism, evident in the rising suicide rate, threatened France with social dislocation, for which he invented the notion of anomie. Although he was identified with socialism, Durkheim took a conservative view of the importance of moral regulation of the individual and state regulation of society, following Rousseau in applauding the functions of a civil religion.

What then is the argument of *The Elementary Forms* of 1912? We can grasp Durkheim's sociology of religion to some extent as a response to the philosophy of Kant, since Durkheim's sociology of knowledge rejected the epistemological arguments of Kant's critique by demonstrating how individual concepts acquire their generality and force from social forces. He rejected the idea that the fundamental concepts of the mind are a priori categories and sought instead to identify universal aspects of classificatory systems in the social structure. In order to understand Durkheim's analysis of aboriginal totemism, we need therefore to start with his theory of classification.

Durkheim's sociology of religion is an application of the arguments put forward with Marcel Mauss in *Primitive Classification*, which first appeared in volume six of the *Annee Sociologique* in 1901–02.[19] Durkheim's study of the principles of primitive totemism as a method of cultural classification has become one of the great classics of sociological thought. His argument is complex and much contested. While the arguments of Durkheim and Mauss have been either neglected by philosophy or treated as unsupportable by anthropologists, we can learn a great deal about the general problem of classification from their work. I take their underlying question to be: How can classifications have any authoritative force? More specifically, if all classification is essentially arbitrary, how can classification ever have any force in social arrangements? Both *Primitive Classification* and *The Elementary Forms* attempt to understand (religious) knowledge from the sociological study of the general forms of classification, especially forms of classification that divide the world into the sacred and the profane or the prohibited and the permitted.

There is a double meaning to Durkheim's notion of the "elementary." At one basic level "elementary" does mean "primitive" and hence Durkheim's sociology was a second-order reflection on the original field work that had been carried out in Australia by Baldwin Spencer and F. J. Gillen, an anthropologist and a colonial magistrate, and published as *Native Tribes of Central Australia* in 1899 and *The Northern Tribes of Central Australia* in 1904.[20] But Durkheim's intention was also to give a more general sociological account of the fundamental forms of the collective structures of consciousness, and hence "elementary" means "foundational" or "constitutive." The subtitle of the earlier work on primitive classification—*A Study of Collective Representations*—perhaps makes their intellectual intentions more transparent. These primitive forms of collective representation are the elementary or foundational principles of cultural classification. Durkheim argues that we cannot understand forms of consciousness by a study of the consciousness of separate individuals in terms of Kantian philosophy. More specifically, we cannot grasp the nature of thought through a psychological study of the contents of human minds. The social comes before and indeed produces the individual, and thus to understand consciousness (and systems of classification) we need to study social forms. The explicit thesis of Durkheim's study is that it is society itself that presents the mind with these "primitive forms," namely, the elementary forms of classification.

What was the originality of Durkheim's study of religion? Durkheim was a rationalist and positivist in his approach to sociology, in which his intention was to understand "social facts," that is, phenomena that are independent of individuals. Despite Durkheim's secular rationalism, he came to see the religious as the wellspring of social life. Talcott Parsons famously observed in *The Structure of Social Action* (1937) that Durkheim at the conclusion of his career came to recognize that it was religion that produced society, not society that produced religion.[21] Durkheim's sociology of religion departed decisively with the intellectual environment of nineteenth-century individualism, evolutionary thought, and cognitive rationalism. Before the development of Durkheim's sociology of religion, rationalist theories of religion treated the religious beliefs of primitive society as irrational or at least as mistaken views of reality. Primitive religion was seen to be animist, because it proposed that natural phenomena were governed or animated by spirits. Natural science would eventually show that primitive magic and mythology were based on false beliefs, and hence the spread of science would lead eventually to the demise of religion. Durkheim was especially critical of such rationalist views, emphasizing the continuing social importance of religion to social cohesion.

It was against that late-nineteenth-century background of individualistic, rationalist, and psychological theories of religion that Durkheim's generic definition of religion was intellectually interesting and influential. According to his famous definition, Durkheim proposed that religion is "a unified system of beliefs and practices relevant to sacred things, that is to say, things set apart and surrounded by prohibitions—beliefs and practices that unite its adherents in a single moral community called a church."[22] Religion does not generically involve a belief in a high

God or gods, but rather a unified system of beliefs and practices based upon a classification of social reality into the sacred and profane. Durkheim thereby redirected attention away from individuals to social groups, or what he called a moral community. Religion as a social phenomenon is thus set apart from magic, which was seen by Durkheim to be an individual activity. There is no church of magic, and religion survives because it satisfies a basic social function, not a psychological one. Thus Durkheim argued there is no society that does not need at regular intervals to sustain and reaffirm its collective emotions and ideas in order to survive as a community.

In this sense there are no false or irrational religions, because religion is the self-representation of society, that is, its collective representation. In these arguments Durkheim was influenced by pragmatism, specifically by William James in his *The Varieties of Religious Experience* of 1902.[23] From a pragmatist position, it does not make sense to ask about the truth of religious classificatory practices; rather, classificatory systems are only more or less useful in helping us to cope with reality rather than true or false in explaining reality. Just as it makes no sense to ask whether cricket as an activity is true or false, so it makes no sociological sense to inquire into the truth or falsity of religious practices. Religion is primarily a collective activity based on a classification of things into the sacred (set apart and forbidden) and profane (part of the everyday world). Because religion is collective, it is experienced as obligatory on the life of the individual. In this sense, religion is what Durkheim called a social fact—a phenomenon outside the individual, existing independently, and exercising moral force over society. Finally it makes little sense to have a strong evolutionary view of religion. In modern society, while the collective sense of the sacred may be less vivid, the same functions can be detected.

The principal implication of his argument is that the collective and emotional character of classificatory practices in modern societies has broken down, and that with modernity there is greater indeterminacy because individuals can become more reflective about classificatory principles. They are no longer taken for granted and they are exposed to the corrosive effects of an individualistic and secular culture. However, under certain circumstances such as revolutionary moments or a collective threat to a society in wartime, collective symbolism once more becomes crucial. The lasting value of Durkheim's work is therefore the insight it gives us into traumatic events, collective emotions, and symbols in modern politics. Why has there been a revival of religion in the public sphere? Why have forms of religious nationalism become so prevalent? One answer is that religious cosmologies and collective symbolization now have a collective force that was not fully available to the secular ideological systems of Stalinism or Maoism, which collapsed after a relatively short period. However, even in the secular climate of communist China, Mao eventually assumed the characteristics of an imperial cult in attracting the devotion of the masses.[24] By contrast to secular politics, religion allows a national community to express its history in deep-rooted myths or sacred time as if that national history had a universal significance, namely, to express the mythical history of a nation in terms of a story of suffering and survival about humanity as a whole. The classical illustrations would be Poland, Mexico, and the Philippines. Poland above all understood itself as the Crucified Nation of Europe. We might note the obvious point that these are Catholic societies in which Roman Catholic symbolism, especially the figures of the Crucified Christ and the lamenting Virgin Mary, is crucial to their historical self-understanding as imagined communities. The Protestant Churches have been more readily the vehicles for expressive individualism and subjectivism and perhaps less able to function as national vehicles of collective action. The exceptions might be Protestant nationalism in Scotland and Northern Ireland. Reading Durkheim's classic study of religion thus continues to offer us a creative sociological insight into these ongoing tensions between nationalism religious revival and individual subjectivity in modern cultures, proving a stimulus to the constant renewal of sociological theory. Religion has a major role in society because it is the foundation of our collective representation, and hence collective memory, of the social.[25]

CONCLUSION: ENLIGHTENMENT OR REVELATION

What in conclusion is the relationship between Weber and Durkheim in the history of the sociology of religion? Weber was unambiguously convinced that the reflecting faith of Kant's philosophy had contributed to the ultimate rationalization of the world, but Weber could not feel comfortable with the bleak world of modern bureaucracies or industrial capitalism. The Protestant Ethic can be understood as a tragic doctrine about the fatefulness of modern life resulting in an "iron cage." If Weber felt that he was under the shadow of Kantian duty, he also recognized the force of Nietzsche's objections to metaphysics as an expression of nihilism and resentment. For Weber and Nietzsche, God was dead, in the sense that religious belief could no longer command any widespread or collective authority, and both men recognized the human cost of this historical event. In this respect, we can interpret Weber's sociology of Protestantism as a Nietzschean account of the Cartesian separation of body and mind in Western metaphysics. By denying the corporeal or sensual character of human existence and elevating duty as the principal characteristic of human freedom, Protestantism ultimately denied Life. Weber's sociology of religion is therefore an account of the unintended consequences of Reformation rationality, namely, the paradoxical creation of a routinized social world. In this regard, Weber's celebration of Life and Nature was consistent with the contemporary German interest in the late nineteenth century for "primal reality" in art, culture, and politics.[26]

Durkheim, while also profoundly influenced by Kantian epistemology, was more concerned with practice than belief. He also recognized that the authority of our fundamental categories was social rather than logical. Durkheim argued that the very existence of society presupposed collective beliefs and emotions that had their roots in something that we ultimately want to call "the sacred." Modern philosophers such as Charles Taylor have claimed that we are living in a post-Durkheimian world, but Durkheim's view of social reality is perhaps more enduring and pertinent than Weber's pessimistic analysis of rationalization.[27] In the shape of religious nationalism, fundamentalism, and public religions, Durkheimian religious effervescence is a significant force in many social and political movements in the modern world.

NOTES

1. Immanuel Kant, *Religion Within the Boundaries of Mere Reason* (Cambridge: Cambridge University Press, 1998).
2. Ernst Cassirer, *Kant's Life and Thought* (New Haven: Yale University Press, 1981), 382.
3. Georg Wilhelm Friedrich Hegel, *Lectures on the Philosophy of Religion* (Berkeley: University of California Press, 1985).
4. Émile Benveniste, *Indo-European Language and Society* (London: Faber and Faber, 1973).
5. Mark Hulliung, *The Autocritique of Enlightenment: Rousseau and the Philosophes* (Cambridge, Mass.: Harvard University Press, 1994).
6. Johnson Kent Wright, *A Classical Republican in Eighteenth-Century France: The Political Thought of Mably* (Stanford: Stanford University Press, 1997).
7. Joachim Radkau, *Max Weber: A Biography* (Cambridge: Polity, 2009).
8. Freidrich Tenbruck, "The Problem of the Thematic Unity in the Works of Max Weber," *British Journal of Sociology* 31, no. 3 (1980): 316–51; Max Weber, *Economy and Society: An Outline of Interpretive Sociology* (Berkeley: University of California Press, 1978).
9. Hans H. Gerth and Charles Wright Mills, eds., *From Max Weber: Essays in Sociology* (London: Routledge, 1991).
10. Bryan S. Turner, "Islam, Capitalism and the Weber Thesis," *British Journal of Sociology* 25, no. 2 (1974): 230–43.
11. Wilhelm Hennis, *Max Weber: Essays in Reconstruction* (London: Allen and Unwin, 1988).
12. Georg Stauth and Bryan S. Turner, *Nietzsche's Dance: Resentment, Reciprocity and Resistance in Social Life* (Oxford: Basil Blackwell, 1988).
13. Leslie Paul Thiele, *Timely Meditations: Martin Heidegger and Postmodern Politics* (Princeton: Princeton University Press, 1995), 221.
14. Hennis, *Max Weber*, 195.
15. Max Weber, *The Protestant Ethic and the "Spirit" of Capitalism, and Other Writings* (New York: Penguin, 2002), 121.
16. Bryan S. Turner, *For Weber: Essays in the Sociology of Fate* (London: Sage, 1996).
17. Max Weber, *The Sociology of Religion* (London: Methuen, 1966), 1.
18. Steven Lukes, *Emile Durkheim: His Life and Work; A Historical and Critical Study* (London: Allen Lane, 1973).
19. Émile Durkheim and Marcel Mauss, *Primitive Classification* (Chicago: University of Chicago Press, 1963).
20. Baldwin Spencer and F. J. Gillen, *The Northern Tribes of Central Australia* (London: Routledge, 1997).
21. Talcott Parsons, *The Structure of Social Action* (New York: McGraw-Hill, 1937).

22. Émile Durkheim, *The Elementary Forms of the Religious Life* (New York: Oxford University Press, 2001), 46.

23. William James, *The Varieties of Religious Experience* (New York: Longmans, Green, 1922).

24. Fenggang Yang, "The Red, Black and Gray Markets of Religion in China," *Sociological Quarterly* 47 (2006): 93–122.

25. Daniele Hervieu-Leger, *Religion as a Chain of Memory* (Cambridge: Polity, 2000).

26. A. K. Wiedman, *The German Quest for Primal Origins in Art, Culture and Politics, 1900–1933* (New York: Edwin Mellor Press, 1995).

27. Charles Taylor, *A Secular Age* (Cambridge, Mass.: Belknap Press of Harvard University Press, 2007).

28

Contemporary Social Theory and Religion

The Misconstrual of Religion in Theories of "Second" Modernity

SIMON SPECK

INTRODUCTION

Since its inception social theory's central concern has been the analysis of modernity.[1] Over the last forty years this engagement with the origins, nature, and assumptions of modernity as a distinct institutional and cultural complex has intensified as the debate over "postmodernity" has waxed and waned across the humanities and social sciences. Simultaneously, this period has witnessed the so-called resurgence of religion as a global phenomenon, characterized by the greater public visibility of religion alongside the emergence of new modes of religious self-expression. In this conjuncture, then, one might expect that anyone seeking to understand the ways in which contemporary society and culture give rise to, and are affected by, these transformations of religious practice and belief—and how these might, in turn, be understood as constituting transformations within "modernity" itself—could turn to social theory for enlightenment. Yet, while the sociology of religion has been galvanized by the impact of modernization on religious life, much of the most important and influential work on modernity has ignored or misunderstood the phenomenon. In the following, I focus on one of the most telling examples of this failure of engagement in the treatment of religion in the work of three leading social theorists for whom modernity is of central concern: Zygmunt Bauman, Anthony Giddens, and Ulrich Beck.[2]

It is instructive to view these theorists synoptically, as it were, inasmuch as they share not only a common focus on but also a similar schematization of the problematic of "modernity." This is to say, Bauman, Giddens, and Beck are united in conceptualizing the contemporary age as constituted by the transition from a "first" modernity (the era of industrial society, classical social theory's object of study) to a "second" modernity (the era whose cultural, economic, and political contours become visible in the West in the late 1960s). In contrast to the notion of "post-" modernity, this historical shift is seen to be *immanent* to modernity—the result of the process of modernization itself, which has the unintended effect of unsettling and destabilizing the fixed certainties and assumptions of industrial society yet thereby radicalizing (rather than replacing) the defining features of modernity. For Bauman, Giddens, and Beck, the social and cultural transformations of the past half-century can best be conceived as a recapitulation of the passage from traditional society to modern society, now occurring "within" the institutional framework of modernity itself. This is the dissolution of the countermodern attitudes on which the key institutions of modernity depended—what Beck refers to as "the tradition-ality inherent in industrialism."[3] Thus, the mainstays of individual and collective identity in the age of "first" modernity—class-communal membership, ascribed gender roles, tribalistic national identity—together with the legal-normative and cognitive framework provided by the nation-state and industrialized techno-science are utterly transformed by the far-reaching consequences of their own implementation. This takes place for better *and* for worse: the certainties of an infallible scientism are undermined yet scientific rationality remains indispensable to social reproduction and human well-being, and the constraints of stratification by status (whether class-communal, gender, or race) are dissolved yet with the ambivalent result that individuals are then set "free" to forge their own destiny in a world of endemic material inequality, without communal supports or self-evident norms. Conceived as a dynamic of thoroughgoing detraditionalization, the passage into a "second" modernity is, therefore, figured not only as the "modernization of modernity" but also as the "secularization of secularity." Hence, the persistence or, indeed, resurgence of religion can only be construed as an attempt to evade the challenges of cognitive and normative relativization and the existential demands of individualization and the economic, political, and cultural implications of global interdependence by taking refuge in the certainty and security provided by unquestionable dogma. In a nutshell: in second modernity religion must take the form of *fundamentalism*. In the course of this essay I will rehearse the broad outlines of this argument as it is presented in the work of Bauman and Giddens while tracing Beck's departure from the consensus with the publication of his important book *A God of One's Own*, where the relationship between religious resurgence and reflexive modernization is reevaluated. While recognizing the advance this represents in the analysis of religion in second modernity, I argue that Beck nonetheless retains the polarized categories of Bauman and Giddens (dogmatic religious fundamentalism versus enlightened-secular moral reason) in his construal of religious modernity as constituted by an intolerant institutionalized religion in opposition to an ecumenical individualized "religiosity." I conclude by adumbrating the ways in which the theories of second modernity provide a theoretical framework for the analysis of contemporary religiosity despite the flaws in their own cursory or prejudiced treatment of the subject.

ZYGMUNT BAUMAN: RELIGION AS THE SOLACE OF FLAWED CONSUMERS

Zygmunt Bauman was born in Poland in 1925 and educated in the Soviet Union. Bauman left Poland in the late 1960s as a result of the upsurge of party-sponsored anti-Semitism, moving to Britain, where he became professor of sociology at the University of Leeds in 1971 and where he has been emeritus professor since his formal retirement in 1990.[4] Bauman's earlier work engaged with questions of social class and socialist politics as well as hermeneutical philosophy and sociological method. Since the mid-1980s, however, he has been an influential voice in the debates in the social sciences around the meaning of "postmodernity." In the last three decades Bauman's work has shifted from a critique of the amorality of rationalization as it was entrenched within Western modernity[5] and a qualified embrace of the ethical potential inherent in postmodern sensitivity to Otherness[6] to providing an unremittingly negative evaluation of the contemporary epoch—now figured as "liquid modernity"—as one in which thoroughgoing commodification and the reduction of all social relations to market-conformity undermine any possibility of individual and collective autonomy.[7] In much of the work of the 1980s and early 1990s Bauman underscored the totalitarian potential of modernity in its deployment of instrumental reason with the aim of constructing the perfect social order. For Bauman, the collapse of these pretensions is, therefore, hardly to be regretted insofar as it enables the reemergence of authentic individual responsibility, the acceptance of ambivalence as constitutive of human experience, and the recognition of the price to be paid for utopian projects seeking to realize heaven on earth. Nonetheless, as Bauman's exploration of the political, cultural, and affective dimensions of "liquid times" has unfolded in the course of the last fifteen years, his estimation of the potential for human emancipation and genuine self-determination has become ever more sanguine. Thus, despite the (moderate) shift of emphasis, Bauman's evaluations of "post-" and "liquid" modernity are unified by their concern with the two key features that bear directly on his view of the place of religion in contemporary society: "second" modernity as an era of radicalized uncertainty and rampant consumerism.[8]

It is in the essay "Postmodern Religion?," published in 1997, where Bauman chooses to discuss the place and character of religion in the contemporary era. He situates it within the social and cultural context of "post-" or "liquid"[9] modernity—an epoch of rapid and disorienting change in which individual orientation and conduct are patterned after what Bauman will later come to call the "consumerist syndrome."[10] Individuals now experience social and psychic life as one of unceasing experimentation and transience—the "solidity" that in the age of industrial society was provided by stable institutions and unquestionably "rational" norms is volatilized and we are cast into a deregulated and privatized existence where "choice" reigns supreme and "everything is or should be handled like a commodity."[11] Existential dilemmas are resolvable problems whose solution is to be found on the shelves of shops,[12] yet the nature of both the solutions and the problems will change with the next change in fashion, leaving people with no sense of permanence, continuity, or firm foundation in a life transformed into a series of episodic choices. This gives rise to two consequences with profound implications for religion in contemporary society: in the first place it effects the dissolution of tradition—as Bauman states matters, "there is a close link between the value of durability and the entrenchment of moral standards"[13]—and in the second place it impels people to look for expert guidance in their choice-making, giving rise to a whole "industry" of counselors and lifestyle gurus. In approaching the understanding of religion, Bauman draws heavily on Leszek Kolakowski's conception of religion as stemming from human insufficiency[14]—religious belief and practice is predicated on the assumption of unalterable human weakness and the acknowledgment of the "noumenal" dimension of existence.[15] Human beings are frail creatures in need of help from a deity whose purposes are ultimately inscrutable. The religious worldview is thereby undermined, in Bauman's construal, by solid modernity's pragmatic concern with providing solutions for the ills of humanity—resulting in an "anti-eschatological revolution,"[16] which places the stress on medicine's extension of life rather than religion's explanation of its meaning. This is radicalized by post- or liquid modernity's sense of total immanence. Thus, Bauman argues that the expression "postmodern religion" is oxymoronic and any identification of postmodernity with the resurgence of religion is an optical illusion. The admission of insufficiency is far from the concern of New Age religiosity whose "peak experiences" are wrongly identified by theorists with the ascetic practices of yore—they are, in fact, part of the consumerist compulsion to develop "experiential potential" and try the next life-enhancing sensation on offer. The message of "spirituality" is, then, *you can do it*. Furthermore, the pursuit of spiritual wisdom in these cases is akin to the need for authoritative guidance in an age of continual change, when choices must be made but individuals' resources for doing so have been undermined. In Bauman's view, people don't need preachers telling them about weakness and insufficiency but counselors providing them with the motivation and confidence to make the most of their opportunities.

Nonetheless, for Bauman there *is* a form of religiosity that is authentically "religious" in its appeal to human insufficiency *and* "postmodern" in its address to individuals afloat in a world of infinite choice: *fundamentalism*. If New Age spirituality is the (pseudo)religion of those in search of guidance, opening up new opportunities for consumerist self-exploration and sensation, fundamentalism is the religion of those left out of the party—it addresses the poor and excluded, those who experience the compulsory individualization that comes with the globalization of free markets and the shriveling of collective provision and welfare protection. It is authentically religious because it embraces the idea of human insufficiency *and* genuinely postmodern because, rather than focus on the human species, it bears on the individual as such: it addresses me in my sense of frailty and consoles me in my sense of weakness. As such it is the religion of "flawed consumers,"[17] for whom it solves the problem of freedom by abolishing it.[18]

Fundamentalism is an attempt to recover what post- or liquid modernity has dissolved—a firm and communal foundation for individual existence. As Bauman summarizes: "The allure of fundamentalism stems from its promise to emancipate the converted from the agonies of choice. Here one finds, finally, the indubitably supreme authority, an authority to end all other authorities."[19] Yet it is not only a dangerous throwback to solid modernity's most dangerous features in its prototo-talitarian construction of a *mappa vitae*—an answer to all aspects of existence[20]—but it is nonetheless undone by its emphatic "postmodernity": Bauman maintains that individuals' "neo-tribalist" affiliation to such religious communities and institutions tends to be as provisional, contingent, and short term as the transient and pragmatic contractual relations from which they are seeking escape.

ANTHONY GIDDENS: RELIGION AS THE REFUSAL OF REFLEXIVITY

If Bauman's view of contemporary modernity is marked by a bleakness that is qualified solely by an acknowledgment of the benefits of emancipation from solid modernity's functionalist ethics, Anthony Giddens's perspective is one that appears to radiate an optimism undaunted by the new challenges of the age. In Giddens's account the "modernization of modernity" is the process that realizes the principles of Enlightenment reason, now educated by the experience of its own (mis)application and self-misunderstanding. Giddens, a British social theorist of world renown, was born in 1938 and is currently emeritus professor of sociology at the London School of Economics. Giddens's career could be said to divide into three stages: His works of the 1970s focusing on classical and contemporary social theory[21] were followed by a period during which his concern was with methodological questions, culminating in his theory of "structuration" in the mid-1980s.[22] With the publication of *The Consequences of Modernity* in 1991, Giddens's attention shifted to the analysis of the contours of "modernity" as an institutional and cultural complex whose capacity for self-reflexivity granted it a globalizing and individualizing dynamic of apparently inexhaustible potential. The political implications of this were explored in his book *Beyond Left and Right: The Future of Radical Politics*, published in 1994, where he sought to develop a "politics of emancipation" that took account of the changed social, cultural, and economic conditions and that was popularized in *The Third Way*, published in 1998—the book that identified Giddens with Tony Blair's New Labor government in Britain and led to his elevation to the House of Lords in 2004.

In Giddens the same key themes are apparent—the loss of tradition and pell-mell "individualization"—that are evident in Bauman's account and, for that reason, despite the radical differences in their evaluation of the emancipatory potential of "second" modernity, both tend to arrive at the same conclusion regarding the place of religion in contemporary society. Religion is, ultimately, a retreat into unquestionable dogma in the face of the challenges of individualization with its demand for reflection and choice-making—the flight from a thoroughly secularized world of provisional and contingent cognitive and normative truths. Giddens's account of second modernity is centered on its emancipatory potential, which resides primarily in its institutionalization of reflexivity. The loss of the "traditional" coordinates of classical modernity, which fixed individual identity and social norms in the certainties of scientistic rationality, class-community, and prescribed gender roles,[23] registers the emergence of an individual autonomy that is paradigmatically modern in its stress upon individual self-determination and the right to demand justification of cognitive and normative authorities. In Giddens's account the global spread of Western modernity was the result of its capacity to maintain and regulate social

interactions across distance—"disembedding" social relations from their dependence on physical and temporal copresence through "time-space distanciation"
effected by technologies that render time and space abstract and quantifiable—
clocks and maps, chiefly.[24] This in turn was made possible by the use of mediating
"symbolic tokens" such as money, and rationalized administrative "expert systems"
functioning independently of direct human intervention and capable of self-
monitoring and correction. Thus, we witness a "stretching" of social relations,
dependent on expert systems in which social agents are required to place their
confidence in the result that *trust* is a fundamental psychic orientation in modernity. Our lives are dependent on the smooth running of expert systems that cannot, however, be completely protected against malfunction or accident: yet this
does not reduce us to a feeling of powerlessness, as if we were thrown back into
a state of anomie and at the mercy of supernatural agencies, for trust is in large
part *rational*—it must be earned. Hence, it implies a democratization of expertise; a process of "re-embedding" must take place whereby the expert systems
and their purpose and rationality are made subject to popular understanding and
consent. This allows us a sense of "ontological security," enabling us to tolerate
and navigate a world of irreducible contingency and change without the loss of
the underlying sense of continuity and integrity of experience.[25]

The "reflexivity" of modernity is, then, the *demand for justification*: the "secularization of secularity" proceeds apace as expertise and administrative power are
viewed with a skepticism that is rational and systematic in its appeal to the stated
principles and aims. We no more "believe in" the wisdom of the scientist and bu-
reaucrat than we do the chieftain or priest. This situation is further intensified with
the emergence of "manufactured risks"—the dangers confronting modern society
that are the result of social action itself (climate change, Bovine Spongiform En-
cephalitis [BSE], avian flu, and so on)—where the risks are of a global-universal *and*
individual-existential nature but also where they reveal the irrationality of scientific
and administrative reason in its failure to anticipate the disastrous side effects of
previous knowledge and policy. The recognition that the narrowly technocratic definition of risk is inadequate means a deepening of the reflexive demand for the
democratization of expertise and an acknowledgment of the ethical implications
of the definition of risk itself whereby "acceptable" risk is inseparable from "a consideration of desired ways of life."[26] The consideration of conduct detached from
a taken-for-granted legitimation by culture and custom also implies a reflexive individualization whereby one's identity is subject to self-scrutiny and revision and
choices have to be made that must be justified on the basis of principles and evaluated in the light of possible outcomes (that is, risks) and for which tradition is an
inadequate guide.

Giddens states emphatically that "modernity destroys tradition."[27] It replaces the
"formulaic notion of truth"—the body of esoteric wisdom rooted in the past and
accessible only to a hieratic authority—with "corrigible knowledge." If classical modernity tended to instrumentalize tradition as a form of legitimation, the reflexivization of modernity issues in the end of tradition concomitant with the "end of
nature":[28] as a result of the Promethean energies of industrial modernity, we

confront a world thoroughly transformed by human agency but not to universal advantage, with the result that human autonomy is key but unquestionable authority is lacking. This gives rise to the liberating *and* disorienting prospect that "in post-traditional contexts we have no choice but to choose how to be and act"[29] but to do so without total certainty of the bases of action, or results. In the face of contemporary risks, there are only multiple and contending authorities but no "super authority." Traditions therefore accommodate themselves to the modern world either by the inflexible reassertion of the formulaic truth without regard to consequences or context *or* by seeking to defend and justify themselves in the light of the very difficulties and demands of living in a state of radical doubt.[30] The latter acknowledges the relativization that results from a world of plural worldviews and multiple authorities: the former is defined by Giddens as "tradition defended the traditional way"[31] and describes how "tradition becomes fundamentalism."[32] As was the case with Bauman, then, second modernity is characterized by a radical individualization whereby people must make choices whose consequences are far-reaching and unclear, without recourse to the unquestionable authority of custom or tradition and in a context of rapid economic, technological, and political change. Again, the resurgence of religion is understood in the light of the shaking of "ontological security." In the more benign and accommodating forms exemplified by New Age spirituality, it involves the reflexively induced manufacture of "sham" traditions[33]—selecting from a range of choices to consciously construct a set of convictions and beliefs that enable one to navigate the challenges of risk society. However, in its fundamentalist guise religion is, for Giddens, akin to addiction—another characteristic feature of reflexive modernity—in its cultivation of stasis, the enabling of a refusal to choose. Thus, "tradition without traditionalism"—tradition in the hostile, posttraditional world of radicalized modernity—amounts to "a repetition which stands in the way of autonomy rather than fostering it."[34] The modernization of modernity is the secularization of secularity and the persistence of religion in second modernity can only be accountable on the basis of psychological need. Giddens, like Bauman, thereby understands religion as a form of solace, a psychological crutch, and an index of anomie. As he states matters,

> Religion in some part generates the conviction which adherence to the tenets of modernity must necessarily suspend: in this regard it is easy to see why religious fundamentalism has a special appeal. But this is not all. New forms of religion and spirituality represent in a most basic sense a return of the repressed, since they directly address issues of the moral meaning of existence which modern institutions tend to dissolve.[35]

ULRICH BECK: DESECULARIZING REFLEXIVE MODERNITY—RELIGION *VERSUS* RELIGIOSITY

Ulrich Beck's conceptualization of religion in second modernity is remarkable for its abrupt and radical change of direction. While maintaining his theoretical framework and basic terms of analysis, Beck's work shifts from a depiction of reflexive modernization as the consummation of secularization to one that argues for the re-newed subjective and political significance of religion—and not solely as reaction-ary consolation or "fundamentalism" but as a vital, progressive, moral constituent of "world risk society."[36] In contrast to Bauman and Giddens, Beck draws on the resources of the sociology of religion to grasp the ways in which the resurgence of religion is a part of the wider cultural reflexivization that is central to the theories of second modernity. In so doing, Beck's work is commendable in its self-critical attention to the "religious deficit" of his own thinking hitherto and of much socio-logical theory in general.[37]

Ulrich Beck, who was born in 1943 and is currently professor of sociology at Lud-wig-Maximillian University in Munich, has probably been the most influential proponent of the idea of a "second" or "reflexive" modernity and his work informs Bauman's notion of "individualization"[38] and Giddens's account of "risk"[39] as the medium of modernity's self-modernization. In his publication *Risk Society*, pub-lished in 1986, Beck set out his account of a second modernity, explaining the transformations in society since the 1960s as stemming from the encounter of mo-dernity with its own (countermodern) side effects. The focus was centered on the environmental consequences of advanced industrialization, the transformed expe-rience of "risk" as temporally and spatially unbounded (with the risks of nuclear power as emblematic), and its potential to delegitimize political and scientific authority—all ideas that, as we have seen, Giddens adopted and adapted. In addi-tion, Beck described how this modernization of modernity was its "reflexivization" as the key institutions of modern society are found to be dependent on tacit, taken-for-granted, unexamined, and therefore *unmodern* assumptions. As with Bauman and Giddens, the central motifs of *individualization* and *globalization* characterize the key features of the contemporary era. No longer understanding their lives as enmeshed in networks of kin and class-communal membership, thanks to the "indi-vidualizing" effects of the labor market and the welfare state, people must take re-sponsibility for their own fate, choose "a life of one's own."[40] Augmented by medico-scientific developments, particularly in the field of contraception, gender and family relations are transformed in a similar fashion as women are no longer fated to the domestic sphere and demand equal status with men. The worldwide expansion of modern economic and political institutions beyond the West has the effect of ren-dering nationally bounded identities and policy-making otiose—with globalization we are put into relations of mutual dependence on "cultural others,"[41] which de-mands a new perspective on the challenges we face in a "world risk society."[42]

At this stage of his thinking, Beck—like Bauman and especially Giddens—presents this modernization of modernity as the secularization of secularity. The tech-nocratic regime of first modernity is one that regards the scientist as a priest pursuing the socially sanctioned aim of "redemption through science."[43] The encounter with the unintended consequences of technoscience leads to the development of an authen-tically "scientific" attitude of skepticism and, in Beck's phrasing, "demystification spreads to the demystifier and in doing so changes the condition of demystifica-tion"[44]—or more emphatically, "truth has taken the usual route of modernity. The scientific religion of controlling and proclaiming truth has been secularized in the course of reflexive scientization."[45] In addition, like Bauman and Giddens, Beck sees religion as a form of consolation for those unable to endure the reflexivization of culture and society with its pervading uncertainty, pluralization, and relativization of lifestyles and cultures and the obligation to choose. Beck too takes fundamentalism as *the* definitive expression of religiosity in reflexive modernity, seeing it as "the choice of unfreedom."[46] In the era of global risk it absolves human beings of responsibility and furnishes a sense of certainty by placing the care of the world in the hands of God alone. With implicit reference to the "climate change deniers' of the US Religious Right, Beck asserts that if "risk enters the global stage after God has made his exit," then "those who believe in God are risk atheists."[47]

Yet Beck gives notice of a view of religion unlike that of Bauman and Giddens when, in his interview with Johannes Willms from 2000, he sets out the possible role that the Catholic Church might play in the era of world risk society by virtue of its supranational institutional identity and doctrinal concern for the poor—it might, in Beck's words, embrace a "cosmopolitan" politics whereby it seeks "to shame globalism before the world, to care for its victims, and the help the world perceive the bad consequences"[48] of neoliberal globalization. This argument comes to fruition when, in 2008, Beck published *A God of One's Own: Religion's Capacity for Peace and Potential for Violence*[49] and emphatically identifies religion as a constituent part of the reflexivization of modernity—no longer solely as its refusal but now also as its spiritual expression. Instead of describing a linear process of secularization, Beck now maintains that structurally the "modernization of modernity" both secularizes *and* desecularizes inasmuch as it is the emancipation of religion from its dependence on public-political authority. Hence, in the face of the crisis of legitimation besetting the political, economic, and scientific authorities in the age of risk, religion—now free from complicity with these institutions—is able to draw on its vast normative resources to criticize the dehumanizing effects of political-technocratic and corporate power.[50] What is more, it is this concern with the individual human being per se that is basic to the moral force of religion in the age of reflexive individualization.

Beck maintains the binary opposition between dogmatic adherence to an inflexible and unchanging truth, on the one hand, and a readiness to reflexively engage with the enlightened-modern norms of universal equality and individual autonomy, on the other, but this is no longer simply the opposition of religion-as-fundamentalism to secular moral reason: instead the division is placed *within* the field of belief as the opposition between fundamentalism (or institutionalized "religion") and individualized "religiosity." The same processes of deinstitutionalization and individualization are observable in religious life as elsewhere in contemporary Western society. Drawing on the sociology of religion,[51] Beck identifies the resurgence of religion of the last five decades with the *individualization* of religion—just as one chooses a life of one's own so one chooses a god of one's own: religious faith and affiliation are constructed by the individual; God is understood as residing in the individual. Thus, what has been described as "believing without belonging"[52]—coterminous with the notion of "the God in me"[53]—is the deinstitutionalization of belief as the burgeoning of a "religiosity" that is sensitized to questions of individual choice, reflection, equality, and mutual respect. This, in turn, encourages Beck to see religion as the seed-bearer of modernized modernity's cosmopolitan ethic—as was tentatively suggested in the interview with Willms in the years before. Religion is addressed to and appropriated by the individual qua human being abstracted from the particularities of nationality, ethnicity, sex, or social status in general. As Beck states, it is Émile Durkheim who "anticipates the union of individualization and cosmopolitanism"[54] in his account of the modern republican-democratic *conscience collective*—the "cult of the individual."[55] In contrast to Bauman's picture of an essentially privatized and depoliticized "individualism" shaped exclusively by consumerism or Giddens's thoroughly secularized view of rational-critical autonomy, Beck carries through Durkheim's idea of a "sacred" individualism wherein "man has become a god for man"[56] and that is now evident in the contemporary preeminence of the idea of human rights. Thus, Beck can maintain Durkheim's inclusive and expanded view of religion to argue that "we 'believe' in human rights because in them man's likeness to God has acquired its secular-cum-sacred form and has even in part been institutionalized in law. Thus, for example, Amnesty International may be said to represent a modern church dedicated to a 'god of its own.'"[57] As a result, Beck goes on to posit a "double religion" wherein religious believers engage with the beliefs and practices of those of other faiths by acknowledging the universal validity of the rules governing interaction: "the relations of cosmopolitan truths to one another call for a cosmopolitanism of the religions that is based not on immutable truths handed down to mankind, but ultimately on rules, treaties, procedures (human rights, the rule of law, etc.) that have been agreed upon by people among themselves."[58] This is characteristic of contemporary individualized religiosity, where the doctrines and beliefs of other faiths are encountered as opportunities for spiritual growth—faith is a "work in progress," the construction of the god of one's own as effectively the embrace of a "subjective polytheism"[59]—but, problematically, not for that of the religious institutions, which for the most part try to maintain their monopoly on truth and guard dogma against dilution or compromise.[60] As Beck's subtitle shows, the reflexive individualism of "religiosity"—the cosmopolitan concern for the human individual—is religion's capacity for peace while the dogmatic insularity of institutionalized religion is religion's potential for violence. Thus, Beck's account of religion is more than a critical-analytical study of its engagement with cultural reflexivization. Rather, Beck, as the theorist of "world risk society," sets out how religion is now central to the survival of the planet and the human race: it can engender the moral resources necessary to averting catastrophe or—as in the case of religiously motivated terrorism—it can constitute another global risk.

RELIGION IN SECOND MODERNITY: FALSE DICHOTOMIES AND USEFUL CONCEPTS

As we have seen Bauman, Giddens, and Beck all figure the political, cultural, social, and economic developments of the last four decades as amounting to the modernization of modernity: a historical process wherein the customary, socially sanctioned obligations and the quasi-traditional supports that sustained classical modernity dissolve, leaving individual men and women compelled to make existential choices without certainty of success and on the basis of criteria whose evidential basis is provisional. The modernization of modernity is also, therefore, the process that reveals the incomplete secularization of an era whose central institutions (and, in particular, the technocratic authority of scientistic reason) reveal a pseudo-religious certainty at odds with an authentic modernity. As a result, Bauman, Giddens, and (until 2008) Beck take the view that secularization extends to the secularizers and the only space left for religion is as a refuge from the "runaway world"[61] of second modernity: religion is in its essence countermodern and in its contemporary form "fundamentalism." Beck's revision, in identifying the resurgence of religion with its "individualization," while breaking with the traditional secularization thesis exemplified by Bauman and Giddens, nonetheless posits the same opposition of a progressive and enlightened reflexive rationality to a reactionary adherence to unquestionable dogma and superstition. What this schema misrecognizes, therefore, is the possibility that the resurgence of religion might "reflexivize" individualism and faith without producing either fundamentalist refugees from second modernity or ecumenical cosmopolitans. Instead, religious reflexivization might also give rise to the stress upon "piety" and on a conception of religion as a system of beliefs and practices providing the moral resource for engagement in a world where individual agency and personal flexibility are at a premium and electronically mediated social networks intensify processes of self-relativization and the problems of choice.[62]

Thus, Bernice Martin, drawing on the example of the rise of Pentecostalism in Brazil, took issue with Bauman's view on account of its Olympian remoteness from the empirical realities, overlooking the ways in which the mass movement of Protestantism in Latin America has provided individuals with the means to engage positively with the social and economic transformation of the continent since the 1980s.[63] To describe Pentecostalism as "fundamentalist" and its appeal as "proto-totalitarian" is, in Martin's view, merely abusive and prevents an understanding of the ways in which evangelical Protestantism provides moral and practical resources for the construction of an energized and entrepreneurial individualism that can navigate the perilous waters of the deregulated, winner-takes-all capitalism. Thus, the "second Reformation in Latin America" is a reaction to and engagement with—but not a retreat from—the insecurities and uncertainties of liquid modernity. The binarism of Bauman's argument is undermined by this "world-accommodating"[64] character of the churches but also by the extent to which, in Martin's account, they combine organizational and doctrinal authoritarianism with the requirement of congregational consent, for, as voluntary associations, there remains the option of seceding. This is a "liquid church" that is neither the self-imploding victim of the culture of short-term transactions, as Bauman maintains, nor the elusive image of a deinstitutionalized and congrationless community, envisaged in Pete Ward's coining of the term.[65] In a similar fashion, the "*de jure* patriarchalism" of the Pentecostal churches is qualified by a "*de facto* feminization" in their insistence on men's familial responsibilities and their refusal to sanction the "traditional" double standard.[66]

Phillip Mellor, meanwhile, took issue with Giddens's opposition of a mutually exclusive "reflexivity" and "tradition" by demonstrating the ultimately untenable nature of the argument while showing that reflexivity illuminates the ways in which traditions are regenerated in response to changed social and cultural conditions. Importantly, such reflexivity is particularly visible in cross-cultural adoptions and adaptations, which are only comprehensible as acts of reconstruction and selection of traditional components suitable to different localities: although these may be exemplary of late-modern cultural patterns in the age of globalization, Mellor notes that it would also fit the description of, for example, Japanese Buddhism as it developed during the sixth century.[67] Reflexivity does not falsify tradition but is rather its very means of survival and "what is characteristic of religious traditions in modernity is that this reflexivity is more expansive and more systematic than in the past."[68] Mellor's concept of "reflexive traditions"[69] has been adopted by other theorists in the sociology of religion to look at the transformations of non-Western religious traditions through their encounter with colonialism, nationalism, and globalization. Thus, John Wallis[70] traces the selective interpretation of Hindu tradition in the development of the teachings and practices of the Brahma Kumaris World Spiritual University. The transformations of, and tensions within, the teachings of the movement demonstrate a high degree of reflexivity on the part of its leaders and adherents and are consequent upon its encounter with other religious and spiritual currents as well as with global secular institutions through its proselytizing efforts further afield. Thus, acknowledging the "reflexivity" at the heart of tradition's response to social change, the sociology of religion can utilize Giddens's concept to explore how, why, and where traditions are contested—and the cultural and political implications thereof.

Instead of denying the very possibility of "religious modernity" as do Bauman and Giddens, Beck's "religious turn" is predicated on the notion that religion is a "co-maker of modernity"[71] in its concern for the universal human individual, and this revaluation of the place of religion in reflexive modernity enables Beck to acknowledge the ways in which religious modernity is shaped by the forces affecting the wider culture of "second" modernity. Beck's awareness of the literature in the sociology of religion enables him to escape the one-dimensional views of Giddens and Bauman and their rehash of the secularization thesis. In grasping the ways in which religious individualization—"religiosity"—and the demise of institutional religion are coterminous with wider patterns of social transformation, Beck usefully shows how social theory might understand contemporary religion as neither consumerist "spirituality" nor reactionary fundamentalism. Yet Beck's opposition of a dogmatic institutionalized religion and a reflexive, individualized religiosity prejudices the case as the political agenda—the need to foreground a pacifist religiosity in keeping with the liberal-ecumenical spirit that would reinforce the cosmopolitan ethic necessary to an age of global risk—conjures up an enlightened religiosity reminiscent of Kant's "reflecting faith," a Protestantism that would augment rational-critical autonomy,[72] and this ultimately determines his construal of religion in the era of reflexive modernity. The emphasis on the political-ethical force of an individualized religiosity set free by the "paradox of secularization"[73] fails to look at the impact of this on the public sphere (the theme of Steve Bruce's work on the subject),[74] just as Beck's account does not explore the reinstitutionalization of religion—the collective expression of religious belief is overlooked in an account that, as I have argued elsewhere, is religion "from the neck-up."[75] Thus, the "piety movements,"[76] which can be sociologically understood as responses to the challenges of second modernity, do not fit into Beck's mold—any more than they accord with the crude polarities of Bauman and Beck. They exemplify a mode of religious expression and experience that is individualized, reflexive, and emphatically globalized (stitched into networks of migration, media, and commerce), whose appeal is enabling of entrepreneurial activity and pragmatic but whose moral code embodies a social conservatism that is, at the same time, ambivalent in its relation to the public-political: the individualization of faith sometimes challenging the privatization of faith (particularly in the context of an elite secularism experienced as repressing the necessarily public expression of sincere faith), at other times maintaining the individual's rights of religious expression in the face of majoritarian sanction. Reflexivity, individualization, and globalization (and in their relationship to neoliberal capitalism, one might add) constitute the parameters within which religious modernity is best conceptualized by social theory, it might be argued, yet the political implications are more complex than Beck allows. Thus, for instance, Olivier Roy's work[77] describes a "deculturation" of Islam resulting from the migration of Muslims to non–Muslim majority societies: removed from its age-old customary and ethno-cultural form of expression and legitimation, Islam becomes increasingly individualized and reflexive as, in a non-Islamic milieu, believers are called upon to explain and justify tenets and dogma that previously would have gone without saying. The social authority of the religion gives way to its individual expression, to *religiosity*, and, furthermore, the individualization of belief is also its universalization: shorn of its particularistic ethno-cultural content, the faith is now relevant to all peoples. In contrast to Bauman and Giddens, then, the reflexivity and individualization induced by globalization and cultural plurality are internalized by religious expression and identity and evident in the distinction between religion and religiosity, as Beck comes to see it, but—in contrast to Beck's "ecumenical" reading of the results—this is yet compatible with a reinforced insistence upon dogmatic purity. The individualization of belief means a renewed focus on the tenets and principles of the religion, but this "religiosity" inclines believers toward an increased concern for dogmatic purity and authenticity—an Islam that is universal because it is uncontaminated by culture, but not thereby "cosmopolitan" in Beck's ecumenical sense. Indeed, Roy argues that the failure of liberal-reformist conceptions of Islam to take hold among diasporic Muslims reflects the appeal of religions in the contemporary age that address the individual and provide encapsulated dogma—"born-again Muslims prefer gurus to teachers, consider that too much intellectualism spoils the faith, and seek a ready-made and easily accessible set of norms and values that might order their daily lives and define a practical and visible identity. Liberal thinkers do not meet the demands of the religious market."[78] As with Martin's Pentecostalists, Roy's

"neofundamentalists"[79] undermine Bauman's construal of a reactionary "fundamentalism" in retreat from the social dislocations of liquid modernity, but, at the
same time, they confound Beck's prospect of a cosmopolitan religiosity engaged in
a critique of the injustice of globalization.

Yet, beyond the failure to account for the burgeoning of "piety," the construal
of religion by the theorists of second modernity is marked by a yet-greater omis-
sion, identified by Beck himself when he admits to the glaring absence of the non-
Abrahamic religions from his account. Tellingly, Giddens and Bauman make little
attempt to extend the discussion beyond the West, and although, as we have seen,
their marginalization of religion is manifest in the level of generality at which they
discuss the phenomenon, it is nonetheless a mark of the Eurocentrism of their accounts of globalized modernity and, thus, of wider significance for the credibility
of their theories. Again, Beck acknowledges this when he confesses that his own exclusive concentration on the monotheisms renders *A God of One's Own* a failure
on its own "cosmopolitan" terms[80] but seeks pardon on the grounds that such a perspective is still under construction. However, at a deeper level, while Beck allows
that the framing of "religion" (and thus secularity) as a distinct cultural formation
is relevant principally to the monotheisms and to Western modernity, he fails to explain the global implications of his fundamental assumption of religious "choice"
as basic to the construction of a "god of one's own," and he does not defend against
the charge that the universalism and egalitarianism that he claims are at the heart of
all religiosity—motivating his depiction of a religion of humanity at the heart of
all particular faiths—root the argument in a profoundly "Christocentric" perspective.
As we have already mentioned, in taking Weber as the key, Beck relies on Protestant
Christianity as the template of individualization, with the historical trajectory
moving from "individualization of religion" to "individualization within religion":[81]
that this may be underway as a result of processes associated with globalization is
of central concern in the sociology of religion, but a characteristic flaw of Beck's
theoretical approach is the eliding of the analytical and the normative such that the
results of social and cultural transformations are prejudged in the light of the preferred political options. In addition, where the absence of the non-Abrahamic religions is noted, Beck tends toward an ahistorical and unsociological invocation of
their inherent plurality and (therefore) pacifism, which displays uncomfortable orientalist traces only too continuous with the shallow consumerist appropriation of
"Eastern wisdom" identified by Bauman and documented by Carrette and King.[82]
Again, the political exigencies that prompted Beck's engagement with religion—the
global threat of jihadist violence—tend to determine and short-circuit the theoretical account.

In conclusion, then, we should separate the flawed depictions of religion in the
contemporary age from the conceptual framework deployed. The positing of reflexivity as alien to religious belief and practice is crude and untenable and at the root
of the construal of religion as a flight from the challenges of radicalized modernity. Beck, commendably, recognizes this and grasps the fact that the resurgence of
religion is a constituent part of reflexive modernity. Yet the credibility of his analysis is undermined by its desire to present a domesticated religiosity that can

nonetheless perform its cosmopolitan duty in the age of global risk. Yet—as is evident from the sociology of religion's productive use of the conceptual framework of "second modernity"—the theories of Bauman, Giddens, and Beck provide significant theoretical resources for an analysis of religious transformation in an age of radicalized uncertainty, cultural reflexivization, and global interdependence. What needs to be explored is the ways in which social transformations associated with the modernization of modernity are shaping religious practice, organization, and doctrine in particular concrete circumstances, as well as how religious institutions, traditions, and beliefs are reconfigured to offer resources for individuals and communities, states and citizens, to make use of political and commercial opportunities, to resist and criticize dehumanizing or alienating social conditions—and not always in ways that might sit comfortably with a progressive liberal-enlightened politics.

NOTES

1. Justin Harrington, ed., *Modern Social Theory: An Introduction* (Oxford: Oxford University Press, 2005), 17.
2. James Beckford, "Postmodernity, High Modernity and New Modernity: Three Concepts in Search of Religion," in *Postmodernity, Sociology and Religion*, ed. Kieran Flanagan and Peter C. Jupp (New York: Palgrave MacMillan, 1999). See Beckford for a still-relevant critique of the absence of any serious engagement with religion in theories of second modernity.
3. Ulrich Beck, *Risk Society: Towards a New Modernity* (London: Sage, 1992), 14.
4. See Zygmunt Bauman and Keith Tester, *Conversations with Zygmunt Bauman* (Cambridge: Polity, 2001).
5. See Zygmunt Bauman, *Modernity and the Holocaust* (Cambridge: Polity, 1989).
6. See Zygmunt Bauman, *Modernity and Ambivalence* (Cambridge: Polity, 1991); Zygmunt Bauman, *Postmodern Ethics* (Oxford: Blackwell, 1993).
7. See Zygmunt Bauman, *In Search of Politics* (Cambridge: Polity, 1999); Zygmunt Bauman, *Liquid Modernity* (Cambridge: Polity, 2000).
8. See Bauman, *Liquid Modernity*; Zygmunt Bauman, *Liquid Love* (Cambridge: Polity, 2003); Zygmunt Bauman, *Liquid Life* (Cambridge: Polity, 2005); Zygmunt Bauman, *Consuming Life* (Cambridge: Polity, 2007); Zygmunt Bauman, *Culture in a Liquid World* (Cambridge: Polity, 2011); Bauman and Tester, *Conversations with Zygmunt Bauman*; Simon Speck, "Religion, Individualisation and Consumerism: Constructions of Religiosity in 'Liquid' and 'Reflexive' Modernity," in *Religion in Consumer Society: Brands, Consumers and Markets*, ed. Francois Gauthier and Tuomas Martikanen (Farnham, UK: Ashgate, 2013).
9. Anthony Elliot, ed., *The Contemporary Bauman* (London: Routledge, 1997). I am treating the terms as synonymous for the purpose of this exposition. See "Editor's Introduction" in *The Contemporary Bauman* for a discussion of Bauman's change of terminology.
10. Bauman, *Liquid Life*, 84.
11. Ibid., 88.

12. Ibid.

13. Bauman and Tester, *Conversations with Zygmunt Bauman*, 95.

14. See Leszek Kolakoski, *Religion: If There Is No God . . . On God, the Devil, Sin and Other Worries of the So-Called Philosophies of Religion* (London: Fontana, 1982).

15. Zygmunt Bauman, *Postmodernity and Its Discontents* (Cambridge: Polity, 1997), 169.

16. Ibid., 173.

17. Ibid., 183.

18. Ibid.

19. Ibid.

20. Ibid., 185.

21. See, inter alia, Anthony Giddens Anthony, *Capitalism and Modern Social Theory: An Analysis of the Writings of Marx, Durkheim and Weber* (Cambridge: Cambridge University Press, 1971); Anthony Giddens, *Politics and Sociology in the Thought of Max Weber* (London: Macmillan, 1972); Anthony Giddens, *Politics, Sociology and Social Theory: Encounters with Classical Contemporary Thought* (Cambridge: Polity, 1995); Anthony Giddens, *In Defence of Sociology: Essays, Interpretations and Rejoinders* (Oxford: Polity, 1996).

22. See, inter alia, Anthony Giddens, *A Contemporary Critique of Historical Materialism*, vol. 1, *Power, Property and the State* (London: Macmillan, 1981); Anthony Giddens, *The Constitution of Society: Outline of a Theory of Stucturation* (Cambridge: Polity, 1984); Anthony Giddens, *A Contemporary Critique of Historical Materialism*, vol. 2, *Power, The Nation-State and Violence* (London: Macmillan, 1985); Anthony Giddens, *New Rules of Sociological Method: A Positive Critique of Interpretative Sociologies*, 2nd ed. (Cambridge: Polity, 1993).

23. See, inter alia, Anthony Giddens, *Consequences of Modernity* (Cambridge: Polity, 1990); Anthony Giddens, *Modernity and Self-Identity: Self and Society in the Late Modern Age* (Cambridge: Polity, 1991); Anthony Giddens, *The Transformation of Intimacy: Sexuality, Love and Eroticism in Modern Societies* (Cambridge: Polity, 1993); Anthony Giddens and Christopher Pierson, *Conversations with Anthony Giddens: Making Sense of Modernity* (Cambridge: Polity, 1998); U. Beck, A. Giddens, and S. Lash, *Reflexive Modernisation* (Cambridge: Polity, 1994).

24. Giddens, *Consequences of Modernity*, 16–17, passim.

25. Ibid., 92.

26. Giddens and Pierson, *Conversations with Anthony Giddens*, 231.

27. Beck, Giddens, and Lash, *Reflexive Modernisation*, 100.

28. Ibid., 77; Anthony Giddens, *Runaway World: How Globalisation is Reshaping Our Lives* (London: Profile Books, 2002), 43.

29. Beck, Giddens, and Lash, *Reflexive Modernisation*, 84.

30. Ibid., 100.

31. Giddens, *Runaway World*, 49.

32. Beck, Giddens, and Lash, *Reflexive Modernisation*, 38.

33. Giddens, *Modernity and Self-Identity*, 38.

34. Beck, Giddens, and Lash, *Reflexive Modernisation*, 70.

35. Ibid., 207.

36. For a more detailed treatment of the "desecularization of reflexive modernity," see Simon Speck, "Ulrich Beck's 'Reflecting Faith': Individualization, Religion and the Desecularization of Reflexive Modernity," *Sociology* 47, no. 1 (2013): 157–72.

37. Ulrich Beck, *A God of One's Own: Religion's Capacity for Peace and Potential for Violence* (Cambridge: Polity, 2010), 1–2.

38. See Elliott, *Contemporary Bauman*, 23; Bauman, *Culture in a Liquid World*, 83.

39. Christopher Bryant and David Jary, *The Contemporary Giddens: Social Theory in a Globalizing Age* (Basingstoke, UK: Palgrave, 2001), 246–47.

40. Ulrich Beck and Elizabeth Beck-Gernsheim, *Individualization* (London: Sage, 2002), 22–30.

41. See, inter alia, Beck, *A God of One's Own*; Ulrich Beck, *The Cosmopolitan Vision* (Cambridge: Polity, 2007); Ulrich Beck, *World at Risk* (Cambridge: Polity, 2009).

42. See, inter alia, Beck, *World at Risk*; Ulrich Beck, *World Risk Society* (Cambridge: Polity, 1999).

43. Beck, *World at Risk*, 218.

44. Beck, *Risk Society*, 156.

45. Ibid., 166.

46. Ulrich Beck, *The Cosmopolitan Vision* (Cambridge: Polity, 2007), 52.

47. Beck, *World at Risk*, 72.

48. Beck, *Cosmopolitan*, 212.

49. Beck, *A God of One's Own*.

50. Ibid., 25.

51. Ibid., 20. Beck is particularly indebted to the work of Peter Berger, Robert Bellah, Jose Casanova, Grace Davie, and Daniele Hervieu-Leger, among others.

52. Grace Davie, *Religion in Britain Since 1945: Believing Without Belonging* (Oxford: Blackwell, 1994).

53. Grace Davie, *The Sociology of Religion* (London: Sage, 2007), 98.

54. Beck, *A God of One's Own*, 96.

55. Émile Durkheim, "Individualism and the Intellectuals," *Political Studies* 17, no. 1 (1969): 19–30.

56. Ibid., 26.

57. Beck, *A God of One's Own*, 97.

58. Ibid., 194.

59. Ibid., 62.

60. Ibid., 173.

61. Giddens, *Runaway World*.

62. See Bryan Turner, *Religion and Modern Society: Citizenship, Secularization and the State* (Cambridge: Cambridge University Press, 2011), 271–91, passim.

63. Bernice Martin, "From Pre- to Postmodernity in Latin America: The Case of Pentecostalism," in *Religion, Modernity and Postmodernity*, ed. Paul Heelas (Oxford: Blackwell, 1998).

64. Ibid., 250.

65. Pete Ward, *The Liquid Church* (Carlisle: Paternoster Press, 2002).

66. Martin, "Case of Pentacostalism," 135.

67. Phillip Mellor, "Reflexive Traditions: Anthony Giddens, High Modernity, and the Contours of Contemporary Religiosity," *Religious Studies* 29 (1993): 119.

68. Ibid.

69. Ibid., 120.

70. John Wallis, "The Problem of Tradition in the Work of Anthony Giddens," *Culture and Religion* 2, no. 1 (2001): 81–98.

71. Beck, *A God of One's Own*, 180.

72. Speck, "Religion, Individualisation and Consumerism," 169–70.

73. Beck, *A God of One's Own*, 24.

74. For example, see Steve Bruce, *God Is Dead: Secularization in the West* (Oxford: Blackwell, 2002).

75. Speck, "Religion, Individualisation and Consumerism," 168.

76. See Bryan Turner, *Religion and Modern Society*.

77. See Olivier Roy, *Globalised Islam: The Search for a New Umma* (London: Hurst, 2004); Oliver Roy, *Holy Ignorance: When Religion and Culture Part Ways* (London: Hurst, 2010).

78. Roy, *Globalised Islam*, 31.

79. Ibid.

80. Beck, *A God of One's Own*, 49.

81. Ibid., 81.

82. Jeremy Carrette and Richard King, *Selling Spirituality: The Silent Takeover of Religion* (London: Routledge, 2005).

29

Classical Anthropological Theories of Religion

RANDALL STYERS

As amply reflected in this volume, the concept of "religion" is a distinctive product of the modern West, a generic umbrella term that only took shape from the sixteenth century forward as European colonists, merchants, missionaries, and soldiers brought new information back to Europe about human cultural diversity. Through the Enlightenment, new forms of cultural analysis and critique took hold, and new humanistic approaches to the study of human identity and society began to emerge. A comparative approach to cultural history was developed by thinkers such as Giambattista Vico (1668–1744), the Baron de Montesquieu (1689–1755), and David Hume (1711–76). Confidence in the value of secular rationality and in the forward trajectory of human social development—represented most vividly in the work of French thinkers such as the Marquis de Condorcet (1743–94) and Auguste Comte (1798–1857)—held sway among Europe's leading intellectuals.

Within this context, "religion" became a significant question. Religion was increasingly seen as one discrete component of the larger social whole, and even if it displayed astounding heterogeneity, it was also widely understood as a cross-cultural aspect of human social organization. Through the seventeenth and eighteenth centuries, new texts appeared in Europe recounting the mystifying practices of non-Christian religions, and a number of these texts began to seek the earliest stage of human religious development in order to identify religion's ultimate nature. As secularism spread among Europe's intellectuals, religion moved from being an obvious fact of life to a mystery in need of explanation. How did religion originate within human culture? What could account for its variety? What functions did it serve in human life? Particularly as religion became less obligatory for European intellectuals—as it became possible to imagine a secularized and disenchanted future—cross-cultural, comparative analysis emerged as a promising route to account for this widespread but highly divergent feature of human culture.

Within Europe, Romanticism spurred interest in folk practices, and new compilations of folklore and popular beliefs appeared. Through the late eighteenth and early nineteenth centuries, European scholars began the study of classical Hindu religious texts, archaeology provided new information about ancient civilizations, and interest in Indo-European languages and cultures grew. New philosophies of history sought to identify the broad developmental principles of human culture, and the great German philosopher Georg W. F. Hegel (1770–1831) produced his *Lectures on the Philosophy of Religion* (from a set of lectures delivered in 1827) utilizing a mass of comparative data to offer an elaborate and detailed account of the development of religion through human history.

By the later half of the nineteenth century, these various developments had coalesced into an evolutionary, historical approach to the study of religion. Scholars such as the German philologist Max Müller (1823–1900), who worked for much of his life in Britain, advocated a new "science of religion" that would use a comparative method to identify the laws governing human religious development. Using his work in comparative Indo-European philology, Müller argued that the source of religion was to be found in nature mythology, as the great phenomena of nature (the sun, the moon, storms, and so on) became personified in mythic form.[1] During the latter half of the nineteenth century a whole new set of scholarly disciplines began to take shape (including comparative philology, folklore, ethnology, and anthropology), and religion was a central feature in various new social-scientific theories aiming to account for human cultural development.[2]

One of the central preoccupations in these early theories of religion was the question of its origins. Auguste Comte, the founder of French sociology, had affirmed the theory put forth by the French writer Charles de Brosses (1709–77) in his *Du culte des dieux fétiches*, published in 1760, that religion had its origin in fetishism— the belief that particular material objects have supernatural power. Through the early decades of the nineteenth century fetishism was commonly seen as the defining feature of the religion of primitive peoples. An important challenge to this argument came from the British archaeologist John Lubbock (later Lord Avebury, 1834–1913), in his *Origin of Civilization and the Primitive Condition of Man* (1870). Lubbock here invoked newly accumulated ethnographic data in an effort to modify and correct Comte's scheme of social evolution. Lubbock identified six stages of religious development (atheism, nature worship [or totemism], shamanism, idolatry [or anthropomorphism], the deity as creator, and finally religion joined with morality), and he argued that human cultures move through these stages in a unilinear fashion. Lubbock concluded that religion was not to be found among the lowest primitives (who were prone to magic and fetishism), since these groups lack the defining feature of real religion, respect for a deity. Rejecting the claim by de Brosses and Comte that fetishism is the origin of religion, Lubbock asserted that fetishism was better understood as an "anti-religion" since it seeks only to coerce and control supernatural power rather than to worship it.[3]

Lubbock's mode of empiricist evolutionism was indicative of his era. Earlier in the nineteenth century, the English geologist Charles Lyell (1797–1875) had provided new empirical confirmation that the earth itself developed by the slow accumulation of small changes and that its history was much older than indicated in the Bible. This empirical foundation coupled with the evolutionary theory of Lyell's friend Charles Darwin (1809–82) and the theories of social evolution put forth by one of their contemporaries, the philosopher and social theorist Herbert Spencer

(1820–1903), to bolster the position of evolutionism as the dominant scientific approach of the later nineteenth century.

Spencer applied his notion of social evolution to the analysis of religion, arguing that religion develops from false speculation first as primitive people identify figures in dreams as ghosts and then as the ghosts of dead ancestors are transmuted into deities. Over time, religion evolves from this simple initial stage of euhemerism (named for the ancient Greek mythographer Euhermeus) into more complex forms of polytheism and on to monotheism, advancing "from the simple to the complex" as do all other aspects of society.[4] Spencer concluded that the final step in this evolutionary path is an agnosticism supported by a positivistic scientific epistemology. Spencer was a leading figure in promoting evolutionism as the key to social analysis, and his account of the origin of religion exemplifies the "intellectualism" that would dominate early social-scientific theories of religion; in this view, the earliest religion was a product of intellectual reflection that led primitive humanity to formulate religious interpretations of human experience.

These various evolutionary trends coalesced in the work of Edward Burnett Tylor (1832–1917), who is commonly identified as the founding figure of modern social anthropology. In his influential two-volume text *Primitive Culture* (1871), Tylor assembled a broad range of ethnographic material to set forth the principles of a new mode of scholarly inquiry into human culture. Anthropology, he said, is the "science of culture," and culture is "that complex whole which includes knowledge, belief, art, morals, custom and any other capabilities and habits acquired by man as a member of society."[5] Tylor acknowledged his indebtedness to prior theorists of evolutionary development (such as Hume, Comte, and Lyell), and in *Primitive Culture* he formulated a theory of cultural evolution that aimed to account for the variation of human cultures as they moved through progressive stages of development.

When Tylor turns to consider religious evolution, he begins by declaring that the "minimal definition of Religion" is "the belief in Spiritual Beings."[6] In line with this definition, Tylor identifies the most primitive form of religion as "animism," the belief in souls and other spiritual beings. He proceeds to offer an account of how primitive people arrive at this belief through the experience of figures in dreams and reflection on the difference between living and dead bodies. Rumination on these experiences leads the primitive thinker to formulate the concept of a "soul." As this concept continues to evolve, religion develops to include the belief in an afterlife and eventually comes to manifest true worship and morality. While later religious systems will demonstrate enormous complexity and diversity, this core religious principle—the belief in souls and spirits—persists as the defining feature of even the most developed religious system. And, Tylor asserts, despite the reports of some writers to the contrary, there is no human culture so primitive that it has not yet attained the stage of animism.[7] Religion, it would appear, is a foundational feature of all human culture.

Before proceeding, it is important to note a few of the most significant aspects of Tylor's formulation here. First, Tylor demonstrates a key concern that will preoccupy early anthropology, the effort to define the contours of religion and to determine its position with the larger cultural whole. Religion is a particularly vexing object of study for these theorists since its boundaries can appear so amorphous, and a great deal of effort will be expended in the attempt to determine exactly what "religion" might be. Second, like many of his predecessors and successors, Tylor defines religion in a manner that is deeply informed by a distinctively Protestant Christian perspective. He localizes religion as a matter of interior belief (as opposed to emotion, behavior, ritual, community, or other features). Belief is the defining feature of religion, he says, and all other aspects are thus rendered ancillary. Tylor's method was indicative of his era, as he compiled a mass of decontextualized data from various reports to support his evolutionary theory and assumed that contemporary "primitive" cultures gave meaningful information about prehistoric life. Further, Tylor's account of how religious belief takes shape is deeply individualistic and deeply intellectual. He attributes a complex mode of conceptual analysis to primitive thinkers, and he asserts that each thinker—in widely different circumstances and cultural contexts—reaches the same fundamental conclusions about the existence of souls and spirits. Tylor will be known as a leading figure in the "intellectualist" anthropological tradition, because of his insistence on the prominence of these intellectual processes at the earliest stages of cultural development. But despite the many obvious conceptual flaws in his approach, it is important to recognize that, unlike many of his contemporaries who emphasized human racial and ethnic difference and the mental deficiencies of "primitives" (often in support of overtly racist colonialist policies), Tylor's approach is premised on the psychic unity of humanity.

While Tylor demonstrates significant appreciation for the importance of animistic religion in the development of culture, he is far less sanguine about the present of magic. Tylor never makes a precise demarcation between religion and magic, but his entire scheme of social evolution depends on the distinction between religious beliefs and magical acts. In his account, magic arises from a misapplication of the principle of association of ideas, as mental connections between coincidental events are misinterpreted as causal connections. Further, he asserts, the spread of magical thinking causes significant intellectual and social disruption throughout history. While magic is chiefly characteristic of the lowest levels of civilization, it persists into more developed cultures as a "survival" (an element of lower culture that persists because of habit, ignorance, or superstition).[8] Phenomena such as astrology and spiritualism, exhibiting new popularity in Victorian England, demonstrate the potential of magical thinking to revive despite scientific and social progress. Indeed, the very notion of cultural survivals poses a deep challenge to Tylor's fundamental evolutionary scheme; he uses the concept in order to account for the variations in cultural evolution, but the persistence of these antiquated beliefs tempers his confidence in human progress. As Tylor acknowledges, while the history of magic is largely a history of "dwindling and decay," the laws guiding this history are so variable that they often appear to be "no law at all."[9]

Tylor's theory that animism was the initial stage of human religious development quickly supplanted the earlier theories of fetishism and nature mythology, and it dominated anthropological theory for almost thirty years. But Tylor was not without his critics. Müller had argued that humanity has a fundamental inclination toward monotheism (a view in easier harmony with the biblical narrative), and this theme was developed by various scholars who proposed theories of primitive high gods. Most prominent among early anthropological theorists in this regard was Andrew Lang (1844–1912). In 1898, Lang published *The Making of Religion*, in which he offered an extended challenge to Tylor's theory of animism by arguing that the earliest forms of religion were actually relatively high in their stage of sophistication. Primitive religion had its roots not in animism, he said, but in the belief in powerful high gods.[10] Lang's theory was based on rather thin evidence, but the theory of primitive monotheism attracted other prominent advocates, most notably the Austrian linguist and anthropologist (and Roman Catholic priest) Wilhelm Schmidt (1868–1954). Schmidt would develop the argument in a twelve-volume work, *The Origin of the Idea of God*, where he argued that monotheism could be found in the earliest stages of human cultural history. Even the most primitive peoples, Schmidt asserted, come to recognize the notion of a supreme being through their reflections on concepts of causation and agency. Magic and mythology, he argued, take shape only in later stages of cultural development, but the materialism and selfishness that characterize magic give it the power to corrupt the originary monotheism and lead culture on a path of degeneration.

Tylor's theory of animism was also challenged by his fellow intellectualist anthropologist James George Frazer (1854–1941). Frazer's major scholarly work was *The Golden Bough*, a study of sacred kingship that grew from its first edition in 1890 to twelve volumes by its third edition (1906–15). From the second edition of 1900 forward, Frazer became particularly engaged with the role of magic and religion in cultural evolution, and he offered an extremely influential typology of different forms of magic. In Frazer's scheme, magic is divided into two basic species, homeopathic or imitative magic (based on the principle of similarity) and contagious magic (based on the principle of contact). In addition, he said, there is an important distinction between positive forms of magic and its negative mode (which he identified as *taboo*).

Frazer formulated a far more rigid scheme of cultural evolution than Tylor. He argued that human cultures move through a fixed set of developmental stages in a linear fashion: magical, religious, and finally scientific. In the initial magical stage, human beings see nature as regular and mechanistic, and they seek methods to control its operations through various ritualistic behaviors and practices. But in this early stage, human beings fail to understand the operative laws of causality, and their magical practices are largely futile. Both of the basic principles of magical thinking (similarity and contact) are misapplications of the proper association of ideas.

Despairing of these initial efforts at controlling nature, the wisest thinkers in a group begin to seek alternative explanations for the flux of nature. They come to surmise that instead of being mechanistic, nature must be under the control of powerful divine beings. As this new idea takes hold, culture moves to a new developmental stage as human beings seek to propitiate or sway these spiritual agents. In this religious phase, the natural world is understood as plastic and variable, subject to the personal intervention of divine beings. While earlier magical practices might persist and intermingle with new religious practices, Frazer argues that over the course of the religious stage, magic comes increasingly to be seen as a vain and vulgar encroachment on the prerogatives of true religion.

As the process of cultural evolution moves forward, the limits of the religious worldview become apparent, particularly to members of the priestly caste with sufficient leisure for observation and reflection. Reverting in part to the earlier magical worldview that looked for mechanistic regularity in nature, the intellectual elite begins to reformulate a new understanding of the laws of nature. Unlike the magical stage, the scientific phase of cultural development takes shape as more sophisticated and patient observation leads to accurate judgments about causality. But like magic, science sees nature as regular and uniform, determined "not by the passions or caprice of personal beings, but by the operations of immutable laws acting mechanically."[11] Through his account of these evolutionary developments, Frazer appears to see religion as a rather unfortunate detour on the path to an accurate understanding of the workings of the natural order.

Both because of the sweep of the material he incorporated into *The Golden Bough* and because of its broader themes, Frazer's work remained extremely influential—particularly among a popular audience—for many decades. Despite the gapping conceptual flaws of his work, *The Golden Bough* had a wide impact in art, literature, psychoanalytic theory, and even various twentieth-century supernaturalist subcultures. Frazer's basic typology of magic is still invoked by various writers, even if the broader contours of his theory of religious development are unsustainable.

A different type of challenge to Tylor's theory of animism came from anthropological theorists who argued that magic and religion should be seen not as successive stages in a path of cultural evolution, but instead as two subsets of a broader category of supernaturalism. In his text *The Supernatural: Its Origin, Nature, and Evolution*, published in 1892, the American anthropologist John H. King argued that primitive human beings observe impersonal physical powers at work in the natural world, and in the face of these mysterious forces they begin to develop various techniques designed to control fate. The most basic human sentiment, said King, is a sense of "luck, fear of uncanny evil or the desire for canny good."[12] As human beings search for means to control these mysterious forces, they develop early forms of magic. Over time, simple varieties of religion begin to develop involving charms and spells, and specialists emerge, leading to the religion of the medicine man. Eventually more developed religious ideas take hold, and concepts of ghosts, spirits, and gods emerge. King thus argued that a sense of impersonal supernaturalism preceded the concepts of souls or spirit; counter to Tylor's theory, magic precedes animism. And, King concluded, all forms of supernaturalism will eventually fade as intellectual development brings effective means of controlling the forces of nature and science comes to predominate.

By the end of the nineteenth century, new anthropological theories began to appear placing the origin of religion and magic in an undifferentiated and impersonal spiritual force (a broad view that some would label "dynamism").[13] R. R. Marett (1866–1943), a close friend of Tylor and his successor as reader in anthropology at Oxford, wrote a series of papers beginning in 1899 arguing that prior to the emergence of animism, there was a stage of preanimism, a wider and vaguer sense of impersonal supernatural power. Marett challenged Tylor's intellectualism, arguing that this preanimistic stage was characterized more by emotion and instinctive motor response than by cogitation. As Marett explained, rather than understanding religion simply as a matter of belief, it is preferable to see religion as "a certain composite or concrete state of mind wherein various emotions and ideas are directly provocative of action."[14] Religion is thus a matter of emotion, thought, and behavior. As Marett framed in his most famous aphorism, "savage religion is something not so much thought out as danced out."[15]

In response to Tylor's methodology, Marett pointed behind animism to a broader, amorphous emotive and behavioral stew that served as the "raw material of religion" long ignored in the search for religion's origins.[16] Marett argued that religion and magic should not be seen as successive stages in a path of cultural evolution, but as two subsets of this broader category of supernaturalism. Magic and religion both arise, he said, from "a common plasm of crude beliefs about the awful and occult," from a fundamental emotional response of awe, fear, and wonder at phenomena of supernatural power.[17] Only as this amorphous sense of supernaturalism develops into more specific and individuated forms can an animistic sense of souls or spirits take shape. But even as Marett pointed toward this undifferentiated sense of supernaturalism that was logically antecedent to animism, he disclaimed any pretense of offering a new theory of the origin of religion. As he explained, the early periods of human development are "in large part indecipherable."[18]

Through the first decade of the twentieth century, Marett seized on the concept of *mana* as his primary idiom for the undifferentiated and impersonal preanimistic force field from which both religion and magic arose. *Mana* had first been introduced to Europe by R. H. Codrington (1830–1922), who in the 1870s served as head of the Anglican mission to Melanesia. In 1891 Codrington published a famous study of Melanesian culture, and *mana* featured prominently in his text. During the subsequent decade a number of ethnographers identified comparable notions of amorphous supernatural power from a range of other cultures, and in 1904 Marett declared that *mana* was "a category of world-wide application" for the scientific study of religion, designating a generalized, nonpersonalized sense of sacred power.[19] *Mana* marks out a fundamental distinction between the sacred (the realm of extraordinary power that elicits awe and wonder) and the profane (the mundane world of ordinary, practical experience), and it designates the positive mode of this extraordinary power or energy (with *taboo* as the negative pole). *Mana* moves through the social field, he said, much like electricity.

Just as Marett rejected Tylor's claim that animism was the initial stage of religion, he also rejected Frazer's sharp differentiation between religion and magic, arguing instead that religious and magic elements are intermingled in the sense of supernaturalism and that only in more developed levels of culture is the human response to the magico-religious realm moralized (and magic stigmatized). Marett also rejected the theory of primitive high gods put forth by Lang and Schmidt, arguing that such a sophisticated religious concept must have a psychological prehistory.

Marett's amorphous notion of supernaturalism became extremely popular during the early years of the twentieth century. It was adapted, in various forms, by theorists as diverse as the founder of psychoanalytic theory, Sigmund Freud (1856–1939), the folklorist Sidney Hartland (1848–1927), the German psychologist Wilhelm Wundt (1832–1920), and the German anthropologist K. T. Preuss (1869–1938). In France, Marett's French contemporaries Marcel Mauss (1872–1950) and Henri Hubert (1872–1927) also adopted *mana* as the preferred term to describe diffuse supernatural power in "Esquisse d'une théorie générale de la Magie," published in 1904. Mauss and Hubert argued that *mana* is the wellspring of both religion and magic and that religion and magic are differentiated only on the basis of the relation of each practice to the social group—religion is a collective and public phenomenon, while magic is secret and individualistic, taking place outside the organized cult.[20]

As developed by Marett, his contemporaries, and his successors, the concept of *mana* moved the origin of religion into a vague, emotional context of differential power, and it appeared to offer a method for recognizing the social contexts and implications of those power differentials. Yet *mana* gave only the illusion of conceptual clarity. The notion offered Marett and his peers a benign idiom with which to acknowledge human agency in relation to the supernatural realm, but it afforded few substantive resources for assessing or conceptualizing power. Thus the vague notion of *mana* served to mystify social relations by cloaking religious agency in an aura of primeval mystery. *Mana* was everywhere and nowhere; it remained potent as *mana* only so long as it remained incomprehensible. As Marett stated this theme, it is "of the very essence of *mana* that it should be indefinite and mysterious in its effect."[21] Any effort to account for *mana* leads to its dissipation. And this bind would appear to include not only the naive practitioner, but also the modern scholar. The mystery of the origin of religion could be explained only by recourse to an indeterminate primeval force.

Further, these various accounts placing the origins of religion in, in a sense, undifferentiated and impersonal spiritual power might dampen down the evolutionary fervor demonstrated by earlier theorists, but at the same time they had the effect of emphasizing the emotional and instinctive aspects of "primitive" lives rather than its intellectual accomplishment. Religion is no longer a great intellectual development but instead a collective emotional response to mystery.

Marett's basic argument that a supernaturalistic emotional sense of the extraordinary produces religion and magic would remain quite popular for a number of decades. In one notable example, the American anthropologist Robert Lowie restated this basic theme in 1924, as he stressed a fundamental dichotomy in human experience between the ordinary and the extraordinary. Distinct from the mundane and ordinary, he said, there is a shared human "sense of the Extraordinary, Mysterious, or Supernatural," and it is in this sense that one finds the roots of religion.[22] He rejected Frazer's effort to differentiate different cultural phases of magic and religion (since, Lowie asserted, both always coexist), and he objected to Mauss and Hubert's claim that magic is always on the margins of society, since just like religion, magical practices require the acceptance of traditional social concepts and practices.

Building on the emotive component of religion's origins, a further competing theory of religion came from late-nineteenth- and early-twentieth-century social scientists who sought the roots of religion in totemism or clan gods. In his *Lectures on the Religion of the Semites*, published in 1889, the Scottish biblical scholar William Robertson Smith (1846–94) developed the work of his teacher J. F. M'Lennan (1827–81) to argue that the earliest form of religion involved the worship of various totemic creatures that were identified as the ancestors of the social group. Religion, Robertson Smith asserted, was born from the sense of reverence for these totemic figures. A number of important scholars came to accept the view that totemism was more fundamental than animism. So, for example, in his *Introduction to the History of Religion*, published in 1896, Frank Byron Jevons (1858–1936) argued that religion emerges through the development of social relations with a clan god (functioning as a totem). Only after religion is established can magic emerge as a transgression of the socially accepted sense of proper human agency and communal connection.

The notion of totemism would find its most influential formulation in *The Elementary Forms of the Religious Life* (1912) by Émile Durkheim (1858–1917), one of the founding figures of French social theory. Durkheim begins by articulating what he sees as the core principle of religion, the division of the world between the sacred and the profane. Since both magic and religion fall within the scope of the sacred, Durkheim invokes the notion of totemism (and the basic conception of religion put forward by Robertson Smith and Mauss and Hubert) in order to define the boundary between them. As he explains, religion is the product of a social group, fostering unity and bringing together the members of a community. Magic, on the other hand, involves the use of sacred power for selfish or socially disruptive ends. Moving forward in this analysis, Durkheim concurs in identifying the "indefinite powers" and "anonymous forces" at work within the totemic principle as *mana*.[23] He concludes that the ultimate focus of religion is actually the totemic social group itself, "since religious force is nothing other than the collective and anonymous force of the clan."[24] Or, more pointedly, in religion, society is worshiping itself. Durkheim's totemistic theory contrasts with the individualism of other early social-scientific theories of the origin of religion by stressing religion's fundamentally communal nature.

Working within these traditions of totemism and *mana*, the French anthropologist and philosopher Lucien Lévy-Bruhl (1857–1939) challenged intellectualist theories such as those from Tylor and Frazer by arguing that primitive thought is fundamentally different from modern thought. Lévy-Bruhl claimed that, far from demonstrating logical or causal thinking, the "primitive mentality" is mystical, instinctive, and emotional, deeply shaped by the communal and highly charged atmosphere surrounding totemism. As he explained it, primitive thought lacks individuality and entails a form of participatory affect that ignores distinctions between subject and object, cause and effect, nature and supernature. The primitive mind is thus unable to grasp even the most basic principles of scientific rationality, and it attributes all types of occurrences to magical and mystical powers.[25] While even Lévy-Bruhl himself eventually dampened down some of his more extreme formulations, this notion of a "primitive mentality" deeply shaped by communal participation and emotion persisted in many quarters of social theory into recent decades.

Through all these competing theories, scholars worked to identify the origin of religion in the hope that by identifying its formative state, the ultimate nature of religion would become clear. But these competing efforts to penetrate prehistory proved futile, and through the early decades of the twentieth century, the preoccupation with identifying the origin of religion began to falter. By the 1920s scholars became more deliberate in separating the question of religion's origin from the question of its essence, and through the 1920s and 1930s increasing numbers of theorists abandoned the search for origins and moved into new modes of social analysis in regard to the nature and function of religion. At the same time, methodologies in anthropology and the social sciences changed dramatically. By the turn of the twentieth century, armchair anthropologists (such as Marett and Frazer) recognized the need for ethnographic fieldwork, and a new generation of ethnographers brought that experience to bear in their theorizing concerning the nature of religion. In the wake of this new ethnographic focus and new forms of linguistic analysis, the evidence on which much of this early anthropological theory was based began to crumble, and the tendency to universalize notions such as *mana* or totemism began to fade.

These shifts in theoretical and methodological focus are readily apparent in the work of the Polish anthropologist Bronisław Malinowski (1884–1942). Malinowski pioneered ethnography among the Melanesians, and in his analysis of Melanesian culture Malinowski abandoned any search for the origin of religion to focus instead on its psychological and social functions. He argued in his essay "Magic, Science, and Religion" from 1925 that religion should be understood as a set of practices promoting social integration and interpersonal attachment among members of a group, providing a ground for psychic and social integration in the face of major life questions (such as death).[26]

This definition of religion is rather amorphous, and Malinowski seeks to give it more clarity by contrasting religion to magic. Unlike religion, which has transcendent and self-realizing objectives, magic is performed to accomplish specific practical objectives in circumstances where ordinary technical skill has reach its limit. Rejecting Lévy-Bruhl's negative assessment of the "primitive mentality," Malinowski stresses that human beings in even the earliest stages of cultural development have significant technical abilities and knowledge. But when that technology fails, magic provides ritual behavior that can increase confidence and optimism in situations of anxiety. Religion, in contrast, is focused on broader, more abstract concerns. It invokes traditions concerning the supernatural (spirits and demons, the power of the totem, ancestral spirits, and notions of life after death) in order to create more abstract social values and promote cohesion.

Through this theory of religion, Malinowski has no concern with religion's origins. Instead, he is focused on its social function, working to identify the particular needs religion addresses in the lives of the members of a social group. In this mode, he identified the essence of religion in its focus on transcendent, nonpragmatic values. Malinowski's stress on the commonalities between "primitive" and modern thought would be followed by a number of important later anthropologists. For example, Alexander Goldenweiser's *Anthropology: An Introduction to Primitive Culture*, published in 1937, highlights the continuing role of superstition and magical thinking in modern society, but rather than see this as a troubling anomaly (in the vein of Tylor and Frazer), Goldenweiser concludes that supernaturalism is a vivid example of primitive ingenuity, "perhaps the most outstanding and certainly the most historically significant achievement" of the human imagination, serving a range of positive social functions.[27]

By the middle of the twentieth century, Marett's most prominent student, E. E. Evans-Pritchard (1902–73), could reject most all the classical anthropological efforts to comprehend "primitive" religion. Evans-Pritchard disparaged these early theories as "just-so stories," and he detailed many of their significant conceptual flaws.[28] Anthropology would move in new directions and develop new methods (often with its early focus on religion supplanted by attention to kinship, economic systems, and other aspects of society). The most significant legacy of these early anthropological theorists lies in their naturalistic approach to the study of religion, as they bracketed questions of the truth of religion and looked instead to empirical data in order to investigate religion's origins and nature. While the large portion of their presuppositions and conclusions about religion are unsupportable, these theorists succeeded in defining a new approach to the study of religion that would focus on its human, social history.

The explicit focus on social evolution that was so central to these early theorists became far more muted in later social-scientific theory, but basic evolutionist currents remain visible. Even today, many social scientists continue to frame human culture in terms of trajectory (a tendency reflected in recent theories of social and religious development, in the persistent theorizing about magical thinking, and even in the basic design of introductory textbooks in anthropology and comparative religion). Various more recent forms of structuralism, sociobiology, and evolutionary psychology follow the path of evolutionary thinking, even if their nuance surpasses their late-nineteenth- and early-twentieth-century predecessors.

NOTES

1. See Max Müller, *Introduction to the Science of Religion* (London: Longmans, Green, 1873).

2. On the emergence and development of anthropological approaches to the study of religion, see generally Brian Morris, *Anthropological Studies of Religion: An Introductory Text* (Cambridge: Cambridge University Press, 1998); and Fiona Bowie, *The Anthropology of Religion: An Introduction*, 2nd ed. (Oxford: Blackwell, 2006).

3. John Lubbock, Lord Avebury, *The Origin of Civilization and the Primitive Condition of Man: Mental and Social Condition of Savages*, 3rd ed. (London: Longmans, Green, 1875), 319.

4. Herbert Spencer, "Progress: Its Law and Cause," in *On Human Evolution: Selected Writings*, ed. J. D. Y. Peel (Chicago: University of Chicago Press, 1972), 45; and see Herbert

Spencer, *Principles of Sociology*, ed. Stanislav Andreski (Hamden, Conn.: Archon Books, 1969), 171–73, 446–49, 575–87.

5. Edward Burnett Tylor, *Primitive Culture: Researches Into the Development of Mythology, Philosophy, Religion, Language, Art and Custom* (New York: Henry Holt, 1889), 1:1, 1:410.

6. Ibid., 2:8.

7. Ibid., 2:4–13, 83–86.

8. Ibid., 1:16, 72, 112–13.

9. Ibid., 1:11, 116, 136–37.

10. See Andrew Lang, *The Making of Religion*, 2nd ed. (London: Longmans, Green, 1900).

11. James George Frazer, *The Golden Bough: A Study in Magic and Religion* (New York: Macmillan, 1922), 59.

12. John H. King, *The Supernatural: Its Origin, Nature, and Evolution* (London: Williams and Norgate, 1892), 1:5.

13. See Gregory D. Alles, "Dynamism," in *Encyclopedia of Religion*, ed. Lindsay Jones, 2nd ed. (Detroit: Macmillan, 2005).

14. R. R. Marett, "Pre-Animistic Religion," in *The Threshold of Religion* (London: Methuen, 1914), 5.

15. Ibid., xxxi.

16. Ibid.

17. Ibid., xi.

18. Ibid., viii.

19. Ibid., 110.

20. See Marcel Mauss, *A General Theory of Magic*, trans. Robert Brain (London: Routledge, 1972).

21. Ibid., 91.

22. Robert H. Lowie, *Primitive Religion* (New York: Liveright, 1948), xiv–xvi.

23. Émile Durkheim, *The Elementary Forms of the Religious Life*, trans. Joseph Ward Swain (New York: Free Press, 1965), 229.

24. Ibid., 253.

25. Lucien Lévy-Bruhl, *How Natives Think*, trans. Lilian A. Clare (New York: Macmillan, 1966).

26. Bronisław Malinowski, *Magic, Science and Religion, and Other Essays*, ed. Robert Redfield (Glencoe, Ill.: Free Press, 1948).

27. Alexander A. Goldenweiser, *Anthropology: An Introduction to Primitive Culture* (New York: F. S. Crofts, 1937), 208.

28. E. E. Evans-Pritchard, *Theories of Primitive Religion* (Oxford: Clarendon, 1965), 25.

30

Defining Religion

Geertz and Asad

JON P. MITCHELL

As a debate rooted in anthropology, the exchange between Clifford Geertz and Talal Asad revolves around universals and particulars. While Clifford Geertz attempts a universal definition of religion that also accounts for the differences between particular religious traditions, Asad particularizes not only the definition of religion, but more fundamentally the very possibility of a universal definition of religion, suggesting that Geertz's universalism is itself particular—rooted in particular modern, Christian-influenced understandings of what religion *is* and what it *does*. While Geertz sees religion as a cultural or symbolic system with distinct properties and functions, Asad sees particular religions as discursive traditions that authorize particular forms of religious practice and knowledge, including the very definition of what qualifies as "religion" in the first place.

GEERTZ AND INTERPRETIVE ANTHROPOLOGY

Alongside Claude Lévi-Strauss, Geertz (1926–2006) was probably the single most influential anthropologist of the twentieth century. His inspiration was drawn, via Talcott Parsons, his Harvard tutor, from Max Weber,[1] and developing Weber's interpretive, *verstehende* methodology, he reconfigured the culture concept as a system of symbols, meanings, and texts that express and govern people's lives.[2] This move was to prove influential across the social sciences and humanities. Unlike Weber, who famously argued against a priori definitions of religion,[3] Geertz proffered a definition of "Religion as a Cultural System" to "provide a useful orientation, or reorientation, of thought."[4] Although he later denied a concern with definition per se,[5] his attempt to define religion nevertheless had an important theoretical purpose: to give analytical priority and *autonomy* to religion as an area of human life and experience. In doing so, he was writing against the prevalent Durkheimian orthodoxy within—particularly British—anthropology, which presumed a direct correspondence between religion and social structure. As such, it was "more of a provocation than anything else, directed toward upending the complacencies at once of structuralism and functionalism, then the reigning paradigms in ethnological research."[6]

His "provocation" saw religion as a cultural, or symbolic, system with a unique and particular feature: an ability to unite or synthesize a people's ethos—the emotional tone or "feel" of their culture, and of their worldview, "the picture they have of the way things in sheer actuality are, their most comprehensive ideas of order."[7] In doing so, they unite the way things *are* (worldview) with the way things *ought* to be (ethos) by showing that ethos represents a way of life ideally adapted to the reality of the worldview, and that the worldview is particularly well arranged to accommodate this way of life. This both objectivizes moral and aesthetic preferences (ethos) and provides deeply felt experiential evidence for the truth of assumptions about the world (worldview): "Religious symbols formulate a basic congruence between a particular style of life and a specific (if, most often, implicitly) metaphysic, and in so doing sustain each other with the borrowed authority of the other."[8]

RELIGION AS A CULTURAL SYSTEM

With this established, he defines religion as (1) a system of symbols that acts to (2) establish powerful, pervasive, and long-lasting moods and motivations in men by (3) formulating conceptions of a general order of existence and (4) clothing these conceptions with such an aura of factuality that (5) the moods and motivations seem uniquely realistic.[9]

He then works through this definition, drawing comparatively from a range of different "religious" contexts, to demonstrate the universal applicability of his definition.

(1) Symbols are public vehicles of meaning, which is itself public. They are organized into integrated systems, which constitute "models" of relations among the entities or processes to which they refer. As such, they are both "models of" and "models for" the world, and how to live in it—they both describe and prescribe: "Unlike genes, and other nonsymbolic information sources, which are only models *for*, not models *of*, culture patterns have an intrinsic double aspect: they give meaning, that is, objective conceptual form, to social and psychological reality both by shaping themselves to it and by shaping it to themselves."[10]

(2) Religious symbols communicate meanings about the world, but also inculcate definitive and distinctive "dispositions"—tendencies, capacities, propensities, skills, habits, liabilities, pronenesses—that motivate and orient social action. Symbols also generate a susceptibility to "fall into certain moods."[11] These are the primary causal and consequential features of what Geertz calls "the religious perspective."[12] Motivations have a causal aspect—they make people act—while moods are a consequence of an actor being "properly stimulated" by symbols.[13]

(3) Religious symbols provide a conceptual framework for explaining circumstances in which the world seems inexplicable—"points at which impasse looms."[14] There are three main points where this may happen: incomprehension, suffering, and evil. When a mysterious toadstool grows "too quickly" in a

Javanese house, when a Navaho seeks a cure from illness, or when Dinka speculate on the moral ambiguities of life, religious symbols are mobilized to give order and meaning to the chaos—in the form of a cosmological explanation, a healing ritual, and a myth that explains the withdrawal of "Divinity" from the material realm:

> The strange opacity of certain empirical events, the dumb senselessness of intense or inexorable pain, and the enigmatic unaccountability of gross iniquity all raise the uncomfortable suspicion that perhaps the world, and hence man's life in the world, has no genuine order at all—no empirical regularity, no emotional form, no moral coherence. And the religious response to this suspicion is in each case the same: the formulation, by means of symbols, of an image of such a genuine order of the world which will account for, even celebrate, the perceived ambiguities, puzzles, and paradoxes in human experience.[15]

(4) Religious symbols demand and command "faith": "The basic axiom underlying what we may perhaps call 'the religious perspective' is everywhere the same: he who would know must first believe."[16] The "religious perspective" differs in this respect from others—the common-sensical, the scientific, the aesthetic—that are based, respectively, on the "given-ness" of knowledge, a systematic skepticism of that "given-ness," and a deliberate disengagement from knowledge. Religious knowledge is not "given," but is absolute; it "deepens the concern with fact and seeks to create an aura of utter actuality."[17] This is achieved through ritual.

Geertz uses the example of the Rangda-Barong ritual in Bali, a cultural performance that sees a terrible witch (Rangda) fighting an endearing monster (Barong) as an enactment or materialization of the balance of moral power within the Balinese universe. The performance brings forth these forces as genuine realities rather than mere representations. It does so by inducing mass trance among both performers and spectators, who themselves "become" the forces:

> The acceptance of authority that underlies the religious perspective that the ritual embodies thus flows from the enactment of the ritual itself. By inducing a set of moods and motivations—an ethos—and defining an image of cosmic order—a world view—by means of a single set of symbols, the performance makes the model *for* and model *of* aspects of religious belief mere transpositions of one another.[18]

(5) Religious symbols—"religion pure"—are engaged with only sporadically, during ritual performances. The transformations that occur in ritual are then taken back into everyday contexts where, as "religion applied," they also transform the everyday, which means that religion does not merely describe or reflect the social order, but also shapes it: "The anthropological study of religion is therefore a two-stage operation: first, an analysis of the system of meanings embodied in the symbols which make up the religion proper, and second, the relating of these systems to social-structural and psychological processes."[19]

ASAD: RELIGION AS AN ANTHROPOLOGICAL CATEGORY

Talal Asad sits alongside thinkers such as Foucault and Said as part of an intellectual tradition concerned with exploring the conceptual assumptions that govern knowledge in "the West"—and particularly "'the West's knowledge about the 'non-West.'"[20] Inspired by Wittgenstein and Foucault, he utilizes a genealogical methodology to examine the authoritative discourses that frame the conditions of possibility for the development and emergence of particular knowledge systems. His critique of Geertz's definition of religion[21] applied this technique to both the definition itself and the conditions of possibility for this particular definition—and indeed the conditions of possibility for the very project of definition.

While Geertz's intention was to establish religion as an autonomous area of cultural life, Asad points toward the location of the possibility of this analytical move in a particular modern Western and ultimately Christian discursive tradition.[22] It only really makes sense, he argues, in the context of post-Reformation Christianity, in which fragmentation and confessional pluralism required a conceptualization of the universal essence behind diverse religious practices.[23] With this in place, religion could be separated out from other areas of life, and different religions classified. Asad questions not only the essence of Geertz's definition, but the very search for essence: "My argument is that there cannot be a universal definition of religion, not only because its constituent elements and relationships are historically specific, but because that definition is itself the historical product of discursive processes."[24]

With that established, Asad takes Geertz to task, drawing on examples from the history of Christianity to demonstrate that Geertz's universalist definition is in fact rooted in particular Christian understandings of what religion is and its (lack of) relationship to other areas of social life. This in turn has fueled an approach to non-Christian societies—and particularly Muslim societies—which are habitually vilified because of an apparent inability to separate religion and politics.[25] Asad argues that in both—and perhaps all—traditions, religion and power are interlinked to the extent that they are analytically inseparable.

RELIGION AS A DISCURSIVE PROCESS

For each of the five stages of Geertz's definition, Asad offers critique.

(1) Asad criticizes Geertz for treating symbols as both vehicles for meaning and meanings in themselves, confusing the communicative and cognitive properties of symbols, so that it is difficult to untangle the processes or practices through which meaning becomes attached to particular symbols. In short, he argues, Geertz fails to offer a theory of how meaning comes into being. Moreover, in emphasizing the correspondence of models *of* and models *for* the world, and viewing the authority of these two types of models lying with each other, he generates a picture of

intrasystemic authorization, which not only fails to account for change in the system, but also misses the point that religious conceptions are authorized by discourses outside the religious sphere: "the authoritative status of representations/discourses is dependent on the appropriate production of other representations/discourses; the two are intrinsically . . . connected."[26]

Asad therefore proposes a shift of emphasis, from systems of symbols to discursive practices: "The conditions [wherein] symbols come to be constructed, and how some of them are established as natural or authoritative as opposed to others."[27]

(2) If symbols invoke "dispositions"—moods and motivations—then the question again this raises is: Under what conditions? Particular religious symbols gain and lose power over time, or more specifically, they come to or cease to embody truth. St. Augustine's elaboration of Christian *disciplina* demonstrates that Christian dispositions are inculcated not merely by symbols, but by power—once more, authorizing processes or practices:

> ranging all the way from laws (imperial and ecclesiastical) and other sanctions (hellfire, death, salvation, good repute, peace) to the disciplinary activities of social institutions (family, school, city, church) and of human bodies (fasting, prayer, obedience, penance). Augustine was quite clear that power, the effect of an entire network of motivated practices, assumes a religious form because of the end to which it is directed, for human events are the instruments of God. It was not the mind that moved spontaneously to religious truth, but power that created the conditions for experiencing that truth.[28]

(3) Geertz makes religious symbols do both too much work and too little. On the one hand, while they produce moods and motivations they also formulate conceptions of a general order of existence. This compounds experiential aspects of religion as practice with more discursive and reflexive aspects, which we might call "theology." Theology and religious practice are not the same thing, argues Asad, and one of the reasons Geertz wants them to be the same is so that he can clearly distinguish between "religious" and other forms of knowledge, in order to grant autonomy to the former. Once more, though, we need to ask questions about the authorizing processes that lead to the creation of "religion" as a separate and separable category.[29] On the other hand, the reassuring "order in chaos" function he attributes to them reduces religious knowledge to a residual of the secular, as in forms of "God of the gaps" theologizing.[30] What science doesn't know, religion fills in. This again, for Asad, is a product of post-Enlightenment Christian thinking, which permits only a limited legitimate space for religion in society.

(4) This space is that of the right to individual *belief*—a concept that, apart from its rootedness in particular, Christian understandings of religion,[31] serves once more to distance religion from the practices that reproduce it. Geertz sees belief as a precondition for religious activity, rather than its result: "Geertz's treatment of religious belief, which lies at the core of his conception of religion, is a modern, privatized Christian one because and to the extent that it emphasizes the priority of belief as a state of mind rather than as constituting activity in the world."[32]

As a prior commitment of faith, belief is seen by Geertz as an optional choice of one perspective among many. However, as Asad points out, these "choices" do not present themselves in equivalent ways in different social contexts. The "choices" might be hierarchized—do we *choose* a scientific perspective in contemporary technological society?—or even nonexistent. As Evans-Pritchard noted of the Nuer: they do not "believe in" God; he is "simply there."[33] Yet Geertz presents this "simply there"-ness of religious conceptions as both a cause and a consequence of religious activity. On the one hand, they are the objects of a prior "belief"; on the other hand, they are brought about by the action of ritual. Asad suggests that we can step out of this circularity by focusing on religious symbols as "one condition for engaging with life" rather than "the precondition for religious experience."[34]

(5) Geertz's final comments about "shifting" or "leaping" from religious to common-sense perspective present religion as a rather fixed system of symbols that can have an effect on the world, but that lie at a remove from that world. There is no scope for a "feedback" effect, in which common-sense engagements can modify religious sensibilities or religious knowledge. To this extent, religion is presented as transcendent over, rather than imminent *within*, everyday social life. We must relocate our understanding of religion as embedded within social practice, argues Asad, rather than presupposing an analytical distinction between religion and other areas of social life, which would then require Geertz's two-stage analysis of (a) identifying systems of religious meaning, and (b) identifying their effects upon society:

> The two stages that Geertz proposes are, I would suggest, one. Religious symbols—whether one thinks of them in terms of communication or cognition, of guiding action or of expressing emotion—cannot be understood independently of their historical relations with nonreligious symbols or of their articulations in and of social life, in which work and power are always crucial. . . . From this it does not follow that the meanings of religious practices and utterances are to be sought in social phenomena, but only that their possibility and their authoritative status are to be explained as products of historically distinctive disciplines and forces.[35]

ISLAM AS A DISCURSIVE TRADITION

Such disciplines and forces constitute a discursive tradition, which serves to establish both orthodoxy and orthopraxy in particular historical contexts.[36] Discourses "instruct practitioners regarding the correct form and purpose of a given practice that, precisely because it is established, has a history."[37] The exploration of this history is the exploration of religion. He develops this conception of religion not only to critique Geertz, but also to formulate a more promising anthropology of Islam. Geertz's comparative work on Islam in Indonesia and Morocco[38] was an exemplification of his earlier theoretical definition of religion, in which ethos and worldview combine to provide models *of* and models *for* the differing worlds of Southeast Asia and North Africa. In very different ways, Geertz argued, Islam provides "frames of perception" and "blueprints for conduct."[39]

In Asad's view, Geertz failed to capture the flow of power within Islam as discourse, because it sees the source of power—the system of symbols—lying outside, and presiding over, its production and reproduction in practice. To this extent, it is an externalist vision of religion, where Asad favors an internalist rendition. This enables him to see not just that symbols mean, or even what symbols mean, but more substantively *how* symbols mean—and this is through the body. His account of discourse, then, is not merely linguistic:

> My concern is with the way the living body subjectifies itself through images, practices, institutions, programs, objects—and through other living bodies. . . . I take the grammar of authority (authoritative discourse) to be rooted in continuously interacting materialities—the body's internal and external constitution, and the energies that sustain them—that make for its *compelling character*. It is not signs in themselves that explain people's recognition of authority; it is how people have learned to do, feel, and remember signs that helps explain it. Or (in another key) how they apprehend signs of the beloved when they "fall in love."[40]

This opens up an approach to religion that focuses on the body, emotion, experience—in which "moods and motivations" are not epiphenomena *caused by* symbolic phenomena that are the substance of religion. Rather, they *are* religion.

NOTES

1. Adam Kuper, *Anthropology and Anthropologists* (London: Routledge, 1983), 188; Adam Kuper, *Culture: The Anthropologists' Account* (Cambridge, Mass.: Harvard University Press, 2000), 70–121; James L. Peacock "The Third Stream: Weber, Parsons, Geertz," *Journal of the Anthropological Society of Oxford* 7 (1981): 122–29.
2. Clifford Geertz, "Thick Description: Toward an Interpretive Theory of Culture," in *The Interpretation of Cultures* (New York: Basic Books, 1973), 5.
3. Max Weber, *The Sociology of Religion* (Boston: Beacon, 1963), 1.
4. Clifford Geertz, "Religion as a Cultural System," in *The Interpretation of Cultures* (New York: Basic Books, 1973), 90.
5. Clifford Geertz, "Shifting Aims, Moving Targets: On the Anthropology of Religion," *Journal of the Royal Anthropological Institute* 11 (2005): 7.
6. Ibid.
7. Geertz, "Religion," 89.
8. Ibid., 90.
9. Ibid.
10. Ibid., 93.
11. Ibid., 97.
12. Ibid., 110.
13. Ibid., 97.
14. Geertz, "Shifting Aims," 7.
15. Geertz, "Religion," 108.

16. Ibid., 110.

17. Ibid., 112.

18. Ibid., 118.

19. Ibid., 125.

20. David Scott and Charles Hirschkind, "Introduction: The Anthropological Scepticism of Talal Asad," in *Powers of the Secular Modern: Talal Asad and His Interlocutors,* ed. D. Scott and C. Hirschkind (Stanford: Stanford University Press, 2006), 1.

21. Talal Asad, "Anthropological Conceptions of Religion: Reflections on Geertz," *Man* 18 (1983): 237–59; Talal Asad, "The Construction of Religion as an Anthropological Category," in *Genealogies of Religion: Discipline and Reasons of Power in Christianity and Islam* (Baltimore: Johns Hopkins University Press, 1993).

22. Ibid., 28.

23. Ibid., 40–42.

24. Ibid., 29.

25. For a discussion of recent critical works in this field, see Filippo Osella, "Islam, Politics, Anthropology," special issue, *Journal of the Royal Anthropological Institute* (2009).

26. Ibid., 31–32.

27. Ibid., 31.

28. Ibid., 35.

29. Ibid., 44–45.

30. Richard H. Bube, "The Failure of the God-of-the-Gaps," in *Horizons of Science,* ed. Carl F. H. Henry (New York: Harper and Row, 1978), 21–35.

31. Jean Pouillon, "Remarks on the Verb 'to Believe,'" in *Between Belief and Transgression,* ed. M. Izzard and P. Smith (Chicago: University of Chicago Press, 1982), 1–8; Malcolm Ruel, "Christians as Believers," in *Religious Organisation and Religious Experience,* ed. John Davis (London: Academic, 1982), 9–31.

32. Asad, "Construction," 47.

33. Jon P. Mitchell and Hildi J. Mitchell, "For Belief: Embodiment and Immanence in Catholicism and Mormonism," *Social Analysis* 52, no. 1 (2008): 79–94.

34. Asad, "Construction," 51.

35. Ibid., 53–54.

36. Ovamir Anjum, "Islam as a Discursive Tradition: Talal Asad and His Interlocutors," *Comparative Studies of South Asia, Africa and the Middle East* 27, no. 3 (2007): 661.

37. Talal Asad, *The Idea of an Anthropology of Islam* (Washington: Center for Contemporary Arab Studies, 1986), 14.

38. Clifford Geertz, *Islam Observed: Religious Development in Morocco and Indonesia* (Chicago: University of Chicago Press, 1968).

39. Ibid., 98.

40. Talal Asad, "Responses," in Scott and Hirschkind, *Powers of the Secular Modern,* 214.

31

Religion, Media, and Cultural Studies

RICHARD FOX

Scholars and pundits alike insist we live in a new age variously described as "the age of information," "the age of interaction," "the network age," "the media age," and even "the second media age." It is, we are told, the age of "postmodernity," "globalization," "late capitalism," "multiculturalism," "hyperreality," and so on. The style of commentary associated with these terms may often seem bombastic or simply confused, when not outright obfuscatory. But, beneath the verbal effluence, lie two related ideas: everything has changed, and media have something to do with it. It is with a critical eye to these ideas that I would like to consider why—and precisely how—attention to media might prove important for an account of religion in the contemporary world.

In pursuing an answer to this question, my point of departure will be the simple observation that any attempt to account for religion will, by necessity, make certain assumptions regarding media, how they work, and why they matter. As we shall see, this observation is as applicable to nineteenth-century philology as to present-day analyses of television and the Internet. The larger point to be taken is that a critical awareness of media theory—broadly construed—is important not only for those interested in new media, but equally so for students and established scholars working with more traditional media, such as scripture, music, and poetry.

It is with this point in mind that we shall turn first to consider briefly the rise of "religion and media" as a new field of scholarly inquiry and reflect on its relationship to earlier approaches to the academic study of religion. We will then examine some of the ways in which this new field has drawn on the legacy of British cultural studies, particularly in theorizing mass-mediated communication. However, on closer inspection, we will find that—in addition to providing a conceptual framework for new research on "religion and media"—this approach reiterates several key assumptions traditionally associated with earlier approaches to theology and religious studies. For this reason, we may wish to reconsider both its claim to novelty and its critical viability.

RELIGION AND MEDIA

"Religion and media" has gained visibility as a new field in the academic study of religions through a growing number of publications, research centers, and thematically focused conferences and workshops. In addition to single-authored monographs[1] and a regularly issued professional periodical,[2] recent years have seen several edited volumes published on the subject.[3] Scholars working in this new field have tended to represent its rise to prominence within the academy as a response to broader developments in contemporary society, as exemplified by a series of events covered extensively in the Euro-American press. These predictably include the attacks of September 11, 2001, but also inter alia the ensuing "war on terror," the invasions of Iraq and Afghanistan, the United States' presidential election of 2004, and debates on legislation pertaining to reproductive and marriage rights. Taken together, these developments are thought at once to mark a rupture with the past (everything has changed) and at the same time to underwrite the urgency of research on religion and media (media have something to do with it). One finds, for example, Stewart Hoover's recently published monograph *Religion in the Media Age* beginning with the following observation: "Religion and the media seem to be ever more connected as we move further into the twenty-first century. It is through the media that much of contemporary religion and spirituality is known."[4]

The mission statement for the NYU Center for Religion and Media opens on a similar note, suggesting that "In the 21st century, religion is difficult to imagine detached from the dizzying array of media that amplify and circulate its ideas and practices."[5] The referent for the term "media" is often left unspecified in such accounts, allowing for a great deal of slippage between different usages, on which more in a moment. Yet, whether emphasizing the idea of "the media" as a social institution (Hoover) or "media" as a form of technology (NYU), the central presupposition generally remains much the same. This is namely that, although the realms of religion and media—however understood—were once readily distinguishable, these days the boundaries between them are becoming increasingly blurred.

Given the emphasis on "the twenty-first century," one might be forgiven for thinking that media are a new problem for students of religion. Yet, here, it is important to bear in mind that it is actually quite difficult to discuss religion at all—during any historical period—*without* reference to media. One finds, for example, that new media were crucial in various ways for the rise and development of movements as disparate as the Buddhist Mahayana (circa first century CE), the Protestant Reformation (sixteenth century CE), and Indian Hindu Nationalism (twentieth century CE). That is to say, for the Mahayana, it is likely the use of written texts that helped new teachings—for example, the ideal of the *bodhisattva*—to be preserved and disseminated without the direct involvement of the monastically based institutions traditionally responsible for the oral transmission of the Buddha's discourses and discipline.[6] Similarly, the invention of the printing press facilitated the rise of a vernacular readership and the related decline of a clerical monopoly on scriptural interpretation in early modern Europe. As a result, for many Christians, a "direct" engagement with scripture came to replace the Latin liturgy as a primary interface with God.[7] Lastly, in late-twentieth-century India, the epic Ramayana was serialized and broadcast on state television as part of a broader campaign to generate popular support for a religiously defined nationalism. Represented as an ancient pan-Indian tradition, the story and images of the divine king Ram were used in the late 1980s and early 1990s to articulate a new "Hindu" political solidarity across divisions of ethnicity, sectarian affiliation, gender, language, and class.[8]

Without wishing to oversimplify unduly, new forms of religiosity and community were in each case related to the rise of a new medium. But what precisely does it mean to interpret the written word, the printing press, or television *as media*? Should the medium be understood primarily in technological terms, as a conduit for the transmission of religious ideology? Or perhaps institutionally, as a structured complex of social relations? Or, again, pragmatically, as constituted by the practices through which it becomes intelligible as an object of historical inquiry? Any one of these approaches might have something to contribute to an account of why a particular medium has mattered for an understanding of religion in a given historical context. But it must be emphasized that each of these approaches constitutes "media" differently as an object of knowledge; and there is no self-evident reason to assume commensurability between them. For reasons that will become apparent, it is my contention that one's assumptions regarding the nature and theoretical significance of media will determine in important ways one's interpretation of a given religious configuration and its history. As an initial step toward understanding why this is the case, I would like briefly to consider the media-related assumptions of a prominent scholar of religion working in the latter half of the nineteenth century. The selection of this particular example is meant to counter the prevailing tendency to associate problems of media exclusively with developments in present-day society, as well as to lay the foundations for our subsequent analysis of more recent work on religion and media and its theoretical dependence on cultural studies.

MÜLLER'S MEDIA

In February and March of 1870, the recently appointed Oxford professor of comparative philology, Friedrich Max Müller (1823–1900), delivered a series of four lectures on "the science of religion" at the Royal Institution in London. Originally collected and published in 1873, and reprinted several times, these lectures have been interpreted retrospectively as a charter for what would later be called comparative religion or religious studies.[9] In an oft-cited passage, Müller declared,

> It becomes . . . the duty of those who have devoted their life to the study of the principle religions of the world in their original documents, and who value religion and reverence it in whatever form it may present itself, to take possession of this new territory in the name of true science, and thus to protect its sacred precincts from the inroads of those who think that they have a right to speak on the ancient religions of

mankind, whether those of the Brahmans, the Zoroastrians, or Buddhists, or those of the Jews and Christians, without ever having taken the trouble of learning the languages in which their sacred books are written.[10]

This brief excerpt brings together several of the central principles underpinning Müller's approach to the study of religion. We have an emphasis on language and textual sources; an ideal of science as characterized by discovery, possession, and custodianship; and an implicit distinction between religion as such and the various forms in which it may present itself. By examining these ideas more closely, we will discover that they are linked at various levels to a general theory of media that is evident, among other places, in his understanding of text, language, and even religion itself.

For our purposes, it is instructive to begin with the idea of "original documents" and "sacred books" as comprising a scholar's primary point of access to "the principle religions of the world." This emphasis on textual sources drove much of Müller's work, from his critical edition of the Rig-Veda to his substantive contributions and editorship of the historic fifty-volume translation series *The Sacred Books of the East*. These editions and translations were not produced as an end in their own right, but were rather meant to provide a textual foundation for the comparative study of "the principle religions of the world."[11]

In pursuing such textually based comparison, Müller was drawing on a broader European philological tradition that grew up around the study of classical antiquity and the Bible, to later include the historical linguistics—or "comparative philology"—associated with figures such as Karl Wilhelm Friedrich von Schlegel (1772–1829) and Franz Bopp (1791–1867). The procedural principle driving this tradition of inquiry may be described in its barest form as the recovery of an originary moment (for example, a word, text, or language) through the comparative analysis of its various transformations through space and time. It was on this basis, for example, that William Jones (1746–94) first proposed the idea of a common Indo-European linguistic ancestor for Sanskrit, Greek, and Latin. As he put it, "no philologer could examine them all three without believing them to have sprung from *some common source*, which perhaps no longer exists."[12] Following Jones's lead, historical linguists refined the comparisons in pursuit of a conjectural proto-Indo-European language from which were descended the various members of a linguistic family stretching from northern India through much of Europe and into western Asia. In short, the idea was that one could work back to the originary form by discerning and eliminating the changes that had occurred in its transmission.

This general principle played out at several levels within Müller's work on the Rig-Veda, the oldest stratum of what he called "the sacred books of the Brahmans." We have first, at a most rudimentary level, the basic philological framework defined by "the text" and "its manuscripts." Prefacing his presentation of one of the Vedic commentaries, Müller noted, "If it were possible to recover the original manuscript of a work, as written by the author himself, there would be no need of criticism."[13] Unfortunately, this was rarely the case, as "generally our manuscripts are much later than the composition of the works which they contain, and, if compared with one another, they are found to differ from each other, partly in mistakes and omissions, partly in corrections and additions, arising, in the course of centuries, from the hands or heads of ignorant or learned transcribers."[14] Here, through the metaphor of container/content, the author's work was represented as a subtle substance transmitted—that is to say, quite literally sent across (Latin, *trans-* + *mittere*) space and time—through the medium of its manuscripts. However, as Müller remarked in a related connection, this originary substance was "always . . . distorted by the medium through which it had to pass."[15] Faced with such a predicament, the comparative procedures of textual criticism were deployed "to restore from the manuscripts a readable and authentic text" by reversing the process of "distortion."[16] As Müller explained,

> if there are, for instance, certain manuscripts which omit a certain number of passages that have been preserved in others, we may safely conclude that the manuscripts which coincide in omitting these passages flow from the same original source. But out of the number of manuscripts which thus coincide in omitting certain sentences, some may again differ in other characteristic passages, and thus form new classes and subdivisions. By carefully collecting a large number of such characteristic passages, all the manuscripts of an author arrange themselves spontaneously, and form at last a kind of genealogical series, where each has its proper place, and commands . . . its proper share of authority.[17]

This procedure mirrors precisely the logic at work in the pursuit of a "common source" for Sanskrit, Greek, and Latin. One restores the original moment by discerning and removing the omissions, additions, and other transformations that characterize its appearance—however distorted—in the various manuscripts (or languages) to which the scholar has access on the contemporary scene. It is worth emphasizing the circularity entailed in such an endeavor. Simply put, a foreknowledge of the original text is implicitly required to recognize its manuscripts as such (that is, as manuscripts *of that text*), while the manuscripts themselves are the sole avenue to a knowledge of the text. Put another way, while scientific comparison was thought to enable a return to origins, one could only enter the interpretive circle through a leap of faith. As European philology and hermeneutics emerged out of the tradition of biblical criticism,[18] it should perhaps come as little surprise to discover a theological foundation undergirding Müller's theory of text.

The more general principle of recovering an originary moment by way of comparison was also evident on a larger scale in Müller's assessment of the Veda itself. Noting that "the mythology of the Veda is to comparative mythology what Sanskrit has been to comparative grammar," he explained, "nowhere is the wide distance which separates the ancient poems of India from the most ancient literature of Greece more clearly felt than when we compare the growing myths of the Veda with the full-grown and decayed myths on which the poetry of Homer is founded. The Veda is the real Theogony of the Aryan races, while that of Hesiod is a distorted caricature of the original image."[19] As with the more narrowly philological framework defined by the text and its manuscripts, here we encounter the trope of "distortion" writ large. The "original image" of the early Veda is constituted as a subtle substance that suffers distortion in the process of its transmission through "the wide distance" of space and time.

Working this figure through yet several more permutations, Müller continued,

> If we want to know whither the human mind, though endowed with the natural consciousness of a divine power, is driven necessarily and inevitably by the irresistible force of language as applied to supernatural and abstract ideas, we must read the Veda; and if we want to tell the Hindus what they are worshipping—mere names of natural phenomena, gradually obscured, personified, and deified—we must make them read the Veda.[20]

On this account, Homer and Hesiod, as well as contemporary Hindus, possess but the distorted image of their Vedic past. As with his model of text, such distortion emerges as an ineluctable consequence of the process of mediation. Müller often referred to this degeneration as a "disease of language," whereby a primitive apprehension of "the Infinite"—as intuited in Nature—would necessarily give way to elaborate mythologies that "gradually obscured, personified, and deified" what had originally been "mere names of natural phenomena." Although for Müller this "irresistible force of language" was universal, he also thought it reversible. For "much of what seems to us, and seemed to the best among the ancients, irrational and irreverent in the mythologies of India, Greece, and Italy, can . . . be removed," thereby revealing "the most ancient, the most original intention of sacred traditions."[21] It was to this end, in the passage cited above, that Müller called for the comparative study of religion "in whatever form it may present itself." The idea was that, by comparing "the principle religions of the world," we might work our way back to the one "true religion." For, "though each religion has its own peculiar growth, the seed from which they spring is everywhere the same. That seed is the perception of the Infinite."[22]

Müller's science was premised on the possibility of approaching the primordial apprehension of "the Infinite" through a comparison of its variously distorted instantiations in "the principle religions of the world." The character of this project was determined by a specific set of presuppositions that we have seen consistently at work in his account of several media, from text and language to religion itself. In each case, a subtle substance—the author's original work, the real Theogony of the Aryan races, and the apprehension of the Infinite—was distorted "by the medium through which it had to pass" as it moved through time and space. It must be emphasized that, from this perspective, the unity of "media" was not to be found in a particular technology or social institution, but rather in the presuppositions underpinning a range of practices, from textual criticism to Müller's uniquely religio-philosophical anthropology. In each case, the same fundamental presuppositions underwrote a deployment of the comparative method to trace a path from distorted transmissions to their common point of origin. The very recognition of distortion— for example, "when religion is not any more what it ought to be"[23]—already presupposed precisely this model. And in this regard we may say, as we may say for us all, that Müller's assumptions regarding media determined in important ways his understanding of religion.

CULTURAL STUDIES: HEADING BACK TO THE FUTURE?

One might expect that some one hundred years later Müller's understanding of religion and media would appear rather dated. Among other developments, the intervening years have seen new approaches to media from figures as diverse in critical and political orientation as Theodor Adorno and Marshall McLuhan, Jürgen Habermas and Jean Baudrillard, Claude E. Shannon and Stuart Hall. Similarly, for nearly half a century, the viability of "religion" as a critical category has been questioned through the work of Wilfred Cantwell Smith, Talal Asad, Jonathan Z. Smith, and others. In contrast to Müller's nineteenth-century approach, which sought to reverse the effects of mediation and reduce the apparent multiplicity of "religions" through recourse to a universal foundation ("true religion" as "the apprehension of the Infinite"), more recent scholarship in the human sciences has—at least in principle—tended to work in the opposite direction. That is to say, for many, the recognition of difference has motivated a radical reassessment of the claim to universality for European and American ways of understanding and being in the world. This reassessment has often entailed acknowledging the possibility of an irreducible disjuncture between scholarly categories (for example, religion, race, gender, culture) and the lives of those they purport to represent.[24] Unfortunately, scholars working on "religion and media" have tended to shy away from the problems raised by this potential disjuncture, instead cleaving to one or another universalizing definition of "religion."

In his analysis of "religious visual culture," for example, David Morgan has drawn on the work of Catherine Albanese to offer a "working definition of religion" as "configurations of social relatedness and cultural ordering that appeal to powers that assist humans in organizing their collective and individual lives."[25] With somewhat different emphasis, Hoover has offered a definition of religion as "rooted in individual consciousness," a position he supported through reference to Clifford Geertz's frequently cited model of "religion as a cultural system."[26] The point here is not simply to take issue with one or other of these definitions, but, rather, to question the very grounds on which definition itself is pursued as an intellectual practice. As Asad argued in his critique of Geertz, "there cannot be a universal definition of religion, not only because its constituent elements and relationships are historically specific, but because that definition is itself the historical product of discursive processes."[27]

There are several possible reasons why this critique has failed to register with scholars of "religion and media." In the first instance, the field is generally characterized by a lack of engagement with pertinent debates long underway in related fields (for example, anthropology, history, postcolonial studies, queer theory), combined with an apparent lack of familiarity with the genealogy of their own ideas (for example, the historical relationship between media theory, hermeneutics, and theology). Second, with notable exceptions, the vast majority of research on "religion and media" is conducted in Anglophone North America and Western Europe. Taken together, these tendencies have shielded scholars of "religion and media" from the challenges that might be posed by a more cosmopolitan approach, their provincialism abetted by a theory of mass-mediated communication adopted—or perhaps adapted—from British cultural studies. For, as we shall see, this account of media is structurally analogous to the model we have already discussed in relation to Müller's account of text, language, and religion—and, as such, it engenders all the circularity and presumption to universality that we discerned there.

We may begin by noting that much of the current scholarship on "religion and media" is organized around the analysis of "media reception" and "meaning-making." Studies have focused, for example, on "the contribution of religious frameworks to meaning making in relation to the media,"[28] "the meaning-making that believers undertake in the visual practices of daily life,"[29] "how local values and conditions mediate the reception and uses of media technology,"[30] and the "ways in which situated media reception occurs according to the logic of individual receivers and audiences."[31] This emphasis on "meaning-making" may be read as a distinctly American—and perhaps even generationally specific (that is, "baby boomer," following Roof)[32]—extrapolation from David Morley's ethnographic work with audiences,[33] which itself drew heavily on Geertz's model of interpretive anthropology.[34] However, more generally speaking, the interest in "individual receivers and audiences" tends to be represented by scholars of "religion and media" as a corrective both to statistically driven studies of "consumption" (associated particularly with the field of Mass Communications) and to more textually oriented analyses of media "products" (associated with various strands of cultural studies and "discourse analysis"). While the former has been judged inadequately sensitive to local contexts of media use, the latter has been deemed similarly incapable of grasping the importance of media as they affect "everyday lived experience." The question is whether such a corrective emphasis on "reception" is capable of producing its desired effect. To understand what is at issue, we must have a closer look at the underlying theory of media on which it is based.

As Clark and Hoover noted in an early bibliographic essay,[35] students of religion and media have tended to follow the lead of British cultural studies in their accounts of mass-mediated communication. These accounts—beginning with Stuart Hall's oft-cited essay on "encoding/decoding,"[36] and subsequently including the work of John Fiske, John Hartley, David Morley, and others—more or less agree on the fundamentals of communication. In short, an encoded message is transmitted from a sender to a receiver, who then decodes the message—or, as it is sometimes called, the "media text"—with varying degrees of fidelity to its original form. The distortion or changes that are detected in the message as it occurs at the site of reception (for example, in interviews with "audience members") are generally attributed to an incongruity—deliberate or otherwise—between the encoding and decoding of the sender and receiver respectively. Various factors are invoked in explanation for what appear to be nonmimetic decodings, ranging from the inherent polysemy of the message to a deliberately aberrant or oppositional posture taken up by the audience.[37]

This account of mass-mediated communication emerged out of a broader series of developments in the analysis of class and ideology in postwar Britain. The latter were associated most prominently with figures including Richard Hoggart, E. P. Thompson, Raymond Williams, and later Stuart Hall and the Birmingham Centre for Contemporary Cultural Studies. The work of the Centre was explicitly political from the outset, with its emphasis on the analysis of media premised on the idea that "any society/culture tends, with varying degrees of closure, to impose its classifications of the social and cultural and political world."[38] Following a broadly Marxian trajectory—and drawing more specifically (if selectively) on the work of the Italian political philosopher and activist Antonio Gramsci (1891–1937)—this was thought to comprise a "process whereby the subordinate are led to consent to the system that subordinates them."[39] Media figured in this account as the primary means toward such imposition, while the imposition itself was cast as the outcome of uncritical media decoding on the part of the audience—that is, the consenting acceptance of the "dominant" or "preferred meaning" that has been encoded in the "media text." So, precisely how is this "decoding" thought to work? And under what conditions does it become accessible as an object of scholarly inquiry?

Although the "preferred meaning" is encoded at the site of production, it seems that it is not always received as sent. Rather, we are told that "the codes of encoding and decoding may not be perfectly symmetrical. . . . What are called 'distortions' or 'misunderstandings' arise precisely from the *lack of equivalence* between the two sides in the communicative exchange."[40] Noting this potential for incongruity, Morley suggested that the "effects" of mass-mediated communication might be measured by "the extent to which decodings take place within the limits of the preferred (or dominant) manner in which the message has been initially encoded."[41] For example, on this approach, the ideological "effectivity" of an advertisement for an American-made pickup truck might be measured by the extent to which viewers identified with and acted on its articulation of masculinity, authenticity, patriotism, and so on. That is to say, the degree of an audience member's consent to the dominant ideology is deemed measurable by the extent to which she or he receives and decodes the mass-mediated message as sent.[42]

On this account, the analysis of any particular decoding would proceed from (and therefore require) a foreknowledge of the "preferred meaning" that is thought to inhere in the "media text." From there, an ethnographic study of audience commentary might comprise the means of establishing "the extent to which decodings take place within [its] limits." Aberrant decoding on the part of the audience—that is, an interpretive departure from the "preferred meaning"—would register as something akin to a "distortion" resulting from a "lack of equivalence between the two sides in the communicative exchange." This, however, raises the question of how one might recognize "distortion" as such.

Morley noted that "the text is never available for analysis except in the context of its activations,"[43] and so it would appear that its "preferred meaning" would have to be sought in a particular "activation." Yet, insofar as such an "activation" would entail decoding—for example, by the cultural studies analyst—the "activated" message will be always already potentially distorted ("the codes of encoding and decoding may not be perfectly symmetrical"). As we have seen in the previous section with respect to Müller, there is an unavoidable circularity entailed in any such process. On the one hand, the analyst's goal of identifying the "preferred meaning" in the "activated" message would ride on the recognition and removal of any distortion brought about in the process of (analytic) decoding. Yet, on the other, the ability to recognize that distortion presupposes a foreknowledge of the undistorted "preferred meaning." As with Müller's recovery of the unitary "apprehension of the Infinite" from its distorted appearance in "the world's principle religions," this mode of inquiry can only reveal something that was already known at the outset.

It is at least in part for this reason that the study of "religion and media" has been able to proceed free from the kinds of doubts currently plaguing older and arguably more mature disciplines. By adopting a theory of media that entails such circularity, one presumes they can rest assured that no challenge will be made to the assumptions from which they have begun. As I have already suggested, this orientation has insulated the process of inquiry from the kinds of challenges and uncertainties that would arise from a more cosmopolitan approach. This is not to suggest that, within the fold, there is no one working on "religion and media" in Asia, Africa, and elsewhere. On the contrary, edited volumes and conference panels frequently incorporate contributions addressing research conducted in other parts of the world. And, to be fair, there is interesting work being done by those with a broader purview.[44] However, for the time being, studies of "the non-Western world" seem to amount to little more than what the French philosopher and cultural critic Roland Barthes theorized in terms of *inoculation*: "One immunizes the contents of the collective imagination by means of a small inoculation of acknowledged evil; one thus protects it against the risk of a generalized subversion."[45] That is to say, we entertain "the Other" as a variation on what we think we already know, thereby reassuring our faith in the universality of our own understanding of the world. This may have been de rigueur in the late nineteenth century. It is surely an embarrassment in the so-called media age.

NOTES

1. See, for example, Marie Gillespie, *Television, Ethnicity, and Cultural Change* (London: Routledge, 1995); Lynn Schofield Clark, *From Angels to Aliens: Teenagers, the Media, and the Supernatural* (New York: Oxford University Press, 2003); David Morgan, *The Sacred Gaze: Religious Visual Culture in Theory and Practice* (Berkeley: University of California Press, 2005); and Stewart M. Hoover, *Religion in the Media Age* (London: Routledge, 2006).

2. The *Journal of Media and Religion*, first published in 2002.

3. See, for example, Chris Arthur, *Religion and the Media: An Introductory Reader* (Cardiff: University of Wales Press, 1993); S. M. Hoover and Knut Lundby, eds., *Rethinking*

Media, Religion and Culture (London: Sage, 1997); Hent de Vries and Samuel Weber, eds., *Religion and Media* (Stanford: Stanford University Press, 2001); David Morgan and Sally M. Promey, eds., *The Visual Culture of American Religions* (Berkeley: University of California Press, 2001); Jolyon P. Mitchell and Sophia Marriage, eds., *Mediating Religion* (London: Continuum, 2003); S. M. Hoover, L. S. Clark, and Diane F. Alters, *Media, Home, and Family* (London: Routledge, 2004); Claire Badaracco, *Quoting God: How Media Shape Ideas About Religion and Culture* (Waco: Baylor University Press, 2005); Birgit Meyer and Annelies Moors, eds., *Religion, Media, and the Public Sphere* (Bloomington: Indiana University Press, 2006); and L. S. Clark, ed., *Religion, Media, and the Marketplace* (New Brunswick, N.J.: Rutgers University Press, 2007).

4. Hoover, *Religion in the Media Age*, 1.

5. New York University Mission Statement for the Center for Religion and Media, www. nyu.edu/fas/center/religionandmedia/?menu=aboutUs&sub=missionStatement.

6. See Richard Gombrich, "How the Mahayana Began," *Journal of Pali and Buddhist Studies* 1 (1988): 29–46.

7. See Lucien Febvre and Henri-Jean Martin, *The Coming of the Book: The Impact of Printing, 1450–1800*, trans. David Gerard (London: New Left, 1976).

8. See Arvind Rajagopal, *Politics After Television: Hindu Nationalism and the Reshaping of the Public in India* (Cambridge: Cambridge University Press, 2001).

9. See Eric J. Sharpe, *Comparative Religion: A History*, 2nd ed. (London: Duckworth, 1986).

10. Friedrich Max Müller, introduction to the *Science of Religion: Four Lectures Delivered at the Royal Institution in February and May, 1870* (London: Longmans, Green, 1893), 26–27.

11. See *The Upanishads: The Sacred Books of the East*, trans. Friedrich Max Müller (Oxford: Clarendon, 1879), 1:xi–xii.

12. William Jones, *The Works of Sir William Jones: With the Life of the Author by Lord Teignmouth* (London: John Stockdale and John Walker, 1807), 2:268; emphasis in original.

13. Friedrich Max Müller, *Rig-Veda-Samitâ: The Sacred Hymns of the Brâmans; Together with Commentary of Sâyanâkârya*, 2nd ed. (London: Oxford University Press, 1890), 1:xvi. NB: The preface to the first edition is dated 1849.

14. Ibid.

15. Müller, introduction to the *Science of Religion*, 53.

16. Müller, *Rig-Veda-Samitâ*, 1:ix.

17. Ibid., 1:xvi–xvii.

18. See, for example, Richard E. Palmer, *Hermeneutics: Interpretation Theory in Schleiermacher, Dilthey, Heidegger, and Gadamer* (Evanston, Ill.: Northwestern University Press, 1969).

19. Friedrich Max Müller "Comparative Mythology," in *Chips from a German Workshop* (London: Longmans, Green, 1867), 2:75–76.

20. Ibid.

21. F. M. Müller, "The Science of Religion: Lecture I," in *The Essential Max Müller: On Language, Mythology, and Religion*, ed. Jon R. Stone (New York: Palgrave Macmillan, 2002), 120.

22. F. M. Müller, "The Perception of the Infinite," in Stone, *The Essential Max Müller*, 188.

23. F. M. Müller, "Buddhist Nihilism," in Stone, *The Essential Max Müller*, 85.

24. On "religion," see Talal Asad, *Genealogies of Religion: Disciplines and Reasons of Power in Christianity and Islam* (Baltimore: Johns Hopkins University Press, 1993). Compare, for example, on "gender," Judith Butler, *Gender Trouble: Feminism and the Subversion of Identity* (London: Routledge, 1999); on "culture," Mark Hobart, *After Culture: Ethnography as Radical Metaphysical Critique* (Denpasar, Indonesia: Duta Wacana University Press, 2000); and on "race," Anne McClintock, *Imperial Leather: Race, Gender, and Sexuality in the Colonial Contest* (London: Routledge, 1995).

25. Morgan, *The Sacred Gaze*, 52.

26. Hoover, *Religion in the Media Age*, 11, 23; Clifford Geertz, *The Interpretation of Cultures* (San Francisco: HarperCollins, 1973).

27. Asad, *Genealogies of Religion*, 29.

28. Hoover, Clark, and Alters, *Media, Home, and Family*, 13.

29. Morgan and Promey, *The Visual Culture of American Religions*, 17.

30. Rosalind Hackett, "Managing or Manipulating Religious Conflict in the Nigerian Media," in *Mediating Religion*, ed. Jolyon P. Mitchell and Sophia Marriage (London: Continuum, 2003) 49, 52.

31. S. M. Hoover, "The Culturalist Turn in Scholarship on Media and Religion," *Journal of Media and Religion* 1, no. 1 (2002): 29.

32. Wade C. Roof, *Spiritual Marketplace: Baby Boomers and the Remaking of American Religion* (Princeton: Princeton University Press, 1999).

33. For example, David Morley, *Television, Audiences, and Cultural Studies* (London: Routledge, 1992).

34. Geertz, *The Interpretation of Cultures*.

35. L. S. Clark and S. Hoover, "At the Intersection of Media, Culture, and Religion: A Bibliographic Essay," in Hoover and Lundby, *Rethinking Media, Religion and Culture*.

36. Stuart Hall, "Encoding/Decoding," in *Culture, Media, Language: Working Papers in Cultural Studies, 1972–1979*, ed. S. Hall (London: Hutchison, 1980). This article is listed as an edited extract from S. Hall, "Encoding and Decoding in Television Discourse," *CCCS Stencilled Paper* no. 7 (1973).

37. This tripartite model of mass-mediated communication—and its notion of "the audience"—naturalizes an industry model associated with the practices of producers. See, for example, John Hartley, *Tele-ology: Studies in Television* (London: Routledge, 1992); and Ien Ang, *Desperately Seeking the Audience* (London: Routledge, 1991).

38. Hall, "Encoding/Decoding," 134.

39. John Fiske, *Television Culture* (London: Routledge, 1987), 40.

40. Hall, "Encoding/Decoding," 131, italics in original.

41. Morley, *Television, Audiences, and Cultural Studies*, 86.

42. For a critique of this approach, see Virginia Nightingale, *Studying Audiences: The Shock of the Real* (London: Routledge, 1996).

43. Morley, *Television, Audiences, and Cultural Studies*, 179.

44. See, for example, contributions to Meyer and Moors, *Religion, Media, and the Public Sphere*; and cf. Charles Hirschkind, *The Ethical Soundscape: Cassette Sermons and*

Islamic Counterpublics (New York: Columbia University Press, 2006); and Faye Ginsburg, Lila Abu-Lughod, and Brian Larkin, eds., *Media Worlds: Anthropology on New Terrain* (Berkeley: University of California Press, 2002).

45. Roland Barthes, *Mythologies*, trans. Annette Lavers (New York: Hill and Wang, 1972), 150.

PART VII

Religion, Ritual, and Action

32

Classic Ritual Theories

ULRIKE BRUNOTTE

The study of rituals and ritualization in cultural studies has grown remarkably as an interdisciplinary and international realm of research in the last decades.[1] Transdisciplinary research projects—especially those encompassing sociology, cultural anthropology and gender theory, theater studies, and religious studies—revolve around the concept of the *performative*. Today, ritual acts are often treated as the primeval scene of the performative.[2] But how is the interdisciplinary concept of the *performative* associated with rituals and ritualization?

The current heterogeneous discourse links the theory of *Speech Acts*,[3] developed in John L. Austin and John R. Searle's linguistics, to the concept of *performance*[4] in theater studies and the notion of *performative acts and gender constitution*,[5] introduced by Judith Butler, and the theories of *social drama* and the *liminal*,[6] advanced by Victor Turner. Common to all of these approaches is a special link between speaking and acting, which hints at the power of the speech act to produce reality. Austin developed the crucial innovations in his lectures *Words and Deeds* (1952–1954) and *How to Do Things with Words* (1955). According to Iris Därmann, he made a distinction between two types of utterance: "one type of utterance stating that which is already the case, and one that does something by saying something, and thereby creates and produces something that did not previously exist."[7]

Although Austin did not incorporate the long religious and legal tradition of performative speech acts into his theory, it is striking "that many of the performative utterances he examines constitute the act of execution or 'part of the execution of a ritual' and/or 'ritual phrases.' "[8] This is particularly true of the central examples he chose, namely, marriage and baptism. On the one hand, Austin had therefore discovered or rediscovered[9] the performative element of certain speech acts; yet, on the other hand, he did not explore their ritual and quite frequently, as in the case of marriage, theatrical framework. Furthermore, he also completely excluded the link between speech acts and nonverbal performative acts (that is, the relationship between myths, magic spells, and rituals) from his considerations, which is significant from more than simply a religious studies perspective.

The theory of the performative as a whole draws crucial impetus from ethnological research into rituals. According to Catherine Bell, performance theory also bridges a gap between so-called indigenous and Western societies. However, referring back to Milton Singer, the pioneer of cultural performance theory, Bell stressed that ethnological performance theoreticians often work on the basis of two initial considerations that are linked and therefore normative:[10] first, from the hypothesis[11] that indigenous societies "think of their culture as encapsulated within discrete performances, which they can exhibit to outsiders as well as to themselves," and, second, that such *performances* "are the most observable units of the cultural structure"[12] for the researcher. Therefore, ritual theories reflect the normative prescriptions of the researchers involved.

All current approaches in ritual theories, which are part of the *performative turn*, are embedded in a broader theoretical discourse and stand in tense relationship with the two preceding turning points in the twentieth-century theory of rituals. Although concepts of the ritual emerged in the 1960s and evolved through the late 1970s, they were already developed around the turn of the twentieth century, especially in the field of *comparative anthropology*, and they moved as a kind of knowledge transfer from the colonial discursive space into European societies.

Current theories of ritual focus less on the ritual performance of structures or symbolic systems but, rather, "in connection with Victor Turner's theories of ritual process, the transformative power of rituals has increasingly moved into the center of attention."[13] This trajectory revolves around symbolic power *and* the corporeal, the processual and communicated *performative* practice of rituals—religious and secular, civil, or artistic: "For ritual theory, a performative mode of observation pushes the completion of the action and the effective ritualized situations, ritual performances, and staged depictions, into the focus of interests."[14] Here, an enterprise is conducted in an interdisciplinary manner, which Ronald Grimes already outlined programmatically in the foreword of his *Beginnings in Ritual Studies* about thirty years ago.[15] In the 1960s and 1970s, pioneering approaches to ritual theory and in practical ritual research merged in the context of "symbolic anthropology," linked to scholars like Victor Turner, Mary Douglas, Stanley Tambiah, Clifford Geertz, and Erving Goffman. In this context, "the theoretical justification of rituals as transformative performative acts goes back to the stimulus provided by Tambiah's 1979 text *A Performative Approach to Ritual*."[16]

The dissociation of ritual research and ritual from theology and religion, as well as the establishment of a broad field of research in cultural studies, has also been fostered by the interdisciplinary forum that Grimes introduced in 1985 with the *Journal of Ritual Studies*.[17]

Already in 1967, Erving Goffman had—with reference to Ernst Simmel—applied the model of the theater and role-play to social everyday life and sociable interaction.[18] The magical dimension of rituals, making something appear or generating something unavailable, indicates its proximity to art and cult.

Starting with his early studies of the North African Kabyles, Pierre Bourdieu (1930–2002) developed the notion of the "performative magic"[19] of ritual practice through the embodiment and enactment of social schemata of thought and

expression. In this notion, he followed Claude Lévi-Strauss by referring to the ritual as a "source and expressive form of social structures"; nevertheless, he showed
how in a ritual "through precarious transcendence of the 'normal' a situationally-
bound synthesis can be created."[20] For Bourdieu's sociology of social praxis, the
habitus is the "social turned into body,"[21] not only in the sense of assimilation of
social disposition, but also with the potential for change or an *ars vivendi*.[22]

Against the backdrop of the antiritualism of the student revolt, Mary Douglas
(1921–2007) rehabilitated the concept of the ritual as *ex opere operato* action in her
Natural Symbols: Exploration in Cosmology (1970). Following Durkheim, Mauss,
and Geertz, she viewed rituals as necessary symbolic communicative forms equipped
with magical efficacy. Ritualism would therefore presuppose a heightened sensitivity to symbolic action. Within Douglas's comparative perspective, this applies to
both indigenous and Western European societies. Douglas vehemently fought against
the shift away from the magical, which she detected in both the Reformation and
the "ecstatic" millenarianism of the rebelling students.[23] She provided a proper
"apology of the ritual."[24] Her comparative study has also become famous for
distinguishing between *grid* and *group*; it allowed the analysis of forms of extreme
antiritualism or ritualism to be made along the lines of diverse "styles" and "lan-
guage-codes" of social organization and not along the dichotomy of modern Western culture versus traditional indigenous societies.

For Douglas, the body is a microcosm of society and what becomes cut into the
individual body during initiation is the image of society. The body as a *natural symbol* also functions as the central symbol for societal differentiation. In *Purity and
Danger*,[25] Douglas emphasized the corporeal side of social drama, with regard to
impurity, purity, and taboo, and elaborated on the social control and embodiment
functions of rituals.

When Erika Fischer-Lichte talks about a twofold *performative turn* in modernity, she situates the first of these turns around 1900.[26] From today's perspective, it
is astounding that the "ritual" as the term for representative symbolic acts only came
to the attention of Religious Studies around the turn of the century (as Jan Bremmer indicated, with reference to Talal Asad).[27] For a long time, ritual was primarily
understood in a semiotic way as a text, script, or scenario. This was due to the influence of theology and its emphasis on text and faith, as well as an idealist-classicist-
oriented Hellenism (whose interests lay primarily in written and poetically fixed
myths). The shift to ritual as a means of action and embodiment and the "discovery" of "rituals" in Religious Studies and culture around 1900 would have been impossible without the knowledge transfer from the colonies.

This "discovery" also became a central engine in the production of the social imagery of European Modernity.[28] David Chidester stated: "A colonized periphery
was also an arena of theory production, with the conquering and colonizing center
itself colonized by reports about religion from missionaries, travelers, colonial administrators, and others on the periphery."[29] A "third space" of exchange was established and a colonial border discourse, whose effects inaugurated an "imaginary
ethnography" in Fritz Kramer's sense,[30] opened up a new awareness of ritualization in European culture. In his book *Discovering Religious History in the Modern*

Age,[31] Hans Kippenberg elaborated on the co-occurrence of the beginning of Religious Studies and European modernization from the perspective of history and the sociology of knowledge. The description of what is labeled as "religion" already entails a cultural political prescription and has to be read, following Kippenberg, as a reflex of modernization. With Catherine Bell, it has to be asked to what extent the theoretical concepts of ritual that accumulated in the late-nineteenth-century colonial border discourse can be read as a part of a *ritual turn* in European cultural studies and as an attempt by European cultures to come to a new self-understanding.[32]

The "discovery" of ritual as an elementary form of religion between 1889 and 1920 was a turn away from the Christian paradigm and was linked to an anti-idealist view of religious practices. Mainstays of this turn were William Robertson Smith's *Lectures on the Religion of the Semites* (1889/1894), Jane Ellen Harrison's books *Mythology and Monuments of Ancient Athens* (1890), *Prolegomena of the Study of Greek Religion* (1903), and *Themis: Study of the Social Origins of Greek Religion* (1912), and James George Frazer's *The Golden Bough* (first edition 1890). Émile Durkheim turned the ritualistic approach in his work *The Elementary Forms of Religion* (1913) into the linchpin of his sociology of religion. In 1890, the Semitist and biblical scholar William Robertson Smith (1846–1894) was the first to view ancient religion not as faith but as social practice.[33]

The first edition of James George Frazer's (1854–1941) *The Golden Bough* (1890) often takes a prominent role in discussions about the Cambridge Ritualists. Indeed, this edition of his monumental work, which revolves around the dying and resurrected god of the year, shows a strong influence from Wilhelm Mannhardt's[34] work on vegetation cults and Robertson Smith's theory of sacrifice on his work.[35] In the first edition of *The Golden Bough*, Frazer gave priority to the archaic ritual as a magical act in contrast to the myth, which derives from it.[36] But the act remains oriented in an individualist and utilitarian fashion: the cult actor is an agent who attempts to control the natural world and to influence the gods by dint of magic and ritual. Nevertheless, the Frazerian concept of the sacred king as the vegetation spirit, whose ritual death and resurrection regulate the entire natural cosmos, influenced all myth and ritual theories in this first phase. However, intellectualism prevailed in his later approaches.

In a case somewhat parallel to that of the Old Testament scholar and Semitist William Robertson Smith, Jane E. Harrison, an archaeologist and expert in ancient Greece (also see "The Myth-Ritual Debate," chapter 33 of this volume), published her ritualistic approach to religion in 1890.[37] Her book *Themis* (1912), with the subtitle *A Social Theory of Greek Religion*,[38] combined the paradigm shift in the theory of religion with a clear turn to the social culture of collective emotions. This approach integrates Frazer's vegetation spirit, but simultaneously socializes it as an initiant. Harrison emphatically established the connection between social emotion, ritual, and myth-making when she wrote: "Strong emotion collectively experienced begets this illusion of objective reality; each worshipper is conscious of something in his emotion not himself, stronger than himself. He does not know it is the force of collective suggestion, he calls it a god."[39]

The ritual actor is no longer the lone manipulator and controller of natural processes as in Frazer's account; rather, "man is *the one who is manipulated*: however
the ritual may relate to external data like fertility of the soil, what occurs is *what the
participant himself experiences*, his own emotion. The mythical images, therefore, are products, first and foremost, of *spontaneous, collective emotions*."[40] In
Robertson Smith's approach and especially in Émile Durkheim's sociology, external nature and vegetation in their seasonal change are already left as a frame of
reference for rituals, and the social space as a performative constituted space is
entered. However, the focus on the ritual process itself stands at the center of
Harrison's theory of culture. In an emphatic sense and in close reference to
Durkheim, rituals are treated as a media for the stimuli of the masses, for festive self-
perception, and for collectivization.

Émile Durkheim (1858–1917) based his functional theory of religion, as is generally known, on the analysis of the symbolic and ritual systems of the Australian
aborigines, especially on the "totemism" that fascinated scholars at the time. However, his heuristic interest was focused on the question of social cohesion in the secular, laicist Third Republic of France. Time and again, this social political interest
appears like a palimpsest through his narratives about the Arrente (Aranda) people. In his early work *The Division of Labor in Society* (1893), his thinking already
aimed at the design of new forms of social solidarity in increasingly differentiated
and rationalized societies. In *The Elementary Forms of the Religious Life* (1912), he
claimed to have found a paradigmatic ritual model in the Australian aborigines' clan
celebrations, which were called *corroboree*. During these celebrations, Durkheim
claimed, the separation of the individuals that atomized during their work in the
space of the profane becomes weaker once an intermediary space has been established. This space alternates between subject and object, a collective space of excitement and affect ordered in and by the ritual:

> Life in Australian (aboriginal) societies alternates between two different phases. In one
> phase, the population is scattered in small groups that attend to their occupation
> independently. . . . In the other phase, by contrast, the population comes together. . . .
> This concentration conducts a religious ceremony. . . . Once the individuals are gath-
> ered together a sort of electricity is generated from their closeness and quickly launches
> them into an extraordinary height of exaltation. . . . Probably because a collective emo-
> tion cannot be expressed collectively without some order that permits harmony and
> unison of movement, gestures and cries tend to fall into rhythm and regularity, and
> from there into songs and dances.[41]

Durkheim used the words "electricity" and "exaltation" to describe a state of
"collective *effervescence*." This collective emotion, which occurs in the frame of the
celebration, has, as the ritual constitutes it, no destructive power; rather, it is the
space for the generation of the *Sacré*: "Sacred time is devoted primarily to ritual."[42] It
is the birthplace of the religious notion of the Divine and of all categories of thought.
Therefore, the ritual defines the core of the social life, without being far from reason.
Its center is the experienced, hallucinated, and imagined *social* unity: the "society."

The individual feels "transcended" and safe in the celebrations. Such a transformation of individuals into a sacred and homogenous collective body can only succeed in ritual when the rituals themselves have contributed to forming the binding collective imagination. For Durkheim, the ritual space is the site for the production of "beliefs" and "representations" and not vice versa:

> The individual minds can meet and commune only if they come outside themselves, but they do this only by means of movement. It is the homogeneity of these movements that makes the group aware of itself and that, in consequence, makes it be. Once this homogeneity has been established and these movements have taken a definite form and been stereotyped, they serve to symbolize the corresponding representations. But these movements symbolize those representations only because they help to form them.[43]

Thereby, the totemic ritual creates and reflects again and again the first social, moral, and epistemological "totality."

In this vein, Robert Bellah, whose theory of *civil religion* was inspired by Durkheim, argued that "Durkheim does not authorize a 'symbolic interpretation' of ritual that attempts to read off symbolic meaning from observed events. . . . Meaning arises from this totality, not as an interpretation of it."[44] Mary Douglas also followed Durkheim in her interpretation and analysis of a Dinka ritual: "It would be absurd to say that their ritual has represented a community meal, when they have just eaten one. Their wish for community to be possessed by divinity is realized (not represented) in the trance of their priest whom the spirit possess."[45] In Durkheim's understanding, the ritual performance of collectivization is primary. Even if he explicated his theories with reference to the totemic symbols, rituals, and cultural celebrations of the aborigines, his *Elementary Forms* revolved, according to Jan Bremmer,[46] around the modern model of the self-celebrating French Republic.[47]

Marcel Mauss (1872–1950), a disciple of Durkheim, critically engaged with Edward Burnett Tylor and Robertson Smith in his *Essai sur la nature et la fonction du sacrifice* (*Sacrifice: Its Nature and Functions*), cowritten with his colleague Henri Hubert in 1899. They developed a theory of sacrifice that can simultaneously be read as a radical theory of the performative power of social action. They first linked the Tylorian theory of sacrifice as a gift to the gods and medium of communication with the concept of sacrifice as a "communion" with the gods and a guarantee of social cohesion, as introduced by Robertson Smith. They then combined these approaches with the Frazerian concept of ritual sacrifice as a performance of the drama of the dying of the vegetation god and the exorcism of the "agrarian evil spirits of Mannhardt."[48]

In contrast to their predecessors, Hubert and Mauss did not interpret the victim and the institution of the sacrifice as substantial facts or institutions. Rather, they thought that the ensemble of collective social acts produces the sacralization or desacralization of the victim: "Contrary to what Smith believed, the victim does not necessarily come to the sacrifice with a religious nature already perfected and clearly defined: it is the sacrifice itself that confers this upon it."[49] For this reason, the sacrificial ritual, as illustrated by examples from indigenous cultures, the Hebrew Bible, Greek antiquity, and Vedic rituals, can sometimes simultaneously serve very different functions.

As Marcel Mauss explicated in his far more famous *The Gift* from 1923–24, cultic giving and taking are about the shaped handling of the ambivalent energies of the sacred (just as in the case of the total consumption of the victim in a burnt offering). The acts of sacrifice create an intermediate zone in which society grapples with its own dangerous energies, tensions, and aggressions: "The sacrificer remains protected: the gods take the victim instead of him. *The victim redeems him.* . . . This is the purpose of the intermediary. Thanks to it, the two worlds that are present—[the sacred and the profane]—can interpenetrate and yet remain distinct."[50] The contents of faith or symbols, which connect the individual or the society with the process of the sacrifice, can be neglected. According to Hubert and Mauss, the analysis of the sacrificial rituals leads directly into the center of the social and into the production sites of religious beliefs:

> Not, doubtless, that society has need of the things which are materials of sacrifice. . . . But the act of abnegation implicit in every sacrifice, by recalling frequently to the consciousness of the individual the presence of collective forces, in fact sustains their ideal existence. These expiations and general purifications, communions and sacralizations of groups, these creations of the spirits of the cities give—renew periodically for the community, represented by its gods—that character, good, strong, grave, and terrible, which is one of the essential traits of any social entity. . . . They confer upon each other, upon themselves, and upon those things they hold dear, the whole strength of society. . . . At the same time they find in sacrifice the means of redressing equilibriums that have been upset...This indicates the importance of sacrifice for sociology.[51]

For a long time, the *Essai sur la nature et la function du sacrifice* had no significant impact or successor. However, the most widely read work of the late twentieth century in this area is *Violence and the Sacred* (1972), written by René Girard, a French scholar of Romance Studies (French literature). In this book, Girard took up the theory of the *ambivalent* notion of the *Sacré* as the center of the Holy. He also stated that ritual sacrifices are purifying regulations of "social violent crises." His approach follows the myth-ritual schema proposed by Robert Segal;[52] however, it takes myths literally to some extent and gives them relevance equal to that of social reality. Girard focused especially on the analysis of *foundational violence*, on rituals and myths of the "scapegoat," and on the role of the sacrifice as "surrogate violence" already emphasized by Huber and Mauss.[53]

Also in 1972, Walter Burkert, a Swiss religious scholar and expert on ancient Greece, published his book *Homo Necans*.[54] It contained a second *ritual-myth* approach that integrated ethology[55] (theories on animal behavior) in order to analyze ancient Greek religion and rituals. This idea gave center stage to the dramatization of ritual sacrifice killings and to the role of repetitions, symbolization, and (archaic) action patterns in rituals.

Like the previously discussed pioneers of ritual theory, the founder of psychoanalysis, Sigmund Freud (1856–1939), also took the construction of a "primitive" collectivity, which he situates in the Darwinian "primal horde," as his starting point. To avoid the charge of *petitio principii*, namely, that the ritual that creates the collective institutions and the sacred always already presupposes them, the psychoanalyst constructed his "scientific myth" of the "primal patricide" and projected this concept to the beginning of the development of the species.[56]

At the same time, he still saw the remaining virulence of aggressive efforts and tendencies left in the modern "masses."[57] Against the backdrop of his experience as an assimilated Jew in the anti-Semitic 1930s in Vienna, Freud granted the masses far fewer constructive qualities than Durkheim had in his time. Sigmund Freud's *Totem and Taboo* first appeared in 1912 and 1913 in serialized form in the journal *Imago*. One year before the outbreak of the First World War, the founder of psychoanalysis presented his pessimistic theory of the irresolvable connection of violence and guilt in modern Judeo-Christian-influenced society in the form of a theory of archaic sacrifice. In his "scientific myth," he championed the thesis, inspired by Robertson Smith, that social organization, moral limitations, and religion began with a murder and ultimately arose from a "creative feeling of guilt": "Society now rests upon the shared responsibility for the mutually committed crime, religion upon the conscience of guilt and the regret, morality partly upon the needs of this society, partly upon the atonements demanded by the guilty conscience."[58] Today, we should no longer read *Totem and Taboo* as an "indefensible" contribution to prehistory or ethnology, but instead as a text about political violence and its ritualization in modern societies.

The archaeologist and Hellenist Jane Harrison (1850–1928) also addressed social cohesion as a focus of collective ritual actions, yet she focused her attention on the reconstruction of concrete ritual sequences and often small face-to-face ritual communities. She used the *thiasos* of intoxicated followers of the mystery god Dionysus as a paradigmatic example for her research in this area. Harrison especially concentrated on the connection between ritual, tragedy, and theatricality in her book *Ancient Art and Ritual* (1913), based on a new acquisition of antique cults and myths. Richard Schechner, one of the leading scholars in early performance studies, viewed Harrison's ritualistic understanding of Greek tragedy as a turning point. He stated: "it was not only novel, it was revolutionary: drama is not just something that occurs on stage, but something full of meaning and operating on many levels in everyday life, in both secular and sacred rituals, play, sports, legal processes, and popular entertainments."[59] Her enthusiastic attention to ancient ritual traditions such as the mystery cults of Dionysus, which have fascinated Hellenists since Friedrich Nietzsche and Walter Pater, contributed to the cultural transformation of the image of antiquity from a textual and visual Apollonian culture to a theatrical and ritual Dionysian culture.

THE INITIATION COMPLEX

Furthermore, Jane Harrison integrated the initiation complex as a social and ritual reality with the study of Greek religion,[60] especially when she combined Arnold van Gennep's (1873–1957) theory in *The Rites of Passage* (1909) with the Durkheimian theory of social practice. Van Gennep moved the question of the ritual formation of individual transformation and the social dynamic into the center of his comparative studies. He noticed that all transitional and critical situations in human life—birth, initiation, marriage, and death, but also war or ordination—utilize a similar ensemble of rituals. His model in *The Rites of Passage* had three parts: (1) rites of separation; (2) liminal or transformative rites; and (3) rites of incorporation. These rites stage the following over and over again: a person dies, is separated from her former status, enters a formless transitional field where she changes, and then reenters society "carried" by a reincarnation drama at a changed location (status). Van Gennep argued that it is important that the symbolism of the transformational ritual aims at spatial transitions as a model for life-historical or social transitions.[61] The middle area of the liminal rituals carries special meaning in the ensemble of rituals because the staging of border crossings belongs in the liminal or "neutral zone."[62] The space in which she moves is a sacred no-man's-land; she floats between the worlds. Van Gennep termed this situation "the threshold phase."

Jane Harrison was the first to turn the connection of social puberty, rites of passage, and initiation into the central complex of ancient religion and mythology. In *Themis* (1912), she interpreted the myths of the tortured, slain, dismembered, and reborn Dionysus Zagreus as an expression of the symbolic death and social rebirth of the neophyte during the initiation ritual. She was prompted to focus her attention on the initiation complex by an archaeological finding in Eastern Crete: the fragments of the "Kourete Hymn." The hymn, which was sung during the ritual dance, praises the Megistos Kouros, the greatest youth of all. He was identified as the young Zeus and invited to head a group of dancers and "rejoice in dance and song and . . . leap for full jars, and leap for fleecy flocks, and leap for fields of fruit, and for our Cities . . . and for goodly Themis."[63] In Harrison's view, the Frazerian year god or the vegetation spirit was no longer at work here: "the initiant," as Versnel wrote, "arose from the dying god's ashes."[64]

For Harrison, the hymn and the dance of the mythical Kouretes were the mythical expression of the real orgiastic dance, the dance of youths during the ritual of initiation.[65] Harrison combined the myths of the threatened children Zeus and Dionysus Zagreus, and added death and rebirth to the ritual dance. It was obvious to her that "the worshippers in the Hymn invoke a Kouros who is obviously but a reflection or impersonation of the [real] body of Kouretes."[66] She worked out the surplus of performance qualities of the ritual processes in her interpretation of the Kouretes hymns and dance:

> We note certain characteristics of a Hymn of Invocation that may help to its understanding. The god invoked is not present, not there in a temple ready waiting to be

worshipped: he is bidden to come, and apparently his coming, and as we shall later see his very existence, depends on the ritual that invokes him. Moreover the words addressed to him are not, as we should expect and find in the ordinary worship addressed to an Olympian, a prayer, but an injunction, a command, "come," "leap." Strangest of all, the god it would seem performs the same ritual as his worshippers, and it is by performing that ritual that he is able to confer his blessings.[67]

With this theory of ritual action, understood as transformative and creative with its multiple magical manifestations, Harrison approximated a minimalist theory of the performative as is topical in recent theories. The interpretation focused on rituals as song and dance *acts* with a performative magical power: they create the "gods" in the same moment when the group of worshipers sings, feels, and dances "the gods."

Jane Harrison's main contribution to the understanding of Greek religion was her focus on the initiation complex in her ritualistic approach to the Dionysian mystery cults. Although it turns out that "the hymn of the Kouretes itself hardly contains any reference to initiation elements,"[68] since 1960 the initiation complex has also become a new research paradigm in the anthropological study of Greek religion. Before the 1960s, A. Brelich's *Paides e Partheno I* (1969) and H. Jeanmaire's *Couroi et Courètes* (1939) "were the first major studies in the classical field in which the initiation scheme was applied to Greek myths and rites in a consistent manner."[69] Influenced by Victor Turner's (1920–83) theory of liminality and ritual as the medium of "conflict" and "social drama" and "transformation," the anthropological approach to Greek antiquity is now focused on ritual dynamics, ambivalence, and reversal. After a first renaissance at the beginning of the twentieth century, the initiation complex was reintroduced into the debate about mythos and ritual by four authors in the 1960s: the religious scholar and expert on ancient Greece Walter Burkert,[70] the religious phenomenologist Mircea Eliade,[71] the psychoanalyst Bruno Bettelheim,[72] and the ethnologist and cultural scholar Victor Turner.

In Victor Turner's work, the middle phase of *The Rites of Passage* and the initiation complex developed into the nucleus of a broad cultural theory, covering indigenous as well as modern societies.[73] Turner's view of ritual processes did not concentrate on their static-repetitive and socially stabilizing functions, but rather on their potential for change. The collective play and "drama" in the rituals of the Ndembu, with whom he lived for a long time, offered him a space of experience in which things could be expressed that could not be negotiated in the normality of everyday relationships and in the ensemble of social positions. In Turner's words, the rituals of transition are the refuge of this "experimental sphere of culture."[74] Turner took up Van Gennep's dynamistic concept of the three-phase ritual in *The Rites of Passage* and focused on the social and religious significance of liminality as unstructured intermediary interstices and mingling spaces: "Liminality may be partly described as a stage of reflection. During the liminal period, neophytes are alternately forced and encouraged to think about their society, their cosmos, and their powers that generate and sustain them. . . . Liminality is the realm of primitive hypothesis, where there is a certain freedom to juggle with the factors of existence."[75]

In his article "Betwixt and Between" (1967), Turner developed the qualities of liminality with the help of boys' initiation rituals. He used these rituals because they show a relatively richly developed and lengthy threshold phase and their mainly collective performance offers an exemplary experimental space for alternative social forms. In the threshold phase, the ritual subject exists in an empty space between all axioms, predetermined polarities, and social structures: between sexes, between rule and servitude, and even, which is decisive, between life and death. The initiant is characterized by ambiguity. The novice is a marginalized commuter across the border. As a socially dead "transient being," he enters the realm of death, chaos (anti-structure), and the terrifying disintegration of form. At the same time, the initiant enters into a relationship; he even merges with the sacred dead. He must pass numerous tests and imitate the foundational deeds of heroic ancestors. At the end, the connection to the motherly world is dissolved, the quality of birth is transferred to male society, and the culturally dominant gender difference is anchored in the next generation.

Still, Turner was no romantic. As an ethnologist, he understood how tightly drawn the borders are within the frame of the liminal phase of an indigenous puberty ritual. In the end, he stressed, the reversal of the world in the threshold phase is "at the same time collectively binding duty";[76] it leads into mechanical solidarity and the affirmation of the given gender, work, and social structures. Nevertheless, he conceived of the ritual process as a "social drama"[77] of conflict resolution and change.

The experience of liminality does not remain without any traces of change for a society as a whole, especially when an age group has experienced it collectively. The explicit theoretical center of the Turnerian account is what he called the second model of human social relationships. In contrast to "society" as a system of social position," Turner stated in 1969, "*communitas* refers to a homogenous, unstructured, other dimension of society."[78] Turner's idea, expressed in 1969 in the United States, that "existential *communitas*" exists apart from every social structure may have owed more to the protest movements of the time than to the "ideal" tribal society or the encounter of equal individuals, men and women. From the Ndembu to the Broadway theater, Victor Turner's "comparative symbology" focused on the liminal leeway of ritual processes and conceptualized social dramas as transformative performances. No other ethnographer has had such a broad influence on the shift from a theory of "representation" or "structure" to the performative turn than Victor Turner.

The performative approach in cultural studies focuses on the bodily, verbal, theatrical, and "transformative" dimension of social practices. In more than one way, the "magical" and "playful" power of ritual and ritualization, the making of an event, the creativity, and the power to embody a collective feeling or to act a social or religious drama point to the nearness of the liminal stage of initiation ritual, and the performative dimension is art. With the help of Victor Turner's theories, we are now able to conceive of "symbols not only as carrier of meaning, but to 'capture' the process of symbolization 'in motion.' "[79]

NOTES

1. Jens Kreinath, Jan Snoek, and Michael Stausberg, *Theorizing Rituals: Issues, Topics, Approaches, Concepts* (Boston: Brill, 2006).

2. Klaus-Peter Köpping and Ursula Rao, eds., *Im Rausch des Rituals: Gestaltung und Transformation der Wirklichkeit in körperlicher Performanz* (Hamburg: LIT, 2000).

3. John L. Austin, *Philosophical Papers*, 2nd ed. (Oxford: Oxford University Press, 1970); John R. Searle, *Speech Acts: An Essay in the Philosophy of Language* (Cambridge: Cambridge University Press, 1969); cf. Uwe Wirth, ed., *Performanz: Zwischen Sprachphilosophie und Kulturwissenschaften* (Frankfurt: Suhrkamp, 2002).

4. Erika Fischer-Lichte, *The Transformative Power of Performance: Re-Enchanting the World; A New Aesthetics* (London: Routledge, 2008); John L. Austin, *How to Do Things with Words* (Oxford: Oxford University Press, 1962); Searle, *Speech Acts*.

5. Judith Butler, "Performative Acts and Gender Constitution: An Essay in Phenomenology and Feminist Theory," in *Performing Feminism, Feminist Critical Theory and Theatre*, ed. Sue-Ellen Case (Baltimore: Johns Hopkins University Press, 1990), 270–82.

6. Victor Turner, *Dramas, Fields and Metaphors* (Ithaca: Cornell University Press, 1974); Victor Turner, *The Ritual Process: Structure and Anti-Structure* (New York: Aldine, 1969).

7. Iris Därmann, *Kulturtheorien: Zur Einführung* (Dresden: Junius, 2011), 75. Both lectures in Austin, *Philosophical Papers*; Searle, *Speech Acts*; cf. also Wirth, *Performanz*.

8. Därmann, *Kulturtheorien*, 78.

9. As Därmann rightly emphasized, "Knowledge concerning the power of speech that is itself action is very old" ["*Ist das Wissen um die Wirkmacht von Reden, die selbst ein Handeln ist, sehr alt*"]. It extends beyond the philosophical teachings of rhetoric into magical religious speech and action itself. Ibid., 75.

10. Catherine Bell, *Ritual Theory, Ritual Practice* (Oxford: Oxford University Press, 1992), 39.

11. Ibid.

12. Milton Singer, ed., *Traditional India: Structure and Change* (Philadelphia: American Folklore Society, 1959), xiii.

13. Ibid., 1.

14. Christoph Wulf and Jörg Zirfas, eds., *Die Kultur des Rituals: Inszenierungen, Praktiken, Symbole* (München: Fink, 2004), 39.

15. Ronald Grimes, *Beginnings in Ritual Studies* (Lanham, Md.: University Press of America, 1982).

16. Köpping and Rao, *Im Rausch des Rituals*, 8.

17. Andrea Belliger and David R. Krieger, eds., *Ritualtheorien: Ein einführendes Handbuch* (Göttingen: Westdeutscher, 1998), 8.

18. Erving Goffman, *Interaction Ritual* (New York: Doubleday, 1967).

19. Pierre Bourdieu, *Language as Symbolic Power* (Cambridge: Polity, 1991), 111; Christoph Wulf, *Das Soziale als Ritual: Zur performativen Bildung von Gemeinschaften* (Opladen: Leske + Budrich, 2001), 8.

20. Karl-Siegbert Rehberg, "Institutionelle Ordnungen zwischen Ritual und Ritualisierung," in Wulf and Zirfas, *Die Kultur des Rituals*, 252.

21. Pierre Bourdieu and Loïc Wacquant, *Reflexive Anthropologie* (Frankfurt: Suhrkamp, 1996), 154.

22. Cf. Beate Krais and Gunter Gebauer, *Habitus* (Bielefeld: Transcript, 2002), 6.

23. Mary Douglas, *Natural Symbols: Explorations in Cosmology* (London: Barrie and Rockliff, 1970), 10–25.

24. Michael Stausberg, "Ritualtheorien und Religionstheorien," in *Ritualdynamik: Kulturübergreifende Studien zur Theorie und Geschichte rituellen Handelns*, ed. Dietrich Harth and Gerrit Jasper Schenk (Heidelberg: Synchron, 2004), 37.

25. Mary Douglas, *Purity and Danger* (London: Routledge, 1966).

26. Erika Fischer-Lichte, "Theater und Ritual," in Wulf and Zirfas, *Die Kultur des Rituals*, 280.

27. Cf. Talal Asad's instructive study on the change in the concept of rituals around 1900—from text to attitude. Talal Asad, *Genealogies of Religion* (Baltimore: Johns Hopkins University Press, 1993), 55–79. Jan N. Bremmer, "'Religion, 'Ritual' and the Opposition 'Sacred vs. Profane': Notes Towards a Terminological 'Genealogy,'" in *Ansichten griechischer Rituale: Geburtstags-Symposium für Walter Burkert*, ed. Fritz Graf (Stuttgart: B. G. Teubner, 1998), 9–32.

28. Cf. recently, Erhard Schüttpelz, *Die Moderne im Spiegel des Primitiven* (Munich: Wilhelm Fink, 2005).

29. David Chidester, *Savage Systems: Colonialism and Comparative Religion in Southern Africa* (Charlottesville: University of Virginia Press, 1996).

30. Fritz Kramer, *Verkehrte Welten: Zur imaginären Ethnographie des 19. Jahrhunderts* (Frankfurt: Syndikat, 1977).

31. Hans G. Kippenberg, *Discovering Religious History in the Modern Age* (Princeton: Princeton University Press, 2002).

32. Cf. Ronald Hutton, *The Triumph of the Moon: A History of Modern Pagan Witchcraft* (Oxford: Oxford University Press, 1999), 114.

33. See Ulrike Brunotte, "The Myth-Ritual Debate," chapter 33 of this volume.

34. Wilhelm Mannhardt, *Die Korndämonen* (Berlin: Borntraeger, 1868); Wilhelm Mannhardt, *Antike Wald- und Feldkulte* (Berlin: Borntraeger, 1875–77).

35. As Frazer clearly stated in his foreword: "I have made great use of the works of the late W. Mannhardt, without which, indeed, my book could scarcely haven been written." Robert Ackermann, *The Myth and Ritual School: J. G. Frazer and the Cambridge Ritualists* (New York: Garland, 1991), 49.

36. Robert A. Segal, "Myth and Ritual," in Kreinath, Snoek, and Stausberg, *Theorizing Rituals*, 105.

37. Brunotte, "The Myth-Ritual Debate."

38. Jane E. Harrison, *Themis: A Study in the Social Origin of Greek Religion* (Cambridge: Cambridge University Press, 1912).

39. Ibid., 46.

40. Henrik S. Versnel, *Transition and Reversal in Myth and Ritual* (Leiden: Brill, 1993), 26.

41. Émile Durkheim: *The Elementary Forms of Religious Life* (New York: Free Press, 1995), 216–18.

42. Robert N. Bellah, "Durkheim and Ritual," in *The Cambridge Companion to Durkheim*, ed. Jeffrey C. Alexander and Philip Smith (Cambridge: Cambridge University Press, 2005), 184.

43. Durkheim: *Elementary Forms*, 232.

44. Bellah, "Durkheim and Ritual," 184.

45. Mary Douglas, "Rightness of Categories," in *How Classification Works: Nelson Goodman Among the Social Sciences*, ed. Mary Douglas and David Hull (Edinburgh: Edinburgh University Press, 1992), 249–51.

46. Bremmer, "Religion, 'Ritual' and the Opposition," 31.

47. Hort Firsching, "Die Sakralisierung der Gesellschaft," in *Religionssoziologie um 1900*, ed. Volkhard Krech and Tyrell Hartmann (Würzburg: Ergon, 1995), 186.

48. Henri Hubert and Marcel Mauss, *Sacrifice: Its Nature and Function* (Chicago: University of Chicago Press, 1964), 4.

49. Ibid., 97.

50. Ibid., 98–99.

51. Ibid., 102–3.

52. Segal, "Myth and Ritual," n32.

53. René Girard, *La Violence et le Sacré* (Paris: Bernard Grasset, 1972), 18.

54. Walter Burkert, *Homo Necans* (Berlin: Walter de Gruyter, 1972).

55. Ethology means the scientific study of animal behaviour and ritualization.

56. Sigmund Freud, *Totem und Tabu: Einige Überseinstimmungen im Seelenleben der Wilden und der Neurotiker*, vol. 9, *Gesammelte Werke*, ed. Anna Freud, 8th ed. (Frankfurt: Fischer Taschenbuch, 2001).

57. Sigmund Freud, *Massenpsychologie und Ich-Analyse*, vol. 12, *Gesammelte Werke*, ed. Anna Freud, 8th ed. (Frankfurt: Fischer Taschenbuch, 2001), 72–161.

58. Sigmund Freud, *Totem und Tabu*, ed. Mario Erdheim (Frankfurt: Fischer, 1991), 201.

59. Richard Schechner, introduction to *Performance Theory* (New York: Routledge, 2003).

60. Walter Burkert, "Griechische Mythologie und die Geistesgeschichte der Moderne," in *Les études classiques aux XIX et XX siècles: Leur place dans l'histoire des idées*, ed. Willem den Boer (Genève: Foundation Hardt, 1979), 175.

61. Douglas, *Purity and Danger*, 126.

62. Arnold van Gennep, *Les Rites de Passage* (Frankfurt: Campus, 1986), 27–28.

63. Harrison, *Themis*, 8.

64. Versnel, *Transition and Reversal*, 49.

65. Harrison, *Themis*, 27.

66. Ibid.

67. Ibid., 10.

68. Versnel, *Transition and Reversal*, 43.

69. Ibid., 49.

70. Burkert, *Homo Necans*.

71. Mircea Eliade, *Myths, Dreams and Mysteries: The Encounter Between Contemporary Faith and Archaic Realities* (New York: Harper and Row, 1967).

72. Bruno Bettelheim, *Die symbolischen Wunden: Pubertätsriten und der Neid des Mannes* (Frankfurt: Fischer Wissenschaft, 1990).

73. His complete works are worth revisiting: Bobby C. Alexander, *Victor Turner Revisited: Ritual as Social Change* (Oxford: Oxford University Press, 1991); Peter J. Bräunlein, "Victor Witter Turner (1920–1983)," in *Klassiker der Religionswissenschaft: Von Friedrich Schleiermacher bis Mircea Eliade*, ed. Axel Michaels (Darmstadt: Beck, 1997), 324–42.

74. Turner, *The Ritual Process*; Victor Turner, *Vom Ritual zum Theater* (Frankfurt: Campus, 1989), 42.

75. Victor Turner, "Betwixt and Between: The Liminal Period in Rites de Passage," in *The Forest of Symbols: Aspects of Ndembu Ritual*, ed. Victor Turner (Ithaca: Cornell University Press, 1967), 105.

76. Turner, *Vom Ritual zum Theater*, 82, 188. The author indicates the tight borders of social tribal liminality (Turner, "Betwixt," 106).

77. Turner, *Dramas, Fields and Metaphors*.

78. Turner, *Ritual Process*, 128.

79. Doris Bachmann-Medick, *Cultural Turns: Neuorientierungen in den Kulturwissenschaften* (Hamburg: Rowohlts Enzyklopädie, 2006), 113.

33

The Myth-Ritual Debate

ULRIKE BRUNOTTE

In its narrowest sense, the myth-ritual debate happened around 1900. Together with the advent of comparative anthropology in England, it marked a turning point in the analysis of classical European religions: the epistemological focus moved from a text-centric approach to the recognition of social practices and performances, and to visual cultures and material artifacts as mediators of religion. Yet still at the beginning of the 1970s, two eminent religious scholars publicly offered two completely contrary approaches to the myth-and-ritual question.[1] In 1971, Geoffrey Stephen Kirk stated in *Myth: Its Meaning and Functions in Ancient and Other Cultures*: "Therefore it will be wise to reject from the outset the idea that myth and religion are twin aspects of the same subject, or parallel manifestations of the same psychic condition just as firmly as we rejected the idea that all myths are associated with rituals."[2] Around the same time, in 1979, the Swiss Hellenist Walter Burkert developed a totally different position in his Sather Lectures, *Structure and History in Greek Mythology and Ritual*.[3] Burkert claimed: "And it was in this way that the complex of myth and ritual, though not indissoluble, became a major force in forming ancient cultures, and as it were, dug those deep vales of human tradition in which even today the streams of our experience will tend to flow."[4]

How and in which context did the notion of a close connection between myths (beliefs, creeds, and symbols) and rituals (action, cult) start to emerge? For a long time, myths were understood as autonomous, sometimes even as a literary edifice of narratives about gods, heroes, and chthonic demons. The interest in rituals developed in Germany, France, and Great Britain roughly at the same time. Around the middle of the nineteenth century, Wilhelm Mannhardt[5] began to conduct empirical surveys "in search of traces of belief in vegetation, grain, and wood spirits and related manners and customs." About the same time Edward Burnett Tylor[6] managed to interest the Anglo-Saxon public in "the peculiar features of primitive cultures outside Europe."[7] Comparative anthropologists created some temporal distance from the "primitives" through their stage model of evolutionism, yet the concepts of *survivals* or *revivals* imply a rather vague concomitancy.

It is no coincidence that the myth-ritual debate unfolded around 1900 in the intellectual center of the largest contemporary European colonial empire. If we follow David Chidester,[8] comparative religious studies in general were not only a product of the Enlightenment, but first and foremost a result of the shock of religious and cultural pluralism experienced in the colonial *contact zone*.[9] However, comparative religious studies, stimulated by the "Other" within colonial contact, also discussed issues of the hierarchy of thought (reason, meaning) and action (social practice) in the myth-ritual debate. In *Ritual Theory, Ritual Practice* (1992), Catherine Bell argued that traditional theories of ritual reproduce a hierarchal dichotomy between thought and action, mind and body. She also emphasized the role of power structures in this discourse, especially the action-thought dichotomy in ritual theories.[10]

If one wanted to develop a rough outline of research positions concerning the changing relationship between myth and ritual, one could determine that mythology research was the predominant paradigm in the eighteenth and nineteenth centuries and was influenced by the Christian, often Protestant coding of the contemporary discourse. This position was captured by one single sentence: "A ritual is an enactment of a myth."[11] However, until the end of the nineteenth century, myths were the central object of research in religious historiography, often disassociated from both their associated rituals and social context. Myths were seen as a mainly prescientific explanation of nature;[12] at the same time, they were perceived as an important source for the study of "primitive mentality." Edward Burnett Tylor, the founder of the English anthropology, proposed an equally evolutionist and rationalist schema in which myths represented a primitive stage of human thought, detached from rituals: "Myth is the ancient counterpart to modern science. . . . It is an explanation of the physical world, not of ritual. It operates independently of ritual. It amounts to creed, merely expressed in the form of a story."[13] Ritual and therefore action were subordinate to mythos, belief, and ethos, and hence to thought: the ritual follows a nonmaterial content, which it enacts.[14] This notion changed radically with the beginning of myth-ritualist theory around 1900.[15]

However, a new anthropological concept of ritual only became possible through a transdisciplinary development in European societies around the turn of the century. This trajectory replaced theories of religion based on the individual and its consciousness with approaches that perceived religion as mainly a social, public, and collective matter.

The first religious scholar who gave the ritual priority over the mythos was the biblical scholar, Semitist, and anthropologist William Robertson Smith.[16] During his analysis of the archaic layers of Semitic religions in his book *Lectures on the Religion of the Semites* (1889/1894), Robertson Smith concluded that rituals are more fundamental than myths (dogma). To him, ritual and practice appeared to be the oldest component of religion. In this context, myths and religious belief are secondary; they are primarily derived from the cult or have an etiological meaning: "So far as myths consist of explanations of ritual, their value is altogether secondary, and it may be affirmed with confidence that in almost every case the myth was derived from ritual, and not the ritual from the myth; for the ritual was fixed and the myth was variable, the ritual was obligatory and faith in the myth was at the creation of the worshipper."[17]

Robertson Smith's search for the oldest layers of religion, which he also tried to find in "survivals" as an ethnographer in the "field," culminated in his then-revolutionary theory of sacrifice. In his opinion, sacrifice is not a gift to the gods but is a "communal performance, in which the participants constitute themselves as a moral community through the consumption of the sacred totem animal."[18] The medium for the cheerful communion and "joyous confidence"[19] between the god and its worshipers is the flesh and blood of the sacrificial animal: "The leading idea in the animal sacrifices of the Semites, as we shall see by and by, was not that of a gift made over to the god, but of an *act of communion*, in which the god and his worshippers unite by partaking together of the flesh and blood of a sacred victim."[20] If all who share the meal are brothers, then the meal results in the recognition of the obligations of friendship and of fraternal relationships in all actions. According to Robertson Smith, all institutions of morality and duty take this ritual as their starting point.

Using the account of an author called Nilus from the fourth century BCE, Robertson Smith believed that he could reconstruct a "survival" of the "reportedly much older public ritual of a camel sacrifice in which all members of the tribe took part in."[21] Even if the historical pillars of his theoretical edifice are somewhat dubious and obsolete today,[22] Robertson Smith's theory of religion had significant ramifications. Its central notion is the creation of social cohesion—the highly emotional process of binding and bonding—through the collective ritual of sacrifice. The theory inextricably welds individuals' bodily and emotional perception, collective ritual practice, and society (collective conceptions and institutions): "His interest in 'Ritual institutions' as *social* instruments influenced Durkheim, Freud,"[23] and Marcel Mauss.

In his work *The Elementary Forms of Religious Life*,[24] Émile Durkheim initially distinguished between "beliefs" and "rites": "Between these two classes of facts, there is all the difference which separates thought from action."[25] However, he then established the collective ritual celebration as the social space in which the individual perception and collective action/affect are integrated and collective representations/conceptions are created. In contrast to Robertson Smith's ideas, Durkheim believed that the "substance" or the "consubstantiality" in which the participants of the totemic sacrificial meal and orgy take part is not merely connected to consuming the "flesh/matter" of the "sacrifice"; "instead it is the corporeal conceived community itself, an apotheosis of the body of the Roman law."[26] For Durkheim, the sphere of the sacred (*Sacré*) coincided here with society and paved the way for scientific research into secular or civil rituals.

Following Wilhelm Mannhardt's theory of vegetation cults and Robertson Smith's theory of sacrifice, James George Frazer developed a significant and influential version of myth ritualism, especially in the first edition of *The Golden Bough*.[27] Frazer focused on the vegetation cycle and the seasonal changes marked by New Year's rituals and the mythical narratives about the dying and resurrection of the vegetation god or holy king. Myths and rituals are closely connected in his account.[28]

Still, Frazer's concept of the relationship between ritual and myth is not congruent in his work: "One can find, strewn through the many volumes and editions of *The Golden Bough*, statements by Frazer supporting at least three different and incompatible theories concerning myth: euhemerism, intellectualism and ritualism."[29] He either preferred a rationalizing method of myth interpretation that means, like the Greek mythographer Euhemerus, that myth is a "supernatural" explanation of a historical event, or he interpreted ancient man as an intellectual who tried to understand and influence "natural law." Admittedly, in Frazer's evolutionary scheme of magic, religion, and science, something like "myth-ritualism [can] be found" only in the transitional stage from magic to religion: "The ritual operates on the basis of the magical law of similarity, according to which the imitation of an action causes it to happen. The ritual directly manipulated the God of vegetation."[30]

In the same year as Robertson Smith, Jane Ellen Harrison,[31] an expert on classical antiquity and the initiator of the Cambridge Ritualists, came to believe that rituals precede myths during her studies of ancient Greek religion. She began to revolutionize the study of antiquity, which had previously focused primarily on texts, literature, and "high culture," by building on archeology, especially on Sir Arthur Evans's[32] discovery of the early Greek Mycenaean-Minoan culture on Crete and some studies of material artifacts and vase images that she interpreted in the light of and as ritual scenes. In *Mythology and Monuments of Ancient Athens*, published in 1890, she developed her first myth and ritual theory: "I have tried everywhere to get at, where possible, the cult as the explanation of the legend. Some of the loveliest stories the Greeks have left us will be seen to have taken their rise, not in poetic imagination, but in primitive, often savage, and I think, always practical ritual."[33]

Together with her colleagues Gilbert Murray and Francis Macdonald Cornford, Harrison established the circle of the Cambridge Ritualists, which was later joined by Arthur Bernhard Cook.[34] Robert Segal explained that "for them, myth-ritualism is likely the earliest stage of religion."[35] Harrison developed her second, much more complex myth-ritual theory in her book *Themis: A Study of the Social Origin of Greek Religion*.[36] She theorized that myths, even collective beliefs, stem from the process of ritual dance; they are no mythical idea, but rather "a projection of group unity,"[37] or an embodiment of collective effects. As she illustrated with regard to an initiation ritual found in the Kouretes hymn, the fact that "the god invoked . . . depends on the ritual that invokes him" does not mean that the ritual takes priority over the myth, the action, the song, or speech: "They probably arose together. Ritual is the utterance of an emotion, a thing felt in *action*, myth in words or thoughts. They arise *pari passu*."[38] In another part of the book, she wrote: "Myth is the spoken correlative of the acted rite, the thing done; it is *to legomenon* as contrasted with or rather as related to *to drômenon*."[39] Because Harrison linked her model of myth directly to the enactment of the cult, to song and dance, her second myth-ritual theory approximated the performative theory of the speech act. The most prominent contemporary religious scholar to take up Harrison's myth ritualism is Walter Burkert.[40] However, in theater studies, Jane Harrison is currently being rediscovered as a pioneer of a performative theory of drama.[41]

The anthropologist Bronisław Malinowski also engaged with myth ritualism and gave it a functional edge. For him, myths work as a charter for customs, rights, rituals, and institutions: "Society depends on myth to spur adherence to rituals."[42] In a similar vein, Clyde Kluckhohn argued in 1942 that there is "an intricate interdependence of myth . . . with ritual and many other forms of behaviour."[43] Edmund Leach came close to Harrison's second myth-ritual theory when he wrote: "Myth implies ritual, ritual implies myth; they are one and the same. . . . As I see, myth regarded as a statement in words 'says' the same thing as ritual regarded as a statement in 'action.'"[44]

In 1933, the Old Testament scholar Samuel Henry Hooke published his programmatic essay "The Myth and Ritual Pattern of the Ancient East." It was a part of his edited volume *Myth and Ritual: Essays on the Myth and Ritual of the Hebrews in Relation to the Culture Pattern of the Ancient East.*[45] Following the title of the anthology, the ensuing academic school was termed the Myth and Ritual School. It assumed that a unified cult pattern existed in the entire Orient, in which kingship played a central role. Hooke focused on the analysis of the Babylonian New Year's festival, which ritually dramatized the appointment of the king with Marduk's mythic fight against the chaos-water snake Tiamat and made it present through the recitation of the myth in the Babylonian creation song *Enuma Elish.* With almost no reference to Frazer or the Cambridge Ritualists, Hooke developed an incoherent myth-ritual theory, which finally placed the myth as the representation of godly deeds *"in illo tempore"*[46] above the ritual: *"It is the story which the ritual enacts. This is the sense in which the term 'myth' is used in our discussion. The original Myth, inseparable in the first instance from its ritual, embodies in more or less symbolic fashion, the original situation which is seasonally reenacted in the ritual."*[47] A number of biblical scholars and orientalists, especially British and Scandinavian scientists, were inspired by Hooke's approach.[48]

Even if one leaves the field of the classical myth and ritual debate, the epistemological tension between thought (myth, symbol) and action (ritual) remains prevalent in newer ritual theories. As Talal Assad[49] and then especially Catherine Bell have argued, the role of ritual is sometimes seen as mediating the dichotomy of thought and action. Nevertheless, in many theories of ritual, the starting point of theorizing ritual is still the tension between action and thought.

For example, Roy A. Rappaport, who took up the work of Durkheim, Austin/Searle, and Levi-Strauss, saw *formalism* as the commonality between performative speech acts and rituals. Rituals provide a basic structure for social existence. They are repetitive acts, "not entirely encoded by the performers,[50] which refer to a 'higher [being].'" In contrast to Durkheim, Rappaport's "transcendental" did not coincide with "society": "Religion's major conceptual and experiential constituents, the sacred, the numinous, the occult, and the divine, and their integration into the Holy, are creations of ritual."[51]

However, his theory of ritual was ambivalent. On the one hand, he tried to focus on the power of ritual actions: as "meta-performative actions," rituals do not perform mythical scripts but they cause something themselves. In their performance, they generate and confirm the cultural codes, conventions, and social rules of society: "I will argue that social contract, morality and the establishment of convention are intrinsic to ritual's form."[52] On the other hand, he conceptualized rituals as "prior" encoded symbolic actions. In ritual acts, those participating submit themselves to "something 'higher,' they are taken up by something higher."[53] Sometimes, Rappaport even compared "intentionless" ritual action with genetically coded animal behavior, which dictates particular gestures.

At times, the dichotomy between act and thought can escalate into the question of the meaning or meaninglessness of rituals. Especially where the construction and analysis of meaning in religious and cultural systems is concerned, as in Clifford Geertz's work, rituals play the role of intermediaries. Combining Durkheimian and Weberian approaches, Geertz first distinguished between "ethos" and "worldview"; "ethos" denotes dispositions like "mood" and "motivations," while "worldview" captures the more cognitive aspects of the "real," such as "ideas" and "notions." In his analysis of the symbolic systems, the ritual space functions as the medium for synthesis: "In ritual, the world as lived and the world as imagined, fused under the agency of a single set of symbolic forms, turns out to be the same world."[54]

If ritual theories define the ritual as action and then separate it from the conceptual-symbolic aspects of culture such as belief, myths, and meaning, then these dichotomist differences can be taken to extremes, according to Catherine Bell: "Ritual is then described as particularly *thoughtless* action—routinized, habitual, obsessive, or mimetic—and therefore the purely formal, secondary, and mere physical expression of logically prior ideas."[55]

In 1979, Frits Staal published his famous article with the programmatic title "The Meaninglessness of Ritual."[56] On the basis of his research on the Vedic ritual of the fire epiphany, Staal reached a radical conclusion: formalist ritual theories focus on the technique and a ritual's exact repetitive sequence of action. According to Staal, a ritual does not refer to something "prior" that was coded symbolically: "It is characteristic of a ritual performance, however, that it is self-contained and self-absorbed. The performers are totally immersed in the proper execution of their complex task. Isolated in their sacred enclosure, they concentrate on correctness of act, recitation and chant. Their primary concern, if not obsession, is with rules. There are no symbolic meanings going through their minds when they are engaged in performing ritual."[57]

For Staal, the ritual is "pure activity."[58] In this sense, his understanding approximates the concept of a ceremony, which is first and foremost about the correct observance of rules. But "if ritual is useless this does not imply it may not have useful side-effects. It is obvious, for example, that ritual creates a bond between the participants, reinforces solidarity, preserves morale and constitutes a link to the ancestors."[59] Staal denoted prelinguistic rituals as early forms of *pure activity* and compared them to bird songs, which, as a succession of sounds or movements, cannot be allocated a direct function.

Following Staal, Caroline Humphrey and James Laidlaw also detached rituals from symbolic or functional meaning in their much-discussed book *The Archetypal Actions of Ritual*, published in 1994. In their study of the Jain *Puja*, they differentiated between ritual action and everyday action through the Jainists' own reversal of intentionality, as "they learn how to perform ritual acts and have them inscribed in their bodies separately from prototypical ideas they may come to have of them."[60] If rituals function at all as a means to convey messages, then they do so through embodied emotional states that are expressed in dance, gestures, or music.

Even within the most recent theories of ritualization, a certain tension remains between opposed concepts: ritual action is seen as, on the one hand, a meaningless and thoughtless repetitive behavior and, on the other hand, the result of a similar focus on unconscious incorporated mechanisms that defines rituals as "making sense" on both levels, physical and cognitive. In these latter theories, rituals represent a creative, *performative* practice. According to Klaus-Peter Köpping, the tension between the two approaches might be resolved by dint of "the *habitus*-concept as the core concept of praxis. If we assume with Bourdieu that people in daily practice demonstrate the unconscious mastering of their system, then ritual performance can be understood as 'regulated improvisation,' which makes possible the 'intentionless' emergence of the unexpected so that the unexpected and involuntary almost appears as a result of the regulatedness of ritual redundancy and formality."[61]

In the production of a "ritual sense" within processes of ritualization, Catherine Bell also saw a kind of embodied or incorporated knowledge that enables us to perform rituals and reproduce dispositions but also to create and shape future transformations. The approach to ritual as ritualization and often-unconscious *habitus* can perhaps overcome the theoretically constructed gap between thought and action, ritual and myth, and body and mind.

NOTES

1. Henrik S. Versnel, *Transition and Reversal in Myth and Ritual* (Leiden: Brill, 1993), 19.
2. Geoffrey Stephen Kirk, *Myth: Its Meaning and Functions in Ancient and Other Cultures* (Berkeley: University of California Press, 1971), 31.
3. Walter Burkert, *Structure and History in Greek Mythology and Ritual* (Berkeley: University of California Press, 1979).
4. Ibid., 58.
5. Wilhelm Mannhardt, *Roggenwolf und Roggenhund: Beitrag zur Germanischen Sittenkunde* (Danzig: Constantin Ziemssen, 1865–66); Wilhelm Mannhardt, *Die Korndämonen* (Berlin: Borntraeger, 1868); Wilhelm Mannhardt, *Antike Wald- und Feldkulte* (Berlin: Borntraeger, 1875–77).
6. Edward Burnett Tylor, *Primitive Culture* (London: J. Murray, 1871).
7. Versnel, *Transition*, 20.
8. David Chidester, *Savage Systems: Colonialism and Comparative Religion in Southern Africa* (Charlottesville: University of Virginia Press, 1996).
9. Mary Louise Pratt, "Arts of the Contact Zone," *Profession* (1991): 33–40.
10. Catherine Bell, *Ritual Theory, Ritual Practice* (New York: Oxford University Press, 1992), 6.

11. Clyde Kluckhohn, "Myths and Rituals: A General Theory," *Harvard Theological Review* 35 (1942): 49.

12. Cf. Robert A. Segal, *Myth: A Very Short Introduction* (Oxford: Oxford University Press, 2004).

13. Robert A. Segal, "Myth and Ritual," in *Theorizing Rituals: Issues, Topics, Approaches, Concepts*, ed. Jens Kreinath, Jan Snoek, and Michael Stausberg (Leiden: Brill, 2007), 103.

14. Cf. the instructive study by Talal Asad on the change of the concept of ritual from text to attitude around 1900. Talal Asad, *Genealogies of Religion* (Baltimore: Johns Hopkins University Press, 1993), 55–79.

15. Segal, "Myth and Ritual," 101.

16. Hans G. Kippenberg, "William Robertson Smith (1846–1894)," in *Klassiker der Religionswissenschaft: Von Friedrich Schleiermacher bis Mircea Eliade*, ed. Axel Michaels (Darmstadt: Beck, 1997), 67.

17. William Robertson Smith, *Lectures on the Religion of the Semites* (London: Transaction, 2002), 18.

18. Hans G. Kippenberg, "Emile Durkheim," in Michals, *Klassiker der Religionswissenschaft*, 108.

19. William Robertson Smith, "Lecture VII," in *Lectures on the Religion of the Semites*, 255.

20. William Robertson Smith, "Lecture VI," in *Lectures on the Religion of the Semites*, 227.

21. Kippenberg, "Robertson Smith," 71.

22. Erhard Schüttpelz, *Die Moderne im Spiegel des Primitiven* (Paderborn: Fink, 2005), 112; Robert Alun Jones, "Robertson Smith, Durkheim, and Sacrifice: An Historical Context for *The Elementary Forms of the Religious Life*," in *Emile Durkheim: Critical Assessments*, ed. Peter Hamilton (London: Routledge, 1990), 3:376–404.

23. Versnel, *Transition*, 21.

24. Émile Durkheim, *The Elementary Forms of the Religious Life*, trans. J. W. Swain (New York: Free Press, 1965).

25. Ibid., 51.

26. Erhard Schüttpelz, "Wunsch, Totemist zu warden: Robertson Smiths totemistische Opfermahlzeit und ihre Fortsetzungen bei Emile Durkheim, Sigmund Freud und Elias Canetti," in *Verschlungene Grenzen: Anthropophagie in Literatur und Kulturwissenschaften*, ed. Annette Keck, Inka Kording, and Anja Prochaska (Tübingen: Narr, 1999), 279. See Kippenberg, "Robertson Smith," 30.

27. James George Frazer, *The Golden Bough*, 1st ed. (London: MacMillan, 1894).

28. Robert Ackermann, *The Myth and Ritual School: J. G. Frazer and the Cambridge Ritualists* (New York: Garland, 1991), 49. As Frazer clearly stated in his foreword: "I have made great use of the works of the late W. Mannhardt, without which, indeed, my book could scarcely haven been written."

29. Ibid., 55.

30. Segal, "Myth and Ritual," 101–21, 105.

31. See Ulrike Brunotte, *Das Wissen der Dämonen: Gender, Performativität and Materielle Kultur im Werk von Jane Ellen Harrison* (Würzburg: Ergon, 2013).

32. For Evan's discoveries and their immediate importance for Harrison, see Jane Ellen Harrison, *Mythology and Monuments of Ancient Athens* (London: Macmillan, 1890).

33. Ibid., iii.

34. Ackermann, *The Myth and Ritual School*, 3.

35. Segal, "Myth and Ritual," 108.

36. Jane Ellen Harrison, *Themis: A Study of the Social Origin of Greek Religion* (Cambridge: Cambridge University Press, 1912).

37. Ibid., 48.

38. Ibid., 16.

39. Ibid., 328.

40. Cf. Henrik S. Versnel, "From Harrison to Burkert," in *Transition and Reversal in Myth and Ritual* (Leiden: Brill, 1993), 51.

41. Erika Fischer-Lichte, *Ästhetik des Performativen* (Frankfurt: Suhrkamp, 2004), 45ff.

42. Segal, "Myth and Ritual," 111.

43. Kluckhohn, "Myths and Rituals," 54.

44. Edmund Leach, *Political Systems of Highland Burma: A Study of Kachin Social Structure* (London: Athlone, 1954), 11–12.

45. Samuel Henry Hooke, ed., *Myth and Ritual: Essays on the Myth and Ritual of the Hebrews in Relation to the Culture Pattern of the Ancient East* (Oxford: Oxford University Press, 1933).

46. Cf. the term by Mircea Eliade.

47. Samuel Henry Hooke, "The Myth and Ritual Pattern of the Ancient East," in *Myth and Ritual* (Oxford: Oxford University Press 1933), 1–14, 3.

48. Cf. Versnel, *Transition*, 35.

49. Talal Assad, "Toward a Genealogy of the Concept of Ritual," in *Genealogies of Religion: Discipline and Reasons of Power in Christianity and Islam* (Baltimore: Johns Hopkins University Press, 1993).

50. Ray A. Rappaport, *Religion and Ritual in the Making of Humanity* (Cambridge: Cambridge University Press, 1999), 27.

51. Ibid., 3.

52. Ibid., 26.

53. Andrea Bellinger and David J. Krieger, eds., *Ritualtheorien: Ein einführendes Handbuch* (Wiesbaden: VS Verlag für Sozialwissenschaften, 1998), 21.

54. Clifford Geertz, *The Interpretation of Cultures* (New York: Basic Books, 1973), 112–13.

55. Bell, *Ritual Theory*, 19.

56. Frits Staal, "The Meaninglessness of Ritual," *Numen* 26 (June 1979): 2–22.

57. Ibid., 3.

58. Ibid., 9.

59. Ibid., 11.

60. Caroline Humphrey and James Laidlaw, *The Archetypal Actions of Ritual* (Oxford: Clarendon, 1994), 266.

61. Klaus-Peter Köpping, "Transformationen durch performative Verkörperung in japanischen Ritualen," in *Im Rausch des Rituals: Gestaltung und Transformation der Wirklichkeit in körperlicher Performanz*, ed. Klaus-Peter Köpping and Ursula Rao (Hamburg: LIT, 2000), 188.

34

From Ritual to Ritualization

JON P. MITCHELL

The Foucauldian turn in the humanities and social sciences led, by the 1980s, to a new, genealogical approach to theoretical debate. As much as focusing on the detailed *content* of particular theoretical argument, theorists began to examine the discursive *conditions* under which particular sets of theoretical assumptions became possible. Both Talal Asad[1] and Catherine Bell[2] take this genealogical approach to the theorization of ritual, arguing that ritual theory has been dogged by the central and problematic assumption that the role of ritual is communicative. This in turn is premised on a separation of action from meaning that sees the former as a vehicle for the latter. Such an assumption not only is ethnocentric—because rooted in a particular, European understandings of the self[3]—but also fails to capture the significance of ritual action: its "action-ness." A focus on action in and of itself suggests a movement, in ritual theory, away from definitional questions—concerned with identifying the formal and functional properties of ritual—toward processual ones. As a result, we shift from a primarily semiotic theory of ritual toward a theory of embodiment. We also shift from "ritual" to "ritualization" as our primary object—the contextual processes through which action becomes "ritual action." Finally, we shift from a conception of ritual as something that is done to people, to one of ritual as something that people themselves do. This in turn opens up the possibility of theorizing ritual change.

A GENEALOGY OF THE CONCEPT OF RITUAL

Asad argues that early modern European changes in conceptions of the self made possible contemporary understandings of ritual as a universal category. He observes a shift, from "ritual" considered as a script or instruction manual for the regulation of everyday practice, particularly in monastic contexts, to ritual "as a type of routine behavior that symbolizes or expresses something, . . . a type of practice that is interpretable as standing for some further *verbally definable*, but tacit, event."[4] This distinction between ritual action and its meaning, as outward sign and hidden or inner meaning, establishes a principle whereby ritual is seen as a primarily communicative act. To this extent, ritual action is opposed to more mundane or everyday action geared toward utilitarian or practical ends. Ritual action is action + symbol, or "action wrapped in a web of symbolism."[5]

This view of ritual displaced medieval monastic notions of disciplined practice—as exemplified in the Benedictine *Rule*—which saw liturgical action (ritual) not as a separate class of action, differentiated from the technical or utilitarian, but as "a practice among others essential to the acquisition of Christian virtues."[6] This conception saw no disjunction between outer behavior and inner sentiment, and so no communicative role for ritual—its meaning, such as we can talk about meaning at all, was inherent in practice. This changed in the early modern period—what Asad calls the Renaissance—which saw an emergent individualism generating concern over the nature of "character," "proper behavior," and "manners":[7]

> In this early modern world, the moral economy of the self in a court circle was constructed very differently from the ways prescribed in the medieval monastic program. Created and re-created through dramas of manipulative power, at once personal and political, the self depended now on the maintenance of moral distance between public forms of behavior and private thoughts and feelings.[8]

The resultant parallax between action and meaning, or action and thought, is a precondition for more contemporary theories of ritual, which, as Catherine Bell has pointed out, frequently see ritual's role as mediating or collapsing this dichotomy. For example, Clifford Geertz, for whom ritual was the "clinching" factor in religious symbolism, making it "uniquely realistic,"[9] saw ritual as action that unites a culture's worldview—its system of everyday knowledge—with its ethos, or emotional orientation, or "feel." In doing so, it also unites culture with social system, and thought with action.[10]

This is one of a number of interrelated manifestations of the action-thought dichotomy that Bell identifies within ritual theory. Such theory has it, first, that ritual "acts out, expresses or performs the beliefs, world view or values of a group."[11] Second, and consequently, the theory has it that ritual integrates individual perception and behavior with socially conditioned, collective conceptions. This is central to Durkheimian understandings of ritual, and indeed his overall theory of religion. Durkheim's *Elementary Forms of the Religious Life* figures the person as *homo duplex*: caught in enduring and inherent tension between the individual and the collective, body and soul:[12] "In this model, ritual activity constitutes the necessary interaction between the collective representations of social life (as a type of mental or meta-mental category) and the individual experience and behavior (as a category of activity)."[13]

Third, the theory has it that ritual is therefore aligned with structure, "provisionally distinguished as the synchronic, continuous, traditional, or ontological in opposition to the diachronic, changing, historical, or social."[14] As a consequence, ritual functions to affirm social unity and transcendence in contrast to the everyday competitions and frictions of social life. In Turnerian terms, it generates enduring *communitas*—a sense of transcendent communal solidarity that, ultimately, contributes to social stability.[15]

To Geertz, Durkheim, and Turner, one might add Bloch, Rappaport, and others, for whom the starting point of ritual theory is a dichotomization of action and thought. For Bloch, ritual accomplishes a symbolic conquest of "vitality"—mundane, everyday, corporeal features of existence—by the "transcendental."[16] Immediate, immanent features of action are pitted against transcendent and conceptual features of thought to ensure the primacy of the latter over the former and, ultimately, the continuity of socioreligious institutions.[17] The theory rests on a prior separation of action from thought, which is then resolved, with thought triumphant, in ritual.

For Rappaport, the action-thought distinction is expressed in terms of *form* and *substance*. While they are inseparable in ritual performance, he argues, they are nevertheless distinguishable analytically, and should be distinguished, if only in order to give priority to the role of form in our definition of ritual.[18] He argues contra Kertzer, for example, but also Turner and La Fontaine,[19] that symbolism is a definitional feature of ritual action. Other types of action are equally—and perhaps better—suited to symbolic communication, and yet there are certain types of message that are best—and perhaps only—communicable through ritual. The reason for this, argues Rappaport, must lie in its *formal* rather than *substantive* qualities: "The ritual form, to say the least, adds something to the substance of ritual, something that the symbolically encoded substance by itself cannot express."[20]

While Rappaport is clearly trying to move toward an analysis of ritual action as action, looking at the "surface" or "obvious" aspects of ritual,[21] he nevertheless falls back into the central assumption, identified by Asad, that ritual is primarily communicative of a set of linguistically expressible and structurally "prior" messages that are encoded into the formal and repeated actions of ritual:

> Messages, although transmitted by the participants [in ritual], are not encoded by them. They are found by participants already encoded in the liturgy. Since these messages are more or less invariant obviously they cannot in themselves reflect the transmitter's contemporary state. . . . In recognition of the regularity, propriety, and apparent durability and immutability of these messages I shall refer to them as "canonical"[22]

This understanding of ritual—like those of Geertz, Durkheim, and Bloch—sees the participants in ritual as objects, rather than subjects, of ritual action, in that even as they perform, they are recipients rather than generators of ritual's messages. As such they are reified, analytically separated out from the practical contexts in which they are performed.

FROM RITUAL TO RITUALIZATION

Humphrey and Laidlaw have questioned the assumption that ritual form is a conduit for canonical messages preencoded in the liturgy. Coming close to Frits Staal's conclusion that the essence of ritual is its meaninglessness, rather than its ability to convey messages,[23] they conclude that if it does convey messages, these messages are not ideas, expressible in language, but, for example, "mental-emotional states conveyed by music and gesture."[24] In other words, the formal aspects of ritual, the action of ritual, does not defer to a deeper-seated repertoire of thought, but generates its own significance by, through, and within action itself.

Similar conclusions are reached by both Asad and Bell, in their attempt to transcend the action-thought dichotomy. Asad enlists the help of Marcel Mauss, who although normally thought of as going hand in hand with Durkheim—he was, after all, Durkheim's nephew—provided a means of resolving the problem of *homo duplex*. In his essay on "Techniques of the Body,"[25] Mauss emphasizes the primacy of the body as both object and means, or subject, of human social competence. He develops the concept of *habitus*, some forty years before Bourdieu's popularizing of the term,[26] to describe the socially derived regularities of "body techniques," which, as Asad points out "are linked to authoritative standards and regular practice. . . . the concept of *habitus* invites us to analyze the body as an assemblage of embodied aptitudes, not as a medium of symbolic meanings."[27] This approach to ritual might transcend the action-thought dichotomy as it transcends the Cartesian dualism of body and mind: "Thus, the possibility is opened up of inquiring into the ways in which embodied practices (including language in use) form a precondition for varieties of religious experience. The inability to enter into communion with God becomes a function of untaught bodies. 'Consciousness' becomes a dependent concept."[28]

This effectively turns Rappaport on his head. Action, not thought, becomes analytically "prior" and in no way subordinate to the conceptual processes of meaning-making or the symbolic messages of liturgy. Rather, it generates or reproduces its own "practical reason"—or "reason of practice"—not in the ethical sense described by Kant, but as a form of reasoned knowledge transmitted by and through bodily practice.[29]

Mauss's notion of *habitus*, though, was not reserved for the analysis of what we might want to call "ritual." On the contrary, the opening passages of "Techniques of the Body" focus on a range of mundane and everyday techniques—swimming, digging, walking—that we would not normally regard as ritual activities. Yet this brings up the question once more of how we are to define ritual activities—or perhaps more suggestively, as Humphrey and Laidlaw suggest, what is *done* to action to make it "ritual action." They suggest that what is *done* to action is that it is "ritualized"—turned into ritual—and that we should shift our focus, in the analysis of ritual, from ritual per se to processes of ritualization: " 'Ritual' can be specified: not as a kind of event or as an aspect of all action, but as a quality which action can come to have—a special way in which acts may be performed. From this perspective theoretical attention focuses on ritualization, the process by which normal, everyday action is endowed with this quality and becomes ritual." Ritualization begins with a particular modification of the normal intentionality of human action. Action that has undergone this modification is ritual action.[30]

This move from ritual to ritualization enables us to focus on action *as* action, rather than mere epiphenomenon, or vehicle of "deeper" symbolic messages. It also enables us to position human actors as the *subjects* of ritual action, rather than its *objects*—ritualization is something people *do*, rather than something people have done to them. Finally, it enables us to formulate a theory that accounts for ritual change. Within accounts that polarize thought and action, it is difficult to see how rituals might be changed through their performance. If their purpose is to reproduce preexisting symbolic messages, then for their form to correspond to this fixed substance, it must also be fixed.

Alongside formality—in the sense of "decorum"—and repetition, the notion of fixity lies at the center of most definitions of ritual. Catherine Bell, who also proposes moving from "ritual" to "ritualization" as our object of study, argues that rather than being definitional features of ritual, conceived as a specific type of action, formality, fixity, and repetition should rather be seen as strategies of ritualization— things people do to action to make it ritual action.[31] This opens out Humphrey and Laidlaw's rather narrow and politically neutral definition of ritualization, to focus on the "texture" of ritualizing practices, seen as fundamentally interested, in a political sense. To this extent, Bell locates ritualization within broader social practice. Ritualization involves "strategies of differentiation through formalization and periodicity, the centrality of the body, the orchestration of schemes by which the body defines an environment and is defined in turn by it, ritual mastery, and the negotiation of power to define and appropriate the hegemonic order."[32] Bell's account of practice is drawn primarily from Bourdieu's theoretical outline, and his own notion of *habitus*: an acquired system of dispositions, which organize perception and classification, but also have a generative aspect, "constituting the social agent . . . as practical operator of the construction of objects."[33] Action that emerges from the *habitus* is interested action, though not necessarily consciously so. It is geared toward the reproduction of the social order, but does not straightforwardly "perform" or "act out" social messages or liturgy. It is "objectively 'regulated' and 'regular' without in any way being the product of obedience to rules."[34] In other words, it is action in and of itself, not as a representation or proxy for some other, deeper meaning. Ritualization, for Bell, is practice in this sense.

Bell goes on to identify the central features of ritualization-as-practice. First, ritualization is always situational. Although ritual is frequently presented, one might say it "presents itself," as transcendent, set apart from the sociopolitical and historical context in which it takes place, the ritualization practices that achieve this "setting aside" emerge directly from that context. Second, ritualization is always strategic. While Humphrey and Laidlaw see ritualization as a process of stripping action of its intentionality, for Bell the intentionality is merely shifted, from the straightforward intentionality of instrumental utility to the practical intentionality inherent in the reproduction of the *habitus*. Such practical and strategic intentionality is as present in ritual contexts that exhibit formal continuity as those that change. The practical "decision" to reproduce past ritualizations is as strategic as the decision to innovate. Third, ritualization is always embedded in a "misrecognition" of what it is doing. Thus, although ritualization is both situational and strategic, it is thought not to be. What appears to drive ritual action is a system of symbolic meanings of which it is both representation and vehicle. This system has acquired a number of different labels—from Rappaport's liturgy, to "tradition" and even "culture." Yet these systems do not exist outside their reproduction in and through action itself. Ritual action is a *modus operandi*, not the product of an *opus operatum*:[35] "By abstracting the act from its temporal situation and reducing its convoluted strategies to a set of reversible structures, theoretical analysis misses the real dynamics of practice."[36]

Fourth, ritualization is always characterized by a form of "redemptive hegemony"— an ability to reproduce or reconfigure a vision of the order of power in the world.[37] It is redemptive, because despite reproducing *habitus*—which is itself rooted in structures of power, as the means by which they are generated—it nevertheless also affords the actor a vision of an emancipatory sphere of action. It enables actors to "discharge their obligations in relation to the moral imperatives of the community"[38]— and to view their own and society's interests and motivations as one and the same. It is hegemonic, because through it are reproduced the conditions within which the structures of power are naturalized as "common sense":

> As a practical construal or consciousness of the system of power relations and as a framework for action, redemptive hegemony suggests that human practice is characterized by relations of dominance and subjugation. These relations, however, are present in practice by means of the practical values, obligations, and persistent envisioning . . . of a state of prestige within this ordering of power. This vision exists as a practical consciousness of the world (common sense) and a sense of one's options for social action. It is also a vision of empowerment that is rooted in the actor's perceptions and experiences of the organization of power.[39]

This vision of ritual practice as both empowered and empowering enables us to develop a theory of ritual that can handle ritual change. If ritual's role is to *communicate* a preexisting system of meanings, then it is difficult to see how ritual—or indeed thought—changes over time. If, on the other hand, the systems of meanings, such as they exist, are immanent properties of ritual action itself, reproduced through the practice of ritualization, then change can occur in and through the act. If ritual participants are the *objects* of ritual action, they are doomed to represent messages of which they are not the authors. However, if they are the *subjects* of ritualization— agents of ritual process—they become shapers of their own destiny.

NOTES

1. Talal Asad, "Toward a Genealogy of the Concept of Ritual," in *Genealogies of Religion: Discipline and Reasons of Power in Christianity and Islam* (Baltimore: Johns Hopkins University Press, 1993).

2. Catherine Bell, "Discourse and Dichotomies: The Structure of Ritual Theory," *Religion* 17 (1987): 95–118; Catherine Bell, *Ritual Theory, Ritual Practice* (Oxford: Oxford University Press, 1992).

3. Asad, "Toward a Genealogy," 67.

4. Ibid., 57.

5. David Kertzer, *Ritual, Politics and Power* (New Haven: Yale University Press, 1988), 9.

6. Asad, "Toward a Genealogy," 63.

7. Steven Lukes, *Individualism* (Oxford: Basil Blackwell, 1973); Alan Macfarlane, *The Origins of English Individualism: The Family, Property and Social Transition* (Cambridge: Cambridge University Press, 1978); Peter Stallybrass, "Shakespeare, the Individual, and the Text," in *Cultural Studies,* ed. L. Grossberg, C. Nelson, and P. A. Treichler (London: Routledge, 1992).

8. Asad, "Toward a Genealogy," 67.

9. Clifford Geertz, "Religion as a Cultural System," in *The Interpretation of Cultures* (New York: Basic Books, 1973).

10. Bell, "Discourse," 108.

11. Ibid., 98.

12. Asad, "Toward a Genealogy," 74–75. See also Anne Warfield Rawls, *Epistemology and Practice: Durkheim's "The Elementary Forms of the Religious Life"* (Cambridge: Cambridge University Press, 2005).

13. Bell, "Discourse," 98.

14. Ibid.

15. Victor Turner, *The Ritual Process: Structure and Anti-Structure* (Chicago: Aldine, 1969).

16. Maurice Bloch, *Prey Into Hunter* (Cambridge: Cambridge University Press, 1992).

17. David Gellner, "Religion, Politics and Ritual: Remarks on Geertz and Bloch," *Social Anthropology* 7, no. 2 (1999): 135–53.

18. Roy A. Rappaport, *Ritual and Religion in the Making of Humanity* (Cambridge: Cambridge University Press, 1999); Roy A. Rappaport, "The Obvious Aspects of Ritual," in *Ecology, Meaning, Religion* (Richmond, Calif.: Northatlantic Books, 1979).

19. Jean La Fontaine, "Introduction," in *The Interpretation of Ritual*, ed. J. La Fontaine (London: Tavistock, 1972).

20. Rappaport, *Religion and Ritual*, 31.

21. Ibid.; Rappaport, "Obvious Aspects."

22. Rapport, "Obvious Aspects," 179.

23. Frits Staal, "The Meaninglessness of Ritual," *Numen* 26, no. 2 (1979): 2–22.

24. Caroline Humphrey and James Laidlaw, *The Archetypal Actions of Ritual* (Oxford: Oxford University Press, 1994).

25. Marcel Mauss, "Techniques of the Body," *Economy and Society* 2 (1973): 70–88.

26. Pierre Bourdieu, *Outline of a Theory of Practice* (Cambridge: Cambridge University Press, 1977).

27. Asad, "Toward a Genealogy," 75.

28. Ibid., 76–77.

29. Ibid.

30. Humphrey and Laidlaw, *The Archetypal Actions*, 64, 71.

31. Bell, *Ritual Theory*, 92.

32. Ibid., 220.

33. Pierre Bourdieu, *In Other Words: Essays Towards a Reflexive Sociology* (Cambridge: Polity, 1990), 13.

34. Bourdieu, *Outline*, 72.

35. Ibid.

36. Bell, *Ritual Theory*, 83.

37. Ibid., 81.

38. Kenelm Burridge, *New Heaven, New Earth: A Study of Millenarian Activity* (New York: Schocken, 1969), 6.

39. Bell, *Ritual Theory*, 84.

Religion and Theories of Action

KOCKU VON STUCKRAD

INTRODUCTION: THE PROBLEM
OF DEFINING "ACTION"

"Action" is one of those categories that seem simple at first glance but that become more and more difficult and complex the more we try to figure out what *exactly* we mean by it. If a person's legs are moving, does this mean that this person moved her legs? And if she indeed moved her legs, was this an intentional action or did it simply happen? And if she indeed performed an intentional action, was the reason for the action conscious to herself or can her intention only be reconstructed from outside? Simple cases such as this one have triggered theoretical thinking in various disciplines, from philosophy to behavioral science, to sociology and psychology. In all these disciplines, there is a tendency to differentiate "action" from "doing something," "happening," or "behavior"—differentiations usually made with reference to *intentionality*, *reason*, or *agency*. A certain behavior becomes "action" as soon as the actor is performing an intentional act that can be interpreted in a situational structure.

For instance, the philosopher Donald Davidson notes that an action ultimately is "intentional under some description."[1] But even then, further clarification is necessary, because otherwise a spider that moves its legs to crawl across a table can also be called an "agent." Intentionality must therefore be conceptualized in relation to knowledge and consciousness. This is what Harry Frankfurt suggests when he argues that volition and freedom of action presuppose that we need to have a concept of "acting on a desire with which the agent *identifies*."[2] But is the conscious identification of an agent really a necessary precondition to call something an action? Particularly in sociological theory, there are attempts at establishing clearly defined structural reasons for intentional (or meaningful) behavior the agent himself does not need to be aware of.

Although there are numerous resonances between general theories of action that have been developed in philosophy and sociology,[3] in what follows I will focus primarily on the categorization and interpretation of *religious* action. This does not mean that religious action is fundamentally different from nonreligious action or that we thus need a special theory for religious action. What is at stake here is the usefulness of theories of action for an analysis of religious behavior.

INFLUENTIAL APPROACHES TO (RELIGIOUS) ACTION: WEBER, PARSONS, LUHMANN

It is reasonable to start our overview with Max Weber (1864–1920). Interested in the impact of religious worldviews on the genealogy of modern Western culture, Weber developed a terminology that became highly important in subsequent scholarship.[4] Against approaches to religion—common in his day—that conceptualized religion as an inner experience and that looked for the "essence" of religion (*Wesen der Religion*), early on Weber insisted on the fact that the object of sociological inquiry can never be a person's internal processes. Already in 1913 he claimed that the object of *verstehende Soziologie* is not every kind of "inner disposition" or "outward habit" but: "*action.*"[5] In *Wirtschaft und Gesellschaft*, Weber notes that the sociology of religion is not dealing with "the 'essence' of religion but with the conditions and the impact of a certain kind of communal action [*Gemeinschaftshandeln*], the understanding of which . . . can only be gained when we start with the subjective experiences, ideas, and intentions of the individual—with the 'meaning' ['*Sinn*']—because the outward order of things is extremely variable."[6] This "meaning" of religious action is something different than the "essence" of religion. It is a meaning that an individual attributes to social action. The sociology of religion identifies this meaning and thus is able to interpret and understand religious action. Consistently, Weber defines action (*Handeln*) as "an understandable response to 'objects' that is specified by some (*subjective*) *meaning* that a person 'has' or 'intends,' even if this meaning is more or less unnoticed."[7] With such a definition, Weber can subsume even Buddhist contemplation or Christian asceticism under the rubric of action because in both cases the actor refers to the subjective meaning of inner "objects."[8] Every form of action or habit (*Verhalten*), be it internal or external, be it active or passive, is subsumed under the sociological category of action. As noted already, this is true even if a person fails to do something at all, because the actor still demonstrates an "inner response," or *inneres Sichverhalten*. Action can be called *religious* action when the subjective meaning of the action is based on religious motives and ideas.

We can see that for Weber the category "action" is intrinsic to his very concept of religion. And because his concept of religion is broader than that of interpretative models of his time, he often uses the term "religiosity" instead of "religion," thus making clear that the attribution of religious meaning to action can easily transgress the borders of institutionalized religion. In the light of Weber's methodological framework, it is important to note that he conceptualizes sociology as an "empiric science of action," contrasting the "dogmatic sciences" such as logic, aesthetics, or ethics.[9] Sociological interpretation reconstructs the "subjectively intended meaning" of an action; it is not interested in establishing an "objectively 'correct' or a metaphysically established 'true' meaning."[10] Religion is only interesting insofar as it influences social action, that is, in its capacity to form a certain response to and positioning vis-à-vis the world. This positioning and response to the world (*Sich-verhalten zu "Objekten"*) is what Weber conceptualizes as *religiosity*.

For the sociology of religion in general and the sociology of religious action in particular, the work of Talcott Parsons (1902–79) is the second major pillar, next to Weber's. In critical dialogue with Weber and other theorists, Parsons developed a complex theory of action and integrated it—combined with a systems theory— into a general sociological theory. It is impossible to review the development of his work, usually divided into several phases, and its high level of theoretical reflection in detail here.[11] But let us have a brief look at his major model of a general theory of action, which Parsons introduced between 1935 and 1939 in his important studies "The Place of Ultimate Values in Sociological Theory," *The Structure of Social Action*, and "Actor, Situation, and Normative Pattern."[12] Underlying his theory of action is a critique of two methodological tendencies in contemporary social sciences. On the one hand, Parsons argues against the dominance of interpretational patterns that try to reduce social phenomena to empirically testable categories. Over against this reduction to causal relations, taken over from the natural sciences, he notes that there are forms of behavior that are not subject to simple, empirically demonstrable causalities; religious action but also actions of art or emotional affection belong to such a category of behavior that transgresses causal patterns of the natural sciences. On the other hand, Parson critiques a social-scientific interpretation that—opposing the paradigm of natural sciences—intends to explain action entirely as a self-referential manifestation of ideas and values, or as a Hegelian "self-realization of the spirit."

Consequently, in his early work Parsons tries to establish a theory of action that is able, first, to demonstrate the causal patterns of action, as long as they are empirically verifiable, second, to include interpretational schemes for forms of action that transgress causal contexts, and finally, to integrate both parts into one theory of action without giving preference to one of them. On a most basic level, Parson notes: "For the purposes of the theory of action the smallest conceivable concrete unit is the unit act."[13] While the unit acts cannot be further divided, they can still be analyzed in their complexity. Parsons differentiates several "concrete elements" that form the referential pattern of his theory of action: (1) Every unit act presupposes the existence of an *actor*. (2) Every unit act refers to a future state that is different from the initial state of the act; it therefore has an *end*. (3) The unit act is taking place within an identifiable *situation*. The situation can further be analytically divided into several components: those that the actor can manipulate, control, and instrumentalize, and those that cannot be changed by the actor. The former Parsons calls the *means* of the unit act; the latter are its *conditions*. (4) Among the elements of the unit act there is a relation of arbitrariness and nonarbitrariness at the same time.[14] For instance, regarding the selection of means we can speak of a certain level of choice between alternatives, but this choice is also dependent on *normative orientations* that are intrinsically forced upon the actor by the situational context of the unit act.

Already in his early versions of this model, Parsons introduced several subschemes and categories. His theory became much more complex in his subsequent work, when he developed what has become known as his *structural functionalism* and his theory of *functionalist systems*. These influential contributions were picked up directly by important theorists such as Clifford Geertz, Anthony Giddens, Robert N. Bellah, and Niklas Luhmann.[15]

For sociological theory, the work of Niklas Luhmann (1927–98) is of special importance.[16] Like Jürgen Habermas and others, Luhmann extrapolated Parsons's social theory, trying to bridge the gap between action theory and social systems theory. While for Parsons the unit of the system's operation was action, Luhmann's social systems theory is analogously construed to Parsons's "structural functionalism." According to this approach, the analysis of social structure should be based not on (the aggregate of) action, but on the interactions between actions. Put differently, whereas Parsons (and Giddens after him) had attributed actions to actors and to aggregates of actors performing via institutions, Luhmann's theory referred to "symbolic interactionism": Luhmann defines human action in terms of its interactive meaning at the network level.[17] This brought Luhmann to a theory of communication that is broader than action. With regard to religion he notes:

> We can, . . . in the context of a sociological theory, think of religion exclusively as a communicative happening [*kommunikatives Geschehen*]. . . . In contrast to statements religions make about themselves, we therefore are not dealing with religious entities (godheads, for instance) that are described as existing. The only thing that interests us is the fact that this is said. (Because if it would not have been said, there would be no reason to mull over the question whether it is true or not.) . . . Hence, religious *belief* always is *confession*. But the happening's *unity* is generated as communication and not as (unavoidably precarious) state of mind of the people involved.[18]

THE IMPACT OF THEORIES OF ACTION
IN RECENT METHODOLOGICAL DEBATES

Classic theories of action, both from philosophy and from sociology, have had an enormous impact on the development of recent theoretical approaches in the study of religion, even if this influence often remains unacknowledged. Let me briefly illustrate this with two examples.

The development of the so-called *rational choice theory of religion* is directly influenced by the theories of action discussed above. The basic idea that is operative in this approach is that (a) human action necessitates a decision between alternatives and that (b) this decision is made in a rational way. While the reduction to rational choices of actors allows us to interpret and analyze much of religious action, doubts have been raised about this theory.[19] For instance, it can be argued that the theory is not open to falsification because according to the theory the benefits of an action (and thus the "rational" reasons) can be unknown to or even unintended by the actors; hence, it is up to the observing scholar to make up the "rational" reasons of specific actions. Making use of theoretical suggestions by Weber, Parsons, and others, more elaborated versions of rational choice theory respond to this problem by establishing a referential framework of individual action that allows for an objective interpretation of social action. Hartmut Esser's concept of *situational logic* (*Situationslogik*) is such an elaborated theory.[20] Following Karl R. Popper's theoretical considerations, Esser makes it clear that this model is not interested in the individual's inner experience or opinion but in the situational context that provides an objective framework for (rational) behavior. What is of interest here is action that is in accordance with the situation (*situationsgerechtes Handeln*). This is reminiscent of Weber's terminology, as well as of Parsons's notions of the "means" and "conditions" of a situation in which a unit act takes place. But now the analytical focus is moved even more into the direction of situational contexts.

Another recent application of classic theories of action is the field of *performance and ritual studies*. James Laidlaw and Caroline Humphrey note: "Not much about ritual is incontrovertible, but that rituals are composed of actions is surely not open to doubt. To view ritual as action might therefore seem to be an obvious and a reasonably promising starting point for analysis, but it has been a comparatively rare one."[21] Interestingly enough, even Laidlaw and Humphrey are referring only to anthropological approaches to action and performance (Émile Durkheim, Victor Turner, and the like), as well as to cognitive theories that have recently entered the stage (Thomas Lawson and Robert McCauley, in particular). The benefit of applying sociological and philosophical models of action to our understanding of ritual dynamics remains more or less unexplored.

As a conclusion, we can argue that large areas of contemporary discussion regarding method and theory in the study of religion are directly or indirectly linked to theories of action that have been developed earlier. When it comes to explaining and understanding human behavior—be it religious or not—the category "action" is the basic component of all interpretational models. Actions of individuals and of groups follow an identifiable pattern, which the academic study of religion has to establish. An explicit response to and application of theories of action in our attempt to interpret religious behavior and its situational structure would be a step forward in many debates that occupy scholars of religion today.

NOTES

Please note that this article contains material also explored by the author in Kocku von Stuckrad, "Action," in *Vocabulary for the Study of Religion*, ed. Robert A. Segal and Kocku von Stuckrad (Leiden: Brill, 2015).

1. Donald Davidson, *Essays on Actions and Events* (Oxford: Oxford University Press, 1980).
2. Harry Frankfurt, *The Importance of What We Care About* (Cambridge: Cambridge University Press, 1988); Harry Frankfurt, *Volition, Necessity, and Love* (Cambridge: Cambridge University Press, 1999).

3. On philosophical theories of action, see George Wilson, "Action," in *The Stanford Encyclopedia of Philosophy (Fall 2008 Edition)*, ed. Edward N. Zalta, http://plato.stanford.edu/archives/fall2008/entries/action/; an overview of sociological theories of action is provided in Ghita Holmström-Hintika and Raimo Tuomela, eds., *Contemporary Action Theory* (Dordrecht: Kluwer, 1997); see also Hans Haferkamp, *Soziologie als Handlungstheorie: P. L. Berger und T. Luckmann, G. C. Homans, N. Luhmann, G. H. Mead, T. Parsons, A. Schütz, M. Weber in vergleichender Analyse und Kritik*, 3rd ed. (Opladen: Westdeutscher, 1976).

4. On the usefulness of Weber's theory of action for subsequent philosophical discussion, particularly in Donald Davidson, see Stephen P. Turner, "Weber on Action," *American Sociological Review* 48 (1983): 506–19; see also Wolfgang Schluchter, *Handlung, Ordnung und Kultur: Studien zu einem Forschungsprogramm im Anschluss an Max Weber* (Tübingen: Mohr Siebeck, 2005).

5. Max Weber, *Gesammelte Aufsätze zur Wissenschaftslehre*, ed. Johannes Winckelmann, 3rd ed. (Tübingen: Mohr Siebeck, 1968), 429, italics in original. All translations of quotations from German are mine.

6. Max Weber, *Wirtschaft und Gesellschaft: Grundriß der verstehenden Soziologie*, ed. Johannes Winckelmann, 5th ed. (Tübingen: Mohr Siebeck, 1976), 245.

7. Weber, *Gesammelte Aufsätze*, 429, italics in original.

8. Ibid.; Weber, *Wirtschaft und Gesellschaft*, 11.

9. Weber, *Wirtschaft und Gesellschaft*, 1–2.

10. Ibid., 1.

11. An excellent analysis is Sigrid Brandt, *Religiöses Handeln in moderner Welt: Talcott Parsons' Religionssoziologie im Rahmen seiner allgemeinen Handlungs- und Systemtheorie* (Frankfurt: Suhrkamp, 1993). On the reception of Parsons's theories, see Renée C. Fox et al., eds., *After Parsons: A Theory of Social Action for the Twenty-First Century* (New York: Russell Sage Foundation, 2005); Helmut Staubmann, ed., *Action Theory: Methodological Studies* (Hamburg: LIT, 2006); On Parsons's response to Weber see Brandt, *Religiöses Handeln in moderner Welt*, 317–52; Thomas Schwinn, "Wieviel Subjekt benötigt die Handlungstheorie? Zur Weber-Rezeption von Alfred Schütz und Talcott Parsons," *Revue internationale de philosophie* 49 (1995): 187–220; Keith Tribe, "Talcott Parsons as Translator of Max Weber's Basic Sociological Categories," *History of European Ideas* 33 (2007): 212–33.

12. Talcott Parsons and Edward A. Shils, eds., *Toward a General Theory of Action*, 5th ed. (Cambridge, Mass.: Harvard University Press, 1962), 3–29; Talcott Parsons, "The Place of Ultimate Values in Sociological Theory," *International Journal of Ethics* 45 (1935): 282–316; Talcott Parsons, *The Structure of Social Action* (New York: McGraw-Hill, 1937); Talcott Parsons, *Actor, Situation, and Normative Pattern: An Essay in the Theory of Social Action* (1939; Münster: LIT, 2010).

13. Parsons, *The Structure of Social Action*, 48.

14. Ibid., 44.

15. For Bellah's own response to Parsons, see Robert C. Bellah, "God, Nation, and Self in America: Some Tensions Between Parsons and Bellah," in *After Parsons: A Theory of Social Action for the Twenty-First Century*, ed. Renée C. Fox, Victor M. Lidz, and Harold J. Bershady (New York: Russell Sage Foundation, 2005), 137–47.

16. See Niklas Luhmann, *Die Religion der Gesellschaft*, ed. André Kieserling (Frankfurt: Suhrkamp, 2000); Niklas Luhmann, *Funktion der Religion* (Frankfurt: Suhrkamp, 1977); Rudi Laermans and Gert Verschraegen, "'The Late Niklas Luhmann' on Religion: An Overview," *Social Compass* 48 (2001): 7–20. Laermans and Verschraegen discuss his later theory of religion.

17. Loet Leydesdorff, "Luhmann, Habermas, and the Theory of Communication," *Systems Research and Behavioral Science* 17 (2000): 273–88.

18. Ibid., 40–42, italics in original.

19. Lawrence A. Young, ed., *Rational Choice Theory and Religion: Summary and Assessment* (New York: Routledge, 1997); Steve Bruce, *Choice and Religion: A Critique of Rational Choice Theory* (Oxford: Oxford University Press, 1999); Roy Wallis and Steve Bruce, *Sociological Theory, Religion and Collective Action* (Belfast: Queen's University of Belfast, 1986).

20. Hartmut Esser, *Soziologie: Spezielle Grundlagen*, band 1, *Situationslogik und Handeln* (Frankfurt: Campus, 1999), 387–403.

21. James Laidlaw and Caroline Humphrey, "Action," in *Theorizing Rituals: Issues, Topics, Approaches, Concepts*, ed. Jens Kreinath, Jan Snoek, and Michael Stausberg (Boston: Brill, 2006), 265.

PART VIII

The Phenomenology of Religion
and Its Critics

36

Phenomenology of Religion

The Philosophical Background

CHARLES E. SCOTT

In this short introduction I will highlight the concept of phenomenology and some of its distinguishing characteristics as distinct from giving summaries of the ideas of leading phenomenologists or accounts of the formation and changes in their thinking. I understand "phenomenology" to name a tradition of thought rather than any one method. This tradition's founding influence is in the work of Edmund Husserl, although a careful historian of "early" phenomenology would include reference to the work of G. W. F. Hegel, Franz Brentano, C. S. Peirce, William James, and other nineteenth-century and early-twentieth-century thinkers. One of the leading characteristics of this tradition, beginning with Martin Heidegger's emphasis on time and history, is careful attention to the canonical works in Western thought. This historical turn led to major transitions away from Husserl's approach within the phenomenological tradition, away from the ideas of transcendental consciousness, a priori and pure forms of consciousness, and the search for timeless essences. This is a turn toward descriptive thought that takes careful account of lineages of interpretation, texts, power, language, and conceptual mutation. The phenomenological tradition became one of considerable dynamism and diversity that stretches from Husserl's transcendental phenomenology to scholars who are sometimes called postmodern. I will point to several of the persistent characteristics that highlight it and that help to define it amid its dynamic, transformative life.

First, the word itself. "Phenomenology" is a word that derives from the Greek deponent *phainesthai* (to show itself). It brings into one word the roots *pha* (*phos*, "light"), *nomos* ("law," "custom"), and *logos*, which in its richness means "word," "thought," "reason," and "account." Phenomenologists thus often interpret "phenomenology" as an account of the usual or required ways things come to light. We can understand "phenomena" to mean "things showing themselves," and phenomenology as careful study of how such showing takes place. If we interpret phenomena as Heidegger does in *Being and Time*, we would emphasize the middle voice construction of *phainesthai* and understand it to mean, in the context of phenomenology, something shows itself from itself. Let's unpack these initial observations.

SHOWING AND BEING SHOWN

Phenomenology began with Husserl as a new, descriptive philosophical method to describe the showing of whatever engages us. The "new" comes in part in the leading question for thought: *How* is something manifest? Not, *What* is it that appears? Or we could ask, How does a manifest event occur as manifest? What makes something apparent? Whether we locate the "how" in a transcendental structure of consciousness, a tradition, language, or community, as phenomenologists we will look for the way something happens manifestly and not for something that stands outside of the event and is represented by it. We do not look for something behind the phenomena: The phenomenon presents itself. A phenomenon shows itself from itself.

The change of thought that is prompted by prioritizing phenomena means that the lives and identities of what we encounter are found in the self-showing events, not in the particular, knowing subject. The meaning and truth of things are found in their disclosive occurrences and not in an a priori structure of perception and understanding on the part of the knower. The priority of subjectivity that has exercised such force in modern Western thought is radically shifted. This shift began with Husserl. Although he posited a conscious transcendental subjectivity in his account of the structures of appearing, he also argued that philosophers must suspend or "bracket" the relative, subjective factors in experience if they are to find access to the transcendental structures of phenomena; and late in his career, as we shall see in a moment, he formulated the idea of life-world that began to move attention away from the knowing subject. Heidegger refined considerably Husserl's trend toward decentering the knowing, experiencing subject as he insisted that phenomenologists must begin with a highly disciplined account of a nonsubjective state of being that he calls *Dasein* (being-there, or being-in-the-world, to which we will return below) as distinct from transcendental consciousness. The point now is that beginning with Heidegger's account of *Dasein*, many phenomenological thinkers developed descriptive methods in which knowing subjects do not "do" the showing. Phenomena are the showing events and prior to conscious acts, knowledge, or theory.

Phenomenologists typically want to follow a disciplined procedure for describing the definitive aspects of phenomenal events, the defining characteristics of manifestation (or disclosure), the "how" of whatever is apparent. Husserl spoke of a *strenge Wissenschaft*, a "strict science or discipline," as the backbone of phenomenology, an approach that included a specialized vocabulary, the cultivation of an art of intuitive perceiving, and a practice of separating out the relative and nonrelative factors in phenomena. Heidegger and many others also formed a specialized vocabulary with a purpose analogous to Husserl's: to provide a new philosophical locale for thinking in an effort to turn appropriately to the living events of things. Heidegger's discipline, in contrast to Husserl's, requires a thorough knowledge of Western metaphysics, a new way of prioritizing time, and the use of an approach he called "deconstruction." I want only to note at this point that according to Heidegger lineages of thought and practice become crucial determinants of the ways things show themselves, and that this aspect of his thought had an enormous effect on many developments in the phenomenological lineage, in the accounts of interpretation in the work of H.-G. Gadamer, the deconstructive thought of J. Derrida, and the genealogical studies of power, institutions, and knowledge by M. Foucault. I will return to this approach that brings together time and deconstruction after considering the phrase "to the things themselves."

TO THE THINGS THEMSELVES

This phrase may be taken as a phenomenologist's motto. First, last, and always phenomenologists emphasize the living events that they study. How do we go about developing knowledge of living things as distinct from knowledge of lifeless objects? That is not a new concern in Western thought but it gained a special urgency as the "natural sciences" grew in sophistication, power, and influence and as the "social sciences" turned to them as models of responsible investigation. Husserl, Heidegger, J. P. Sartre, E. Levinas, Derrida, Foucault, and many others in the phenomenological tradition share this passionate concern for knowledge appropriate to living things in their diverse ways of occurring. They do not want to constitute their thought as theory, as controlled forms of objectifying sight and analysis. They want to develop disciplines of thought and language that turn them to things themselves in ways that are not circumscribed by objectification, and as we have seen, "things themselves" means the self-showing of whatever shows up. In a manner of speaking, phenomena speak for themselves. How do we learn to hear them and speak appropriately of them?

That kind of discipline is not easy in a lineage largely governed by types of gazing, analyzing, and categorizing, by "logics" into which things are required to fit. In order to provide an option to deeply ingrained habits of thought with their subjective, rational laws for things, Heidegger developed a "deconstructive" approach to instances of traditional philosophical thinking. "Deconstructive" refers to a process of uncovering and putting in question a text's or way of thinking's formative assumptions and claims. Deconstruction brackets to a certain extent the force of thinking in the grand sweep of Platonic and Aristotelian lineages. Deconstructive thinkers' goal is to take apart ideas and assumptions and to let what traditional ideas are actually talking about—the definitive phenomena—shine through the theoretical layers that have covered over the subject matter. The real issues and questions for thinking appear hidden in major aspects of traditional metaphysics, and the deconstructive goal is to let them gain clarity as they come to pass in obscuring logics and ideas, to find a language and manner of thought that addresses their own phenomenal occurrences. These thinkers are not looking for timeless structures of disclosure. Heidegger, for example, is interested in the prime mover of Western thought, which he thinks is a question that is constitutive of people's lives, one that requires response but is not subject to definitive answer: the question of being. For him that is a question that arises in disclosure as such. Gadamer, on the other hand, intends to describe the way texts and interpretations happen in the context of the history of interpretation, while Derrida in one aspect of his work describes the way deconstruction happens in the very structure of written language. In each case, the phenomenal quality of time and historical developments plays crucial roles in the appearing of whatever appears.

Whatever the virtues and limitations of Heidegger's question of being, it had the effect of unseating an image of truth as something that can be achieved or found. Heidegger develops an important implication in Husserl's thought that truth happens as disclosure, as the living event of self-showing. It had the further effect of weakening the value of certainty—something that people can possess—as a philosophical goal. Many people in the phenomenological lineage have felt, in addition to the force of Husserl's groundbreaking thought, the impact of Heidegger's deconstructive work and his positive agenda of turning to things themselves, although most of those philosophers (such as M. Merleau-Ponty, Levinas, M. Blanchot, Derrida, Gadamer, Foucault, L. Irigaray, J.-L. Nancy, G. Deleuze, and J. Lacan) have adopted only parts of his specialized language and have not prioritized the question of being. The turn to things themselves—the formation of disciplined alternatives to metaphysical thinking, and language and concepts in which living, self-disclosive events trump the importance of theoretical certainty—characterize the major works in the phenomenological tradition.

LIFE-WORLD, BEING-IN-THE-WORLD, AND BEYOND

A crucial distinction in Husserl's and Heidegger's thought is one between accounts of the occurrence of disclosure as such and accounts of particular regions of occurrence. Each in his own way wanted to account for the logos of phenomena, the essence, for Husserl, or truth of manifestness as such, for Heidegger. This is a distinction that is sometimes blurred by people who understand their phenomenological work in regional terms: accounts of, for example, religious events and experiences or of specific social worlds. Perhaps Husserl and Heidegger are right in saying that without a well-conceived understanding of the *nomos* of coming to light we will inevitably fall into a kind of theorizing that loses its phenomenological edge. We can provide, however, an emphasis on regional events, locate our thinking in engagements with them, orient ourselves by reference to a particular and well-conceived understanding of disclosure, and meet some of the obligations of phenomenological work without developing our own account of disclosure.

Husserl developed a strong notion of the life-world in order to emphasize the situated concreteness of phenomena. It is the world of manifest events that we experience as given prior to reflection. We always engage things in perspectives—they show their excessiveness of our situated experience of them by indicating their availability for different accounts and perspectives. Spaces, times, events are not initially objective. They are lived. Whether we are carrying out manual labor, writing a poem, or doing research in physics, we live in an encompassing, suffusing world that is given in our lives before we do anything in its regard. We are always with and in the world, infused by a vast complex of associations, senses, connections, and meanings. We are worldly to the core of our existence. Our ways of being disclose a pretheoretical world that operates in all dimensions of people's lives.

If we know ourselves and the objects of our study carefully in the context of being-in-the-world, we will be able to give regional accounts of phenomena while appreciating the limits of our work in connection with the vast, nonobjective dimensions of the lived world. Concretely speaking, if we give phenomenological accounts of such regions of occurrence as religious experiences, communities of faith, or ritual practices with a clear understanding of being-in-the-world, we will be disposed to language and concepts that recognize their limitations. There will likely be caution in our work regarding generalization, a marked disinclination to universalizing claims, and an overtone of appreciation for the dimension of disclosure in the phenomenal quality of our subject matter.

We might think and feel that way, that is, if we are under the strong influence of Husserl or Heidegger. If, however, we take a more deconstructive (Derridian, for example) or hermeneutical (Gadamerian, for example) turn, we will probably pay more attention to the ways the lives of texts and language forestall our ability to establish text-free meanings without violating the very occurrence of meanings. Many people who think deconstructively are most attentive to the liveliness of texts and connections of words and signs. It is a liveliness that gives disconnection simultaneously with significant connections, nonsense with sense, a textual life quite other to human consciousness, good sense and everyday understanding. The phenomenological turn to things themselves—be those things connections among signs, power relations, transmissions of meaning, or states of mind—has produced an emphasis on the "other quality" of what engages us, on the differences that infuse kinships and permeate self-showing. Self-showing comes with an otherness, a differential quality, a kind of integrity that refuses to be fully absorbed into appropriations of it. It comes with a range and depth that allow perspectival variation and elude complete grasp; it happens with hiddenness as well as presence, with secrecy as well as public significance. The self-showing of things themselves offsets any presumed dominance by subjective appropriation or by imposed logics of good sense.

ETHOS AND DWELLING

I have said that phenomenology is a highly diversified tradition of thought and scholarship that requires self-aware discipline based on careful knowledge of the major texts in both its own lineage and the broader Western philosophical lineage. I pointed to the following hallmarks of the lineage:

1. Phenomenology is focused by the self-showing of phenomena. This means that phenomena do not appear primarily as objects.
2. Although Husserl is the founder of phenomenology, his method of discovery and thought does not define the entire lineage. A phenomenologist might or might not follow his approach.
3. Phenomenology is guided by the question of how something manifests itself, not by the question of what something is. This means that phenomena are events that present themselves as distinct to re-presenting something else.

4. The priority of the knowing subject is consequently displaced in this lineage. Phenomena, not knowing subjects, are the sites of original manifestation.

5. An emphasis on time and history had an explosive, transformative effect in phenomenology.

6. Phenomenologists typically are guided by disciplined accounts of the occurrence of disclosure that provide the philosophical context for their work.

7. Such discipline usually requires specialized language and concepts.

8. The motivation for phenomenology is expressed in the motto "to the things themselves." "Things themselves" names living, self-disclosive events, not objects of knowledge.

9. Deconstruction developed in this lineage as a way to enhance the clarity of definitive, originary phenomena that gave rise to questions, meanings, and conflicts in Western thought and practice.

10. Truth in the phenomenological tradition is found as the manifestness of things— as the *nomos* of coming to light—as distinct from the correspondence of mental formations and objects of experience.

11. The concepts of life-world and being-in-the-world in the lineage point out the definitive aspect of worldly relations in all dimensions of human existence. This shifting, pretheoretical field orients phenomenological thinking.

12. This lineage has produced a strong emphasis on the differential quality of phenomena. In showing themselves, phenomena are excessive to perspectives on them or identities assigned to them. Self-showing establishes a quality of otherness and difference in our experiences of phenomena.

People who have recognized and appreciated this differential quality of phenomena are often moved to give priority to ways of living that place a high value on the singularity of lives and cultures. We can carry out such an evaluation by giving importance, for example, to the singularity of texts and traditions, to *their* self-showing and hiddenness as we then engage them as much as possible in their own terms and histories. We might pay special attention to the ways the silencing of different voices happens, the forms that the colonization of other lives takes, or the types of power that affirm or suppress human and nonhuman lives. Those who study religious phenomena might pay attention to what appears as different and outside of structures of identity in those phenomena as well as to formations of religious identity and formulations of common belief. Is the uncommon a dimension of the disclosure of what is common? Do religious phenomena show themselves as other to the meanings that define them? If they do, how are we to speak appropriately of them? How are we to understand our knowledge of them?

Such questions are among those that arise in thought in the phenomenological lineage. The variety of approaches and manners of speech that respond to such questions suggests that phenomenology itself is not reasonably subject to one, overarching identity, that the name designates a historical process of uncovering what has been covered over by forms of usage, clarification, and identification. A further suggestion is that the way we address such questions constitutes a manner of dwelling with phenomena, an ethos at the heart of which are the lives that show themselves and make up our animated worlds.

37

The Phenomenology of Religion

JAMES L. COX

The phenomenology of religion, alongside the history of religions, forms part of a larger field initially associated with the comparative study of religions but nowadays frequently referred to in academic institutions simply as religious studies. Movements to conduct research on religious communities using contemporary scientific methods originated in the late nineteenth and early twentieth centuries from disciplines as diverse as linguistic and textual studies, anthropology, sociology, archaeology, economics, and political studies. The phenomenology of religion, as a specific branch of the science of religion, was influenced from two main sources: the philosophical phenomenology of Edmund Husserl and liberal Christian theology as it developed at the end of the nineteenth century. Ultimately, phenomenologists of religion distinguished their methodology from that employed by theologians, philosophers, and social scientists by arguing that religions must be interpreted according to a unique methodology. Although the social sciences were regarded as integral to contributing to an understanding of religion, scholars in the phenomenological tradition insisted that a method needed to be developed that would identify and interpret the uniquely *religious* elements that were interwoven into historical and social contexts. Philosophy was employed inconsistently in phenomenological writings, with most scholars selecting basic concepts derived from philosophical phenomenology without attempting to employ its methods in depth. As we will see, only Gerardus van der Leeuw attempted to apply Husserl's epistemological analyses directly to a methodology for the study of religion. Theology, since it originated from within specific traditions, was regarded as forming part of the phenomena of religion, which, alongside other phenomena such as myths, rituals, and beliefs, comprised part of the data for the study of religion itself.

EARLY HISTORICAL BACKGROUND

C. P. Tiele (1830–1902), the Dutch theologian and scholar of ancient Egyptian religions, was a foundational figure in the formation of the comparative study of religions. Tiele promoted a comparative study of religions as a way of distinguishing a "science of religion" from "confessional theology."[1] Tiele argued that the study of religion begins with accurate and scientifically verifiable descriptions of religious behavior. Comparisons of religions are made possible by the scholar initially grouping the religious phenomena described into typical patterns, then identifying the origins of each class of religious practice, and finally ranking the types according to their place in the evolution of human religious development. Tiele believed this step-by-step methodology would show that religions evolve in phases from nature religions through mythological religions through doctrinal religions and finally to the world religions. Key to the transition from the nature stage to the mythological stage is the capacity for humans to think symbolically. Throughout this progression, the scholar identifies the abiding core of religion as it is expressed at every level of development. Tiele believed that discovering the essence of religion could only occur at this final stage in the process. Otherwise, preconceived notions of religion would render the entire method unscientific.

The first thinker to employ the term "phenomenology of religion" was another Dutch scholar, Pierre Daniel Chantepie de la Saussaye (1848–1920).[2] Chantepie defined the phenomenology of religion as a method for classifying and comparing religious beliefs and practices, which would produce a new discipline, falling midway between the history of religions and the philosophy of religion. Among the phenomena of religion he included "religious acts, cult, and customs," particularly as they are expressed in rituals, which he believed provided the "richest material" for the phenomenology of religion. Chantepie defined religion as focusing on beliefs in "superhuman powers," the universal character of which confirmed that religions everywhere originate from a divine source.[3] When scientists of religion observe, describe, and classify religious phenomena, therefore, they actually are recording the revelations of God. By affirming the universality of natural revelation, Chantepie, like Tiele, separated the science of religion from confessional theology, the latter being confined largely to a study of the special revelation of God in Christ. This meant that for scholars to understand religion scientifically, they must note variations in the human responses to God, compile them historically, and classify them for comparative purposes according to phenomenological typologies.

The German theologian Rudolf Otto (1869–1937) also played a critical formative role in the phenomenology of religion, particularly through his landmark book *The Idea of the Holy* (first published in 1917 as *Das Heilige*, with its English translation appearing in 1923).[4] One of the most important concepts in Otto's thinking derived from his description of the core of religion as an unknown and unknowable "holy," which is expressed and hence becomes observable in religious experience. In his discussion of the "elements of the 'numinous,'" Otto referred to the experience of "creature feeling," which he defined as "the emotion of a creature, abased and overwhelmed by its own nothingness in contrast to that which is supreme above all creatures."[5] The numinous is objective, outside the self, and responsible for the intensity of feelings produced within an individual who responds to it. The "nature of the numinious," described by Otto as the *mysterium tremendum*, is manifested in the feelings it produces in humans, which vary in intensity and mood depending on how it is apprehended by the individual. By calling the source of these experiences a mystery, Otto implied that the cognitive content of the numinous remains "hidden" and lies beyond the ability of humans to conceptualize it or put it into words. In this sense, the mysterious numinous reality is couched in negative terms as something unknown in itself, but it can be seen positively in the feelings it produces in human experience, such as awe, majesty, dread, fear, urgency to be in relation with it, and concurrent emotions of fascination and revulsion.[6]

Although the comparative study of religion, as conceived by Tiele, Chantepie, and Otto, ultimately was motivated by their shared conviction that Christianity would be shown in the light of science to be superior to other religions, we find in their writings the main components that formed the basis for the thinking of later phenomenologists. These include the requirement for accurate descriptions of religious behavior both historically and in contemporary practice, the classification into typologies of the descriptive material, the use of comparative studies to discern the core or essence of religion, and, finally, the recognition that religion as a universal phenomenon shares a common source which can be understood only by a scholar who possesses religious sentiments.

KEY PHENOMENOLOGISTS OF RELIGION

One of the earliest thinkers to develop a phenomenological approach to the study of religions was Tiele's student, W. Brede Kristensen (1867–1953), who for thirty-six years beginning in 1901 held the chair of the history of religion in Leiden University. Kristensen defined phenomenology quite simply as a method that places characteristic data of religion into groups in a systematic way in order to provide insight into the human religious disposition.[7] Kristensen's description of the role of phenomenology as a science of classification resulted in the general portrayal of phenomenology in academic circles during the first third of the twentieth century primarily as a method for identifying religious typologies, by which the scholar organizes the vast diversity of human religious beliefs and behaviors into orderly categories for comparative purposes.

Kristensen also introduced the notion into the phenomenology of religion that the scholar must privilege the believer's point of view in any interpretation of religious data. The primary technique Kristensen advocated to achieve this was "empathy," by which he meant that a scholar must cultivate a feeling for what is unfamiliar by relating it to one's own experience. This involved more than a hypothetical "as if," since it is virtually impossible for a scholar of religion to employ this technique unless the scholar has some personal experience of religion. Kristensen thus thought that the use of empathy would deepen and strengthen the personal faith of the researcher. Whether or not a genuinely scientific methodology has been applied would be disclosed only by research findings, which are based on such an empathetic approach. By giving priority to the adherents' perspectives, Kristensen offered a resolution to the problem of evaluating religions, which he had inherited from Tiele. He rejected any form of evaluative comparison that presupposes an a priori ideal or standard whereby one religious act, belief, or practice is judged as better, higher, or more valuable than another act, belief, or practice. Instead of judging by what the believers of the religion in question identify as the key to understanding their own beliefs and practices, the scholar who engages in evaluative comparison uses an alien interpretative key or prejudgment imposed from without. Over against evaluative comparison, Kristensen advocated the practice of an informed comparison based on historical data, a method that leads to understanding rather than judgment. Historical evaluation does this by helping the scholar discern what is important and lasting in religion and helps avoid wasting time on fleeting movements or transitory events. By leading to informed, as opposed to evaluative, comparisons, history becomes the servant of phenomenology and ensures that it retains a fully scientific methodology.

Kristensen's version of phenomenology of religion had a lasting impact on his student Gerardus van der Leeuw (1890–1950), whose name by the mid-1940s was virtually synonymous with the phenomenology of religion. Van der Leeuw's main contribution to the field is found in his substantial book of over seven hundred pages *Phänomenologie der Religion*, first published in German in 1933, and translated into English in 1938 as *Religion in Essence and Manifestation*.[8] Van der Leeuw defined phenomenology initially as a method for outlining the proper relationship between subjects and objects. In the study of religions this relationship defines the role of the scholar as one who seeks to understand the behaviors of religious practitioners, who in various ways respond to supernatural forces. This starting point is intended in van der Leeuw's phenomenology to provide sympathetic insight into the way devotees experience religion, while at the same time allowing scholars to study objectively the manifold religious apprehensions of the supernatural.

Van der Leeuw drew explicitly on the philosophy of Edmund Husserl to describe what he meant by the relationship between the subject and the object. He explained that phenomenology as a way of knowing deals with what "appears," but this is complicated by the fact that what appears manifests itself to someone, implying that "appearance" is ambiguous in that it refers equally to what appears and to the person to whom it appears.[9] This classical Husserlian analysis of perception led van der Leeuw to assert that what appears is not a pure object, since it results from the interaction between subject and object. This does not mean that the objective reality of the phenomenon that appears is determined or "produced" by the subject, but it is important nonetheless to emphasize that it appears to "someone." When this "someone" begins to talk about what has appeared, to analyze it, and to give it objective meaning, phenomenology, the study of phenomena, arises. By speaking of the phenomena, the observer attempts to make sense of otherwise "chaotic" data by sketching an outline of them, that is, by giving them a structure. The structure of what is observed does not appear directly in experience, nor does it result from logical analysis. It is somehow "understood" in its totality by the observer, in a way that draws us back to the primary relationship between the subject and the object. The subject-object distinction in this sense translates into a relationship between "understanding" and "intelligibility," which van der Leeuw asserted is connected in a way that is "unanalyzable" because it is an "experienced connection."[10]

In order to make sense of this analysis for the study of religion, van der Leeuw identified five stages that ultimately came to define the phenomenological method in the study of religion as a step-by-step process, although van der Leeuw admitted that the stages in practice occur simultaneously.[11] First, the phenomenologist assigns names to that which is observed in order that various phenomena can be identified, separated, and classified. Certain practices fit into one classification and other practices do not, but each must be assigned a different designation for purposes of clarification. Hence, one act might be called "purification" and another "sacrifice," since they are distinguishable in kind. Second, the phenomena must be interpolated into the scholar's own experience in order to avoid misunderstanding religious practices with which one is not familiar. The foreign character of religions other than one's own is complicated by the fact that what appears and that which is named are always mediated through symbols and language that must be interpreted through the personal experience of the researcher. This requires a sympathetic understanding, much more akin to art than to pure logic. Interpolation thus is employed to promote understanding by inserting what is unusual or unfamiliar into the researcher's own experience. Third, the phenomenologist performs the *epoché*, that is, bracketing out or suspending one's own prior assumptions or potentially distorting biases. Van der Leeuw referred to *epoché* as observing "restraint" by concerning itself only with phenomena and not by assuming what is "behind" appearances. It is precisely all such prior assumptions that are restrained, or put within brackets, thereby suspending judgments about their reality or their value. Fourth, the scholar allows the phenomena to speak for themselves in a way that clarifies their meaning. The phenomenological clarification refers to structural relations and connections, in which ideal types are identified and arranged to reveal their comparative significance. Finally, the end of this process, when stages one through four are combined, produces understanding in the sense of comprehending deeply, thoroughly, and intuitively.

Van der Leeuw thus defined the principal role of the phenomenology of religion as making sense out of otherwise chaotic religious phenomena that "appear" to the observer. Although this may sound entirely subjective, even mystical, phenomenology, like all sciences, seeks understanding that has resulted from an interpretative or hermeneutical analysis of data. In the final analysis, for van der Leeuw's phenomenology of religion, the use of the twin techniques, *epoché* and sympathy, led to a unique understanding (*Verstehen*) of religion, a result that he contended established phenomenology as a genuinely scientific discipline.

No figure has exercised such an extensive influence over the academic study of religions in North America, and arguably elsewhere, as Mircea Eliade (1907–86). Even today, over twenty years after his death, his writings are read and debated among students of religion in numerous international settings. Eliade, who was born in Bucharest, Romania, went to India to study at the University of Calcutta as a young man. Although he remained in India for just three years, his experience there had a lasting effect on his eventual theory of religion. In 1958, after having spent over a decade in Paris following the Second World War, Eliade was appointed chair of the history of religions in the University of Chicago, where he made substantial contributions to the study of religion. Some of his most important books include *Patterns in Comparative Religion, The Sacred and the Profane, Rites and Symbols of Initiation, Shamanism: Archaic Techniques of Ecstasy*, and *The Quest: History and Meaning of Religion*.[12]

Eliade's theory of religion depicts the religious person as focused on a time when the world came into being through an initial creative act of sacred manifestation. The religious person imagines a primeval moment, before the foundation of the world, dominated by the terror of profane homogeneity, where there were no indications of sacred orientation. In a homogeneous universe, everything is the same; no points of demarcation can be located. This is equivalent to being lost, where a person cannot identify any familiar landmarks and experiences utter despair and hopelessness as a result. In like manner, for the religious person, homogeneity, the inability to recognize sacred points of orientation, results in a sense of absolute meaninglessness and total chaos. In the beginning, *in illo tempore*, sacred intrusions broke into the homogeneity of space and time, revealing what would otherwise (following Otto) remain unknown and unknowable and providing life with meaningful points of cosmic orientation by "founding" the world.[13] As religions develop in history, these primordial hierophanies become expressed symbolically chiefly through cosmogonic myths and their ritual reenactments. The history of religions thus becomes a study of sacred manifestations (hierophanies), uncovering how they have been enshrined in myths and how they are brought into the present through rituals. For the religious person, myth and ritual are replete with symbolic meaning and provide the scholar with the tools necessary for interpreting religious experience. As a result, the scholar of religion can best be described as a "hermeneutist," one who identifies hierophanies within the history of religions and deciphers their meanings for believers.

Because religion primarily is about orientation, certain symbols recur in various forms throughout the world and across history. These primarily have to do with cosmic centers, which connect the layers of the world, the upper levels reaching to the heavens and hence to the gods and the lower levels extending to the foundations of the earth, often inhabited by murky figures, devils, and demons, what Eliade called "the infernal regions."[14] Such centers result from hierophanies, but for Eliade these not only provide points of orientation for religious people; they primarily facilitate "communication" between the "cosmic planes," that is, between the upper world, the earth, and the lower world.[15] This explains why myths and symbols frequently refer to natural objects extending to the sky, such as mountains, trees, birds, sun, and moon. It also explains why the shaman constitutes such a central and universal religious figure, since the shaman primarily travels to the upper and lower worlds and converses directly with the gods on behalf of the religious community. Although some hierophanies do not convey meanings beyond their own cultural contexts, the universal pattern whereby the sacred discloses itself can be discerned everywhere.

Clearly, on this model, Eliade has constructed a dichotomy between the sacred and the profane, what he calls "the dialectic of the sacred."[16] To understand this, we need to note that anything at all can become a hierophany, a conduit for manifesting the sacred, but not everything does. A particular entity becomes sacred precisely because it has manifested what otherwise would remain unknowable. A mountain may be selected because it is the highest in the region and hence nearest the abode of the gods, or a tree may be identified because of its unusual shape indicating the presence of a mysterious force. The hierophany thus implies a choice: not every tree, mountain, pool, or river is sacred; only those that are associated with hierophanies obtain such significance. The sacred object also possesses a certain ambivalence, since potentially it can be dangerous if it is not treated in a prescribed fashion, or if it becomes polluted by contact with profane objects. Its ambivalence is also enhanced by its mundane character; a stone or a tree remains what it is even while manifesting the "wholly other." By understanding the dialectic of the hierophany, the scholar gains insight into the way the religious person apprehends and experiences the world, and thus is able, as a hermeneutist, to disclose for academic understanding the structure of the religious consciousness.

The structure of the religious consciousness can be made objective through the categories of sacred and profane, and in the typologies of myth and ritual, but the symbolism that infuses both cannot be grasped by the scholar or interpreted to outsiders without the scholar adopting an entirely empathetic attitude toward the religious worldview. To understand in the fullest sense is to articulate that, for the religious person, symbols convey reality, meaning, and being. The religious person thus longs to be as near as possible to the sacred, to the moment when everything became new, and the only way to do this is to reexperience the creation by telling the story of beginnings and reenacting it in powerful and symbolic ritual dramas. The scholar simply cannot communicate the potent strength of a religious symbol without understanding it religiously. We see clearly from this analysis that Eliade's hermeneutical method suggests a thoroughly religious interpretation of the world. His investigations into "religio-historical facts" were intended not only to enhance the understanding of religion academically, but in the end to commend religion as the only way to achieve a sense of meaning in life and to attain what he called "access to the world of spirit."[17]

By 1970, as exemplified through the writings of Kristensen, van der Leeuw, and Eliade, the influence of phenomenology as a methodology for the study of religion had reached its apex, the primary characteristics of which can be summarized in the following points:

Religion constitutes a subject matter in its own right, and thus must insist on its own unique methodology.

The methodology peculiar to religion clarifies the relationship between historical data and the interpretation of the data by the researcher and distinguishes phenomenology, understood in a partnership with the history of religions, from all other academic approaches.

Testing interpretations from phenomenological research always takes place by recourse to the data of the religions themselves.

Phenomenological interpretations privilege the perspectives of believers, which are conveyed appropriately and academically only by scholars who cultivate a personal sensitivity to the religious experience of adherents.

Evaluating data is to be distinguished from interpreting meanings and delineating structures; evaluation does not belong within a scientific approach to the study of religions, whereas interpretations leading to understanding define its fundamental purpose.

PHENOMENOLOGY AS SURREPTITIOUS THEOLOGY

Since its heyday in the 1970s, serious methodological questions have been asked about the assumptions that motivated many of the key thinkers in the phenomenology of religion. Increasingly today phenomenologists are being criticized for combining theological assumptions with a simplistic understanding of Husserl's phenomenology in support of their claim that religion constitutes a unique subject matter, irreducible to any other dimension within human experience. In this light, the phenomenology of religion, although pretending to be a genuine science of religion, actually masks the fact that its aims are theological at their root. The related philosophical problem to the theologizing of the study of religion, particularly as it was expressed by van der Leeuw, resulted from the classical formulation of the subject-object dichotomy. When translated into religious studies, this has been formulated in terms of the personal faith of the scholar of religion and how that faith influences the scholar's understanding and interpretation of religious data. This has resulted in the phenomenological emphasis on a sympathetic approach to the study of religious communities by identifying the core of religion as something akin to Eliade's "sacred," which is expressed through its observable manifestations. The manifestations can be described, classified, and compared, but never understood apart from the scholar's possessing some personal sense of the essence of religion itself.

The critique of phenomenology forms part of a larger debate over a properly conceived methodology in the study of religion, which has developed over the past twenty-five years, often in polarized forms, initiated by scholars of religion, such as Donald Wiebe, Robert Segal, and Ivan Strenski, who assert that religion is not an autonomous subject.[18] As a *religious* study, they argue, it is best placed within theology, and in its scientific form, it is best dealt with in the social sciences. More recently, Timothy Fitzgerald has developed a damning critique of the term "religion," arguing that it is a Western invention, closely associated with colonialism, and that it should be replaced in academic circles by the more appropriate term "culture."[19] Fitzgerald's scathing analysis of the term "religion" as a category does not spare the phenomenology of religion in the process. According to Fitzgerald, phenomenologists erred not by carefully describing religious practices and classifying them, but by insisting that for something to qualify as religion it must refer to a sacred or transcendental entity. This makes the category religion indistinguishable from theology, since the study of religion is maintained as a distinct category, sui generis, in a classification of its own, requiring its own methodologies and its own department within universities on the basis of one criterion only: its numinous, sacred, transcendental core. If scholars want to avoid the problems they have inherited from phenomenology and study religion nontheologically, Fitzgerald insists, they must focus on the real object of study: the social, "understood as the values of a particular group and their institutionalization in a specific context, including the way power is organized and legitimated."[20] Fitzgerald concludes that the social is not some dimension of religion, some aspect that can be studied as if it were an "optional extra," but "the actual locus of a nontheological interpretation."[21]

Motivation beneath the phenomenology of religion has produced unintended consequences.[22] By emphasizing the central importance of interpreting subjective states, conveyed in terms of numinous experience, faith, or inner enlightenment, the study of religion has been transformed from an empirical science into the study of religious "consciousness." This is especially clear in the case of Eliade, who derived his notion of the sacred from Otto's definition of religion as a "creature feeling" for the "wholly Other." Paradoxically, this grants to the phenomenologist what Flood calls an "epistemic privilege" since it is the researcher who maintains control of describing subjective religious states, thereby veiling the power relations between the researcher and the communities that are being researched.[23] By performing the phenomenological bracketing to eliminate every type of prejudice, the scholar of religion remains in control of knowledge and thereby dictates the rules for interpreting religious phenomena. This makes phenomenology, at the very least, vulnerable to the charge that it actually promulgates a method for maintaining power over the objects of academic study, notwithstanding the virtual unanimity among phenomenologists that their personal religious experience provides them with privileged access to the mind of the religious practitioner.[24]

The line of thinking expressed by Fitzgerald and Flood suggests that the phenomenology of religion is outdated in the light of contemporary postmodern and postcolonial thinking. The postmodern emphasis on specificity and cultural contexts flies in the face of the phenomenological search for the essence or core of religion, which at best suffers from a naive application of Husserl's eidetic intuition but at worst surreptitiously advocates inserting into an ostensibly empirical study what Fitzgerald calls a liberal, ecumenical Christian theological agenda.[25] Flood's critique points to the lack of awareness by phenomenologists of the scholar's role in the hermeneutical process, who, by using empathy to cultivate a "feeling for" the practices of religious people, either naively or dishonestly pretends to experience what believers themselves experience in order to promote understanding. This stinging criticism is closely aligned with Fitzgerald's assertion that phenomenologists of religion, who have campaigned forcefully for a unique academic category called "religion," are implicated historically with the hegemonic power of the Western colonial enterprise.[26]

A MODIFIED PHENOMENOLOGY AS A VIABLE METHOD IN THE STUDY OF RELIGION

Very few scholars of religion today would advocate a return to the pure phenomenologies of van der Leeuw and Eliade or other classical thinkers in the phenomenological tradition. In this sense, some contemporary critiques of phenomenology are misplaced, since a case can be made that principles modified from phenomenology can make a viable contribution to the academic study of religions today. For example, the critical assessment of the term "religion" as advocated by Fitzgerald conforms to one central phenomenological tenet, originally advanced by Husserl, that naive assumptions should not go unchallenged. The way phenomenologists have applied the *epoché* can be interpreted to mean that the scholar needs to bring unexamined presuppositions to consciousness, to expose them to the full light of day and at the very least put them into brackets or suspend them so new perspectives can be explored and tested. This is precisely what Fitzgerald is doing when he calls for a historical reinterpretation of the term "religion."

This may lead us in the direction of reconceiving what is meant by religion, and to consider if indeed it would be better to replace it with a different term. By definition, phenomenology as a method does not foreclose consideration of such a proposal, but I would argue that such a reexamination must be conducted in light of the fact that people around the world form communities, and have done so throughout history, as direct responses to what they postulate to be an alternate reality or realities. The alternate realities do not translate into a transcendent being necessarily, but they define one of the primary reasons such communities claim to exist. The term "alternate reality or realities" suggests that the focus of each community's attention is something that is perceived by adherents to interact with them in mundane time and space but clearly represents a different kind of time and space from that which is ordinarily experienced, and thus is often expressed in ritual contexts. That communities exist and that they promulgate beliefs and rituals around such alternate realities are undeniable. Of course, they do other things: they construct power structures within their communities; they relate to one another economically; they often adhere to strictly enforced social relations. Nonetheless, a discipline that focuses on how communities understand and organize themselves in relation to their postulated alternate realities would seem to conform to what phenomenologists of religion traditionally have defined as their primary academic task.[27]

Insofar as phenomenologists stressed the importance of transcendence within human experience and identified a sacred reality as the source for religion, they strayed into theological discourse, but the attempt to describe, understand, and interpret how communities conceive themselves in relation to postulated alternate realities, in my view, qualifies unequivocally as academic research. What phenomenology today sacrifices, in the light of postmodern and postcolonial critiques, is its attempt to provide all-encompassing interpretations of religion that derive from an alleged empathetic understanding of the religious consciousness. A more dialogical method, whereby the researcher and the researched combine to produce interpretations, is likely to emerge—or as Gavin Flood calls it, a narrative approach to hermeneutics that allows the stories of communities to come to the fore rather than following a model based strictly on a subject-object dichotomy.[28] Awareness of power relations in constructing knowledge, a suspicion of grand theories, and an admission of the traditional complicity of phenomenology with theology, although affecting changes in the way research is undertaken and understood, need

not result in wholesale rejection of the potent insights phenomenologists historically have contributed to the disciplinary formation of religious studies.

NOTES

1. C. P. Tiele, *Elements in the Science of Religion* (Edinburgh: W. Blackwood, 1897–99).

2. P. D. Chantepie de la Saussaye, *Manual of the Science of Religion* (London: Longmans, Green, 1891).

3. Ibid., 69.

4. R. Otto, *The Idea of the Holy: An Inquiry Into the Non-Rational Factor in the Idea of the Divine and Its Relation to the Rational* (London: Oxford University Press, 1923).

5. Ibid., 8.

6. Ibid., 10–13.

7. W. B. Kristensen, *The Meaning of Religion*, trans. J. Carman (The Hague: Martinus Nijhoff, 1960).

8. G. van der Leeuw, *Religion in Essence and Manifestation: A Study in Phenomenology* (London: G. Allen and Unwin, 1938).

9. Ibid., 671.

10. Ibid., 672–73.

11. Ibid., 646.

12. M. Eliade, *Patterns in Comparative Religion* (London: Sheed and Ward, 1958); M. Eliade, *The Sacred and the Profane: The Nature of Religion* (New York: Harcourt Brace, 1989); M. Eliade, *Rites and Symbols of Initiation: The Mysteries of Birth and Rebirth* (New York: Harper and Row, 1966); M. Eliade, *Shamanism: Archaic Techniques of Ecstasy* (London: Routledge, 1964); M. Eliade, *The Quest: History and Meaning of Religion* (Chicago: University of Chicago Press, 1975).

13. Eliade, *The Sacred and the Profane*, 20–22.

14. Ibid., 36–37.

15. Ibid., 63.

16. Ibid., 32.

17. Ibid., 210.

18. D. Wiebe, *The Politics of Religious Studies: The Continuing Conflict with Theology in the Academy* (London: Macmillan, 1999); I. Strenski, *Religion in Relation: Method, Application and Moral Location* (London: Macmillan, 1993); R. Segal, "In Defense of Reductionism," *Journal of the American Academy of Religion* 51, no. 1 (1983): 97–124.

19. T. Fitzgerald, *The Ideology of Religious Studies* (New York: Oxford University Press, 2000).

20. Ibid., 71.

21. Ibid.

22. G. Flood, *Beyond Phenomenology: Rethinking the Study of Religion* (London: Cassell, 1999).

23. Ibid., 168.

24. Ibid., 92–108.

25. Fitzgerald, *The Ideology of Religious Studies*, 63.

26. See, T. Fitzgerald, ed., *Religion and the Secular: Historical and Colonial Formations* (London: Equinox, 2007).

27. See J. L. Cox, *From Primitive to Indigenous: The Academic Study of Indigenous Religions* (Aldershot, UK: Ashgate, 2007), 75–93; and J. L. Cox, *A Guide to the Phenomenology of Religion: Key Figures, Formative Influences and Subsequent Debates* (London: Continuum, 2006), 236–42.

28. Flood, *Beyond Phenomenology*, 154–57.

38

Mircea Eliade

GREGORY ALLES

Mircea Eliade (1907–86) was one of the most influential historians of religions in the second half of the twentieth century. Following three years spent studying in India with the philosopher Surendranath Dasgupta as well as in an ashram in the Himalayas, he became intensely involved in the political and cultural struggles of Romania prior to World War II. He spent the majority of the war years as a cultural attaché in Portugal. After the war he accepted positions in the history of religions in Paris (beginning 1946) and Chicago (beginning 1957). His goal, as formulated in his maturity, was to foster a "new humanism." By this he meant a humanism that differed from its Renaissance precursor in recovering the wisdom of a global rather than merely a European antiquity. Put differently: Eliade sought to redress what he perceived as the meaninglessness of secular modernity by recovering, through both scholarship and belletristic fiction (novels and short stories), fundamental religious forms that had been lost to modern consciousness. His major scholarly publications include (citing the first editions in English) *The Myth of the Eternal Return* (1954; also published as *Cosmos and History* in 1959), *Patterns in Comparative Religion* (1958), *Yoga: Immortality and Freedom* (1958), *Shamanism: Archaic Techniques of Ecstasy* (1964), *The Sacred and the Profane* (1959; a once popular textbook), *The Quest: History and Meaning in Religion* (1969), and *A History of Religious Ideas* (three volumes, 1978–85). He also served as general editor of the first edition of the Macmillan *Encyclopedia of Religion* (sixteen volumes, 1987).

The connection between Eliade's belletristic writings and his scholarship is intimate and complex, but our concern here is specifically with his theory of religion. What follows sketches out a system abstracted from Eliade's mature scholarly writings. It cannot include every facet of Eliade's thought. It also neglects changes that occurred over time, but perhaps that reflects the character of Eliade's project. Eliade self-consciously attempted to produce an oeuvre, a unified life's work, as well as to escape the ravages of time or, as he put it, the terrors of history.

STRUCTURE AND HISTORY

As a scholar, Eliade represented himself as a historian of religions. In part he was simply reflecting common linguistic conventions. During the nineteenth century in Europe and somewhat later in North America, historians and philologists had by and large developed the study of the religions of literate people.[1] Their efforts helped constitute a field that became known as *Istoria religiilor* in Romania, *l'histoire de religions* in France, and "the history of religions" at some institutions in North America, such as the University of Chicago. At the same time, Eliade also used the designation "historian of religions" to distinguish himself from theologians. The latter could develop abstract systems of thought on the basis of key claims about God, human beings, and the universe. Historians of religions always had to ground their claims in an empirical investigation of what human beings actually said and did. Nevertheless, with the exception of the three volumes of *A History of Religious Ideas*, Eliade's "history of religions" is not history in the ordinary sense of the word. Indeed, the lesson he drew from Freud was that a historian of religions was entitled to articulate the meaning of a symbol, regardless of whether any of the people using the symbol had ever consciously formulated that meaning as such. It can be difficult, then, to discern precisely how Eliade's claims are grounded in empirical, historical data.

In addition, Eliade insisted that in the matter of discerning or deciphering religious meaning, the history of religions is superior to all other academic pursuits. He did recognize the need for work by philologists, historians, ethnographers, and others who carefully interpret documents and other data within their cultural contexts, but he faulted such specialists for being unable to recognize the more general structures that are accessible to historians of religions. He acknowledged that other disciplines such as psychology, sociology, and economics cast light on some dimensions of religious phenomena, but he faulted them for "reducing" religion to something that it is not, for example, psychological processes. In doing so, these scholars missed what makes religion religion. Finally, Eliade faulted other historians of religions for their philosophical timidity. In controversial phrases, he contended that in order to truly understand religion, one must understand the sacred on its own plane of reference. He compared historians of religions to art historians and literary scholars, who sought to understand art as art and literature as literature.

One may question to what extent understanding religion is identical with understanding the sacred, but even granting that identity, one needs to specify what it means to understand the sacred on its own plane of reference. Eliade was fond of citing Rudolf Otto's account of religious experience as the experience of a wholly other that is both terrifying and attractive. For him, however, understanding the sacred involved something different from analyzing a religious person's internal feelings and intuitions. He maintained that "the sacred" manifested itself through specific forms or patterns that appeared repeatedly throughout human history. Through what he called morphology he sought to identify the structure and meanings of these forms. (Because Eliade's morphology resembles what others, such as Gerardus van der Leeuw, were calling "phenomenology," Eliade is often considered a phenomenologist.) Furthermore, Eliade was not entirely clear about the ontological status that he assigned to the sacred. It is possible to read him as simply describing structures of the human mind, analogous to Kant's a priori categories, such as time, space, and cause. This reading is compatible with Eliade's insistence that the sacred is a structure of human consciousness. Nevertheless, to speak of the sacred as manifesting itself—as distinct from the mind constructing, projecting, or imagining the sacred—also seems to attribute ontological reality and independent agency to an object that exists separately from human mental activity.

In any case, Eliade's writings do not generally share a historian's concern for particularity, change, and subtle contextual analysis. Most of his writings in the history of religions focus instead on general forms or structures and propound a two-stage philosophy of history. The first stage is the stage of "archaic man," the paradigmatic *homo religiosus*, "religious man." The second stage is the era of modern humanity, whose relation to religion is more complex. In modernity people consciously reject religious structures but also retain them subconsciously, so that they appear in film, literature, comic books, and other artistic products. Such a two-stage model hardly makes for subtle history. In fact, one of Eliade's defenders, Guilford Dudley, once suggested that Eliade would do well simply to stop presenting his work as history.

THE SACRED AND ITS MANIFESTATIONS

Eliade's theory of religion centers on the experiences of "archaic man," the paradigmatic *homo religiosus*. It is redolent with neologisms and Latin phrases that may give the impression of arcane, out-of-the-ordinary knowledge but that may also make reading difficult for those not trained in classical European languages.

The heart of Eliade's theory of religion is the claim that the sacred manifests itself in the profane. (Aside from the observations that the sacred is the opposite of the profane but also that the sacred unites opposites, technically known as the *coincidentia oppositorum*, the meanings of these terms emerge only as they are used.) He refers to the manifestation of the sacred as a "hierophany," a term coined from the Greek adjective *hieros, -a, -on*, "sacred," and the Greek verb *phainomai*, "to appear." In one particular type of hierophany, the theophany, the sacred manifests itself as a divine being. In another, the kratophany, it manifests itself as a powerful force. In any case, Eliade calls the process of hierophany "the dialectic of the sacred and the profane." While the sacred is the opposite of the profane, it also always manifests itself through the profane. Thus, worshipers of Viṣṇu may find manifestations of the sacred in certain black stones known as *śālagrāmas*. Christians may find manifestations of the sacred in certain pieces of bread and certain cups of wine. In principle, Eliade claims, anything at all may and, over the millennia, probably has at some time or other served as a vehicle for the sacred. "Archaic man" desires to live in proximity to these manifestations of the sacred, for "he" finds in them the source of meaning, being, and truth.

As a historian of religions, Eliade seeks to decipher the meanings of the religious symbols through which the sacred repeatedly manifests itself. He finds symbols rooted in nature particularly important. Thus, *Patterns in Comparative Religion* discusses in turn the symbolism of the sky, the sun, the moon, the waters, stones, the earth (along with women and fertility), vegetation, agricultural fertility, sacred places, and sacred times. For example, water is an amorphous, ambivalent substance. Its shapelessness emblematizes the primal chaos, but it is also the source from which life and ordered existence emerge. To take another example: When the sacred manifests itself in space, it provides orientation. It marks out a sacred center that may be elaborated in terms of cardinal directions, an *axis mundi* (a vertical extension of some sort that unites various planes of existence, such as earth, atmosphere, and sky), or an *imago mundi* (an "image of the world"). Recall that in Eliade's mind, Freud's discovery of the unconscious means that historians of religions do not need to establish that any religious person was ever consciously aware of these symbolic meanings. Even if the meanings were never explicitly formulated, they are nevertheless present. Eliade also refers to these basic patterns as "archetypes," inviting comparison with C. G. Jung. Somewhat at odds with his treatment of Freud, Eliade maintains against Jung that his archetypes do not reside in a collective unconscious. They are, rather, structures of human consciousness.

The forms through which the sacred manifests itself to human beings become realities in the lives of *homo religiosus* through myths and rituals. For Eliade the irruption of the sacred into the profane is a creative event; it produces cosmos (order) amid chaos (disorder). Here we encounter a different sense of the word "archetype": *homo religiosus* finds in these irruptions the archetypes or models for his existence. He associates these archetypes with a special time, discontinuous from the profane duration of everyday life. This time is the time of beginnings, which Eliade refers to as *illud tempus* ("that time"). The events in myths take place *in illo tempore* (in better Latin, *illo tempore*, "at that time"), for, Eliade maintains, the primary myth in every archaic society is the cosmogony, the story of creation. Moreover, every creative act is a replication of the cosmogony. In this way, *homo religiosus* models "his" life on the patterns that were established at the foundations of the world.

If myth recalls the time of beginnings, ritual returns participants to it. It overcomes the disintegrative effects of profane duration and renders *homo religiosus* and his world present at the time of origins, the *fons et origo* (fount and origin) of the world. In other words, in Eliade's view ritual effects a return of all of existence to its initial, pristine state. It brings about a *regressus ad uterum* (return to the womb), not just for human beings but for the cosmos as a whole. This "eternal return" endows *homo religiosus* with a distinctive understanding of time. Religious time is not linear, as in a ceaseless progression from past to future, but cyclical. It is an ongoing series of returns to the origin. In this way *homo religiosus* escapes from a world of secular, profane duration and eludes the terrors of history. Eliade finds such structures quite clearly in initiatory rituals, which utilize the symbolism of death and rebirth to return initiates to the womb and then "rebirth" them as new creatures.

Not all religions exhibit these archaic patterns. Many forms of Christianity do not, although Eliade insists that the "cosmic Christianity" of Romanian peasants does. Above all, however, it was the prophets of ancient Israel that effected a change from time characterized by repeatedly returning to the beginning to time as progression from beginning to end, the time of history and (for Eliade) its terrors. This shift in time would seem to have been the first step along the path to secular modernity, which no longer recognizes the manifestations of the sacred. Eliade calls this lack of recognition the second Fall. (The first Fall is the inevitable shift from the *illud tempus* of origins, mythical events, and rituals to profane duration.)

ASSESSMENT

A balanced assessment of Eliade's thought has proven difficult. His ideas have provoked both sharp criticism and spirited defense. It is impossible to review all of the critiques and rejoinders here. What follows is intended only as a sampling.

Especially since Eliade's death, much attention has focused on his youthful involvement in politics and its relation to his theory of religion. Among others, this work has been pursued by Ivan Strenski, Adriana Berger, Steven Wasserstrom, Daniel Dubuisson, and Russell McCutcheon. In various ways critics have tried to link Eliade's views as an alleged ideologue for Romanian fascism in the form of the Iron Guard and his later analysis of religion.

Some of Eliade's cultural and political writings from the 1930s are indeed shocking, even chilling, in their blindness to the potential for evil in fascism, their antagonism toward minority populations, including but not limited to Jews, and their bald advocacy of what we have come to know as ethnic cleansing. It is especially troubling that, despite the extensive publication of his journals and autobiography, Eliade never clarified his early complicity in one of the most heinous movements of the twentieth century, much less apologized for it. It is reasonable, although not inevitable, to read his assumed apoliticism after the war as hiding, perhaps even from himself, a past tainted by support for fascism and "Hitlerism" (his term). It is equally reasonable both to read his desire to escape the terrors of history as the longings of a guilty conscience and to postulate that there is some continuity between his early, political attempts to redress modernity and his later attempts to do so as a historian of religions. Furthermore, that Eliade makes Jews ultimately responsible for the terrors of history is suspicious, especially when read against the Romanian context.

Nevertheless, while not denying the significance of political criticism, one should also note that even if Eliade were the most politically admirable person of the twentieth century, one could still raise serious questions about his views on religion. The problems are both methodological and theoretical.

In terms of methodology, critics have called into question Eliade's interpretive procedures, his opposition to history, his rejection of reductionist explanations, and what appear, despite his claim to be a historian, to be his theological interests. Consider, for example, Eliade's claim that historians of religions are better positioned to understand religion than historians, philologists, ethnographers, or social scientists, because they alone seek to understand religion as a universal sui generis on its own plane of reference. It is far from clear that this is true. Take Eliade's *Yoga*, a more specialized book that has been relatively well received. Scholars such as Richard Gombrich have charged that the book distorts Buddhism. The last chapter, on aboriginal India, shows almost no awareness of the work that had been done on "aboriginal" India by 1958, when the book appeared. The early parts of the book consist largely of close readings of Sanskrit texts, but even—or especially—in these parts it is not clear that Eliade's perspective as a historian of religions is particularly illuminating. Nothing would seem to be gained, and arguably much muddled, when, after summarizing in the manner of philology the basic views of the Sāṃkhyakārikā in chapter 1, Eliade assumes his identity as a historian of religions and identifies *puruṣa* with the sacred and *prakṛti* with the profane.[2] This identification, like much of Eliade's analysis, simply seems to schematize other people's beliefs and practices in his own terms.

The difficulty is not that Eliade has read the texts hastily or superficially; it is rather that his presuppositions about religion distort the interpretive process. Eliade has misconceived of religion as a natural kind, that is, as a universal object defined by an essence and so one whose properties can be inferred to be present wherever it is found. Moreover, the properties that interest Eliade seem to reflect very particular theological or religious interests. It is difficult to overlook the manner in which his view of religion resonates with the Christian idea of the incarnation (hierophany), the Orthodox Christian account of icons (cf. Ansgar Paus), the apostle Paul's baptismal theology (death and rebirth), and Eliade's own representation of the Christianity of Romanian peasants (an ahistorical openness to the meaning of the cosmos)—all combined with elements of a Platonizing esotericism (the archetypes). Somewhat predictably, the result is a schematization of the world's religions in terms of what would seem to be a particular, complex religious vision.

Perhaps the most careful and powerful critic of Eliade's theory, as well as of his methods and politics, has been Jonathan Z. Smith, a former colleague of Eliade's at the University of Chicago. Taking up Eliade's work with centers and sacred space, Smith suggested that, far from representing religion as a whole, Eliade's account presented "a self-serving ideology which ought not to be generalized into the universal pattern of religious experience and expression."[3] Specifically, Smith offered an alternative to Eliade's "locative" view of religious space, which he called "utopian." In this orientation, always present as a possibility in opposition to Eliade's locative view, human beings do not long for the unity defined by the sacred center but rebel against it, seeking escape and liberation. Not only does Eliade's account of the sacred conceive of religion entirely in a conservative mold, but it makes that view normative, excluding much that otherwise goes by the name of religion. Smith also noted that these two options, locative and utopian, are insufficient, because on a number of occasions religious people occupy a middle position between the conservative establishment of order and its revolutionary overturning, a position represented by playfulness and celebration. Sam Gill has elaborated further upon this critique. He suggests that what Smith's critique of Eliade has identified are not three different maps or conceptualizations of the world but three different attitudes toward it. The attitude that Eliade's essentialist approach to religion has the most difficulty with is the one that, on some views, most characterizes human religious behavior: an attitude of playfulness.

It remains difficult to discern what Eliade's long-term legacy will be. His dominance in the 1960s and 1970s has now generally given way to widespread rejection and antagonism. Nevertheless, it remains possible that his rich production, while not initiating the new humanism that he desired, will continue to exercise an effect.

NOTES

1. This is not to overlook the major contributions of ethnographers, ethnologists, and anthropologists, from whom most theories of religion derived.
2. Sāṃkhya is a dualistic philosophy that analyzes our experiences in terms of the intermingling, under conditions of mistaken identity, of a multiplicity of conscious observers (*puruṣas*) and a single, complex object-of-observation (*prakṛti*), which is the source not only of material nature but also of internal objects such as thoughts and desires. In less technical but also less serviceable terms, our world consists of a multiplicity of people, all of whom observe the same universe.
3. Jonathan Z. Smith, *Relating Religion: Essays in the Study of Religion* (Chicago: University of Chicago Press, 2004), 17.

39

Critical Responses to Phenomenological Theories of Religion

What Kind of Category Is "Religion"?

WILLIAM ARNAL

The conception of religious studies as a discipline, or even as a coherent area of study, requires not only that "religion" be *capable* of some kind of reasonable definition, but that it correspond to a specific set of entities that are, in some fashion, *worth* demarcating for some intellectual purpose. This need to define and defend an academic subject matter creates a pressure to fabricate religion as an autonomous and more or less "natural" or universal aspect of human existence.[1] Nearly all modern theories of and approaches to religion therefore have tended to take for granted the given-ness, and the cultural universality, of religion, even when, as with, for example, Marx or Freud, religious phenomena are reduced to aspects of other (universal) human processes.[2] Insofar as the dominant approach to religious studies today (at least as it affects the teaching and the organization of departments and professional associations) remains phenomenological in its orientation, this tendency is greatly exacerbated, and the purpose of study is imagined to be understanding religion *as* irreducibly *religious*. But there has been an increasing dis-ease with this set of assumptions for decades, beginning almost fifty years ago with the demurrals of Wilfred Cantwell Smith,[3] and gathering increasing momentum in the almost thirty years since the publication of Jonathan Z. Smith's *Imagining Religion*.[4] Since that time, dozens of scholars have, in a variety of different and at times incompatible ways, questioned the cogency, validity, and utility of "religion" as a concept.[5] Such is the present mood that Stanley Stowers asserts that "the rhetoric of despair about 'religion as an object of study' has become nearly hysterical."[6] This "despair" merits examination: Is there something odd, something misleading or problematic, about "religion" as a category? In fact, in my view, there is: the idea of "religion" as a bounded entity and a natural type not only represents an imposition on non-Western and nonmodern cultures (an imposition that could be tolerated if it bore intellectual fruit), but is an analytically incoherent concept, an idea that inhibits, rather than facilitates, our understanding of those phenomena we designate "religious." "Religion" is not fundamentally a scholarly, academic, or analytic category (at least not usefully); it is a political and legal category demarcating cultural territory on which the modern secular state will not tread.

I

Wilfred Cantwell Smith's dis-ease about the category of religion represents, in many ways, the limits of phenomenology, the approach's pursuit to its ultimate conclusions. He takes seriously the phenomenological dictum that religion must be handled on its own (sui generis) terms.[7] He likewise adopts the phenomenological viewpoint that observable religious phenomena are but historically variable expressions[8] of the underlying force that motivates them, that is, a faith in, and relationship to, deity:[9] "A lively faith involves a limpid sincerity of relationship to one's fellow men, and to oneself, and to the Creator or ground or totality of the universe. For these things the formalities of one's religious tradition are at best a channel, and at worst a substitute."[10] In addition to rather less important claims,[11] this observation forms the backbone of Cantwell Smith's critique of "religion" as a notion—it diminishes the experience and claims of the practitioner, and it confuses the manifestation or phenomenon (religion) with the invisible essence (faith, deity) of which the phenomenon is but the contingent shadow.[12] Thus does phenomenology's insistence on apprehending its subject matter "as it presents itself" render that subject matter invisible and impervious to investigation.[13] This paradox also reveals to some degree the *theological* tendentiousness of the idea of religion, insofar as the very notion refers itself to and defines itself in terms of its own commitment and claims to transcendence, and, at the same time, manifests the ambivalence associated with the concept by the religious themselves, insofar as the notion is inadequate to the ineffable "reality" to which it purportedly refers.[14]

Jonathan Z. Smith, more recently and with greater effect, has turned Cantwell Smith's arguments inside out, preserving the insight that classifying phenomena as religious involves a dimension of artificiality and even distortion, but defending the taxon nonetheless. J. Z. Smith agrees with Cantwell Smith that "religion" does not correspond to something "really there" in the world, apart from our formulation of it:

> But man, more precisely western man, has had only the last few centuries in which to imagine religion. That is to say, while there is a staggering amount of data, phenomena, of human experiences and expressions that might be characterized in one culture or another, by one criterion or another, as religion—there is no data for religion. Religion is solely the creation of the scholar's study. It is created for the scholar's analytic purposes by his imaginative acts of comparison and generalization. Religion has no existence apart from the academy.[15]

J. Z. Smith's comments represent an important and influential effort to denaturalize the Idea of "religion." But J. Z. Smith does not draw the conclusion from this that religion as a category should be avoided, cannot be defined, or must not be imposed on the data. Quite the contrary: if our goal is to *understand* those data we designate religious, such an active mental process must, of necessity, involve a transformation and manipulation of those data, classifying them according to *our* questions and agenda rather than merely describing them as they appear to insiders. Cantwell Smith's observation that the religious individual would not recognize our characterizations is for Jonathan Smith not an argument *against* the concept's utility, but an argument *for* it. In a variety of places, J. Z. Smith uses the metaphor of a map to defend and even actively promote the distorting effects of our efforts at classification and explanation. Just as a map's utility consists *precisely* in its schematizing and condensing the territory it represents, in order to make that territory more cognitively apprehensible in particular ways, so also does scholarship necessarily do violence to the data it translates: "it is the very distance and difference of 'religion' as a second-order category that gives it cognitive power."[16] Thus the effect of denaturalization is not a repudiation of the concept, but rather increased self-consciousness about what intellectual processes might be served by demarcating some data as religious data. Cantwell Smith is found standing on his head, and is turned right side up: "religion" is *not* an insider category, but it is for that very reason a valuable intellectual tool for reconfiguring data in intellectually constructive ways.

II

Since the publication in 1982 of J. Z. Smith's *Imagining Religion*, the idea that religion is not a universal, cross-cultural, or natural category has proliferated widely. While many (perhaps still the majority of) students of religion—not only phenomenologists, but also the more recent and quite radical cognitive approaches to religion[17]—continue to treat it as a given and essentially self-evident cross-cultural universal, more and more theoretically and methodologically self-conscious scholars have observed that religion as a category is a culture-specific, historically fixed, and perhaps ideologically loaded fabrication of more or less recent time, one that does not necessarily find parallels in non-Western or nonmodern cultures, and one that taxonomizes the world in ways that separate things those cultures associate, and associate things those cultures separate.[18] More importantly, it may also be that such a division separates things whose association would provide analytical leverage, and associates things that convey no explanatory advantage at all.[19] In the field of anthropology, from which religious studies has traditionally derived its more influential definitions of religion,[20] more sophisticated understandings of religion as a culturally specific, recently fabricated, and perhaps misleading taxon are being explored, especially by Webb Keane and Maurice Bloch.[21] Bloch asserts that "anthropologists have, after countless fruitless attempts, found it impossible to usefully and convincingly cross-culturally isolate or define a distinct phenomenon that can analytically be labeled 'religion.'"[22] Within religious studies as well as anthropology, Talal Asad's earlier challenge to modern assumptions about religion has proven very influential.[23] For Asad, the view of religion as distinctively personal-individual, interiorized, and focused on sincerity of belief is a direct reflection of the modern invention of the secular state:

with the triumphant rise of modern science, modern production, and the modern state, the churches would also be clear about the need to distinguish the religious from the secular, shifting, as they did so, the weight of religion more and more onto the moods and motivations of the individual believer. Discipline (intellectual and social) would, in this period, gradually abandon religious space, letting "belief," "conscience," and "sensibility" take its place.[24]

To some degree the *lineage* of "religion" as a taxon and the *agenda* behind its formulation (and the construction of the academic study thereof) are at issue in these more recent discussions. The problem is not merely that the category of religion fails to "carve nature at the joints," but rather that it carves our data in accord with some misleading, mischievous, or at least nonacademic project.[25] These more recent criticisms agree with Jonathan Z. Smith that religion is a fabricated category, but disagree that it is a *scholarly* fabrication. For those who take this position, "religion" imposes on the non-Western or premodern data normative, or political, or theological undertakings alien to them, reads those endeavors into the data, and turns them into little more than reflections of sociopolitical projects or conclusions native to the European West.

The problem may simply rest in an ethnocentric misreading of *our* issues as *their* issues, a problem not because it fails to take an insider viewpoint "seriously," but because it distorts the data in unhelpful ways. Daniel Dubuisson frames the issue with admirable precision:

> has this notion [that is, religion] nevertheless acquired, thanks to critical studies conducted by the history of religions for more than a century, an indisputable and rigorous definition, capable of aiding us in discovering and understanding . . . anthropological invariables . . . or, on the contrary, captive to its origins and history, has it instead remained a kind of native concept, typically European, gathering and summarizing under its aegis the struggles of a Western consciousness grappling with itself?[26]

His own answer is that "the human sciences (and among them the history of religions) have frequently been content, often unknowingly, sometimes naively, at other times arrogantly, consciously to revive a prejudice—and one of our dearest native categories."[27] Analogously, Daniel Boyarin, locating the origin of the Western notion of religion in the Christianity of the Patristic era,[28] sees in it a potential Christian imposition on other cultures, a projection of *one* religion's own self-image *as* a religion onto those other data sets it chooses to so designate—in the case of Boyarin's analysis, Judaism.[29] Similar claims have been made for Hinduism[30] and Buddhism,[31] among others. If these views have merit, the primary vector for what J. Z. Smith decries as the imposition of theological categories onto the analysis of religious data[32] could be the notion of religion itself.

III

More may be going on, however, than mere oblivious ethnocentrism. Some scholars, particularly those focused on the study of religions of "the East," have argued that "religion" is used as a stalking horse for colonial agenda, as is the identification of variegated national-ethnic traditions as reified and single "religions" (for example, "Hinduism"). Influenced the discourse criticism of Michel Foucault and by postcolonial theorists such as Edward Said, the very act of classification itself is seen as an act of power, an imposition on native cultural patterns and types of knowledge.[33] The fact that it is first the colonial administrator and then secondarily the Western scholar who gets to classify types of native discourse as "religious" (or conversely as something else: "philosophical," "legal," "magical," "terrorist," and so on) or as manifestations of *this* and not *that* tradition shows this act of classification for what it is: a political activity, and one particularly related to the colonial and imperial situation of a foreign power rendering newly encountered societies digestible and manipulable in terms congenial to its own culture and agenda.

According to such views, the very point of religious studies as a field may be to process the data generated by the colonial project, implicating the scholar deeply in the mechanisms of state. Such a view of religion is nicely exemplified by Tomoko Masuzawa: " 'World religions' as a category and as a conceptual framework initially developed in the European academy . . . quickly became an effective means of differentiating, variegating, consolidating, and totalizing a large portion of the social, cultural, and political practices observable among the inhabitants of regions elsewhere in the world."[34]

Likewise, Daniel Dubuisson sees something insidious involved in the application of this native European category to outsiders: a mode of affirming our own sense of superiority. Insofar as "religion" is a Western and European concept, it will find its clearest and most developed manifestations in European avatars. As a result, to universalize the category is to create a universal *human* quality or characteristic that is, in fact, best manifested in the European person, hence marking that person's superiority. Dubuisson describes this process as leading to overt rationalizations for imperialism:

> The majority of other religions were henceforth viewed as rough drafts, archaic or primitive forms of our religion. The universal undeniably exists, but at different stages of development. By having these religions succeed one another along a single temporal axis, where the West clearly occupied the terminal position, the differences that were observed lost all capacity to subvert. . . . At a single stroke, imperialism and colonialism were equally justified and even, with the impetus of missionary activity, received an unanticipated moral guarantee.[35]

Or again, Timothy Fitzgerald sees the creation of "religion" as a way of sidelining and deprecating native traditions, while simultaneously naturalizing the functioning of the modern Western state and economy.[36]

According to such readings as these, the category religion and the choice to use that category to make sense of data derived from other cultures represent not the map-making of self-conscious scholarship, but at *best* the distorting and un-self-conscious imposition of native European categories onto cultures that do not share the same organizational principles of those of European modernity, making those cultures into little more than mirrors for our own prejudices and self-understanding. At *worst*, it represents a deliberate and self-interested exercise of discursive power, an imperial dissection of others' cultures into manageable bits, and their relegation to the irrelevant realm of the supernatural. At issue, then, in much of the current discussion is not so much the artificiality of the category of religion as its implication in political agendas of questionable merit.

IV

With all of this in mind, my own view is that the most useful way of thinking about the category of religion is as a historically specific, emic product of the West, an anthropological folk category tied up with the development of the modern state, and the ways in which the modern state has defined itself as *secular*, and thereby needed to generate a shadow image of itself, a realm of collective voluntary commitment rooted in (irrational, variable, and uncompelled) personal belief, that the state would not partake of or constrain.[37] Thus we may answer the question as to what kind of category religion is by asserting that religion is first and foremost a *political* category, albeit an ambivalent one, with its apotropaic function of referring to qualities from which the state seeks to *dissociate* itself. This fundamentally political role is reinforced by the fact that the most consequential and efficacious definitions of religion are those of the state, embodied in the tax code and in judicial decisions about what does and does not constitute religious observance. As Winnifred Sullivan points out, this means that the government itself defines the realm in which "religious freedom" is allowed to operate, thus making that "freedom" paradoxically subject to the edict of the state.[38]

Historically, this concept of religion is secondary to the development of states that dissociated themselves from ecclesiastical institutions to the point of distinguishing citizenship independently of church affiliation, a process begun in the Reformation and culminating in revolutionary secular states in America (1776) and France (1789). The idea of religion as a bounded, independent, distinguishable, and above all universal aspect of human sociality is the product of a specifically Western history.

It is true of course that there are periods for which and cultures in which concepts akin to our modern notion of religion do surface. Daniel Boyarin, for instance, points to expressions of identity in late antiquity that appear to revolve around types of allegiance to the divine.[39] Or again, the category might be applied to any number of premodern discussions of observances with respect to the gods or cult (for example, Cicero's *de legibus* and *de natura deorum*, Plutarch's *de superstitione*). But it takes until the modern period for the notion of religion to be generalized. Only in the last five centuries or so, and with increasing force in the last two hundred years, has the liberal notion of the state as a *negative* entity developed, that is, the belief that the role of the state is to *protect* individual self-expression, rather than constitute it. Religion is created as the shadow image, the denied other, of that secular state, as the personal self-construction of an identity imagined as *distinct* from national identity; and this state of affairs is naturalized and universalized as the common condition of the human race. What we call "religion" is not theorized as an invariable and cross-cultural feature of human nature—never mind a feature with the kind of deracinated, apolitical, otherworldly force we moderns accord it—until the institutionalized secular state established as semipermanent its "religion's" condition of possibility.

That condition of possibility can be elaborated more precisely. Maurice Bloch notes that those kinds of phenomena we tend to categorize as "religion" are in themselves little more than (an arbitrary subset of) representations of the social abstract, a "transcendental social consist[ing] of essentialized roles and groups."[40] As such they do not constitute a natural clade at all—they are intertwined with and to be understood alongside and as functionally identical to other varying forms of imaginative social self-reference such as nationalism,[41] prejudice, kinship groupings, and so on. It is only on those occasions when *some types* of social self-reference— the mythology and symbology of who "we" are—for one reason or another come to be detached from the mechanisms and conception of the state, whatever those may be, that the strange deracinated cultural signifier we moderns call "religion" seems to rear its head. It is precisely for this reason that we do encounter phenomena that *look* like our notion of "religion" long before the invention of religion as an important modern taxon. At any time or in any place in which for one reason or another the coercive state power is detached from other types of social self-signification, we misrecognize the latter as a *thing*, "religion." Again, however, it is only with the advent of the modern nation—in which the ecclesiastical frameworks for expressing the social imaginary are expelled from the purview of the state, or from state compulsion and discipline—as the normative state of affairs that this distinction comes to be permanent and institutional, and, hence, comes to be generalized as a universal and crucial category of human experience.

Religion has thus come to be, as a result of the Western invention of a form of state that deliberately dissociates itself from certain aspects of social identity (that is, those it identifies as "religious," in part because of their past association with ecclesiastical institutions), a central cultural tool that we—modern, Western heirs to Reformation, Enlightenment, revolution, and the secular nation-state—use to describe and make sense of ourselves: our history; our commitments, subjectivities, and identities; and (above all else) our circumscribed political institutions as distinct from other types of social activity. Moreover, "the separation of religion from the transcendental social in general is, even in the places where it appears at first to exist, superficial and transient."[42] The unstable and arbitrary historical accident that creates a sharp division *within* the field of the social imaginary has thus generated a rather ambivalent and incoherent conceptual tool, a category that gets justified, demarcated, and defended in self-contradictory ways. Religion is identified with the quintessence of the human self, the most ineffable interiority, the ultimate concern so powerful as to be immune from criticism or coercion; and simultaneously it is peripheralized as irrational, as subject to individual and arbitrary choice, and as positively ruled out of state activity and effective social potency. It comes to refer to a realm of human desire that is simultaneously ideal and unreal; in fact, the category *as* a category implicitly asserts that what is ideal *is* unreal, is unrealizable socially. It is precisely for this reason that the religiously committed cannot concede that what they are doing is in fact "religion," as Cantwell Smith noted. They are wary of the devil's bargain that they are permitted complete freedom to pursue whatever "religious" practices and beliefs they wish,[43] in exchange for which they must assent to the cost of those practices and beliefs being utterly irrelevant. The price of religious freedom is eternal insignificance.

V

This conclusion has ramifications for the role the imposition of "religion" as a discursive element might have had in European colonialism. In my view, postcolonialist readings of religion as itself a tool for colonization or as the direct product of reflection on newly "discovered" cultures' (various) doctrines of and practices related to the gods may be somewhat overstated. The European West *always* had contact with peoples of differing views and cultural practices: Muslims and Jews, most obviously, but also pagan Europeans well into the Middle Ages (and beyond, in epic literature and the like), the classical pagans via history, literature, and philosophy, and even (albeit more problematically) Christian heretics and apostates. So it is not as though Europe lived in a dreamland of borderless Christian totality, like water in water, until the shocking discovery of Columbus that some people did not believe in Jesus. Certainly overseas exploration contributed data and additional impetus to develop categories with which to relate "their" practices to "our" practices, but it did not introduce the European awareness of religio-cultural difference. Nor again can the sometimes-romantic characterizations of precontact non-Europeans be sustained. It is not as though prior to the onslaught of Enlightenment disenchantment all the world lived in an undifferentiated cultural soup, a kind of unmediated, undivided integrity of spirit infusing all of daily life. *All* cultures and *all* societies carve up the world, make distinctions, classify both objects and social practices, albeit in different ways.[44] So it avails us little—aside from producing a frisson of moral horror and self-loathing—to imagine the incursion of European conquistadors as a kind of Freudian trauma, a radical shock to a body politic earlier marked by primordial integration. Besides being excessively romantic, such an argument against religion as a category can (somewhat ironically) provide a high-minded rationalization for a return to the phenomenological insistence on taking "religion" as it presents itself, that is, as incomparable, transcendent, and ultimately unanalyzable. As Bruce Lincoln notes incisively, "When one permits those whom one studies to define the terms in which they will be understood, [and] suspends one's interest in the temporal and contingent, . . . one has ceased to function as historian or scholar."[45]

The European application of "religion" to societies first encountered in the modern period via voyages of exploration is probably not in the first instance a deliberate effort to *dominate* but to *understand*. This involves the simple, if flawed, process of Europeans somewhat naively applying their own (limited and culture-specific) categories onto "strange" data. The effect *is* ethnocentric, and can be unhelpfully distorting; among other things, such wholesale imposition of one's own native categories can make one blind to the strangenesses of the data, to the genuinely illuminating *differences* between "us" and "them." Moreover, it is certainly true that knowledge, manifested in taxonomizing the novelties one encounters, does express a will to power. But the main work being done with the category religion seems to concern *European* subjectivity, states, and self-identity. The imposition of these self-images on others,[46] while distorting and even oppressive, is fundamentally a claim that those others are in some important way "like us," are, in a word, human (and hence understandable). In fact, such likeness was seriously open to question among explorers of the early modern period, and some in fact denied "religion" to "the natives,"[47] a position that, as Dubuisson notes, was openly dehumanizing.[48] The use of religion as a cross-cultural category implies by contrast that the other is not sheer incomprehensible difference.

In fact, in light of what was said above about the origins of the idea of "religion," it is easy to see why the imposition of colonial rule would bring with it a greater tendency to identify religion among those colonized: the state power has been seized by outsiders, but a persistent sense of "us" remains within the culture thus dominated. In this sense, then, colonialism—Western or not!—really does *create* "religion." It does so not simply or primarily by imposing a Western taxon on non-Western cultures, but by creating a kind of ideological lacuna, a situation in which the social body is divided against itself and is imagined in a kind of bifurcated condition. The disempowered side of that bifurcation will then look to us moderns like what we call religion. The flaw or misconception at the heart of "religion" as a category is thus probably not to be found primarily in its oppressive importation into non-Western contexts by modern colonialism. Rather, the concept's weakness derives from its origins as a political creation rather than an academic one, as well as the fact that the political agenda expressed in the concept is self-contradictory, confused, and ambivalent, making the concept itself enormously incoherent. As Maurice Bloch vividly expresses it: "To explain religion is therefore a fundamentally misguided enterprise. It is rather like trying to explain the function of headlights while ignoring what motorcars are like and for. What needs to be explained is the nature of human sociability, and then religion simply appears as an aspect of this that cannot stand alone."[49]

VI

In sum, then, we might conclude that Jonathan Z. Smith is at least partly wrong: "religion" is *not* a scholarly category or construct.[50] Most scholarly efforts to define religion have in fact simply been efforts to identify the natural type to which this Euro-Western folk category (perhaps imperfectly) must surely refer.[51] At the same time, though, Jonathan Z. Smith is also partly right: we are trying to *understand* our data, and to do so requires us to some degree to frame that data in terms of the categories that make sense to us, even if in so doing we distort them somewhat or offend those whom we seek to understand. Self-critical reflection on the taxonomies of religious studies should not become an excuse for resorting to simple repetition and description of insider claims.

The value of "religion" will not depend on its isometry with the data it delineates and shapes,[52] or on the validity of its claims to universal applicability. Rather, it will depend on the capacity the category might continue (or not) to have to surprise, to clarify, and to shape and transform our own organization of the human universe. If "religion" as an idea forces upon us new and helpful understandings of familiar data, if it leads to us juxtaposing phenomena we might not otherwise think to compare, and if in the process it leads us continually to rectify the taxonomy from which we started, it serves a valuable intellectual purpose, even if it does not refer to anything "real." If, by contrast, the category does little more than provide a justification for comparing things we already see to be similar (or, worse, identical), if it simply reinforces our prejudices or turns foreign cultural data into evidence for the naturalness of our own practices and assumptions, then it is not simply intellectually unhelpful—it is positively pernicious. Which of these judgments is closer to the truth is a matter for debate. What is important—and what is promising about the present juncture in the field of religious studies—is that the question does get raised.

NOTES

Please note that a modified version of this article also appears as chapter 6 of William Arnal and Russell McCutcheon, *The Sacred Is the Profane: The Political Nature of "Religion"* (Oxford: Oxford University Press, 2012). Reprinted with permission from Oxford University Press.

1. So, for example, Russell T. McCutcheon, *Manufacturing Religion: The Discourse on Sui Generis Religion and the Politics of Nostalgia* (Oxford: Oxford University Press, 1997), 202; Tomoko Masuzawa, *The Invention of World Religions; Or, How European Universalism Was Preserved in the Language of Pluralism* (Chicago: University of Chicago Press, 2005), 316–17.

2. Durkheim constitutes something of an exception here; his definition of religion, whatever its problems, remains rigorously and thoroughly sociological, and hence leaves little "religious" in place to anchor it to the transcendent. See, for example, Émile Durkheim, *The Elementary Forms of Religious Life*, trans. Carol Cosman (Oxford: Oxford University Press, 2001), 36: "The division of the world into two comprehensive domains, one sacred, the other profane, is the hallmark of religious thought. . . . A rock, a tree, a spring, a stone, a piece of wood, a house, in other words anything at all, can be sacred."

3. Wilfred Cantwell Smith, *The Meaning and End of Religion: A New Approach to the Religious Traditions of Mankind* (New York: Mentor, 1962).

4. Jonathan Z. Smith, *Imagining Religion: From Babylon to Jonestown* (Chicago: University of Chicago Press, 1988).

5. For example, Talal Asad, *Genealogies of Religion: Discipline and Reasons of Power in Christianity and Islam* (Baltimore: Johns Hopkins University Press, 1993); Daniel Dubuisson, *The Western Construction of Religion: Myths, Knowledge, and Ideology*, trans. William Sayers (Baltimore: Johns Hopkins University Press, 2003); Russell T. McCutcheon, *The Discipline of Religion: Structure, Meaning, Rhetoric* (London: Routledge, 2003); Timothy Fitzgerald, *The Ideology of Religious Studies* (Oxford: Oxford University Press, 2000); and others.

6. Stanley K. Stowers, "The Ontology of Religion," in *Introducing Religion*, ed. Willi Braun and Russell T. McCutcheon (London: Equinox, 2008), 434. Interestingly, Stowers echoes here the observation of Cantwell Smith (Cantwell Smith, *Meaning and End of Religion*, 110) that the term "religion" carries a sense of malaise with it.

7. See, for example, Smith, *Meaning and End of Religion*, 154–55.

8. Ibid., 155.

9. Ibid., 114–17.

10. Ibid., 117.

11. That is, that religion as a concept is a culturally bounded notion specific to Islam and Christianity (Cantwell Smith, *Meaning and End of Religion*, 110–14), and that the term "religion" and, even more so, the names (and ideas) of individual "religions" (that is, Islam, Buddhism, Christianity) reify and make monolithic what are in fact extremely complex and historically changeable phenomena. Such an argument neglects the extent to which category formation is something we undertake precisely in order to simplify matters.

12. Cantwell Smith, *Meaning and End of Religion*, 124. This is stated clearly by Cantwell Smith, who claims that the student of religion runs the risk of "omitting not only the vitality but the most significant of all factors in that vitality, namely its relation with transcendence. The observer's concept of a religion is by definition constituted of what can be observed. Yet the whole pith and substance of religious life lies in its relation to what cannot be observed." Jonathan Z. Smith likewise characterizes Cantwell Smith's argument as boiling down to this claim. See Jonathan Z. Smith, "Bible and Religion," in *Relating Religion: Essays in the Study of Religion* (Chicago: University of Chicago Press, 2004), 214*n*28.

13. The similarities between the claims of phenomenology of religion about its subject matter and those of Calvinist theology about the Eucharist are striking and bear further investigation. For both, outer form is a vector for immaterial, spiritual content, which must not be confused or conflated with that content. See Webb Keane, *Christian Moderns: Freedom and Fetish in the Mission Encounter* (Berkeley: University of California Press, 2007), 61–65.

14. Strangely, Cantwell Smith's demurrals are paralleled today in the popular phenomenon of individuals claiming to be "spiritual, not religious." This suggests that Cantwell Smith, perhaps, is just as much a religious datum in need of explanation as are the self-described "spiritual." On this terminology and its significance for our understanding of religion,

see Janet M. Klippenstein, "Imagine No Religion: On Defining 'New Age,'" *Studies in Religion* 34, nos. 3–4 (2005): 391–403.

15. Smith, *Imagining Religion*, xi.

16. Smith, "Bible and Religion," 208.

17. This is a fatal weakness of the otherwise-promising cognitive approaches: their tendency to treat "religion" as a given, rather than the artificial and, especially, culturally specific (that is, Western and modern) category that it is. Note, for example, the title of Pascal Boyer, *The Naturalness of Religious Ideas: A Cognitive Theory of Religion* (Berkeley: University of California Press, 1994). This weakness of cognitive approaches is discussed brilliantly in Maurice Bloch, "Why Religion Is Nothing Special but Is Central," *Philosophical Transactions of the Royal Society* 363 (February 2008): 2055–61.

18. See the helpful discussion in Malory Nye, *Religion: The Basics* (London: Routledge, 2003), 12–18; cf. Dubuisson, *Western Construction*, 112–15.

19. In other words, religion is a *polyphyletic* category—it associates and confuses objects that range across different categories. An excellent example of such categorization is found in the discussion of *zebras* offered under the rubric of "What, if anything, is a zebra?" in Stephen J. Gould, *Hen's Teeth and Horse's Toes* (New York: Norton, 1983), 355–65.

20. Especially that of Clifford Geertz, "Religion as a Cultural System," in *Anthropological Approaches to the Study of Religion*, ed. Michael Banton (London: Tavistock, 1985), 1–46. I also note that the variety of attempts to cut the Gordian knot by resorting to more "common-sense" and abrupt definitions of religion as discourse pertaining to "nonobvious" or "counterintuitive" beings is little more than a restatement of E. B. Tylor's—also anthropological—definition of religion as discourse pertaining to "spiritual beings."

21. See, for example, Bloch, "Religion Is Nothing Special"; Keane, *Christian Moderns*.

22. Bloch, "Religion Is Nothing Special," 2055.

23. Asad, *Genealogies of Religion*.

24. So ibid., 39; cf. also Talal Asad, *Formations of the Secular: Christianity, Islam, Modernity* (Stanford: Stanford University Press, 2003), 181–94; William E. Arnal, "Definition (of Religion)," in *Guide to the Study of Religion*, ed. Willi Braun and Russell T. McCutcheon (London: Cassell, 2000), 30–33; Keane, *Christian Moderns*, 213–14; McCutcheon, *Manufacturing Religion*, 127–57; and others.

25. Plato, *Phaedrus*, 265d–266a.

26. Dubuisson, *Western Construction*, 5–6.

27. Ibid., 115.

28. See Daniel Boyarin, "The Christian Invention of Judaism: The Theodosian Empire and the Rabbinic Refusal of Religion," in *Religion: Beyond a Concept*, ed. H. de Vries (New York: Fordham University Press, 2008), 152–54, citing, among others, Gregory Nazianzen, Eusebius, and Epiphanius. This early identification of the "invention" of religion is somewhat odd, but not unique—a number of theorists see in the initial separation of ideological commitments from the state, found in nascent Christianity in part due to its illegality and in a definition of cultural entities in terms of commitments to and modes of worship of a given deity, a foreshadowing or even an initial fabrication of the modern notion of religion.

29. So, ibid.

30. See, for example, Richard King, *Orientalism and Religion: Postcolonial Theory, India and "the Mystic East"* (London: Routledge, 1999).

31. See the discussion in Masuzawa, *Invention of World Religions*, 121–46.

32. See, for example, his comments in Jonathan Z. Smith, *Drudgery Divine: On the Comparison of Early Christianities and the Religions of Late Antiquity* (Chicago: University of Chicago Press, 1990), 34.

33. See, for example, Nye, *Religion*, 12–15.

34. Masuzawa, *Invention of World Religions*, 20; cf. 29. For an example of how native political actions in a colonial context can be redrawn as "religious" and, in the process, attenuated, see McCutcheon, *Manufacturing Religion*, 167–77.

35. Dubuisson, *Western Construction*, 114–15.

36. For example, Fitzgerald, *Ideology of Religious Studies*, 8.

37. For an elaboration of this view, see, among others, Asad, *Genealogies of Religion*; Arnal, "Definition"; William E. Arnal, "The Segregation of Social Desire: 'Religion' and Disney World," *Journal of the American Academy of Religion* 69, no. 1 (March 2001): 1–19; Timothy Fitzgerald, "Encompassing Religion, Privatized Religions and the Invention of Modern Politics," in *Religion and the Secular: Historical and Colonial Formations*, ed. Timothy Fitzgerald (London: Equinox, 2007), 211–40; Fitzgerald, *Discourse on Civility and Barbarity: A Critical History of Religion and Related Categories* (Oxford: Oxford University Press, 2007); McCutcheon, *Discipline of Religion*, 230–90.

38. Winnifred F. Sullivan, *The Impossibility of Religious Freedom* (Oxford: Oxford University Press, 2005).

39. So Boyarin, "Christian Invention of Judaism."

40. Bloch, "Religion Is Nothing Special," 2056.

41. Cf. Benedict Anderson's characterization of nation as an "imagined community." Benedict Anderson, *Imagined Communities: Reflections on the Origin and Spread of Nationalism*, rev. ed. (London: Verso, 2006).

42. Bloch, "Religion Is Nothing Special," 2060.

43. With the important caveat, noted earlier, that this "freedom" is in fact circumscribed by the state itself, insofar as a practice or belief must be legally defined as religion to be thus protected—the initial gesture of state noninvolvement is state definition.

44. Note, too, that among other things this means that cultural influences never move simply from the dominating to the dominated culture, but are *reciprocal*. This is a point made perhaps most forcefully by Marshall Sahlins, although others have noted it as well; see especially Marshall Sahlins, *Islands of History* (Chicago: University of Chicago Press, 1987).

45. So Bruce Lincoln, "Reflections on 'Theses on Method,'" in *Secular Theories on Religion: Current Perspectives*, ed. Tim Jensen and Mikael Rothstein (Copenhagen: Museum Tusculanum Press, 2000), 120–21. See also his comments in the same piece specifically addressing the scholar's descriptions of other cultures (ibid., 119): "Reverence is a religious, and not a scholarly virtue. When good manners and good conscience cannot be reconciled, the demands of the latter ought to prevail. Many who would not think of insulating their own or their parents' religion against critical inquiry still afford such protection to other people's faiths, via a stance of cultural relativism. One can

appreciate their good intentions, while recognizing a certain displaced defensiveness, as well as the guilty conscience of western imperialism."

46. Often in the deeply misleading form of "human nature," on which see Marshall Sahlins, *The Western Illusion of Human Nature: With Reflections on the Long History of Hierarchy, Equality, and the Sublimation of Anarchy in the West, and Comparative Notes on Other Conceptions of the Human Condition* (Chicago: Prickly Paradigm, 2008).

47. For example, Jonathan Z. Smith, "Religion, Religions, Religious," in *Relating Religion: Essays in the Study of Religion* (Chicago: University of Chicago Press, 2004), 179, refers to Pedro Cieza de León's *Crónica del Péru* (1553) as denying religion to Andean indigenous peoples; Nancy Senior, " 'Sathans Inventions and Worships': Two 17th-Century Clergymen on Native American Religions," *Studies in Religion* 35, no. 2 (2006): 279–80, refers to Samuel de Champlain's *Des sauvages* (1603) and Gabriel Sagard's *Le grand voyage du pays des Hurons* (1632) for the idea that while North American natives may believe in God, they have no systemic worship.

48. Dubuisson, *Western Construction*, 114.

49. Bloch, "Religion Is Nothing Special," 2060.

50. It may be used as such, as it clearly is in Smith's own work, but this seems more the exception than the rule.

51. This, in my view, is all that is accomplished, for instance, by the excruciating definitional efforts of Geertz, "Religion as a Cultural System."

52. As Smith stresses, it is precisely the difference between analytic concepts and the self-presentation of the data that gives those concepts explanatory force. So, for example, Smith, "Bible and Religion," 208.

40

Critical Religion

"Religion" Is Not a Stand-Alone Category

TIMOTHY FITZGERALD

It is well known that religion is essentially peace-loving, nonviolent, nonpolitical, concerned with the inner spiritual life and the other world. Religion is kind, tolerant, gentle, nonpolitical and nonprofit-making. Religion is a matter of personal faith and piety, essentially separated from the nonreligious secular state, from politics, and from economics. Religion is concerned with personal and family morality, but not with laws, which are the affair of the state. Religion is essentially that domain of private experience in which the individual soul concerns itself with the rewards and punishments of an afterlife in another world.

On the other hand it is equally well known that religion is essentially barbarous, violent, and irrational, causing conflicts through religious terrorism and religious nationalism. This view of religion as essentially violent and irrational is popular today, especially since 9/11. It is said—frequently said—that if religion is confused with politics it becomes dangerously unstable, like a Molotov cocktail. It ceases to be true (pure) religion, and becomes a compound of incompatible elements that will blow up in our face.

This is also a matter of rationality and irrationality, of civility and barbarity. A benign, reasonable religious group understands the logic of separation, as any decent chemist understands that certain chemical elements should not be mixed. Being reasonable, such groups or individuals sensibly accept religion's voluntary and private status, and generally subscribe to the sentiment that one should give unto Caesar the things that are Caesar's, and unto God the things that are God's. Whether one can honestly say that the pope's status conforms to this modern logic is arguable. He is, after all, Pontifex Maximus, a title he inherited directly from the divine Roman emperor. This is one of the reasons why Protestants used to refer to the pope as the Whore of Babylon. But Catholicism has a certain respectability even in the citadels of secular capital. It is at least European and Christian after a fashion. Sadly, barbarous "religious" foreigners do not understand the distinction between Caesar and God, and they do not grasp rational (secular) politics. However, though irrational and fanatical, religious terrorists are cunning, more cunning than their nonreligious cousins. From the point of view of State power, whether US, Chinese, or other, some religious leaders—mullahs, imams, the Dalai Lama, Buddhist monks in Vietnam and Burma, Jesuit priests in Latin America, or whoever cleaves to a powerful alternative view of the world that challenges the values and institutionalized practices of capitalism—pretend to be religious but are *really* political. They *use* religion illegitimately for what are truly political ends.

Classifying groups and their leaders as religious, or as genuinely religious, or as pretending to be religious but really being political, is a widespread practice that is parasitic on an ideological fiction, a discourse supported by courts of law, academics, and politicians, and reported widely in the media.

In all these discourses there is a tacit idea that the nonreligious secular State is (to paraphrase William T. Cavanaugh) essentially peace-loving and reasonable, and only reluctantly violent, as in "the war on terror." The contemporary flourishing of the military-industrial complex and the vast outreach of US military power should not lead us to confuse the rational and reluctant political violence of the peace-loving secular state with the mad acts of savagery perpetrated by "religious" fanatics who cannot see the wisdom of markets or the rational inevitability of private property.

If, however, we take account—with writers such as King and Carrette in their book *Selling Spirituality* (2005)—of the unlimited devotion to capital and the ideology of "free" markets that the modern State serves and protects, then we can ask if capitalism is not itself a religion.[1] Liberal capitalism has many of the characteristics that are typically attributed to "religion." This observation leads me to propose that, instead of uncritically assuming a universally valid binary distinction between religious and nonreligious secular practices, we instead see a vast network of human practices that have both distinctive characteristics and overlapping resemblances. Thus, *buddha dhamma* (usually mistranslated as the religion Buddhism) as it is practiced in southeast Asia is profoundly different from the Catholic faith, so much so that their simultaneous classification as "religions" stretches the credibility of the category. Yet some versions of the liberal Protestant faith seem closer to faith in money, progress, and market salvation. And again in turn the science of economics looks suspiciously more like astrology in its predictive practices than, say, yoga.

If liberal capitalism fulfills many of the usual criteria of a "religious faith"— arguably as many characteristics as other human practices—then what are the implications for our classification systems? The very idea of secular courts and constitutions, secular schools and universities, secular knowledge, including the so-called science of economics, becomes problematic. For the claim that such domains are nonreligiously secular depends on a parasitical relation to the idea of the religious as something essentially different. Embedded in our daily language and our institutions is the presumption of an essential difference between secular and religious experiences or practices. By reclassifying as "religious" our faith in capital and its ritual management by state and city functionaries, we have trouble locating the imagined domain of the nonreligious secular at all. Meanwhile, the term "religion" becomes so all-inclusive as to fade into useless abstraction. This kind of radical instability in usages of the term "religion" and its relation to these other categories, taken as a globalizing

Anglophone discourse that is rhetorically manipulated by specific agents in specific power contexts, leads to a consideration of the term "critical religion."

"CRITICAL RELIGION" AS A TERM

I use the term "critical religion" as shorthand for the critical study of the category "religion" and its discursive formations in relation to other categories, such as "pagan" in the older discourse and the nonreligious secular in the prevailing dominant mode. Clearly, if religion is not a stand-alone category but wedded inescapably to the nonreligious secular, then critical religion amounts to a project for bringing to light the interlinked ideological functions of the so-called nonreligious domains that are parasitic on the invention of religion for their conceptualization. The categories with which "religion" has historically and significantly been linked in various ways can be discovered through the analysis of texts and other discursive media. A category can be linked to others in various ways, for example by identity, or simile, or separation, or encompassment. Some obvious candidates of categories related to "religion" in one or another way are "ecclesiastical," "spiritual," "temporal," "pagan," "civil," "civility," "barbarity," "secular," "politics," "the state," "science," "economics," "sacred," and "profane." These are all English-language terms with close readings in some other European languages; and they all have an Anglophone or widely Europhone history.[2] None of these terms has any essential, ahistorical meaning that can be captured, for example, by a stable and enduring definition that does not itself represent some interest. However, some categories have greater scope for generating ideological illusion than others. Some of these terms are ancient but have taken on significantly new meanings in modern discourses. Some are modern inventions. All of these words are and have been controlled in their dominant usages by powerful interests of one kind or another, and are not therefore simply neutral players in a language game. If by game we mean something played for fun, then language games are not really games at all (though what is a game?) but are possible constructions of the world that have been prioritized because they serve powerful and dominant interests.[3] The expression "politic state of the nation" has a significantly different nuance from "the nation is a political state," even though there are shared significant terms.

To give a simple but powerful example to which I return in more detail below: the dominant discourse on "religion" for centuries concerned Christian Truth, and on this meaning, Religion was related by mutual exclusion with pagan barbarity. However, pagan barbarity was also defined *by* Christian Truth at the moment that it was being posited as its "other"; and the meaning of Christian Truth was tightly controlled by the ecclesiastical and civil authorities. I suggest that the idea of "religions" in the plural, though evident in discourses going back at least to the late sixteenth century or early seventeenth, was an ironic conceit until the late eighteenth century (and probably still is in many contemporary discourses). A non-Christian "religion," if the expression was used, meant an irrational pagan substitute for Truth, in other words a sign of being lost to barbarity and damnation. Only since relatively recently has the supposedly neutral idea of generic "religion"—that is, religion as universally manifested in different "religions," languages, and cultural contexts at all times of history and even prehistory—become dominant. These older and more recent constructions of "religion" are fundamentally antagonistic to each other. Yet the older discourse of religion as Christian Truth (of which presumably there could only be one) and also the modern, more dominant discourse of generic religion as a universal aspect of human nature and society are both current and entangled together in texts across the humanities and social sciences. I shall argue that this ambiguity enhances the rhetorical power of a category such as religion-secular.[4] The border between them is thoroughly permeable, and what gets to be included or excluded can depend on the rhetorical needs of the writer or speaker at any given time. I suggest that the main function of contemporary discourses on religion is not to report what is there, but to embed without question the supposed natural rationality and disinterestedness of the nonreligious secular. The secular is the authoritative ground from which the judge, scholar, politician, and scientist claim to make her or his pronouncements.

RELIGIONS ARE NOT OBJECTS THAT EXIST IN THE WORLD, BUT COLLECTIVE IMAGINARY CONSTRUCTIONS

Many experts on the religions of the world talk and write as though these are observable entities that can be empirically investigated for their properties. Some academics push further and write as though religion is not only an observable object but even a transcendental agent that manifests him- or herself in different "religions." Religion is depicted as an agent with an agenda, central to which is the unjust harassment of the peace-loving secular state.

Jonathan Fox, in his article in the *Journal of Peace Research*, "The Rise of Religious Nationalism and Conflict: Ethnic Conflict and Revolutionary Wars, 1945–2001," claims to be able to prove statistically that religion has a special relation to violence. This assumption derives in part from the popular but misleading narrative about how the Peace of Westphalia of 1648 brought the Wars of Religion to an end and established the modern nation-state. Religion, which at that time meant mainly Catholic or Protestant Christian claims to truth, legitimacy, and civility, became associated with intolerance and fanatical violence, and the story has it that, as a result, the neutral, nonreligious secular state had to be invented to keep the peace. Religion was sent into "exile," banished from public life, disciplined by rational government, privatized, and transformed into a purely personal faith practice concerned with God, with the inner, with judgment in the other world.

From this point on, the general progress of humankind, securely founded on natural secular reason instead of wild faith, was able to surge ahead, until suddenly and inexplicably since the late 1970s, and especially with 9/11, "religion" in various forms—the Iranian revolution, Hindu or Sikh nationalism, Islamic jihad, and others—awoke from its slumbers in exile, where it had refused to die, and resurged as a global agent in the world.

The author uses statistics from two databases, Minorities at Risk (MAR) and State Failure (SF). He is interested in why "religion" was so comprehensively ignored by IR theorists as an important factor in world politics before around 1980, and why it suddenly became such a major concern. Fox answers the first question in the following way:

> Rather than having a theory as to why religion was not important, international relations tended to focus on factors that did not include religion. Paradigms like realism, liberalism, and globalism placed their emphasis on military and economic factors as well as rational calculations, all of which left little room for religion. . . . This trend can be traced to the fact that the academic study of international relations was founded upon, among other things, the belief that the era of religion causing wars was over.[5]

Note that, according to this passage, paradigms that focus on rational calculation, and on military and economic issues, leave "little room for religion."

Why, then, was there a dramatic upsurge in the place of religion in international affairs in the thinking of IR specialists? All of these assumptions began to be questioned from the late 1970s and early 1980s as a result of such events as the Iranian revolution, the rise of the "religious right" in US politics, the events in Waco, Texas, in 1993, and of course 9/11. These events had a galvanizing effect such that "by the beginning of the 21st century, a considerable body of theory developed, positing that religion remains important in the modern era. To an extent, this body of theory was inspired by the facts on the ground. Simply put, real world events have disproved the theories of religion's demise."[6]

Here, explicitly, the continued existence of "religion" is a matter of empirical observation: "facts on the ground" in the "real world." One thing that becomes apparent from Fox's summary is that, in IR and related disciplines, and presumably for Fox himself, "religions" are observable objects. Empirical observation tells one that religion is still alive and active, and that the previous empirical data that religion had met its demise has proved illusory. This is expressed as a witness statement. We saw what we thought was a body lying on the ground, either asleep or dead. But suddenly it started moving. Then it sprang to its feet and attacked us.

Furthermore, according to other experts such as Mark Juergensmeyer, this living corpse wears many masks: not only is religion a universal agent, but it incarnates in specific religions.[7] It is a fact on the ground that Islam is a *religion* that inspires rebellion and terrorism in multiple locations, Al-Qaeda is a *religious* terrorist organization, the Iranian revolution was a *religious* revolution, and so on. In contrast, Juergensmeyer himself, his academic practice of naming, and the nation-state of which he is a privileged citizen are tacitly constructed as everything that these "religious" fanatics are not: secular, rational, objective, liberal, neutral but peace-loving.

In the act of classifying other peoples' practices as "religious"—a practice that the scholar Arvind Pal Mandair has described as an act of "epistemic violence"[8]—academic and nonacademic experts such as politicians and civil servants embed the assumption that religions exist and cause things to happen in some real and observable sense. Through these acts of rhetoric we have been persuaded, and continue to persuade ourselves and others, that we can occupy a disinterested and objective point of observation from which to make true statements about these phenomena. We deal in facts; we leave value judgments to others. But this in turn implies a value judgment: that our supposed neutrality and objectivity make us tolerant and sane, as well as intellectually superior.

But "religions" are not observable objects in the world. They are collective constructions of the imagination. Nobody has ever seen a religion, much as nobody has ever seen a "nation-state" or a "society." None of these words refers to, or picks out, something like an object in the world that can be described, analyzed, compared, or made the object of neutral classification. People who tell us that there is a religion called "Christianity" and another one called "shinto" with such and such defining features are not really telling us what exists in the world, but attempting to persuade us to classify the world in a particular and peculiar way. Somehow this historically unique way of imagining the world, which emerged in a particular historical context of Christian European imperialism, has been rhetorically transformed into the real and unanswerable order of things. It is important for us secular moderns to believe in the existence of religions, just as it is important to believe in the existence of nations.[9] Our act of faith in the existence and even agency of religion and religions makes other things possible.

RELIGIONS AS USEFUL WAYS TO CLASSIFY HUMAN PRACTICES AND INSTITUTIONS

Some experts, sensing that they might be in danger of committing the fallacy of misplaced concreteness, or reification, say instead that, though it is true that religions are merely general categories, they are *useful* general categories. They help to bring a large number of practices, institutions, beliefs, and experiences under one class. What we have are a range of practices and experiences that hold enough in common to be conveniently classified as being of one distinct kind—"*religious* practices." These can be distinguished from those belonging to a fundamentally different kind, "nonreligious" practices such as political, economic, scientific, legal, academic, or artistic. Thus according to this line of thinking we can talk helpfully about religious experiences as a common type of experience had by people everywhere and at all times and places. This kind of position allows that these experiences, or the practices that they are supposed to explain, may admittedly be different from one another, because they are mediated by different languages and cultural or historical contexts. However, they hold sufficient similarities for it to be strategically useful to classify them all as "religious," rather than nonreligious, for example, "political" or "scientific." In this way we break up the world into manageable sections without which we would be unable to think or act at all.

This kind of argument does not solve the problem. For one thing, we need to remember that what counts as "religious" and "nonreligious" is not an innocent exercise of an abstract category that we, as individual academics, can make mean what we want. It is of great constitutional importance and frequently involves legal processes and the identities and rights of people. How are we to identify what does and does not usefully get included as "religious" or "nonreligious," and why is it a better way to classify human experiences or practices than another? For example, by what criteria shall we decide that a particular act of violence is "religious" terrorism, another act is "political," and a third is *really* "political" but merely *masquerading* as "religious"?[10] Immediately one can see with these examples that the way we decide to classify our own or other people's actions can have very serious consequences indeed. As Cavanaugh has shown in a number of works but also in chapter 54 of this volume, these ideologically determined usages underlie the modern myth that, whereas the violence of "religious extremists" is irrational, barbaric, and meaningless, the violence of the (Western) secular state is reluctant and rational.[11]

We can also see in these examples that some putatively *essential* distinctions have become embedded in the way that acts of violence get classified, even though the distinctions are really quite arbitrary. The idea that an act of violence is *really* political while *masquerading* as religious, or that religion and politics are getting mixed up and need to be kept separate, embeds their essential distinction in the very act of rhetorical construction. Yet some scholars have not only made successful careers from framing their books in these terms, but compound their reputations by assuming the further authority of being neutral and objective observers, themselves disinterested in power and above the squalid conflict of ideological imperatives.

Many historians who are experts in early modern history write as though our modern Anglophone or more widely Europhone ways of ordering the world were already established in the seventeenth or even sixteenth centuries. Yet it can surely be argued that people thinking in English would not have distinguished religious from nonreligious practices, or religious violence from political violence. This was not because they were more stupid or backward than us, but because the dominant discourse of those days, Religion as encompassing Christian Truth, did not allow such distinctions to be made. The idea of "the State" or "politics" as it is understood in today's terms did not exist, and these words were only beginning to emerge (in English at least) in the seventeenth century, and did not take on their modern usage until the late eighteenth century. Even in the nineteenth and well into the twentieth century the idea of the State as a distinct, nonreligious entity defined by a written constitution and "religion" as a generic private right and voluntary association was not a fait accompli but was still in the making. Indeed, the point of this argument is that these configurations of categories are still in the making, they are continuing acts of persuasion, and academics are not describing independent realities as much as reconvincing themselves and others that they exist as such. We are deluded by our own rhetorical constructions. We are all collectively involved in making and remaking these imagined domains as though they somehow exist as independent realities.

Some historians have shown us how we have invented traditions and made them appear as old as the hills.[12] Similarly I suggest we have invented religion and religions as religious traditions that are essentially different from nonreligious secular domains. The modern invention of religion in this sense is analogous to the point that Gellner has made about modern nationalism and nations: "Nationalism is not the awakening of nations to self-consciousness: it invents nations where they do not exist."[13]

But many historians seem resistant to the idea that categories like "religion" and "politics" and the putative differences between them are modern inventions, and not timeless domains inherent in human nature and fixed in the order of things. The uncritical habit of some modern historians who reconstruct the past in today's categories, and who talk as though "religion" and "politics" are domains eternally embedded in the nature of European history, is engaged in an ideological act at the very moment that they represent themselves as disinterested observers. This kind of misrepresentation seems even more obvious when scholars claim to be writing about the religion and politics of the Incas or fourteenth-century China (to take arbitrary examples). Today's powerful controllers of language in the media and the political domains, enthusiastically helped by un-self-critical academics, deploy these distinctions in culturally and linguistically complicated situations where clear communication and accurate representation are urgently required to solve problems of human conflict.

THE POWER OF RHETORIC

Another term we can use for powerful discourses is rhetorical constructions. Richard Roberts and J. M. M. Good in their *The Recovery of Rhetoric: Persuasive Discourse and Disciplinarity in the Human Sciences* (1993) argue that "rhetoric has played a central part in the formation, development and legitimation of the emerging human sciences. . . . If we are to understand the present-day classifications and hierarchies of the various disciplines in the human sciences, then it is essential to understand their rhetorical constitution."[14] One of the key points they make about rhetoric, in concordance with their contributor Michael Cahn, is that rhetoric not only constructs disciplines and domains of discourse but also disguises their origins in ways that make them appear as commonplaces, as part of the common order of things.[15] I suggest that writers in the late seventeenth and early eighteenth centuries such as John Locke, William Penn, and Bishop Hoadly (there were many others) were rhetorically constructing the meaning of "religion" in a new way, a contested discourse that through time has come to appear as a natural truth that it is counterintuitive to challenge. They were attempting to subvert the dominant idea of Religion as Christian Truth, a Truth that encompassed the whole of reality, and to persuade us to think that religion is essentially private and personal, and that "religious organizations" are merely voluntary associations of like-minded believers. In the process they promoted the idea of "politics," civil society, and the State as essentially nonreligious. Instead of encompassing Christian Truth, the opposite of which was falsehood and irrationality, they made an essential distinction between the religious and the nonreligious. To strengthen this rhetorical act of persuasion they deployed a number of backup dichotomies such as private and public, inner and outer, this world and other world, natural and supernatural, faith and scientific knowledge, metaphysics and empiricism, so that each binary can stand in for the others in a chain of substitutions in a constant deferral of meaning, each being used in circular fashion to define and thus to substantiate the others. This new idea of the essential distinction between the religious and the nonreligious caught on powerfully in North America, for reasons that need to be explored, and became incorporated into the Bills of Rights and state constitutions.

As I have been arguing, "religion" is not a stand-alone category. It is joined at the hip with "secular politics," the state, and other supposedly nonreligious domains such as economics. This new imagining of "religion" was simultaneously the invention of a new binary, forming the basis for two new essentialized domains, "religion" and "nonreligion." In a complex historical process, the older binary between Christian Truth and pagan falsehood was replaced as the dominant trope by the binary opposition between generic religion and the nonreligious, scientifically rational secular. The world dominance of Euro-America came to be largely expressed in the orientalist binaries of secular rationality as against the irrational traditions of religious backwardness.[16]

ENCHANTMENT AND DISENCHANTMENT

This formulation is encoded in the thesis of secularization: for example, in the distinction between the magical enchantments of primitives (including our own pre-Protestant ancestors) as against the progressive disenchantment of true rational knowledge of the world. Our own fetishistic enchantment with the circulation of commodities, self-regulating markets, money, private property, and capital, for example, is represented as a rational and factual confrontation with the real order of things, freed at last from the centuries of irrational superstition. I suggest instead that we moderns are knee-deep in superstitions, which we proudly proclaim to be a brave confrontation with the really real.

This basic opposition typically gets formulated in various binary terms like "religion and politics," or "religion and the state," or "religion and science." The widely understood meanings of all these terms became radically changed or newly invented. They came to denote domains with clear differences, all of which could be classified under the more general categories "religious" and "nonreligious." And this presumption is tacit in every claim that religion can be studied scientifically, or that religion and politics sometimes come dangerously into conflict, or that religion is a private right that in any civilized society ought to be guaranteed by the secular state.

The rhetorical origins of these distinctions, while well known, were also strategically forgotten, because they became normalized in Enlightenment reason, along with a range of other essentialized dichotomies: soul and body, spirit and matter, supernature and nature, rational science and irrational or nonrational faith. The modern academic discipline of religious studies and the much wider academic discursive deployment of "religion" and "spiritualities" were formulated within this hegemonic discourse. But the same can be said for the modern invention of "science" or "politics" or "economics." In principle we could take any of these categories as our starting point. Thus, when we talk about "religion" as a rhetorical construction, we are also always tacitly talking about what is being constructed as *outside* religion. When a historian told me recently that he wasn't interested in religion, I pointed out to him that his self-identity as a secular historian is historically and conceptually parasitic on the modern invention of religion and religions. You could not have a category and powerful discourse of the nonreligious secular without simultaneously having a category of the religious. They mutually implicate each other. There is no secular history without the *exclusion* of religion, or its transformation into an object of secular knowledge.

AN OLDER DISCOURSE: RELIGION AS CHRISTIAN TRUTH

Yet at the same time there is an older discourse of Christian Truth, in which both church and state were encompassed and which I shall refer to as the totalizing Church-State or Commonweal. This rhetorical construction was hegemonic long before the modern binary became progressively articulated. Religion emerged as a distinct and separated domain in the context of colonialism and the nation-state as it was emerging as a distinct, abstract, rational, nonreligious, imagined entity. This older discourse, along with its partial replacement by the modern one, has been generally suppressed from the collective memory. This is one of the functions of rhetoric, to make a particular *imaginaire* seem eternal, natural, incontestable, part of the order of things. This is achieved through the suppression of historical memory. Ironically historians are important actors in this process, frequently reconstructing the past in today's dominant categories and thus making our contemporary assumptions—the distinction between religious and political practices, for example—seem inherent in human nature.

I said that the older discourse on religion as Christian Truth, along with its replacement by a new dominant paradigm of religion as a universal, private right, has been generally suppressed from memory. However, there are quite obvious domains, pockets of resistance if you like, in which it still operates, such as evangelical Protestantism. Actually, if you carefully analyze the rhetoric of contemporary academics and politicians, and the analytical models of anthropologists and sociologists, or the language used by evangelical Christian missionaries, you can quickly detect vestiges of the older discourse mixed up and confused with the more dominant modern one. If the modern invention of the religious and the secular was remembered as a historical process connected with the growth of colonial wealth and power, the whole religion industry, which promotes rhetoric on religion and religions as though it is obvious what is meant, would come to seem untenable. This confusion of discourses operates to obscure the assumptions about the rhetorical construction not of "religion" alone, as though that category refers to something of and in its own right, but simultaneously of "religion" in problematic relation to "state," "politics," and other modern categories of "secular" rationality such as "economics" or "science."

THE IDEOLOGY OF RELIGIOUS STUDIES

Religious studies departments typically justify their existence by claiming either that religions are important objects in the world that need to be studied or that there is a distinct class of religious experiences and practices that are essentially different from nonreligious ones such as political, scientific, economic, or aesthetic ones. While some theorists will claim that these are merely heuristic distinctions, and should not be taken to imply essential differences, a study of the actual usages of languages shows this to be a shallow claim. Whatever conscious methodological intentions the writer may or may not have, the recycling of discourses on religion and religions in hundreds of books, journal articles, and conference papers marks out and constructs religion and religious things as distinct and different from the nonreligious ones. These latter are in turn classified as secular political, economic, or aesthetic, and thus mystified as essentially distinct from "religious" practices. From behind our closed departmental doors, political scientists, historians, lawyers, educationalists, economists, anthropologists, and social scientists construct the religion-secular dichotomy in their own contexts in accordance with their own research interests and funding requirements.

In religious studies this tacit distinction between the religious and the nonreligious is reproduced as though it were a fact of nature in special journals, conferences, university lecture courses, school curricula, research seminars, and symposia. The very act of writing a secular account of religion quietly embeds the distinction without anyone really noticing. This in turn underwrites the presumption that science is essentially different from religion, just as "knowledge" is essentially different from "faith," or "nature" is essentially different from "supernature." I can hear some readers shouting denials, but once one has looked at how language is actually used one can find that religion is rhetorically constructed as essentially different from other so-called nonreligious domains.

Yet a look at the practices of so-called secular institutions can throw doubt on the validity of this powerful discourse. For instance one could argue that there is nothing essentially different about the American Academy of Religion, which is supposed to be a secular academic event, from the annual hajj at Mecca. To attend the AAR is to engage in a kind of pilgrimage, to participate in a vast liturgical chant, to congregate in smaller chapels of specialized devotion, to adopt demeanors of pious confession, to observe taboos, obey disciplinary abstentions, and submit to hierarchical pronouncements.

All these reproductions of discourses on religion have a fundamental ideological function of embedding "religion" as part of human nature, and thus making it seem difficult to question. Perhaps even more importantly, by embedding "religion" as ubiquitous, we simultaneously embed the nonreligious. When cognitive scientists claim that "religion" can be explained scientifically by evolutionary theory, and even posit a special gene for "it," we can see mystification at work. The very form of this claim tacitly embeds "religion" (which as we have seen is an inherently confused category with powerful and contradictory meanings) as a distinct kind of "thing" that can be defined according to its universal characteristics. But the other side of this embedding is the unquestioned assumption not only that the term "religion" can be made to stand for a specific aspect of evolutionary behavior (as if, for example, counterintuitive beliefs are typically religious, but could not be found in science), but that science is a distinctly nonreligious kind of activity that can explain religion. This illusory assumption, which depends on an arbitrary decision about what some group of researchers has decided they want to mean by religion, has many powerful implications, for example, the way government funding gets channeled. That observation, however, still leaves us with the question of why governments should want to assume that there is an obvious class of practices that are nonreligious.

MEANINGS OF THE ANGLOPHONE TERM "RELIGION" IN HISTORICAL PERSPECTIVE

When, where, and how did the modern English-language discourse of "religion" and "religions" arise?

Religion as Christian Truth

For many centuries after the Reformation the term "Religion" meant Christian Truth, more frequently one of the Protestant versions. The opposite of Religion was not "the secular," but Superstition. In the powerful Roman Catholic Church discourse, significant aspects of which were incorporated into the new Anglican church-state, Latin *religio* was sparingly used, for example, as a minor virtue subordinate to "justice."[17] In Protestant countries such as England, the term "Religion" emerged as Protestant Christian Truth encompassing the whole of reality. This Protestant conception reclassified the Catholic Church as part of the pagan world of superstition. But this change did not immediately lead into the modern religion-secular binary. Despite the significant reconfigurations of power heralded by the rise of Protestant power formations that challenged the Catholic status quo, the powerful *imaginaire* of the encompassment of Christian Truth persisted in the new national churches, and extended throughout the colonial empires. What was outside Religion could not properly exist: falsehood, ignorance, evil, all destined for hell, for a kind of limbo or nonbeing. True, there were disagreements about what constituted Christian Truth, not only between Catholics and Protestants but also between Lutherans, Calvinists, and others. But in the early modern period few doubted that the truth about the meaning of life was revealed through Christ, the Bible, and the church-state authorities. And, regardless of whether Catholic or

Protestant, few doubted that Christian Truth encompassed all aspects of life, including what we have subsequently separated out as "the state" and as distinct spheres of political, economic, or scientific practice.

The "Religious" as a Status

The term "religious" (as distinct from "the religious") is difficult to find in texts before the seventeenth century. It was generally only used in the sense of "the religious"—monks, nuns, friars, and also "the religious houses," for example, monasteries, convents, and abbeys. "The religious" was a status within Christendom. These were abolished in England and other Protestant countries, such as Holland and some German states, though the term still persists in such contexts as Catholicism and high Anglicanism. At around the same time Catholicism was condemned by Protestants as "superstition," along with "Mahometanism" (Islam) and Paganism. Thus in one early-seventeenth-century text, I found the Protestant expression "the superstitious religious," a deliberate Protestant satirical play on words to describe the Catholic monastic orders.[18] But this play is also an indication of a significant shift in nuance.

However, it should be noted that the adverb "religiously" seems to have a very ancient sense, possibly going back to the Roman *religio*.[19] It was the *religio* of a soldier to serve the glory of Rome and extend her conquests, or of a senator to serve the Senate. One could say that the soldier and the senator honored their duties religiously—with religious attention to the tasks at hand. Today we catch an echo of that usage when we say, in everyday English, that the opera singer is devoted to her art and religiously practices Mozart every day. Such examples indicate the dedicated performance of duties regardless of any further and additional Christian monotheistic preoccupation with belief in God or in theistic doctrinal orthodoxy. Thus, while most English-Latin dictionaries and concordances will consistently define "religion" as "belief in God," they usually also include this other, quite different sense of the performance of a practice "religiously," such as "faithfully, strictly, exactly, conscientiously, scrupulously."[20] This meaning decouples the concept from the overdetermined Protestant associations of "religion" with "belief in God," or "religious practice" with "worship of God," and shifts the semantic weight to practices in a more inclusive sense. In this sense, the dedicated service of a Roman citizen to Rome, or a contemporary craftswoman to her craft, is not *essentially* different from the religious dedication of a Christian renouncer to the discipline of his order. They are *different* practices, and their differences can be specified; but they also share important qualities such as devotion, dedication, treating a practice as sacrosanct, or setting some things apart as special. The populist choreography and democratic liturgy behind the media-framed swearing-in of a new president of the United States are presumably as faithful, strict, exact, conscientious, and scrupulous in their attention to detail as the performance of any Vatican ceremony or any devoted opera singer.

The "Secular" as a Status

For centuries the "secular" referred either to "secular priests" or to civil powers such as the courts. None of these was *nonreligious* in the modern sense of "secular." Priests and kings were sacred and anointed by God through the powers of the Church;[21] the secular or civil courts, which were distinguished *not* from the religious courts but from the ecclesiastical courts, were encompassed by Christian Truth, which defined their ends. They served Christ, and cooperated with the ecclesiastical courts in punishing heretics. The "civil" did not have the nuance of the modern "secular," since even for Luther and Calvin the civil was only relatively profane, was encompassed by Christian Truth, and served the purposes of God. It is significantly different in this context to say that the civil courts of Christendom were separated from the ecclesiastical courts, and to say that the civil was separated from religion. These two distinctions, when placed in their proper context, have different meanings.

Even following the demise of the power of ecclesiastical courts, the procedures of the modern civil courts are highly ritualized, solemn, and invested with a dignity and importance that can be called sacred or sacrosanct without any strain on the ordinary use of language—just as we can say today in ordinary English that the conscientious judge religiously interprets each case according to evidence and precedence.

Christian Truth as Commonweal

Religion understood as Christian Truth was frequently expressed in terms of a sacred order—one could use the anthropological term "ritual order"—sometimes called the Commonweal or Commonwealth. This was based on an analogy with the human body. It was a holistic metaphor. Every limb is necessary for the whole, but some limbs are more important than others: the monarch as the heart, his learned advisors as the head, great soldiers as the arms, laborers as the feet. This was a powerful metaphor, a utopian discourse widely disseminated and fixing hierarchy in the order of things, that is to say, God's order. Everyone is born into a specific degree, station, and vocation. Duty is sacred. Thus the ritual order of England was sacralized. By serving the king or one's master, one served God. By serving the whole Body Politic, one served the divine well-being and harmony of God's Providence.

Analogy Between God, King, and Father

The Commonweal, based on the analogy with the human body, was also an analogy for the Creation: As God is the Dad and Progenitor of All, so the King is the Lord and Head of the Commonweal, and the Father is the Head of the family. The organic metaphor at the level of the Commonweal included church and government, ecclesiastical and temporal, bishop and prince, the spiritualty and the commonalty, and all orders and degrees. All were encompassed by Christian Truth. This was the meaning of Religion. This metaphor legitimated male authority, patriarchy, paternalism, obedience, duty to one's superiors as part of the natural order. The relatively profane tasks, such as laboring or grave digging, were still sacralized in official rhetoric as God-given duties. The maintenance of pure and prestigious rank was dependent on the pollution-removing offices of the laboring poor. The relative profanity of aspects of the world, which required separation to an acceptable ritual distance, did not amount to the modern "secular" as something dichotomized and separated from an entirely different domain named "religion." It is therefore in my view necessary to keep the idea of the profane separate from the modern essentialized idea of the secular as the nonreligious.

The Encompassment of Church-State by Religion

The distinction between church and government was not the modern church-state opposition, nor was it the same as the modern distinction between religion and politics. Both church and state were encompassed by Religion. The historian of political theory Quentin Skinner, in *The Foundations of Modern Political Thought* (1978), argues that the first conception of the State in something like the modern sense was articulated by Jean Bodin in around 1570.[22] By this he means that Bodin conceived of the State as an abstract entity in and for itself, and as distinguishable from the person of the king and the older organic idea of the Commonwealth as the king's body. This, however, cannot be the end of the story, because we do not yet have an idea of "religion" as something in and for itself, as a domain essentially distinct from some other putatively nonreligious domain, even though that idea was possibly at an early stage of emergence. And I argue that until "religion" has also been separated off into a separate, distinct, essentialized domain, we cannot have the modern idea of the secular nonreligious State. We are still looking at a process, the rhetorical construction of modern categories through new discourses that suppress their own recent origins and that claim to be as old as the hills. The illusion of primordial continuity embeds categories in the mythological nature of things.

Politics as "Nonreligious" and Separated from "Religion": From Where?

The other side of this question is: Where does the idea of politics as essentially non-religious come from?[23] The term "politics" in English occurs before the seventeenth century, but infrequently. A much more usual term was "politic." Politic (like the words "policy" or "civil") did not refer to a domain separated from "religion." The politic body was the well-ordered (Godly) Commonweal. Any action could be described as "politic" if it was appropriate, fitting, useful, and conducive to harmony and good order. It had a nuance also of diplomacy. Henry VIII and his ministers used it to refer to the church rituals of which they approved. This term did not become a discourse on modern politics as "secular" in the sense of "separated from and neutral towards religion" until there also existed a discourse on religion as a discrete domain separate from secular politics.

There is a historical transition from the adjectival "politic" to the noun "politics" especially around the later seventeenth century. Two examples of influential late-seventeenth-century rhetorical reformulations of the meaning of "religion" and the invention of modern politics as a distinct domain were William Penn and John Locke. William Penn, founder of Pennsylvania and writer of early liberal constitutions, urged on his readers the following:

> Religion and Policy, or Christianity and Magistracy, are two distinct things, have two different ends, and may be fully prosecuted without respect one to the other; the one is for purifying, and cleaning the soul, and fitting it for a future state; the other is for Maintenance and Preserving of Civil Society, in order to the outward conveniency and accommodation of men in this World. A Magistrate is a true and real Magistrate, though not a Christian; as well as a man is a true and real Christian, without being a Magistrate.[24]

Here we can clearly see a distinctly new rhetoric of the essential difference between religion and policy, a word that is at this time beginning to become interchangeable with politics. For Penn is rhetorically constructing a notion of religion as private, individual, concerned with the next life, and "policy" or "magistracy" as concerned with a distinct public domain of civil society.

Similarly John Locke,[25] in his *A Letter Concerning Toleration*, argued:

> I esteem it above all things necessary to distinguish exactly the Business of Civil Government from that of Religion, and to settle the just Bounds that lie between the one and the other. If this be not done, there can be no end put to the Controversies that will be always arising, between those that have, or at least pretend to have, on the one side, a Concernment for the Interest of Mens Souls, and on the other side, a Care of the Commonwealth. . . . *The Commonwealth* seems to me to be a Society of Men constituted only for the procuring, preserving, and advancing of their own *Civil Interests*. *Civil Interests* I call Life, Liberty, Health, and Indolency of Body; and the possession of outward things, such as Money, Lands, Houses, Furniture, and the like.[26]

The duty of the Civil Magistrate "by the impartial Execution of equal Laws" is to defend through the fear of punishment and the possession of force "the civil interests of his Subjects."

Locke seeks to persuade his readers—and himself—that "the whole Jurisdiction of the Magistrate reaches only to these civil Concernments . . . it neither can nor ought in any manner to be extended to the Salvation of Souls."[27]

> All the Power of Civil Government relates only to Men's Civil Interests; is confined to the care of the things of this World; and hath nothing to do with the World to come. . . . A Church I . . . take to be a voluntary Society of men, joining themselves together of their own accord, in order to the publick worshipping of God, in such a manner as they judge acceptable to him, and effectual to the Salvation of their Souls.[28]

The church is a free and voluntary society; no one can inherit religion from their parents in the way that "Temporal Estates" are inherited; it is purely individual, voluntary, to do with inner belief and salvation. If the individual makes an error of judgment, he is free to leave that church or sect and join another. We can see clearly here the rhetorical construction of "religion" and "politics" (also referred to as civil society or the magistracy) as essentially different in terms of ends and purposes, organization, and functions.

Furthermore, one is private and the other public. Both Penn and Locke influenced the development of state charters and constitutions.

Benjamin Hoadly was an Anglican bishop who was frequently cited and quoted in American radical pamphlets, especially his *The Original and Institution of Civil Government, Discuss'd* and *The Measures of Submission to the Civil Magistrate Consider'd. In Defence of the Doctrine. Deliver'd in a Sermon Preach'd Before the Rt. Hon. the Lord Mayor, Aldermen, and Citizens of London, Sept. 29, 1705.*[29] In these works, Hoadly pursues a distinction between religion and the polity that is close to the kind being argued by Penn and Locke. For example, he directly attacks what he calls the Patriarchal Scheme of Government, referring implicitly to Filmer, whom Locke critiqued in his first *Treatise*.[30] Bernard Bailyn says in his *The Ideological Origins of the American Revolution* (1967) that Hoadly "was widely held to be one of the most notable figures in the history of political thought" in the colonies.[31] This is another indication of the importance of the colonization of America in the formation and clarification of this modern ideological construct. Locke, Penn, and Hoadly were among the most often cited and quoted theorists in North America in the eighteenth century, and influenced the state charters, the bills of rights, and the various constitutions, which fed into the US Constitution of 1789–90. Bailyn, after reviewing specific instances of the influence of the Constitution globally, concludes that, "in the generations that have followed, that influence has remained pervasive—not merely in the design of specific constitutions but mainly and increasingly, as America's power has grown, in its embodiment of established western values."[32]

I have suggested that the success of the modern discourse on religion and religions as a special kind of human practice essentially distinct from nonreligious ones has a significant connection to the history of European colonialism and the birth of capitalism. The myth of "religion" as an essentially private inner experience or special psychological state derives in part from some forms of Protestant Christianity, though today it is also a commodity for consumption.[33] But the development of those forms of Protestant Christianity, particularly nonconformist groups, is not self-evident or merely generated internally from some inherent logic of abstract ideas. As the concept of elective affinity suggests, ideas have to be adaptable to the actual interests of emergent classes and their practices for them to survive and prosper. The essentialization of "religious" as distinct from "secular" practices can partly be understood in terms of a dialectical relation with new powerful interests in banking, trading, and manufacturing, with the transformation of land-use rights into private property, and with the commodification of human beings in the forms of slavery or wage labor. The crucial connection is the clothing of faith in capital with an aura of factuality such that, in contrast to religion, the workings of capital and commodity markets can appear to be part of rational knowledge rather than the blind faith of superstition. This process entailed a radical transformation of the old status quo. In this sense we can see the US Constitution as a dominant ritual proclamation that embeds white, male, literate, Europhone categories and rationality as being in the nature of things. Women and men who today turn this wheel of "religion" are unknowingly pump-priming the (male) myth of this paradigmatic discourse on the unavoidable operations of capitalism.

It might be, and sometimes is, argued that this modern ideology is not wholly bad. The development of an ideology of interiority has not resulted only in the shallow individualism of consumer capital and the exploitation of vulnerable people as machines for the extraction of surplus value. It has (arguably) also offered less powerful people such as women and subjugated minorities a significant space to be treated with respect and dignity as human beings, providing some protection against the quantitative exploitation of their material productive power. Constitutional rights have also historically and to some degree provided a space for labor to unionize for the promotion of the common good of the working classes. It is, however, essential to notice (as many feminists, subaltern theorists, and labor historians have pointed out) that constitutional human rights legislation is mainly the invention of white wealthy literate males who owned slaves, switched to wage labor as more economical and profitable, and continue to pursue ambitious and lucrative careers on such grounds as that greed is good, wage labor is a fact of life, and lending money for interest is naturally rational and has nothing inherently to do with moral values—in short, that the secular state and politics were invented to "other" (render marginal) a range of powerful moral discourses in order to more effectively represent and protect the interests and privileges of male private property.

It is on these kinds of grounds that I argue that the category "religion" is complex, is unstable, and holds contradictory meanings, making its supposedly neutral and disinterested employment for analytical and descriptive purposes illusory and dangerous. Religion discourse is deeply ideological, all the more so for being disguised and mystified as neutral, as merely descriptive, or as intellectually satisfying.

NOTES

This chapter was written several years ago when this book was in an early stage of production. Since then I have developed the argument in a range of publications, including a monograph, *Religion and Politics in International Relations: The Modern Myth* (London: Continuum, 2011); an edited volume, Trevor Stack, Naomi Goldenberg, and T. Fitzgerald, eds., *Religion as a Category of Governance and Sovereignty* (Leiden: Brill, 2015); and several articles and book chapters. See, for a recent example, "'Postcolonial Remains': Critical Religion, Postcolonial Theory, and Deconstructing Modern Categories," in *The Postcolonial World*, ed. Jyotsna Singh and David Kim (London: Routledge, 2016).

1. Richard King and Jeremy Carrette, *Selling Spirituality: The Silent Takeover of Religion* (London: Routledge, 2005).

2. Timothy Fitzgerald, *Discourse on Civility and Barbarity: A Critical History of Religion and Related Categories* (New York: Oxford University Press, 2007); William T. Cavanaugh, *The Myth of Religious Violence* (New York: Oxford University Press, 2009). I am not concerned with the etymology of the terms but with the way they have been used historically in a range of discourses. For example, much has been made of the derivation of "religion" from *religio*; but I am not convinced that in either Roman Latin or Medieval Latin *religio* had the same usage and meaning; and both of these were different from early modern "Religion" in post-Reformation Holland, Germany, France, and England. This early modern usage, while still deployed, has been largely superseded by a distinctly modern discourse on religion and religions. I have traced typical usages of these terms since the late sixteenth century in England in *Discourse on Civility and Barbarity*. William T. Cavanaugh has provided an important analysis of the different meanings and usages of these terms in *The Myth of Religious Violence*.

3. See Timothy Fitzgerald, *The Ideology of Religious Studies* (New York: Oxford University Press, 2000), 72–97.

4. I use the singular expression "a category such as religion and secular" deliberately, to indicate a mutually parasitic binary, in order to problematize the idea that "religion" and the "nonreligious secular" are two separate categories, discreet and independent of each other. These categories are rhetorically deployed *as if* they refer to essentially different things, domains, or concepts. This is an ideological illusion.

5. Jonathan Fox, "The Rise of Religious Nationalism and Conflict: Ethnic Conflict and Revolutionary Wars, 1945–2001," *Journal of Peace Research* 41, no. 6 (November 2004): 716–17.

6. Ibid., 715–31.

7. Mark Jeuergensmeyer is a major promoter of this myth; see, for example, Mark Jeuergensmeyer, *The New Cold War? Religious Nationalism Confronts the Secular State* (Berkeley: University of California Press, 1993). And more recently Mark Jeuergensmeyer, "Is Religion the Problem?," *Hedgehog Review* 6, no. 1 (Spring 2004): 1–10.

8. Arvind Pal Mandair, *Religion and the Specter of the West: Sikhism, India, Postcoloniality, and the Politics of Translation* (New York: Columbia University Press, 2009).

9. For an interesting analysis of the coexistence of nationalism with skepticism about the existence of the nation, see G. Aloysius, *Nationalism Without a Nation in India* (Oxford: Oxford University Press, 1999).

10. See Fitzgerald, *Discourse on Civility and Barbarity*.

11. Cavanaugh, *The Myth of Religious Violence*, passim; Fitzgerald, *Religion and Politics in International Relations*, passim.

12. Eric Hobsbawm and Terence Ranger, *The Invention of Tradition* (Cambridge: Cambridge University Press, 1983).

13. Quoted in Benedict Anderson, *Imagined Communities: Reflections on the Origin and Spread of Nationalism*, rev. ed. (London: Verso, 1991), 5.

14. R. H. Robert and J. M. M. Good, *The Recovery of Rhetoric: Persuasive Discourse and Disciplinarity in the Human Sciences* (Charlottesville: University Press of Virginia, 1993), 4.

15. Michael Cahn, "The Rhetoric of Rhetoric: Six Tropes of Disciplinary Self-Constitution," in Roberts and Good, *The Recovery of Rhetoric*, 61–84.

16. See Fitzgerald, "'Postcolonial Remains.'"

17. For a detailed historicization of *religio* and religion, see Cavanaugh, *The Myth of Religious Violence*.

18. Samuel Purchas, *Purchas, His Pilgrimage; Or, Relations of the World and the Religions Observed in All Ages* (London, 1626); analyzed in Fitzgerald, *Discourse on Civility and Barbarity*, chap. 7.

19. William Cantwell Smith, *The Meaning and End of Religion* (Minneapolis: Augsburg Fortress, 1962); S. N. Balagangadhara, *"The Heathen in His Blindness": Asia, the West, and the Dynamic of Religion* (Leiden: Brill, 1994); Richard King, *Orientalism and Religion: Postcolonial Theory, India and "the Mystic East"* (London: Routledge, 1999); Timothy Fitzgerald, ed., *Religion and the Secular: Historical and Colonial Formations* (London: Equinox, 2007).

20. Oxford English Dictionary, s.v. "religion" and "religiously."

21. This point still holds with the 1953 coronation liturgy of the present Queen of England.

22. Quentin Skinner, *The Foundations of Modern Political Thought*, vol. 2, *The Age of Reformation* (Cambridge: Cambridge University Press, 1978), 352–53; see a discussion in Fitzgerald, *Discourse on Civility and Barbarity*, 149–50.

23. The same question can be asked about "political economy" or "economics," for example.

24. William Penn, *The Great Question to Be Considered by the King, and This Approaching Parliament, Briefly Proposed, and Modestly Discussed: (To Wit) How Far Religion Is Concerned in Policy or Civil Government, and Policy in Religion?* (London, 1680), National Library of Scotland, Edinburgh Microfiche, 4.

25. My argument seems to converge in some respects with that of Jakob de Roover and S. N. Balagangadhara, "The Secular State and Religious Conflict: Liberal Neutrality and the Indian Case of Pluralism," *Journal of Political Philosophy* 15, no. 1 (2007): 67–92.

26. John Locke, *A Letter Concerning Toleration*, 2nd ed. (London, 1689), 8–9.

27. Ibid., 9.

28. Ibid., 13.

29. Benjamin Hoadly, *The Measures of Submission to the Civil Magistrate Consider'd: In Defence of the Doctrine. Deliver'd in a Sermon Preach'd Before the Rt. Hon. the Lord Mayor, Aldermen, and Citizens of London, Sept. 29, 1705* (London, 1710); Benjamin Hoadly, *The Original and Institution of Civil Government, Discuss'd*, 2nd ed. (London, 1710).

30. Sir Robert Filmer, *Patriarchy, and Other Writings*, ed. Johann P. Sommerville (Cambridge: Cambridge University Press, 1991).

31. Bernard Bailyn, *The Ideological Origins of the American Revolution* (Cambridge, Mass.: Harvard University Press, 1967), 37.

32. Bernard Bailyn, *American Constitutionalism: Atlantic Dimensions* (London: Institute of United States Studies, University of London, 2002), 25.

33. Jeremy Carrette, *Religion and Critical Psychology: Religious Experience in the Knowledge Economy* (London: Routledge, 2007); Carrette and King, *Selling Spirituality*.

PART IX

Religion and Contemporary
European Thought

41

Post-Marxism and Religion

NELSON MALDONADO-TORRES

Post-Marxism" is widely known today, following Ernesto Laclau and Chantal Mouffe, as the effort to "reappropriate" the Marxist intellectual tradition and "as the process of going beyond it."[1] While it is possible to identify these gestures in a number of Marxist figures all throughout the twentieth century, if not before, it will be difficult to find a consensus that all those figures represent a particularly noticeable post-Marxist stance.[2] Post-Marxism in the most restricted contemporary definition, and in the way that I will use it here, refers to a number of intellectual positions that emerged in the context of widespread skepticism toward Marxism in the late twentieth century, and that respond to a multiplicity of challenges coming from poststructuralism, postmodernism, second-wave feminism, critiques of Eurocentrism, and multiculturalism, among other philosophical and cultural tendencies in that period. Post-Marxism also responds to post-1968 social movements, politics, and economics, as well as to discourses about the end of philosophy and the end of history. Post-Marxists attempt to rescue the critical power of Marxism and the usefulness of its tools in diagnosing capitalism in a context of massive disillusion with leftist discourse, a mood that became all the more widespread after the fall of the Soviet Union but that preceded it.

Marx and Marxism are known for an antipathy toward religion, or as presupposing a devastating critique of religion, but Marxism and religion have come together in varied forms and a good number of Marxists have also been religious followers.[3] There have been Marxists who are religious followers, as well as intellectuals who appropriate or redefine Marxist ideas and incorporate them into their own religious worldview. Others have argued that Marx's thought itself was heavily influenced by religious ideas and categories, notwithstanding his rejection of religion.[4] "Post-Marxism" contributes further to this complex relationship between Marx's thought, the critique of capitalism, and religious discourse.

This chapter will focus on post-Marxism and religion, as they come together in the works of Alain Badiou, Antonio Negri, and Slavoj Žižek. They are arguably the main representatives of a certain "theological turn" within post-Marxism.[5] Throughout the chapter, I will be using the distinction made by Laclau and Mouffe between *post*-Marxism and post-*Marxism*.[6] The former refers to the end of certain Marxist orthodoxy based on the idea of the applicability of Marxism in the understanding of the economy and society, and the other to the refashioning of elements already existing within Marxism. Laclau and Mouffe state that they are both *post*-Marxists and post-*Marxists*. The same arguably holds true for Badiou, Negri, and Žižek. But here I will add that if Badiou, Negri, and Žižek are post-*Marxists*, their approach to religion, and more specifically Christianity, also leads them to a position that could be referred to as *post*-Christian. *Post*-Christianity affirms the vital importance of Christianity or of certain Christian ideas and figures, while it simultaneously defies the foundations of Christianity as a religion and at points even proposes its overcoming. While Badiou and Negri are often associated with appropriating elements from Christianity and translating them into radical materialist ideas, Žižek goes a step further by comparing religions and suggesting a typology and a hierarchy among them. With Žižek, *post*-Christian post-*Marxism* achieves the status of a theory of religion, which is combined with the introduction of a new orthodoxy, now at the heart of Žižek's post-*Marxism*.

ALAIN BADIOU

Perhaps the earliest and probably most important, or at the very least most ambitious, post-Marxist text that addresses religion in a fundamental way is Alain Badiou's *Being and Event*. *Being and Event* was published in French in 1988. Badiou saw the end of the 1980s as a moment of "full intellectual regression."[7] According to him, it was a time when moral philosophy, based on a return to Kant's ethics and a formal defense of respect to others and human rights, "disguised as political philosophy." This "flabby reactionary philosophy" was a "companion to the dissolution of bureaucratic socialism in the USSR, the breakneck expansion of the world finance market, and the almost global paralysis of a political thinking of emancipation."[8] Badiou rejected Kantian formalism, as he also criticized the collapse of philosophy into historical and literary discourse, which opened up the door for relativism and calls for the end of philosophy.

In his response to this context, Badiou pursued a reflection that combined philosophical currents that are often opposed to one another: (1) an interest in ontology (the science of being qua being), which, following Heidegger, he saw as fundamental for any philosophical enterprise; (2) a recognition of the revolutionary character of Cantor's set theory and Frege's logic; and (3) insights of the critique of the subject associated to figures like Marx and Lacan.[9] For Badiou, these three lines of inquiry marked the "closure of an entire epoch of thought and its concerns."[10] He sought to draw a "diagonal" through these three intellectual positions and offer a philosophical framework that provides a way to better understand being, truth, and militancy.[11] His philosophical account can be understood as providing an alternative to widespread views that, according to Badiou, lead to either relativism or formalism, which he believes are not up to the task of critically engaging capitalism or providing tools to ground or understand political action.

The fundamental thesis of *Being and Event* is that being is nothing other than pure multiplicity, by which Badiou means that "situations are nothing more, in their being, than pure indifferent multiplicities."[12] And if being is infinite multiplicity the best way to understand it is through mathematics, and specifically set theory. In short, "mathematics *is* ontology."[13]

If being is best elucidated through mathematical discourse, it means that ontology is not centrally concerned with historical events or the interpretation of meaning. These are ways in which ontology has been understood in the past, and, according to Badiou, root causes of the embrace of relativism and the collapse of philosophy into history or literature. By describing being as infinite indifferent multiplicity, Badiou also undercuts the viability of philosophical discourses grounded in the alleged normative value of difference, since for him ontology is indifferent to differences and is rather concerned with truth. Truth, however, should not be understood as consensus or the discovery of laws, but rather in relation to subjects and situations. Truths are an "incalculable emergence" in a rupture with a given order. Badiou refers to this rupture as "the event," which also marks the beginning of "authentic philosophy."[14] This relates to subject theory in that for Badiou, "a subject is nothing other than an active fidelity to the event of truth."[15] To become a subject is thus to be a militant of a truth, which can take place in politics, science, art, and love.

While religion does not appear alongside politics, science, art, and love as one of the areas where subjects can become militants in their fidelity to an event, Badiou is not shy about admitting that his proposal finds parallels in religious views, particularly in Christianity. In *Being and Event* he writes:

> Lacan used to say that if no religion were true, Christianity, nevertheless, was the religion which came closest to the question of truth. This remark can be understood in many different ways. I take it to mean the following: in Christianity and in it alone it is said that the essence of truth supposes the evental ultra-one, and that relating to truth is not a matter of contemplation—or immobile knowledge—but of intervention. For at the heart of Christianity there is that event—situated, exemplary—that is the death of the son of God on the cross. By the same token, belief does not relate centrally to the being-one of God, to his infinite power; its interventional kernel is rather the constitution of the meaning of that death, and the organization of a fidelity to that meaning. . . . All the parameters of the doctrine of the event are thus disposed within Christianity; amidst, however, an ontology of presence—with respect to which I have shown, in particular, that it diminishes the concept of infinity (Meditation 13)."[16]

Christianity approximates the theory of subject and truth that Badiou aims to formulate. It makes truth fundamentally connected with an event, and it conceives subject formation as fidelity to that event and its truth. But Badiou argues that Christianity does this only within an "ontology of presence" that objectifies the infinite in the figure of the being-one of God. *Being and Event* can thus be seen as an effort to secularize being, truth, and philosophy itself by rendering ontology not as metaphysics—as that which elucidates the reality of what is beyond the physical world—but as mathematics. It is there, in mathematics, and not in relation to religion or metaphysics, that infinity can be properly spelled out.

Here we see not only that *Being and Event* touches on themes that were central in the immediate social, economic, political, and intellectual context when it was written, but that it also aims to provide fresh views about centuries-old questions concerning the relation between philosophy and religion and about the secular character of modern European thought and society. Not surprisingly, these themes are also connected to the legacy of Marxism and to Badiou's understanding of Marx's lessons about capitalism. In *Manifesto for Philosophy*, a book that Badiou published shortly after *Being and Event*, he writes:

> What Marx brings to the fore is especially the end of the *sacred* figures of the bond, the lapsing of the symbolic guarantee granted to the bond by productive and monetary stagnation. Capital is the general dissolvent of sacralizing representations, which postulate the existence of intrinsic and essential relations. . . . Yet, for Marx, and for us, desacralization is not in the least nihilistic, insofar as "nihilism" must signify that which declares that the access to being and truth is impossible. On the contrary, desacralization is a *necessary condition* for the disclosing of such an approach to thought. It is obviously the only thing we can and must welcome within Capital: it exposes the pure multiple as the foundation of presentation; it denounces every effect of One as a simple, precarious configuration; it dismisses the symbolic representations in which the bond found a semblance of being. That this destitution operates in the most complete barbarity must not conceal its properly *ontological* virtue. . . . To think over and above Capital and its mediocre prescription (the general computation of time), we must still have as *a departure point* what it has revealed: Being is essentially multiple, sacred Presence is a pure semblance and truth, as with anything if it exists, is not a revelation, much less so the proximity of that which withdraws itself. It is a regulated procedure resulting in a supplementary multiple.[17]

Capitalism, and not only science, Badiou argues here, contributed to a process of desacralization that facilitated the proper conceptualization of being as multiplicity. In that sense, the use of religious ideas and examples does not disguise the fact that Badiou conceives his project in line with Marx's critique of both religion and capitalism. What he adds here is that capitalism itself provided the means for a more consistent critique of religion, and particularly of Christianity. And, thus, we find Badiou clearly stating the axioms of his "a-religious" thinking in a way that is consonant with his opposition to the Christian view of being as the One:

> Let us posit *our* axioms. There is no God. Which also means: the One is not. The multiple "without-one"—every multiple being in its turn nothing other than a multiple of multiples—is the law of being. The only stopping point is the void. The infinite, as Pascal had already realized, is the banal reality of every situation, not the predicate of a transcendence. For the infinite, as Cantor demonstrated with the creation of set theory, is actually only the most general form of multiple-being. In fact, every situation, inasmuch as it is, is a multiple composed of an infinity of elements, each one of which

is itself multiple. Considered in their simple belonging to a situation (to an infinite multiple), the animals of the species *Homo sapiens* are ordinary multiplicities. . . . Infinite alterity is quite simply *what there is*. Any experience at all is the infinite deployment of infinite differences.[18]

In summary, Christianity, for Badiou, is the religion that is closest to the proper understanding of truth, yet it is skewed by an ontology of presence that limits infinity. Capitalism devours any semblance of substance and reveals the world as multiplicity. It treats the entire world as profane and deflates views that endow the world with more significance than exchange value. In so doing, capitalism helps to open up views that help both to further desacralize the world and to oppose capitalism itself. Authentic philosophy is the inheritor of this desacralizing impulse and it opposes "religion" by disposing "compossible truths with the void as background."[19] Philosophy "subtracts thought from every presupposition of Presence."[20]

And yet, desacralization does not mean that Christianity is not important, since it, like capitalism, also contributes with elements that serve to overcome its limits. From here Badiou would later focus on a Christian figure, Saint Paul, to elucidate important elements of fidelity to the event, particularly the avoidance of relativism by a strict commitment with universality. In *Saint Paul: The Foundation of Universalism* (French original published in 1997), Badiou approaches Paul not as a saint or as an apostle, but rather as a "poet-thinker of the event, as well as one who practices and states the invariant traits of what can be called the militant figure."[21] Badiou seeks in this book to "reactivate" important lessons from Paul in the context of "a widespread search for a new militant figure."[22] This goal reminds one of the post-Marxist' attempt to "reappropriate" and "go beyond" Marx in the context of the massive skepticism of the Left, and introduces what one could call a *post*-Christian stance.

Badiou's *post*-Christianity consists in recentering Christian sources in the understanding of (French) universalism, in a way reversing the terrain gained by Jewish philosophers like Emmanuel Levinas and others, who pointed to limits in Christianity and Western secularism and argued for the importance of Jewish sources. Intentionally or not, this recentering similarly helps to erode claims for significance from other religions in the context of struggling to gain legitimacy in secular democratic governments that perceive themselves as universalist.

In his analysis, Badiou objects to positions that interpret universalism in terms of the formalism of the law (abolished by the Christ-event) and its opposite, the disintegration of truth into communitarian perspectives and differences. Indeed, the book is largely a manifesto against ethnic and national identitarian fanaticism as well as against the rise of communitarian perspectives and the struggle for recognition and the rights of difference. He notes a relation between the homogenizing character of capitalism and "the identitarian and cultural logic of communities or minorities" in that capitalism "demands a permanent creation of subjective and territorial identities" and thus forms "an articulated whole" with the logic of minorities "that never demand anything but the right to be exposed in the same way as others to the uniform prerogatives of the market."[23] Capitalists and minorities who affirm their identities are seen as part of the problem that a concept of militancy based on Saint Paul's view of fidelity to the Christ-event can help to confront.

While Badiou's post-*Marxism* is shown in his continued critique of capital, his French *post*-Christian posture is characterized by the impossibility of seeing viable political possibilities beyond the examples provided by republican principles, such as France's conception of universality and its opposition to communitarianism, and beyond Christianity. To the extent that Badiou's thinking is grounded or seeks to ground specifically these French and Christian notions, one could raise the question of the extent to which his own perspective has communitarian elements disguised as universalism and clothed in mathematics. This raises the question of whether post-*Marxism* properly considers the critique of Eurocentrism that is implicit or explicit in the "communitarian" perspectives that it rejects, a question that is also relevant when assessing the work of other post-*Marxists*.

ANTONIO NEGRI

Contemporary Italian philosophy has been centrally important for post-Marxism for at least the last ten to fifteen years, but one can find serious post-Marxist efforts before. Indeed, before Laclau and Mouffe used the concept of "post-Marxism" in their *Hegemony and Socialist Strategy* (1985), the renowned Italian Marxist Antonio Negri published a book entitled *Marx Beyond Marx* (Italian original published in 1979), where he made explicit what we would today call his post-*Marxist* agenda: "Some say we must modernize, that we must reposition, at the present phenomenological level of capital and within the social development of capital, the fundamental concepts of the Marxist traditions: the concept of capital, of working class, of imperialism. How can we respond other than in the affirmative? All of my discourse is located on this terrain of modernization."[24]

Yet, Negri is quick to clarify, this "modernization" of Marx doesn't imply an abandonment of Marx, but rather a reformulation of his categories so as to "liberate the revolutionary content of the Marxist method," something that Negri aims to do in his text by rereading Marx's *Grundrisse*.[25]

Later on, in 1997, Negri would reaffirm his post-Marxist leanings when referring to "the practical experience of living 'with' and 'beyond Marx' (that is, in the area of historical materialism) that has always guided [his] philosophical and political thinking, for better and for worse."[26] Among other important linkages, this post-Marxist project relates to Marx's thought and to Badiou's post-Marxism by adhering to perhaps one of the fundamental impulses of historical materialism, briefly stated as "enough with transcendentalism," which is another way of referring to desacralization.[27] Unlike Badiou, though, who uses a reconceptualization of the concept of infinity to oppose what he sees as Christianity's ontology of presence, Negri focuses on the idea of eternity, but not the eternity of a supernatural being but that of matter itself. Indeed, for Negri "the guiding light of materialism is the eternity of matter."[28] Referring to the transcendental use of the concept of infinity, he writes: "Although transcendental philosophy has assumed the infinite as the ground of all of its maneuvers, it has in reality paid little attention to it. Like a suit that is only worn on special occasions, the idea of the infinite is useful to poetry, theology, mysticism and all confused reasoning."[29]

As in Badiou, the rejection of Christian ontology is coupled with a reappropriation of Christian themes or examples, arguably making Negri also not only a post-*Marxist*, but also *post*-Christian. Two Christian themes that are important in Negri's work are poverty and love. For Negri, the poor person "is naked on the edge of being, without any alternative." The poor person is "the naked eternity of the power of being."[30] This ontological character of poverty is linked to Negri's conceptualization of philosophy: "If you are not poor you cannot philosophize. For poverty is an immeasurable place where the biopolitical question is posed in an absolute way."[31]

Like Badiou, Negri is not afraid to make explicit the Christian examples that partly inspire his reflections: "From Christ to Saint Francis, from the Anabaptists to the Sans-culottes, from the communists to the Third-World militants, the needy, the idiots, the unhappy (i.e., the exploited, the excluded, the oppressed), it is they who exist under the sign of the eternal. Their resistance and their struggles have opened the eternal to the immeasurableness of the *to-come*. The teleology and the ethics of materialism have always been related to this naked and powerful community whose name is 'poverty.' "[32] Truly, for Negri, "poverty has always been the salt of the earth."[33]

Poverty represents for Negri not only the point of origin of philosophy, but also "the place where ethics is born."[34] The ethical significance of poverty lies in that "poverty is given as resistance. There exists no experience of poverty that is not at the same time one of resistance against the repression of the desire to live."[35] The ethical action of the poor is nothing other than love. And here, again, while appropriating Christian themes, Negri makes a point to mark the difference between his materialist interpretation and Christianity:

> One of the greatest evils perpetrated by Christian philosophy consists in considering the poor person not as the subject but as the object of love. It is true that Christ's mysticism and theology overturns this proposition, such that in each poor person one discovers the figure of Christ. But in common usage, traditionally and in the triumphal history of Christianity, the hegemonic affirmation is that of the object-like status of the poor. The very name of the poor is rendered unusable by pity. On the contrary, the corporeality of the poor, their immediate relation . . . is given a subjective determination in love. The latter, after being animated by poverty, puts poverty in relation to the common.[36]

For Negri, poverty is the foundation of love, and love "is the ontological power that constructs being."[37]

Negri's conceptualization of poverty and love is rooted in his materialist ontology, which, as in Badiou, ultimately aims to provide a vantage point for the critique of capitalism as well as a conceptual bedrock for political activism. Against capitalist individualism, exploitation, and the expropriation of earth resources, Negri argues that the poor is the point of entry to think about a politics that seeks to establish a world where we hold things, values, and ideas not as private property, but in common. For Negri, "the experience of poverty introduces one to the constitution of the common; the experience of love is an activity of construction of the common."[38]

The creation of the common is both an ethical and a political act, which means that Negri, like Badiou, also wishes to establish a firm ground for the legitimization of political activity and militancy. In *Multitude* (2004), a text cowritten with Michael Hardt, Hardt and Negri complain that "people today seem unable to understand love as a political concept."[39] And they go on to explain:

> There is really nothing necessarily metaphysical about the Christian and Judaic love of God: both God's love of humanity and humanity's love of God are expressed and incarnated in the common material political project of the multitude. We need to recover today this material and political sense of love, a love as strong as death. This does not mean you cannot love your spouse, your mother, and your child. It only means that your love does not end there, that love serves as the basis for our political projects in common and the construction of a new society. Without this love, we are nothing.[40]

A political sense of love is also what Badiou finds essential for a proper understanding of fidelity to an event, which "*addresses* the love of self universally."[41] Not surprisingly, both Badiou and Negri find the best-known examples of such loving action in Christian saints.

While Badiou focuses on Saint Paul because of his fidelity to the Christ-event, Negri highlights the importance of Saint Francis for his legendary appreciation of the dignity of poverty, his identification with the poor, and his actions as poor. The final lines of his most famous work, *Empire* (2000), also cowritten with Michael Hardt, celebrate Saint Francis and propose him as a model of communist militancy. It is impossible to miss the religious tone of the passage:

> *There is an ancient legend that might serve to illuminate the future life of communist militancy: that of Saint Francis of Assisi. Consider his work. To denounce the poverty of the multitude he adopted that common condition and discovered there the ontological power of a new society. The communist militant does the same, identifying in the common condition of the multitude its enormous wealth. Francis in opposition to nascent capitalism refused every instrumental discipline, and in opposition to the mortification of the flesh (in poverty and in the constituted order) he posed a joyous life, including all of being and nature, the animals, sister moon, brother sun, the birds of the field, the poor and exploited humans, together against the will of power and corruption. Once again in postmodernity we find ourselves in Francis's situation, posing against the misery of power the joy of being. This is a revolution that no power will control—because biopower and communism, cooperation and revolution remain together, in love, simplicity, and also innocence. This is the irrepressible lightness and joy of being communist.*[42]

Empire becomes to some extent the gospel of a "material mythology of reason" and a "material religion of the senses" that separate "the multitude" from the capitalist ethos and sovereignty. These forms of religiosity that take place "on the imperial surfaces where there is no God the Father and no transcendence" can alone, for Negri, bring about "the earthly city that is strong and distinct from any divine city."[43] Allusions to the division between the divine and the earthly city make reference to yet another saint, Saint Augustine, and make more obvious the connection between Negri's post-*Marxism* and a *post*-Christianity informed by Spinoza's and Marx's materialism.

SLAVOJ ŽIŽEK

Perhaps there is no better example today of a theological turn in post-Marxism than Slavoj Žižek's work. Like Badiou, Žižek is interested in formulating universalist responses to capitalism and is opposed to what he sees as postmodern relativism and multicultural politics of recognition and difference. Like Badiou and Negri, he also wishes to provide a philosophical account of subjectivity and reality that makes anticapitalist militancy not only possible, but also necessary. And like both of them, he finds important examples and conceptual clues in Christianity for articulating his discourse. Žižek, however, goes to a larger extent than Badiou and Negri into exploring the value of Christianity for a materialist intervention into contemporary philosophy and politics.

Žižek is well known for a trilogy of books where he offers a materialist reading of Christianity. They are *The Fragile Absolute* (2000), *On Belief* (2001), and *The Puppet and the Dwarf* (2003). But already in his *Ticklish Subject* (1999) he had laid out the basis of his post-*Marxist* and *post*-Christian agenda: "While this book is philosophical in its basic tenor, it is first and foremost an engaged political intervention, addressing the burning question of how we are to reformulate a leftist, anti-capitalist political project in our era of global capitalism and its ideological supplement, liberal-democratic multi-culturalism."[44] And, in conversation with Badiou, he states: "what we need today is the gesture that would undermine capitalist globalization from the standpoint of universal Truth, just as Pauline Christianity did to the Roman global Empire."[45]

Where Žižek's goes further than Badiou in his reappropriation of Christian themes is, first and foremost, in the absolute interconnection that he sees between Christianity and Marxism, understood as dialectical materialism. In *The Puppet and the Dwarf* he spells out the implications of his approach: "My claim . . . is not merely that I am a materialist through and through, and that the subversive kernel of Christianity is accessible also to a materialist approach; my thesis is much stronger: this kernel is accessible *only* to a materialist approach—and vice versa: to become a true dialectical materialist, one should go through the Christian experience."[46]

The idea that one can only "become a true dialectical materialist" by going "through the Christian experience" makes Christianity not only absolutely central for Marxism, but also superior to other religions when it comes to the point of articulating a critique of capitalism and alternatives to it. And Žižek is not shy about distinguishing and separating what he sees as the "Christian breakthrough" with apparently less radical religious forms, including paganism, Judaism, and "Oriental spirituality."[47] He also calls for Marxism and Christianity to join forces, as they "*should* fight on the same side of the barricade against the onslaught of new spiritualisms."[48]

In Žižek, the lines that distinguish the post-*Marxist* theorist of subjectivity and politics and the *post*-Christian theologian seem to disappear, giving rise to a post-*Marxist* and *post*-Christian theorist of religion. Like most of the early theorists of religion, Žižek is interested in the extent to which Christianity and other religions, but particularly Christianity, have a place not simply in modern civilization, but more particularly in the thought and praxis that can counter capitalism in the twenty-first century. This is important and to some extent intriguing since Marx was on the side of those who wished Christianity to wither away in modernity. But a different attitude toward Christianity emerged among Žižek and other post-*Marxists* when, more than a hundred years later, the major forces of opposition to Marxist discourse were not capitalism and Christianity, but, presumably, capitalism and discourses of difference and multiculturalism. In this context, Christianity passed from being the paradigm of alienation, as in Ludwig Feuerbach, to being an indispensable resource for the practice of true dialectical materialism. And both, Marxism and Christianity, are called upon to resist capitalism and multiculturalism. To be sure, both Marx and Feuerbach, as well as Žižek and the other *post*-Christians, are, in a way, Christiancentric. The main difference is that, while the former questioned Christianity's right to existence in the modern world, for the latter, or at least for Žižek, "Christianity is, from its very inception, THE religion of modernity."[49]

Antipathy toward the value of cultural difference is one of the points that make post-*Marxism* different from other positions such as liberation theology, which is to some extent an irony because most liberation theologians were committed Christians. In this case, the *post*-Christians seem to be more invested in the uniqueness or superiority of Christianity than the militant Christians of the 1960s and 1970s, who, on the one hand, thought that militant praxis could emerge and be exercised through different languages and cultural themes (orthopraxis), and who, on the other, were influence by rising ecumenism. Žižek, instead, sides with other theologians who defend orthodoxy, and elaborates a theory of religion that only gives space to Christianity and Marxism in effectively responding to the gravest problems of the age.

Žižek identifies a number of ideas in Christianity that for him give it uncontested superiority when it comes to determining access to a true dialectical materialism, which in his case is infused with Lacanian insights. As in Badiou and Negri, Žižek's materialism is opposed to the idea of transcendence or metaphysical difference. And he sees this message in Christianity itself: "*it is the epochal achievement of Christianity to reduce its Otherness to Sameness*: God Himself is Man, 'one of us.' If, as Hegel emphasizes, what dies on the Cross is the God of beyond itself, the radical Other, then the identification with Christ ('life in Christ') means precisely the suspension of Otherness."[50] Christianity undermines the idea of an Other beyond, and focuses on the community of believers themselves, represented in the idea of the Holy Spirit. And just as the incarnation and death of Christ represent in a way the death of God as Other, the Holy Spirit represents the break with otherness at the level of the community, that is, with "communitarianism" and the politics of difference.

> "Holy Spirit" designates a new collective held together not by a Master-Signifier, but by fidelity to a Cause, by the effort to draw a new line of separation that runs "beyond Good and Evil," that is to say, that runs across and suspends the distinctions of the existing social body.[51]

> The suspension of Otherness at the metaphysical and the social level gives way to the formation of communities united by their purpose or fidelity to a cause. It is there that true love can emerge.[52]

The suspension of transcendence and any big Other, be it God in Christianity, or History in Stalinism or certain forms of Marxism, can only lead to materialism and love. This is what Žižek refers to as the subversive kernel of Christianity. This subversive kernel leads to materialism in ontology, to love in ethics and politics, and to post-*Marxism* and *post*-Christianity in theory and theology. And for Žižek, this kernel is so powerful that it claims the end of Christianity as a religious form itself. While Žižek goes at great length to demonstrate the superiority of Christianity and the uniqueness of its kernel, he also believes that the kernel of Christianity demands Christianity's own death. As he puts it,

> it is possible today to redeem this core of Christianity only in the gesture of abandoning the shell of its institutional organization (and, even more so, of its specific religious experience). The gap here is irreducible: either one drops the religious form, or one maintains the form, but loses the essence. That is the ultimate heroic gesture that awaits Christianity: in order to save its treasure, it has to sacrifice itself—like Christ, who had to die so that Christianity could emerge.[53]

Žižek's *post*-Christianity is truly "post," and like a good dialectician he finds the imperative for Christianity's overcoming in Christianity itself. And yet, Christianity preserves an aura of truth that no other religion provides, evinced precisely in the fact that the truth of Christianity's overcoming is found in Christianity itself. Christianity appears in Žižek's theory of religion as the only religion that provides the elements to criticize every religion, including itself.

In their contribution to the edited volume *Theology and the Political: The New Debate*, Creston Davis and Patrick Aaron Riches write: "After the given failure of Soviet scientific materialism and the seeming triumph of capitalist hegemony, socialism by its own force must (re)turn to the theological. Socialism, as the true and beautiful alternative to capitalist barbarism, must recapture the force of its own political desire. To do so, it must finally and irrevocably jettison its alliance with modernity, progressivism, and atheism. Socialism's theological turn is necessarily the (re)turn to political desire as spontaneous liberation." Then they go into not only rejecting the modern prejudice against theology, but proposing an "immanent operation" in order to "recover the intrinsically revolutionary implications of Christianity that have recently attracted the scrutiny of Marxists like Alain Badiou, Slavoj Žižek, Antonio Negri, and others."[54] This chapter has aimed to clarify some of the most basic points in the post-Marxist theological turn of Badiou, Negri, and Žižek.

The new rapprochement between Christianity and Marxism has renewed the critical discourse of capitalism and put in question the viability of postmodern and multicultural discourses, even as it tends to take as an object of critique the less sophisticated versions and more water-downed liberal expressions of anti-Eurocentric discourses and defenses of cultural difference. It is therefore not surprising that the project takes the form of a new orthodoxy in Žižek's work. This orthodoxy counters the influence of Judaism in contemporary European critical discourse after the wide influence of Jewish figures like Emmanuel Levinas and Jacques Derrida and opposes the "onslaught of new spiritualisms." Only time will tell if these theoretical *movidas* will mark post-*Marxism* as a necessary and important source in the struggle against myriad forms of domination and exploitation, or if they will further isolate this discourse and make it ultimately as irrelevant as the Marxism that it is trying to replace.

NOTES

1. Ernesto Laclau and Chantal Mouffe, *Hegemony and Socialist Strategy*, 2nd ed. (New York: Verso, 2001), 4.

2. Simon Tormey and Jules Townsend, *Key Thinkers from Critical Theory to Post-Marxism* (London: Sage, 2006); Stuart Sim, ed., *Post-Marxism: An Intellectual History* (London: Routledge, 2000). Simon Tormey and Jules Townsend, for example, argue that "post-Marxism" is only relevant in reference to the post-1968 generation, while Stuart Sim uses it to refer to those and previous figures.

3. Roland Boer, *Criticism of Heaven: On Marxism and Theology* (Leiden: Brill, 2007); Alasdair MacIntyre, *Marxism and Christianity*, 3rd ed. (London: Duckworth, 2010).

4. Enrique Dussel, *Las metáforas teológicas de Marx* (Marx's theological metaphors) (Estella, Navarra: Verbo Divino, 1993); MacIntyre, *Marxism and Christianity*.

5. Göran Therborn, *What Does the Ruling Class Do When It Rules? State Apparatuses and State Power Under Feudalism, Capitalism and Socialism* (London: Verso, 2008), 131; Creston Davis and Patrick Aaron Riches, "Metanoia: The Theological Praxis of Revolution," in *Theology and the Political: The New Debate*, ed. Creston Davis, John Milbank, and Slavoj Žižek (Durham: Duke University Press, 2005), 22.

6. Laclau and Mouffe, *Hegemony and Socialist Strategy*, ix–x, 4.

7. Alain Badiou, *Being and Event*, trans. Oliver Feltham (London: Continuum, 2006), xi.

8. Ibid.

9. Ibid., 1.

10. Ibid.

11. Ibid., 3.

12. Ibid., xii.

13. Ibid., 4.

14. Ibid., xii–xiii.

15. Ibid., xiii.

16. Ibid., 212.

17. Alain Badiou, *Manifesto for Philosophy*, trans. Norman Madarasz (Albany: State University of New York Press, 1999), 56–57.

18. Alain Badiou, *Ethics: An Essay on the Understanding of Evil*, trans. Peter Hallward (London: Verso, 2001), 25.

19. Badiou, *Manifesto for Philosophy*, 143.

20. Ibid.

21. Alain Badiou, *Saint Paul: The Foundation of Universalism*, trans. Ray Brassier (Stanford: Stanford University Press, 2003), 2.

22. Ibid.

23. Ibid., 11.

24. Antonio Negri, *Marx Beyond Marx: Lessons on the Grundrisse*, trans. Harry Cleaver, Michael Ryan, and Maurizio Viano (New York: Autonomedia/Pluto, 1991), 187.

25. Ibid., 189.

26. Antonio Negri, *Time for Revolution*, trans. Matteo Mandarini (New York: Continuum, 2003), 143.

27. Ibid., 146.

28. Ibid., 181.

29. Ibid., 181–82.

30. Ibid., 194.

31. Ibid.

32. Ibid., 195.

33. Ibid., 199.

34. Ibid., 204.

35. Ibid., 201.

36. Ibid., 209–10.

37. Ibid., 210.

38. Ibid.

39. Michael Hardt and Antonio Negri, *Multitude: War and Democracy in the Age of Empire* (New York: Penguin, 2004), 351.

40. Ibid., 351–52.

41. Badiou, *Saint Paul*, 90.

42. Michael Hardt and Antonio Negri, *Empire* (Cambridge, Mass.: Harvard University Press, 2000), 413, italics in original.

43. Ibid., 396, 411.

44. Slavoj Žižek, *The Ticklish Subject: The Absent Centre of Political Ontology* (London: Verso, 1999), 4.

45. Ibid., 211.

46. Slavoj Žižek, *The Puppet and the Dwarf: The Perverse Core of Christianity* (Cambridge, Mass.: MIT Press, 2003), 7.

47. Ibid., 25–33, 115–21.

48. Slavoj Žižek, *The Fragile Absolute; Or, Why Is the Christian Legacy Worth Fighting For?* (London: Verso, 2000), 2.

49. Slavoj Žižek, *On Belief* (London: Routledge. 2001), 150.

50. Žižek, *The Puppet and the Dwarf*, 130.

51. Ibid., 131.

52. Žižek, *The Fragile Absolute*, 129–30.

53. Žižek, *The Puppet and the Dwarf*, 171.

54. Davis and Riches, "Metanoia," 23.

42

Pierre Bourdieu on Religion

TERRY REY

OVERVIEW

Although the French sociologist Pierre Bourdieu wrote relatively little about the subject, religion was one of the most fundamental influences on his understanding of how society works.[1] Institutional religion, especially the Roman Catholic Church, provided Bourdieu with a most serviceable paradigm for identifying and critiquing all institutionalized "systems of meaning." Such systems help create, legitimate, and reproduce social distinctions (for example, of race, class, gender, and sexuality) and all forms of social inequality predicated thereupon, which was Bourdieu's chief preoccupation as a scholar. As such, religion was Bourdieu's model par excellence of an institution that engenders in people a "practical sense" of the social world, of their positions therein, and of what they can expect from life. He thus affirms the awesome historical influence that religion has enjoyed in the creation and reproduction of the *doxa*, or "the pre-verbal taking-for-granted of the world that flows from practical sense."[2] For this reason it is for more than just a sarcastic effect when Bourdieu frequently uses religious language (for example, "orthodoxy," "heresy," "sacred," "consecration," "priest," "prophet," "sorcerer," "heresiarch," "dogma," "doctrine," "transubstantiation," "sacraments," "veneration," and "theodicy") in theorizing a whole range of "secular" social institutions and practices.

How is it that religion got to become the paradigmatic producer and reproducer of *doxa* in the first place? Bourdieu's answer is that religions "impose" worldviews upon people by "inculcating" into them (into their *habitus*, to be precise)[3] modes of perception and thought, as well as values and dispositions. Religions are thus prolific producers of people's "misrecognition" that the social word is only unequal because of karma, God's will, or some other "euphemistic" linguistic construct that "legitimizes" (by "naturalizing")—an act of "consecration"—the order of things, the status quo: "religion conserves the social order by contributing . . . to the 'legitmation' of the power of 'the dominant' and to the 'domestication of the dominated.'"[4] Religion's demonstrable capacity to inspire charity, compassion, and well-being, however, seemingly never struck Bourdieu as important. On a personal level, furthermore, though churched in his childhood, "Bourdieu himself was not religious" and he "manifested no inclination for religious activity."[5] On a scholarly level, meanwhile, Bourdieu argued that any meaning that we find in life, whether derived from religion, politics, the arts, or what have you, is socially produced and thus artificial.

In such an intrinsically meaningless world, one into which we are "born determined" with but "a small chance of ending up free," religion is little more than a desperate attempt to create meaning: "religion is a systematic answer to the question of life and death . . . the death of people we love, the 'ultimate' questions, illness, human suffering.[6] Questions to which humans never find answers on their own; religion provides them answers to such ultimate questions."[7] But the answers that religion provides are, for Bourdieu, entirely groundless because "man is a being without a reason for being. It is society, and society alone [and *not* religion], which dispenses, to different degrees, the justifications and the reasons for existing," resulting in the "wretchedness of man without God or any hope of grace."[8] And so, any attempt "to save spiritual values from the threat of science" is, for Bourdieu, "ridiculous."

Bourdieu's own negative reading of and disposition toward religion notwithstanding, an increasing number of religion scholars and even a few theologians[9] have been employing Bourdieusian theory with much profit, and generally in ways that are *not* negatively disposed to their subject. Basically they fall into two general categories, even if in some instances inevitably straddling them: (1) those concerned with religion and social class; and (2) those concerned with religion and human perception. I will summarize an example of each momentarily, but first a thumbnail sketch of Bourdieu's trademark theory of practice is in order.

BOURDIEU'S THEORY OF PRACTICE

Bourdieu's theory of practice is a highly complex yet subtle collectivity of "thinking tools," a systematic network of concepts that is designed to provide us with a broadly applicable paradigm for the interpretation of human subjectivity's relationship to social structures and of how *practice* (what people do) emerges out of that relationship. Toward understanding Bourdieusian theory, it is helpful to briefly define its three signature concepts and provide an explanatory sketch of what each one does and how they work together: (1) *habitus*; (2) *field*; and (3) *capital*.

1. *Habitus*—fundamental to human subjectivity, *habitus* is both one's "matrix of perceptions" and the generator of one's dispositions, inclinations, and cultural tastes and tendencies.
2. *Field*—the social world is divided into specific and interrelated fields, which are arenas or subspaces of social action (such as the political field, the economic field, the religious field, and so on) in which individuals are positioned in a competitive struggle over the production and consumption of forms of capital.

3. *Capital*—taking various forms relative to specific fields, capital is a socially produced possession or resource, either material or symbolic, that functions as power to secure or improve one's status or station in society, or as a "weapon of symbolic violence"[10] to cement others in lower stati or stations.

Put simply, practice takes place in any number of the interrelated and sometimes overlapping fields that together constitute society. In Bourdieu's model, most of what we do as social agents boils down to perceivably self-interested pursuits of forms of capital, whether material or symbolic, relative to the respective fields in which our practice unfolds. Furthermore, the ways in which we perceive of and pursue capital are chiefly generated by the practical sense that resides in our *habitus*, which is that part of our personal subjectivity that filters our perceptions, molds our cultural tastes, and casts our inclinations, dispositions, and desires.

As a sustained exercise in "fieldwork in philosophy," the most ambitious objective of Bourdieu's theory of practice is to settle once and for all the entire free will *versus* determinism debate. Theological considerations have, for Bourdieu, no place in this debate because God's supposed position therein is occupied by society itself: "God is never anything other than society. What is expected of God is only ever obtained from society, which alone has the power to justify you, to liberate you from facticity, contingency, and absurdity."[11] And so the fundamental question about human practice is whether our actions as "social agents" are in the main determined by social structures or by our own free will. Although he is often criticized for opting for the former and therefore being deterministic in his social thought, Bourdieu's theory of practice in fact quite effectively answers that human subjects are both structured and structuring, for which reason he identifies his approach as a form of "generative structuralism."[12] Thus the key to understanding human practice lies in the *intergenerative* relationship between *habitus* and social structures, or *fields*: the world makes us, just as we make and remake the world through internalizing it and objectifying it and, as such, in (re)-creating it, naturalizing it, and believing it to be real. In other words, "the field structures the habitus" while "habitus contributes to constituting the field as a meaningful world."[13]

Despite variations in the kinds of capital that they feature and in the interests, strategies, and positions that agents employ or occupy within them, all social fields are situated within the metafield of power and are thereby structurally "homologous." By this, Bourdieu means that all fields are characterized by the same (*homo*) principle (*logous*), operating, in this sense, according to a uniform logic, and thus fields can be said to share certain "structural homologies." As such, individual fields (for example, the economic field, the political field, the religious field) are only "relatively autonomous," interpenetrating and influencing one another and interrelating through flows of power within and across them. The structural homology and relative autonomy of fields allow for the transferability of capital from one field to another, a process that Bourdieu refers to as "transubstantiation"![14] To illustrate with a specific example, if I succeed in obtaining an MBA from a prestigious university, which is clearly a highly coveted piece of academic capital (a form of symbolic capital), I will be in a position of greater potential (that is, em*power*ed) to succeed in the economic field and augment my sum of economic capital (a form of material capital), namely, money. Furthermore, my MBA degree is a piece of symbolic capital that contributes to the "misrecognition" that we who hold such degrees are "smart," "hard-working," and "entrepreneurial," and thus deservedly have high incomes, and that's just the way it is; issues such as inheritance, privilege, and racial injustice that clearly play a role in access to quality education are thereby effectively masked, thus clearing the way for the injustices of the world to be reproduced.

We now proceed to take a closer look at some examples of how these and other Bourdieusian ideas have been put to work in the interpretation and analysis of religion.

TWO BOURDIEUSIAN INTERPRETATIONS OF RELIGION

As noted above, most Bourdieusian interpretations of religion fall into either one of two general categories: (1) those that are concerned with religion and social class; and (2) those that are concerned with religion and human perception. Exemplary of the former is Otto Maduro's sociohistorical interpretation of Latin American religion, while exemplary of the later is Thomas Csordas's "cultural phenomenology" of Catholic Charismatic ritual.

Maduro's early work is an important precedent for scholars interested in understanding the sociopolitical role of religion in colonial and emergent postcolonial societies. Taking its cue from Bourdieu, it outlines how the arrival and establishment in the Americas of Spanish and Portuguese colonizers under Vatican sanction created a radically unequal division of labor (including religious labor) and distribution of capital, both material and symbolic. As a result of such divisions and the establishment of the hierarchical and increasingly monopolistic Church of the colonizer, "religion was no longer a product arising directly out of the interest of indigenous Latin American communities."[15] This occurred because the Church "*dispossessed*" colonized subjects of religious capital, forcing them in turn "to have recourse to the clergy to satisfy their religious interests," their *habitus* having been inculcated with the belief in the Church as the unique purveyor of those paramount forms of religious capital called "sacraments," which are of course requisite for salvation. A complementary part of the Church's strategy was to also inculcate into the Native American religious *habitus* the misrecognition that indigenous religious traditions are not religious at all but are heretical and therefore illegitimate and unworthy of pursuit.

Here we see how the transubstantiative capacity of symbolic capital makes Bourdieusian theory so well suited for interpreting the relationship between religion, class, and power, especially in societies that are characterized by stark class divisions. Maduro answers Bourdieu's call for a field analysis that focuses on the struggle over forms of religious capital that enable religious institutions to produce (and consecrate) "salvation goods," such as sacraments and ecclesial sanction. Once transferred into other fields and transformed (that is, transubstantiated) into other forms of capital, "legitimate" religious capital of this kind furthermore enables elite agents or institutions to enhance or augment their holdings of economic and political capital and thereby solidify or improve their positions in the economic and political fields, and thus to dominate in the metafield of power. For Maduro, this has been precisely the case in Latin America. Power requires consecration, after all, and religion is the prototypical possessor of the authority to consecrate, having historically done so in ways that inform Bourdieu's entire understanding of the very nature of society.

In addition to the rich use that scholars like Maduro have made of Bourdieusian theory in the analysis of religion and class, a number of equally impressive studies have emerged that explore the corporal implications of Bourdieu's notion of *habitus* for the study of religion and perception. One's *habitus* is *perforce* embodied in such a way that makes one's body a "socially informed body." Thomas Cordas rightly reads Bourdieu to mean that structures of the social world, including of course the structures of ritual, issue from and are reproduced by "'a dialectic of objectification and embodiment' that makes it *the locus* for the coordination of all levels of bodily, social, and cosmological experience."[16] *Habitus* is thus so useful for the analysis of religious ritual and practice "because it focuses on the psychologically internalized content of the behavioral environment" and because of its resolute "groundedness in the body."[17] Charismatic ritual, for example, features "somatic images" (for example, the laying on of hands, tongues of fire, and the like) that are "inculcated as *techniques du corps* that will embody dispositions characteristic of the religious milieu."[18] One such "*technique du corps*" that is common in Charismatic healing rituals is falling, which usually is caused by the laying on of hands during faith healing: "The act of falling is spontaneously coordinated in such a way that, following Bourdieu, it can be described as a disposition within the ritual habitus."[19]

In the language of Csordas's cultural phenomenology, the images of the Incarnation (God in flesh) and of Grace (God giving the gift of tongues) are embodied and reside in "the matrix of perception" of the Charismatic habitus. Thus when a believer perceives the person in the pew in front of her speaking in tongues, she perceives this to be a manifestation of divinity and not the gibberish of a madman. In this way is seen how the *habitus* is both the generator of this form of ritual behavior in the speaker and the matrix of perception in the hearer/viewer that makes sense of something that would otherwise be senseless.

In different ways, Maduro and Csordas demonstrate that Bourdieusian theory has great analytical power for the understanding of human perception and its function in religious belief and practice. Taken together, they suggest that, thanks to Bourdieu, we can finally say that religious belief has a home: the religious *habitus*, which is as much bodily as mentally constructed through the negotiation of the social. By carefully tracing the implications for the interpretation of religion of the dialectical relationship of *habitus* and field, Maduro and Csordas respectively demonstrate how incisive Bourdieusian theory is for the study of religion, whether for scholars seeking to understand the relationship between religion and politics or for scholars concerned with the place of the human body in religious experience and practice. They suggest, for one crucial example, that everything that one might observe people do in their religious practice is chiefly the manifestation of perceptions and dispositions that are embodied in the religious *habitus* of practitioners (of believers), which is itself (re)generatively structured by the religious field. This is perhaps the most important insight to emerge thus far out of the Bourdieusian interpretation of religion.

CLOSING THOUGHTS AND NEW DIRECTIONS

The foregoing brief discussion of the landmark work of Maduro and Csordas is not intended to suggest that Bourdieu has had the same resounding impact on the study of religion as he has on other human sciences. In two of the leading academic fields concerned with religion, Religious Studies and the sociology of religion, his influence has in fact been relatively marginal, though this is beginning to change, and the theoretical dialogues that are emerging hold tremendous promise. One such emergent dialogue places Bourdieusian thought in conversation with rational choice theory of religion, a model taken from economics that is a dominant approach in the sociology of religion today. In reading its leading proponents, such as Rodney Stark and Roger Finke, I've often wondered why rational choice theorists of religion pay virtually no attention to the most widely cited social scientist of our time, Pierre Bourdieu, who himself also used economic logic and terminology to investigate religion. It may very well be that such proponents of the microeconomic interpretation of religion have not engaged Bourdieu because they consider him to be emblematic of what R. Stephen Warner identifies as "the old paradigm metanarrative of religion": "There was only one provider of religious meaning and religious services, only one place to approach God and only one institution to confer legitimacy on rites of passage. Since the church was a protected monopoly, assent was assured by the fact that there were no ideological alternatives, and the church's viewpoint, it is said, was unquestionably taken for granted."[20]

Alternatively, or additionally, the aversion to Bourdieu in most sociology of religion might be a reaction to Bourdieu's own explicit criticisms of rational choice theory. For Bourdieu clearly opposes the thoroughgoing subjectivity and freedom of individual choice upon which rational choice theory and the new paradigm are predicated: "Thus, against the scholastic illusion which tends to see every action as springing from an intentional aim . . . the theory of habitus has the primordial function of stressing that the principle of our actions is more often practical sense than rational calculation."[21] One among a small but growing cadre of sociologists of religion who are beginning to notice this perplexing rift,[22] Roland Robertson[23] helpfully suggests how Bourdieu's theory of practice, despite some measure of structuralist rigidity that many scholars have assailed,[24] can help counter the "complete absence of constraint on consumers" in rational choice theory of religion, thereby affirming that "choices are formed by circumstances"—by the dialectic of *habitus* and field, as it were.[25]

In closing, I would like to suggest that there is abundant potential for synthesizing aspects of Bourdieu's theory of practice with rational choice theory and other leading scholarly interpretations of religion. Though tempted to demonstrate by explaining in detail how *habitus* could help elucidate Mircea Eliade's notion of "hierophany" or the "moods and motivations" in Clifford Geertz's influential definition of religion, I'll end here with a brief Bourdieusian word on William James instead.[26] James understands religion ultimately to be about "pure ideas" of "remoter fact": "in general our whole higher prudential and moral life is based on the fact that material sensations actually present may have a weaker influence on our action than *ideas of remoter fact*. . . . The whole force of . . . religion, therefore, . . . is in general exerted by the instrumentality of *pure ideas*."[27] By "pure ideas" James means notions that are unmitigated by "sense impressions," to use the language of the seventeenth-century British Empiricists, or ideas that are rooted *purely* in intuition, "sixth sense," mystical experience, imagination, and the like, which of course are often understood and transmitted to be the essence of religious tradition. Pure ideas of remoter facts thus largely make up that which Bourdieu calls the "religious habitus": "a lasting, generalized and transposable disposition to act and think in conformity with the principles of a (quasi) systematic view of the world and human existence," and "the principal generator of all thoughts, perceptions and actions consistent with the norms of a religious representation of the natural and supernatural worlds."[28] As the subjective site of belief, or the repository of our pure ideas of remoter facts, and the "principal generator" of practice, so much about the nature and function of religion can be explained via consideration of the religious *habitus* and its *inter-(re)generative* relationship with the social.

NOTES

1. Bourdieu's most important essays on religion are: Pierre Bourdieu, "Genèse et structure du champ religieux," *Revue française de sociologie* 12, no. 2 (1971): 295–334; Pierre Bourdieu, "Une interprétation de la théorie de la religion selon Max Weber," *Archives européenne de sociologie* 12, no. 1 (1971): 3–21. For a review of all of Bourdieu's essays on religion, see Terry Rey, *Bourdieu on Religion: Imposing Faith and Legitimacy* (London: Equinox, 2007). For a discussion of the foundational influence of religion on Bourdieu's social theory, see Erwan Dianteill, "Pierre Bourdieu and the Sociology of Religion: A Central and Peripheral Concern," in *After Bourdieu: Influence, Critique, Elaboration*, ed. David L. Swartz and Vera L. Zolberg (Dordrecht, Netherlands: Kluwer, 2004), 65–85.

2. Pierre Bourdieu, *In Other Words: Essays Towards a Reflexive Sociology*, trans. Matthew Adamson (Stanford: Stanford University Press, 1990), 68.

3. Pierre Bourdieu, *Outline of a Theory of Practice*, trans. Richard Nice (Cambridge: Cambridge University Press, 1977), 82–83.

4. Pierre Bourdieu, "Genesis and Structure of the Religious Field," trans. Jenny B. Burnside, Craig Calhoun, and Leah Florence, *Comparative Social Research* 13 (1991): 1–44, 4.

5. David Swartz and Vera L. Zolberg, eds., "Introduction," in *After Bourdieu: Influence, Critique, Elaboration* (Dordrecht, Netherlands: Kluwer, 2004), 5; Dianteill, "Pierre Bourdieu and the Sociology of Religion," 84.

6. Anne-Marie Lesourret, *Bourdieu* (Paris: Flammarion, 2008), 455.

7. Pierre Bourdieu, *Das religiöse Feld: Texte zur Ökonomie des Heilsgeshehens*, trans. Andreas Pfeffer (Konstanz, Germany: Universitätsverlag Konstanz, 2000), 123. I gratefully acknowledge help in translating this passage from the German from my good friends Gereon Kopf, Claudia Schippert, and Alfons Teipen.

8. Pierre Bourdieu, *In Other Words*, 196, 15.

9. For a discussion of recent Bourdieusian studies of religion, see Terry Rey, "Pierre Bourdieu and the Study of Religion: Recent Developments, Directions, and Departures," in *The Oxford Handbook of Pierre Bourdieu*, ed. Jeffrey J. Sallaz and Thomas Medvetz (New York: Oxford University Press, forthcoming).

10. Pierre Bourdieu, *Pascalian Meditations*, trans. Richard Nice (Stanford: Stanford University Press, 2000), 170. Symbolic Violence is another key concept in Bourdieu's social thought, which he defines as "the coercion which is set up only through the consent that the dominated cannot fail to give to the dominator (and therefore to the domination) when their understanding of the situation and the relation can only use instruments of knowledge that they have in common with the dominator, which, being merely the incorporated form of the structure of domination, makes this relation appear as natural."

11. Bourdieu, *In Other Words*, 196.

12. Cheleen Mahar, Richard Harker, and Chris Wilkes, *An Introduction to the Work of Pierre Bourdieu: The Practice of Theory* (London: Palgrave Macmillan, 1990), 33–34.

13. Pierre Bourdieu and Loïc J. D. Wacquant, *An Invitation to Reflexive Sociology* (Chicago: University of Chicago Press, 1992), 127.

14. Pierre Bourdieu, "The Forms of Capital," in *Handbook of Theory and Research for the Sociology of Education*, ed. J. Richardson (New York: Greenwood, 1986), 242.

15. Otto Maduro, *Religion and Social Conflicts* (Maryknoll, N.Y.: Orbis, 1982), 86.

16. Thomas J. Csordas, *The Sacred Self: A Cultural Phenomenology of Charismatic Healing* (Berkeley: University of California Press, 1994), 97.

17. Ibid., 66. El-Sayed el-Aswad makes similar use of Bourdieu's notion of corporal-hexis (without using the term itself) in theorizing popular cosmology in contemporary rural Egypt. El-Sayed el-Aswad, *Religion and Folk Cosmology: Scenarios of the Visible and the Invisible in Rural Egypt* (London: Praeger, 2002), 91–92.

18. Csordas, *The Sacred Self*, 70.

19. Ibid., 233.

20. R. Stephen Warren, "More Progress on the New Paradigm," in *Sacred Markets, Sacred Canopies: Essays on Religious Markets and Religious Pluralism*, ed. Ted G. Jelen (Lanham, Md.: Rowan and Littlefield, 2002), 2.

21. Bourdieu, *Pascalian Meditations*, 63–64.

22. For more recent considerations of this disconnect in the sociology of religion, see Jean-Pierre Bastian, "La nouvelle économie religieuse de L'Amérique latine," *Social Compass*

53, no. 1 (2006): 65–80; and Jörg Stoltz, ed., *Salvation Goods and Religious Markets: Theory and Applications* (Bern: Peter Lang, 2008).

23. Roland Robertson, "The Economization of Religion? Reflections on the Promise and Limitations of the Economic Approach," *Social Compass* 39, no. 1 (1992): 151.

24. For a review of stated limitations of Bourdieusian theory and their specific relevance to the study of religion, see Rey, *Bourdieu on Religion*, 120–31.

25. Robertson, "The Economization of Religion," 155.

26. Mircea Eliade, *The Sacred and the Profane: The Nature of Religion* (San Diego: Harvest, 1957), 11; Clifford Geertz, *The Interpretation of Cultures* (London: Hutchinson, 1975), 90. Eliade defines hierophany as "the *act of manifestation* of the sacred. . . . that *something sacred shows itself to us.*" Geertz defines religion as "a system of symbols which acts to establish powerful, pervasive, and long-lasting moods and motivations in men by formulating conceptions of a general order of existence and clothing these conceptions with such an aura of factuality that the moods and motivations seem uniquely realistic."

27. William James, *The Varieties of Religious Experience* (New York: Penguin, 1952), 63.

28. Pierre Bourdieu, "Legitimation and Structured Interest in Weber's Sociology of Religion," in *Max Weber, Rationality, and Modernity*, ed. Scott Lash and Sam Whimster, trans. Chris Turner (London: Allen and Unwin, 1987), 124; Bourdieu, "Genèse et structure du champ religieux," 319.

43

Jacques Derrida on Religion

ELLEN ARMOUR

A philosopher by profession, Jacques Derrida's work was imported into the United States through literary criticism, where he became known as the "father of deconstruction." Originally Derrida's term for a reading strategy that inquired after the limits of a text's explicit logic, deconstruction became in America a program—and a controversial one, at that. What some saw as a fresh approach to scholarly inquiry seemed to others at best esoteric nonsense and at worst dangerous nihilism. Derrida was either hailed or vilified as a harbinger of postmodernity, an epochal shift marked by the death of God, of reason, and of the knowledgeable subject.[1] As such, his work was viewed largely as a threat to religion. Scholarly consensus on Derrida's work since, however, has rejected this view.[2] Derrida disavows any association with postmodernism and neither advances nor announces the demise—timely or untimely—of any of these central features of Western thought.[3] He does, however, explore the extent of their reach and expose their boundaries.

The linchpin in this negative view of Derrida's work was what early readers took to be deconstruction's key claim, "there is nothing outside the text." Insofar as moral, epistemological, and religious language presumed to speak of reality, Derrida seemed to allege that they were illusory. Derrida's actual claim, however, is far more specific, for one thing: there is nothing outside the text *of Western metaphysics*. That "text" is the context within which we in the West speak, know, and do. Derrida calls it a text in part to alert us to its linguistic character. Like all languages, this (con)text has a basic grammar and logic that take on flesh in the form of what can and cannot be thought, done, and seen. Its grammar is ontotheological. That is, it revolves around the notion of absolute presence, unadulterated unity, and pure being—that is, God. This God, as the source of all that is (the *theos* that grounds *ontos*), serves as the guarantor of truth because his Word (*logos*) is reality.

The masculine pronoun for God is not coincidental, for the text of Western metaphysics is not just ontotheological, but also phallogocentric, Derrida claims (drawing here on psychoanalytic theorist Jacques Lacan).[4] It is sustained by an economy of desire that circulates around the phallus, the standard of truth and value. Our ability to mean what we say depends on our proximity to the phallus. Those who believe they have the phallus, a position marked as masculine, are better able to approximate truth. Those who believe they are the phallus, a position marked as feminine, are assigned to the realm of the inchoate and incoherent. That the text's grammar extends beyond "mere language," though, is reflected in our heteronormative sexual economy. The desiring subject is masculine and the object of desire feminine.

This economy is religious in two senses. Not only is it ontotheological, but it is sustained by belief. The phallus is a phantasmatic object; no one can *really* have—or be—the phallus. In that sense, its existence is a matter of faith. Believing we have or are the phallus sustains the sexual economy as well as the linguistic one. Being a man or a woman may lack ultimate ontological grounding, but such positions are far from illusory. A substantial infrastructure has grown up around them and continues to support them. This system trades in certain "currencies" (truth, language, desire) and involves the circulation and accumulation of cultural and financial "capital." So to acquiesce to the roles available to us in this system is to accrue whatever cultural or financial capital (if any) is accorded to them.

To the degree that this (con)text is coextensive with Western discourse and culture, what lies outside it is rendered largely invisible, illegible, and unintelligible—nonexistent in any meaningful way, it would seem; nothing fully escapes it. That we can trace its boundaries, however, suggests that what lies "outside" is something other than empty space or absolute nothingness. Derrida's interest lies not in simply exposing the text's boundaries, but in evoking and invoking what lies at its boundaries: what is "othered" by it and thus "other" to it, yet what often grounds it.[5] Here, too, religion and religious motifs figure prominently. In various places, Derrida takes up and takes on "the Abrahamic," his term for the nexus of religions (Christianity, Islam, and Judaism) that trace their roots to this common ancestor.[6] Religious motifs do not arise merely in explicitly religious contexts, however, and so with Derrida's work. In part because religion serves as a placeholder for radical transcendence in Western discourse and culture, Derrida turns to religious motifs as routes to the outside. Much has been made of the resemblance of deconstruction (as a reading and writing strategy) to so-called negative or apophatic theology.[7] In texts such as *Specters of Marx*, Derrida adopted the figure of the messianic to name an orientation to the yet-to-come that carries Western metaphysics beyond itself.[8] He also took up the themes of forgiveness and hospitality as markers of the claims of the unconditioned in and on this context.[9]

In 1994, Derrida participated in a colloquium on religion hosted by the Italian philosopher Gianni Vattimo. Titled "Faith and Knowledge: the Two Sources of 'Religion' at the Limits of Reason Alone," his contribution to the subsequent volume is a useful index to the general tenor of Derrida's work on and with religion. As one might guess, given its title, Derrida challenges the Western narrative of its religiosity.[10] This narrative, which marks modernity's emergence with religion's decline and secularism's rise, presumes that modernity dethroned religion by consigning its two sources, faith and knowledge of the sacred, to the irrational or arational.

Derrida's inquiry begins with a question of language and naming, the etymology and definition of "religion" itself. Embedded therein he finds a set of presuppositions with deep and wide reach. The very occurrence of a scholarly colloquium on religion presumes that the meaning of religion is self-evident and transcends any particular historical or cultural form (of which there are many). Thus, the colloquium takes for granted the term's universality. And yet such an assumption—or belief—belies the specific historico-cultural and linguistic origins of the term, which lie within the Greco-Latinate-Christian idiom (shared, he notes, by the colloquium's participants, Europeans all). The success of religion's ability to name what it claims to name rests on its ability to transcend its original idiom—a promise whose fulfillment Derrida calls into question.[11]

Derrida singles out for particular attention—quite appropriately, given its centrality to modern accounts of religion—Kant's philosophy of religion. Kant cordons religion off from speculative or "pure" reason (that which produces, for example, scientific knowledge) and locates it in the sphere of practical reason. He recognizes two forms of religion: cultic religion, directed toward achieving divine favor, and moral religion, directed toward living rightly in communion with others. Both have their source in faith, but where cultic religion's faith is dogmatic and mistakes divine revelation for genuine knowledge, moral religion's faith is (self-)reflective and issues in action. Reflective faith allows the human being to exercise its capacity for freedom governed by reason, a capacity that distinguishes the human species from its fellow creatures. Thus, in Kant's scheme, true religion is universal, rational, and moral. While one may find true religion practiced by adherents of any particular revealed religion, divine revelation is not necessary to the exercise of true religion—that is, the cultivation of the ethical life. Anyone may access religion's truth via the exercise of the human facility for practical reason.

This does not mean that all religions are equal. In *Religion Within the Boundaries of Reason Alone*, Kant establishes self-reflective faith as the truth of religion not only through his account of the moral life, but through demonstrating its essential kinship to Christianity.[12] Kant's analysis reveals Christianity as the mirror image of rational religion, thus confirming rational religion's claim on religiosity and ipso facto establishing Christianity as itself true. But how universal is this account of the truth of religion? Insofar as Christianity and rational religion are mirror images of each other, only religions that resemble Christianity will be truly moral. Thus, says Derrida, "a mission would thus be reserved exclusively for it and it alone: that of liberating a 'reflecting faith.' "[13]

Modern Christianity arguably took up that mission with a vengeance. One thinks first of Christianity's labors as an ally of colonialist expansion. But the emergence of the academic study of religion is itself arguably a product of this same mission (and history).[14] This indissociable association is reflected in what Derrida calls *mondialatinization* (translated as "globalatinization"). In many ways coincident with globalization, *mondialatinization* renders explicit the cultural and linguistic (as well as economic) forces that have rather literally (re)made the world as a network. "Latinization" calls attention not only to current Western dominance but to that dominance as a reflection of the legacy of Roman imperialism, a prior occasion of world (re)making to which the West (and Christianity, the last religion of the Roman Empire) is heir and by which it remains haunted. Insofar as that heritage helped inspire and sustain previous Western imperialisms—also world-(re)making enterprises—*mondialatinization* recalls a long legacy of exploration, expansion, and colonization.

With that long and complex history in mind, Derrida asks us to consider "what is *said* and *done*, what *is happening* at this very moment, in the world, in history, in [religion's] name."[15] Ours is a time, we say, of renewed religious warfare, he notes (some ten years before 9/11). But lest we identify religious wars only with "them"— whether Al-Qaeda, the Taliban, or the Christian Right, to name some immediate concerns here in the United States—Derrida also asks whether the "military 'interventions,' led by the Judaeo-Christian West in the name of the best causes (of international law, democracy, the sovereignty of peoples, of nations or of states, even of humanitarian imperatives) . . . are not also, from a certain side, wars of religion."[16] To answer in the negative presumes one can isolate "the religious" from "the political, the economic, the juridical"—a project that a consideration of faith's role in politics, economics, and law renders problematic.

Fiduciary trust has made the world go around since the advent of modern capitalism and democracy. The signature, guarantor of the signatory's now absent presence, not only makes checks legal tender, but makes bills into laws; yet it rests ultimately on faith in its genuineness.[17] The juridical system, likewise, is founded on faith. Testimony is given under oath. The witness promises to respond truthfully; the oath sets apart (renders "holy") the speech acts that will constitute this testimony. And insofar as the juridical system rests on a notion of justice as unconditioned and absolute, outside the order of calculation, it too rests on faith. To be just is to do justice, that is, justice is instantiated in its performance, and its performance is a response to a "call to faith" in its unconditionedness.[18]

Insofar as the foundations of justice, democracy, and testimony give rise to justice, democracy, testimony, and the institutions they undergird, they are not themselves just, democratic, truthful, and so on. Insofar as they exceed those orders of naming and being—indeed, of nameability and the ability to be per se—they require leaps of faith. But while the moment of singularity is critical here, such leaps do not (only or simply) wrest one out of the company of others and the values and practices that sustain oneself (as with Kierkegaard's solitary knight of faith). Rather, they ground as well as unground all that life-in-community requires and aspires to be.[19]

Given the foundational role of faith, the modern project of fencing off the secular from the religious seems misguided, if not doomed from the start. Moreover, such a project is itself religious, that is, it proceeds in the name of the pure, the set-apart, the holy, Derrida notes. That religions refuse to cooperate—and that they "return" in the form of so-called fundamentalisms that turn violent and, in turn, provoke violence—registers as an autoimmune response, he suggests.[20]

Clearly, then, religion is not a matter of merely theoretical interest for Derrida. In the years immediately preceding his death, Derrida's work treated the topics of religion and politics, democracy and justice, in published interviews as well as formal presentations and publications.[21] One finds therein further insights not only into the work of a complex and thoughtful philosopher, but into the all-too-real religious terrors of our own day.[22]

NOTES

1. See, for example, the first volume to emerge on deconstruction and religion: Thomas J. J. Altizer et al., eds., *Deconstruction and Theology* (New York: Crossroads, 1982).

2. In Christian studies, see, for example, John Caputo, *The Prayers and Tears of Jacques Derrida: Religion Without Religion* (Bloomington: Indiana University Press, 1997); many of the volumes produced out of Caputo's conferences on religion; and Kevin Hart, *The Trespass of the Sign: Deconstruction, Theology, and Philosophy* (New York: Fordham University Press, 2000). For a selection of recent engagements with Derrida's work from a variety of subdisciplines in Religious Studies, see Yvonne Sherwood and Kevin Hart, eds., *Derrida and Religion: Other Testaments* (New York: Routledge, 2004). I list other resources in the notes that follow.

3. For example, "I try to keep myself at the *limit* of philosophical discourse. I say limit and not death, for I do not at all believe in what today is so easily called the death of philosophy (nor, moreover, in the simple death of whatever—the book, man, or god, especially since as we all know, what is dead wields a very specific power)." Jacques Derrida, "Implications: Interview with Henri Ronse," in *Positions*, trans. Alan Bass (Chicago: University of Chicago Press, 1981), 6. For Derrida on postmodernism, see Jacques Derrida, "Response to David Tracy," in *God, the Gift, and Postmodernism*, ed. John D. Caputo and Michael J. Scanlon (Bloomington: Indiana University Press, 2000), 181–84.

4. On Lacan, see the editors' introductions to Jacques Lacan, *Feminine Sexuality: Jacques Lacan and the École Freudienne*, trans. Jacqueline Rose, ed. Juliet Mitchell and Jacqueline Rose (New York: Palgrave McMillan, 1982), 1–58.

5. For a more substantial version of the aspects of Derrida's work discussed to this point, see Ellen Armour, *Deconstruction, Feminist Theology, and the Problem of Difference: Subverting the Race/Gender Divide* (Chicago: University of Chicago Press, 1999).

6. See Jacques Derrida, *Acts of Religion*, ed. Gil Anidjar (New York: Routledge, 2002). See also Gil Anidjar, *The Jew, the Arab: A History of the Enemy* (Stanford: Stanford University Press, 2003).

7. See, for example, Hart, *The Trespass of the Sign*; and Thomas A. Carlson, *Indiscretion: Finitude and the Naming of God* (Chicago: University of Chicago Press, 1999). For Buddhist, Hindu, and Christian engagements with this aspect of Derridean thought, see Harold Coward and Tony Foshay, eds., *Derrida and Negative Theology* (New York: State University of New York Press, 1992). See also Jacques Derrida, "*Différance*," in *Margins of Philosophy*, trans. Alan Bass (Chicago: University of Chicago Press, 1982); Jacques Derrida, *On the Name*, ed. and trans. Thomas Dutoit (Stanford: Stanford University Press, 1995). On Derrida and Judaism, see Bettina Bergo et al., eds., trans., *Judeities: Questions for Jacques Derrida* (New York: Fordham University Press, 2007).

8. Jacques Derrida, *Specters of Marx: The State of the Debt, The Work of Mourning, and the New International* (New York: Routledge, 1994).

9. Jacques Derrida, *Of Hospitality* (Stanford: Stanford University Press, 2000); Jacques Derrida, "On Forgiveness," in *On Cosmopolitanism and Forgiveness*, trans. Mark Dooley and Michael Hughes (New York: Routledge, 2002).

10. Jacques Derrida, "Faith and Knowledge: The Two Sources of Religion at the Limits of Reason Alone," in *Religion*, ed. Gianni Vattimo and Jacques Derrida (Stanford: Stanford University Press, 1998).

11. Indeed, the colloquium itself betrays such a promise insofar as its participants are all men (and only men) of Jewish or Christian background, he notes.

12. For a recent translation, see Kant, *Religion Within the Boundaries of Mere Reason, and Other Writings*, ed. Allen Wood and George di Giovanni (New York: Cambridge University Press, 1998).

13. Jacques Derrida, "Faith and Knowledge," 10.

14. See, for example, Tomoko Masuzawa, *The Invention of World Religions; Or, How European Universalism Was Preserved in the Language of Pluralism* (Chicago: University of Chicago Press, 2005).

15. Derrida, "Faith and Knowledge," 23.

16. Ibid., 25.

17. For more on the signature (as part of his exchange with John Searle on speech act theory), see Jacques Derrida, "Signature Event Context," in *Limited Inc* (Evanston, Ill.: Northwestern University Press, 1988), 1–23.

18. See Jacques Derrida, "Force of Law," in *Acts of Religion*, ed. Gil Anidjar (New York: Routledge, 2002), 241.

19. For Derrida's own discussion of these matters in relationship to Kierkegaard's *Fear and Trembling*, see Jacques Derrida, *The Gift of Death*, trans. David Wills (Chicago: University of Chicago Press, 1995).

20. As I understand it, the term "fundamentalism" originated with the twentieth-century American Christian movement that was quite explicitly a reaction to conflicts between religion and modern science and history. Its leaders identified a set of "fundamentals" deemed essential to Christian faith (including, for example, biblical inerrancy and Christ's virgin birth), thus becoming known as "fundamentalists." The term is applied by analogy to forms of other religious traditions (Islam, for example) that are deemed "conservative" or antimodern. That naming practice is emblematic of the dynamics Derrida here analyses.

21. See, for example, Jacques Derrida, *Rogues: Two Essays on Reason*, trans. Pascale-Anne Brault and Michael Naas (Stanford: Stanford University Press, 2004); Jacques Derrida, *The Animal That Therefore I Am*, trans. David Wills (New York: Fordham University Press, 2008); Moustafa Chérif, *Islam and the West: A Conversation with Jacques Derrida* (Chicago: University of Chicago Press, 2008); Giovanna Borradori, *Philosophy in a Time of Terror: Dialogues with Jürgen Habermas and Jacques Derrida* (Chicago: University of Chicago Press, 2004).

22. This essay is a much condensed version of Ellen Armour, "Thinking Otherwise: Derrida's Contribution to Philosophy of Religion," ed. Morny Joy (New York: Springer, 2011), 39–60. My thanks to Professor Joy and Springer for permission.

44

Foucault and the Study of Religion

JEREMY CARRETTE

Michel Foucault (1926–84) was chair in the history of systems of thought at the Collège de France from 1970 until his untimely death from AIDS. He had previously held various academic positions in Europe and North Africa, but rose to public attention on the wave of structuralist and poststructuralist thinking in Paris in the 1960s, not least with his work *The Order of Things*, published in 1966. Foucault is best understood in the Parisian context of poststructuralism, rather than through the obfuscating notion of postmodernism, which covers over the historical location of his thinking, his specificity within French intellectual life, and his normative assertions, which resist a simple relativist critique. It is important to note that Foucault resisted attribution of his work as either structuralist, poststructuralist, or postmodernist.[1] Recognizing that he had been perceived in so many different ways by so many different people, he stated in an interview in 1984: "I think I have been situated in most squares on the political checkerboard, one after another and sometimes simultaneously. . . . None of these descriptions is important by itself; taken together, on the other hand, they mean something. And I must admit that I rather like what they mean."[2] He enjoyed the enigmatic and silent play that refused simple positions and established thinking that was strategic and contextual.

THREE WAVES OF ENGAGEMENT WITH FOUCAULT

Foucault is a central critical resource for the field of religious studies. The engagement with his thinking in the field of religion has followed the three distinct waves of interpretation and translation within Foucault scholarship.[3] The first phase of engagement (late 1970s to the late 1980s) was marked by the first reception of Foucault's ideas outside France. Although this was mainly in the areas of French studies, philosophy, history, sociology, and political theory, there was some tentative mapping in religious studies. For example, David Chidester outlined the central theoretical apparatus of Foucault's thought, showing how his thinking could be used to theoretically reshape the study of religion. Other studies showed the critical value of his thinking on early Christianity and sexuality.[4]

The second wave of studies (late 1980s to early 2000) was shaped by the response to Foucault's death in 1984 and the publication of the definitive collection of his articles and interviews, *Dits et écrits*, in 1994.[5] It saw a stronger and more sophisticated application of his ideas and a deeper historical appreciation of knowledge across all fields of study. At this time there was an explosion of studies on Foucault across the humanities and social sciences. The interdisciplinary field of religious studies deployed Foucault's genealogical method to its great advantage, supported by studies in feminist theory, cultural studies, and queer theory. His work was used to read religious history and ideas, not least through a critical rethinking of key concepts such as mysticism, religion, power, and gender.[6]

In the second wave, there was also a deeper textual appreciation of Foucault, inspired by *Dits et écrits*. This drew a distinction between scholars who sought to reveal Foucault's own engagement with religious and theological ideas—through his Catholic context in France and engagement with Christianity and religious ideas—and those studies that utilized his work without primary concern for his own texts; there was, however, some crossover between these two approaches.[7]

The third phase was shaped by the reception of the posthumous publication of Foucault's Collège de France lectures from early 2000 onward. At this time there was a growing appreciation of the "late Foucault," a critical appreciation of his use of the concept "spirituality," and a sharper appreciation of the issue of translation and secondary elaboration.[8] In this phase, the study of Foucault in religious studies went through a consolidation after the initial disciplinary excitement. His work was positioned alongside other critical methods, such as postcolonial and gender theory. It was also located more strongly and more effectively within the domain of poststructural methods, alongside Derrida and Lacan.[9] In this phase the struggle between textual specialist and secondary developments became increasingly apparent. As Clare O'Farrell makes clear: "There is a mythical Foucault that often bears little resemblance to the Foucault who appears in his own writings. . . . There now exists entire books which purport to be about Foucault, but which scarcely refer to his original work—focusing instead on what others have had to say about him."[10]

Each of these stages of engagement with Foucault's thinking has established him as a central figure in the postphenomenological wave of critical scholarship in religious studies.[11] In order to appreciate fully how Foucault moves religious studies beyond phenomenological thinking we can look more closely at his critical methods.

THINKING DIFFERENTLY

I would like my books to be a kind of tool box which others can rummage through to find a tool which they can use however they wish in their own area.[12]

Foucault offers the study of religion a series of critical tools, which emerge from his own historical-philosophical method. He takes the study of religion to central questions of its truth-claims and epistemology. His work questions the given assumptions about knowledge and representation of the world. It shows how wider social and historical forces drive different forms of knowledge. Each study "profoundly changes the terms of thinking" about the issue.[13] As he famously declared late in his career, the challenge was to "think differently."[14] Arguably, just as he saw the nature of the philosophical life as "transformation"—a new ethicopolitical spiritual practice—so his own thinking was an act of seeking transformation.[15] The transformation was necessary because the relations of power that shape a subject of knowledge can be altered by what is refused or concealed.

His work is shaped by methods that allow scholars to reveal the unseen in a field of knowledge or in a social or political context. All of his work rests between history and philosophy, uncovering problems of knowledge in historical circumstances.[16] He explored issues historically in order to make a political comment about contemporary problems. In some ways his work is best described, as he noted in his work *Discipline and Punish* (1975), as a "history of the present."[17] A greater appreciation of how Foucault can be a resource, or tool, for critical scholarship in the study of religion can be found by providing a brief synopsis of his critical methodology as it moved from archaeology to genealogy and problematization.[18]

ARCHAEOLOGICAL CRITIQUE

What, in short, we wish to do is to dispense with "things." To "depresentify" them. To conjure up their rich, heavy, immediate plenitude, which we usually regard as the primitive law of discourse that has become divorced from it through error, oblivion, illusion, ignorance, or the inertia of beliefs and traditions, or even the perhaps unconscious desire not to see and not to speak.[19]

Foucault is best situated in a tradition of historical thinking from the French history of science that sees knowledge as historically determined by longer patterns of thought, and in a tradition of philosophical critique that raises questions about the limits of knowledge, a line of thinking that engages both Kant and Nietzsche.[20] His archaeological works—*History of Madness* (1961), *The Birth of the Clinic* (1963),[21] *The Order of Things* (1966), and *The Archaeology of Knowledge* (1969)—all seek to find a "positive unconscious of knowledge."[22] They are all framed by his distinctive style of taking graphic images from history to capture the imagination and then unraveling the texts and practices of a tradition through grafting different, and what appears at first to be disconnected, ideas together.

His history of madness begins with the image of the "ships of fools" and reveals the processes of silencing and the institutionalization of the mad. His history of medicine begins by showing how the medical gaze was constructed through the "stable" objects of death and the corpse, an archaeology of medical perception. His work *The Order of Things* (1966) begins with exploring the painter's gaze in Diego Velasquez's painting *Las Meninas* (1656). It unravels the archaeology of the human sciences and shows how the human sciences are constituted through the figure of "man" in modern thought. He demonstrates how there was a shift within knowledge from the "Classical period" (sixteenth and seventeenth centuries), based on systems of *taxinomia*, such as wealth analysis, natural history, and general grammar, to a system of knowledge built around the figure of "man." The new configuration of knowledge around the idea of "man" makes the discourses of economics (notions of labor), biology (notions of the organic structure of life), and philology (notions of language) possible. However, he then makes the stronger assertion that with the end of metaphysics, the notion of "man" emerges as a new philosophical problem. In Foucault's view it was another temporary historical construction that would disappear. As Foucault explained: "One thing in any case is certain: man is neither the oldest nor the most constant problem that has been posed for human knowledge."[23]

In an attempt to explain his particular historical method, Foucault wrote *The Archaeology of Knowledge*, his most theoretical study. His aim was to question the unities within knowledge and the "ready-made syntheses, those groupings that we normally accept before any examination."[24] He sought to suspend the "continuities" and highlight the "discontinuities" of knowledge by examining the network of statements within a discursive regime or field of knowledge. Each discourse is a historical formation. According to Foucault, discourses constellate to form a specific "episteme," the network of relations that make it possible to say something at a certain time. In this sense, religious studies is involved in a double task of understanding the values behind its representation of the object of study and how the traditions and cultures of study are carrying forward specific social orders and hidden interests. Foucault's work was particularly concerned with the "rules of exclusion" within a discipline and the "principles of classification, ordering and distribution."[25] Following Foucault, scholars working within religious studies can no longer be seen as engaging in a neutral enterprise. They are rather caught inside a politic of classification and representation. This does not undermine the field or reduce it to relativism, but rather sharpens the awareness of scholars to articulate the values behind the methods and understand the historical processes in which ideas and practices are inevitably caught.

GENEALOGICAL CRITIQUE

I am supposing that in every society the production of discourse is at once controlled, selected, organized and redistributed according to a certain number of procedures, whose role is to avert its power and its dangers, to cope with chance events, to evade its ponderous, awesome materiality.[26]

In *The Archaeology of Knowledge* he recognized that a "preconceptual" realm, the "nondiscursive" and "nondiscursive systems," shaped discourse.[27] After 1971, when he embraced a Nietzschean genealogy, he recognized that these "nondiscursive" dimensions were the power-knowledge regimes of institutional practices.[28] In the post-1968 atmosphere of French thought, Foucault developed the idea of discourse as practice and linked them to the more specific operations within society. He began to see how specific discourses emerge within institutional contexts as ways of regulating and shaping life.[29] This shifted his concern to "the relations of power, not relations of meaning."[30] The postphenomenological shift in religious studies can be seen precisely at this point when the statements of fact, forms of representation, and types of meaning are shown to be reflections of a system of power relations.

Foucault's genealogical method can be seen most clearly in his mid-1970s works, *Discipline and Punish* (1975) and *The History of Sexuality, Volume 1: An Introduction* (1976)—the latter best captured with its French title *La volonté de savoir* (The Will to Knowledge), a deliberate echo of Nietzsche. Genealogy seeks to examine forms of domination and power. It seeks a form of "counterdiscourse" by examining truth in relation to the body. For Foucault, "it is always the body that is at issue—the body and its forces, their utility and their docility, their distribution and their submission."[31] Knowledge (*savoir*) is power (*pouvoir*) and the body reveals how this is manifest.

In *Discipline and Punish* Foucault examined the historical transition from punishment by torture to incarceration and discipline in the eighteenth and nineteenth centuries. He sought to illustrate how the modes of subjection and control of the body shifted from external forces to internal processes of subjection. He showed how the history of the prison was built on other forms of subjection in monasteries, army barracks, and schools. Power in these contexts was not just a negative force, but something that constructed individuals. As Foucault made clear, the subjection to power also creates subjectivity.

While power was a central concern for Foucault, it was not power in a hierarchical or judicial sense, a top-down model of power. "Power," for Foucault, "is everywhere" and "exercised from innumerable points."[32] This can be seen in Foucault's discussion of "bio-power": the regulation and control of the population through the body.[33] Power is a complex network of relations within a society, which shapes the very habits and practices of life.

In his work *The History of Sexuality, Volume 1* Foucault showed how "sexuality" (not sex as such) was a discourse of power. As a form of bio-power it was a way to control and order the population. These processes of power Foucault traces back to the monastic practices of confession: "The Christian pastoral prescribed as a fundamental duty the task of passing everything having to do with sex through the endless mill of speech."[34] By putting sex into speech (discourse) the body could be controlled. In Western societies, life was controlled through a scientific technical knowledge of the sexual body, the *scientia sexualis* of the modern world. It created the boundaries of the normal and pathological. As Foucault made clear in his study of sexuality: "Sexuality must not be thought of as a kind of natural given which power tries to hold in check, or as an obscure domain which knowledge tries gradually to uncover. It is the name that can be given to a historical construct."[35]

During the period of the mid- to late 1970s Foucault was very interested in Christian practices related to the control and ordering of the body. He even completed a draft manuscript *Les aveux de la chair* (*Confessions of the Flesh*), but due to exploring the Greco-Roman traditions this was never published, although fragments appeared in various lectures.[36] During this time he was very interested in religious modes of subjectivity, which led him to extend his interests outside his usual Western, Christian focus. He explored the spirit of resistance during the Islam Revolution in Iran, generating much controversy.[37] He also explored Japanese Zen Buddhism and expressed a sense of the end of European imperialism. As he explained in an interview while staying in a Japanese Zen temple, "It is true, European thought finds itself at a turning point. This turning point, on an historical scale, is nothing other than the end of imperialism. The crisis of Western thought is identical to the end of imperialism. . . . There is no philosopher who marks out this period. For it is the end of the era of Western philosophy. Thus, if philosophy of the future exists, it must be born outside of Europe or equally born in consequence of meetings and impacts between Europe and non-Europe."[38]

PROBLEMATIZATION: THE CONDITIONS OF EMERGENCE

In 1983 Foucault characterized his work as "problematization" (or *problematiques*). The idea sought to capture his method of trying to show how and why issues become constituted at certain historical moments. This also signified a shift in his thinking from the issue of domination to government and self. In Foucault's Collège de France lectures from 1980 there is a shift from concerns of the government of the body and technologies of domination to the ethical government of self or what he called "technologies of self." Foucault's last two publications show this change in approach to problematization. He later admitted that although he had "never isolated this notion sufficiently," it was applicable to all his work.[39]

In his later work, influenced by the thinking of Pierre Hadot, Foucault was drawing out the conditions under which sex and the body were problematized in the ancient world.[40] In *The Uses of Pleasure*, he examined the ethics of pleasure in Greek writings, exploring codes of austerity toward the body (dietetics), marriage (economics), and the love of boys (erotics). In his final published volume, *The Care of the Self*, he explored a variety of different texts, including such writers as Epicurus, Seneca, Plutarch, and Marcus Aurelius, to examine the understanding of pleasure in the arts of self-formation.[41] His underlying argument was that many of the ethical themes in the Christian period were established in the Greco-Roman period. Christian practices were an extension or intensification of earlier practices of the self, something that can be seen in his lectures from 1980 on Christian baptism and confession.[42]

In his examination of the "arts of existence" in the ancient world, one of his aims was to show how philosophy in the modern period had lost the link to such practices of the self, or what he called "spirituality." Though his thinking remains indebted to Christian frameworks, Foucault's idea of "spirituality" does not imply some modern, quasi-religious experience; it rather seeks to capture the process of "a subject acceding to a certain mode of being and to the transformations which the subject must make of himself in order to accede to this mode of being."[43] As

McGushin explored, he was concerned with a philosophical *askesis*, that is, "an exercise of oneself in the activity of thought," that brings about transformation.[44] His work was seeking to explore the relation between truth and self-governance in the ancient world as a way to offer challenges to the modern construction of knowledge and the subject.

CONCLUSION: RELIGION STUDIES AFTER FOUCAULT

Foucault's legacy of critical engagement has sharpened and continues to sharpen methodological debates within religious studies. His work is part of a wider critical and cultural turn from the 1980s that has witnessed the end of phenomenological methods and the domination of social science. Even when Foucault is not appealed to directly, his historical-philosophical methods have been integrated into many aspects of the study of religion, reshaping feminist, gender, race, and postcolonial studies. What he offers is the end of innocence in the representation of knowledge. He transforms the field of religious studies by turning the subject toward its various disciplinary regimes and supporting apparatus. His work shows not only how the "discipline" of religion orders and classifies, but how religious traditions are themselves caught inside complex networks of power. If Foucault's approach is accurate, then these regimes of power will be most evident where there are distinct claims to truth and where the body is shaped by different social and cultural traditions. Foucault's various historical-philosophical critical frameworks offer opportunities to return the study of religion to its very foundations as a body of knowledge and intellectual practice.

NOTES

1. Michel Foucault, "Polemics, Politics and Problemizations: An Interview," trans. Lydia Davies, in *The Foucault Reader*, ed. Paul Rabinow (London: Penguin, 1984), 383.
2. Ibid., 383–84.
3. J. McSweeney, "Foucault and Theology," *Foucault Studies* no. 2 (2005): 117–44; Jeremy Carrette, review of *Michel Foucault*, by Clare O'Farrell, *Foucault Studies* 4 (2007): 164–68.
4. D. Chidester, "Michel Foucault and the Study of Religion," *Religious Studies Review* 12, no. 1 (1986): 1–9; E. A. Clark, "Foucault, the Fathers and Sex," *Journal of the American Academy of Religion* 56, no. 4 (1988): 619–41.
5. Michel Foucault, *Dits et écrits: 1954–1988*, 4 vols., ed. D. Defert and F. Ewald (Paris: Gallimard, 1994).
6. R. McCutcheon, *Manufacturing Religion: The Discourse on Sui Generis Religion and the Politics of Nostalgia* (Oxford: Oxford University Press, 1997); R. King, *Orientalism and Religion: Postcolonial Theory, India and "the Mystic East"* (London: Routledge, 1999); G. Jantzen, *Power, Gender and Christian Mysticism* (Cambridge: Cambridge University Press, 1995); G. Jantzen, *Becoming Divine: Towards a Feminist Philosophy of*

Religion (Manchester: Manchester University Press, 1998); G. Jantzen, *Foundations of Violence* (London: Routledge, 2004).

7. J. W. Bernauer, *Michel Foucault's Force of Flight: Towards an Ethics for Thought* (London: Humanities, 1990); J. W. Bernauer and J. Carrette, *Foucault and Theology: The Politics of Religious Experience* (Aldershot, UK: Ashgate, 2004); J. R. Carrette, *Foucault and Religion: Spiritual Corporality and Political Spirituality* (London: Routledge, 2000); Foucault, *Religion and Culture*, ed. J. R. Carrette (New York: Routledge, 1999).

8. E. F. McGushin, *Foucault's Askésis: An Introduction to the Philosophical Life* (Evanston, Ill.: Northwestern University Press, 2006); C. O'Farrell, *Foucault: Historian or Philosopher?* (London: Macmillan, 1989); J. R. Carrette, "Rupture and Transformation: Foucault's Concept of Spirituality Reconsidered," *Foucault Studies* 15 (February 2013): 52–71; D. Taylor and K. Vintges, eds., *Feminism and the Final Foucault* (Chicago: University of Illinois Press, 2004).

9. J. R. Carrette, "Religion and Post-Structuralism," in *The Routledge Companion to the Study of Religion*, ed. John Hinnells (London: Routledge, 2009), 274–90.

10. C. O'Farrell, *Michel Foucault* (London: Sage, 2005), 9–10.

11. Carrette, "Religion and Post-Structuralism."

12. Michel Foucault, "Prisons et asiles dans le mécanisme du pouvoir," in *Dits et écrits*, 2:523–24.

13. Michel Foucault, *Remarks on Marx*, trans. R. James Goldstein and James Cascaito (New York: Semiotext[e], 1978), 27.

14. Michel Foucault, *The Uses of Pleasure*, trans. Robert Hurley (London: Penguin, 1984), 9.

15. Michel Foucault, *The Hermeneutics of the Subject: Lectures at the Collège de France, 1981–1982*, ed. Frédéric Gros, trans. Graham Burchell (New York: Palgrave Macmillan, 2005).

16. See O'Farrell, *Foucault: Historian or Philosopher?*

17. Michel Foucault, *Discipline and Punish: The Birth of the Prison*, trans. Alan Sheridan (London: Penguin, 1975), 31.

18. Michel Foucault, *Histoire de la folie à l'âge classique* (Paris: Plon, 1961); Michel Foucault, "Nietzsche, Genealogy, History," in *Language, Counter-Memory and Practice: Selected Essays and Interviews*, ed. D. F. Bouchard, trans. D. F. Bouchard and Sherry Simon (New York: Cornell University Press, 1971), 139–64; Michel Foucault, "Critical Theory/Intellectual History," in *Politics Philosophy Culture: Interviews and Other Writings, 1977–1984*, ed. Lawrence D. Kritzman, trans. Jeremy Harding (London: Routledge, 1983), 17–46.

19. Michel Foucault, *The Archaeology of Knowledge*, trans. A. M. Sheridan (London: Routledge, 1991), 47.

20. Michel Foucault, "What Is Enlightenment?," trans. Catherine Porter, in *The Foucault Reader*, 43.

21. Michel Foucault, *The Birth of the Clinic: An Archaeology of Medical Perception*, trans. Alan Sheridan (London: Routledge, 1991).

22. Michel Foucault, *The Order of Things: An Archaeology of the Human Sciences*, trans. Alan Sheridan (London: Routledge, 1991), xi.

23. Ibid., 386.

24. Foucault, *Archaeology of Knowledge*, 22.

25. Michel Foucault, "The Discourse on Language," in *The Archaeology of Knowledge*, trans. Rupert Swyer (New York: Pantheon, 1972), 216, 220, 222.

26. Ibid., 216.

27. Foucault, *Archaeology of Knowledge*, 63, 68, 162.

28. Foucault, "Nietzsche, Genealogy, History."

29. Foucault, "The Discourse on Language," 219; Michel Foucault, "Truth and Power," in *Michel Foucault: Power/Knowledge*, ed. and trans. Colin Gordon (New York: Harvester Wheatsheaf, 1976), 112.

30. Foucault, "Truth and Power," 114.

31. Foucault, *Discipline and Punish*, 25.

32. Michel Foucault, *The History of Sexuality: An Introduction*, trans. Robert Hurley (London: Penguin, 1976), 93, 94.

33. Ibid., 139.

34. Ibid., 21.

35. Ibid., 105.

36. See Foucault, *Religion and Culture*.

37. Michel Foucault, "Iran: The Spirit of a World Without Spirit," in *Politics Philosophy Culture*, 211–24; J. Afray and K. B. Anderson, *Foucault and the Iranian Revolution: Gender and the Seductions of Islamism* (Chicago: University of Chicago Press, 2005).

38. Michel Foucault, "Michel Foucault and Zen: A Stay in a Zen Temple," in *Religion and Culture*, 113.

39. Michel Foucault, "The Concern for Truth," in *Politics Philosophy Culture*, 257.

40. Pierre Hadot, *Philosophy as a Way of Life*, ed. A. I. Davidson (Oxford: Blackwell, 1995).

41. Michel Foucault, *The Care of the Self*, trans. Robert Hurley (London: Penguin, 1984).

42. Michel Foucault, *On The Government of the Living: Lectures at the Collège de France, 1979–1980*, ed. Michel Senellart and trans. Graham Burchell (New York: Palgrave Macmillan, 2014); J. R. Carrette, "'Spiritual Gymnastics': Reflections on Michel Foucault's 1980 Collège de France Lectures," *Foucault Studies* 20 (December 2015).

43. Michel Foucault, "The Ethic of the Care of the Self as a Practice of Freedom," in *The Final Foucault*, ed. James Bernauer and David Rasmussen (Cambridge, Mass.: MIT Press, 1988), 1.

44. McGushin, *Foucault's Askésis*; Foucault, *The Uses of Pleasure*, 9.

45

Contemporary Continental Philosophy and the "Return of the Religious"

RANDALL STYERS

For much of medieval European history, there was little boundary between philosophy and theology. Through the high and late Middle Ages, major figures debated such foundational issues as the relationship between reason and revelation. Thinkers like Ibn Rushd (1126–98) and Thomas Aquinas (1224–74) sought to defend philosophical inquiry by arguing for a fundamental harmony between the truths of reason and revelation; their opponents argued for the independence (or subordination) of reason in relation to revelation. But throughout the medieval period many of Europe's most important thinkers understood their teaching and writing as the study of divine law and the interpretation of divine revelation, as the clarification of theological doctrines and concepts.

This relative synthesis began to break in the fifteenth and sixteenth centuries, as Renaissance humanists began to move their philosophizing in new directions and as leaders of the Protestant Reformation questioned the need to bolster theology with philosophic support. Through the seventeenth century, controversies emerged over the findings of the new scientific methods that were taking hold among natural philosophers. But through the early modern period, at least until near the end of the eighteenth century, most European philosophers professed belief in the existence and activity of God, and most framed their work within a theological context. Many thinkers of this era were convinced that theology could find rational validation in philosophy. At the same time, though, a new skeptical tradition emerged (represented most vividly in England by Thomas Hobbes [1588–1679]), and the rupture between theology and philosophy became far more acute through the European Enlightenment.

The Enlightenment was a period of massive intellectual transformation and ferment. The seventeenth and eighteenth centuries saw dramatic transformation in Europe's economic order and the rise of new forms of scientific inquiry. Natural philosophy and the newly emerging sciences came to share a view of the material world as governed by mechanical laws wholly independent of divine intervention. While the natural order might give some indication of the existence of a creator, that creator was decisively separated from the material world. This scheme saw nature as godless and disenchanted, and it left the material world open to unfettered measurement, dissection, and manipulation by natural science and then to unbridled commodification in new capitalist markets. Amid this social and material change, important thinkers such as Pierre Bayle (1647–1706) came to advocate for the separation of philosophy from theology and for open intellectual inquiry, particularly in matters of religion.

By the eighteenth century, Enlightenment philosophers moved away from theological questions, fueled by a new confidence in critical reason and social and scientific progress, a confidence often defined in explicit contrast to tradition, authority, and clericalism. Particularly through the late eighteenth century, a number of major Enlightenment thinkers were adamantly antireligious. Despite his revulsion at superstition and fanaticism, Immanuel Kant (1724–1804) defended a rationalized form of religion, but in *The Conflict of the Faculties* (1789), Kant explicitly subordinated the claims of theology to philosophy.[1]

In the nineteenth century, mainstream Western philosophy moved into regions distant from overtly religious or theological concerns. The notable exceptions were prominent attacks on traditional religion by important continental thinkers such as Ludwig Feuerbach (1804–72), Karl Marx (1818–83), Friedrich Nietzsche (1844–1900), and Sigmund Freud (1856–1939). By the twentieth century, the dominant strands of continental philosophy were no longer engaged with questions about the divine or religious belief, moving in new directions and focusing particularly on issues such as language and subjectivity.

Christian theology largely acquiesced to this configuration. Through the early modern period, theologians had turned to natural philosophy for proofs of the existence of God, but the God deduced through those proofs was a transcendent "perfect" being, a static, aloof, and utterly impassive creator.[2] As Max Weber (1864–1920) argued, Protestant versions of this view of divine transcendence were well aligned with the interests of new forms of Western science, capitalism, and liberal democracy. A broad range of theologians came to stress divine transcendence and alterity, placing the divine, in Richard Rorty's phrase, "beyond the reach not only of evidence and argument but [also] of discursive thought."[3]

The comparative study of religion emerged as a new academic discipline in the late nineteenth and early twentieth centuries, deeply informed by the dominant trends of modern culture. Religion was understood by the major voices in this new scholarly enterprise as private, interior, focused on purely transcendent concerns. Many of the founding figures in this discipline were descendants of the Enlightenment who saw religion as a regressive survival from superstitious primitive culture, and a number of these thinkers elaborated theories of how religion would inevitably fade in the wake of rationalization, secularization, and scientific and social progress. Others more modestly set about the task of trying to constrain religion into a tame and domesticated form that could better align with the interests of the modern world.

Liberal social theory sought explicitly to constrain religion, since religion was seen as a threat to the modern state, a venerable social formation offering competing visions of the social good and competing demands for loyalty. This domestication of religion played a pivotal role in producing the notion of a secular realm, a public sphere that claimed to be shielded from the irrationality, disruption, and violence of religion and under the "rational" control of politics, science, and capitalism. To the extent such scholars saw any place for religion in contemporary culture, that role was limited to thin psychological comfort, properly removed from practical concerns and material objectives.

At the same time, this interiorizing of religion could serve other agendas as well. Configuring religion as a transcendent, suprarational sphere helped insulate it from reductionist rationalist attack. Through the early twentieth century, theologians were joined by a number of philosophers, avant-garde artists, and other humanists reacting against the drive toward technological and rational regimentation by seeking to configure an idealized zone of spiritualized freedom immune from scientific reductionism and beyond the objectification of technology and markets.

Yet this framing of religion as private and otherworldly was always beset by a number of deep conceptual flaws. The Protestant roots of this notion have long been apparent, and applying such a provincial construction of religion to disparate cultural landscapes runs roughshod over meaningful cultural difference. At the same time, configuring religion as a realm of transcendent and spiritualized values—as the ultimate, idealized site for human meaning decisively removed from mundane human difference—serves to deflect attention away from the significance of the material and social worlds. Such a notion of the divine serves as a potent tool for political mystification, encouraging believers to identify the amorphous realm of the sacred as the site of their deepest values and meaning, while at the same time rationalizing the hardships and inequities of the present socioeconomic regime.[4] As with other ideological stratagems of liberal humanism, sentimental talk of the religious as the transcendent serves to misdirect attention away from the actual realities of capitalist modernity and to neutralize the potency of religion as a social force. And so religious practitioners have themselves regularly refused to conform to this idealized notion of religion as transcendent, sensing that as religion becomes more ethereal and abstract, more spiritualized and absolute, it becomes drained of meaning.

Yet with this framing of religion dominant in the modern West, for much of the twentieth century many forms of continental thought and critical theory remained rather skittish in relation to religion. If religion was framed simply as a matter of private, transcendent, otherworldliness, it had little relevance to the cultural tasks at hand. But something more seemed to be going on. As William Arnal has put it, religion remained "a strange . . . anti-liberal in-between land,"[5] a realm colored both by its connotations as an anachronistic survival and by its anomalously disconcerting social potency.

Despite the overt secularism of the dominant traditions of continental thought through the twentieth century, religion was never far from the surface. There was important analysis of the workings of religion in a host of important critical thinkers spanning the last century: Georges Bataille (1897–1962), Antonio Gramsci (1891–1937), Theodor Adorno (1903–69), Emmanuel Levinas (1906–95), Roland Barthes (1915–80), Michel de Certeau (1925–86), René Girard (1923–2015), and many others. And then especially over the past three decades, religion has become much more prominent, emerging as a central theme of theorists such as Jacques Derrida (1930–2004), Gianni Vattimo (1936–), Slavoj Žižek (1949–), Giorgio Agamben (1942–), Alain Badiou (1937–), Julia Kristeva (1941–), and Terry Eagleton (1943-). This new, overt turn to religion has created substantial commentary both within the scholarly study of religion and within continental philosophy more broadly.

What might we make of this phenomenon? After so much intellectual labor devoted for so long to marginalizing religion within a broader philosophical frame, how did it reemerge as such a prominent theme, particularly among scholars who might appear to be unlikely champions? There are many different aspects to this phenomenon, and many possible responses to these questions.

At a foundational level, this development turns on the basic nature of postmodernism itself. A central theme of postmodern thought has been the end of all the major Western master narratives.[6] Modern secularist triumphalism was one of those metanarratives, with no firmer a foundation than any of the others. If we no longer concede foundational status to Marxism, Freudianism, or positivistic scientism, then we no longer have a coherent reason for peremptorily dismissing religion.[7] As Gianni Vattimo has stated, "disenchantment has also produced a radical disenchantment with the idea of disenchantment itself. . . . demythification has finally turned against itself, . . . recognizing that even the ideal of the elimination of myth is a myth."[8]

As the limits of the secularization metanarrative came into view, a renewed intellectual space emerged for exploring the workings of religion and even for speaking theologically. This site has been mined with particular enthusiasm by various postliberal theologians, especially Christians. For example, an influential group of British theologians spearheaded by thinkers such as John Milbank, Graham Ward, and Catherine Pickstock responded to this opening with a movement they labeled Radical Orthodoxy. Milbank in particular has proudly trumpeted the self-refutation of the metanarratives of Western modernity, and he has used that opportunity to reassert the legitimacy of older Christian understandings of truth and virtue.[9] Yet new forms of orthodoxy seeking to redefine or reinvigorate sectarian boundaries are not the only contenders staking claim to this intellectual opening. We can also see various new modes of creative—and decidedly unorthodox—religious reflection in play.[10]

While some thinkers have used this opening in continental thought as an opportunity for renewed religious reflection, other recent theorists have sought to identify resources in religion that might be of value to critical philosophy itself. In response to developments in critical thought over recent decades, a number of important thinkers have turned to religion as an idiom for gesturing toward the absolute or universal, toward alterity, or for reimagining the ethical. If many forms of postmodernism and neoliberal politics offer only what Amy Hollywood has called "the depoliticizing particularisms of liberal-democratic multiculturalism,"[11] if theory and identity politics seem to leave us in some unsatisfying space of quietism, or impotence, or moral relativism—particularly since global capitalism seems so triumphant—then perhaps religion might offer conceptual resources to resist that tide.

A number of recent thinkers have identified religion as a site of enormous affective and social power. Marx was surely correct that religion often serves as an opiate of the masses, but subsequent generations of philosophers and social theorists have recognized religion as a potent force for social change, an invaluable mechanism for a critique of the alienations of commodity culture and the dehumanizing effects of technological rationalization. At the same time, theorists have also recognized the strategic mistake in ignoring religion and thus leaving it in the hands of the most reactionary social agents; as religion continues to roil global politics, its political and theoretical significance is manifest.

The potency latent in religion is a central theme of Terry Eagleton's recent reflections on religion. As Eagleton states it, "reason alone can face down a barbarous irrationalism, but . . . to do so it must draw upon forces and sources of faith which run deeper than itself."[12] Religion, he asserts, "has proved far and away the most powerful, tenacious, universal symbolic form humanity has yet come up with, " and theology can school us in "a process of self-dispossession and radical remaking" that might lead to a better future.[13] Or, as Simon Critchley has recently asserted, "when it comes to the political question of what might motivate a subject to act in concert with others . . . reason has to be allied to questions of faith and belief that are able to touch the deep existential matrix of human subjectivity."[14]

Religion thus seems to offer a means of mobilizing aspects of affect and social power that might help to counteract the fragmentation or quietism of postmodernity. But religion has also had a great appeal to continental thinkers at a more subtle intellectual level—because of theology's vast archive of reflection on themes of identity and difference, the particular and the universal, the immanent and the transcendent. Recognizing the richness of these theological traditions, a number of recent continental thinkers have worked to rearticulate core religious ideas and themes in the service of contemporary ethics and politics.

So, for example, religious concepts were long a major focus in the work of Emmanuel Levinas and Jacques Derrida. Levinas regularly explored theological themes, and early in his career Derrida offered important critical commentary on Levinas's configuration of alterity (both divine and worldly).[15] Yet despite their differing assessments of the prospects of alterity, Levinas and Derrida both saw religion as offering an invaluable idiom for posing the question of the absolute in relation to crucial questions of cultural politics.[16]

Other recent theorists have deployed religion in related ways. Alain Badiou has turned to the Christian Saint Paul as a "poet-thinker of the event."[17] Giorgio Agamben has valorized Paul as a precursor of Walter Benjamin, in their shared preoccupation with messianic time.[18] And Slavoj Žižek has joined Badiou in seeing religion as illuminating how the singular, particular Event can serve as the path toward a new universal— Žižek also cites Paul as exemplifying how a concrete universal can pass through the particular.[19] Theology offers these thinkers and many others a storehouse of conceptual resources that can be enlisted in the effort to analyze identity and difference and, at the same time, to reenergize a sense of political agency and moral responsibility.

A particularly illuminating example of the effort to reimagine the interplay of religious transcendence and immanence appears in the recent work of Gianni Vattimo. Vattimo has sought to reconfigure a sense of the sacred both to clarify the nature of late modern culture and to deploy key religious principles as a force for progressive political engagement.[20] He argues that no aspect of the contemporary West can be understood without acknowledging the deeply formative role of Christianity. Christian theology has permeated Western history and cultural institutions, shaping them to such a degree that Vattimo reaffirms Benedetto Croce's assertion that "we cannot not call ourselves Christians."[21] Vattimo argues that all the defining features of Western modernity—liberalism, democracy, modern notions of equality and social and political rights, the fragmentation of individual subjectivity, the instrumental organization of society, even the theoretical and practical manifestations of rationality—are deeply rooted in the Judeo-Christian monotheistic tradition: Western modernity is, he declares, secularized Christianity.

Rejecting configurations of the divine as transcendent or absolute, Vattimo has worked to relocalize the sacred immanently within the human world. He argues that the core message of Christianity—embodied in the immanence of Jesus's incarnation—is realized in the faltering of strong structures, the dispersal of authority, and the dissolution of the stable subject.[22] The dissolution of metaphysical objectivity means that religious faith itself becomes open to reinterpretation: it is no longer plausible to claim that the truths concerning the existence and nature of the divine have been definitely fixed. Thus, Vattimo has engaged in active and self-conscious reinterpretation of key Christian concepts. In his view, a properly postmodern recovery of Christianity must not seek a return to dogmatism or literal truth-claims, but instead must affirm "the task of rethinking revelation in secularized terms in order to 'live in accord with one's age.'"[23]

Vattimo argues that the formulation of an antifoundational, postmetaphysical religious ethics is ethically and politically essential. This path, he concludes, points toward true human possibility, not a static circling of the illusions of a transcendent Other, but a movement toward "alterity pure and simple, forever beckoning us toward a horizon of salvation, promising not the tranquillity of a value finally attained, but an interminable negotiation of the self, in which resides the very essence of ethics as our tradition has handed it down to us."[24] Vattimo thus frames his reinterpretation of the sacred as a tool for actualizing new human possibilities. Here we see an intriguing effort to relocate the sacred immanently within the human world and to constrain talk of divine transcendence in the service of political and ethical engagement.

Other continental thinkers as well have interrogated the binary of immanence and transcendence in the effort to formulate a new religious sensibility focused squarely on the concerns of the human world. Žižek has sought to reformulate a version of Christian themes that is profoundly immanent and mobilizing for progressive politics.[25] And the French feminist theorist Luce Irigaray and the British philosopher Grace Jantzen have both worked to reenvision the nature of the divine not as a stable metaphysical entity, but as a horizon pulling human imagination forward.

In this context Jantzen invokes Irigaray's notion of a "sensible transcendental." Jantzen explains that this formulation aims to signal "a transcendence [that] is wholly immanent, not in opposition to the [world] but as the projected horizon for . . . (embodied) [human] becoming."[26] Rather than reject all talk of transcendence, Jantzen prefers to reconfigure the concept and to stress its immanent relation to the world of human becoming. In this frame, we move from talk of polarities to talk of diversities, breaking from a vertical binary of transcendence and immanence into a more active and proliferating sense of human potentiality and promise. This reconfiguration of a sensible transcendental functions as a mobile horizon for human becoming and flourishing.[27] A newly configured sense of transcendence can serve to destabilize human pretensions to comprehend or master the absolute, challenging the human status quo and offering a sense of unimagined possibilities.

What we see in the turn to religion among these continental thinkers and cultural theorists is a twofold effort. On the one hand, they seek to harness the affective and social potency of religion, and at the same time, they seek to utilize the intellectual resources of rich theological traditions to illuminate the nature of the present moment and its possibilities for transformation. In his *Savage Systems*, published in 1996, David Chidester declared that "*religion* and *religions* are not objects but occasions for analysis."[28] That insight should guide our reflection on this turn to religion, since the turn is itself an extraordinarily rich occasion for cultural analysis. Religion is not an ahistorical formation but a concept that arrives with a freighted historical genealogy, and its deployment is often aimed to produce significant rhetorical and strategic effects. As these continental thinkers invoke religious concepts and themes in their efforts to promote cultural change, critical scholarship on religion can illuminate central dynamics in the construction of liberal modernity, and it can resist the many forms of sentimentalism and mystification that can appear in the contemporary invocation of religion.

NOTES

1. See, in this regard, Amy Hollywood, "Saint Paul and the New Man," *Critical Inquiry* 35 (Summer 2009): 868.
2. See, generally, Michael J. Buckley, *At the Origins of Modern Atheism* (New Haven: Yale University Press, 1987).
3. Richard Rorty and Gianni Vattimo, *The Future of Religion*, ed. Santiago Zabala (New York: Columbia University Press, 2005), 34.
4. See, for example, Russell T. McCutcheon, *Manufacturing Religion: The Discourse on Sui Generis Religion and the Politics of Nostalgia* (New York: Oxford University Press, 1997); and Timothy Fitzgerald, *The Ideology of Religious Studies* (Oxford: Oxford University Press, 2000).
5. William Arnal, "The Segregation of Social Desire: 'Religion' and Disney World," *Journal of the American Academy of Religion* 69, no. 1 (2001): 5.
6. See Jean-Francois Lyotard, *The Postmodern Condition: A Report on Knowledge*, trans. Geoff Bennington and Brian Massumi (Minneapolis: University of Minnesota Press, 1984).

7. See, in this regard, Phillip Blond, ed., *Post-Secular Philosophy: Between Philosophy and Theology* (London: Routledge, 1998); Niels Grønkjær, ed., *The Return of God: Theological Perspectives in Contemporary Philosophy* (Odense, Denmark: Odense University Press, 1998); and Hent de Vries, *Philosophy and the Turn to Religion* (Baltimore: Johns Hopkins University Press, 1999).

8. Gianni Vattimo, *Belief*, trans. Luca d'Isanto and David Webb (Stanford: Stanford University Press, 1999), 28–29.

9. See John Milbank, *Theology and Social Theory: Beyond Secular Reason* (Oxford: Basil Blackwell, 1990).

10. See, as just one example, Richard Kearney and Jens Zimmerman, eds., *Reimagining the Sacred* (New York: Columbia University Press, 2016).

11. Hollywood, "Saint Paul and the New Man," 869.

12. See Terry Eagleton, *Reason, Faith, and Revolution: Reflections on the God Debate* (New Haven: Yale University Press, 2009), 161. And see Terry Eagleton, *On Evil* (New Haven: Yale University Press, 2010); and Terry Eagleton, *Culture and the Dead of God* (New Haven: Yale University Press, 2014).

13. Eagleton, *Reason, Faith, and Revolution*, 165, 168.

14. Simon Critchley, *The Faith of the Faithless: Experiments in Political Theology* (London: Verso, 2012), 19.

15. For important texts by Emmanuel Levinas in this regard, see Levinas, *Time and the Other*, trans. Richard A. Cohen (Pittsburgh: Duquesne University Press, 1987); Levinas, *Of God Who Comes to Mind*, trans. Bettina Bergo (Stanford: Stanford University Press, 1998); Levinas, *Entre Nous: Thinking-of-the-Other*, trans. Michael B. Smith and Barbara Harshav (New York: Columbia University Press, 1998); and Levinas, *Alterity and Transcendence*, trans. Michael B. Smith (New York: Columbia University Press, 2000). And see Jacques Derrida, "Violence and Metaphysics: An Essay on the Thought of Emmanuel Levinas," in *Writing and Difference*, trans. Alan Bass (Chicago: University of Chicago Press, 1978), 79–153; and Jacques Derrida, "At This Very Moment in This Work Here I Am," in *Re-Reading Levinas*, ed. Robert Bernasconi and Simon Critchley, trans. Simon Critchley (Bloomington: Indiana University Press, 1991), 11–48.

16. For a number of Jacques Derrida's major texts in this regard, see Derrida, *The Gift of Death*, trans. David Wills (Chicago: University of Chicago Press, 1992); Derrida, *Aporias*, trans. Thomas Dutoit (Stanford: Stanford University Press, 1993); Derrida, *Adieu to Emmanuel Levinas*, trans. Pascale-Anne Brault and Michael Naas (Stanford: Stanford University Press, 1999); and Derrida, *Acts of Religion*, ed. Gil Anidjar (London: Routledge, 2002). See also Jacques Derrida and Gianni Vattimo, *Religion* (Stanford: Stanford University Press, 1998).

17. Alain Badiou, *Saint Paul: The Foundations of Universalism*, trans. Ray Brassier (Stanford: Stanford University Press, 2003); and see Alain Badiou, *Infinite Thought: Truth and the Return of Philosophy*, trans. Oliver Feltham and Justin Clemes (London: Continuum, 2003).

18. Giorgio Agamben, *The Time That Remains: A Commentary on the Letter to the Romans*, trans. Patricia Dalley (Stanford: Stanford University Press, 2005).

19. For important texts by Slavoj Žižek in this regard, see Žižek, *The Fragile Absolute: Or, Why Is the Christian Legacy Worth Fighting For?* (London: Verson, 2000); Žižek, *On*

Belief (London: Routledge, 2001); and Žižek, *The Puppet and the Dwarf: The Perverse Core of Christianity* (Cambridge, Mass.: MIT Press, 2003).

20. See Randall Styers, "Gianni Vattimo and the Return of the Sacred," *Annali d'Italianistica* 25 (2007): 47–75.

21. Gianni Vattimo, *Nihilism and Emancipation*, trans. William McCuaig (New York: Columbia University Press, 2004), 30–31, 36; and Rorty and Vattimo, *The Future of Religion*, 53–54. See also Gianni Vattimo and René Girard, *Christianity, Truth, and Weakening Faith: A Dialogue* (New York: Columbia University Press, 2010).

22. Gianni Vattimo, *After Christianity*, trans. Luca D'Isanto (New York: Columbia University Press, 2002), 80.

23. Vattimo, *Belief*, 75.

24. Vattimo, *Nihilism and Emancipation*, 69–70.

25. See, in this regard, Slavoj Žižek and John Milbank, *The Monstrosity of Christ: Paradox or Dialectic* (Cambridge, Mass.: MIT Press, 2009).

26. Grace M. Jantzen, *Becoming Divine: Towards a Feminist Philosophy of Religion* (Bloomington: Indiana University Press, 1999), 271; and Luce Irigaray, *An Ethic of Sexual Difference*, trans. Carolyn Burke and Gillian C. Gill (London: Athlone University Press, 1993), 32–33. See also Julia Kristeva, *This Incredible Need to Believe*, trans. Beverley Bie Brahic (New York: Columbia University Press, 2009).

27. Jantzen, *Becoming Divine*, 271–72.

28. David Chidester, *Savage Systems: Colonial and Comparative Religion in Southern Africa* (Charlottesville: University of Virginia Press, 1996), 260, emphasis in original.

PART X
Religion, Gender, and Sexuality

46

Feminist Approaches to the Study of Religion

DARLENE JUSCHKA

This essay is a genealogy of feminism and feminist approaches to the study of religion.[1] It is genealogical in the sense that I wish to speak to the development of feminist theorizing and its engagement in the work of feminists in the study of religion. To do this I first provide a processual narrative and locate the "events" of feminism (proposing series rather than unity) in the conditions of possibility that allowed for the acceptance of feminist "waves" one through three, as they are often times referred.[2] The conditions of possibility are, as Michel Foucault wrote, "particular stages of [social] forces" that support, either positively or negatively, the discourse(s). In my development of a genealogy of feminism, I consider some successes but also important prohibitions in feminist discourses, and their manifestation in the feminist narratives generated in the study of religion.[3] These prohibitions, or places where feminist voices sometimes cease, are important to make apparent if only to remind ourselves that feminists too have not arrived at the end of history.

WAVE ONE

Many years prior to the formation of women's clubs and organizations in the nineteenth century were found the works of protofeminists like Christine de Pisan (1364–circa 1430), whose disputation against misogyny (*The Book of the City of Ladies*) was published in 1405. With the assistance of Ladies Reason, Virtue, and Justice, the text challenges dominant representation of women of the time.[4] Locating her textual voice in the period's authoritative narrative form, disputation, she challenged the normative and misogynistic view of the female/feminine.[5] She was not, however, part of a larger group or movement seeking to change the "world" for women, and so her voice was silent for a time, but happily revivified in the narratives of feminists 550 years later.

By the mid-nineteenth century and into the twentieth, across Europe, North America, and Australia, in South America and the Middle East, groups of women sought to have the capacity to shape the worlds they found themselves living within. But barred from formal education, they were also blocked from taking up explicit public roles in civil, political, and social institutions. They could of course operate behind the scenes, or provide supporting roles, but they could not stand front and center. In order to change this social inequality, women's organizations, presses, and the like were formed. In Egypt, for example, Islamic women founded organizations for the intellectual improvement of women such as the Society for the Advancement of Women, founded in 1908, and in 1914 the Intellectual Association of Egyptian Women emerged and included among its founders Huda Sha'rawi, the preeminent feminist leader of the 1920s and 1930s, and Mai Ziyada, a feminist intellectual and writer.

In the feminist struggle to bring those marked as female/feminine into what was thought of as human history, an identity, the "new woman" (largely white and of European descent), was proffered by early feminists. The figure of the "new woman" represented the female/feminine as autonomous, intelligent, and self-reliant; given the vote, the legal ability to own property, and access to education, the new women would, and did, develop a history of their own.[6] Included with social rights were claims to the freedom to enjoy sexuality, seen in the Free-Love Movement with proponents such as the feminist anarchist Emma Goldman (1869–1940), and to develop a spirituality in the feminine as played out in the spiritualism movement of the nineteenth and early twentieth centuries.[7] However, challenging female/feminine autonomy were many masculine-dominated social institutions, for example, Christianities, and the new woman was made to figure as a threat to current social organization; she was the "vamp" in need of subjugation, or the coldhearted or neglectful mother needing to regain her maternal instincts, the latter nicely represented by the character Mrs. Banks in the film *Mary Poppins*, released in 1964.[8] Even Bram Stoker in *Dracula* (1897) contributed to the negative casting of the "new woman" as a threat not only to women, but to a normative, masculine-dominated social body.[9] "She," when independent, had been (in witch hunts) and would be again the vulnerable site where evil—in whatever form—finds its way into the social body.

Progress, the progress of society and the progress of "man," informed most theories of the human species and nature in the late nineteenth and early twentieth centuries. At this time progress and social Darwinism had been imaginatively linked, suggesting that "man's" progress could be halted by his own lack of control—the lack of which could be seen in the fate of the poor, the lower classes, the subjugated peoples under colonialist empires, and the hysterical woman. The individual who leads a licentious life, the Christian physician and university professor John Cowan wrote in his popular book *Science of a New Life* (1869), "causes a great strain on his vitality—such a drain as required the whole life force of his system to supply."[10] Consequently a sexually "spendthrift" man (and in this equation onanistic boys) "does in part or in whole, weaken his nervous system . . . and dyspepsia, rheumatism, apoplexy, paralysis and a score of other diseases, assert their way."[11]

In his ideology of the seed Cowan wrote that men who succumb to the allures of female sexuality without thought of conservation (or who, equally, are sexually active with men or by themselves) disorganize their brain tissue so that memory, perception, and reflective power are weakened, bringing about imbecility, indecision, and effeminacy, which ultimately ensavages and impoverishes men. Equally, such behavior meant these kind of men lacked vitality so that, Cowan wrote, his offspring "will be sickly, scrofulous, deformed, and die prematurely."[12]

Interestingly, Elizabeth Cady Stanton, an important first-wave Christian feminist, endorsed the text, writing in the preface: "I have read Dr. Cowan's work, and made it my text-book in lectures, 'to woman alone,' for several years. As it is far easier to generate a race of happy, healthy men and women than to regenerate the disease and discordant humanity we now have, I heartily recommend the study of 'The Science of a New Life' to every mother in the land."[13]

Stanton, like the other white feminists Margaret Sanger (1879–1966) and Nellie McClung (1873–1951), and like the British scientist, women's rights activist, and founder of the first birth control clinic in England Marie Stopes (1880–1958), supported eugenics, a class- and race-based Euro-Western applied science of the time period. Although certainly not unanimously, this early movement's discourses were shaped by racism, colonialism, and class, even as many suffragettes struggled against the ruthless tactics of governments and police, the like of which resulted at times in their physical harm.[14]

Operating in a paradigm of normative colonialism and colonization, white women, some as settlers and some as missionaries, traveling to the West, for "wild," "open," and "unsettled" spaces, were oblivious to its current human occupants, who were represented in their travel journals and diaries as part of the fauna of the "natural world," eminently dangerous but equally exploitable. In Montana, indigenous peoples, the Blackfoot, Pegan, and Siksika, among other linguistic and cultural groups, were represented as the threat to settlers, that is, to "humans," much like other large mammals. In the frontier expressions of "Indian country" and "bear country" we see a conceptual and linguistic link that makes apparent the locating of indigenous peoples as part of the space of "nature" and outside of civilization. On the Canadian side of the border, equally problematic, the tendency was to also locate indigenous peoples in nature, but less as a threat and more as absence from that which is perceived as human.[15]

The efforts of white feminists of wave one tended to be shaped by racism and colonialism, and so it was often up to feminists marked by race and colonization to speak to these issues and to make apparent that more than just gender/sex was used as a tool of oppression. Anna Cooper, born a slave but dying a free black woman with three degrees, one being a PhD from the Sorbonne in Paris, wrote, "The colored woman of today occupies, one may say, a unique position in this country. . . . She is confronted by both a woman question and a race problem, and is as yet an unknown or an unacknowledged factor in both."[16]

Elizabeth Cady Stanton (1815–1902) of the North American Woman Suffrage Association produced with a committee of women *The Women's Bible* in 1895 and 1898, writing in the preface, "The object is to revise only those texts and chapters directly referring to women, and those also in which women are made prominent by exclusion."[17] The effort was to reclaim this text for those Christians marked as female/feminine, but the "woman" imagined was white, of European descent, and middle and upper class so that those marked by gender/sex *and* colonization, race, class, and sexuality were not part of this imagined community of women.

Wave one of feminism developed in the context of Enlightenment ideals, the Industrial Revolution, the rise of unions, and the abolitionist movement, and operated in tandem with the notion of societal progress: indeed, many saw feminism as a necessary outcome of this imagined progress. These early feminists operated within the knowledge of the time, and although at times they called it into question, they tended to stay within its parameters. However, within the nineteenth-century spiritualism movement, although some continued to adhere to conservative ideas about women, many supported the feminist movement and indeed it has been argued that spiritualism was a significant site for the development and communication of feminist critical engagement with the masculine-oriented hegemonies of wave one.[18]

WAVE TWO

Feminism did not disappear after wave one; rather, when the First World War began in 1914, feminists decided this was as good a place as any to show their masculine-oriented and -dominated governments and social systems that they too were soldiers and therefore able citizens. Some women enlisted—some as women and some disguised as men—and as the war dragged on women necessarily took up work defined as masculine in munitions factories, maintained infrastructures, and acted on the ground in defense capacities, ensuring the safety of neighborhoods. In these activities women demonstrated themselves to be citizens, and in many Euro-Western locations they achieved the vote by 1920, although often countries dominated by Catholicism tended to be later in giving women the vote, for example, the vote was given federally in Canada in 1920, but not until 1940 in Quebec, and in Spain it was given in 1931 and in Italy in 1945.

Between the wars, some women, more often than not those with resources, continued to struggle for women's rights. In 1929 in Canada the "famous five," Nellie McClung among them, won the right of personhood for women so that women could participate in the political and legal overseeing of the social body. Margaret Sanger continued her struggle for women's access to birth control, specifically the pill by the 1940s, the use of which was made legal for married women in the United Kingdom and Canada in 1961 and the United States in 1965. Feminists were working hard, but the conditions that created their concerns regarding reproductive justice, violence against women, and the continued social and economic inequality of those marked as female/feminine did not allow for a significant public hearing. Feminists like McClung and Sanger drew attention to these injustices, and indeed made gains for women, but the gains (for white-settler women) were sporadic and infrequent between and shortly after the world wars.

However, by the 1960s the conditions of the possibility for feminist discourses to make sense came into play and the feminist movement was off for its second large effort. Sharing the stage with wave two, and indeed with marked crossover, were the Civil Rights (beginning in 1955) and anti–Vietnam War movements (beginning in 1964) in United States, the student uprising in 1968 in France, decolonization around the globe and the establishment of human rights over and above citizenship rights, the Cultural Revolution in China (beginning in 1966), and the American Indian movement in the United States (with members in Canada), which began in 1968. The conditions for the possibility of these movements were the increase of communication technology, postmodernity (also known as late capitalism), the Vietnam War, the Cold War and escalating nuclear armament, globalization, and neocolonialism.

Second-wave feminism in its early manifestation sent a clarion call to all women to challenge the social conditions that oppressed the female/feminine. As feminism of wave one drew on the ideas of equality and rights that inflected the social movements of the time, wave two drew on the ideas of oppression and liberation. Those marked as female/feminine supposedly had equal rights with those marked as male/masculine. However, they continued to be locked out of many professions and were paid significantly less money for their labor, which then meant their continued dependence on male relatives; violence against the female/feminine either was considered normative or was something "she" brought on herself; and they were held accountable for reproduction but lacked the rights and resources to be responsible. Equally, even as the rights of those marked as female/feminine were severely limited in masculine hegemonies, the female/feminine, her body and sexuality, continued to be represented as problematic and too often as the site/source of potential and sometimes realized social disease.

In the face of the negative and too often misogynistic representations of the female/feminine, feminists in the practice of or study of systems of belief and practice set about rereading, reconceiving, and rewriting canonical texts, much as was being done in history, science, literature, philosophy—all locations where knowledge is produced. The late 1960s marked the beginning of the production of the work of feminists in the Academy such as Mary Daly, who wrote *The Church and the Second Sex* (1968), which was a challenge to the ruling masculine hegemony of the Catholic Church.[19] Judith Plaskow published *Women and Religion* (1974) and later *Standing Again at Sinai* (1991), both of which challenged patriarchal texts and patriarchal readings of texts.[20] In this effort their intent included bringing to the forefront the female/feminine and bringing her doings to the historical texts of humankind. To read against the grain of the patriarchal text and see women again, a feminist hermeneutics, a term coined by Elisabeth Schüssler-Fiorenza in her text *In Memory of Her* (1983), was employed to challenge representations and figurations of the female/feminine as problematic due to sin, sexuality, rationality, the female body, and so forth in canonical texts and their subsequent interpretations.[21]

This effort to reread, rethink, and then rewrite occupied feminists in all disciplines well into the 1980s (and continues now), although throughout this period of time, particularly in the 1970s, it became very clear that women as a homogenous group were the master's tool that feminists had unthinkingly adopted. White, elite, heterosexual, and first world feminists were challenged for their blindness to the social dimensions of the categories of race, class, sexuality, and geopolitical location and their *intersection* with gender/sex. Black feminists in the United Kingdom, the United States, and Canada had been making significant contributions to feminist theorizing at the outset of wave two, but their works were often marginalized insofar as their studies were seen only to apply to the localized group of marked women (that is, marked by race, class, and the like) under study and not all women. Socially privileged feminists, then, even as they demanded that masculine hegemonies accept women's knowledge as applicable to all humans, denied this to feminisms of color and of the third world and considered "theirs" a discourse too particular to represent the oppression of all women. The irony was not lost on marginalized feminists and indeed is a theme of the text *This Bridge Called My Back*, edited by Cherríe Moraga and Gloria Anzaldúa and published in 1982.[22] This internal racism operated more or less without impingement throughout the 1970s in feminism, and equally could be found in most if not all academic disciplines. The normativity of racism and the view that antiracism and feminism were in competition haunted white feminism (liberal, radical, socialist, and Marxist), as they were understood at the time. Audre Lorde's "Open Letter to Mary Daly," responding to her *Gynecology: The Metaethics of Radical Feminism* (1978) and the continued erasure of race, class, and geopolitical location therein, asks: "So the question arises in my mind, Mary, do you ever really read the work of Black women? Do you ever read my words."[23] Written in 1979, and published in 1982, this letter indicted all feminists who had assumed that gender/sex was the preeminent category of oppression and exploitation—it wasn't.

The 1980s and 1990s saw the continued production of feminist work, now enriched by the insights and keen observations of feminists who intersected gender/sex with other social categories of inequality such as race and colonization. At the outset of this period, however, sex, sexualities, and pornography had also become a site of contestation and indeed a struggle for power—the power to speak and say the feminist view of "good" sexuality (that is, erotic and nonoppressive) versus "bad" sexuality (that is, pornographic and oppressive).

Feminists, in large measure, divided into two groups: one group pushed for government intervention and the criminalization and eradication of pornography. Andrea Dworkin, Adrienne Rich, and Catharine McKinnon, among others, viewed the kind of sex and sexuality operative in masculine hegemonies as oppressive for those marked as female/feminine since she is "other" (alterity) to his "same" (ipseity) and therefore always carries negative value in a masculine hegemonic system.[24] All heterosexual relations, then, and those homosexual relations that mimic heterosexual relations are relationships shaped by misogyny. Catharine McKinnon argued that "sexuality is the linchpin of gender inequality" in her article "Feminism, Marxism, Method, and the State. An Agenda for Theory."[25] She, among others, argued that laws were required to protect women from rampant misogynistic heterosexuality: laws prohibiting rape, sexual harassment laws, and the criminalization or censorship of sexually explicit images called pornography. In Britain and Europe the divide between lesbian and heterosexual women increased with the presentation at a conference in 1978 of "Political Lesbianism: The Case Against Heterosexuality" by the

Leeds Revolutionary Feminism Group, which implied that heterosexuality and feminism were incommensurable.[26] While in France Monique Wittig published her article "The Straight Mind" and in it declared that lesbians were not "women" since they rejected heterosexual relations and subsequently lived outside of the "patriarchal class system."[27] Both of these positions implied that heterosexual women were either co-opted by masculine hegemonies (called patriarchy at this juncture) or were in collusion with it.

In the other camp were feminists who felt sexuality was already repressed and the free expression of sexuality by women was a good thing. In their view not all sexual images were pornographic and therefore effort must be made to distinguish between erotica and pornography, a possibility that Dworkin and McKinnon rejected. It was furthered argued that one person's pornography was another person's erotica and censorship itself was simply a tool of oppression regularly used against women, and indeed was a mechanism to control female sexuality, like reproduction and fornication laws throughout the nineteenth century up until the 1960s and the continued criminalization of sex work. Women have been prevented from experiencing different and alternative forms of sexuality as their sexuality has always been limited to reproduction. As Ann Ferguson wrote in her piece "The Feminist Sexuality Debates," published in the preeminent feminist journal *Signs*:

> These issues have come to a head recently in disagreements regarding radical feminists' condemnation of pornography and sadomasochistic sexuality, particularly by such groups as Women against Pornography and Women against Violence against Women. Some of the spokeswomen for libertarian feminism are self-identified "S/M" lesbian feminists who argue that the moralism of the radical feminists stigmatizes sexual minorities such as butch/femme couples, sadomasochists, and man/boy lovers, thereby legitimizing "vanilla sex" lesbians and at the same time encouraging a return to a narrow, conservative, "feminine" vision of ideal sexuality.[28]

The debates were never resolved, and indeed would emerge again, but this time as a catalyst for the feminisms of wave three in the late 1990s, but more about that later.

Feminism in the study of religion participated in the endeavors of second-wave feminism and were similarly shaped and motivated. Many began to openly challenge their religious institutions, calling for the inclusion of women in leadership roles and the recognition of women as active participants in their respective systems of belief and practice. Rosemary Radford Ruether, Jacquelyn Grant, Rita Gross, Judith Plaskow, Susan Sered, and Yvonne Haddad, among many others, challenged canons and institutions and made significant contributions to the study of women in systems of belief and practice.[29] But, as with wave one, race and geopolitical location too often acted as a determinant as to which feminist perspectives gained a hearing. Feminists in the study of religion, troubled that their feminism evinced an absence of attention to the privileges accorded to those deemed unmarked by race, class, geopolitical location, and sexuality, realized that they could not speak for all feminists, let along all humans marked as female/feminine. Therefore, by the mid- to late 1980s, instead of a disregard for feminist analyses coming from the margins, their work gained a hearing, and feminism in the study of systems of belief and practice was enriched.

Feminist spirituality- and goddess-centered systems of belief and practice emerged once again during wave two of feminism. The spiritualism linked to wave one was replaced with a feminist spirituality that focused on a Mother Goddess or Earth Goddess, a deity that tended to be singular, or a female deity operating in conjunction with a male deity, the latter either as an equal or as a subordinate. Wiccan groups and individuals began to articulate their own theological views, views that were strongly feminist insofar as the human and the divine, represented as in primary relationship, were both female/feminine. In the 1970s and 1980s feminist ritual, mythology, and symbolic ideation developed, providing texts like Barbara Walker's *The Woman's Encyclopedia of Myths and Secrets* (1983) and others written by Zsuzsanna Budapest, Riane Eisler, Merlin Stone, and Starhawk.[30] However, the feminist spirituality movement had also been hedged in by unexamined privilege, and feminist spirituality and its expressions of ultimate truths were equally shaped by white privilege.

Sex, sexuality, and erotica, however, fared differently in feminist spirituality than they did among feminists studying and practicing mainstream systems of belief and practice. The breach in feminism of wave two on the subject of sexuality was subtly mirrored in the study of religion, so that the "sex-positive" and "censure-positive" split ran along the lines of feminist spirituality (and nonnormative systems of belief and practice such as Vudou) and more normative systems of belief and practice, respectively. Feminist spirituality had in general embraced sexuality in the majority of its manifestations: same-sex, sex-play including domination, multiple partners, ritual sex, and so forth, as long as no harm was not done. In a number of manifestations sexuality—seen as life-giving and affirming—was also linked directly to deity(ies).[31] Interestingly, it is feminist spirituality that was brought into and embraced by wave three of feminism,[32] a feminist movement that had diversified and consisted of feminisms, made up as it was of a number of emergent feminist epistemological locations influenced by postmodern, poststructural, and postcolonial theories and their accompanying tools of analysis.

WAVE THREE

The end of the Second World War saw the rise of global agreements such as the one signed at the Bretton Woods Conference in 1944 and institutions such as the World Bank and the International Monetary Fund, both outcomes of this conference. These institutions were said to have been established to reduce poverty in what were called underdeveloped countries, under the sway of Keynesian economics and the Rostovian takeoff model.[33] These events shaped the future to come and laid the groundwork for neoliberalism and resistance to it. This resistance was engendered by feminists in so-called underdeveloped countries and joined by Euro-Western feminists; once the latter got over the notion that they had to "save" other women from the horror of their lives, not having recognized that those living thoughtlessly in their so-called developed worlds had contributed to some of that horror. (The worlds were developed for the settlers but not for the indigenous peoples in colonized countries.) By the 1990s the full implications of so-called development and the rapacious nature of neo-Keynesian capitalism became clear. Feminists from multiple geographical locations and of differing cultures, languages, and systems of belief and practice engaged in discussions regarding how to stand against inhumane structural adjustment programs that had been lowered onto countries that were resource-rich but heavily in debt to global financial institutions. Feminists working internationally coming from China, India, Australia, and Africa— from numerous geographical locations—joined forces in an effort to challenge neoliberalism and its accompanying privatization of public services and to mitigate as best as possible the worst of its effects.

These efforts made very apparent to feminists that the category of women as single and unified was a problem and indeed had distorted feminist analyses and ensured they were partial at best. Needed was the recognition that racism, colonization, heterosexism, and other categorizing that ensured the delimitation of societal privilege intersected with gender/sex as Kimberlé Crenshaw had argued in her development of critical race and feminist intersectionality theories.[34] The 1990s, although understood to mark the onset of a backlash against feminism, as Susan Faludi wrote in 1991, still marked a time of the growth and diversification for feminism. As younger people came into their adulthood, feminism of wave two didn't resonate strongly for them. Faced with an increasing technological and consumer-oriented existence, young people began to shape their own movements, some of which came to represent wave three of feminism. Wave three rejected the fixity and homogenization of the category of "women" while it embraced postcolonial, poststructural, and queer theorizing. The addition of theoretical lenses meant the complexification of feminist analyses and resulted in the troubling of fixed categories, such as "the body," which was analyzed as historically, culturally, and discursively constructed, as well as evincing multiple sexualities. Influenced by the work of Judith Butler, the French feminists Christine Delphy, Luce Irigaray, and Julia Kristeva, and the postcolonial work of feminists like Gayatri Spivak, Pompa Banerjee, Aihwa Ong, and Gloria Anzaldúa, among many others, third-wave feminisms turned to cultural analysis, embracing difference, fluidity, and uncertainty.

Feminism in the study of systems of belief and practice demonstrated much of the same shifts as feminism in general. The late 1980s and 1990s saw an increase of texts published by feminists in non-Euro-Western locations; indeed, some like the American Letty Russell assisted in this process.[35] Equally, there was the multiplication of feminist positions when standpoint feminist epistemology, which had dominated wave two, was augmented or replaced by insights from postmodernism, poststructuralism, and postcolonialism.[36] With the movement into the new millennium and under the influence of wave three, feminist analyses in the study of religion shifted and thematic analyses, comparative, genealogical, and cultural in orientation, emerged. Interesting and edifying texts that demonstrate this shift are Pompa Banerjee's *Burning Women* (2003), which compares the narrative representation of witch burning in early modern Europe with widow burning in colonized India, showing how colonizers were blind to the similarities in practices; Todd Penner and Caroline Vander Stichele's edited text *Mapping Gender in Ancient Religious Discourses* (2006), in which the discursive formations of gender and sexuality and their intersection in the ancient Greco-Roman Mediterranean world are examined; and Ellen Armour and Susan St. Ville's *Bodily Citations: Religion and Judith Butler* (2006).[37] The enrichment of feminist analyses in the study of systems of belief and practice under the influence of wave three (which includes poststructuralism, postcolonialism, and queer theories) has been in evidence since the 1990s. Feminists in the study of religion have become even more careful and detailed in their analyses and in marking differences, and in so doing they are less prone to making sweeping generalizations about feminisms, peoples, and systems of belief and practice.

To conclude this genealogy, limited as it is, I want to say feminism is not dead. There is no end to history until there is an end to humanity, and therefore no end to injustice of one kind or another. Each generation is faced with injustice, however coded, and each must deal with it. In the new millennium we find reference to postfeminism and wave-four feminism; both share the tenets of wave three, such as the critical engagement with wave-two feminism, thematic analysis, cultural studies, and the recognition of difference. Wave four, like wave three, has made a place for feminist spirituality as a means to affirm bonds across borders, and has also included an engagement with and reverence for the earth and its inhabitants, something seen as early as wave two in the work of Rachel Carson or Vandana Shiva.[38] Wave-four feminism has yet to be established in a robust way, and so its development by feminists in the study of religion is relatively new. However, instances of posthumanism shaping their work, seen in Kim Patton and Paul Waldau's *A Communion of Subjects: Animals in Religion, Science, and Ethics* (2006), speak to some of the new directions to come. Gaps continue to exist in feminist analyses because feminists, like all theorists, are bound by the social and historical conditions of their contexts.[39] New conditions of possibilities, such as environmental degradation and robust environmental movements, increasing distrust of government, and a radical doubting of current institutionalized religious and social structures, have a way of ensuring that new discourses emerge, the outcomes of which have yet to be conjectured.

NOTES

1. In this essay "religion" acts as a collective noun for systems of belief and practice.
2. Because I tend not to see a deep divide between the "church and state" insofar as Christianity inflects Euro-Western democracies, the Christianities I reference in this chapter are sometimes implicit as they act to shape the norms, morals, rules, and regulations in accordance with central and core beliefs. In other instances I make references to specific systems of belief and practice.

3. Michel Foucault, "Nietzsche, Genealogy, History," in *The Foucault Reader*, 1st ed., ed. P. Rabinow (New York: Pantheon, 1984), 83.

4. Pisan lived in the French court with her father until her marriage. She took up the pen in earnest upon her husband's death, faced as she was with the necessity to support herself and children.

5. Disputation is a formalized method of debate in the Middle Ages of Europe wherein the effort was to uncover truth, often theological.

6. A. Richardson and C. Willis, eds., *The New Woman in Fiction and in Fact: Fin de sie'cle Feminism* (New York: Palgrave, 2001).

7. A. Braude, *Radical Spirits: Spiritualism and Women's Rights in Nineteenth Century America* (Boston: Beacon, 1989).

8. B. Dijkstra, *Evil Sisters: The Threat of Female Sexuality and the Cult of Manhood* (New York: Alfred A. Knopf, 1996). In the film Mrs. Banks is shown putting on a suffragette sash and leaving her children, intent on her own selfish ends, much as the capitalist Mr. Banks. When the family is "reunited" in the film, Mrs. Banks is shown dropping the sash in the umbrella stand.

9. B. Stoker and B. Allen, *Dracula*, ed. G. Stade (New York: Barnes and Noble, 2005). Stoker's female protagonists, Lucy and Mina, both dally with the identity of the new woman and find themselves at the business end of both tooth and stake. Lucy, the more inquisitive of the two, is the first to succumb, but Mina, who evinces a Christianity not present in Lucy, is saved by the ministrations of Christian symbols and text by her masculine keepers.

10. J. Cowan, *The Science of a New Life* (New York: Source Book Press, 1970), 120.

11. Ibid., 118.

12. Ibid., 119.

13. E. C. Stanton, *The Women's Bible: A Classic Feminist Perspective* (Mineola, N.Y.: Dover, 2002).

14. S. Rowbotham, *A Century of Women* (London: Penguin, 1999), 11–12.

15. S. McManus, *The Line Which Separates: Race, Gender, and the Making of the Alberta-Montana Borderlands* (Lincoln: University of Nebraska Press, 2005), 151, 154. Sheila McManus notes that the landscape of the "West" figured in multiple ways in the diaries and letters of early white-settler Christian women as they journeyed from the east to Montana, in the United States, and Alberta, in Canada. For example, Mary Douglas Gibson wrote of her journey from Minneapolis to Fort Benton in Montana in 1882, "Everything seemed strange and wild to me. I had never slept in a tent before, to say nothing of being in a country of Indians and wild animals," while in Canada arriving in Calgary in 1883 Mary Inderwick wrote in her diary that "the town was very nice but it is a village of tents framed in Indians and Squaws in a plenty"; the first is a threat, the other a backdrop, as McCanus convincingly argues in her text.

16. G. Lerner, ed., *Black Women in White America: A Documentary History* (New York: Vintage, 1972), 572–73.

17. Stanton, *The Women's Bible*, 6.

18. Braude, *Radical Spirits*.

19. M. Daly, *The Church and the Second Sex* (New York: Harper and Row, 1968).

20. J. Plaskow, ed., *Women and Religion: Papers of the Working Group on Women and Religion, 1972–73* (Missoula, Mont.: Scholar's Press, 1974); J. Plaskow, *Standing Again at Sinai: Judaism from a Feminist Perspective* (New York: HarperCollins, 1991).

21. E. Schüssler-Fiorenza, *In Memory of Her: A Feminist Theological Reconstruction of Christian Origins* (New York: Crossroads, 1990).

22. C. Moraga and G. Anzaldùa, eds., *This Bridge Called My Back: Writings by Radical Women of Color* (New York: Kitchen Table Press, 1982).

23. A. Lorde, "Open Letter to Mary Daly," in ibid.; Mary Daly, *Gynecology: The Metaethics of Radical Feminism* (Boston: Beacon, 1978).

24. A. Dworkin, "Pornography," in *The Feminism and Visual Cultural Reader*, ed. A. Jones (London: Routledge, 2003), 387–89; A. Rich, "Compulsory Heterosexuality and Lesbian Existence," *Signs* 5, no. 4 (1980): 631–60; C. McKinnon, "Feminism, Marxism, Method, and the State: An Agenda for Theory," *Signs* 7, no. 3 (Spring 1982): 514–44.

25. McKinnon, "Feminism, Marxism, Method, and the State," 533.

26. S. Jackson and S. Scott, eds., *Feminism and Sexuality: A Reader* (New York: Columbia University Press, 1986), 14.

27. M. Wittig, "The Straight Mind," *Questions Féministes* 1, no. 1 (1980): 103–11.

28. A. Ferguson, "Forum: The Feminist Sexuality Debates," *Signs* 10, no. 1 (1984): 107.

29. Rosemary Radford Ruether, *Gaia and God: An Ecofeminist Theology of Earth Healing* (New York: HarperCollins, 1992); J. Grant, *White Woman's Christ and Black Woman's Jesus: Womanist Response* (Atlanta: Scholars Press, 1989); R. Gross, *Buddhism After Patriarchy: A Feminist History, Analysis, and Reconstruction of Buddhism* (Albany: State University of New York Press, 1993); Plaskow, *Standing Again at Sinai*; S. S. Sered, *Priestess, Mother, Sacred Sister: Religions Dominated by Women* (New York: Oxford University Press, 1994); Y. Haddad and E. Findley, eds., *Women, Religion, and Social Change* (Albany: State University of New York Press, 1985).

30. B. G. Walker, *The Woman's Encyclopedia of Myths and Secrets* (San Francisco: Harper and Row, 1983); Z. Budapest, *The Holy Book of Women's Mysteries: Feminist Witchcraft, Goddess Rituals, Spellcasting and Other Womanly Arts* (Berkeley: Wingbow Press, 1989); R. Eisler, *The Chalice and the Blade: Our History, Our Future* (New York: Harper and Row, 1987); M. Stone, *When God Was a Woman* (New York: Harcourt Brace Jovanovich, 1978); Starhawk, *Dreaming the Dark: Magic, Sex and Politics* (Boston: Beacon, 1988).

31. M. Adler, *Drawing Down the Moon: Witches, Druids, Goddess-Worshippers, and Other Pagans in America Today* (Boston: Beacon, 1986).

32. See, for example, Chris Klassen's edited text *Feminist Spirituality*: C. Klassen, ed., *Feminist Spirituality: The Next Generation* (Lanham, Md.: Lexington, 2009).

33. The Keynesian free market economic model was developed by J. M. Keynes (1883–1946), while the Rostovian takeoff model (traditional society, preconditions for takeoff, takeoff, drive to maturity, and age of mass consumption) was developed by W. W. Rostow (1916–2003). Both models shaped global interaction between countries and were central to the logic of the World Bank and the International Monetary Fund. See Gilbert Rist for an extended examination of the rise globalization and so-called development. G. Rist, *The History of Development: From Western Origins to Global Faith* (London: Zed, 2002).

34. K. Crenshaw, *Critical Race Theory: The Key Writings That Formed the Movement* (New York: New Press, 1995).

35. L. Russell, ed., *Inheriting Our Mothers' Gardens: Feminist Theology in Third World Perspective* (Philadelphia: Westminster, 1988).

36. There continue to be feminists who engaged differing systems of belief and practice, for example, Islam, using the tools of standpoint feminism, particularly when the concept of "women's experience" is central to their analyses. Equally, in wave two there were feminists in the field who did not engage standpoint feminism, such as Mieke Bal, whose work operated in line with narrative analysis and its outcomes rather than treating characters in texts as historical persons with historical experiences. See, for example, M. Bal, *Death and Dissymmetry: The Politics of Coherence in the Book of Judges* (Chicago: University of Chicago Press, 1988) and *Murder and Difference: Gender, Genre, and Scholarship on Sisera's Death*, trans. M. Gumpert (Bloomington: Indiana University Press, 1988).

37. P. Banerjee, *Burning Women: Widows, Witches, and Early Modern European Travelers in India* (New York: Palgrave Macmillan, 2003); T. Penner and C. Vander Stichele, eds., *Mapping Gender in Ancient Religious Discourses* (Leiden: Brill, 2006); E. Armour and S. M. St. Ville, eds., *Bodily Citations: Religion and Judith Butler* (New York: Columbia University Press, 2006).

38. R. Carson, *Silent Spring* (Greenwich, Conn.: Fawcett, 1970); V. Shiva, *Staying Alive: Women, Ecology, and Development* (London: Zed, 1988).

39. P. Waldau and K. Patton, eds., *A Communion of Subjects: Animals in Religion, Science, and Ethics* (New York: Columbia University Press, 2006).

47

French Feminism and Religion

MORNY JOY

There are two anomalies that need to be observed before there can be any detailed examination of the life and work of three women scholars—Hélène Cixous, Luce Irigaray, and Julia Kristeva—who feature as exemplars of "French feminism." These are that (1) none of these women was born in France, and (2) none of them subscribes to the term "feminism." There is also one further discrepancy that is crucial to any consideration of the relevance of their work for religion. This is that none of the three women can be regarded as religious in the traditional sense of the term. Yet their early lives, though varied, did provide them with exposure to diverse religious orientations. Cixous, from a Jewish Algerian family, spent her formative years in Algeria. Irigaray is from a Belgian Catholic background, while Kristeva, in an autobiographical reminiscence, tells of her adolescent rebellion against her Eastern Orthodox upbringing in Bulgaria. What is remarkable is that the work of all three resonates with religiously related discussions about the nature of god or the divine, with notions of the sacred, with questions regarding the "feminine" and the debased role of women in religion. Most especially, however, they inquire into the nature of love, with its extravagant desires and displacements. For all three scholars, religion's symbols and representations continue to have long-lasting formative emotional and psychic effects.

Religion, then, still features as a potent and pervasive phenomenon in twentieth-century secular Europe. This is especially evident in their discussion of maternal and paternal figures, of both divine and human provenance, whose focal influence continues even after their psychoanalytic exposure. God's guise as an omnipotent Father and his Virgin Mother/Bride have been demonstrated to be lavish projections of human beings' deepest needs and longings, stemming from unrequited infantile love. Cixous, Irigaray, and Kristeva all concur that these symbolic representations reinforced certain behavioral and psychological patterns at the same time that they mediated deep emotional traumas. These patterns now need to be "reprogrammed": the psychic pain involved should be assuaged by other, more conscious means. Thus, these scholars' respective explorations can only be comprehended through the lens of psychoanalytic theory. Nevertheless, their work is extremely interdisciplinary, ignoring the boundaries and methodologies that are usually associated with specific disciplines. The following presentation can only highlight a selection of their extremely rich and, at times, provocative reflections on the subject of religion.

Perhaps the reason for the recent appeal of their work lies in their respective investigations and evaluations, in the wake of the death of God, of the search for satisfactory therapeutic substitutes. All three, from different perspectives, are preoccupied with the elaboration of an ethics of intersubjective relationships. Though each thinker has her own distinctive position, all three seek to articulate the ways that love can find expression, once freed from instinctive urges and unconscious fantasies of fulfillment. All emphasize the rehabilitation of women—who are all too often obscured or relegated to an inferior position by traditional religious doctrines and practices. The reaction to their work has been mixed. Though acclaimed by many feminists, they have also been criticized for having introduced either a feminine essentialism or a maternal/gynocentric ethics. Yet a closer look at each of their principal concerns is extremely instructive as it provides three very different options for appreciating the tasks of women within a renegotiated understanding of religion.

JULIA KRISTEVA

When she came to Paris from Bulgaria in 1965 at the age of twenty-five, Kristeva's early training had been in linguistics, but this changed after her arrival. She became part of a circle of scholars associated with the avant-garde group Tel Quel, which produced a journal featuring the work of thinkers such as Jacques Derrida, Michel Foucault, and Philippe Sollers (later her husband). She also became interested in psychoanalysis. (At that time, Jacques Lacan's seminars and writings were having a dramatic influence on French intellectual thought.) In 1978, Kristeva qualified as an analyst herself, with a particular interest in object-relations theory. She then began to write about religious texts in which she detected a type of latent revolt against constricting ideologies, as was the case in the communist Bulgaria of her youth. There she witnessed religion as providing emotional solace, if not psychic survival tactics, even if she did not accept its tenets. Such a thesis was not particularly attractive to the secular scholars of Europe who interpreted this turn in Kristeva's work as basically nostalgic.

In 1976, Kristeva gave birth to a son, which stimulated her interest in the maternal role—a central focus of object-relations theory. All of her previous interests coalesced in a unique manner in one of Kristeva's most important works, "Stabat Mater," originally published as "Héréthique d'amour" in *Tel Quel* (1977).[1] Kristeva divides each page of this text into two distinct columns. The two columns represent what she appreciates respectively as the semiotic and symbolic dimensions. The term "semiotic" is derived from the Greek work *semion*, meaning a "trace, mark or distinctive feature."[2] It indicates those traces of the maternal voice that have been muted in the official structures of Western culture. (This latter dimension of culture is named by Lacan the "symbolic" and is also associated with linguistic competence.) Thus, the left-hand column, with its impressionistic images and expressions, is basically a semiotic evocation of a woman's (possibly Kristeva's) experience in giving birth to a child. This is juxtaposed with a highly theoretical text that examines the symbolic cult of the Virgin Mary. It describes the cult's seeming exaltation of women that, at the same time, negotiates a domestication of the anguish, love, and hatred that are associated with the primal mother/child relationship. Although she allows that the semiotic and symbolic realms are not absolutely separate, Kristeva indicates that the "semiotic," when aligned with maternity/women, indicates a repressed yet potentially disruptive force that can interrupt the civilized surfaces of the symbolic, including religion.

Kristeva's work, however, contains a somewhat mixed message for women. It would seem that, on the one hand, she is advocating the rehabilitation of the maternal role, yet, on the other, she still endorses the Freudian necessity of the rejection of the mother—which she terms "abjection." Kristeva advocates interruption of the maternal symbiosis by the classic third, a father figure. She nonetheless introduces a revision of this Freudian postulate with the "the father of individual prehistory,"[3] who is described as a phantasm of a father who is the object of the mother's love. She even proposes a merger of the two as a loving mother/father composite. The transference to this "Other" love object, in the guise of a paternal God, is graphically described by Kristeva in her book *In the Beginning Was Love* (1987).[4] This study is a reworking of Freud's *The Future of an Illusion*.[5] Here she posits that Christianity's message reenacts, even remedies, the dynamics of a problematic initial transference in the switch to this loving mother/father composite: "God was the first to love, God is love."[6]

Given the death of God, however, Kristeva is concerned about the growing manifestation in contemporary society of the narcissistic wounds caused by the absence of such religious means of compensation. These involve problems of self-representation and personal relationships that stem from a defective transference. Kristeva's solution is to propose the psychoanalyst as a substitute for the original transference object who, as a surrogate loving parent, allows a therapeutic enactment of unresolved conflicts. Such a process liberates a space that encourages conscious imaginative reconstructions. Yet religion is not entirely banished. In *New Maladies of the Soul* (1995), Kristeva even suggests the reading of the Bible.[7] This is not to reawaken the religious impulse itself but to introduce an educative process for the impoverished contemporary secular imagination. By illuminating the way that religion and the biblical narratives can provide retrospective cathartic relief through their "necessary fictions"—either as revolt, as in communist Bulgaria, or as a resolution of residual Oedipal conflicts—Kristeva encourages the redirection of the energies that were formerly invested there into creative alternatives. In this way, interpersonal relationships of love are fostered, without illusions and without excessive demands or expectations of others.

LUCE IRIGARAY

Luce Irigaray came to Paris from her native Belgium in 1960. Her education and interests are multifaceted, embracing psychoanalysis, philosophy, literature, social thought and politics, and religion. She is famous for having been expelled by Jacques Lacan from his École Freudienne, where she trained, after the publication of her doctoral thesis, *Speculum of the Other Woman*.[8] This was a major study of the exclusion of women from participation in those institutions and practices of Western culture that decided matters concerning their own identity and destiny. Such institutions are associated by Lacan with the symbolic, which he also calls the Law of the Father, and which Irigaray aligns with a God made in man's image. Irigaray's work primarily concerns critical discussions of such a God and of alternative constructive modes of the divine, and the ensuing implications for women.

In the development of her ideas on God, Irigaray takes different approaches. First, in both *Speculum* and *This Sex Which Is Not One*, she attempts to subvert the absolute ideal of the transcendent male God and father figure that has dominated Western religious traditions.[9] To achieve this, in the essay "La Mystérique," which appeared in *Speculum*, Irigaray deliberately adopts the role of a female mystic/hysteric and implies that women may share a mode of affinity with God in a dimension that exceeds the capabilities of language and expression—tools that are necessary for communication. She explores this extraneous zone of *jouissance*—suggestive of both excess and eroticism. The female mystic is portrayed as not sexually repressed, but as protesting by means of her body against religious regulations that have excluded women from full participation in religion's official institutions of learning and in public sacred rituals.

In continuing her eulogy honoring women's eccentricity, Irigaray introduces her infamous motif of the two lips of women's sexuality as indicative of nonduality or a fluidity that allows women to resist traditional philosophical maneuvers such as objectification and appropriation. Irigaray also intends to use the two lips as an emblem of women's alternative constructive abilities that are infinite in their possibility. In time, however, Irigaray became dissatisfied with this strategy. She came to believe that, if women are to effect religious and social change, their expressions cannot remain restricted to the nonrepresentable realm of mystical experience.

In "Divine Women," an essay in *Sexes and Genealogies*,[10] Irigaray depicts a new mode of relationship of women with God, whom she now refers to as the "divine." Her project is to propose that women should themselves become divine. For Irigaray, God can no longer continue to be located on high as a remote authoritarian figure or as an unknowable Other. God must be appreciated as an integral part of a process of becoming, instead of confined to the static metaphysical categories of Being. The modes of the divine that Irigaray seeks to express will be both incarnate and inherent in creation. She proposes that, by abandoning a transcendent God, as well as the primacy of faith and dogma, "a new chapter in history"[11] will thus be born, involving an intimate relation with the natural world.[12] At the same time, Irigaray advises women to undertake an exercise of conscious self-reflexivity that questions definitions of "femininity" inculcated by patriarchal religious norms. Irigaray later elaborates on these ideals to include consciously disciplining one's instinctual reactions and curbing one's desires—what has been named women's "natural immediacy."[13] Such practices have definite spiritual implications.

It soon becomes obvious, however, that Irigaray holds some rather explicit ideas about what mode of divine might now be realized by women. This is because Irigaray has become fascinated with a purported gynocratic age that predated patriarchy. Irigaray identifies this mythological period as a time of love, peace, and tenderness, where there was respect for the body and nature, and where people lived in communion with the divine. It is such virtues that Irigaray now endorses as appropriate for contemporary women to incorporate in their process of becoming divine. In *An Ethics of Sexual Difference*, Irigaray affirms that, if she cultivates these virtues and disciplines her impulses, a woman will also be able to experience spirituality as a form of transcendence, or become divine, in her physical body.[14] In this same work, however, Irigaray takes a somewhat unexpected step in delineating another new manifestation of the divine. She introduces a model of irreducible sexual difference that will take on ontological proportions in her work.[15] Irigaray recommends that once a woman has attained a state of personal integrity, she can enter into a relationship with a male in a manner previously not possible. Such a relationship will also foster a realization of embodied human love as divine. It will also usher in "a new epoch of History."[16] Irigaray expands on this vision of divine love in *I Love to You*, where she proposes that this new era will be one that honors the couple. Thus, after the respective ages of the Father (the Jewish religion) and of the Son (Christianity), there is "the era of the spirit and the bride."[17]

This suggestion should not be understood to imply only a revival of Christianity, as Irigaray has also turned toward Eastern religions. Since *I Love to You*, Irigaray has described her own personal spiritual quest.[18] Her various practices of yoga and breathing, as well as an attitude of detachment, have been informed by selective readings of Hindu and Buddhist texts. One can appreciate Irigaray's adoption of the tantric symbol of male and female figures in an embrace of disciplined sexual ecstasy as a fitting symbol of the divine love she advocates—a symbol lacking in the Western religious repertoire. The spiritual discipline that Irigaray now prescribes consists of an intriguing amalgam of Eastern and Western religious elements.

Unfortunately, however, Irigaray does not question the place of women in Eastern religions as critically as she engaged with Christianity. As a result, it appears that she may be simply reintroducing exalted ideals of womanhood that reinforce typical stereotypes. Irigaray will also make some unsubstantiated sweeping generalizations regarding women's close relations to myth, to Eastern religions, and to the Buddha, "who venerates the feminine spiritual."[19] Perhaps the most questionable aspect of Irigaray's advocacy of this path occurs when she proclaims the spiritual superiority of women. The consequence of such a romantic idealization of women is highly debatable.

Thus, while Irigaray's work in *Speculum* and *This Sex Which Is Not One* was a critical denunciation of the injustice enacted upon women in traditional religions—most dramatically in the delimitation of women's potentiality to be divine—her solutions are problematic.[20] The introduction of a worldview based on a dualist sexual differentiation, the emphasis on heterosexual relationships as the ideal locus of a new era of spiritual history, as well as the recommendation of specific values and conduct for women to become divine all have a prescriptive tone. These elements diminish the fine achievement of her diagnosis of the continuing plight of women in religion—most especially Christianity.

HÉLÈNE CIXOUS

Hélène Cixous grew up in French-occupied Algeria, appreciating her own situation as that of an outsider in multiple senses—as a Jew, as a women in Judaism, as a colonial. She recognizes this state, referring to herself as a "Jewwoman."[21] Her family came to France at the outbreak of the Algerian war in 1956, where she pursued her studies, completing a doctorate on the work of James Joyce in 1968. Her subsequent academic career has been mainly in English literature at the University of Paris VIII, Vincennes. From her first writings, a collection of short stories titled *The First Name of God*,[22] religious themes have suffused her work, as a "constant 'poetico-philosophical' companion."[23] Cixous coined the phrase *écriture feminine* to describe her own style of writing, influenced as much by Derrida as by psychoanalysis. This style, employed in many genres of literature (poetry, prose, and drama), is at once allusive and evocative. It is also visceral and finely attuned to nuances that have barely come to consciousness. While not entirely in a "stream of consciousness" form, this style of writing allows for associations and interruptions in a train of thought that avoids the logic of binary oppositions with its exclusions and closure. Cixous views the latter type of presentation as symptomatic of a "masculine" mode of thought, although she allows that men also use *écriture feminine*—Joyce himself being a prime example.

In Cixous's work, the themes of the father, God, divinity, and religion interweave in complex patterns that constantly reformulate her preoccupation with attaining a state of integrity that is faithful to her own sense of openness to others and an affirmation of her own existence as a woman. In Cixous's view, traditional religion, with its unitary God, imposes a rigidity that obscures, even denies, her own more fluid orientation. In her writing, Cixous seeks to discover another understanding of God, or gods, who reveal the multiple possibilities of "our own divinity."[24] For Cixous, such a notion of God is redolent not just of repressed memories, but "of what escapes us and makes us wonder. Of what we do not know but feel."[25]

It is in her work *Promethea*, a feminine retelling of the myth, that Cixous presents a portrait of a mode of human relationship that is in keeping with her vision.[26] It is a love between women that she presents as escaping the constraints of possessive and exploitative desire. Instead, love is an invitation to a noncalculative form of exchange that is open to extemporaneous variations from the basic expectation of recompense, characteristic of most gift giving. Above all, in its rejection of projections, and in its fostering of the unpredictable, such love summons each person to surpass their own previous assumptions and complacency. Such a love is in harmony with Cixous's earlier evocation of God. Ultimately, for Cixous, God is a love or yearning that impels a human being to venture into the perilous unknown—be it in writing, in life, or in relationships. Such divine love is at once the impetus and gift of Cixous's own writing.

NOTES

1. Julia Kristeva, "Stabat Mater," in *Tales of Love*, trans. L. S. Roudiez (New York: Columbia University Press, 1987), 234–64.
2. Julia Kristeva, *In the Beginning Was Love: Psychoanalysis and Faith*, trans. A. Goldhammer (New York: Columbia University Press, 1987), 5.
3. Ibid., 25.
4. Ibid.
5. Sigmund Freud, *The Future of an Illusion* (New York: Norton, 1975).
6. Kristeva, *In the Beginning Was Love*, 25.
7. Julia Kristeva, *New Maladies of the Soul* (New York: Columbia University Press, 1995).
8. Luce Irigaray, *Speculum of the Other Woman*, trans. G. C. Gill (Ithaca: Cornell University Press, 1985).
9. Luce Irigaray, *This Sex Which Is Not One*, trans. C. Porter with C. Burke (Ithaca: Cornell University Press, 1985).
10. Luce Irigaray, *Sexes and Genealogies*, trans. G. C. Gill (New York: Columbia University Press, 1993).
11. Ibid., 72.
12. Ibid., 52.
13. Luce Irigaray, *I Love to You*, trans. A. Martin (New York: Routledge, 1996), 64.
14. Luce Irigaray, *An Ethics of Sexual Difference* (Ithaca: Cornell University Press, 1993).
15. Luce Irigaray, *Between East and West: From Singularity to Community* (New York: Columbia University Press, 2002), 98–99.
16. Irigaray, *An Ethics of Sexual Difference*, 98.
17. Ibid., 148.
18. Irigaray, *I Love to You*.
19. Irigaray, *Between East and West*, 79.
20. Irigaray, *This Sex Which Is Not One*.
21. Hélène Cixous, *Coming to Writing, and Other Essays*, trans. S. Cornell et al. (Cambridge, Mass.: Harvard University Press, 1991), 101.
22. Hélène Cixous, *Le Prénom de Dieu* (Paris: B. Grasset, 1967).
23. Sal Renshaw, "The Thealogy of Hélène Cixous," in *Religion in French Feminist Thought: Critical Perspectives*, ed. M. Joy, K. O'Grady, and J. Poxon (London: Routledge, 2003), 173.
24. Cixous, *Coming to Writing*, 129.
25. Ibid.
26. Hélène Cixous, *The Book of Promethea*, trans. B. Wing (Lincoln: University of Nebraska Press, 1991).

48

Queer Theory Meets Critical Religion

Are We Starting to Think Yet?

NAOMI R. GOLDENBERG

What is most thought-provoking is that we are still not thinking.
—*Heidegger,* What Is Called Thinking

Both "sexuality" and "religion" are words that refer to important characteristics of individuals, groups, countries, and cultures. However, a cloud of uncertainty surrounds the common usage of both terms. Consider the following two quotations from two well-known authors whose works address these themes: "In my view, the whole idea of 'having a sexuality' is a wild and improbable locution, not because we are without sex or sexuality but because sex is something that has its way with us, even when we think we are having our way with it, even when (precisely when?) we are at our most lucid and agentic."[1] And "Religion is fundamental to human experience, history, and culture, but it is difficult to define. No single, universally valid definition applicable across all cultures can be given, although many have been attempted."[2]

Indeed, one of the most significant points about sexuality and religion is the instability of meanings attached to each one. Perhaps, at present, confusion is more apparent in regard to sexuality. Although there is agreement that "sex" and "sexual" are words pointing to qualities pertaining to gender, and to the erotic relationship of genders vis-á-vis one another, not much more can be said definitively. There is not even agreement about what constitutes gender, how or if it differs from sex, or even how many genders there are. As "queer theory"—that is, literature and scholarship about the complex construction of sex and gender—proliferates, notions of sexuality expand further to encompass more variation and ambiguity. We are becoming increasingly aware of the fluidity and mutability of whatever it is that is called "sexuality"—something that, as Butler says, we speak of as "having."

A similar awareness of complexity and contradiction might be developing in regard to the concept of religion—something we also often speak about as "having." As readers of this volume know, the term has no consistent referent. Social and political agendas and institutions construct "religion" in different times and places in relation to other equally unstable concepts such as secular and profane.

The notion that Ursula King expresses that there is something we can call religion that "is fundamental to human experience, history and culture" is being eloquently and effectively challenged. Such analysis is the substance of the emerging branch of theory called "critical religion."

Any work that combines queer theory and critical religion ought to analyze and critique frameworks of thought and experience built up around the linkages of the emotionally charged and difficult-to-define notions of both sexuality and religion. "Critique," states Butler, can be "understood as an interrogation of the terms by which life is constrained in order to open up the possibility of different modes of living."[3] This essay will attempt to further both queer theory and critical religion by arguing that "sexuality" and "religion" have to be thought about together within religious studies in order to advance critique about each one.

Even though there is a huge and growing body of academic work about sexuality and religion under the headings of women and religion, gender and religion, feminism and religion, lesbian and gay studies and religion, queer theory and religion, feminist theology and queer theology, little of it interrogates "religion" and its attendant categories such as "secular," "sacred," "spiritual," and "divine."[4] Almost every text about sexuality and religion shows how religious ideas and institutions influence the construction of various aspects of sex and gender while leaving religious terminology unanalyzed.

Likewise, with few exceptions, texts within the comparatively new field of critical religion argue for the necessity of scrutinizing the historical origin and political motivation behind all religious vocabulary but tend not to discuss sexuality as a topic of central importance to the project of critique. This silence is ironic since, as Richard King writes in his introduction to this volume, the move to "denaturalize" the concept of religion as a category "received much of its initial impetus from the impact of feminist criticism upon the academy and its canons of knowledge."

In order to frame the argument that critical religion and queer theory need each other to go places that neither has gone before, I will offer an overview of theories about religion and sexuality. My focus will be on the constraints placed on such theories in regard to their political and ideological scope and implications.

The phrase "feminist studies in religion" is probably a good-enough label to refer to the work that has so far been done about religion and sexuality. I am employing the term as a shorthand phrase despite the fact that many scholars prefer to classify their work under one of the more precise headings mentioned above. The panoply of available descriptions is one sign of the strength and diversity of the subject area. In order to point out what I judge to be the self-imposed limits of existing discourses about religion and sexuality, I will focus on distinctions between two pairs of terms: feminist theory vs. queer theory and feminist theology vs. queer theology.

Feminist studies in religion are based on the application of feminist theory and women's studies to the academic study of religion. The field originates in the 1970s in tandem with what is known as the second wave of women's liberation—the first wave being generally identified with the struggle for women's suffrage in Europe and North America in the early decades of the twentieth century. A significant characteristic of second-wave feminism is said to be its broad scope. Instead of focusing on one issue, activists and theorists extended their reach to include all facets of life and thought that are pertinent to women's oppression. A key slogan is "the personal is political"—an axiom proclaiming that every facet of a woman's life is influenced by politics and is thus a legitimate subject for feminist analysis.

There is most likely no sentence in all of feminist theory that is as important as these four words. It inspired critical theorists to explore spheres of life that had heretofore been considered private and personal. Since much of women's experience had been thought of as separate from public domains, huge parts of female lives had not been investigated politically. And because women's lives were relatively unanalyzed, men's lives in relation to women were also poorly understood. Feminist theory opened up huge vistas for critical thought and social reform. Not only did such topics as domestic violence, sexual abuse, and wages for housework become subjects of study, but so did every idea, image, and representation having to do with women, femininity, and relationships between men and women become fair game for thorough academic scrutiny. The rich and varied expansion of critical thinking about all aspects of sex and gender continues unabated.

The intellectual energy and activist spirit of feminist theory has been a significant influence on the development of theory throughout the academy. Because entrenched and seemingly eternal concepts and behaviors related to "man and woman," "male and female," "masculine and feminine," and "girl and boy" were discussed as contingent, mutable, and dependent on social and political factors, other categories thought to be universal, "natural," timeless, and unchanging—such as "race," "body," and now "religion"—could be deconstructed as well.

Queer theory is one expression of the radical vitality of both feminist theory and LGBT (lesbian, gay, bisexual, and transgender) studies. It enters academic vocabulary in the early 1990s on the heels of Queer Nation, the creative US activist movement that effectively advanced gay and lesbian political agendas. Derogatory associations to the word "queer" were challenged and the term was reborn as a label for work that interrogates the production and organization of all sexuality. Dominant and so-called normal expressions connected with heterosexuality are scrutinized and deconstructed in regard to behaviors and representations labeled as marginal. That which is considered normal receives just as much analytic attention as what is thought of as peripheral or alternative. Interestingly, the word "queer" is sometimes used as a verb to initiate critical thinking about concepts without an explicit connection to sex and gender. To "queer" something now means to begin to unmoor it from a fixed position in discourse and thus to start thinking about it in new ways.

The differences between queer theory and feminist theory are difficult to pin down. Because of the diversity of both subject matter and approaches, only observations about dominant trends can be made with any accuracy. In a general sense, queer theorists have explored and contested formulations of categories of identity connected with sexuality, while feminist theorists have concentrated on critiquing the conditions that bring about women's oppression. The subject matter of both bodies of thought overlaps considerably.

Queer theorists are concerned with how cultural formations such as language and representational norms produce what we understand as "sex," "gender," and "body." The work of Judith Butler is a cornerstone of queer theory. In 1993, in *Bodies That Matter: On the Discursive Limits of "Sex,"* Butler argues that bodies are made intelligible through a chain of citation that invokes and reinforces social norms by performing them.[5] Resistance to norms is expressed when cultural conventions are performed differently, thereby altering the process of citation. Butler adheres to the poststructural position that there is no concept in culture that exists nonrelationally. Because all ideas and social categories are constructed through language, they are dependent on other linguistic categories to be intelligible. For example, ideas about what "male" means are related to that which a culture considers "female." (Likewise, the word "sacred" can only mean anything at all in relation to a concept such as "profane.") Notions about what male (or sacred) might mean will change if and when concepts to which they are related take on new or altered meanings.

Furthermore, in Butler's work, no concept is considered to be "pre-discursive." That is, there is no idea present within language that has not grown out of other previous language. For example, ideas about what constitutes a "family" are linked to the contingencies of specific histories and social practices rather than to unchanging "nature" or to essential conditions of biology. Since history and social contingency are full of complexity and contradiction, opportunities for variation and innovation are always present. Thus, at any given moment in culture, the concept of "family" can refer to an array of behaviors and arrangements that can serve to support innovation. Citation of suppressed, covert, or unnoticed aspects of social practices to expand ways of living is what Butler has called "working the norm."[6] She interprets culture as rife with fissures of new possibilities in what can appear to be the solid bedrock of unyielding traditions.

Some feminist theorists have disparaged queer theory for being too obscure and insufficiently concerned with "real" issues such as poverty or violence against women.[7] Likewise, some queer theorists have minimized the complexity of feminist theory in regard to issues of identity, sexuality, and cultural constructions. Currently, however, work is being done to merge the two subfields.[8]

The application of feminist and queer theories to religion has a rich history of variety and debate. In the last decade, a plethora of accounts about the evolution and taxonomy of the subject has become available in the form of dictionaries, encyclopedias, and textbooks.[9] Although it is hazardous to generalize about the content of this large and growing body of scholarship, I will do just that in order to present my argument that the field is being circumscribed along conservative boundaries.

Literature in the field of gender and religion is characterized by one of two tendencies: a passion for description or an impetus to reform. The former is fueled by a desire to gather overlooked data. Because women's lives within religious traditions and institutions have received much less attention than their male counterparts, there is a gap in information and knowledge about what religious women actually do, say, write, and think. Scholarship that describes and investigates women's religious behavior has brought to light copious material about how women cope within traditions to enhance their lives as best they can. The argument that is framed explicitly or implicitly through such descriptive work is that "religion" cannot be said to be either detrimental or beneficial to women in any universal sense because women make use of religious material in highly varied and creative ways.

In contrast, the feminist impetus toward reform of religious traditions is directed toward both minimizing sexism and improving women's lives. Descriptive scholarship about heretofore unrecognized women's history is mined for the purpose of discovering material that contemporary women could use to have more influence in their religious institutions and to interpret their religious heritage more advantageously.

There is a wide range of substantial scholarship and theory that supports feminist reform of religious institutions and ideologies. Three examples indicate the breadth of such work. One is a body of theory inspired by the work of Elisabeth Schüssler-Fiorenza, who cites the history of the early Jesus movement to uncover traditions of women's religious authority and resources for feminist theologizing within Christianity. She reveals precedents for the formation of what she terms "woman-church" in the present.[10] A second example is the work of Judith Plaskow, who urges Jewish women to understand themselves as reformers of Judaism who are, as she says, "standing again at Sinai" to move Jewish tradition in more inclusive, progressive directions.[11]

In her "thealogical" writings, Carol Christ also argues for religious reform by attending to traditions linked to ancient goddesses rather than reinterpreting established institutions linked to masculine deities and male religious leaders.[12] Christ, along with others such as Starhawk and Z. Budapest, explains why "women need the goddess" on which to base an effective feminist ethics and to feel at home in the world.[13]

Like most feminist theologians, Schüssler-Fiorenza, Plaskow, and Christ are interested in suggesting new ways for women to be religious. Despite the radical and highly controversial thrust of their work, each one sees herself and is seen by others as a representative of a particular religion. At present, feminist theology is a field that functions along sectarian lines, as if it were a parliament of world religions comprising theorists and activists who are delegates standing for their own (reformed and reformable) traditions. Edited collections about women and religion as well as conferences in the field tend to be compiled and organized in accordance with the ideal of religious diversity. At times, the hegemony of Christianity is decried with the usual result that a greater effort is made to be more inclusive in relation to "other" religions.[14]

Thus does feminist theology both participate and reinforce the "world religions discourse" that Tomoko Masuzawa identifies in *The Invention Of World Religions*. Masuzawa raises a provocative and important question about this well-intentioned way of thinking, speaking, and writing. She asks "whether the idea of the diversity of religion is not . . . the very thing that facilitates the transference and transmutation of a particular absolutism from one context to another." Or, more specifically, is an "overtly exclusivist and hegemonic version" of "Christian supremacist dogmatism" simply being expressed in another form, namely, that of "the openly pluralistic one" of "world religious pluralism"?[15]

By leaving the concept of religion unanalyzed, feminist theorists in religious studies support religion as a standardized category of identity that is natural and appropriate for women to think of themselves as having or of being. Such work does not interrogate the assumption that religion is a unique sphere of life, a thing in itself, and thus does not ask how promoting this idea influences the way women function as political subjects and agents. Instead, the favored goal is to purge religion of sexism in order to enhance it.

Like feminist theologians, those applying queer theory to religion are interested in reinterpreting religious traditions in liberating directions. At present queer thought about religion is animated by a lively passion to show how Christianity can be understood as encompassing and endorsing a wide and sometimes wild range of sexual imaginings and practices. A vivid example is Lisa Isherwood's essay "Fucking Straight and the Gospel of Radical Equality" in the anthology she edited with Marcella Althaus-Reid titled *The Sexual Theologian: Essays on Sex, God and Politics*.[16] Isherwood discusses Margery Kempe's condition of being "married to God." Kempe describes her "sexual play" with divinity (that Isherwood interprets as being both female and male) as "more satisfying than with her husband and sire of her fourteen pregnancies." In a conversation with Jesus that Kempe relates, she is told "that Jesus himself wished to go to her bed as both son and husband."[17] Isherwood concludes that

> Margery appeared to be without boundaries, she moved beyond fucking straight, this is perhaps her gift to us as individuals and her challenge to us as queer theologians. . . . While we allow the enactment of fixed binary oppositions, stable and unequal categories on our bodies through sexual stereotyping and sexual intimacy we fail to open to the diverse/surprising wonder of radical incarnation. Fucking straight has no part in the embodiment of a gospel of radical equality.[18]

In "Queering Death," in the same volume, Elizabeth Stuart argues that Christian ritual contains within it a program for the expansion of all embodied identifications.[19] "The Christian story," she writes, "is a comedic drama: every act involving a dance with death; every act resounding with the laughter of resurrection; every act orientating us beyond our constructed identities, beyond our sexual desires, beyond death towards a life which is not strange to us but experienced in every Eucharist. It is all very queer."[20]

These quotations from Isherwood and Stuart exemplify a dominant objective of contemporary queer theology: to expand Christian ideas of norms about sex and indeed about all embodied experience. This is an urgent and massive political task, given the way conservative groups cite Christianity and other religions to justify oppression of persons and groups deemed to be "deviant." However, deconstructing the concept of religion itself might prove to be an equally pressing objective for queer work in religious studies.

In "Religion Trouble," his essay about three anthologies that apply queer theory to religion, Mark Jordan points out how "disciplinary troubles" in the field of religious studies sow confusion in emerging queer-focused literature. The indeterminateness about what constitutes religion in *Que(e)rying Religion: A Critical Anthology*, edited by Gary Comstock and Susan Henking, renders it difficult for a reader to "judge the project of the anthology itself." He wonders if endorsing an "extended sense of the religious" in an effort to avoid making any one religion normative is a wise strategy. Such a vague use of "spirituality" might prove to be "complicit with the most institutionalized regimes for the production and management of selves—in just the way that Foucault claimed movements of sexual liberation were."[21]

In the postscript of *Gay Religion* (a volume about gay communities' efforts at innovation in American religion, edited by Scott Thumma and Edward Gray), Jordan quotes an observation referring to an essentialism adhering to religious terminology. R. Marie Griffiths asks if the categories used in the book "suggest that human beings have inherent religious impulses" instead of recognizing "the social and cultural production of these kinds of needs."[22]

If queer theorists continue to use religious language without queering it, that is, if they cite religion as if it were an essential and nonpolitical constituent of culture, they might well accomplish nothing more than a reinforcement of religious authority. Because, as Jordan says, "memories of an old theocracy are tirelessly reactivated in the 'Christian' discourses around many of us—and in the discourses of other religious regimes elsewhere," religious terminology itself warrants thorough critique by theorists whose goal is to open up social space traditionally policed by ecclesiastical forces. [23]

"Religion Trouble" foregrounds pivotal questions regarding queer forays into religious studies. Jordan notes that "many contemporary writers on queer religion" seem to have "the desire to dethrone the hegemonic claims of privileged religions while retaining the power, the *aura* of the category."[24] He recalls that Michel Foucault once suggested that discourse about sexuality was formed in the lacuna left by the death of God. The title of David Halperin's classic text *Saint Foucault: Towards a Gay Hagiography* is an example of the religious rhetoric employed by queer theorists—a rhetoric indicating that queer theory occupies some of the discursive territory now claimed by "theology" and "religion."[25]

Like Jordan, I too have noticed a tendency among queer theologians to describe their work in religious language. Consider this passage from Althaus-Reid and Isherwood's introduction to *The Sexual Theologian*. "Queer theory," they write,

> impacts on theology and opens its horizons. . . . Theology has, over the years, forgotten that it is a brave subject and one that should lead the way as "queen of the sciences." It has become self-referential and therefore cut off, afraid to look outside itself in case its own irrelevance becomes abundantly clear. Sadly this becomes a self-fulfilling prophecy: the less it looks and ventures out, the more irrelevant it becomes. This can never be acceptable, particularly for a theology that declares incarnation to be at the heart of its reflections. Those engaged in queer theology are stating publicly their faith in the relevance of theology in all areas of life.[26]

This declaration—that queer theory has a mission to save theology from itself—indicates, like Halperin's choice of title, that the topic of sexuality has a soteriological grandeur and scope in the thinking of at least some prominent theorists. Such expressions of emotion about the calling of queer theory might intuitively underline a kinship between sex and religion that is deeper than metaphor or rhetoric. "Queer is a continuing moment, movement, motive—recurrent, eddying, *troublant*," writes Eve Kosofsky Sedgwick in a passage from *Epistemology of the Closet* that is often cited in reference to the destiny of queer theory. "The word 'queer' itself means *across*—it comes from the Indo-European root *twerkw*, which also yields the German *quer* (transverse). . . . The immemorial current that *queer* represents is antiseparatist as it is antiassimilationist. Keenly, it is relational, and strange."[27]

Queer theory's future relationship to religion is indeed likely to be very troubling and strange. It will be characterized by efforts at both separation and assimilation because both fields contest the same discursive territory. "Theology in (once) hegemonic traditions," Jordan writes, "knows something of what it is to be an urgent discourse of power over sex-linked identities."[28] It is very possible that the linguistic and social institutions that are now identified as "religions" are recognizable historically and culturally because of their regulation and standardization of sex and gender. Likewise, what is understood to be sexuality might be genealogically and ideologically bound to what has been thought about religion. Sexuality and religion thus could well be discursive products of each other. Thus, if critical analysis of both religion and sexuality continues, the categories will continue to intersect, collide, and displace each other.

Such adventures in deconstruction would disturb concepts that are now powerful markers of identity as well as fundaments of public policy and government. It is not at all apparent that religious studies as an academic discipline is a site in which this sort of far-reaching theory can flourish. The idea that religion is a thing in itself—religion *an sich*—still animates much of the field.[29] That the very concept of "religion" depends on normative constructions of sex and gender is a view that conflicts with seeing religion as separable from the to and fro of cultural movement. Furthermore, many academic units devoted to religious studies are housed in divinity schools whose mission is to train pastoral personnel committed to work within religious institutions and not to rethink the theories on which the institutions are founded. In both divinity schools and secular universities and colleges, specific denominational communities fund chairs promoting "studies" of particular world religions. Radical questioning of the religious categories themselves is not likely to be part of the job description of those who hold these academic appointments. Like feminist studies in religion, queer work in religious studies will be subject to similar pressures to be contained as a reformist movement within what are seen to be established religious traditions.

I want to conclude this essay with a type of case study to illustrate what I have said about the critical potential and unsettling politics involved in doing queer theory in religious studies. The groundbreaking work of Howard Schwartz shows how radical thought about sexuality and religion can open up troubling trajectories for theory. Furthermore, Schwartz's truncated academic career might serve as a cautionary tale about just how troubling such trajectories can be.

In 1994, Howard Schwartz, an ordained rabbi and an assistant professor of religious studies at Stanford University, published a highly original, carefully argued analysis about masculinity and Judaism titled *God's Phallus and Other Problems for Men and Monotheism*. Three years earlier, Schwartz had gained recognition for his outstanding scholarship in religious studies by winning the coveted American Academy of Religion's Award for Excellence for *The Savage in Judaism*. In his introduction to *God's Phallus*, Schwartz explains how feminist thought about religion had inspired him:

> Feminist and gender criticism convinced me that gender is not just another subject that intersects with religion, but is central to the work that religion accomplishes and the ways in which it goes about it. I have learned to take very seriously the ways in which symbols are gendered and the ways such gendered images influence conceptions of men and women. At the same time, I have found that gendered images themselves are inextricably entangled in issues of sexuality, desire, and the body. More specifically, feminist criticism and gender theory impressed me with the importance of taking seriously the gender of God. God's imagined masculinity is critical to understanding many central rituals and myths of monotheism.[30]

Schwartz's hypothesis that gender ought to be considered as a product of religion sets up a provocative agenda for theory in religious studies. His work in *God's Phallus* focuses on one idea that is a component of the systems labeled religions—namely, that of a sexed deity. Schwartz notes that although Mary Daly and other feminist critics have elaborated the problems that a masculine godhead raises for women—"Briefly," writes Daly, "if God is male, then Male is God"—the conundrum a male god poses for men themselves remains undertheorized.[31]

Schwartz points out that although a male god functions, perhaps primarily, to legitimate male power, it also "generates all kinds of tensions for men and masculinity."[32] Because it is men who are presented as being in an intimate and passionate relationship with a male God, homoeroticism is encouraged even though ancient texts explicitly forbid homosexual acts and utilize heterosexual metaphors to describe God's bond with his people. Schwartz believes that anxiety about sexual feelings between men and a male God is expressed in several ways in both Judaism and Christianity. He interprets scriptures about veiling, disguising, and otherwise disappearing the body of God as showing discomfort with too-literal representations of God's sexuality.

In addition to hiding God's body, Jewish and Christian traditions have a tendency to feminize men—perhaps to make them more desirable to the father God or possibly to further occlude images of more explicit homosexual affiliations between men and God. Both traditions displace their apprehension about God's body on to women. Impregnating women is especially fraught because if God does it, human men are rendered irrelevant. However, if men do it, God is somewhat desexed and men risk being seen as unlike a sexless deity. Thus do male deities express and foster profound unease around procreation. In Judaism, Schwartz thinks this anxiety is the motivation for making the production of Torah more important than physical reproduction. In Christianity, he thinks it is key to the ambivalence about both Jesus's conception and his corporeality.

These are intriguing ideas about how specific religious ideas create basic notions about gender and sex and accordingly about how imagination about sexuality provides an impetus for the construction of religious traditions. However, the ideas Schwartz sets out have not yet been widely discussed by queer theorists in religious studies. Nevertheless, it can be said that his radical and provocative text did have a notable and possibly chilling impact on the field: Howard Schwartz, whose permanent appointment at Stanford once appeared to be a foregone conclusion, was denied tenure and eventually left the academy entirely. If he could have continued writing and speaking about his work on sexuality and religion, analysis of the intersections between queer theory and religion might be more advanced.

In her entry titled "Queer Theory" in the *Encyclopedia Of Women and World Religion*, Claudia Schippert muses about whether "queering" religion will be "subversive and transgressive, and not merely an extension of existing projects" or whether it will "reinscribe normalizing rhetoric."[33] In this essay, I have argued that queer theory and critical religion need each other to creatively displace conventions of thought and practice that adhere to both religion and sex. Judith Butler, in her "Afterword" to *Bodily Citations*, a book that applies her work to religious topics, notes that "whether or not God exists" is a question that she has come to understand "that most of religious studies" sets aside.[34] I suggest that a more important lacuna persists in the subfield of the study of gender and religion. If most of queer and gender studies about religion continue to set aside the question of the existence of religion, that is, if scholars doing work on gender within religious studies do not ask how religion is created historically and politically as a category constructed in relation to sex and gender, the opportunity to start to think will have to be taken up somewhere else.[35]

NOTES

1. Judith Butler, "Wittig's Material Practice," *Gay and Lesbian Quarterly* 13, no. 4 (2007): 531.

2. Ursula King, "Religion," in *Encyclopedia of Women and World Religion*, ed. Serinity Young (New York: Macmillan Reference, 1999), 2:837.

3. Judith Butler, *Undoing Gender* (New York: Routledge, 2004), 4.

4. Janet R. Jakobsen and Ann Pellegrini, eds., *Secularisms* (Durham: Duke University Press, 2008); Laura S. Levitt, "Other Moderns, Other Jews: Rereading Jewish Secularism in America," in Jakobsen and Pellegrini, *Secularisms*, 107–38; Janet R. Jakobsen and Ann Pellegrini, *Love the Sin: Sexual Regulations and the Limits of Religious Tolerance* (New York: New York University Press, 2003); Daniel Boyarin, *Unheroic Conduct: The Rise of Heterosexuality and the Invention of the Jewish Man* (Berkeley: University of

California Press, 1997). There are some important exceptions. Jakobsen and Pellegrini have collected essays that explore the construction of gender and sex in regard to changing concepts of religion and secularism. For example, Levitt's essay shows how Jewish women learned to behave in ways that would be recognized as religious in a US context. This volume follows Jakobsen and Pellegrini's coauthored text, which shows how progressive directions in US law regarding sexual orientation could occur by specific strategic use of religious and secular categories. In addition, Boyarin has explored the interrelationship of secular and religious factors in the construction of Jewish masculinity.

5. Judith Butler, *Bodies That Matter: On the Discursive Limits of "Sex"* (New York: Routledge, 1993).

6. Judith Butler, "Afterword," in *Bodily Citations: Religion and Judith Butler*, ed. Ellen T. Armour and Susan M. St. Ville (New York: Columbia University Press, 2006), 286.

7. Martha Nussbaum, "The Professor of Parody," *New Republic* (February 22, 1999): 37–45. Nussbaum's criticism of Butler's work is the best-known example of such disparagement.

8. Diane Richardson, Janice McLaughlin, and Mark E. Casey, eds., *Intersections Between Feminist and Queer Theory* (New York: Palgrave Macmillan, 2006).

9. Carol Christ and Judith Plaskow, eds., *Weaving the Visions: New Patterns in Feminist Spirituality* (San Francisco: Harper and Row, 1989); Carol Christ and Judith Plaskow, eds., *Womanspirit Rising: A Feminist Reader in Religion* (San Francisco: Harper and Row, 1979); Rita Gross, *Feminism and Religion: An Introduction* (Boston: Beacon, 1996); Rosemary Skinner Keller, R. R. Ruether, and Marie Cantlon, eds., *The Encyclopedia of Women and Religion in North America* (Bloomington: Indiana University Press, 2006); Janet M. Soskice and Diana Lipton, eds., *Feminism and Theology* (New York: Oxford University Press, 2003); Letty M. Russell and J. Shannon Clarkson, eds., *Dictionary of Feminist Theologies* (Louisville: Westminster John Knox Press, 1996); Serinity Young, ed., *Encyclopedia of Women and World Religion* (New York: Macmillan Reference, 1999); Marcella Althaus-Reid and Lisa Isherwood, eds., *The Sexual Theologian: Essays on Sex, God and Politics* (London: T and T Clark International, 2004); Daniel Boyarin, Daniel Itzkovitz, and Ann Pellegrini, eds., *Queer Theory and the Jewish Question* (New York: Columbia University Press, 2003); Gary David Comstock and Susan E. Henking, eds., *Que(e)rying Religion: A Critical Anthology* (New York: Continuum, 1997); Scott Thumma and Edward R. Gray, eds., *Gay Religion* (Walnut Creek, Calif.: AltaMira, 2005). Two edited collections by Christ and Plaskow offer foundational and now classic essays about feminist studies in religion. More recent texts providing overviews are Gross, *Feminism and Religion*; Keller, Ruether, and Cantlon, *Encyclopedia of Women and Religion*; Soskice and Lipton, *Feminism and Theology*; Russell and Clarkson, *Dictionary of Feminist Theologies*; and Young, *Encyclopedia of Women and World Religion*. Queer theory and religion is the subject of collections by Althaus-Reid and Isherwood, *The Sexual Theologian*; Boyarin, Itzkovitz, and Pellegrini, *Queer Theory and the Jewish Question*; Comstock and Henking, *Que(e)rying Religion*; and Thumma and Gray, *Gay Religion*.

10. Elisabeth Schüssler-Fiorenza, *Bread Not Stone: The Challenge of Feminist Biblical Interpretation* (Boston: Beacon, 1984); Elisabeth Schüssler-Fiorenza, *In Memory of*

Her: A Feminist Theological Reconstruction of Early Christian Origins (New York: Crossroads, 1983).

11. Judith Plaskow, *Standing Again at Sinai: Judaism from a Feminist Perspective* (San Francisco: Harper and Row, 1990); Judith Plaskow, *The Coming of Lilith: Essays on Feminism, Judaism and Sexual Ethics, 1972–2003* (Boston: Beacon, 2005).

12. Carol Christ, *Laughter of Aphrodite: Reflections on a Journey to the Goddess* (San Francisco: Harper and Row, 1987); Carol Christ, *Rebirth of the Goddess: Finding Meaning in Feminist Spirituality* (Reading, Mass.: Addison-Wesley, 1997); Carol Christ, *She Who Changes: Re-Imagining the Divine in the World* (New York: Palgrave Macmillan, 2003).

13. Starhawk. *Dreaming the Dark: Magic, Sex and Politics* (Boston: Beacon, 1982); Starhawk, *The Spiral Dance: A Rebirth of the Ancient Religion of the Great Goddess* (San Francisco: Harper and Row, 1979); Zsusanna Budapest, *The Holy Book of Women's Mysteries: Feminist Witchcraft, Goddess Rituals, Spellcasting and Other Worldly Arts* (New York: HarperCollins, 1993).

14. Peggy Schmeiser, "Wanting More Change: A Few Reflections from a Secular Menace," *Journal of Feminist Studies in Religion* 23, no. 2 (Fall 2007): 121–26; Naomi R. Goldenberg, "What's God Got to Do with It? A Call for Problematizing Basic Terms in the Feminist Analysis of Religion," *Feminist Theology* 15 (2007): 275–88; Rita Gross et al., "Roundtable Discussion of 'Feminist Theology: Religiously Diverse Neighborhood or Christian Ghetto?,' " *Journal of Feminist Studies in Religion* 16, no. 2 (Fall 2000): 73–131.

15. Tomoko Masuzawa, *The Invention of World Religions* (Chicago: University of Chicago Press, 2005), 326–27.

16. Althus-Reid and Isherwood, *The Sexual Theologian*, 48–57.

17. Ibid., 47.

18. Ibid., 56.

19. Elizabeth Stuart, "Queering Death," in Althaus-Reid and Isherwood, *The Sexual Theologian*, 58–70.

20. Ibid., 69–70.

21. Mark D. Jordan, "Religion Trouble," *Gay and Lesbian Quarterly* 13, no. 4 (2007): 567.

22. Ibid., 571.

23. Ibid., 574.

24. Ibid., 568.

25. Ibid., 564.

26. Althus-Reid and Isherwood, *The Sexual Theologian*, 13.

27. Eve Kosofsky Sedgwick, *Epistemology of the Closet* (London: Penguin, 1993), xii.

28. Jordan, "Religion Trouble," 569.

29. Timothy Fitzgerald, *Discourse on Civility and Barbarity: A Critical History of Religion and Related Categories* (Oxford: Oxford University Press, 2007); Timothy Fitzgerald, *The Ideology of Religious Studies* (Oxford: Oxford University Press, 2000); Russell McCutcheon, *Critics Not Caretakers: Redescribing the Public Study of Religion* (Buffalo: State University of New York Press, 2001) Russell McCutcheon, *Manufacturing Religion: Discourse on Sui Generis Religion and the Politics of Nostalgia* (Oxford: Oxford University Press, 1997).

30. Howard Eilberg-Schwartz, *God's Phallus and Other Problems for Men and Monotheism* (Boston: Beacon, 1994), 5.

31. Mary Daly, *The Church and the Second Sex* (New York: Harper, 1975), 37.

32. Eilberg-Schwartz, *God's Phallus*, 16.

33. Claudia Schippert, "Queer Theory," in Young, *Encyclopedia of Women and World Religion*, 2:826.

34. Butler, "Afterword," 278.

35. David Chidester, *Savage Systems: Colonialism and Comparative Religion in Southern Africa* (Charlottesville: University Press of Virginia, 1996), 266. Chidester suggests that "something new" can happen in the study of religion—particularly in comparative religion—through analysis of the "situational, relational and strategic practices" that "have produced *religion* and *religions* as objects of knowledge and instruments of power." I heartily agree. However, I argue that sex and gender must always be taken into account in order for such analysis to go forward most radically.

PART XI

Religion, Coloniality, and Race

49

Religion, Modernity, and Coloniality

NELSON MALDONADO-TORRES

The concept of religion most used in the West by scholars and laypeople alike is a specifically modern concept forged in the context of imperialism and colonial expansion.[1] Postcolonial theory has made some contributions to the understanding of the links between religion, modernity, and coloniality, but it has tended to side with modern secularism in its characterization of religion, and it has equally privileged conversations with European and, to some extent, Third World secular authors. That is, the views of religious thinkers themselves, and experiences grounded in religious practices, rituals, narratives, or forms of organization, tend to be less present than the perspectives of secular authors in the understanding of the meaning of religion, modernity, or coloniality.

Another tendency in postcolonial theory, due in part to the collective impact of renowned theorists such as Edward Said, Gayatri Spivak, and Homi Bhabha, has been to identify sources for postcolonial theorizing in the specific histories of eighteenth- and nineteenth-century English and French colonialism and in the regions of the Middle East and South Asia. Less attention has been paid to fifteenth- to seventeenth-century formations of coloniality, and to colonies in the West, where the Spanish, the Portuguese, the Dutch, and more recently the United States, among other imperial powers, have had enduring influences. One of the consequences of this is that religious studies scholars who are in conversation with postcolonial theory tend to be well versed in the postcolonial critique of Orientalism, but much less informed about the theorization of Occidentalism or Americanity.

"Occidentalism" is a term coined by the Venezuelan anthropologist Fernando Coronil to refer to Western conceptions of the West that are presupposed in the characterization of the non-West. "Occidentalism," he states, "is . . . not the reverse of Orientalism but its condition of possibility, its dark side (as in a mirror)."[2] For Walter Mignolo, Occidentalism is important for the understanding of the West and its conceptualizations of the non-West, particularly Latin America, since, from the very emergence of the "Indias Occidentales" (West Indies) to the very idea of Latin America, the entire region has been casted as an ambiguous zone that must always see itself in relation to the West but without never obtaining that stature.[3] The relation between Europe and the Americas is therefore as important as that between Europe and the "Orient," or as that between the West and other regions in the "Old World." In the last five hundred years, such differentiations have taken place as part of a process of intensive European colonial expansion that began with the so-called discovery of America.

Americanity, in its turn, refers to the gradual globalization of a model of power, knowledge, social organization, and geopolitical formation that came about in the invention and administration of the "New World." Aníbal Quijano and Immanuel Wallerstein introduce and elaborate the concept in the context of the five hundredth anniversary of the "discovery" of the Americas.[4] For them, Americanity "has always been, and remains to this day, an essential element" in modernity, which means that the concept is not only relevant to the Americas, but to the entire world.[5] For Quijano and Wallerstein, what was "new" in the "New World" was not a geographical location, but new forms of geopolitical and interpersonal relations as well as new aspirations and criteria for "modernization." For them, "The newnesses were fourfold, each linked to the other: coloniality, ethnicity, racism, and the concept of newness itself."[6]

Of the four forms of newness that are contained in the concept of the "New World" and that come to define key aspects of modernity and modernization, perhaps the least understood is coloniality, which has also served theorizations about power, knowledge, and being by a number of Latin American and Latina/Latino intellectuals.[7] In the essay by Quijano and Wallerstein, coloniality is defined as "the creation of a set of states linked together within an interstate system in hierarchical layers. Those at the very bottom were the formal colonies. But even when formal colonial status would end, coloniality would not." They argue that coloniality "continues in the form of a socio-cultural hierarchy of European and non-European." And they add that "the hierarchy of coloniality manifested itself in all domains—political, economic, and not least of all cultural"—and that it "reproduced itself over time."[8] In this way, Americanity requires a consideration of knowledge, ideology, and culture, but also of political economy and institutions, while also considering historical change within the parameters of an expanding model of power that has often gone with the name modernity. This means that the analysis of Americanity and modernity resists the split between culture and structure that is still so common in the humanities and the social sciences.

An understanding of the relations between modernity and coloniality, therefore, requires an engagement with Occidentalism and Americanity, in addition to Orientalism. But Quijano and Wallerstein go further. They believe that "because Americanity has existed longest in the Americas, because its circuitous consequences have led to so much politico-intellectual turmoil over four centuries, Americanity has exposed itself to critical regard, and first of all in the Americas."[9] They call attention to the prominence of core-periphery analysis in Latin America, and antiracist mobilizations in North America.[10] In subsequent writings, Quijano combines these two elements, that is, international capitalism with core and peripheries, on the one hand, and race and racism, on the other, to characterize the most fundamental character of what he refers to as the coloniality of power.[11] This concept critically engages capitalism and racism simultaneously, while it also brings out the importance of the Americas in relation to the expansion of colonial logics. In that sense, coloniality's main object of critique is not just European empires or imperialism, but the enduring cultures and structures of colonialism that have sedimented in the Americas and elsewhere. This is a reason why this discourse is particularly challenging to audiences in the United States, for example, where the critique of European empires and the examination of domination in faraway places is much more acceptable than a combined critical engagement with the multiple legacies of racism and dehumanization in the nation, with the long history of interventionism in the region, and with the position of the country in the capitalist system.

Coloniality brings modern national projects and not only imperialism into question without losing sight of the density of colonial legacies and their impact on modern forms of life. Modernity, however, is often looked at in relation to the European Enlightenment, the French Revolution, and the Industrial Revolution, which is a reason why it is typically less difficult to understand the relevance of the critique of nineteenth-century Orientalism for the understanding and critique of modernity than reflections about the Americas. Race and racism are usually considered in a similar light, as being the offspring of Enlightened naturalism and taxonomies that aimed to classify the diversity of organic and inorganic life. Much of the previously unknown biological life and human diversity were present in colonial territories, and race and racism were as much ideologies for sustaining domination as theories for understanding diversity. But race and racism only emerged at the point when Europeans had found increasing forms of diversity in multiple colonial sites, and when there existed a secular naturalistic framework that rendered biblical stories about origins secondary or irrelevant.

By contrast, the sixteenth- and seventeenth-century Americas often appear as too dominated by religious discourses and old European monarchies for them to deserve serious consideration in this regard. But this only means that theorists of coloniality and Americanity, along with others who follow similar perspectives or insights, have to contend with how religious discourses contributed not only to the expansion of the existing empires, but also to the legitimization of ideas such as race. Perhaps the most prominent figure in this line is the Caribbean writer and theorist Sylvia Wynter.

Wynter is a specialist in the Spanish Renaissance and the early period of Spanish colonization. She published her views about the fundamental character of the Americas for the understanding of modernity and for its proper critical assessment not only independently from the theories of Quijano and Wallerstein, but before the theories of Americanity and Occidentalism had appeared.[12] She also later engaged that literature as well, and contributed to it.[13] Wynter argues that racial difference finds a ground in the transformation of the "sacred geography of feudal-Christian Ideology," according to which the earth is divided between habitable and unhabitable zones, into a new anthropological divide that posed some subjects as fundamentally superior to others. She describes late-fifteenth-century Europe as a region in transition where the Church's intolerance grew, but so also resistance to established dogma by monarchs who were seeking "to challenge the decision-making power of the Papacy," by Christian humanists, by emerging "mercantile, artisan and lay professional categories," and by "religious movements of apocalyptic millenarianism."[14]

Christopher Columbus belonged to the last two groups. His apocalyptic millenarianism combined with his professional vocational interest led him to believe, contrary to established dogma, that all the seas were navigable. Thus, even though a key part of the motivation for his voyage across the Atlantic was to extend the reach of Christianity and finance expeditions with the purpose of "rescuing" Jerusalem from the Muslims, the geographical conception that emerged after the "discovery" and the forms of governance and social organization that began to become normative not only were different from established Christian dogma, but also challenged the authority of Christianity. The "discovery" and colonization of the New World put in question Christian medieval geographical conceptions and forms of power in a similar way to how Copernicus's theories challenged Ptolemaic-Christian astronomy and the authority of theology. Wynter puts it elegantly: "The same path opened up to a scientific geography would also open onto the phenomenon of what was to be the increasingly global colonization of the peoples of the earth by the modern post-feudal European state. It would come to act increasingly in the name of its own power and this-worldly goal of competitive expansion, rather than acting merely as before, as the temporal arm of the Church, or as a vehicle for the spread of its faith."[15]

For Wynter, then, parts of the fifteenth and the sixteenth centuries cannot be described simply as religious. These centuries were going through a transition and it is best to consider them as religious-secular. The "discovery" of the Americas played a significant role in the humanist and scientific challenge to theocentric models of creation and salvation, and helped to open the path to see the earth as having been made by God "on behalf of, and for the sake of humankind (*propter nos homines*)."[16] This more secular point of view was accompanied by the idea that "humanity" was not entirely homogeneous, and that Europeans should not take the humanity of others for granted. Likewise, emerging European nation-states and empires seemed the ones for whose sake God had truly made the world for them to enjoy and exploit its resources. In short, a racist and imperial religious-secular humanism was at the heart of Western modernity before formal categories of race emerged. It was the unfolding of this civilization project and worldview that necessitated, as it were, the formal invention of race. The process was contingent, to be sure, and it was and has been challenged by multiple sectors, but there is no doubt that we have seen a gradual strengthening and globalization of the secular, imperial, and racial project that has come to be known as European modernity.[17]

The "new poetics of the *propter nos*," that is, the new discourse, symbols, and sensibility that became an imprint of European modernity in the context of the "discovery" and colonization of the Americas, animated racism as much as it gave meaning and sense to an emerging capitalism. It did so because the earth was simultaneously seen as a territory to be explored and exploited for the well-being of the emerging European nation-states. The exploitation of resources was coupled with the slavery of human beings (a slavery that was gradually naturalized) and the colonization of vast lands, leading up to the accumulation of capital, which became the substitute of otherworldly salvation.

The idea that the spread of capitalism could be related to "the new poetics of the *propter nos*" and therefore to a transition from a theocentric view of the world to a more secular one in a context of national and imperial building runs counter to the Weberian thesis about the Puritan grounds of capitalism.[18] Before the spirit of capitalism was animated by Puritan ethics, it found support in the suspension of ethics that was characteristic of "discoverers" and conquerors and the new worldview that was opened up with the "New World."[19] The spirit of conquest within a "new poetics of the *propter nos*" served as a common ground for capitalism and for racism, a link—between coloniality, modernity, racism, and capitalism—that is lost from view if one adheres to the Weberian thesis.

Weber's lack of attention to what modernity and capitalism owed to the relation between Europe and the Americas, and his attention in this respect to intra-European social processes, could be considered part of his general belief that in Western civilization, "and in Western civilization only, cultural phenomena have appeared which (as we like to think) lie in a line of development having *universal* significance and value."[20] Weber makes this statement in the very introduction to *Protestant Ethics and the Spirit of Capitalism*. It is, of course, not surprising that the idea about the significance of European history, science, and culture in respect to all other cultures and civilizations on the globe enters in direct conflict with analyses that are often made by theorists of modernity and coloniality, and by intellectuals who focus on decolonization. The retort from the position of postcolonial and decolonial analysis is that the very idea of Europe, and Europe alone, having a history and cultural elements of universal significance is part and parcel of the very colonialism that contributed to the sedimentation of capitalism and modernity in the West and beyond it.

Weber's statement about the universal character of European culture is the point of entry for Walter Mignolo's reflections about subaltern knowledges and the imaginary of the modern/colonial world system in his seminal *Local Histories/Global Designs: Coloniality, Subaltern Knowledges, and Border Thinking*.[21] Mignolo explores the colonial constitution of "the West" and "Western knowledge" and highlights the importance of what he refers to, following the Chicana writer and theorist Gloria Anzaldúa, as "border thinking."[22] Border thinking denotes the epistemological character of subjects who have been forced to think through differently situated and colonially inflected registers and languages. It is an epistemological operation that is characteristic of colonial subjects and other subjects whose subjectivity is split by the effects of coloniality. To the "*universal* significance" of European history, science, and culture, Mignolo opposes the epistemic potential of border thinking, which addresses the contradictions and limits of European thought while it also facilitates the proposal of new approaches about central problems created by modernity/coloniality as well as appreciation of solutions that have been kept out of modernity's discursive boundaries.

The first example that Mignolo uses to oppose Weber's characterization of knowledge and to explain the idea of "border thinking" is Tu Wei-ming's reflections about Confucianism, in particular, his explicit objection to the idea that commitments with concepts such as equality and liberty require an endorsement of views of private property and the self as found in classical Western philosophers and theoreticians.[23] Tu Wei-ming simultaneously points to the epistemological limits of Western thought and to the epistemological potential of Confucianism, viewed "as sustainable knowledge and not as a relic of the past to be 'studied' and 'fixed' from the perspective of Western disciplines."[24]

The second example that Mignolo uses is the work of the Native American scholar Vine Deloria Jr., who made similar points about the existence, viability, and sustainability of indigenous views about time, space, religion, knowledge, and other key concepts in theory. Mignolo concludes his discussion with reference to religious studies: "Tu Wei-ming and Deloria are not interpreting, translating from the Western hegemonic perspective, or transmitting knowledge from the perspective of area studies. Their analytic critical reflections (rather than 'religious studies') are engaged in a powerful exercise of border thinking from the perspective of epistemological subalternity."[25] And, then, in a final blow to Weber and to critical theorists whose only sources are European, Mignolo states: "Alternatives to modern epistemology can hardly come only from *modern* (Western) epistemology itself."[26]

The combined contributions here from Wynter and Mignolo indicate that modernity/coloniality is strongly connected to an emergent secular and increasingly naturalistic point of view, and that alternatives to it need to consider border forms of thinking that challenge the strict divide between the religious and the secular. One can find some parallels between Mignolo's interest in sustainable epistemologies that defy the secular/religion distinction and works such as Richard King's *Orientalism and Religion: Post-Colonial Theory, India, and "the Mystic East,"* which is one of the most sophisticated expressions of the postcolonial theory of religion.[27] Yet, Mignolo has not seriously explored the depth of the proposal for a decolonized spirituality that is arguably part of authors such as Gloria Anzaldúa, who inspires his views on the subaltern cognitive subject.[28] The same applies to the other figures featured in this chapter.

Here, scholars such as Jacqui Alexander, Sylvia Marcos, and Laura Pérez, along with a number of authors who work within the tradition of liberation theology and philosophy, and those who are trying to introduce postcolonial studies and feminism more strongly to religious studies, become important contributors and crucial interlocutors to further advance an understanding of religion, modernity, and coloniality.[29] A number of these authors, such as, once again, Anzaldúa herself, also take gender and sexuality more centrally in consideration within a framework centered on the concept of decolonization or decoloniality than those who focus on Orientalism, Occidentalism, or Americanity; and this represents yet another area of necessary engagement and discussion in relation to a discourse that defies the boundaries of religious studies and might help to decolonize the field.

NOTES

1. Jonathan Smith, "Religion, Religions, Religious," in *Critical Terms for Religious Studies*, ed. Mark C. Taylor (Chicago: University of Chicago Press, 1998), 269–70; Nelson Maldonado-Torres, "Religion, Conquest, and Race in the Foundations of the Modern/Colonial World," *Journal of the American Academy of Religion* 82, no. 3 (2014): 636–65.

2. Fernando Coronil, "Beyond Occidentalism: Toward Nonimperial Geohistorical Categories," *Cultural Anthropology* 11, no. 1 (1996): 56.

3. Walter Mignolo, "Postoccidentalismo: El argumento desde América Latina," in *Teorías sin disciplina (latinoamericanismo, poscolonialidad, y globalización en debate)*, ed. Santiago Castro-Gómez and Eduardo Mendieta (México DF: Miguel Angel Porrúa, 1998), 31–58.

4. Aníbal Quijano and Immanuel Wallerstein, "Americanity as a Concept; or, the Americas in the Modern World-System," *International Social Science Journal* 134 (1992): 549–57.

5. Ibid., 549.

6. Ibid., 550.

7. Santiago Castro-Gómez and Ramón Grosfoguel, eds., *El giro decolonial: Reflexiones para una diversidad epistémica más allá del capitalismo global* (Bogotá, Colombia: Siglo del Hombre Editores, IESCO-Universidad Central, and Instituto Pensar, Pontificia Universidad Javeriana, 2007); Ramón Grosfoguel, Nelson Maldonado-Torres, and José David Saldívar, eds., *Latin@s in the World-System: Decolonization Struggles in the 21st Century U.S. Empire* (Boulder: Paradigm, 2006); Edgardo Lander, *La colonialidad del saber: Eurocentrismo y ciencias sociales; Perspectivas latinoamericanas* (Caracas, Ven.: Facultad de Ciencias Económicas y Sociales [FACES-UCV]; Instituto Internacional de la UNESCO para la Educación Superior en América Latina y el Caribe [IESALC], 2000); Walter Mignolo and Arturo Escobar, eds., *Globalization and the Decolonial Option* (New York: Routledge, 2009); Catherine Walsh, Freya Schiwy, and Santiago Castro-Gómez, eds., *Indisciplinar las ciencias sociales: Geopolíticas del conocimiento y colonialidad del poder; Perspectivas desde lo andino* (Quito, Ecuador: UASB/Abya Yala, 2002).

8. Quijano and Wallerstein, "Americanity as a Concept," 550.

9. Ibid., 552.

10. Ibid.

11. Aníbal Quijano, "Coloniality of Power, Eurocentrism and Latin America," *Nepantla: Views from South* 1, no. 3 (2000): 533–80.

12. Sylvia Wynter, "Columbus and the Poetics of the *Propter Nos*," *Annals of Scholarship* 8, no. 2 (Spring 1991): 251–86.

13. Sylvia Wynter, "Unsettling the Coloniality of Being/Power/Truth/Freedom: Towards the Human, After Man, Its Overrepresentation—An Argument," *CR: The New Centennial Review* 3, no. 3 (2003): 257–337.

14. Wynter, "Columbus and the Poetics of *Propter Nos*," 252.

15. Ibid., 257.

16. Ibid., 256.

17. Nelson Maldonado-Torres, "Secularism and Religion in the Modern/Colonial World-System: From Secular Postcoloniality to Postsecular Transmodernity," in *Coloniality at Large: Latin America and the Postcolonial Debate*, ed. Mabel Moraña, Enrique Dussel, and Carlos A. Jáuregui (Durham: Duke University Press, 2008).

18. Max Weber, *The Protestant Ethic and the Spirit of Capitalism*, ed. Anthony Giddens (New York: Routledge, 1992).

19. Nelson Maldonado-Torres, *Against War: Views from the Underside of Modernity* (Durham: Duke University Press, 2008).

20. Weber, *The Protestant Ethic*, 13; Walter Mignolo, *Local Histories/Global Designs: Coloniality, Subaltern Knowledges, and Border Thinking* (Princeton: Princeton University Press, 2000), 3.

21. Mignolo, *Local Histories/Global Designs*.

22. Ibid., 5–6.

23. Ibid., 6.

24. Ibid.

25. Ibid., 9.

26. Ibid.

27. Richard King, *Orientalism and Religion: Post-Colonial Theory, India, and "the Mystic East"* (New York: Routledge, 1999).

28. Gloria Anzaldúa, *Borderlands/La frontera*, 2nd ed. (San Francisco: Aunt Lute, 1999).

29. Jacqui Alexander, *Pedagogies of Crossing: Meditations of Feminism, Sexual Politics, Memory, and the Sacred* (Durham: Duke University Press, 2005); Sylvia Marcos, ed., *Gender/Bodies/Religions* (Mexico DF: IAHR-ALER, 2000); Sylvia Marcos, *Taken from the Lips: Gender and Eros in Mesoamerica* (Leiden: Brill, 2006); Laura Pérez, *Chicana Art: The Politics of Spiritual and Aesthetic Altarities* (Durham: Duke University Press, 2007); Laura Pérez, "Decolonizing Spiritualities: Spiritualities That Are Decolonizing and the Work of Decolonizing Our Understanding of These," in Grosfoguel, Maldonado-Torres, and Saldívar, *Latin@s in the World-System*, 157–64; Enrique Dussel, *Religión* (Mexico DF: Edicol, 1977); Enrique Dussel, *The Invention of the Americas: Eclipse of the "Other" and the Myth of Modernity* (New York: Continuum, 1995); Laura Donaldson, *Decolonizing Feminisms: Race, Gender, and Empire-Building* (Chapel Hill: University of North Carolina Press, 1992); Laura Donaldson and Kwok Pui-lan, *Postcolonialism, Feminism, and Religious Discourse* (New York: Routledge, 2002); Kwok Pui-lan, *Postcolonial Imagination and Feminist Theology* (Louisville: John Knox, 2005).

50

Apartheid Comparative Religion in South Africa

DAVID CHIDESTER

The term *apartheid*, meaning "separation," became notorious in South Africa as a political policy of exclusion and incorporation, a policy for excluding the majority black population from citizenship while incorporating black people as exploitable labor within a capitalist economy. Drawing on earlier British colonial policies of racial segregation, urban townships, native reserves, and indirect rule through African chiefs, the white Afrikaner nationalists who came to power in 1948 sought to transform all of South Africa into separate spheres that were defined not only on the basis of race but also by differences of language, ethnicity, culture, and religion.

Economic historians have argued that apartheid secured a labor supply for white-controlled mining and manufacturing, for white-controlled farming and banking, or for competing interests among different factions of white Afrikaner nationalists who were struggling for control over the South African economy. At the same time, apartheid was underwritten by ideological justifications that ranged from an apartheid theology of racial separation, through scientific racism, to moral appeals for respecting the right to self-determination of separate nations, languages, cultures, and religions. Although some advocates of apartheid were influenced by the racism of Nazi Germany, others were informed by the history of racial discrimination and segregation of the United States.[1]

For our purposes in thinking about theory in the study of religion, we can regard apartheid as a term of exclusion and incorporation, a term of exclusion in marking, making, and policing boundaries, and a term of incorporation in absorbing everyone into an all-encompassing system of classification. On this basis, we can understand apartheid comparative religion to refer to the intellectual work of distinguishing among separate and perhaps even pure religions within an overarching system of classification for identifying distinct and separate languages, cultures, and religions. However, we will need to refine this preliminary definition of apartheid comparative religion.

On the one hand, we must situate it within a local history of engaging religious difference in South Africa. As I have argued elsewhere, intercultural contacts, relations, and exchanges in South Africa resulted in a proliferation of comparisons about religion within contested frontier zones.[2] For European travelers, explorers, missionaries, soldiers, settlers, and administrators, frontier comparative religion generally began with denial, with the insistence that indigenous Africans lacked any trace of religion. Once a frontier was brought under European control, however, colonial agents discovered that Africans had a religious system, just like a colonial administrative system, that kept them in place. Accordingly, apartheid comparative religion needs to be understood against the background of this longer history of colonial denial, discovery, and containment.

On the other hand, we must situate apartheid comparative religion within broader European and even global developments in the academic study of religion. In the emergence of the study of religion in Britain, we can discern an imperial comparative religion that its putative founder, F. Max Müller, advanced under the slogan "classify and conquer."[3] Here also was a system of classification that was based on distinguishing separate languages, cultures, and religions. Although it was global in scope and produced through complex mediations between imperial centers and colonized peripheries, this imperial comparative religion lacked the local policing power that is one of the defining features of apartheid comparative religion. Although apartheid theorists incorporated many aspects of imperial theory in assuming an animistic core of primitive religion, an evolutionary progression from primitive to civilized, and a general classification of separate and distinct world religions, they applied these theoretical principles by directly intervening in political policy, social engineering, education, and other areas of public and personal life.

Along these lines, I want to propose that we can consider apartheid comparative religion as a generic term for making and enforcing separations. As Daniel Boyarin has observed, this understanding of apartheid comparative religion can be useful in understanding the making and enforcing of the separation between two distinct religions, Christianity and Judaism, in late antiquity. Second-century religious theorists, such as Justin Martyr, deployed the term "heresy" to mark distinctions but also to police new boundaries between two religions. These new borderlines, Boyarin has argued, were produced through a kind of apartheid comparative religion in which the "heresiologists of antiquity were performing a very similar function to that of students of comparative religion of modernity." In their intellectual work of identifying "pure" religions and their political work of legislating against religious mixtures or exchanges as illicit syncreticism, experts on heresy policed the emerging border lines separating Judaism and Christianity. Accordingly, as Boyarin concludes, their marking and policing of heresy should be understood as "a form of apartheid comparative religion, and apartheid comparative religion, in turn, is a product of late antiquity."[4]

While appreciating Daniel Boyarin's analysis of the deep history of apartheid comparative religion in late antiquity, here I will focus on South Africa, recalling the historical roots and extensions of apartheid in the study of religion and concluding with postapartheid prospects.

FRONTIER, IMPERIAL, AND APARTHEID COMPARATIVE RELIGION

In the emergence and implementation of apartheid in South Africa, the anthropologist Werner Eiselen played a prominent role. An expert on indigenous African religion, Eiselen was an apartheid theorist and administrator, marking and enforcing boundaries. As the South African anthropologist Isaac Schapera recalled in an interview at the end of the 1980s, "Eiselen [was] the son of a missionary in the civil service. He became Secretary for Native Affairs and drafted the original blueprint of apartheid."[5] Fifty years earlier, however, Schapera had praised Eiselen for his in-depth knowledge of the indigenous religious beliefs and practices of Africans in South Africa. As Schapera noted in 1932, "Eiselen is now engaged in writing a book on the religious life of the Southern Bantu which . . . should make this aspect of Bantu life one of the best known."[6] Although this book was never written, Eiselen nevertheless wrote extensively on African religious life, trying to recover its "primitive" forms and endeavoring to assess the impact of Christianity and civilization. In his research findings, Werner Eiselen replicated a history of frontier denials and imperial assumptions about social evolution that fed into apartheid comparative religion in South Africa.

Within open and contested frontier zones, European observers had consistently reported that Africans lacked any trace of religion. Although they might have an abundance of superstition, the defining opposite of religion, Africans allegedly had no religion. This denial, which was repeated over and over again by European travelers, missionaries, and colonial agents, was a comparative observation that served to call into question the full humanity of Africans and thereby challenge their human rights to land, livestock, or control over their own labor within fluid and contested frontier zones. During the 1920s, Werner Eiselen, expert on African religion, began with such a denial as his point of departure, insisting that Africans actually did not have beliefs and practices that should be designated as religion. Insisting that the term "religion" should be reserved only for people of an "elevated culture," Eiselen found that Africans did not qualify. Since they lacked the "higher" culture supposedly developed by Europeans, Africans could not be credited with such a cultural accomplishment as religion. Accordingly, he argued, Africans might very well have "forms of belief" (*geloofsvorme*); but they had no religion (*godsdiens*).[7] In his earliest research, therefore, Eiselen argued that Africans had no religion, recasting the frontier denial of African religion and culture.

Drawing on imperial comparative religion, however, Werner Eiselen found that Africans were not merely an absence of religion; they also represented a point of origin for the evolution of religion. A variety of British imperial theorists, developing this evolutionary theme, had traced the origin of religion back to "primitive" fetishism, animism, or totemism. For example, John Lubbock, in 1870 in his *Origin of Civilization*, had tracked a developmental sequence—atheism, fetishism, totemism, shamanism, idolatry, polytheism, and theism—in the origin and evolution of religion.[8] Eiselen was interested in placing indigenous African religion within such an evolutionary trajectory from the primitive to the civilized. Placing Africans in South Africa on this scale, Eiselen observed, "The Bantu is no longer primitive in the true meaning of the word." Although this might at first glance seem to be a positive judgment, Eiselen only meant to suggest that he had detected some evolutionary progression from a primitive origin to totemism. "The level of development that he has reached," Eiselen continued, "we usually call the Totem-culture."[9] Having advanced one stage above fetishism, the primitive and promiscuous worship of objects, Africans in South Africa according to Eiselen had evolved to the next evolutionary stage of worshiping emblems of collective identity or tribal solidarity. In this finding, we can only suspect, Werner Eiselen was anticipating the importance of the totemic group, the *volk*, in the blueprint of apartheid.

As an architect of apartheid, Werner Eiselen claimed that he only intended to facilitate "the creation of effective arrangements for the peaceful existence of different ethnic groups."[10] The policy of "separate development," which created fictional nations for African ethnic groups, was an integral part of this apartheid plan for peaceful coexistence. But Eiselen's policy bore traces of both the frontier and the imperial heritage of comparative religion in South Africa.

Maintaining frontier denials, Eiselen's research denigrated Africans as if they represented an absence. The Bantu, according to Eiselen, were not rational. For evidence of this alleged lack of rationality, he compared European and African methods in agriculture. According to Eiselen, white Afrikaans-speaking farmers made use of rational techniques, such as irrigation and storage, although they might also draw on religious resources of prayer. African farmers, however, not being rational, knew nothing of such rational techniques, so they only resorted to prayer or its functional equivalent, rainmaking ritual.[11] Ironically, this apartheid denial seemed to reverse the frontier assertion that Africans lacked religion. Instead, Africans allegedly only resorted to religion. But South African frontiers did not only produce denials; they also resulted in discoveries that Africans had religious systems, perhaps irrational systems, which kept them in place. Clearly, Eiselen and other ideologues of apartheid were interested in assigning, maintaining, and enforcing separate places for Africans in South Africa.

At the same time, drawing on his own missionary background and the Christian interests invested in apartheid, Eiselen recast the evolutionary scheme of imperial comparative religion. Accordingly, when he outlined the next stage of African evolution, Eiselen foresaw an evolutionary trajectory guided by Christian civilization. "Christian education," he concluded, "is the only way to make [the African] a useful inhabitant of our Union."[12] This version of evolutionary progression, turning Africans into "useful" subjects of a Christian state, was symptomatic of an apartheid comparative religion based on denigrating but also incorporating people in theory and practice.

BEYOND APARTHEID

As it was developed by Werner Eiselen and other apartheid ideologues in South Africa, apartheid comparative religion drew upon earlier ways of understanding religion, including frontier denials and containments, imperial theories of primitive mentality and social evolution, and even Émile Durkheim's thesis that religion reflects society. Making explicit reference to Durkheim, Eiselen argued that "the South African tribes had a very rigid structure and so we can expect to find a fairly clear replica thereof in the structure of their religion."[13] Rigid and unchanging, African religion supposedly reinforced a "tribal solidarity" that kept everyone in their place. As secretary of native affairs, Eiselen played a crucial role in carrying out apartheid policies of exclusion and incorporation, marking and enforcing spatial boundaries, such as separate urban areas defined by race and separate African "homelands" defined by tribal solidarity, while also seeking to incorporate everyone within the domain of a single "Christian nationalism" enforced by a self-professed Christian state.

Under apartheid, the study of religion in South African universities displayed a specific division of labor, with Afrikaner theologians, biblical scholars, and missiologists claiming expertise not only in Christianity but also in "other" religions from a Christian perspective, while Afrikaner anthropologists, developing the science of *volkekunde*, claimed expertise in the "tribal" religions of indigenous Africans in South Africa.[14] Generally, Christianity was regarded as a dynamic force, capable of converting and transforming, but African indigenous religious life was depicted as static repetition of the past. Following the nonracial democratic elections of 1994, these highly politicized approaches to the study of religion, privileging Christianity, organizing religious diversity for Christian conversion, and denigrating African religious heritage, were rejected by the government of a postapartheid South Africa. New initiatives in affirming religious diversity, especially in education, and valuing African indigenous heritage as a basis for cultural renewal were also political strategies.[15] But they sought to engage religion in ways that might redress the religious divisions and Christian hegemony entrenched in South Africa under apartheid.

As a generic term for marking and enforcing religious boundaries, apartheid comparative religion highlights the role of power in the production of knowledge about religion and religions.

Reflecting on the workings of hegemonic power, Talal Asad has observed that dominating regimes of knowledge are not necessarily based on dissolving differences into an overarching unity. They are not necessarily dependent upon achieving uniformity. Rather, in marking and enforcing boundaries, "dominant power has worked best through differentiating and classifying practices."[16] Clearly, in South Africa, apartheid comparative religion was a science of differentiating and classifying, producing knowledge about religion and religions that served a dominating political project. But the South African case drives us to ask: How have such practices registered in others colonial situations? How have imperial theorists of religion produced, even if they have not echoed Max Müller's flamboyant motto "classify and conquer," knowledge about the religious diversity that underwrote European hegemony.[17] While colonial denials and containments, differences and classifications, have influenced knowledge about religion and religions all over the world, the imperial notion of separate and distinct "world religions" sometimes resembles the divisions of apartheid. Going beyond apartheid might be helped by research that goes back through colonial and imperial histories to uncover enduring legacies of marking and enforcing boundaries in the study of religion.

Moving beyond apartheid also requires recovering what apartheid denied. In the name of purity, seeking to identify and maintain the purity of separate races, ethnic groups, languages, cultures, and religions, apartheid ideologues tried to prevent any mixtures. Religious mixtures, condemned as syncretism, were particularly decried when they appeared to weave together religious resources of indigenous and Christian traditions. Arguably, this apartheid obsession with purity was already subtly inscribed in European theories of "families" of world religions and ethnic religions. Such organic models, as Robert Young has observed, were "designed to deny the more obvious possibilities of mixture, fusion, and creolization."[18] Postapartheid possibilities in the study of religion have been opened by attention to indigenous religion as a dynamic, fluid, and contested set of resources that have been deployed in transcultural contact zones.[19] Certainly, this understanding of religion as resources and strategies could be extended more broadly to the analysis of any religious form of life. In the case of indigenous religions, however, such a situated and dynamic rendering is necessary to counteract colonial, imperial, or apartheid formulations of these resources and strategies as "religious systems" that can be contained or controlled.

A postapartheid study of religion, like recent initiatives in postcolonial anthropology, can be critical of the links between knowledge and power, analyzing the ways in which disciplinary knowledge might be "embedded in certain social, cultural and political dynamics that unfold in contexts which are differently and historically structured by changing power relations."[20] But such a project can also be creative in exploring the vitality of religious resources and the dynamics of religious strategies within the changing power relations of local, regional, and global contact zones.

NOTES

1. Hermann Giliomee, "The Making of the Apartheid Plan, 1929–1948," *Journal of Southern African Studies* 29, no. 2 (2003): 373–92.

2. David Chidester, *Savage Systems: Colonialism and Comparative Religion in Southern Africa* (Charlottesville: University Press of Virginia, 1996).

3. David Chidester, "'Classify and Conquer': Friedrich Max Müller, Indigenous Religious Traditions, and Imperial Comparative Religion," in *Beyond Primitivism: Indigenous Religious Traditions and Modernity*, ed. Jacob K. Olupona (London: Routledge, 2004), 71–88; David Chidester, "Real and Imagined: Imperial Inventions of Religion in Colonial Southern Africa," in *Religion and the Secular: Historical and Colonial Formations*, ed. Timothy Fitzgerald (London: Equinox, 2007), 153–76.

4. Daniel Boyarin, *Border Lines: The Partition of Judaeo-Christianity* (Philadelphia: University of Pennsylvania Press, 2004), 14.

5. John Comaroff and Jean Comaroff, "On the Founding Fathers, Fieldwork, and Functionalism: A Conversation with Isaac Schapera," *American Ethnologist* 15, no. 3 (1988): 555.

6. Isaac Schapera, "The Present State and Future Development of Ethnographical Research in South Africa," *Bantu Studies* 8 (1934): 258.

7. W. M. Eiselen, "Geloofsvorme van Donker Afrika," *Tydskrif vir Wetenskap en Kuns* 3 (1924–1925): 84–98.

8. John Lubbock, *The Origin of Civilization and the Primitive Condition of Man*, 5th ed. (London: Longmans, Green, 1889), 205–10.

9. W. M. Eiselen, "Die Seksuele Lewe van die Bantoe," *Tydskrif vir Wetenskap en Kuns* (1923–24): 166, 174.

10. W. M. Eiselen, "Die Aandeel van die Blanke in Afsonderlike Ontwikkeling," *Journal of Racial Affairs* (1965); quoted in T. Dunbar Moodie, *The Rise of Afrikanerdom* (Berkeley: University of California Press, 1974), 275.

11. W. M Eiselen. "Die Eintlike Reendans van die Bapedi," *South African Journal of Science* 25 (December 1928): 387–92.

12. W. M. Eiselen, *Stamskole in Suid Afrika: 'n Ondersoek oor die funksie daarvan in die lewe van die Suid-Afrikaanse Stame* (Pretoria: L. J. van Schalk, 1929), 76.

13. W. M. Eiselen, "Christianity and the Religious Life of the Bantu," in *Western Civilization and the Natives of South Africa: Studies in Culture Contact*, ed. Isaac Schapera (London: Routledge, 1934), 66–67.

14. John Sharp, "The Roots and Development of *Volkekunde* in South Africa," *Journal of Southern African Studies* 8, no. 1 (1981): 16–36.

15. David Chidester, "Unity in Diversity: Religion Education and Public Pedagogy in South Africa," *Numen* 55 (2008): 272–99.

16. Talal Asad, *Genealogies of Religion: Discipline and Reasons of Power in Christianity and Islam* (Baltimore: Johns Hopkins University Press, 1993), 17.

17. Tomoko Masuzawa, *The Invention of World Religions; or, How European Universalism Was Preserved in the Language of Pluralism* (Chicago: University of Chicago Press, 2005).

18. Robert Young, *Colonial Desire: Hybridity in Theory, Culture, and Race* (London: Routledge, 1995), 19.

19. David Chidester, "Dreaming in the Contact Zone: Zulu Dreams, Visions, and Religion in Nineteenth-Century South Africa," *Journal of the American Academy of Religion* 76, no. 1 (2008): 27–53.

20. Gustavo Lins Ribeiro, "World Anthropologies: Cosmopolitics for a New Global Scenario in Anthropology," *Critique of Anthropology* 26, no. 4 (2006): 363; see Gustavo Lins Ribeiro and Arturo Escobar, eds., *World Anthropologies: Disciplinary Transformations Within Systems of Power* (Oxford: Berg, 2006).

51

Theorizing Race and Religion

Du Bois, Cox, and Fanon

WILLIAM DAVID HART

Through the pursuit of India's wealth, the agents of colonial modernity constructed India, Africa, and America as a complex object of imperial desire. White supremacy, the transatlantic slave trade, and African colonization, as artifacts of that desire, are foundational events in the emergence of theories of religion. Constructed as contemporary embodiments of primitivism, the aboriginal religions of Africa, America, and Australia represented an evolutionary stage that Western religions had left behind. I construe the "race critical" theories of W. E. B. Du Bois, Oliver Cromwell Cox, and Frantz Fanon as responses to this history, even though religion is rarely conceived as their primary object. Their analyses of race, with varying degrees of attentiveness to religion as a social force, pivot on the subordination of black people. Du Bois is most attentive to the constitutive relation between race and religion. Cox is least attentive; but he understands best how the black-white axis stereotypes racial thinking, and he creates a rank order with whites at the top, "intermediate races" in the middle, and blacks at the bottom. Fanon understands the depth dimensions of race better than the others but does not explore the relations within psychoanalytic theory between race and religion.

W. E. B. DU BOIS

What then is a race? It is a vast family of human beings, generally of common blood and language, always of common history, traditions and impulses, who are both voluntarily and involuntarily striving together for the accomplishment of certain more or less vividly conceived ideas of life.[1]

"The Conservation of Races" is the fullest expression of Du Bois's racial theory. At the time of its publication in 1897, it was virtually impossible to speak outside the discourse of race. Thus Du Bois crafted a theory designed to protect the interests of black people in sheer physical survival during the nadir of their post-Emancipation experience: a period of unprecedented forms of antiblack

violence—neoslavery, riots, lynching, and the "racial cleansing" of entire munici-
palities and counties. In Du Bois's theory, race is simultaneously the superficial
reality of gross morphological difference and the deeper reality of spiritual difference. On this Herder-derived view, religious expression, if not a propensity for
religion, is the distinctive manifestation of the black *Volksgeist*. One can trace a
straight line from the claims that Du Bois makes in this essay to his *The Souls of
Black Folks* (1903), in which he argues that black people cannot be understood
apart from religion, and where he explicitly affirms that religiosity is the preeminent
expression of black people's "racial genius."[2] He made similar claims in *Black
Folks: Then and Now* (1939). Indeed, he continued to make such claims as late as
1947, more than a decade after the Marxist-inspired *Black Reconstruction* (1935).[3]
DuBois's Herderian views shaped his concepts of religion and race, and their
interrelations.

While the old function of race was to create ever-larger social groups less tied to
kinship and clan, its new function, as Du Bois described it, is the social expression
of racial gifts, the flowers of a long period of germination. Each race embodies a
distinctive message for humankind. The conservation of races would ensure that
these messages are not lost, that the special gift, "racial genius," of each group is
expressed. If the English have a genius for "constitutional liberty and commercial
freedom," Germans for "science and philosophy," and Romance nations for art and
literature, then surely the Negro has its own genius, which has not been fully expressed.[4] The Negro is an artist by nature. The distinctive "gift of black folks," as
Du Bois described it elsewhere, is a special spiritual sensitivity that ranges across
the full spectrum of American life.[5] As I remarked above, the most obvious *racial
gift* of "black folks," their distinctive spiritual contribution, was a genius for religious expression. Just to be clear, this religious genius simultaneously distinguished
their racial essence. In some respects, Du Bois's description of the black gift resembles the primitivist discourse of the Harlem Renaissance, of which he otherwise
was a critic. As one commentator remarks, his view "could as easily [have] been
stigmatized by hostile racialist[s] as esteemed by admiring racialists."[6] And so it
has been.

Du Bois's theory of race is confusing and confused, reflecting the kudzu-like
history of the idea. In the first instance, race is what we see. Beneath, and more
important than, gross morphological differences are historical and cultural differences. However, these differences are somehow rooted, nontrivially, in biological difference. Thus we have a bizarre circle: gross morphological differences are signs of
spiritual differences, which are rooted in biological difference; but biological differences are superficial! Furthermore, spiritual differences appear simultaneously as
artifacts of history *and* as metaphysically stable. This is confusing: it is virtually
impossible to distinguish racial difference from historical, cultural, ethnic, and
national differences. On second thought, the confusion is less Du Bois's theory
than the very history of "race." Historically and conceptually, there is no cordon
sanitaire between history, culture, nationality, ethnicity, and race. Race is a motley
crew, and that motley crew includes religion. Religion is constitutive of race.

OLIVER CROMWELL COX

> *Our hypothesis is that racial exploitation and race prejudice developed among Euro-*
> *peans with the rise of capitalism and nationalism, and that because of the world-wide*
> *ramifications of capitalism, all racial antagonisms can be traced to the policies and*
> *attitudes of the leading capitalist people, the white people of Europe and North*
> *America....*
>
> > *Race prejudice is an attitudinal instrument of modern human, economic*
> > *exploitation....*
>
> > *We cannot defeat race prejudice by proving that it is wrong. The reason for this is*
> > *that race prejudice is only a symptom of a materialistic social fact....*
>
> > *There will be no more "crackers" or "niggers" after a socialist revolution because*
> > *the social necessity for these types will have been removed.*[7]

These epigraphs capture Cox's racial theory in a nutshell. As reflected in the title of his monumental study *Caste, Class, and Race* (1948), Cox sees race as part of a three-termed conceptual economy. His basic thesis is that modern capitalist class relations rather than ancient Indian caste relations explain race relations. While caste is a cultural phenomenon, race is produced by the political economy of capitalism.

Cox gets the definitional problem out of the way by refusing to defer to scientific accounts. Whatever reservations or enthusiasms scientists may have about the concept, race is preeminently a sociological phenomenon. Just as linguistics will always be subordinate to how we actually use language, the scientific meaning of race (including the notion that it is scientifically meaningless) will always be subordinate to its larger social meanings. Race is a social concept, and its meanings are determined by its use. As a material reality (relations of dominance and subordination expressed attitudinally as racism), the concept of race will not disappear merely because scientists prove that it is not a "natural kind," or because philosophers show through elegant argument that it is incoherent. Even if we stop using the word "race," the phenomena it designates do not evaporate as conceptual reductionists and romantics might imagine. On the contrary, Cox asserts that those phenomena are produced and sustained by the labor demands of modern capitalism. To put it bluntly, "race relations," the ensemble of practices we call white supremacy, racism, and racial ideology, make it easier to exploit black labor, white labor, and—beyond the black-white binary—every other kind of labor. I am agnostic on the question of whether Cox's analysis should be taken as applicable to all forms of capitalism or to specific types.

Cox identifies seven racial regimes. They range from situations where the numbers of "colored" people is so small that they constitute "strangers" to "amalgamative situations," where there is extensive intermarriage; from "original contact situations," especially those that result in the genocide of the "colored" population, to "slavery"; from "ruling class situations," in which a small white population rules a large "colored" population, to the "nationalistic situation," in which the colored population has seized power from the white ruling class. Finally, there is the "bipartite situation," such as South Africa and the United States, where the white ruling class segregates a large "colored" population. Thus there are stranger, original contact, slavery, bipartite, amalgamative, and nationalistic racial regimes. Curiously, Cox does not explore religion as an "ideological apparatus" or as a site of "struggle for hegemony" within these regimes. In a "fugitive" remark he construes religion as a potential competitor of capitalism.[8] This recalls Marx's description of religion as both opium *and* protest.

Having argued that race is a tool of capital deployed in seven "situations of race relations," Cox attacks *the caste school of race relations*, that is, the claim that race relations are class relations. Race cannot be assimilated to caste because racial difference cuts across caste difference: Indians have both a caste identity vis-à-vis each other and a racial identity in relation to their English colonizers. Unlike race pride, "Caste pride is based upon internal invidiousness." *Caste conflict* strengthens the caste system, while racial conflict destabilizes racial regimes. Occupational choice is governed by different criteria—"purity considerations" in caste, "income and personal adaptability" in race relations. Hypergamy (marrying up) has fundamentally different effects within caste and race relations; it poses no threat to the former but is deeply threatening to the latter. Further, "caste is a truly endogamous social entity," while "race is not a closed endogamous unit." In a racial situation, subordinate races regard their status as unjust, while in the caste system, members of lower castes regard their status as "natural," that is, questions of justice and injustice do not arise.[9] The concept of "outcasting," of expelling someone from a caste, is incompatible with the logic of race.[10] A person cannot be expelled from her race any more than she can convert from one race to another. Between the two, difference is conceived differently—different material realities, different conceptual universes. The caste school of race relations, whether old or new, whether represented by luminaries such as Robert E. Parks, Ruth Benedict, and Gunnar Myrdal or by anonymous academics, is wrong. Race is not caste.

In the sixty years following Cox's argument (1948–2008), the socialist project has virtually collapsed, especially in its actually existing and once-existing communist formats (or *deformations*, for those who remain hopeful). It is now doubtful that race relations remain tied, necessarily, to the capitalist exploitation of labor, or that the ties are as strong as Cox believed. Whether race relations have the same material logic that they did during the period of capitalist ascendancy is an open question. Perhaps the biggest deficiency in Cox's analysis is his failure to understand the role of religion in systems of social hierarchy, whether caste or race. Because Cox does not tell us explicitly what he thinks about religion, we have to interpret its place in light of its absence. In his economistic brand of Marxism, religion, like race, is little more than a dependent variable, a subterfuge for the operations of capital. Cox conforms to the dominant if not classical view in which religion, as the aboriginal form of fetishism, is false consciousness. In the history of theorizing religion, fetishism is a thoroughly racialized idea based on the misperceptions of the Portuguese during the fifteenth century who thought that Africans worshiped rocks and other "fetishes." This view construes African religious practices—in counterdistinction to European practices—as exemplifying "prelogical" thinking.

FRANTZ FANON

I am not the slave of the Slavery that dehumanized my ancestors.

I, the man of color, want only this: That the tool never posses the man. That the enslavement of man by man cease forever. That is, of one by another. That it be possible for me to discover and to love man, wherever he may be.[11]

Black Skin, White Masks is the principal source of Fanon's racial theory. Originally published in French, under the title *Peau Noire Masques Blancs* (1952), it appeared four years after Cox's *Caste, Class, and Race*. In contrast to Cox's sociology of racial formations, Fanon's text is a psychoanalytic study. But, with roots in social analysis, it shares Cox's broad Marxist ideology, if not its analytic frame. Fanon's thesis is that black identity is an artifact of white identity. Both identities are forms of estrangement between humans, with black alienation rooted in white alienation. The Europeanization of the world (modern imperialism) beginning in the fifteenth century was the first move in a Kabuki dance between black and white "races" that constitutes what Fanon describes as "a massive psychoexistential complex."[12] "The black man wants to be white. The white man slaves to reach a human level."[13] This perverse struggle for recognition is the psychoexistential complex.

Fanon was schooled in the French tradition of psychoanalysis, which includes the huge presence of Jacques Lacan, and his racial theory has five foci: language, interracial love, phenomenology, psychopathology, and the problem of recognition. The language of white people—the master, the colonizer—bifurcates the black self, producing a subject whose desire to be white, whose "whiteness idolatry," divides her against herself. The master's language is part of the white mask that the black subject wears in the presence of white people. Fanon remarks that "to speak a language is to take on a world, a culture."[14] The black subject cannot help but be estranged from herself. At the very least, she must work hard to combat alienation. Thus she is angered when addressed in pidgin, as if the Negro, the black person, were infantile, developmentally retarded, or suffered from dementia. Conversely, the surprise that white people often express—"You speak French so well"[15]—when they encounter a well-spoken black person is also a source of estrangement-producing anger, presupposing, as it does, black people's inability to master the language. Every element of the psychoexistential complex, which Fanon wishes to destroy, is rooted in the master/colonizer's language: in the world, culture, and assumptions about the status of black people implicit in language.

Fanon believes that "authentic love" between black women and white men and between black men and white women is possible. (He does not consider same-sex love; I do not believe he can conceive it as other than perverse.) However, white supremacy pathologizes interracial love. White men and women are constructed as objects of desire, prizes to be won, the possession of which elevates the black person who possesses them. Mayotte Capécia and Jean Veneuse are exhibits A and B. Both are racially elevated, transfigured through their relations with white lovers. Capécia becomes beautiful and virtuous like a white woman. Veneuse acquires the dignity and prerogatives of a white man.

Fanon's insights are often deep. Had he connected his account of race to the religiously derived category of idolatry to which the tradition of ideology critique is indebted, he might have provided even deeper insights. He might have recognized, for example, the way in which the "white obsession" of Mayotte Capécia and Jean Veneuse exemplifies idolatry. The deification of whiteness screams for psychoanalytic critique. Indeed, it calls for a kind of anticolonial, psychoanalytic, Marxist analysis that Fanon was best qualified to provide. If only he had.

It is no coincidence that Fanon devotes more space to "The Negro and Psychopathology" than to any other topic. White supremacy is pathogenic. It makes blacks and whites sick. We saw this in the cases of Mayotte Capécia and Jean Veneuse, who, through their white lovers, sought to become white. Again, this *religious desire* for radical transformation—metamorphosis, rebirth, transfiguration—is ripe for an investigation that Fanon gestures toward but does not provide. We see it in white people's superiority complex and in the inferiority and dependency complexes of black people. Much of this psychopathology has to do with constructions of black people as sexual athletes, if not beasts, reduced to unconstrained desire, to genitalia. The black male is a penis: hence the importance of castration in lynching rituals. "In the collective unconscious of *homo occidentalis*, the Negro—or, if one prefers, the color black—symbolizes evil, sin, wretchedness, death, war, famine." To put it crudely, black people will fuck, kill, and eat you. As speakers of the master/colonizer's language, black people are possessed by this same imagination. They are divided within themselves against themselves. "Hence a Negro is forever in combat with his own image."[16] Fanon wishes to destroy these social arrangements that make a choice between equally untenable alternatives necessary.

Insofar as he is a philosophical thinker, Fanon is part of the French tradition of phenomenology—the tradition of Jean-Paul Sartre and Maurice Merleau-Ponty—and a contemporary of soon-to-be-emerging thinkers such as Michel Foucault and Jacques Derrida. In a chapter titled "The Fact of Blackness," Fanon analyzes the black experience of objecthood, of blacks as object of the white gaze. "Look, a Negro!" When describing the reaction of a young white boy to his presence and his own reaction to the white gaze, Fanon does not exploit the religious idea of a "panoptic God" that empowers the very concept:

> I am given no chance. I am overdetermined from without. I am the slave not of the "idea" that others have of me but of my own appearance.
>
> I am being dissected under white eyes, the only real eyes. I am *fixed*.
>
> Shame. Shame and self-contempt. Nausea. When people like me, they tell me it is in spite of my color. When they dislike me, they point out that it is not because of my color. Either way, I am locked into the infernal circle.[17]

If only Fanon had subjected the central narrative of psychoanalytic theory to a religio-racial critique. What he would have discovered are the historical and conceptual relations among the primitive, immature, rationally deficient, and black people. These associations color (pun intended) Freudian-derived accounts of culture, especially religion. The persistence of religion is a form of evolutionary failure, of

arrested development. On this view, no people exhibit this psychosexual immatu-
rity more than black people. If the "id" is the psychoanalytic primitive, then black
people are the historical primitive. In Freud's theory, the Marxist concept of the
fetish receives a psychoanalytic makeover. In any case—whether attributing to inani-
mate objects powers they do not have, mystifying commodities, or obsessing sexually
about women's feet—the concept of the fetish is rooted in Kant's religio-moral theory of Enlightenment, the colonial encounter, and white supremacy. Fanon employs
the theory without exploring this genealogy.[18]

Du Bois asked the question, "How does it feel to be a problem?"[19] Cox shows
that the "Negro problem" is an ideological instrument of capitalism. Fanon describes what it is like to be a problem, an object—phenomena subject to the white
gaze. Such is the fact of blackness. According to Fanon, the system of white supremacy presents black people with a bad either-or: either they can ask that others ignore the symbolic meaning of their skin color or they can ask that others be aware
of their color while inverting or otherwise resignifying its meaning. Rejecting both
options, Fanon advocates a universal humanism beyond racial classification. Is this
possible? I have my doubts.

To theorize religion is simultaneously to theorize race. Theories of religion—
especially evolutionary theories, whether Humean, Hegelian, or post-Darwinian—
presuppose and channel white supremacy and the rank ordering of "races." The
metaperspectives of Du Bois, Cox, and Fanon (Herderian, Marxist, and psychoanalytic) are complicit with these hierarchical assumptions insofar as they fail to
identify and repudiate them. As a critical theorist of race, Cox is the most thorough,
clear-eyed, and systematic, if not sophisticated. He is also the shallowest. Cox avoids
Du Bois's romantic Herderian metaphysics and Fanon's psychoanalytic narrowness
but at the cost of a certain depth. Though Cox may be correct when he claims that
racism is the offspring of capitalism,[20] there is no good reason to believe that racial
ideology will disappear if capitalism disappears. Cox ignores the extent to which
racial ideology is rooted in the religious imagination. (Indeed, I suspect that racism
has many fathers. Only when we imagine religion making love to capitalism and to
other lovers will we get a firm handle, if we ever do, on the origins of racism.) Besides, capitalism is incredibly robust and flexible, and it is unlikely to disappear any-
time soon. A more credible claim, I submit, is that the racial genie is out of the bottle.
We must learn to live with her until a more powerful metaphor, a more compelling
system of classification, takes place. As Lévi-Strauss and others have shown, classification is a basic human activity. Among other things, race and religion are systems of
classification. However tenacious, each is historically contingent; religion and race
mutually construct and inflect each other.

Under modern/postmodern conditions religion has mutated. We should expect
no less of race: the concept is in the process of transformation as purely social
notions displace the biogenetic meanings that the idea acquired in the nineteenth
and twentieth centuries. But there is no good reason to think that the idea will simply
disappear, any more than we believe that the state will wither away (postcapitalist
societies will find the state too useful to let go). The category of race will continue to
mutate: Du Bois's dream of racial conservation and Fanon's vision of a postracial,

humanist future seem equally unlikely to me. The Roman cross did not simply disappear; rather, Christians adopted it as their symbol and subverted its shameful meaning. When testifying, males no longer grab their testicles to certify the truth of their claims but a residual association between the words "testes" and "testify" persists. The premodern, prescientific meanings of the word "testify" continue to signify but in a thoroughly harmless, if not humorous, manner. We can only hope that the same will be true of the category of race. Though we disavow any *nontrivial*, biogenetic meaning and disconnect the idea from orders of rank and invidious distinctions, race is likely to remain a powerful metaphor for human difference even if the Marxist-oriented social restructuring advocated by Fanon, Cox, and an older Du Bois is achieved. Like kudzu in America, race is an invasive species within the ecology of modern/postmodern thought. Race's complicated imbrication with religion only intensifies its social power. Despite the predictions of modernist, especially evolutionary, analysts, religion persists in a world they thought would make it obsolete. Why should race be any different? Though no species is invulnerable to extinction, racial thinking, which was taken up, transformed, and put to new uses by capitalist modernity/postmodernity, has secured a niche, *for the foreseeable future*, in our world.

NOTES

1. Philip S. Foner, ed., *W. E. B. Du Bois Speaks* (New York: Pathfinder, 1970).
2. W. E. B. Du Bois, *The Souls of Black Folks*, ed. Henry Louis Gates Jr. (New York: Norton, 1999), 123–29.
3. David Levering Lewis, *W. E. B. Du Bois: The Fight for Equality and the American Century, 1919–1963* (New York: Henry Holt, 2000), 456, 528.
4. Foner, *W. E. B. Du Bois Speaks*, 74–78.
5. W. E. B. Du Bois, *The Gift of Black Folk* (New York: Oxford University Press, 2007), xxvii–viii.
6. Lewis, *W. E. B. Du Bois*, 95.
7. Oliver C. Cox, *Race: A Study in Social Dynamics* (New York: Monthly Review, 2000), 6.
8. Oliver C. Cox, review of *Separation of Church and State in the United States*, by Alvin W. Johnson and Frank H. Yost, *American Sociological Review* 14, no. 3 (June 1949): 437.
9. Cox does not qualify this claim but perhaps we should.
10. Cox, *Race*, 120, 123–24, 140, 142, 145, 154.
11. Frantz Fanon, *Black Skin, White Masks* (New York: Grove, 1967), 230, 231.
12. Ibid., 12.
13. Ibid., 9.
14. Ibid., 38.
15. Ibid., 35.
16. Ibid., 190–91, 194.
17. Ibid., 116.

18. See Charles H. Long, "Primitive/Civilized: The Locus of a Problem," *History of Religions* 20, nos. 1–2 (August–November 1980): 43–61. See also Celia Brickman, "Primitivity, Race, and Religion in Psychoanalysis," *Journal of Religion* 82, no. 1 (January 2002): 53–74.

19. Du Bois, *The Souls of Black Folk*, 3.

20. Cedric J. Robinson, "Oliver Cromwell Cox and the Historiography of the West," *Cultural Critique* 17 (Winter 1990–1991): 5–19.

52

Black Cultural Criticism, the New Politics of Difference, and Religious Criticism

VICTOR ANDERSON

Cultural criticism is a confused idea, meaning different things to different people. It describes expressive acts such as music, art, literature that constitute creative forms of life. It also exposes ways that the "real interests" of people and their social aspirations are advanced by their cultural productions and operations of power and privilege. So, cultural criticism can be both descriptive, insofar as it describes expressive activities, and socially constructive, insofar as it commends activities worthy of pursuing in the interest of a person's and group's cultural fulfillment.

I take culture as a social system of interconnected and interdynamic practices that include economic, political, moral, religious, artistic, and linguistic formations that are socially symbiotic, mutually assuring. This description theoretically commits the critic to reject any account of cultural criticism that divides cultural meanings between the "real" and "ephemeral" or "epiphenomenal." Following Clifford Geertz: "Believing . . . man is an animal suspended in webs of significance he himself has spun, I take culture to be those webs, and the analysis of it to be therefore not an experimental science in search of law but an interpretative one in search of meaning. It is explication I am after, construing social expressions on their surface enigmatical."[1]

The social practices that constitute culture operate as a system of signs and symbols that communicate human interests and purposes, which are open to interpretation and analysis, given methodologies appropriate to distinct cultural spheres. Any dichotomous critique of culture that positions the subjective over the material basis of social life or the material over the subjective needs of individuals is inadequate. Rather, cultural criticism requires a phenomenological grasping of the intersubjective meanings of our cultural practices. It recognizes that these practices are reflexive, integrative systems of purposive activities. They are social projects and culture makers themselves. Therefore, the critique of culture is oriented toward analyzing the ways that culture both "forms" and "expresses" our socially imagined, socially articulated, and socially constructed needs, ends, and values that operate throughout the cultural spheres.

The formative and expressive aspects of culture are mobilized in discursive and nondiscursive practices within differentiated social spaces that range from simple to very complex formations that include clans and families, religions and societies, classes and castes, labor and markets, and states and governments. While culture displays complex organizations of social practices, their formations are directed toward satisfying the basic needs, ends, and values that culture-producers require for a fulfilled life. As a communicative system of interests, needs, ends, and values, culture integrates the satisfaction of persons' basic needs (life, safety, work, leisure, knowledge) with their subjective needs (friendship, peace of mind, integrity of conscience, and spiritual strivings). I call this reflexive integration of persons' basic and subjective needs "cultural fulfillment."[2]

Cultural criticism is concerned with the processes of successful cultural fulfillment and the conditions by which it is either satisfied or frustrated. Cultural criticism is an interpretative, that is, hermeneutical, discipline, but if it is only descriptive, it will not be very emancipatory of the creative powers of persons directed toward correcting and advancing their projects of cultural fulfillment. Therefore, cultural criticism is also a socially constructive discipline that renders ambiguous social relations meaningful and maps social problems and contexts for the purpose of establishing a common moral universe.[3] An adequate theory of cultural criticism is not merely content to describe the dark sides of our cultural formations but also affirms creative possibilities for cultural fulfillment by seeing within social regimes of power possibilities for realizing our political, social, and spiritual strivings. Theory: imagining, articulating, and socially constructing such forms of transcendence in the worlds of black experience are the work of black cultural criticism.

Black cultural criticism emerged from insurgent movements within black culture itself such as Black Power, the New Black Arts, and the Black Student Movements. A number of factors contributed to the possibility of these movements. They include: (1) increasing social and economic differentiation within black culture itself due to higher enrollments of black students in American colleges and universities beyond the traditional sites of two-year community colleges, trade-technical schools, and historically black colleges and universities (HBCUs); (2) greater access to higher education through the GI Bill and progressive liberal reforms in federal funding by guaranteed students loans and other grants; and (3) the media explosion of televised violence, genocide, race riots, and assassinations of political and religious leaders in the United State and South Africa.

From the shadow of black insurgent movements in the late 1960s and 1970s emerged black studies, Afro-American studies, African American studies or Africana studies, and black cultural studies. Black cultural studies is intrinsically interdisciplinary and has developed greatly since the late 1960s from a few black studies programs and departments at notable universities such as San Francisco State, Cornell, University of California (Berkeley), Harvard, Wesleyan University, and Yale.[4] While only a few universities actually have departments of black studies or African American studies (for example, Yale, Temple, Indiana-Purdue), Black cultural studies is largely located in departments of language, literature, communications, sociology, and American studies. Consequently, what is loosely called black cultural criticism is the deployment of critical theories immanent within these humanities and social science fields to create a counterdiscourse on the politics of *Difference*. Black cultural criticism is regulated by hegemonic regimes of discourse that define and subjugate black experience under the representational force of white supremacy and its formations in the social and cultural productions of race. Black cultural studies produced a new politics of race, symbolized by *Blackness*. Difference equaled Black: Black Power, black arts, black expressive culture, the black church, and a black theology of liberation.

However, a certain irony prevailed in the countercultural discourse of the black arts movement and black cultural studies as they critiqued the dominant literatures and representations of black experience overtheorized by assimilation and decadence or pathology and retheorized by asserting a new radical, militant, and Africanized black consciousness. The black feminist critic Barbara Christian argues that black cultural criticism and its politics of difference turned back on itself, replicating and reinscribing forms of black identity that totalized into a singular set of cultural images in the Afro, Dashikis, and head dress and Motown's productions of Aretha Franklin's "R.E.S.P.E.C.T.," James Brown's "Say it Loud, I'm Black and I'm Proud," and Marvin Gaye's "What's Going On."

Black expressive culture registered signs and symbols of black empowerment and a near "monolithism" of blackness itself. "It is true that the Black Arts Movement resulted in a necessary and important critique both of previous Afro-American literature and of the white-established literary world. But in attempting to take over power, it, as Ishmael Reed satirizes so well in *Mumbo Jumbo*, became much like its opponent, monolithic and downright repressive," says Christian.[5] She continues: "Inevitably, monolithism becomes a metasystem, in which there is a controlling ideal, especially in relation to pleasure. Language as one form of pleasure is immediately restricted, and becomes heavy, abstract, prescriptive, monotonous."[6] Black cultural criticism and its politics of race consciousness displayed not only a tendency toward monolithism but also a repressive monotheism, says Christian. It formed an iconography of an essentialized blackness that raised "Blackness" itself to the divine and registered all other expressive modes of difference in black culture as manifestations of Black Power.

By the late 1980s and early 1990s, black cultural criticism was in search for a new politics of difference, and the philosopher and cultural critic Cornel West theorized it. The new cultural politics of difference points toward the rejection of "the monolithic and homogeneous in the name of diversity, multiplicity and heterogeneity; a rejection of the abstract, general, and universal for the concrete, specific and particular; and it signifies commitment to writing that privileges the historic, contextual, and plural by emphasizing the contingent, provisional, variable, shifting, and changing."[7] It points toward the celebration of tradition, but it also celebrates multiculturalism. It recognizes that no adequate account of the self can be gained from a grand narrative about the nature and destiny of humanity in general. Rather, the new cultural politics of difference privileges the historical, cultural context as the locus for self-understanding and meaning. Politically, it sets itself in opposition to the politics of domination. It enables openings in our political culture that provide the vocabulary and vision for the self-determination, self-realization, and self-conscious reflection of the situated subject. Therefore, the new cultural politics of difference is not satisfied with the cultivation of a critical consciousness that only sets itself to the task of disclosing the dark side of modernity.

Rather, it proposes a political praxis that results not only in critical enlightenment but also in emancipatory practices that celebrate the potentialities of situated subjects. In the new cultural politics of difference, multiplicity of cultural expressions contributes to a transformation of our life together and explodes our preoccupation with the so-called Other, while celebrating difference: race, gender, sexuality, cultural, national, political, and religious.

However, a word of caution is in order for those of us who make the symbol of *difference* controlling in our theorizations of black cultural criticism. As the philosopher Kwame Anthony Appiah cautions, even difference itself can dangerously slip over into reifications, monolithisms, and monotheisms. He warns that difference, including the politics of race, "can harden into something fixed and determinate, a homogeneity of Difference. But I don't know what to do about such perils, aside from pointing them out, and trying to avoid them."[8] When race discourse marshals a politics of difference that reifies race itself into a monolith, a monotheism, the new cultural politics of difference enters black cultural criticism as a mode of "religious criticism."

In religious criticism, the critic's thoughts and actions, explanations and judgments of culture, are informed by, but not necessarily derived from, his or her appropriations and interpretations of their particular religious community's beliefs and ritual practices. This is not to determine the black religious critic as a black theologian or a professional theologian concerned with the explication and transmission of a religious community's beliefs and faith; in the case of the black theologian such a community is the black church. However, religious criticism may draw interpretative and critical judgments about formations of the social economy by making use of theological and religious vocabularies in the critique of a society's cultural formations.

There are some postmodern critics who would separate cultural criticism from any form of religious criticism altogether and exorcise the "religious" from cultural criticism by means of a thoroughgoing secular criticism. The philosopher Richard Rorty, for instance, suggests that cultural critics who want a hearing today would do well to show that the divine is worldly and that what parades as religious objectivity, including our social constructions of race, is permeated thoroughly by textuality. Social and cultural critics would do well to see their discourse as "descriptive" and "edifying," if not cognitively or morally regulative. Rorty proposes that "we try to get to the point where we no longer worship anything, where we treat nothing as a quasi divinity, where we treat everything—our language, our conscience, our community—as a product of time and chance. To reach this point would be in Freud's words, to 'treat chance as worthy of determining our fate.'"[9]

Rorty is joined by the literary critic Edward W. Said, who sees the religious as the privatization of spiritual ends, otherworldliness, epistemological certainty in morals, the dogmatism of group solidarity and communal belonging, and the cultural products and institutions whose purposes are to successfully perpetuate such religious intentions. Religious intentions are not necessarily and exceptionally expressed in religions and theology; they are also expressed as cultural motives widely open to other spheres—even in the dogmatism of so-called militant secularists from Marx and Walter Benjamin to Daniel Bell, radical feminists, psychoanalysts, neopragmatists, and other so-called promoters of edifying discourses who may stress "the private and hermetic over the public and social," says Said.[10] For him, wherever we see the tendency for "the secure protection of systems of belief (however peculiar those may be) and not for critical activity or consciousness," we are met with the religious.[11] Said's aims are to promote a form of secular criticism that eschews the temptations of religiosity, whether in politics, literary criticism, morals, or the politics of race. He envisions a form of cultural criticism that will rob "Culture" itself of totalizing possibilities.

However, I propose that religious criticism cannot be successful if it regards itself as radically oppositional to rather than expressive of linguistic openings, not only in the black cultural critic's own culture but also in his or her own religious community and tradition. Religious criticism shares much with secular criticism insofar as it is guided by an iconoclastic rigor that robs every mode of discourse, whether race, sexuality, gender, nation, or other formations of culture, of totality, monolithism, or monotheism. It fulfills its iconoclastic role by exposing the demonic present even in those forms of theology that parade as liberating and revolutionary projects, including black preaching, black theology, womanist theology, or black church studies. In black cultural criticism, religious criticism remains suspicious both of black cultural heroism and idolatries of black expressive culture that mark performances of music, art, poetry, and literature with a distinct black essence or genius. However, because religious criticism is a form of black cultural criticism, it also attempts to disclose emancipatory aspects of individuality or difference that every person has a legitimate right to expect of cultural fulfillment. In this regard, religious criticism can be both iconoclastic and utopian. But the iconoclastic role of religious criticism can be so overdetermined that its operations can breed nihilistic traits that would foreclose, in our democratic society, the prospects of African American cultural fulfillment in whose interest it is theorized.

What is the relation of religious criticism to theology? Religious criticism is not theology, except in a loosely defined sense in which every theologian who possesses faith in some object that he or she finds worthy of ultimate devotion and loyalty can be said to be generally religious. However, as a vocation, theology requires more to establish the legitimacy of its discourse than loose generalities about religious languages. If all that is meant by theology is the general understanding that anyone who has ever held beliefs about what is of ultimate concern, devotion, and value is a theologian, then nothing particularly exceptional about theology is advanced beyond more general philosophical claims about the world and human life. Theology requires more than a general, ordinary preoccupation with religious matters and languages, that is, unless the theologian understands herself to be a philosopher of religion or an academic religionist, whose specialty lies in explaining the phenomena of religion under methodologies peculiar to sociology, cultural anthropology, cultural linguistics, and history. Black theology, however, is associated with at least two normative and specific tasks that are not required of religious criticism. It reflexively integrates the differences of black Christians' beliefs under governing categories that isolate object(s) of ultimate concern, devotion, and loyalty, such as God's preferential option for the poor; and it gives meaning to black Christians' individual practices in light of black solidarity in common beliefs and liturgical practices. Black theology serves the black church, symbiotically assuring its identity as a community of liberation and social justice.

The form of religious criticism that I defend may be described as a religious pragmatism that does not require that religious criticism be congruent with the beliefs and practices of the black church, although some of the doctrinal and ritual actions that characterize that institution may inform the critical vocabulary of the black cultural critic. In religious criticism, the black cultural critic is organically related to the particular beliefs and moral vocabularies that may define his or her religious community and may bring his or her own faith to bear on the critique of culture. The insights, prejudices, fears, anxieties, hostilities, affirmations, and ground motives that black cultural critics acquire by participation in religious community are all viable sources for black cultural criticism. However, the legitimacy of religious criticism is not justified in terms of the critic's ecclesiastical affiliation or by whether the belief system with which the critic identifies is internally satisfying. Moreover, the legitimacy of black cultural criticism does not depend on the critic's devotion to forms of difference, racial, sexual, or gendered, that commend a "monolithism" and "monotheism" as marks of the cultural authenticity and solidarity that signified the politics of difference in the Black Power, the black student, and the black arts movements and their corresponding black church with its black theology of liberation. Rather, the legitimacy of black cultural criticism, its new politics of difference, and its iconoclastic and utopian forms of religious criticism depend on whether it genuinely contributes to or frustrates the social and cultural conditions, processes, and possibilities for cultural fulfillment. This is the test of adequacy in theorizing black cultural criticism.

NOTES

1. Clifford Geertz, *The Interpretation of Cultures* (New York: Basic Books, 1973), 5.
2. Victor Anderson, *Beyond Ontological Blackness* (New York: Continuum, 1995), 27.
3. Mostafa Rejai, "Ideology," in *Dictionary of the History of Ideas*, ed. Philip Wiener (New York: Scribner's, 1973), 2:558.
4. Nathan Huggins, *Afro-American Studies* (New York: Ford Foundation, 1985), 5–30.
5. Barbara Christian, "The Race for Theory," in *The Black Feminist Reader*, ed. Joy James and T. Denean Sharpley-Whiting (Malden, Mass.: Blackwell, 2000), 18.
6. Ibid., 19.
7. Cornel West, "The New Cultural Politics of Difference," in *The Cornel West Reader* (New York: Basic Civitas, 1999), 119.
8. Kwame Anthony Appiah, *The Ethics of Identity* (Princeton: Princeton University Press, 2005), xvi.
9. Richard Rorty, *Contingency, Irony and Solidarity* (New York: Cambridge University Press, 1989), 22.
10. Edward W. Said, *The World, the Text and the Critic* (Cambridge, Mass.: Harvard University Press, 1983), 292.
11. Ibid.

53

Theorizing Black Religious Studies

A Genealogy

VICTOR ANDERSON

Black religious studies, sometimes called African American religious studies, is the academic study of black religion. The two nomenclatures significantly mark two trajectories in the study of black religion. According to the critical theorist William D. Hart, African American religious studies form the standard narrative of black religion. "In this narrative, the black protestant Church is virtually coterminous with Black Religion. It defines Black Religion. Every other form of black religious expression is normatively peripheral and culturally suspect."[1] By contrast:

> Black Religion is a consequent not an antecedent—primordial—reality, an artifact not an essence. Produced by people identified as "Negro," "colored," "black," or "African American," Black Religion emerged from a violent intercultural encounter under the conditions of conquest, slavery, and white supremacy. Black people transformed the traditions they encountered by "bluing the note" and producing a sound that was recognizable but different. . . . Black Religion is an act of improvisation; it is also a provocation.[2]

Whether one theorizes black religion as a narrative of the black church and black Christianity or as the biography of encounter, conquest, and self-making, genealogy is the clue toward theorizing, that is, imagining, articulating, and socially constructing black religious studies. Michel Foucault makes genealogy the tool of criticism itself. "Genealogy is gray, meticulous, and patiently documentary. It operates on a field of entangled and confused parchments, on document that have been scratched over and recopied many times."[3] So it is with theorizing black religious studies.

From the radical identity politics of the Black Power, the New Black Aesthetic, and black student movements of the 1960s, the Negro Church (signified as such for a century), which marked black religious movements and religiosity in the United States, met its greatest challenges in this new climate of racial and political consciousness. A number of factors aggregated in black culture itself from insurgent militancies of Black Power, black nationalism, and black disenchantment with the perceived quietism of black Christianity made the "Negro Church" ripe for social, political, cultural, economic, and ideological criticism. The ideological critique of the Negro Church and the historical and sociological theories that funded its preeminence in the study of black religion determined the work of black religious studies.

For much of the first half of the twentieth century, black religion was almost singularly registered and understood by North American Christianity and its peculiar divide between white Christianity and the Negro Church. The Negro Church was celebrated as an epochal, messianic event, a moral light to the world, and Ethiopia's rising from its shadowy negation in world universal history. It was a shadowy existence determined by a world-historical consciousness that rendered Africa invisible in Europe's cultural formation of civilization. The Negro Church was theorized, that is, imagined, articulated, and socially constructed, as God's providential hand directing history toward its fulfillment in a kingdom of love and justice. Such a theorization of black religion evidences an understanding of the Negro Church as an epochal event of world-historical significance, articulated as cultural, Ethiopian, and progressive millenarianisms in the nadir of post-Reconstruction and Jim Crow legislations.[4] Cultural millenarianism imagines the great expectation of freedom being worked out in images of the United States as the "redeemer nation of the world" through forces of Western civilization, education, and democracy. Ethiopian millenarianism articulates a pan-African "future golden age connected to a great African past accompanied by God's judgment over white society and Western civilization." Progressive millenarianism socially constructs the role of the church, evangelicalism, missions, and social reform as keys to the earthly kingdom of God, displaying great optimism in power of Christianity to transform and correct the social ills of America.[5]

Black religious studies of the Negro Church were historical and sociological. This is not surprising since the religious and moral questions guiding its inquiry concerned the historical and cultural legitimacy of the Negro Church not as a Christian entity, but as a distinctively "Negro" or "black" manifestation. The historical and cultural significance of this question is adequately presented in two contrasting progressive and pan-African millenarian articulations:

> Happy for the great country, happy for the negro and the nation when the great principles upon which our government is founded, when the genius of liberty as understood by the fathers, shall permeate this whole land, mold the opinions of statements, fix the decrees of judges, settle the decisions of Supreme Courts and executed by every law officer of this broad land; then there will need be no more discussion as to what of the negro problem. . . . There will be one homogeneous nation governed by intellectual, moral worth and controlled by Christian influences. Then there will be no East, No West, no North, no South, no Black, no White, no Saxon, no Negro, but a great, happy and peaceful nation.[6]

While such a progressive millenarianism signifies an assimilationist black religion, pan-African millenarianism offers a contrasting theorization. Imagining and articulating Hamite superiority in the building of Egypt and the pyramids, one J. Augustus Cole detested educated blacks who referred to themselves as American or Afro-American and not "African" or "Negro" (black). Articulating pan-African commitments, Cole contends:

> There is no reason why the distribution of the Negro in America and the West Indian Islands should impede the progress of African advancement, if all could labor for one end and keep the integrity of the race. . . . It is in the Christianity of the Negro that this destiny will be realized. But in embracing Christianity the Negro has made a very sad mistake, which will always hinder his progress. When we accept Christianity from the white man, we do not regard it so much as the religion of Christ, as the "white man's religion." Consequently we have imitated the white man instead of imitating Christ, and we have retained both the white man's vices as well as his virtues.[7]

Mapping the spiritual, moral, and distinct contribution of black religion and religiosity to world universal historical significance was the primary method of black religious studies in the first half of the twentieth century, and *tracking* the social role of the Negro Church in racial uplift and democratic progressive social reform was its socially constructive aim. Both emphases define the works of eminent twentieth-century black religious historians and sociologists such as W. E. B. Du Bois, Carter G. Woodson, and E. Franklin Frazier and C. Eric Lincoln.[8] Their emphases continue on in the late-twentieth-century works in black religious studies: Gayraud Wilmore, Lincoln and Lawrence H. Mamiya, and Stacey Floyd Thomas.[9]

With ethnographers' tools for observing practices, rituals, and ecstatic expressions of spirited life prior to Emancipation, black religious scholars tracked the distinctive contribution of the African presence in black religious experience to the spiritual and moral significance of black religion. What spiritual, moral, and cultural influence have the African presence and religiosity prior to Emancipation on the institutional Black Church? What religious meanings are expressed in spirituals, shouting, and dancing, all bearers of the African presence?

> These were the characteristics of Negro religious life as developed up to the time of Emancipation. Since under the peculiar circumstances of the black man's environment they were the one expression of his higher life, they are the deep interest to the student of his life, both socially and psychologically. Numerous are the attractive lines of inquiry that have grouped themselves. What did slavery mean to the American savage? What was his attitude toward the World and Life? What seemed to him good and evil,—God and Devil? Whither went his longings and strivings and wherefore were his heart-burnings and disappointment? Answer to such questions can come only from the study of Negro religion as a development, through its gradual changes from the heathenism of the Gold Coast to the institutional Negro Church.[10]

Ethnography disclosed the theological and moral meanings of black religion by analyzing black folk religion. Of great importance for theorists of black religion were the spirituals, black preaching, and surviving slave tales. Black religion not only imagined, articulated, and socially constructed the Black Church but overly determined the whole of black expressive culture as well. This double signification of black religion, in the production of black expressive culture as organic, expressive, and performed displays of black folk religiosity constituting the soul of the institutional Black Church, would come to situate the most significant and lasting debate on the theorization of black religious studies for the second half of the twentieth century. Even today the influence of this debate is everywhere acknowledged in contemporary theories of black religion and its distinct "Africanisms" in the Black Church. The debate eventually erupted in the social sciences themselves, sociology and anthropology, between Melville Herskovits and E. Franklin Frazier. The debate centralized slave culture and slave religion in black religious studies in the second half of the twentieth century.

Radical cultural deprivation and assimilation theorists, such as those of Robert E. Park and Frazier, argued that transplanted Africans to the United States were geopolitically landless. Therefore, they were unable to provide a conducive environment for preserving and cultivating an ongoing tradition of "Africanisms" or "African retentions" in their religious experience, as was evident in the Caribbean Basin, including Brazil, where distinct African forms provided continuity with an continental West and South African past. This was not a new idea for historians and sociologist of the late nineteenth and early twentieth centuries. However, it found its most explicit voices in Park, of the Chicago school of sociology, and Frazier, his student and the one-time president of the American Sociological Association:

> My own impression is that the amount of African tradition, which the Negro brought to the United States was very small. In fact, there is every reason to believe, it seems to me, that the Negro, when he landed in the United States, left behind him almost everything but his dark completion and his tropical temperament. It is very difficult to find in the South today anything that can be traced directly back to Africa.[11]

In 1939, Frazier made more explicit the ramification of Park's cultural deprivation and radical assimilation thesis in his account of the Negro family, which was reiterated in the infamous Moynihan Report (1965). Frazier's thesis would ideologically and politically reposition black religious studies in opposition to the thesis. In its starkest articulation, Frazier observes:

> Probably never before in the history has a people been so stripped of its social heritage as the Negroes who were brought to America. . . . Through force of circumstances, they had to acquire a new language, adopt new habits of labor, and take over, however imperfectly, the folkways of the American environment. Their children, who knew only the American environment, soon forgot the few memories that had been passed on to them and developed motivations and modes of behavior in harmony with the New World. Their children's children have often recalled with skepticism the fragments of stories concerning Africa, which have been preserved in their families. But, of the habits and customs as well as the hopes and fears that characterized the life of their forbearers in Africa, nothing remains.[12]

In the *Myths of the Negro Past* (1941), Melville Herskovits challenged Park's and Frazier's cultural deprivation and radical assimilation thesis by correcting five myths supporting it and articulating a comparative method of ethnography that determines the African presence in the religious experience and imagination of black Americans.[13] By comparing black religion in the United States with the distinctive religious cultures of the Caribbean Basin and West Africa, persistent African traits of practices and thought in slave religion and culture could be measured in contemporary black Christianity. By targeting American "Negro religion" as the most decisive site for mapping "Africanisms" in black cultural formation, Herskovits challenged the cultural deprivation thesis of black cultural inferiority and acculturation. He argued that the cultural deprivation thesis was "a misrepresentation of the richness of the African cultural past and a denial of the tenacity of that culture in the life ways of Afro-American people."[14] Under Herskovits's influence, black religious studies contends that the African presence in black religion is located where one looks for it and knowing how to decode its often-coded significations in black folk culture and slave religion is the clue toward understanding the tenacity of the African presence in black religion.

In distinction from early-twentieth-century black religionists, black folk culture (tales, songs, spirituals, conjuring, root medicine, wit and humor, signifying, playing the dozens, dancing, ring dancing, shouting, call and response, clothing, material culture, even dialect and language) all became measurements of the African presence in black religion in the Caribbean Basin, most distinctively, and in the United States, to a lesser extent. And it is the work of black religious studies to track, identify, and interpret these instances of Africanisms in black religion, thereby determining it as a distinct field of study from the mainstream history of Protestant Christianity in America, including Black Church history and its evangelical formations. The discourse on African retentions transformed our understanding of the Negro Church of the nineteenth century and first half of the twentieth. The Negro Church metamorphosed, under the Black Power, black student, and black studies movements into the Black Church in America with its distinctive black theology. Black Church studies became the point of departure for theorizing black religious studies.

In the last half of the twentieth century, black religious studies produced two distinct imaginations, articulations, and social constructions of black religion. The one theorizes "African American religious studies" as a "theological discourse" (Wilmore, Lincoln and Mamiya, Floyd-Thomas et al.). The other theorizes "black religious studies" as a "critical discourse" (Cornel West, Eddie S. Glaude). In *African American Religious Studies: An Interdisciplinary Anthology*, the discourse is framed by rubrics of theological studies: "Origins, Context, and Conceptualization"; "Biblical Studies"; "Theological and Ethical Studies"; "Historical Studies"; and "Missions and Ministry."[15] The majority of contributors are theological educators. The theological curriculum structures African American religious studies within the geopolitical constructions of the North American Black Church experience, nearly equivocating African American religious studies with Black Church studies.

The best religious scholarship in the Black academy is, perforce, "believing scholarship," accepting all the risks that such a position entails. It could not be other wise. The centuries-old struggle for Black humanity in a racist environment has not encouraged the development of a dispassionate, armchair science of religion for preparing the leadership of the Black Church in North America.[16]

In *African American Religious Thought: An Anthology* (2003), Glaude and West imagine, articulate, and socially construct black religious studies within historical and critical interdisciplinary projects in eight parts: "Prehistory of African American Religious Studies"; "Theorizing African American Religion"; "Slavery and a Black Religion Imagination"; "Black Destiny and the End of the Nineteenth Century"; "The Interwar Period: Migration, Urbanization, and Black Religious Diversity"; "Black Religion and the 1960s"; "Black Theology and Its Critics"; and "African American Religion and Cultural Criticism."

> With this historical periodization and these three extant categories in mind (politics, cultural criticism, and the study of a variety of black institutions that intersect with black religion), this volume aims to broaden our conception of the field and to take seriously the importance of interdisciplinary approaches to African American religious practices. History, theology, and what can be called cultural criticism remain constitutive subareas of the field. One of our major tasks is to urge that we think about these areas within a broader framework that is not reducible to theological claims.[17]

The state of black religious studies today remains entrenched within the tensions mapped out by Hart, between "Black Church studies" and "black cultural studies," in theorizing of black religion. The tensions ought best to be understood within the genealogy of the twentieth century's imaginations, articulations, and social constructions of the spiritual and moral meanings of the Black Church in America, on the one hand, and, on the other, the generativity of the African presence and its cultural influences not only in black religion but also in black expressive culture. What is suggested by this genealogy is that black religious studies is never reducible to purely academic interests alone. Rather, at its best, black religious studies theorizes: imagines (sees connections), articulates (makes explicit), and socially constructs (contributes to) formations of the cultural fulfillment of Black Americans and their global connections with the wretched of the earth. This genealogical insight provides the clue toward theorizing black religion and black religious studies.

NOTES

1. William David Hart, *Black Religion: Malcolm X, Julius Lester, and Jan Willis* (New York: Palgrave, 2008), 8.
2. Ibid., 193.
3. Michel Foucault, "Nietzsche, Genealogy, History," in *Language, Counter-Memory, Practice*, ed. Donald F. Bouchard (Ithaca: Cornell University Press, 1977), 139.

4. Timothy E. Fulop, "The Future Golden Day of the Race: Millennialism and the Black American in the Nadir, 1877–1901," in *African American Religion: Interpretive Essays in History and Culture*, ed. Timothy E. Fulop and Albert J. Raboteau (New York: Routledge, 1997), 231.

5. Ibid.

6. AME Bishop R. H. Cain, quoted in Fulop, "The Future Golden Day of the Race," 80–81.

7. J. Augustus Cole, quoted in Fulop, "The Future Golden Day of the Race," 238.

8. W. E. B. Du Bois, *The Souls of Black Folk* (New York: Penguin, 1969); Carter G. Woodson, *The History of the Negro Church* (Washington, D.C.: Associated Publishers, 1921); E. Franklin Frazier and C. Eric Lincoln, *The Negro Church/The Black Church Since Frazier* (New York: Schocken, 1974).

9. Gayraud Wilmore, *African American Religious Studies: An Interdisciplinary Anthology* (Durham: Duke University Press, 1989); C. Eric Lincoln and Lawrence H. Mamiya, *The Black Church in the African American Experience* (Durham: Duke University Press, 1990); Stacey Floyd-Thomas et al., *Black Church Studies: An Introduction* (Nashville: Abingdon, 2008).

10. Du Bois, *The Souls of Black Folk*, 212.

11. Robert E. Park, quoted in Johnnetta B. Cole, "Africanisms in the Americas: A Brief History of the Concept," *Anthropology and Humanism Quarterly* 10, no. 4 (1985): 121.

12. E. Franklin Frazier, quoted in Cole, "Africanisms in the Americas," 121.

13. Melville Herskovits, *The Myth of the Negro Past* (New York: Harper and Brothers, 1941).

14. Cole, "Africanisms in the Americas," 121.

15. Wilmore, *African American Religious Studies*.

16. Ibid., xii.

17. Cornel West and Eddie S. Glaude Jr., *African American Religious Thought: An Anthology* (Louisville: Westminster John Knox, 2003), xviii.

PART XII

Religion/Nation/Globalization

54

Religion and Violence

WILLIAM T. CAVANAUGH

When I recently gave a talk titled "Does Religion Cause Violence?" at a college, someone scrawled on a poster for the lecture the single word "Duh!" The idea that religion has a peculiar tendency to cause or aggravate violence has taken on the status of a truism in Western society. The idea is constantly repeated in the academy, court decisions, media coverage, and everyday parlance. The political corollary of this idea is the notion that religion must be tamed, removed to the private from the public sphere for the sake of peace. In the United States, for example, the dangers of religion in public have been cited repeatedly by the Supreme Court in banning public school prayer and public aid to parochial schools. In US foreign policy, the assumption is often made that Muslim social orders are especially prone to violence because they have not yet learned to domesticate religion in public life.

The idea that religion is essentially prone to violence depends on the idea that there is an essence of religion that is unchanging over time and space. Religion is seen as a transhistorical and transcultural feature of human life, whose outward forms exhibit a bewildering variety, but whose inward essence permits the identification of religion as such wherever and whenever it is found. A preference for secular social orders appears in this view as natural, because it corresponds to a universal and timeless truth about the inherent dangers of religion.

What happens to the idea that religion has an inherent tendency to promote violence, however, if we find that there is no such transhistorical and transcultural feature of human life, and religion is in fact a constructed reality of a peculiarly modern and Western vintage? Constructivist views of religion, such as those found throughout this volume, have opened us up to seeing that the concept of religion as such has a history that is tied up with the modern West, and therefore also carries with it a certain politics. In this chapter I will explore the history and politics of the idea that there is a transhistorical and transcultural feature of human life called "religion" that is inherently prone to violence. In the first section, I will argue that the religious/secular distinction arose as an ideological accompaniment of the triumph of the modern state over the medieval ecclesiastical order. In the second section, I will discuss the origins of the idea of religious violence in the tale of the "Wars of Religion," a tale that does not stand up to historical scrutiny. In the third section, I will argue that the modern nation-state, rather than marginalizing the sacred, took on its trappings, especially in establishing a monopoly on violence. In the fourth and final section, I will contend that a constructivist view of religion can help to analyze and resist the violence done by the religious/secular distinction. This chapter is only a brief précis of ideas I develop at much greater length in my book *The Myth of Religious Violence*.[1]

WHY WAS RELIGION CREATED?

The primary use of the term *religio* in the medieval period was to distinguish religious from secular clergy, that is, clergy that belonged to orders from diocesan clergy. This is the meaning religion had when it entered the English language. In 1400, the religions of England were the various orders—Benedictines, Franciscans, and so on.[2] A secondary use of *religio* in the medieval period was to refer—as in Aquinas—to one of the nine subvirtues attached to the cardinal virtue of justice.[3] In this sense, *religio* approximated "piety," but only as a bodily habit embedded in a complex set of practices within a Christian social order. *Religio* was not a universal genus of which Christianity was a species, it was not a system of beliefs, it was not merely interior to the human person, and it was not something separable from politics, economics, and other pursuits deemed "secular" in modernity.

The concept of religion as a universalized and interiorized human impulse, expressing itself in beliefs held on a nonrational basis, and essentially different from secular pursuits like politics, is a creation of Europe between the fifteenth and seventeenth centuries, which, not coincidentally, is also the period of the rise of the modern state. Nicholas of Cusa, Marsilio Ficino, Herbert of Cherbury, John Locke, and many others contributed to the creation of a religious/secular distinction into which all human activities should be divided. The creation of religion was a product of the early modern struggle between civil and ecclesiastical authorities for power in Europe. Whereas medieval Christendom had subordinated civil to ecclesiastical authorities, at least in theory, in the early modern period civil authorities were largely successful in curbing ecclesiastical power and establishing the modern reality of state sovereignty. Key to this process was the confinement of the church's proper area of concern to an interiorized human impulse called "religion" that is essentially distinct from politics, the proper concern of the state.

For Locke, for example, religion was a matter of "opinion" not adjudicable by public reason. Locke wanted a sharp separation between the "outward force" of the state and the inward persuasion of religion, which is the province of the church. "The end of a religious society . . . is the public worship of God and, by means thereof, the acquisition of eternal life. All discipline ought therefore to tend to that end, and all ecclesiastical laws to be thereunto confined. Nothing ought nor can be transacted in this society relating to the possession of civil and worldly goods."[4] Locke does not appear to think that his attempt to "distinguish exactly the business of civil government from that of religion"[5] is involved in the creation of something new. He sees himself as trying to separate two essentially distinct types of human endeavor that have gotten mixed up together, mainly by the ambitions of churchmen. The church, whose only business is religion, has overstepped its boundaries: "The church itself is a thing absolutely separate and distinct from the commonwealth. The boundaries on both sides are fixed and immovable. He jumbles heaven and earth together, the things most remote and opposite, who mixes these two societies, which are in their original, end, business, and in everything perfectly distinct and infinitely different from each other."[6]

In fact, Locke was witnessing a very new configuration of power, the birth of the modern state, which was proving that the boundaries were certainly not fixed and immovable. Locke's claim that they are essentially fixed gives legitimacy to the new order by making it appear natural. The idea of religion as transhistorical and transcultural and the idea that the religious/secular boundary is fixed and immutable are themselves part of the new configuration of power that comes about with the birth of the modern state. In this view, religion appears not as what the church is left with once it has been stripped of earthly power, but as the timeless endeavor to which the church's pursuits should always have been confined. We might want to say that the modern separation of church and state is a good thing. But we should not ignore the way that the term "religion" carries not merely descriptive but normative political power.

THE BLACK LEGEND OF THE "WARS OF RELIGION"

The idea that religion has a tendency to promote violence followed closely upon the creation of the idea of religion as an essentially private and nonrational human impulse. The labeling of the European wars of the sixteenth and seventeenth centuries as "Wars of Religion" is found already in Spinoza, Hobbes, Locke, Voltaire, Rousseau, and other early modern theorists of the modern state. For all of them, the chief reason for the wars was pointless squabbling between Catholics and Protestants over religious doctrine. As Locke put it, the unwillingness to tolerate the religious opinions of others "has produced all the bustles and wars that have been in the Christian world upon account of religion."[7] These disputes would be harmless but for the way that the churches have sought to use coercive political power to enforce their doctrinal opinions. The solutions offered by political theorists vary, but they tend to center on the state's appropriation of powers hitherto claimed by the church. Hobbes would do away with doctrinal dispute by absorbing the churches into the state and making the state the undisputed arbiter of doctrinal disputes. Similarly, Spinoza's state would absorb the church, while putting greater emphasis on the individual's complete liberty to believe whatever he or she would about mere doctrine. Voltaire and Rousseau would favor a compulsory civil religion of public cult and morals, while leaving the individual similarly free in matters of belief. Locke would establish clear boundaries between the proper business of the church, which is religious doctrine and rites, and the proper business of the state, which claims a monopoly on violence and jurisdiction over the civil interests of society. What they all have in common is a significant reduction of the public power of the church, and a complementary augmentation of the power of the state, justified by the need to defuse the threat of further religious wars.

Although they continue to use the phrase "Wars of Religion," historians often note that the tale of religious zealotry run amok told by political theorists hardly does justice to the actual wars of the sixteenth and seventeenth centuries. The most oft-reviled "War of Religion," the Thirty Years' War (1618–48), for example, was largely a struggle between Catholic France and the Catholic Habsburgs of Germany and Spain. The Catholic Cardinal Richilieu of France supported Lutheran Sweden, which in turn attacked Lutheran Denmark. Historians tend to deal with such facts by recognizing the presence of political and economic factors alongside religion in these wars. What a constructivist view of religion helps us to see, however, is that it is pointless to try to divide up responsibility for the violence of sixteenth- and seventeenth-century Europe among different discrete factors called "politics," "economics," "religion," and so on, because such distinctions are anachronistic. The Eucharist, for example, was not a purely "religious" phenomenon, but was a powerful locus of social and political cohesion. When King Francis I of France reacted violently to anonymous Calvinist placards attacking the Catholic Eucharist in 1534, it was not a purely "religious" controversy; Francis saw the placards as a threat to social order and to his authority. In the sixteenth century, there simply was no neat distinction between religion and politics. According to John Bossy, religion is not fully formed as a separate concept until around 1700.[8] Any attempt to assign the cause of the wars in question to "religion"—as opposed to politics or other "secular" causes—will get bogged down in hopeless anachronism. The same, of course, is true of attempts to pin the blame on political and economic causes as opposed to religion. We might best say something like what Axel Oxenstierna—Gustavus Adolphus's chancellor and architect of the Swedish intervention in the Thirty Years' War—told the Swedish council of state in 1636: the war was "not so much a matter of religion, but rather of saving the *status publicus*, wherein religion is also comprehended."[9] There is simply no way to isolate "religion" as the source of the conflict from the whole fabric of the *status publicus*. It is clear that the standard narrative of the "Wars of Religion" will not stand up to scrutiny of the term "religion."

The point is not that the concept of "religion" was simply absent in the sixteenth and seventeenth centuries, but that the distinction between religion and social or political factors was in the process of development as new forms of power—what would become known as the "state"—were developing. The modern idea of religion as a realm of human activity inherently separate from politics and other "secular" matters depended upon a new configuration of Christian societies in which many legislative and jurisdictional powers and claims to power—as well as claims to the devotion and allegiance of the people—were passing from the church to the new sovereign state. The secular/religious binary helped facilitate this shift. The noun "secularization" as it first appeared in France in the late sixteenth century meant "the transfer of goods from the possession of the Church into that of the world."[10] The new conception of religion helped facilitate the shift to state dominance over the church by distinguishing inward religion from the bodily disciplines of the state. The new subject is thus able to do due service to both church and state, without conflict. Certain interests promoted this process, while others resisted it.

If this is true, then the idea put forth by political theorists that the rise of the modern state rescued Europe from the scourge of religious wars becomes highly dubious. The modern state was not simply a response to the advent of religious difference in the Reformation and the subsequent violence that religious difference unleashed. If the Reformation itself was at least in part an effect of the ongoing struggle for power and authority between church and civil rulers—which had been going on for quite some time before Luther nailed his ninety-five theses on the door at Wittenberg—then the transfer of power from the church to the state was not so much a solution to the wars in question, but a *cause* of those wars. The so-called Wars of Religion were fought by state-building elites for the purpose of consolidating their power over the church and other rivals. The point here is *not* that these wars were really about politics and not really about religion. The point is that the very distinction of politics and religion made possible by the rise of the modern state against the decaying medieval order—the transfer of power from the church to the state—was itself at the root of these wars.

There is a great deal of evidence to suggest that the aggregation of power by the emergent state was a cause, not the solution, to these wars. The process of state-building, begun well before the Reformation, was inherently conflictual. Beginning in the late medieval period, the process involved the internal integration of previously scattered powers under the aegis of the ruler, and the external demarcation of territory over against other states. As Heinz Schilling comments, the invention of sovereignty demanded both the "integration and concentration of all political, social, economic and other power under the supremacy of the ruler," and "at the same time the process of state-building meant territorial integration and a dissociation from the 'outside' world, which as a rule was implemented in an offensive, not infrequently even aggressive manner. All the states of the early modern age aimed to augment their state territory through expansion and the annexation of as much territory as possible." Schilling continues:

> The internal process of state-building was no different to the external one and the accompanying birth of the early modern Europe of the great powers was accompanied by massive disruptions. Internally the rulers and their state elites used violent means against the estates, cities, clergy and local associations which laid claim to an independent, non-derived right of political participation which the early modern state could no longer grant under the principle of sovereignty. Externally in addition to the above-mentioned tendencies of territorial adjustment between the states, conflicts were mainly over "rank," since at this stage there was no generally acknowledged system of states. Therefore, at the end of the middle ages, Europe entered a long phase of intense violent upheaval both within and between states.[11]

The link between state-building and war has been well documented by historians of the early modern state. Charles Tilly has shown how building a state depended on the ability of state-making elites to make war, and the ability to make war in turn depended on the ability to extract resources from the population, which in turn depended on an effective state bureaucracy to secure those resources from a recalcitrant population. As Tilly puts it, "War made the state, and the state made war."[12] Much of the violence of the so-called Wars of Religion is explained in terms of the resistance of local elites to the state-building efforts of monarchs and emperors. As Michael Howard writes,

> The attempts by the dominant dynasties of Europe to exercise disputed rights of inheritance throughout the fourteenth and fifteenth centuries became consolidated, in the sixteenth century, into a bid by the Habsburgs to sustain a hegemony which they had inherited over most of western Europe against all their foreign rivals and dissident subjects, usually under the leadership of France. The result was almost continuous warfare in western Europe from the early sixteenth until the mid-seventeenth centuries.[13]

THE RELIGION OF THE STATE

Constructivist readings of religion help us to see not only that religion has a history, but also that religion has a politics. Constructivism argues that there is no transhistorical and transcultural religion out there; what counts as religion in any given context depends upon how power is configured in that context. The idea that there is a transhistorical and transcultural feature of human life called "religion" that has a tendency to promote violence is not only historically false; it is also politically useful. The creation of religion and the myth of religious war helped facilitate the transfer of power and loyalty to the state in early modern Europe, and helped establish the idea that the rise of the state was the solution to the wars, rather than a significant cause of them.

The common myth of religious violence claims that the modern state tamed religion by removing it from the public sphere. In fact, however, the state was not secularized but sacralized in the sixteenth and seventeenth centuries. As John Neville Figgis wrote, "the religion of the State has replaced the religion of the Church."[14] The end of the so-called Wars of Religion found the rapidly aggrandizing states of Europe appropriating the trappings of sanctity from the church, a process that had already begun in France well before the Reformation. What David Potter calls a "royal religion" developed in France in which the king was seen as both priest and the image of God on earth.[15] In England, Elizabeth I suppressed celebrations of Corpus Christi and appropriated significant symbolic aspects of the feast with herself substituting for the Eucharistic Host.[16] At the same time, martyrdom *pro patria* eclipsed martyrdom *pro fide*.[17] In short, the transfer of power from the church to the state that occasioned the creation of religion also accompanied what Bossy calls the "migration of the holy" from the church to the state.[18]

Even if we concede that the early modern state took on the trappings of the sacred, is it not now the case, with the advent of liberal, secular, social orders in the last two centuries, that the Western world has finally vanquished religion? To the contrary, there is a large body of scholarship that considers modern nationalism as a religion, and the debate over "civil religion" in the United States captures the same sense that liberal nation-states reproduce some of the same dynamics as confessional states. For example, Carlton Hayes, author of the book *Nationalism: A Religion*,[19] argues that the decline in public Christianity with the advent of the modern state left a vacuum for the religious sense that was filled by the sacralization of the nation, the "enthronement of the national state—*la Patrie*—as the central object of worship."[20] Robert Bellah famously identified "an elaborate and well-institutionalized civil religion in America" that "has its own seriousness and integrity and requires the same care in understanding that any other religion does."[21] Bellah argued that the civic rituals of American life revolve around a unitarian God that underwrites America's sense of purpose in the world. This God, however, is not the Christian God. References to Christ and the church are kept to a private, voluntary sphere of worship.[22] The implication of Bellah's argument is that the separation of church and state in America is *not* the separation of religion and state. Similarly, Carolyn Marvin and David Ingle identify the flag as the totem object of American civil religion and argue that "nationalism is the most powerful religion in the United States, and perhaps in many other countries."[23]

According to Marvin and Ingle, the transfer of the sacred from Christianity to the nation-state in Western society is seen most clearly in the fact that authorized killing has passed from Christendom to the nation-state. Christian denominations still thrive in America, but as optional, inward-looking affairs. They are not publicly true, "For what is really true in any community is what its members can agree is worth killing for, or what they can be compelled to sacrifice their lives for."[24] The nation and the flag are the only things publicly recognized as worth killing and dying for. For most American Christians today, for example, it would be inconceivable to kill for Christianity, but the occasional necessity of organized slaughter on behalf of the nation-state is generally taken for granted.

If this is true, then there is simply no good reason to accept the notion that there is something called "religion" which is inherently prone to violence in ways that "secular" ideologies and institutions are not. The supposedly secular nation-state can and does inspire violence on a massive scale. What the World War I poet Wilfred Owen called "the old Lie" came back with a vengeance in the twentieth century: "Dulce et Decorum est / Pro patria mori." Although it may be true that Christians, for example, profess that God is absolute in a way that the nation-state is not, what matters is behavior—especially behavior during wartime—and not simply belief. In other traditions and other contexts, what people will kill and die for may be different. The point is simply that there is no a priori reason to assume that ideologies and institutions that are commonly identified as religious inspire more violence than those identified as secular. People use violence for all sorts of reasons. An adequate approach to the question of violence would be resolutely empirical: Under what circumstances do ideologies and institutions of all kinds encourage violence? We should examine *jihad* and the sacrificial Christian theologies, but we should also examine ideologies of freedom and the "invisible hand" of the market and the role of the United States as worldwide liberator.

A CONSTRUCTIVIST APPROACH

Is the term "religion" helpful at all in such an investigation? Carlton Hayes and Marvin and Ingle continue to use the term in a functional way to argue that nationalism really is a religion because it functions to reinforce a certain kind of social order. For functionalists, what matters is not *what* people believe but *how* they believe. It does not matter that the flag does not refer to a god; if it is treated as a sacred object and is a central symbolic point for the configuration of power in a society, then it is a religious object.

Functionalist approaches to religion and violence are helpful because they don't rely on arbitrary religious/secular distinctions. Functionalist approaches expand our critical lenses beyond the usual lists of "world religions"—Christianity, Islam, Sikhism, and so on—to include other ideologies and institutions like "secular" nationalism that also focus killing energies in similar ways. However, insofar as functionalism continues to regard religion as a transhistorical and transcultural phenomenon—albeit a much more inclusive one than previously thought—functionalism is less helpful. A constructivist approach would not bother with trying to decide, once and for all, what is and is not a religion. What matters for the constructivist in any given context is why some things are called religion and some things are not. What configurations of power are authorized by the different ways that "religious" and "secular" are used?

Supreme Court Justice Rehnquist acknowledged, in supporting a proposed amendment against "desecration" of the flag, that the flag is regarded by Americans "with an almost mystical reverence."[25] Here the word "almost" is crucial, for American civil religion must deny that it is religion. Marvin and Ingle ask, and attempt to answer, the key question:

> If nationalism is religious, why do we deny it? Because what is obligatory for group members must be separated, as holy things are, from what is contestable. To concede that nationalism is a religion is to expose it to challenge, to make it just the same as sectarian religion. By explicitly denying that our national symbols and duties are sacred, we shield them from competition with sectarian symbols. In so doing, we embrace the ancient command not to speak the sacred, ineffable name of god. The god is inexpressible, unsayable, unknowable, beyond language. But that god may not be refused when it calls for sacrifice.[26]

Marvin and Ingle treat nationalism as a real religion, according to their definition.[27] But whether or not nationalism is *really* a religion is beside the point. What is crucial is the question they ask: Why deny it is a religion? Why affirm it? What is authorized by either the denial or the affirmation? Why is it acceptable in some contexts for Abraham Lincoln to say that reverence for the Constitution is "the political religion of the nation"?[28] Why, in other contexts, is the American constitutional order held as the model of "secular" government? With regard to the question of violence, why is violence on behalf of the Muslim *umma* religious, but violence on behalf of the American nation-state is secular? What is gained or lost by the insistence that violence on behalf of America is of a fundamentally different nature from violence on behalf of Islam?

To answer these types of questions is simply to trace the uses to which the myth of religious violence has been put. For example, since 1940 the idea that public religion is dangerous and divisive has been invoked by the US Supreme Court in case after case, in decisions banning school prayer, forbidding voluntary religious instruction on public school property, forbidding state aid to parochial school teachers, and so on. One such case is the 1963 *Abington* decision forbidding public school prayer. In dissent, Justice Potter Stewart famously warned that the decision would be seen "not as the realization of state neutrality, but rather as the establishment of a religion of secularism."[29] Stewart noted the long history of government religious practice in the United States, including the fact that the Supreme Court opened its sessions with "God save this Honorable Court." In their concurring opinion in *Abington*, however, Justices Goldberg and Harlan addressed this objection by drawing a sharp line between patriotic invocations of God and "religious" ones.

There is of course nothing in the decision reached here that is inconsistent with the fact that school children and others are officially encouraged to express love for our country by reciting historical documents such as the Declaration of Independence that contain references to the Deity or by singing officially espoused anthems that include the composer's professions of faith in a Supreme Being, or with the fact that there are many manifestations in our public life of belief in God. Such patriotic or ceremonial occasions bear no true resemblance to the unquestioned religious exercise that the state has sponsored in this instance.[30]

Goldberg and Harlan offer no reason why patriotic invocations of God bear no true resemblance to religious invocations. But it is clear that, for them, what separates religion from what is not religion is *not* the invocation of God. God may be invoked in public ceremonies without such ceremonies thereby becoming religious exercises, provided such ceremonies express "love for our country." Separating religion from nonreligion in this case depends not on the presence or absence of expressions of faith in God, but on the presence or absence of expressions of faith in the United States of America. Again, we see how the religious/secular distinction and the myth of religious violence are part of the legitimating conceptual apparatus of the modern Western nation-state.

The idea that religion must be separated from public power for the sake of peace also influences much American foreign policy. Muslim societies are seen as essentially problematic because they lack a proper separation between religion and the secular. Indeed, to call Islam a "religion" is immediately to mark it as an abnormal religion, because it does not make a neat distinction between religion and politics. Conflicts between Western and Islamic social orders can be explained by the inherently pathological nature of the latter. The myth of religious violence can then justify Western military action in the Islamic world. We will have peace once we have bombed the Muslims into being reasonable.

A constructivist approach to the question of religion and violence will always take a hard look at what counts as religion and what does not in any given context, and see what kinds of power—good and bad—different uses of the term authorize. A constructivist approach will be critical of all kinds of violence, taking a hard look *both* at Muslim-inspired violence *and* at the things—flags, markets, "freedom"— to which secular social orders sacrifice lives.

NOTES

1. William T. Cavanaugh, *The Myth of Religious Violence: Secular Ideology and the Roots of Modern Conflict* (New York: Oxford University Press, 2009).

2. *Oxford English Dictionary*, 2nd ed., s.v. "religion."

3. Thomas Aquinas, *Summa Theologiae*, ed. Blackfriars (New York: McGraw-Hill, 1964), 2–2.80–81.

4. John Locke, *A Letter Concerning Toleration* (Indianapolis: Bobbs-Merrill, 1955), 22–23.

5. Ibid., 17.

6. Ibid., 27.

7. Ibid., 57.

8. John Bossy, *Christianity in the West, 1400–1700* (Oxford: Oxford University Press, 1985), 170–71.

9. Axel Oxenstierna, quoted in Geoffrey Parker, ed., *The Thirty Years' War* (London: Routledge, 1984), 122.

10. Walther von Wartburg, "Saeculum, séculariser," in *Französiches etymologisches Wörterbuch* (Basel, 1964), 11:44–46, quoted in Jan N. Brenner, "Secularization: Notes Toward a Genealogy," in *Religion: Beyond a Concept*, ed. Hent de Vries (New York: Fordham University Press, 2008), 433.

11. Heinz Schilling, "War and Peace at the Emergence of Modernity: Europe Between State Belligerence, Religious Wars, and the Desire for Peace," in *1648: War and Peace in Europe*, ed. Klaus Bussmann and Heinz Schilling (Münster: Westfälisches Landesmuseum, 1998), 14.

12. Charles Tilly, "Reflections on the History of European State-Making," in *The Formation of National States in Western Europe*, ed. Charles Tilly (Princeton: Princeton University Press, 1975), 42.

13. Michael Howard, *The Invention of Peace: Reflections on War and International Order* (New Haven: Yale University Press, 2000), 15.

14. John Neville Figgis, *From Gerson to Grotius, 1414–1625* (New York: Harper Torchbook, 1960), 124.

15. David Potter, *A History of France, 1460–1560: The Emergence of a Nation State* (New York: St. Martin's Press, 1995), 43, 285.

16. Richard McCoy, *Alterations of State: Sacred Kingship in the English Reformation* (New York: Columbia University Press, 2002), 58–66.

17. Ernst H. Kantorowicz, *The King's Two Bodies: A Study in Medieval Political Theology* (Princeton: Princeton University Press, 1957), 232–72.

18. Bossy, *Christianity in the West*, 153–71.

19. Carlton J. H. Hayes, *Nationalism: A Religion* (New York: Macmillan, 1960).

20. Carlton J. H. Hayes, *Essays on Nationalism* (New York: Macmillan, 1926), 100.

21. Robert N. Bellah, "Civil Religion in America," in *American Civil Religion*, ed. Donald E. Jones and Russell E. Richey (San Francisco: Mellen Research University Press, 1990), 21.

22. Ibid., 28–30.

23. Carolyn Marvin and David W. Ingle, "Blood Sacrifice and the Nation: Revisiting Civil Religion," *Journal of the American Academy of Religion* 64, no. 4 (Winter 1996), 767.

24. Ibid., 769.

25. William Rehnquist, quoted in Carolyn Marvin and David W. Ingle, *Blood Sacrifice and the Nation: Totem Rituals and the American Flag* (Cambridge: Cambridge University Press, 1999), 30.

26. Marvin and Ingle, "Blood Sacrifice and the Nation," 770.

27. Ibid., 768. "By 'religion' we mean a system of cosmological propositions grounded in a belief in a transcendent power expressed through a cult of divine being and giving rise to a set of ethical prescriptions."

28. Abraham Lincoln, quoted in Emilio Gentile, *Politics as Religion*, trans. George Staunton (Princeton: Princeton University Press, 2006), 2.

29. Abington Township School District v. Schempp, 374 U.S. 203 (1963), 313.

30. *Abington Township*, 374 U.S at 307–8.

55

Religion and Economy

GREGORY ALLES

In the past the term "economy" has had a number of meanings in religious contexts that may seem odd today. For example, within English-speaking Christianity it has referred to the manner in which God governs the world, to a careful presentation of religious teachings or doctrines, and to presumed relations between the various persons of the Trinity.[1] The word "economy" may also be used, however, in a sense that approximates its contemporary meaning within nonreligious contexts, namely, the organization and operation of interactions between different parties or agents, especially interactions that involve exchange. A religious economy in this sense may encompass interactions and exchanges between human beings and postulated religious agents, such as gods, ancestors, or spirits, as when one speaks of an economy of salvation linking devotees and saints. The term may also refer to specific interactions and exchanges among human beings or of humans with other universally perceived beings or objects, such as animals. One example of this second type of religious economy would be exchanges between laypersons and *bhik-khus* in Theravāda Buddhism.

At the end of the twentieth and the beginning of the twenty-first century, the study of religions in economic terms has attracted some attention. This interest may reflect contemporary developments. For example, after the end of the Cultural Revolution and then the reintegration of Hong Kong almost a quarter century later, the People's Republic of China has emerged as a global economic powerhouse. During the same period, more books by Rodney Stark, a rational-choice sociologist, have been translated into Chinese than into any other language (as of December 2008). Roughly simultaneously but less directly, in the United States a general shift has taken place in the financing of retirement. Since the establishment of 401k tax shelters in 1980, defined-benefit retirement plans, in which a provider promises a fixed benefit upon retirement, have been disappearing in favor of defined-contribution plans, in which an individual receives a certain sum at regular intervals that she or he must manage in the hopes of having sufficient retirement savings. One wonders to what extent such a shift has stimulated interest in economics among professionals, including scholars of religions. Perhaps it is best to leave such questions to future historians.

One should also note that the economic study of religion is not without its detractors. Although as a matter of methodological principle scholars of religions do not particularly care about God or gods, they often care a great deal about Mammon, or, rather, about systems of economic organization and their distributional effects. Anecdotal evidence would suggest that most scholars who have chosen to study religions professionally have also rejected, at least in part, the values and aspirations of those who have chosen to study business and economics. The result may be a very deep chasm between humanistic values and materialistic ones, between orientations to communal interest and orientations to self-interest, evidenced, for example, in a divide between a celebration of altruistic activity and a denial that such activity is possible. Conflicting values also divide those who would engage in economic analysis. Although much attention has been paid to ways in which religious differences fracture the global human community, economic convictions are at least as divisive. For example, in October 2008, the former US secretary of state Colin Powell asserted publicly that it should make no difference whether a candidate for the US presidency was a Christian or a Muslim. It is difficult to imagine him expressing the same indifference about whether a candidate was a Marxist or a capitalist.[2] Similarly within the academy, adherence to a particular kind of economic analysis may resemble commitment to a religious belief system.

In such a fractious environment economic theorizing about religion should be seen more as a general trend or tendency than as a unified approach to the study of religions, unless one is willing, as many are, to ignore movements and modes of analysis that violate one's own chosen economic faith. What follows aspires to greater pluralism. It discusses the rather different contributions of three classical theorists, Adam Smith (1723–90), Karl Marx (1818–83), and Max Weber (1864–1920), then turns to more contemporary work.

THE CLASSICAL THEORISTS

Depending upon a scholar's orientation, Smith, Marx, and Weber occupy different places in the genealogy of the economic study of religion. Those trained in the study of economics, along with economically inclined social scientists, tend to see themselves as standing in the tradition of Smith; they acknowledge Weber's contributions but condemn Marx. Scholars trained in the humanistic study of religions see things quite differently. They tend to embrace Weber; many are also attracted to the younger Marx, but they are largely unaware of Smith's ideas about religion.

Some of Smith's most important comments on religion are found in *The Wealth of Nations*, book 5, chapter 1, part 3, article 3.[3] This article's topic is not religion per se but "institutions for the instruction of people of all ages." Despite the title, Smith is thinking primarily of religious institutions, not vertically integrated schools. He makes several general points and then turns to a historical account of Western

Christianity. Thus, what is presented as a general account of human behavior turns out to be a generalized preface to a limited range of data from European Christianity. Smith's focus is on the compensation of religious professionals. His basic thesis is that religious institutions are healthiest when religious professionals are compensated poorly and by means of private, voluntary contributions.

Smith analyzes religion within a two-tiered, class-based model of society that in many ways idealizes what he calls "the common people" as distinct from "people of fashion." He contrasts relatively well-off clergymen (there were few if any clergywomen at the time), supported by steady incomes from benefices and the like, with members of the clergy who depend upon popular support and voluntary contributions. Religious professionals with a secure income tend, he says, to be comfortable, educated, and attracted to a sophisticated life of "loose" morality. As a result, they both lack religious fervor and are inattentive to the arts that inspire the "common people." Commoners, by contrast, are always the main support of religion. They admire clergy who are persuasive and inspirational and who embody the strict morality that by necessity defines their lives. Smith's economics of religion, then, theorizes competition among various groups for membership and support. New, independent churches always have a competitive advantage over traditional, state-supported rivals.

Although Smith assigns independent groups a competitive advantage in the religious marketplace, he does not see them as unequivocally beneficial to the community. They pose threats associated with fanaticism and overbearing zeal, for which Smith proposes remedies. On the one hand, the state should require that anyone who holds office should have an education in philosophy and science.[4] On the other, the state should support religion as little as possible. Without state support one can expect to find within a state, Smith says, not two or three major religious bodies but a vast multiplicity of small sects, whose leaders will find it expedient to temper their zeal because they will need to coexist with many fellow religionists.

In addition to discussing religious institutions, Smith finds a lesson about educational institutions in his observations, specifically, a lesson about the university. He claims, perhaps correctly for his day, that the vast majority of "men of letters" belong to the clergy. In countries like France, where the clergy have access to permanent, generous livings, men of ability will prefer those posts and remain outside of the universities. In countries like England, in which the clergy must depend upon modest contributions, men of genuine intellectual ability will enter the universities as a way to better their lot. So far as I can see, he does not consider whether a comfortable life in the university would be any less conducive to indolence than one in an ecclesiastical office.

Like Smith, Marx thinks within the parameters of a rather simple, hierarchically tiered view of society, although one more complex than Smith's division between "common people" and "people of fashion." Unlike Smith, his concern is not with the competitive advantages of various religious groups within a religious marketplace. It is with the adverse economic consequences of religion among the urban industrial proletariat and the need to eliminate religion as a prerequisite to the elimination of poverty among urban laborers.

Marx actually gives religion relatively little attention. His general philosophical stance deliberately shifts attention away from heaven to earth: from ideas to reality, from human beings as disembodied, atomized intellects to human beings as social agents who need to work in order to live and who do so within a society characterized by severe economic disparity. Since Marx sees religion as a veil protecting idealized views of humanity, he is willing to embrace as a strategic move the left-wing Hegelian critique of religion developed, for example, by Ludwig Feuerbach as a prerequisite to the broader, more important shift that he sees as necessary. It is in this context that he makes his best-known comments about religion.

For Marx, religion is a misguided response to life's miseries among the poor. This view resembles what Rodney Stark and William Sims Bainbridge have called a "compensator." Instead of working to improve their lives here on earth, religious people seek a resolution to their misery in the alienated forms of religion. They believe that, as sinners, they should accept their fate and thank God for whatever gifts God bestows upon them. They further believe that if they trust in God and act appropriately, they will receive rewards not here on earth but after death. Marx differs from Stark and Bainbridge, however, in thinking that religious compensators substitute for goods that are in fact available in this life. Religion becomes, then, both an analgesic and a distraction. Rather than pursuing religious rewards, people should abandon them and seek to improve their material lot in life. Émile Durkheim, standing in a long line of thinkers who critique Marx by detecting elements of religion in his thought, would later apply Marx's view of religion more or less to Marxism itself. Socialism, he said, was the desperate cry of a trapped animal. By contrast, one might see in Smith a person of privilege viewing the lives of the less privileged through unrealistically positive lenses.

Max Weber is best known in the context of an economic study of religion not for work on the relation between religion and economic stratification in particular societies but for work on the varying relationships between religion and economic ethics and practices. These interests reflect his context: he wrote in the heyday of European colonialism and as a liberal member of the German cultured but nonaristocratic upper class (*Bildungsbürgertum*), which was wrestling at the time with historical and cultural plurality (for example, historicism, Ernst Troeltsch on the "absoluteness" of Christianity). His writings explored the extent to which religious ideals and values shaped economic practice in a variety of global contexts.

Weber's groundbreaking and still controversial work was *The Protestant Ethic and the Spirit of Capitalism* (1904).[5] He began from observations about religious and economic differentiation in the Germany of his day: Protestants tended to be more involved in business and wealthier than Catholics; they also tended to work and save more. He used these observations as a lever with which to pry open the box of the historical origins of capitalism. What he found was that these origins lay in Calvinistic values. With its emphasis on the majesty of God and God's election (in Calvinism, whether one is saved or damned is solely God's choice, regardless of human action), Calvinism created anxiety about one's eternal fate. It taught that human beings should acknowledge God's majesty and conform to His will. In response, Calvinists adopted an ethic of "inner worldly asceticism." They rejected extravagant expenditure as sinful, emphasized hard work, and saw in prosperity a possible sign of God's favor. The result was a religiously motivated style of economic behavior that emphasized making money and reinvestment, the seeds from which capitalism grew. Weber did not claim that only Protestants are capitalists. He claimed that Calvinism was the catalyst that gave rise to capitalism. The latter has since broken free from its religious bonds and spread throughout the world. Having stated this thesis, Weber then set out to examine the economic ethics of other "world religions."

Rationality figures prominently in economic analysis, and it does so in Weber's thought as well. Unlike some views of economic rationality, however, Weber did not presuppose that rationality is universally identical. Instead, he identified in history a trend that he called rationalization. To describe the attraction of religious leaders like Jesus or the Buddha, he had introduced the notion of "charisma." Upon the death of the charismatic founders, he noted, religious communities undergo a process of rationalization, at least if they are to survive. Furthermore, Weber saw rationalization in the spread of modern capitalism. With this spread, the world is becoming disenchanted; it is losing its "magic" and "mystery." Now the dominant rationality is instrumental; attempts to maximize utility pervade all spheres of life. Like the German Romantics, Weber did not see this development as progress. Rather, it had created an iron cage of social organization in which we are now trapped. The less pessimistic form of the "secularization thesis," the contention that, as rational modernity advances, religion inevitably declines, was until recently canonical within the sociology of religion.

One major objection to Weber's view of the origin of capitalism has been empirical. Although committed Weberians may see medieval economic institutions as protocapitalistic at most, others find that capitalistic institutions predate the Protestant Reformation. Recently Rodney Stark has argued that it was not Calvinism that created capitalism but Christianity with its emphasis on rationality. He has also been among the staunchest critics of Weber's claim that modernity necessarily leads to secularization.

RECENT TRENDS

As is true of the classical theorists, more recent thinkers have pursued various projects in the economics of religion. They have done so with very different orientations and with more or less attention to the classical thinkers.

Rational Choice Theorists

Those who identify with the social sciences have tended to develop Adam Smith's concern with competition between groups in the religious marketplace. Many scholars have worked in this direction. They include Robert Ekelund and colleagues, who have analyzed the medieval Catholic Church as a multidimensional firm. This approach is, however, most closely associated today with the work of Rodney Stark, Roger Finke, and Laurence Iannaccone.

Stark began his career as a sociologist who studied conversion. Working in collaboration with John Lofland, he focused upon an early missionary effort of the Unification Church in the San Francisco bay area. What he and Lofland discovered is that (in Stark's later formulation) converts are not attracted so much by a religious group's teachings, which at first usually seem bizarre, as by personal connections with people already in the group. Religious conversion should be seen, then, as a process of maximizing benefits from interpersonal relationships, given one's place within networks of such relationships. Later Iannaccone would theorize conversion in terms of the maximization of benefit from religious capital, such as knowledge of rituals and teachings acquired over time. Iannaccone postulated that those with less religious capital—the young, those with less attachment to religion—would have less to lose from conversion than those with more religious capital; therefore, they would be more likely to convert. He noted further that a person changing affiliation from one group to another similar group would preserve more religious capital than someone converting to a radically different group. Therefore, he suggested, reaffiliation, as the less costly option, should be more common than conversion.

As these examples show, Stark, Finke, and Iannaccone develop a "rational-choice" theory of religion. They are staunch spokespersons for the view that religion is neither irrational nor nonrational but rational. Although the word "rational" can have a number of meanings, in the context of rational-choice theories it means that people act to further their interests. They seek to gain what they desire—to maximize utility—and avoid what they do not desire. As Stark and Finke have put it, "Within the limits of their information and understanding, restricted by available options, guided by their preferences and tastes, humans attempt to make rational choices." Although the mention of preferences and tastes allows room for social goals and thus for behavior that seems self-sacrificial and altruistic, the rational-choice theorists of religion, like most thinkers in the tradition of Adam Smith, have tended to focus on atomized agents and their individual wants and desires rather than social utility.

Rationality has figured prominently in theories of modernity and, along with them, theories of secularization. The alleged irrationality of religion was one reason why the "secularization thesis" predicted that, with advancing modernity, religion would disappear. Stark, Finke, and Iannaccone have vehemently rejected this thesis. They contend that as modernity increases, religion may become privatized, but it does not diminish or disappear. Rather, they maintain, the demand for religion is constant and variations in religious practice must be explained from the supply side. One prominent advocate of the secularization thesis from the 1960s, Peter Berger, has conceded that it was wrong, but other scholars, notably Steve Bruce, whose primary location is in the United Kingdom rather than the United States, have strongly rejected both the antisecularization thesis and its rational-choice underpinnings. Since 2000 Robert Barrow and Rachel McLeary as well as Pippa Norris and Ronald Inglehart have undertaken empirical surveys that were global in scope. Their results have not provided unqualified support for either the secularization or the antisecularization position.

In pursuing a supply-side approach to religion, Stark and Finke have theorized the competitive advantages enjoyed by various religious groups. Their basic example is the growth of conservative churches in the United States in the last third of the twentieth century, although they also invoke the spread of Pentecostalism during the same period in much of Africa and Latin America. They explain this growth by claiming that such groups provide more religious value. Specifically, conservative religious groups stand in greater tension with their environments, and so attract people who are looking for greater religious commitment and conviction than are represented in mainstream church groups. (This would seem a difficult proposition to maintain universally, since there have been times when conservative religiosity has been extremely dominant and liberals highly marginalized.) From this perspective Stark and Finke reformulate a standard developmental model that strongly reflects its origins in the study of US American Protestantism: movements begin as high-tension "sects" but as a result of attracting members eventually become low-tension "churches"; they then begin to lose members. Stark and Finke add that it is possible for low-tension churches to become vital once again by recovering their sectarian roots and becoming stricter.

Laurence Iannaccone, who is trained in economics per se, has developed complementary analyses of religion that Stark and Finke accept without reservation. Besides the notion of religious capital, Iannaccone has introduced the "free-rider problem" into the study of religion. According to this well-known economic problem, when rational agents participate in a group, they tend to perform suboptimally. They reason that regardless of the effort they expend, overall benefit will remain roughly the same; as a result, groups will seriously underperform. Iannaccone invokes these dynamics to account for the many onerous demands that religious groups make upon their members, such as costly moral strictures and door-to-door proselytizing. He suggests that people are willing to incur such costs because they have the effect of eliminating free riders and thus ensuring greater religious benefit. Invoking another well-known economic topic, the free market, Iannaccone explains the European trend toward secularization not in terms of the advancement of modernity but in terms of market dynamics. In Europe the establishment of religion has created a regulated religious market and, as in all regulated markets, put a damper on religious activity. In the United States, where disestablishment has created a free market in religion, religion thrives.

In many respects all of this work is a continuation of Adam Smith's concern with religious marketplaces in which individual religious agents choose between religious providers. In the late 1980s, however, Stark was engaged in a more ambitious theoretical project in collaboration with William Sims Bainbridge. The two attempted to develop a hypothetical-nomological theory of religion in terms of rational choice that rested upon seven basic axioms about human thought and behavior. Their key move was the observation that the goods people desire are scarce (a commonplace in economic theory) and sometimes nonexistent. As a result, people acquire religious goods as "compensators," a term Stark has since abandoned. In other words, religious people settle for goods allegedly received from divine beings that they would not otherwise enjoy. Although from this starting point analysis could go in a number of different directions, the theory quickly turns to the dynamics of the religious marketplace.

Within the social-scientific study of religion, Stark's, Finke's, and Iannaccone's work has exerted a great deal of influence, especially in the United States, the structures of whose religious situation their theorizing reflects closely. Indeed, in the first decade of the twenty-first century Stark has become an apologist for conservative, evangelical US American Christianity, endorsing such positions as intelligent design and identifying Islam as a retrograde movement. Whatever one's attitudes to these moves, they should not necessarily stand as a criticism of the general theoretical position. It may be worth noting three weaknesses in the work to date. First, there is a problem with what Germans refer to as the *Religionsbegriff*, the way in which religion is conceptualized. It is not at all clear to what extent the terms in which the analysis is framed are appropriate to what we call religion outside the United States. For example, to speak of "churches" and "sects" in Islamic and Hindu contexts is problematic at best. To suggest that liberal Protestants like David Friedrich Strauss and his colleagues stood in low tension with their environments is to ignore history. They all lost their jobs, and when Strauss was hired at the University of Zurich, the citizens overthrew the government. Second, the rational-choice postulate is questionable in terms of actual human decision-making. In its most careful form, economics does not claim that human beings are rational agents but that economic activities measurable in monetary terms, such as the exchange of scarce goods and services, can be modeled with a fair degree of accuracy by presupposing that agents are rational. Even so, work done within the last few decades has revealed the limits of the rationality postulate in economic models by demonstrating the relevance of risk, uncertainty, framing effects, and incomplete information, among other factors. To date, rational-choice theorists of religion have resisted taking these developments into account. Third, the rational-choice theorists have adopted a rather heavy-handed approach toward empirical evidence. Stark in particular has been quick to reject as flawed studies that raise questions about his claims. In one notorious instance it was revealed only after ten years that he and his critics had obtained contradictory results because, despite Stark's self-confident bluster in print, he and Iannaccone had made a basic mathematical mistake. Furthermore, in dealing with empirical evidence the rational-choice theorists have tended to embrace a verificationist fallacy, according to which the discovery of an instance, or a series of instances, in which their theoretical postulate works "confirms" the theory. Their use of sophisticated statistical analysis notwithstanding, this is not the way in which the best science determines which theories it will embrace.

Other Trends

To date, the rational-choice theorists present the most thorough and consistent attempt to develop explanatory accounts of religion in economic terms. Work in other traditions has been more diffuse. A brief overview such as this will necessarily be selective and superficial.

For decades Marcel Mauss's *The Gift* was a must-read for aspiring scholars of religion as well as for those in various fields of anthropology.[6] It treated the gift as a "total prestation," one that must be understood not as an isolated act but in its full social context. The book had the effect of popularizing Franz Boas's material on the potlatch among indigenous people of the northwest coast of North America. As a wanton act of the destruction of property, the potlatch might seem to present a major violation of rational-choice postulates; indeed, the French thinker Georges Bataille used it in advocating a "transcendence" of economic rationality. The rebuttal from the rational-choice side is, however, self-evident. Another influential example from the early twentieth century, although one that is not particularly religious, is the account of the *kula* exchange in the Trobriand Islands by the Polish-British anthropologist Bronisław Malinowski. Malinowski described this exchange as a circular system in which two different kinds of ceremonial objects, armbands and necklaces, traveled in two different directions, clockwise and counterclockwise. The effect was to establish relationships between parties to the exchange.

One may find a continuation of Mauss's and Malinowski's approaches in analyses of religion from the perspective of neoinstitutional economics, represented by contemporary German scholars such as Ronald Brinitzer. Neoinstitutionalism is a variety of economic contextualism or holism that, instead of trying to develop universally applicable models on the basis of a common desiderative-ratiocinative mechanism, sees economic values and behavior as determined by the institutions within which they are found. Neoinstitutionalists are not alone in problematizing a universal rational-choice calculus. Some feminists have also rejected it, although not always on neoinstitutional grounds. They have seen cost-benefit calculation as an approach to life more characteristic of men than of women, women tending, perhaps by biological programming, to be more self-sacrificial, at least in regard to their children. To date, little actual work in the economics of religion has been done from this perspective, perhaps because it seems antithetic to the economic enterprise itself.

Until the rise of rational-choice theory, Max Weber's influence dominated the sociology of religion. Indeed, rational-choice sociology of religion was in many respects a response to Weberianism. Weber's influence tended, however, to shape work in sociology and anthropology (for example, Peter Berger, Clifford Geertz) rather than in an economics of religion per se. Weber continues to be influential, again apart from the economic focus, among contemporary scholars of religions such as the German Hans G. Kippenberg. A more ambivalent utilization of Weber, and one of greater interest here, has been the work of a French scholar who toward the beginning of his career sought to think "with Weber against Weber," namely, Pierre Bourdieu. In *Outline of a Theory of Practice*, a book nominally devoted to a study of the Kabyle of Algeria, Bourdieu developed a complex model of social practice.[7] Extending economic analysis well beyond the traditional domain of scarce goods and services, he aimed "to abandon the dichotomy of the economic and the non-economic which stands in the way of seeing the science of economic practices as a particular case of a *general science of the economy of practices*, capable of treating all practices . . . as economic practices directed towards the maximization of material or symbolic profit." Symbolic profit and capital have emerged as major themes in Bourdieu's work, as has the notion of the *habitus*, a traditional, internalized pattern for action that is less deterministic and thus provides more room for innovation than the notion of institution. At the same time, Bourdieu's attention to social reality is much more class- and context-sensitive than the rational-choice approach. In his analysis, agents in any number of fields or areas of life are entrepreneurs who, given the *habitus* (in this case plural) that they share but also the consistent possibility of innovation, seek to maximize their positions, in particular, to maximize their symbolic capital. Unfortunately, Bourdieu developed these ideas after he had largely turned his attention away from religion. He has also been much less utilized in the study of religions than his French compatriots Jacques Derrida and Michel Foucault. Although some work in the study of religions has been done from a Bourdieusian perspective, room remains for much more.

As is true of the Weberian tradition, Marxian influence within the study of religions has been largely social and cultural. If one takes the distinctive Marxian contribution to the study of religions to be a correlation between economic organization and religious practice, with economic organization being the independent variable, then one might say that in the twentieth century a kind of Marxianism was quite common within the study of religions. It was customary to describe distinctive religious complexes for various modes of subsistence: hunters and gatherers, pastoralists, early agriculturalists, the early city dwellers, and so on. Similarly, it is possible to see Marxian overtones in Peter Berger's contention that religion provides a "sacred canopy"; it misrepresents a reality that is socially constructed and thus contingent as if it were natural and necessary. In spirit, however, none of this work was Marxian in one important respect: none of it shared Marx's distinctive emphasis on social critique.

More recent scholars have adopted a much more critical attitude toward social forms, including forms of economic organization, often under the label of cultural studies or critical theory. They have been inspired not only by Marx but by a host of Marxian thinkers, among them Georg Lukacs, Walter Benjamin, Max Horkheimer, Theodor Adorno, and Antonio Gramsci. As the name "cultural studies" indicates, these thinkers have not been concerned so much with economic analysis as with cultural critique. Such critique, however, can and often does target forms of economic organization. One manifestation within religion rather than religious studies was the rise of liberation theology during the 1980s, especially Christian liberation theology in Latin America and Africa. Much of this thinking was done by priests, monks, and nuns within the Roman Catholic Church, and it was suppressed by Pope John Paul II, a Pole active in the resistance to Polish Communism. Within religious studies itself, a recent book by Richard King and Jeremy Carrette, *Selling Spirituality*, is more focused on economic issues than many cultural-critical studies. The authors criticize the commodification of religion, especially religions appropriated from Asia under the guise of "spirituality," by Europeans and North Americans living within the structures of late capitalism or postmodernity.[8] Clearly, there is a normative component to this argument. Some consider it inappropriate to the study of religions to distinguish genuine or proper religion from inauthentic, improper religion or, in this case, "spirituality." It is also possible, however, to view a value-neutral approach to the study of religions as an essentially conservative undertaking.

FINAL REFLECTIONS

Elsewhere I have suggested that there is an important difference between classical and contemporary thought in the economics of religion. The classical theorists conceptualized "religion" and "economy" as two distinct domains that interacted; contemporary thinkers tend to treat "religion" and "economy" as two species of the same genus of human thought and behavior, species that we conventionally distinguish as religious and secular or symbolic and material but that are susceptible to analysis in parallel terms. This move is clearly seen in the passage from Bourdieu quoted above. Such a move, made in conjunction with Melford Spiro's well-known definition of religion as "an institution consisting of culturally patterned interaction with culturally postulated superhuman beings," could lead to the interrogation of the extent to which interactions with culturally postulated superhuman beings manifest the same regularities that appear in interactions between human beings. Made in conjunction with a broader notion of religion that includes interaction between people, such as the Manichean elect or Buddhist *bhikkhus* and *bhikkhunis* and their supporters, in search of goods that are always only symbolic (*karma*, *nirvāṇa*, the purification of light from dross matter), such a move could lead to the interrogation of the extent to which interactions between people for such nonempirical goods follow patterns identified in the case of material goods. While such work, taking full account of the complexity of human economic thought and behavior, can be envisioned within current conceptualizations of religious studies and economics, it has at most only begun.

NOTES

1. *Oxford English Dictionary*, s.v. "economy."
2. Powell's remarks are rooted, of course, in a liberal concept of the state that sees religion as a private matter to which government should take a stance of principled indifference. Not all would agree.
3. Adam Smith, *The Wealth of Nations*, ed. Edwin Cannan (New York: Random House, 1994 [1776]).
4. Smith does not advocate universal public education. He thinks people will find much better teachers privately on the open market, and he does not consider the adverse effects of disparities between parents' resources and children's intellectual aptitudes.
5. Max Weber, *The Protestant Ethic and the Spirit of Capitalism*, ed. Talcott Parsons and Anthony Giddens (London: Unwin Hyman, 1930).

6. Marcel Mauss, *The Gift*, trans. Ian Cunnison (London: Cohen and West, 1966).

7. Pierre Bourdieu, *Outline of a Theory of Practice*, trans. Richard Nice (Cambridge: Cambridge University Press, 1977).

8. Jeremy Carrette and Richard King, *Selling Spirituality: The Silent Takeover of Religion* (New York: Routledge, 2005).

56

Globalization and Religion

JEREMY CARRETTE

Globalization is a word that has risen to dominance in academic and popular public discourse, in both the media and politics and across different languages, since the 1980s. It is a complex and contested category that can both reveal and conceal the world, because it is both used to promote political agendas and used as an attempt to theorize new social realities. Globalization is therefore a concept that reveals the very overlapping tensions between the political, the theoretical, and the empirical. It is a concept that requires critical analysis in the field of religion, not least because it is caught inside the limits of disciplinary analysis, logical tensions, and polemical debates.

There are distinct discourses on globalization across the areas of politics, sociology, economics, ecology, and media, but with little coherence. As Manfred Steger correctly notes, "there exists no scholarly agreement on a single conceptual framework for the study of globalization. Academics remain divided on the validity of available empirical evidence and for the existence and extent of globalization, not to mention its normative and ideological implications."[1] The very complexity of the idea reflects the multivalence of the term and its diverse application. However, the concept can still carry out critical work and identify substantial changes in human consciousness, social relations, and lifestyle, not to mention new orders of power and influence that change the understanding, classification, and conceptualization of religious phenomena.

THE CONTESTED CATEGORY

True, much talk of globalization is muddled, redundant, unsubstantiated and hyped. However, the concept can be constructed in such a way that it brings to light important circumstances of contemporary social relations that other vocabulary and analysis does not reveal.[2]

There is no definitive meaning of the word "globalization." The very nature of the term opens it up to the plurality and multiplicity of the processes and subjects that it seeks to capture. It attempts to map a complex and ever-changing set of phenomena of increased interrelations and networks of different orders of life, which reinforce a sense of living in an interconnected world. Rather than seeking to find a fixed meaning to the word, it is more effective to examine its use and application within the various fields of use and to understand its conceptual deployment and resistance.

There are three main problems in the attempt to make sense of globalization theoretically. First, as many scholars have noted, there is the issue of its extent and influence. It is easy to make a hegemonic (elitist and power-driven) application of globalization, which does not appreciate that globalization is in part an oxymoron. Its theoretical field of application undermines itself. The very global diversity and complexity defy easy reduction to a single process. Let me give some examples. The idea, in part, seeks to articulate a new ordering of space and time in human experience when the experience of space and time is never determined in one dimension. For example, Scholte seeks to make a distinction between different historical waves of global activity, including empire and industrialization, and wishes to mark out advanced technologically driven global activity by referring to "supraterritoriality," which conveys a form of "accelerated globalization" and something unique to the post-1980s information technology revolution.[3] While this application has distinct value with its historical specificity, it is important to note that compression of space and time does not negate seasonal time and space. International business-technological time and space are always layered on top of other modes of experiencing. For example, migrating tribal people in Mongolia can never be captured entirely in terms of global-mediated twenty-four-hour news activity, but all groups of people are still caught in solar and lunar cycles of time and space and the time-space reality of human birth cycles. The reduction of globalization to territorial and spatial ideas misses the central cultural hegemony of the concept and its differentiation across different layers of experiencing time and place.

The problem is when globalization is made into a "thing," as a reified single process operating in the world, rather than deconstructing its diverse processes that are historically contingent and that interrelate in diverse ways in any specific place. As commentators with very different concerns like to indicate, the forms of "globalization" are not equally distributed; we find rather peaks and troughs and varied relational distributions. Tulasi Srinivas, in an insightful attempt to reconfigure thinking about religion and globalization from the perspective of the Indian subcontinent, indicates that we need to consider where we locate the "centre" and "periphery."[4] She sees rather a "two-way" process and a much more "plastic" understanding of global processes that refuses any simple Western capitalistic view in the creation of, what she calls, an "engaged cosmopolitan" picture. This process and fluid conception are also usefully addressed by J. Glenn, who argues that we could describe "the world as globalizing rather than globalized."[5] But this use still opens the issue of whether globalization is principally a socioeconomic and political problem, rather than a geophysical order (that is, environmental and biological), which involves volcanic ash, weather patterns, and panepidemics. The question is how useful it is to use the word for all processes that underline the connected nature of the world and whether we need to differentiate types or periods of globalization.

A second problem of globalization relates to its paradoxical character. Roland Robertson made this point with his notion of "glocalization," the idea that the global is always caught inside local processes.[6] This tension has been captured most effectively by Paul James in his retheorizing of globalization alongside nationalism and tribalism.[7] He identifies the "contradictory processes" involved in globalization and, importantly, recognizes that it "cannot be understood in terms of itself." He attempts to understand these tensions by returning to a layered and ontological understanding of embodied-local and abstract-global, which in part responds to the first problem of extent and influence. Globalization is always a double process. As James effectively articulates: "Our world is experiencing powerful processes of globalization that are contributing to reconstituting the local, but at the same time globalization is making people more aware of the meaning of local embeddedness."[8]

A third major problem is the conceptual overlap and blurring. Globalization merges, often with deliberate political slippage, to capture related issues. It is often fused with geopolitical influences and mixed with other terms such as "Americanization" and "Westernization." There are clear links between imperialism and global political empires but global interconnections can be wider. However, some may wish to argue that technological advances are related to American capitalism. Here we see the problem of the multiple layers captured by the term. In addition to these conceptual overlaps, Leslie Sklair also recognizes the problem of making distinctions between other related words.[9] He draws attention to the difference between "inter-national" (what he defines as "the changing nature of states and their relationship"), "trans-national" (what he calls the "institutions not founded upon state system"), and "global" ("a position of influence across all territorial boundaries"). Ulrich Beck also makes a useful distinction between "globality," "globalism," and "globalization" to make a distinction between three realms: the social/culture realm, the realm of markets, and the realm of the political shift from national to transnational networks.[10] This tripartite structure of culture, economy, and politics can be seen in most textbooks on globalization, but it raises problems of the disciplinary frame of globalization and whether old disciplinary structures are sufficient to capture new forms of knowledge in a globally interconnected environment.[11]

DISCIPLINING GLOBALIZATION

Globalization falls outside the established academic disciplines, a sign of the emergence of a new kind of social phenomenon as much as an index of the origins of those disciplines in nineteenth-century realities that are no longer ours.[12]

Theories of globalization are caught inside disciplinary perspectives about the issue, which seek to give priority to one dimension, rather than map wider orders of global connection and disconnection. The term is used in different ways to capture processes of economic, political, social, and cultural developments, but the disconnection of disciplinary knowledge to assess the increased connection of the world creates a paradox in the study of globalization. The main problem is that globalization theory is caught within old paradigms of industrial knowledge and its related disciplines.[13] Globalization emphasizes that the epistemic structures of knowledge and theory created in the colonial and industrial period of the late nineteenth century are now weakened. Steger recognized the same problem of traditional disciplines "losing their old rationales in a globalizing world."[14] In response to such problems, Paul James's model of immediate-abstract and embodied-disembodied attempts to find a way to theorize a new set of social relations.[15] The phenomena of globalization require a fluidity of knowledge to register its complex processes. As B. S. Turner and H. H. Khondker argue, it "almost certainly requires a high degree of interdisciplinarity."[16]

Technology is often seen to be the pivotal feature allowing the reduction of time-space and making extended communication possible. It is seen as the central feature of globalization theory, as can be seen in Manuel Castells's study of the information age.[17] But as W. E. Murray indicates, "Globalization processes are *facilitated* by technological change but are driven by much more fundamental forces."[18] Murray usefully makes a distinction between "processes and political-economic agendas." In his work, Murray tries to capture how the multiple "spheres" of geography are changed by globalization and how it is the constant redefinition of fields of knowledge that globalization demands.

Appadurai earlier on in globalization debates referred to the different "flows" such as ethnoscapes (movement of people), technoscapes (internet messages), financescapes (capital flows), mediascapes (information), and ideoscapes (political ideology).[19] Appadurai enables us to see the "dynamic" nature of global processes and their disjunctions and irregularity.[20] All these fields force us to challenge subject boundaries to make sense of the complexity of global phenomena, but the literature on globalization still falls distinctively into disciplinary engagements, mainly across sociology, politics, and economics.

In the field of sociology there has been an attempt to understand globalization as part of the wider processes and extension of modernity. Giddens showed "the intensification of worldwide social relations" and Tomlinson carries out a similar analysis in seeking to show how culture is caught inside the "complex connectivity" of "global modernity."[21] Sociological analysis of globalization grew out of Wallerstein's world-systems theory, which recognized in the changing nature of capitalism that "the only kind of social system is a world-system."[22] Responding to Wallerstein, Roland Robertson, a key voice in globalization theory, not only recognized the importance of the local and global with his idea of "glocalization," but sought to bring an understanding of history and consciousness to the concept.[23] He strongly upholds the view that globalization is a sense of living in a "single place," something supported by ideas of the "global village."[24]

The economic analysis of globalization is perhaps the most dominant, not least because in the post–Cold War era the rise of neoliberalism (the unrestricted world market) led to new orders of power that radically changed aspects of social life. The Austrian economist Friedrich Hayek, in his postwar analysis of the problems of totalitarianism and the nation-state, believed that the markets would bring greater freedom and liberty. His ideas were adopted by Reagan and Thatcher in the 1980s and this allowed the opening up of world markets and increased the power of transnational corporations. The advance of neoliberalism increased global power to nonstate actors and in consequence increased the power of global capitalism. This entailed radical shifts in the social and global order. As the economist Karl Polanyi rightly observed: "Instead of economy being embedded in social relations, social relations are embedded in the economic system."[25] Social orders were now driven by efficiency and productivity demands in a global economic system. The political idea of TINA (There Is No Alternative) represented the force of these economic ideas as inevitable. Much of the literature around the social resistance to globalization assumes this dimension as central, and it is possible to argue that the extension of globalization theory is part of the knowledge apparatus that sustains this economic agenda through a cultural extension of its central ideals.

The structures of both social and economic globalization in the end rest upon political forms of globalization. The increasing range of transnational issues and the rise of international relations theory reflect the underlying drive of political and policy issues behind the processes. J. Baylis, S. Smith, and P. Owens's *The Globalization of World Politics* (2008) reflects this analysis with consideration of issues from global trade to human rights.[26] The political process of internationalization and the creation of institutional political institutions, such as the World Trade Organization, the World Bank, and the United Nations, reflect a widening of structures of political influence. Indeed, the United Nations commissioned its own report, *Our Global Neighbourhood* (1995), to reflect on the new conditions of the world.[27] While this was a positive attempt to understand global governance, there was also anxiety. It is this aspect that led M. Hardt and A. Negri to suggest that there is now a new form of global sovereignty, a decentred and deterritorialized empire, not unrelated to the US Constitution.[28] It is in resistance against these forms of globalization that social movements and antiglobalization groups emerged.[29]

THE ETHICS OF GLOBALIZATION AND THE GLOBALIZATION OF ETHICS

While there are movements fighting against the realities of political-economic globalization, scholars have also tried to correct the theoretical assumptions behind the concept. A. Cameron and R. Palan exposed the "imagined economies" of globalization, Smith exposed the "hidden agenda" of humiliation (lack of freedom, agency, security, recognition), and John Glenn challenged the ideas of globalization by looking at the North-South perspectives, showing that the South has few choices in the adoption of global neoliberal policies.[30] Jan Nederveen Pieterse argued for a "wider and deeper" understanding of globalization not as a simple homogenization but as "cultural hybridization"; and Turner and Khondker raised its East-West dimensions, not least resisting the simplistic and extreme model of Samuel Huntington's "clash of civilizations" thesis.[31] Following a different political vein, R. Munck drew out the "contestation" from social movements such as the Zapatistas in Mexico.[32] A similar line of resistance can also be seen in M. Woodin's and C. Lucas's green alternatives to globalization.[33]

All these perspectives, and many more being generated as the processes and implications of the political and economic issues unfold, still generate their discourses according to the industrial and postwar disciplinary models of the world, but there is also a widening out of globalization theory. There is increasingly an appreciation of deeper historical processes, of movements and cultural exchanges, not only in terms of cosmic visions of the world and desires for universal salvation, but in terms of the exchange of cultural artifacts, aesthetics, rituals, music, and dance. This drive to share ideas and habits of cultural practice, albeit not unrelated to the logic of imperialism and empire, at least adds greater theoretical depth to an analysis of globalization. It is not just the logic of conquest and violence that creates globalization, but also the logic of communication and curiosity.

Any discourse on globalization cannot avoid that it is embedded inside a set of normative evaluations, and even the attempt to map global flows empirically is still trapped in a value of ordering and selecting from the myriad of phenomena. The reaction to globalization is, of course, muddied by a confusion of what is being critiqued or celebrated. The three positions, often outlined by commentators, of globalists (the supporters), antiglobalists or "skeptics" (those against), and the "moderates" or "modifiers" (those who reject the excesses but accept the reality) can obscure the layered and contested nature of the debate.[34] It is thus possible to reject neoliberal globalization and accept the global connectedness of the environment, communication, and trade. One may also follow James in seeing different ongoing phases according to "traditional" globalization and "modern" globalization and accept one but not the other.[35] The normative evaluation of globalization is thus reflected within the norms of globalization theory. This is made even more complex by recognizing those attempts to build a global ethical perspective in response to the pluralistic conditions of a global world.[36] However, there is here another double movement. Human rights discourse and the values of international law can at the same time allow a camouflage for a sociopolitical drive for a globalization of ethics, with all its neocolonial aspirations for a universal system.[37] Here we see the constant shift between globalization as a descriptive category and as a normative category and how the empirical claim of globalization is already caught within a value-driven theoretical assertion.

THREE MODELS OF RELIGION AND GLOBALIZATION

The blurring of the empirical and theoretical in globalization theory is nowhere more apparent than in the field of religion. The question of the period of historical emergence, the link of globalization to technology, and its value as an ethical or unethical process are all given additional complexity when we consider the history of religions. Robertson is rightly "discontent with a truncated, economic version of globalization" and attempts to show the importance of religious factors within a model of a "single place" notion of globalization.[38] The recognition of multiple global processes, independent of economic realities, is important and insightful, but there is an unavoidable normative question about how far-reaching the political-economic forces are in determining other areas of life. Indeed, the relation to the economic model of neoliberal globalization is one that reveals not just the competing importance of historical and noneconomic global flows, but the political position one takes in relation to the economic domination of neoliberalism. *There can be no neutral position in relation to globalization.* It is this dimension that makes the field so complex.

The appeal to the cosmic and universal in religious discourse illustrates how it can enhance the "abstract" processes that James showed were a necessary part of globalization.[39] Ideas can be transported from the embodied locality, and religions have resources from premodern global flows of ideas. This can be seen in Olivier Roy's reading of Islam and globalization and how the notion of the "umma" allows Islam to be transported from its geographical historical roots to a global order.[40] The metaphysical systems inside religious traditions bring a profound framing of a single global-spiritual order prior to modernity, and these were easily transported along trade roots. These studies follow what James called "traditional globalization," part of what he called "sacred universalism," which, as he observes, is not necessarily the same as (modern) globalization.[41] But spiritual abstractions are radically transformed and intensified through the sociopolitical aspects of late-modern globalization, such that Internet technology increases the transmission of premodern (global) abstractions. The key issue here is that even if we differentiate forms of globalization we cannot ignore the interaction between these different forms.

The study of globalization and religion can be framed according to how far scholars acknowledge the force of the socioeconomic process and how far they seek to bracket out other types or disciplinary forms of globalization. Increasingly disciplinary exclusion only serves to diminish the picture of analysis. Scholars of religion are therefore divided not only in terms of their use of the terminology of the global, but also in terms of how far they are prepared to entertain the politic-economic implications of neoliberalism or the economic model. This is not to assume economic determinism, but rather to argue that neoliberalism is a neocolonial metaphysical order built inside something portrayed as economic or political. In this respect, we can identify three main models of analyzing religion and globalization according to how they relate to the dominant political-economic paradigm, how they respond to the fear of economic reductionism, and, in consequence, where they stand on the related issue of periodization.

First, the Global "World Religions" Model, which argues that there is a distinct and separate process of globalization from economic globalization. This position sees religious exchange as existing prior to the developments of advanced technology and as something that is part of a longer set of evolving processes. Second, the Religion *of* Globalization Model, which integrates the sociopolitical-economic model into religious discourse and shows globalization as a religious force. According to this model globalization carries both premodern and modern dimensions. Third, there is the Religion *Within* Political-Economic Globalization Model. This position argues that the processes of neoliberal globalization are radically transforming religion (as both category and a corresponding empirical reality). This position sees globalization as a late-modern event connected to specific post-1980s technological and political developments. Let us explore each in greater depth.

Global "World Religions" Model

In the first model, the move in the study of religion is to avoid specific commitment to the sociopolitical-economic analysis by using the adjective "global" as a new contextual framework of analysis. The global dimension of religion is seen as a new context of empirical sampling without recourse to technical processes. Religion can now be studied according to a spatial context in terms of global mission, cosmic message, and universal salvation or in terms of the intersexes of local practices in global political and economic processes, such as commodification of artifacts or media representation.

There is an obfuscation and avoidance of complex globalization theory in this approach. First, there is an intriguing shift from a discourse of "world religions" to "global religions."[42] In these approaches there is little evidence of engagement with globalization as a contested category and distinct undertheorization. The "global" functions as little more than a descriptive update of the aging semantic operations of the category "world," or, worse, as an endorsement of the neoliberal ideals by a refusal to theorize the problems of the concept of globalization. In some cases it carries the additional problem of confusing associations with the postmodern.[43]

By arguing that religion "has always been global" because of its "permeable boundaries," Juergensmeyer brackets out the complexity of the processes.[44] He thus discusses "diasporas," "transnational religions," and "global societies" without the force of political transparency. This is exacerbated by the fact that religion is seen as an "expression of a transnational culture and society," without any reflection of how culture and society are politically and economically ordered.[45] A slightly different separation occurs in Csordas, where engagement with global economics is separated from religion to avoid a "reductionism" of religion to economic processes.[46] There is recognition of "economic constraints" to religion but a bracketing of its domination. Religion is one of many layers of globalization. Csordas therefore talks of the "globalization *of* religion," examining the global flows of religion in terms of what is "portable," "transposable," "mobile," or "mediated."[47] This process deliberately disconnects the economic globalization from the analysis and attempts a return to an uncritical phenomenological position.

We may also note how there is a constant obscurity in the analysis. Take, for example, Juergensmeyer's analysis. He makes reference to "the era of globalization," "the globalization of religion," and "the religion of globalization" in the context of introducing thinking about "global religions."[48] The problem here is that "globalization" is never integrated and easily merges with the word "global" as a new contextual frame. The essays in the book maintain the "world religion" paradigm of looking at each "world" religion and how it is changing in a new global context, but we do not know how the "global" is theoretically distinct from the category "world" in this analysis. This elision is key, because it shows the way a new order maps the "global religions" model onto the "world religion" model without much theoretical difference. If, as King and Masuzawa illustrate, there are colonial aspirations with the universal model of "world religions," then we can easily see how "global" religions carry a second layer of imperial ambition from the new colonial order of neoliberal ideology.[49] Behind the notion of world and global we find the shadows of imperialism and a new neocolonial representation of religion.

Let me illustrate the point in greater detail with reference to one of the most extraordinary events in the study of religion. At the pinnacle of the Industrial Revolution and the colonial expansion of the world in the 1890s, the world trade fair experiment was extended yet further when it arrived in the United States. After equally great trade fairs in Crystal Palace, London, in 1851 and Paris in 1889, the Chicago trade fair in 1893 included a gathering of the "world religions." As Seager's study illustrates, it was a meeting shaped and determined by world trade and American imperialism in the late nineteenth century.[50] The language of the time was distinctively the language of the "world"—the welcoming speaker talks of the "world's first" parliament.[51] There are also references to "universal" as a religious aspiration, not least in terms of the Protestant agenda. The event in 1893, by virtue of its time, could not be dominated by the language of "global" religions, but by the time of late-twentieth-century scholarship examining the event there were references to the "global reach" of the World's Parliament of Religions and its "global significations."[52]

This shift in register is not surprising, but tells us something important about how the register of the "global" can create a new layer to the industrial-colonial framing of the world. "World" and "global" appear to refer to the same sense of space, but both refer to conditions shaped by external economic and colonial orders. The notion of the "global" appears to map onto the "world" without any descriptive problem, but it hides the forces shaping the representation. When we make the shift to "globalization," there is a more open acknowledgment of the sociopolitical agenda, though some wish to cover this analysis. The signifier "global" thus hides the latent political drives behind this conception of the world and the neocolonial dimensions of neoliberalism. By the time of the centennial gathering of the World's Parliament of Religions in 1993, the language of the global had started to shape the agenda and reference to global economy, ecology, and politics is evident.[53] There is even acknowledgment and concern about the state of the "global" world. To fuse and confuse the global and the world and to continue the world religions model inside a global religions perspective reflect the neocolonial picture of such theories of religion. Quite simply, to use the phrase "global world" is to deploy the adjective in ways that indicate not just the same spatial territory but a different consciousness of the world created by distinct political forces. It is my contention that the post-1980s use of the adjective "global" cannot be disentangled from the politic-economic power that shapes a new consciousness of the world, and to use it uncritically is at best a refusal of the politics of knowledge and at worst an endorsement of such a viewpoint.

The Religion of Globalization Model

In contrast to the global world religion model, we find a set of theories that deliberately seek to displace the religious and economic idea of globalization. The abstract processes of premodern transmissions of religion are now shown to operate *within* the economic force of globalization. This alternative way of thinking of religion and globalization can be seen in Dwight Hopkins's provocative essay "The Religion of Globalization." Here Hopkins models globalization on a structure of an idealized notion of religion as "a system of beliefs and practices." Hopkins works on the assumption that globalization relates to the "the concentration of monopoly, finance capitalist wealth" and shows how the institutions, rituals, and ideas of transcendence require a faith and commitment. They create a distinct theological anthropology and regulate behavior. For Hopkins globalization is a "religious system of capitalist wealth."[54]

Many would dispute this modeling of globalization, but while there are problems with the category of religion and its essentialization of rituals and practices, it does convey Polyani's point that culture is now driven by economy rather than economy being part of the world. There are, of course, many others who have made this move of blurring economy and religion, although for some this is a strategy to reveal the power of neoliberalism rather than assuming a given idea of religion.[55]

Interestingly, Juergensmeyer also refers to the idea of a "religion of globalization" in his own modeling of the relation between religion and globalization, but he uses a slightly different phrase, referring to the "*religions* of globalization."[56] This indicates how new forms of religion are created within a globalized world, which is a very different ordering. However, to acknowledge that there are new forms of religion, or even that new religions exist, requires some engagement with the political-economic understanding of globalization. To refuse such theorization, and fail to map how religions are involved in socioeconomic and political process, only maintains an inadequate disciplinary isolation.

Religion Within Political-Economic Globalization Model

If we accept that there are distinctively different social and organizational processes operating in the world due to globalization and that late-modern global flows are different from premodern or modern, then there is a need to understand the specific factors that redefine and perhaps transform religion, but also to understand how religion can be a form of resistance against such processes.[57] We can map five key areas for an analysis of globalization and religion: (1) transnational media, (2) Internet technology, (3) international governance, (4) markets/business, (5) markets/consumption. These areas are, however, already overlapping and interconnecting.

Religious experience and practice are redefined through these five areas. In the limits of this analysis we cannot cover all aspects of these area, but merely provide some examples: Beaudoin and Lynch illustrate how spiritual practices are transformed through media culture, with pop culture and dance music; Dawson and Hojsgaard and Warburg have done work mapping the changes cyberspace makes to religious experience and practice; Berger makes clear the increasing profile of religious NGOs in international governance; and Carrette and King have shown the ways spirituality has been incorporated into global business and world markets.[58] All these process are reflections of a new political economy of religious engagements and behavior brought about through neoliberal ideology. They show that globalization transforms religions and indeed transforms how we must conceive of religion outside a "world religions" model as it moves into a cultural-economy. In such a process the very basis, form, and construction of "religion" are renegotiated.

Conclusion: Globalization, Plurality, and the Same

Globalization requires the rethinking of the study of religion in its entirety. It challenges us to move outside of the industrial methods and its "world religions" model. It encourages us to move toward new geographies of the imagination, not to think of "traditions" and "religions" as distinct categories, but to think of the category of "religion" in terms of cultural-economic flows, regional influences, and political interconnections. It enables us to see how processes of abstraction are central to global flows of information within the study of religion and the fusion of types of knowledge. In this new atmosphere of theorizing and the new consciousness of global diversity in theory and practice, we need to challenge our presumptions and develop critical engagement with the concept and its deployment in the study of religion.

Scholte rightly notes that globalization "is very much what we make it."[59] Its vagueness requires us to develop critical precision and to understand how knowledge carries a normative register. In this sense, the contestation to frame religion in terms of the category of globalization is one that signals the politic order of knowledge itself. It takes us back to the post-1968 site of knowledge-power.[60] Globalization is the new frontier that will redefine the study of religion, but the tensions, paradox, and double movements inside the term signal that it carries the tension of abstract, hegemonic, and totalizing forces against the local and embodied nature of lived everyday practices. It is because of these tensions that we need to find ways to think and theorize that can capture plurality and diversity inside the imagined order of the same. Singular theories in a global world reveal the problem of thinking about a single-space full of multiple dimensions and possibilities. Globalization is the tension of the one and the many, the single and the plural, and its binary tension is the moment for contestation and critique.

NOTES

1. Manfred Steger, *Globalisms*, 3rd ed. (Lanham, Md.: Rowman and Littlefield, 2009), 47.
2. J. A. Scholte, *Globalization: A Critical Introduction* (New York: Palgrave Macmillan, 2000), 3; T. Schirato and J. Webb, *Understanding Globalisation* (London: Sage, 2003), 2–3.
3. Scholte, *Globalization*, 62.
4. T. Srinivas, *Winged Faith: Rethinking Religion and Globalization in the Sathya Sai Movement* (New York: Columbia University Press, 2010).
5. J. Glenn, *Globalization: North-South Perspectives* (London: Routledge, 2007), 67.
6. Roland Robertson, *Globalization: Social Theory and Global Culture* (London: Sage, 1992).

7. Paul James, *Globalism, Nationalism, Tribalism: Bringing Theory Back In* (London: Sage, 2006), 5, 16.

8. Ibid., 44.

9. Leslie Sklair, *Globalization: Capitalism and Its Alternatives*, 3rd ed. (Oxford: Oxford University Press, 2002).

10. Ulrich Beck, *What Is Globalization?* (Cambridge: Polity, 2000).

11. F. J. Lechner and J. Boli, eds., *The Globalization Reader*, 2nd ed. (Oxford: Blackwell, 2004); D. Held and A. McGrew, eds., *The Global Transformations Reader*, 2nd ed. (Cambridge: Polity, 2004).

12. F. Jameson and M. Miyoshi, eds., *The Culture of Globalization* (Durham: Duke University Press, 1998), xi.

13. Jeremy Carrette, *Religion and Critical Psychology: Religious Experience in the Knowledge Economy* (London: Routledge, 2007).

14. Manfred Steger, ed., *Rethinking Globalism*, 3rd ed. (Lanham, Md.: Rowman and Littlefield, 2004), 3.

15. James, *Globalism, Nationalism, Tribalism*, 3, 67.

16. B. S. Turner and H. H. Khondker, *Globalization: East and West* (London: Sage, 2010), 7.

17. Manuel Castells, *The Information Age: Economy, Society and Culture* (Oxford: Wiley-Blackwell, 1996–98).

18. W. E. Murray, *Geographies of Globalization* (London: Routledge, 2006), 8.

19. A. Appadurai, "Disjuncture and Difference in the Global Cultural Economy," *Public Culture* 2, no. 1 (1990): 1–19.

20. J. Beynon and D. Dunkerley, *Globalization: The Reader* (New York: Routledge, 2000), 27.

21. A. Giddens, *The Consequences of Modernity* (Cambridge: Polity, 1990), 64; J. Tomlinson, *Globalization and Culture* (Chicago: University of Chicago Press, 1999), 32. See also P. Beyer, *Religion and Globalization* (London: Sage, 1994).

22. I. Wallerstein, *The Modern World System*, vol. 1, *Capitalist Agriculture and the Origins of the European World-Economy in the Sixteenth Century* (New York: Academic, 1974).

23. Robertson, *Globalization*.

24. R. Robertson, "Antiglobal Religion," in *Global Religions: An Introduction*, ed. Mark Juergensmeyer (Oxford: Oxford University Press, 2003), 110–23; M. McLuhan, *Understanding Media* (London: Routledge, 1964); M. McLuhan and B. R. Powers, *The Global Village* (Oxford: Oxford University Press, 1989).

25. Karl Polanyi, *The Great Transformation: The Political and Economic Origins of Our Time* (Boston: Beacon, 1944), 57.

26. J. Baylis, S. Smith, and P. Owens, *The Globalization of World Politics*, 4th ed. (Oxford: Oxford University Press, 2008).

27. UN Commission on Global Governance, *Our Global Neighbourhood: The Report of the Commission on Global Governance* (Oxford: Oxford University Press, 1995).

28. M. Hardt and A. Negri, *Empire* (Cambridge, Mass.: Harvard, 2000).

29. A. Starr, *Global Revolt: A Guide to the Movements Against Globalization* (London: Zed, 2005).

30. A. Cameron and R. Palan, *The Imagined Economies of Globalization* (London: Sage, 2004); D. Smith, *Globalization: The Hidden Agenda* (Cambridge: Polity, 2006); Glenn, *Globalization.*

31. J. N. Pieterse, *Globalization and Culture: Global Mélange* (Lanham, Md.: Rowman and Littlefield, 2009); Turner and Khondker, *Globalization*; Samuel Huntington, *The Clash of Civilizations and the Remaking of the World Order* (New York: Simon and Schuster, 1996).

32. R. Munck, *Globalization and Contestation* (London: Routledge, 2007).

33. M. Woodin and C. Lucas, *Green Alternatives to Globalization: A Manifesto* (London: Pluto, 2004).

34. Scholte, *Globalization*, 17–18; Manfred Steger, *Globalization: A Very Short Introduction* (Oxford: Oxford University Press, 2003), 93–130; Steger, *Rethinking Globalism*, 24–28.

35. James, *Globalism, Nationalism, Tribalism*, 22.

36. Hans Kung and H. Schmidt, *A Global Ethic and Global Responsibilities: Two Declarations* (London: SCM, 1998).

37. W. Sullivan and W. Kymlicka, eds., *The Globalization of Ethics* (Cambridge: Cambridge University Press, 2007).

38. Robertson, "Antiglobal Religion," 123.

39. James, *Globalism, Nationalism, Tribalism.*

40. Oliver Roy, *Globalized Islam* (New York: Columbia University Press, 2004).

41. James, *Globalism, Nationalism, Tribalism*, 22–23.

42. L. Kurtz, *Gods in the Global Village* (Thousand Oaks, Calif.: Pine Forge Press, 1995); J. L. Esposito, D. J. Fasching, and T. Lewis, *Religion and Globalization: World Religions in Historical Perspective* (Oxford: Oxford University Press, 2008); Juergensmeyer, *Global Religion.*

43. Esposito et al., *Religions and Globalization.*

44. Juergensmeyer, *Global Religion*, 5.

45. Ibid., 9.

46. T. J. Csordas, ed., *Transnational Transcendence: Essays on Religion and Globalization* (Berkeley: University of California Press, 2009), 2.

47. Ibid., 3.

48. Juergensmeyer, *Global Religions*, 4, 10, 5.

49. Richard King, *Orientalism and Religion: Postcolonial Theory, India and "the Mystic East"* (London: Routledge, 1999); T. Masuzawa, *The Invention of World Religions; or, How European Universalism Was Preserved in the Language of Pluralism* (Chicago: University of Chicago Press, 2005); Alfredo Saad-Filho and Deborah Johnston, *Neoliberalism: A Critical Reader* (London: Pluto, 2005).

50. R. H. Seager, *The World's Parliament of Religions: The East/West Encounter, Chicago, 1893* (Bloomington: Indiana University Press, 1995).

51. R. H. Seager, *The Dawn of Religious Pluralism: Voices from the World's Parliament of Religions, 1893* (La Salle, Ill.: Open Court, 1993), 29.

52. Seager, *The Dawn of Religious Pluralism*, 6; Seager, *The World's Parliament of Religions*, 5.

53. Kung and Schmidt, *A Global Ethic and Global Responsibilities*.

54. D. N. Hopkins, "The Religion of Globalization," in *Religions/Globalizations*, ed. D. N. Hopkins et al. (Durham: Duke University Press, 2001), 19.

55. R. H. Nelson, *Economics as Religion* (University Park: Penn State University Press, 2001); Phillip Goodchild, *Capitalism and Religion* (London: Routledge, 2002); Jeremy Carrette and Richard King, *Selling Spirituality: The Silent Takeover of Religion* (London: Routledge, 2005).

56. Juergensmeyer, *Global Religion*, italics added.

57. Carrette and King, *Selling Spirituality*; G. Lynch, *The New Spirituality: An Introduction to Progressive Belief in the 21st Century* (New York: I. B. Tauris, 2007).

58. T. Beaudoin, *Virtual Faith: The Irreverent Spiritual Quest of Generation X* (San Francisco: Jossey-Bass, 1998); Lynch, *The New Spirituality*; L. Dawson and C. Cowan, *Religion Online* (London: Routledge, 2004); M. Hojsgaard and M. Warburg, eds., *Religion and Cyberspace* (London: Routledge, 2005); J. Berger, "Religious Nongovernmental Organizations: An Exploratory Analysis," *Voluntas* 14, no. 1 (March 2003): 15–39; Carrette and King, *Selling Spirituality*.

59. Scholte, *Globalization*, 7.

60. Carrette, *Religion and Critical Psychology*.

Contributors

GREGORY ALLES is professor and chair of religious studies at McDaniel College, Westminster, Maryland, and coeditor, with Olav Hammer, of *Numen*, the journal of the International Association for the History of Religion. He has written extensively on Rudolf Otto and edited the volume *Religious Studies: A Global View* (Routledge, 2008). In recent years his scholarly interests have focused on the religion and cultural of the Rathvas, adivasis (indigenous people) who live in eastern central Gujarat.

VICTOR ANDERSON is Oberlin Theological School Professor of Ethics and Society at Vanderbilt University, the Divinity School, and professor of African American and diaspora studies in the College of Arts and Sciences. His research areas include philosophy and ethics, black studies, American philosophy and religious thought, and African American religious and cultural studies. He is author of *Beyond Ontological Blackness: An Essay on African American Religious and Cultural Criticism* (1995), *Pragmatic Theology: Negotiating the Intersections of an American Philosophy of Religion and Public Theology* (1998), and *Creative Exchange: A Constructive Theology of African American Religious Experience* (2008).

EDWARD P. ANTONIO is Harvey H. Potthoff Associate Professor of Christian theology and social theory and associate dean of diversities at Iliff School of Theology in Denver, Colorado. He has published a number of scholarly articles in these areas and is currently working on two book projects. Previously he taught at the University of the Witwatersrand in Johannesburg, South Africa, where he also served as the treasurer of the South African Academy of Religion and as a Consultant for the World Council of Churches Project on Ecumenical Hermeneutics. Dr. Antonio was the 1997 Louise Iliff Visiting Professor. In 2009, he was appointed an American Academy of Religion (AAR) Luce Fellowship in Theologies of Religious Pluralism and Comparative Theology. In 2010, the Center for Interfaith Action on Global Poverty (CIFA) named Antonio to lead a process in Nigeria for theological reflection and evaluation of the experience of Muslim and Christian faith leaders mutually engaged in interfaith action on malaria prevention throughout the country.

ELLEN ARMOUR holds the E. Rhodes and Leona B. Carpenter Chair in feminist theology at Vanderbilt Divinity School and directs the Carpenter Program in Religion, Gender, and Sexuality there. She is the author of *Deconstruction, Feminist Theology, and the Problem of Difference: Subverting the Race/Gender Divide* (University of Chicago Press, 1999) and coeditor of *Bodily Citations: Judith Butler and Religion* (Columbia University Press, 2006). Her latest book, *Signs and Wonders: Theology After Modernity* (Columbia University Press, 2016), uses photographs to diagnose and respond to shifts in our relationship to biodisciplinary power as channeled by a fourfold of "man" and "his" others (sexed/raced, animal, and divine). Her research interests include theology's relationship to continental philosophy, theories of gender, race, sexuality, and disability, as well as visual culture.

WILLIAM ARNAL is professor and head of the Department of Religious Studies at the University of Regina. He received his doctorate in the study of religion from the University of Toronto in 1997. His research mainly focuses on the New Testament and the earliest forms of Christianity in the context of the religions of Mediterranean antiquity. His articles have been published in a variety of books and academic journals, and his books include *Jesus and the Village Scribes* (2001), *The Symbolic Jesus* (2005), and, most recently, *The Sacred Is the Profane* (2013). He lives in Regina with his partner, Dr. Darlene Juschka, and three cats (none of whom is university educated).

TINA BEATTIE is professor of Catholic studies at the University of Roehampton, London, and director of the Digby Stuart Research Centre for Religion, Society, and Human Flourishing. Professor Beattie's academic research and publications include work on Catholic theology and psychoanalytic theory (*Theology After Postmodernity: Divining the Void*, Oxford University Press, 2013); theologies and theories of gender and sexuality (*New Catholic Feminism: Theology and Theory*, Routledge, 2005); the cult of the Virgin Mary (*God's Mother, Eve's Advocate*, Continuum, 2002); theology and art (contributions to a number of books and journals); atheism and religion (*The New Atheists: The Twilight of Reason and the War on Religion*, Darton, Longman and Todd, 2011), and religion and women's rights (contributions to a number of books and articles). She is currently researching issues of marriage, the family, gender, and women's rights, with a particular focus on maternal well-being in sub-Saharan Africa.

WARD BLANTON is reader in biblical cultures and European thought at the University of Kent, having spent most of his early career at the University of Glasgow. He received his PhD in religious studies from Yale University in 2004, working with biblical scholars, historians of ideas, and continental philosophers to try to map new ways of understanding the shared genealogies and competitive struggles of biblical studies and philosophy within European academic contexts. His first book *Displacing Christian Origins: Philosophy, Secularity, and the New Testament* focused on the ways common tags like critical thought, modernity, or the secular seemed to slip into something more rhapsodic, religious, or strangely biblical than we tend to imagine. More recently he has explored this ancient/modern issue of "Jerusalem and Athens" (often by way of Berlin, Paris, and Rome) through a focus on Paul the apostle as a figure of continental philosophy and psychoanalytic cultural theory (cf. *Paul and the Philosophers, A Materialism for the Masses: Saint Paul and the Philosophy of Undying Life*, and his work on Stanislas Breton and Pier Paolo Pasolini). He is currently working on an ancient philosophical commentary on Paul's letter to the Romans and trying also to develop a new philosophical and religious genealogy of the "securitization" of religion or the militarization of affective sociality (for example, with logics of autoimmunity). This work is deeply engaged with the writings of Hegel and Heidegger, as well as with encounters with this tradition in Jacques Derrida, Peter Sloterdijk, Slavoj Žižek, Roberto Esposito, and Alain Badiou.

LOURENS VAN DEN BOSCH was an associate professor of comparative religious science and history at Groningen University before his retirement in 2002. His work explores Indian and Islamic traditions and he is the author of *Friedrich Max Müller: A Life Devoted to the Humanities* (Brill, Numen ok Series, vol. 94) and coeditor with Jan Bremmer of *Between Poverty and the Pyre: Moments in the History of Widowhood* (Routledge, 1995).

DANIEL BOYARIN is the Taubman Professor of Talmudic Culture at the University of California at Berkeley. His most recent books are *Imagine No Religion,* with Carlin Barton (Fordham University Press, 2016) and *A Traveling Homeland: The Talmud as Diaspora* (University of Pennsylvania Press, 2015). He currently holds an Alexander von Humboldt Forschungs Preis and will spend the academic year 2016–17 in Germany at the Max Weber Kolleg and the Freie Universitaet, working on a book titled "'Judaism': A Genealogy."

ULRIKE BRUNOTTE is associate professor for gender and cultural history at the Faculty of Arts and Social Sciences and the Center for Gender and Diversity of Maastricht University. She completed her PhD (summa cum laude) in religious studies (philosophy and literature) at the Free University in Berlin and her habilitation at Humboldt-University Berlin in 2000. Since 2013 she has been chair of the international research network Rengoo: "Gender in Orientalism, Occidentalism and Antisemitism," www.rengoo.net (promoted by NWO). She is the coeditor of the book series Diskurs Religion (ERGON, twenty volumes published). Her areas of research include Orientalism, gender/sexuality and postcolonial studies, aesthetics of religion, and history of religious studies. Selected publications include the edited volume *Orientalism, Gender, and the Jews: Literary and Artistic Transformations of European National Discourses* (de Gruyter, 2015), *Das Wissen der Dämonen: Gender, Performativität und materielle Kultur im Werk Jane E. Harrisons* (Ergon, 2013); *Helden des Todes: Studien zur Religion, Ästhetik und Politik moderner Männlichkeit* (Ergon, 2015); "From Nehemia Americanus to Indianized Jews: Pro- and Anti-Judaic Rhetoric in Seventeenth-Century New England," in *Journal for Modern Jewish Studies* (2015): 1–20.

JEREMY CARRETTE is professor of religion and culture at the University of Kent. He works in the interdisciplinary study of religion across the fields of philosophy, psychology, politics, and the history of ideas. He has written on a wide array of themes in the study of religion and has published studies on Michel Foucault, William James, the politics of spirituality, and the philosophy of religion.

His publications include *Foucault and Religion* (Routledge, 2000), *Religion and Critical Psychology: Religious Experience in the Knowledge Economy* (Routledge, 2007), *William James's Hidden Religious Imagination: A Universe of Relations* (Routledge 2013) and, edited with Hugh Miall, *Religion, NGOs and the United Nations: Visible and Invisible Actors in Power* (Bloomsbury, 2017).

WILLIAM T. CAVANAUGH is director of the Center for World Catholicism and Intercultural Theology and professor of Catholic studies at DePaul University. His degrees are from the universities of Notre Dame, Cambridge, and Duke. He is the author of seven books, including *The Myth of Religious Violence* (Oxford, 2009) and, most recently, *Field Hospital: The Church's Engagement with a Wounded World* (Eerdmans, 2016). He has lectured on six continents, and his writings have been published in eleven languages.

DAVID CHIDESTER is professor of religious studies and director of the Institute for Comparative Religion in Southern Africa (ICRSA) at the University of Cape Town in South Africa. The author or editor of over twenty books in North American studies, South African studies, and comparative religion, his major publications include *Salvation and Suicide: Jim Jones, the Peoples Temple, and Jonestown* (Indiana University Press, 1988; revised edition, 2003); *Authentic Fakes: Religion and American Popular Culture* (University of California Press, 2005); *Savage Systems: Colonialism and Comparative Religion in Southern Africa* (University of Virginia Press, 1996); *Wild Religion: Tracking the Sacred in South Africa* (University of California Press, 2012); and *Empire of Religion: Imperialism and Comparative Religion* (University of Chicago Press, 2014).

JAMES L. COX is emeritus professor of religious studies in the University of Edinburgh and adjunct professor in the Religion and Society Research Cluster, Western Sydney University. His primary research interests focus on the study of indigenous religions and on theory and method in the study of religion. He is the author of *The Invention of God in Indigenous Societies* (Routledge, 2014), *An Introduction to the Phenomenology of Religion* (Continuum, 2010), *From Primitive to Indigenous: The Academic Study of Indigenous Religions* (Ashgate, 2007), and *A Guide to the Phenomenology of Religion* (Continuum, 2006).

DANIEL DUBUISSON is professor emeritus at the French National Scientific Research Centre (CNRS) and a member of the editorial board for the journal *Method and Theory in the Study of Religion*. He achieved his Docteur ès lettres in 1983, and is director of research emeritus at the CNRS and University of Lille in France. His main publications in English are *The Western Construction of Religion: Myths, Knowledge, and Ideology* (Johns Hopkins University Press, 2003); *Twentieth Century Mythologies: Dumézil, Lévi-Strauss, Eliade* (Equinox, 2006); *Wisdoms of Humanity Buddhism, Paganism and Christianity* (Brill, 2011); *Religion and Magic in Western Culture* (Brill, 2016).

STEVEN ENGLER is professor of religious studies at Mount Royal University in Calgary, affiliate professor of religion at Concordia University in Montréal, and professor colaborador at the Pontifícia Universidade Católica de São Paulo. He studies religions in Brazil, theories of religion, and methodology in the study of religion. He is the coeditor, with Michael Stausberg, of the journal *Religion*,

The Routledge Handbook of Research Methods in the Study of Religion (2011), and *The Oxford Handbook of the Study of Religion* (2016), and coeditor, with Bettina E. Schmidt, of *Handbook of Contemporary Religions in Brazil* (Brill, 2016). See http://stevenengler.ca.

TIMOTHY FITZGERALD was reader in religion at the School of Languages, Cultures, and Religions at the University of Stirling, Scotland, before his retirement in 2016. His research interest include: anthropology of Japan; anthropology of India; meditation; analysis of discourses on "religion and the secular," "religion and politics," "religion and the State," and other such rhetorical constructs; history, theory, and method in the study of religion; Orientalism as a theory; and problems of representing others. Dr. Fitzgerald is the author of a number of books including: *The Ideology of Religious Studies* (Oxford University Press, 2000), *Discourse on Civility and Barbarity: A Critical History of Religion and Related Categories* (Oxford University Press, 2007), *Religion and the Secular: Historical and Colonial Formations* (editor, Equinox, 2007), and *Religion and Politics in International Relations: The Modern Myth* (Continuum, 2011).

RICHARD FOX teaches in the Institut für Ethnologie at the Ruprecht-Karls Universität Heidelberg, where he is also a member of the collaborative research project on Material Text Cultures. His primary teaching and research interests focus on the ethnographic and historical study of religion, media, and performance in South and Southeast Asia, with a special emphasis on Indonesia and the wider Malay region. In addition to a monograph on religion and media in contemporary Bali, and coedited volumes on both entertainment media and textual culture in Indonesia, his most recent publications have appeared in *Bijdragen tot de Taal-, Land- en Volkenkunde*, *Archipel*, *Modern Asian Studies*, *Asian Journal of Communication*, and *Jurnal Kajian Bali*.

MARK QUENTIN GARDINER is an associate professor of philosophy at Mount Royal University in Calgary. He is the author of *Semantic Challenges to Realism: Dummett and Putnam* (University of Toronto Press, 2000) and has published, often in collaboration with Steven Engler, on the intersection of theory and the study of religion in such journals as *International Journal for Philosophy of Religion*, *Journal for the Cognitive Science of Religion*, *Journal of Ritual Studies*, *Method and Theory in the Study of Religion*, *Religion*, and *Religious Studies*.

VOLNEY GAY is professor of religious studies, professor of psychiatry, and professor of anthropology at Vanderbilt University and Vanderbilt University Medical Center. He was certified in adult psychoanalysis in 1990 by the American Psychoanalytic Association and was made a training and supervising analyst in December 1994. His book *Freud on Sublimation* won the Heinz Hartmann Award from the New York Psychoanalytic Institute. His recent books are *Progress in the Humanities* and *Neuroscience and Religion*. His newest book is *On the Pleasures of Owning Persons: The Hidden Face of American Slavery* (IP Books, 2016). He twice won the Outstanding Teacher Award from the Vanderbilt Department of Psychiatry, and he has won the Outstanding Service Award from the American

Psychoanalytic Association, and the Distinguished Psychoanalytic Educator Award from the International Forum for Psychoanalytic Education.

JAY GELLER is associate professor of modern Jewish culture at Vanderbilt Divinity School and Vanderbilt University's Program in Jewish Studies. The cofounder and former cochair of the American Academy of Religion's Critical Theory and Discourses on Religion Group, he is the author of *On Freud's Jewish Body: Mitigating Circumcisions* (2007), *The Other Jewish Question: Identifying the Jew and Making Sense of Modernity* (2011), and *Bestiarium Judaicum: Unnatural Histories of the Jews* (2017), all from Fordham University Press.

NAOMI R. GOLDENBERG is professor of religious studies in the Department of Classics and Religious Studies at the University of Ottawa in Ottawa, Canada. Her research interests include religion and popular culture, religion and gender, and religion and psychoanalysis. Her publications include *Resurrecting the Body: Feminism, Religion and Psychoanalysis* (Crossroads, 1993), *The End of God* (University of Ottawa Press, 1982) and *Changing of the Gods: Feminism and the End of Traditional Religions* (Beacon, 1979). She is currently working on a book exploring the intersection of critical debates about the category of religion and gender.

WILLIAM DAVID HART (PhD, Princeton, 1994) is the Margaret W. Harmon Professor of Religious Studies at Macalester College. He is the author of three monographs: *Edward Said and the Religious Effects of Culture* (Cambridge, 2000), *Black Religion: Malcolm X, Julius Lester, and Jan Willis* (Palgrave, 2008), and *Afro-Eccentricity: Beyond the Standard Narrative of Black Religion* (Palgrave, 2011). His research interests included relations among slavery, race, animality, and criminality within ethical rhetoric and a comparative exploration of human sacrifice as a religious and political practice.

JUN'ICHI ISOMAE completed his PhD in 2010 at the University of Tokyo. He is a professor at the International Research Center for Japanese Studies in Kyoto. His English-language publications include *Religious Discourse in Modern Japan: Religion, State and Shinto* (Brill, 2014) and *Japanese Mythology: Hermeneutics on Scripture* (Equinox, 2010). His main research interest is in how to listen to the disquieting voices of the dead and the subaltern.

MORNY JOY is university professor in the Department of Religious Studies at the University of Calgary, Canada. Her research has been published in the areas of philosophy and religion, postcolonialism, and intercultural studies in South and Southeast Asia, as well as in diverse aspects of women and religion. Her recent publications include *Women and the Gift: Beyond the Given and the All-Giving* (Indiana University Press, 2013), *Continental Philosophy and Philosophy of Religion* (Springer, 2011), and *After Appropriation: Explorations in Intercultural Philosophy and Religion* (University of Calgary, 2011).

DARLENE M. JUSCHKA teaches in women's and gender studies and religious studies at the University of Regina. Her areas of interest are semiotics, critical theory, feminisms, and posthumanism. Some of her more recent work includes "Feminism and Gender," in The Oxford Handbook of the Study of Religion, edited by Steven Engler and Michael Stausberg (Oxford, 2016); "Responding to

Intimate Partner Violence: Challenges Faced Among Service Providers in Northern Communities," *Journal of Interpersonal Violence* (May 2016): 1–21; "Enfleshing Semiotics: The Indexical and Symbolic Sign-Functions," *Religion* 44, no. 1; and "The Category of Gender in the Study of Religion," in *Theory and Method in the Study of Religion: Twenty Five Years On*, edited by Aaron W. Hughes (Brill, 2013). She has also published *Political Bodies, Body Politic: The Semiotics of Gender* (2009, translated and published in Chinese in 2015) and *Feminism in the Study of Religion: A Reader* (2001). She is currently working on a book titled "Contours of the Flesh: The Semiotics of Pain," a case study focused on intimate partner violence in a northern Saskatchewan community, and "Indigenous Women and Reproductive Freedom," in *Listening to the Beat of Our Drum*, edited by C. Bourassa and Elder B. McKenna. Juschka is the Saskatchewan lead for the four regional research project Rural and Northern Community Response to Intimate Partner Violence.

AHMET T. KARAMUSTAFA is professor of history at the University of Maryland, College Park. His expertise is in the social and intellectual history of Sufism in particular and Islamic piety in general in the medieval and early modern periods. His publications include *God's Unruly Friends* (University of Utah Press, 1994) and *Sufism: The Formative Period* (Edinburgh University Press and University of California Press, 2007).

RICHARD KING is professor of Buddhist and Asian studies at the University of Kent. Before that he worked at Glasgow, Vanderbilt, Derby, and Stirling universities. He writes on Hindu and Buddhist philosophy, the implications of postcolonial theory for concepts of religion, and the comparative study of mysticism. He is the author of a number of books including *Orientalism and Religion* (Routledge, 1999), *Indian Philosophy* (Edinburgh University Press and Georgetown University Press, 2000), *Early Advaita Vedanta and Buddhism* (State University of New York Press, 1995), and *Selling Spirituality: The Silent Takeover of Religion* (Routledge, 2004, coauthored with Jeremy Carrette). He also was the coeditor (with John Hinnells) of *Religion and Violence in South Asia* (Routledge, 2006). His current research explores the issues involved in the classification of apophatic literature as forms of "mysticism" and also a critical examination of modern constructions of "mindfulness" meditation in the neoliberal sociopolitical context of the early twenty-first century.

YA-PEI KUO is university lecturer at the University of Groningen, the Netherlands. She is an intellectual historian by training, and has published articles on the concept of religion and its formation in modern China. Her book *Debating Culture in Interwar China* is forthcoming from Routledge. She has also held fellowships from several research institutions in the Netherlands and Germany. Her research focuses on the formation of key concepts, such as "religion" and "culture," in late-nineteenth- and early-twentieth-century China.

DAVID LAMBERTH is professor of philosophy and theology in the Faculty of Divinity at Harvard. His interests include Western liberal theology and philosophy of religion and the interconnections between theological and philosophical reflection in American and continental thought. His *William James and the*

Metaphysics of Experience (1999) exhibits his interest in the revival of pragmatism and demonstrates the inherent engagement with religion in James's philosophical system, as well as James's pluralism. He is currently preparing two books: "Religion: A Pragmatic Approach," which analyzes both historical and contemporary treatments of religion in the pragmatic tradition, and the volume on William James for the Routledge Philosophers series.

NELSON MALDONADO-TORRES is associate professor in the Department of Latino and Caribbean Studies and the Program in Comparative Literature at Rutgers University, as well as Research Fellow in the College of Human Sciences, University of South Africa. His research interests include decolonial thinking, comparative ethnic studies, postcolonial studies, and modern and contemporary philosophy and religious thought. He is the author of *Against War: Views from the Underside of Modernity* (Duke University Press, 2008), and guest editor of two special issues on the "decolonial turn" for the journal *Transmodernity* (2011), among multiple other publications. His work on modernity/coloniality, the coloniality of being, and the decolonial turn has also appeared in *Journal of the American Academy of Religion*, *Journal of Religious Ethics*, *Cultural Studies*, and the *C. L. R. James Journal*, among other academic publications.

ARVIND MANDAIR teaches at the University of Michigan, where he is associate professor of Asian languages and cultures and holder of the SBSC Endowed Chair in Sikh Studies. Though grounded in South Asian studies, his research interests cut across a number of disciplines and fields of study, including comparative and continental philosophy, the intersection between translation and religion, violence and religion, and postcolonial theory. His book publications include *Religion and the Specter of the West: Sikhism, India, Postcoloniality and the Politics of Translation* (Columbia University Press, 2009); *Secularism and Religion-Making* (with Markus Dressler, Oxford, 2011); *Sikhism: A Guide For the Perplexed* (Bloomsbury, 2013), and a major volume of translations, *Teachings of the Sikh Gurus: Selections from Sikh Scripture* (with Christopher Shackle, Routledge, 2005). He edits the journal *Sikh Formations: Religion, Culture and Theory*, published by Routledge. His current phase of research looks at the political stakes of conceptual encounter.

JON P. MITCHELL is professor of social anthropology at the University of Sussex. He is principally an anthropologist of religion and ritual and has worked mainly in Catholic Malta on themes ranging from the relationship between religion and politics; Europeanization, modernity, and secularization; and the phenomenology of religious visions. His most important books in this area are *Ambivalent Europeans: Ritual, Memory and the Public Sphere in Malta* (Routledge: 2002), *Powers of Good and Evil: Moralities, Commodities and Popular Belief* (edited with Paul Clough, Berghahn, 2002), and *Ritual, Performance and the Senses* (edited with Michael Bull, Bloomsbury, 2015).

HUGH NICHOLSON is associate professor of theology at Loyola University Chicago. He is the author of *Comparative Theology and the Problem of*

Religious Rivalry (2011) and *The Spirit of Contradiction in Christianity and Buddhism* (2016).

ILKKA PYYSIÄINEN is docent of theology, University of Helsinki, Finland. He specializes in cognitive science of religion.

TERRY REY, formerly professeur de sociologie des religions at l'Université d'État d'Haïti, is associate professor of religion at Temple University. He works primarily in the anthropology and history of African and African diasporic religions and is author or editor of a half-dozen books, including *Bourdieu on Religion: Imposing Faith and Legitimacy* (Routledge, 2007) and *The Priest and the Prophetess: Abbé Ouvière, Romaine Rivière, and the Revolutionary Atlantic World* (Oxford University Press, forthcoming).

TYLER ROBERTS is professor of religious studies at Grinnell College, in Grinnell, Iowa. He works at the intersection of continental philosophy and Western religious traditions and has a particular interest in how the categories of the religious and the secular shape the theory and practice of criticism and ethics. In 1998, he published *Contesting Spirit: Nietzsche, Affirmation, Religion.* More recently, he published *Encountering Religion: Responsibility and Criticism After Secularism* (Columbia University Press, 2013).

CHARLES E. SCOTT is distinguished professor of philosophy emeritus and research professor of philosophy at Vanderbilt University. He is also professor of philosophy (fixed term) at Penn State University. His most recent books are *The Lives of Things* and *Living with Indifference.*

YVONNE SHERWOOD has been professor of biblical cultures and politics at the University of Kent since 2013, having worked previously at the Universities of Glasgow, Roehampton, King's College London, and Sheffield. Professor Sherwood is active in the field of biblical studies (Old Testament/Hebrew Bible) and is currently the coeditor of the *Biblical Interpretation* monograph series (published by Brill) and the *Journal for the Study of the Old Testament.* Her research also explores religious studies (more expansively defined), and a range of cross-disciplinary research contexts. Recent publications include *The Invention of the Biblical Scholar: A Critical Manifesto* (cowritten with Stephen Moore) and *Biblical Blaspheming: Trials of the Sacred for a Secular Age.* Past publications include *Derrida's Bible* and *Derrida and Religion: Other Testaments.* She is currently completing a major research project, *Between Abraham and "the Modern": Religion, Secularity, Authority, and Critique.*

SIMON SPECK teaches sociology at the University of Derby. His research interests include the construal of modernity in classical and contemporary social theory, the sociology of religion, and the significance of comic phenomena in contemporary culture. He has published on the place of religion in the social theories of Ulrich Beck and Zygmunt Bauman and is currently researching the ubiquity of humor in "reflexive modernity."

KOCKU VON STUCKRAD is professor of religious studies in the Faculty of Theology and Religious Studies at the University of Groningen, the Netherlands. Kocku von Stuckrad has written eight books, which have been translated into five

languages. He has published ten edited volumes, including two leading dictionaries of religion. He is the founding editor of the *Journal of Religion in Europe*
(Brill), as well as coeditor of the *Numen Book Series* (Brill), the *Texts and Sources
in the History of Religions* series (Brill), the *Supplements to Method and Theory
in the Study of Religion* series (Brill), and the *Religion and Society* series (de
Gruyter). He is on the advisory board of *GNOSIS: Journal of Gnostic Studies*
(Brill, 2015), *Sapienza sciamanica* (Nuova Cultura), and *Zeitschrift für Anom-
alistik* (Society for Anomalistics/Forum Parawissenschaften). His books include
Western Esotericism: A Brief History of Secret Knowledge, translated and with
a foreword by Nicholas Goodrick-Clarke (Equinox, 2005), *Locations of Knowledge in Medieval and Early Modern Europe: Esoteric Discourse and Western
Identities*, Brill's Studies in Intellectual History 186 (Brill, 2010) and *The Scien-
tification of Religion: An Historical Study of Discursive Change, 1800–2000* (de
Gruyter, 2014).

RANDALL STYERS is associate professor and chair of the Department of Religious Studies at the University of North Carolina at Chapel Hill. His research
focuses on religion in modern Western culture, including the cultural history of
the study of religion and religion in various aspects of American law and politics (including such topics as gender politics and debates over the relation between
religion and science). He is the author of *Making Magic: Religion, Magic, and
Science in the Modern World* (Oxford, 2004) and the coeditor of volumes on the
notion of dualism and on magical subcultures in the modern world.

BRYAN S. TURNER is professor of sociology at the Australian Catholic University and the Max Planck Professor at Potsdam University Germany. He is a
founding editor of the journals *Citizenship Studies*, *Journal of Classical Sociology*, and, most recently, *Journal of Religious and Political Practice*. His most recent publication is *The Religious and the Political* (Cambridge, 2013), and, with
Oscar Salemink, he edited the *Routledge Handbook of Religions in Asia* (2015).
His current research interests include legal pluralism, citizenship and religion, and
the social consequences of ageing. With Alex Dumas, he published *Antivieillisse-
ment: Vieillir a l'ere des novelles biotechnologies* (Les Presses de l'Universite La-
val). He holds a doctor of letters from the University of Cambridge.

LUDGER VIEFHUES-BAILEY is distinguished professor of philosophy, gender, and culture at LeMoyne College in Syracuse, New York. His work analyzes
the intersection of globalization and theories of religion, gender, and epistemology. He is the author of *Beyond the Philosopher's Fears: A Cavellian Reading of
Gender, Origin and Religion in Modern Skepticism* (Ashgate, 2007) and of *Between a Man and a Woman? Why Conservatives Oppose Same-Sex Marriage*
(Columbia University Press, 2010). Currently, Viefhues-Bailey is working on a
project titled *Why Religious Violence? Democratization and the Politics of Religion in Secular States*.

Index